김대균은 안다! 토익에 나올 문제

김대균
KING'S TOEIC
실전 유제
모의고사 RC

6 회분

김대균 KING'S TOEIC 실전 유제 모의고사 RC 6회분

지은이 김대균
초판 1쇄 인쇄 2017년 3월 20일
초판 1쇄 발행 2017년 4월 1일

발행인 박효상 **총괄 이사** 이종선 **편집장** 김현 **기획·편집** 박혜민 **디자인책임** 손정수
표지디자인 싱타디자인 고희선
마케팅 이태호, 이전희 **디지털콘텐츠** 이지호 **관리** 김태옥

종이 월드페이퍼 **인쇄·제본** 현문자현

출판등록 제10-1835호 **발행처** 사람in **주소** 121-839 서울시 마포구 양화로 11길 14-10 (서교동) 4F
전화 02) 338-3555(代) **팩스** 02) 338-3545 **E-mail** saramin@netsgo.com
Homepage www.saramin.com

책값은 뒤표지에 있습니다.
파본은 바꾸어 드립니다.

ⓒ 김대균 2017

ISBN
978-89-6049-626-2 14740
978-89-6049-625-5 (세트)

사람이 중심이 되는 세상, 세상과 소통하는 책 사람in

김대균은 안다! 토익에 나올 문제

김대균
KING'S TOEIC
실전 유제
모의고사 RC

6회분

김대균 지음

사람in

머리말

〈대균 KING'S TOEIC 실전 유제 모의고사 LC 6회분〉〈대균 KING'S TOEIC 실전 유제 모의고사 RC 6회분〉을 세상에 자신 있게 내놓는다. 예전에 비해 전체적으로 어려워진 토익에 대비하려면 시험 출제 의도를 제대로 파악한, 실전에 가장 가까운 문제를 많이 풀어 봐야 한다. 그런 문제를 만들기 위해 필자는 일본 토익에 응시하러 일본에 두 번이나 다녀왔고 신토익에 대한 분석을 빠짐없이 해 왔다. 그런 과정을 통해 나오게 된 본서의 모든 문제는 신토익 경향을 정확하게 반영하고 있다. 그렇게 철저한 분석을 통해 알아낸 신토익의 변화와 대처 방법은 이렇다.

PART 1 어려운 단어들을 미리 숙지하고 있어야 하고, 사진을 볼 때는 인물보다는 사물을 중심으로 파악하는 것이 유리하다.
PART 2 질문을 듣고 바로 답을 고르기보다 한번 더 생각을 해야 하는 간접적인 답변이 정답으로 많이 출제되고 있다.
PART 3 리스닝 점수를 좌우하니 충분히 연습해야 한다.
PART 4 구토익과 난이도는 비슷하지만 성우들이 빨리 읽으므로 속도에 주의해야 한다.

* 〈대균 KING'S TOEIC 실전 유제 모의고사 LC 6회분〉은 성우의 음성 샘플을 필자가 직접 들어본 후 선별하였다. 속도는 시험과 비슷하게 EBS FM Jooch 선생님의 주도 하에 실전에 최대한 근접하도록 진행해 좋은 녹음이 나왔다.

PART 5 구토익과 비슷한 난이도이다.
PART 6 문장 넣기 문제가 어렵게 출제된다. 본서를 통해 충분히 연습하자!
PART 7 리딩 점수를 좌우하는 부분이다. 본서의 시험 문제와 흡사한 문제들로 충분히 연습하여 좋은 결과가 있길 빈다.

필자는 230여 회에 이르는 토익 최다 응시 만점 강사로 지금도 시험을 꾸준히 보고 있다. 14년 간 EBS FM 〈김대균 토익킹〉의 집필 및 진행도 맡아 오고 있다. 아프리카 TV에서는 〈김대균 토익킹〉이 토익 방송으로 콘텐츠를 인정받아 BJ 대상 프로 콘텐츠상을 수상했고 Best BJ 자격도 갖추게 되었다. 또 김대균 어학원에서 수강생들을 잘 관리하여 수강생들이 꾸준히 만점을 받는 결과를 낳고 있다. 토익 만점, 남의 얘기가 아니다. 여러분도 그 주인공이 될 수 있다. 여러분과 함께 호흡하면서 이 책이 가장 효과적으로 토익 점수를 올리는 데 크게 도움이 될 것이라 약속드린다.

역사는 만들어 가는 것이다.
토익계의 살아 있는 전설로 더욱 더 크게 발전해 나갈 것을 약속드린다.

하나님과 독자들에게 감사드린다.

김대균

차례

머리말	4
신토익 문제 구성 한눈에 보기	6
신토익 PART별 최신 경향 따라잡기	8
이 책의 구성과 학습 순서	16

문제지

1회	19
2회	53
3회	85
4회	119
5회	153
6회	189

해설지

1회	227
2회	277
3회	327
4회	377
5회	425
6회	475

신토익 문제 구성 한눈에 보기

PART 1

	신토익	구토익
유형	사진 묘사	사진 묘사
문항수	총 6문항	총 10문항

사진을 묘사하는 4개의 보기가 등장하는 유형 유지

 문항수 감소

PART 2

	신토익	구토익
유형	질의 응답	질의 응답
문항수	총 25문항	총 30문항

질문에 대한 적절한 응답을 찾는 유형은 유지

 문항수 감소

PART 3

	신토익	구토익
유형	짧은 대화	짧은 대화
문항수	13개 대화(대화당 3문항) 총 39문항	10개 대화(대화당 3문항) 총 30문항

- **NEW** 3명의 화자가 대화를 나누는 신유형 추가
- **NEW** 대화와 문항수 증가

PART 4

	신토익	구토익
유형	설명문	설명문
문항수	10개 설명문(설명문당 3문항) 총 30문항	10개 설명문(설명문당 3문항) 총 30문항

- **NEW** 제시된 정보를 참고하는 신유형 추가

PART 5

	신토익	구토익
유형	단문 공란 채우기	단문 공란 채우기
문항수	총 30문항	총 40문항

단문에 있는 공란에 적절한 단어/표현을 채우는 유형 유지

- **NEW** 문항수 감소

PART 6

	신토익	구토익
유형	장문 공란 채우기	장문 공란 채우기
문항수	총 16문항	총 12문항

- **NEW** 문제 형태 변화
- **NEW** 문항수 증가

PART 7

	신토익	구토익
유형	단일 지문	단일 지문
문항수	10개 단일 지문 지문당 2–4문항 총 29문항	9개 단일 지문 지문당 2–5문항 총 28문항
유형	이중 지문	이중 지문
문항수	2개 세트 지문 세트당 5문항 총 10문항	4개 세트 지문 세트당 5문항 총 20문항
유형	삼중 지문	
문항수	3개 세트 지문 세트당 5문항 총 15문항	
문항수	총 54문항	총 48문항

- **NEW** 신유형인 삼중 지문 유형 추가
    기존 독해 문제 풀이 방식 유지
- **NEW** 문항수 증가

신토익
PART별 최신 경향 따라잡기

전체적으로 토익이 어려워졌다. 이 사실을 인정하고 공부해야 좋은 결과가 나온다. 시험 출제 경향을 정확히 분석해서 반영한 본서를 중심으로 충분히 연습하면 반드시 좋은 결과가 있을 것이다!

PART 1 핵심 전략

동사 중심으로 잘 들으면 풀 수 있는 문제들이 많지만 다소 어려운 단어와 독특한 묘사가 출제되고 있다. Part 1은 신토익에서도 여전히 holding, display, casting a shadow(그림자를 던지다), lead to, occupied, unoccupied 등이 들리면 정답이다. 하지만 어려운 단어가 함께 들리기도 하므로 주의해야 한다.

1

(A) A woman is holding an oar. 여자가 노를 잡고 있다.
(B) A woman is tying a boat to a pier. 여자가 부둣가에 보트를 줄로 매고 있다.
(C) A woman is getting out of the boat. 여자가 보트에서 나오고 있다
(D) A woman is swimming across a lake. 여자가 수영을 해서 호수를 건너고 있다.

정답 (A)

Part 1에서 holding이 들리면 정답이 잘 된다. 또 oar(노)와 같이 어려운 단어가 들리는 선택지 역시 답이 잘 된다. Part 1의 단어들이 쉽다고 만만하게 보지 말고 발음에 주의하자. vase는 보통 /베이스/로 들리지만 토익에서 영국 발음으로는 /바즈/에 가깝게 들린다.

2

(A) A knife has been placed on the chair. 칼이 의자 위에 있다. → 칼도 없고 의자도 없다.
(B) Flowers have been put in vases. 꽃들이 화병에 꽂혀 있다.
   → 여기서 vases는 /바지즈/로 발음된다 (영국 발음). vase는 /베이스/라고 발음되기도 하지만 영국식 발음 /바즈/로 정답이 자주 되니 꼭 기억하자!
(C) A woman is watering some flowers. 여자가 꽃에 물을 주고 있다. → 사람도 없고 동작도 없다.
(D) A woman is buying some flowers. 여자가 꽃을 사고 있다. → 사진에 사람은 보이지 않는다.

정답 (B)

3

(A) People are gathered at the entryway. 사람들이 입구에 모여 있다.
(B) A door is beneath a staircase. 계단 아래에 문이 있다.
(C) A man is repairing the stairs. 남자가 계단을 수리하고 있다.
(D) Some pictures are propped against a wall. 몇몇 사진들이 벽에 기대어 있다.

정답 (B)
이전보다 더 독특하고 정교하게 묘사되는 사진이 출제된다. 독특한 묘사가 정답으로 나오는 추세이다.
Part 1에서 5번, 6번 문제는 사람이 사진에 나오지만 선택지에서는 사물만 묘사하는 문제가 종종 출제되고 있다는 것도 알아 두자.

PART 2 핵심 전략

Part 2 때문에 고민하는 수험생들이 많다. Part 2는 그저 문제가 다섯 개 감소한 것이 아니라는 사실에 주목해야 한다. 더욱 정교하게 어려워지고 있다. Read between the lines. 즉, 언외의 뜻을 읽어내야 정답을 알 수 있는 '간접적인 대답'이 많이 나오는 추세이다. 이런 문제들은 선택지를 듣고 한번 더 생각해야 풀 수 있는 문제이므로 잘못하면 다음 문제를 놓치기 쉽다. 간접적인 대답에 익숙해지도록 연습해야 한다.

7. Sales of the newly published books are higher than we expected.
신간 매출이 생각보다 더 높네요.
(A) We want to **hire** her. 우리는 그녀를 고용하고 싶어요.
→ higher - hire 유사 발음이 들리면 오답이다.
(B) I know they are very popular. 나는 그 책들이 인기가 있는 것을 알아요.
→ 그래서 잘 팔렸다는 의미로 적절한 답변이다.
(C) What is the bottom line? 핵심이 뭐죠?

정답 (B)

8. How will the new members be selected?
새 회원이 어떻게 선정되죠?
(A) They've already **been chosen**. 이미 선정되었어요.
→ selected = chosen 바꿔 표현한 정답이다.
(B) Jane has a monthly membership. 제인은 월 회원권을 가지고 있어요.
(C) Is **it** on the third floor? 그것이 3층에 있어요?
→ 수 일치(members 복수, it 단수) 오류이므로 오답이다.

정답 (A)

9. Why don't you sign up for the TOEIC workshop with us?
같이 토익 워크샵에 등록하는 게 어때요?
(A) I don't have time to go. 갈 시간이 없어요.
→ 퉁명스러운 대답은 정답이 잘 된다.
(B) There is a shop around the corner. 코너를 돌면 상점이 있어요.
→ workshop - shop 유사 발음이 들리면 오답이다.
(C) At the auditorium. 강당에서요.

정답 (A)

10. Have you made any progress on the merger and acquisition meeting?
　　인수합병 회의에 진전이 있었어요?

(A) The company's office. 회사 사무실이요.
(B) We're getting together again next Monday. 다음 주 월요일에 다시 모여요.
→ 계속 진행해 나갈 거라는 의미의 정답이다. 한번 더 생각이 필요한 경우이다.
(C) Acquired immune deficiency syndrome. 후천성 면역 결핍증이요.
→ acquisition - acquired 유사 발음이 들리는 선택지는 오답이다.

정답 (B)

11. What restaurant did you choose to host the retirement party?
　　은퇴 기념 파티를 주최하기 위해 어떤 레스토랑을 선택했어요?

(A) He said he will retire next year. 그는 내년에 은퇴할 것이라고 말했어요.
(B) Mark is the host of the show. 마크가 그 쇼의 주최자예요.
(C) I'm still waiting for some **price quotes**. 제가 아직 견적들을 기다리고 있어요.
→ quote는 '인용하다'라는 의미도 있지만 명사로 '견적'의 의미가 있다는 사실을 기억하자. quote = estimate

정답 (C)

12. Didn't Susan already fill an order for this?
　　수잔이 벌써 이 주문을 이행하지 않았어요?

(A) That was for December. 이 주문은 12월 것이었어요.
→ 생각을 해야 풀 수 있는 고난이도 문제이다. 이런 선택지가 (A)인 경우 마음에 세모 표시를 하고 더 들어봐야 한다.
(B) Fill her up with unleaded, please. (차에) 무연 휘발유를 가득 넣어 주세요.
→ fill이 질문의 단어와 동일하기 때문에 정답이 아닐 가능성이 크다.
(C) In chronological order. 연대기 순서대로요.
→ order가 단어 중복이라 정답이 아닐 가능성이 크다.

정답 (A)

PART 3 핵심 전략

Part 3는 긴 대화보다 빨라진 대화 속도에 주의해야 한다. 32번부터 호주 '그 놈 목소리'가 빠른 속도로 들린다. 실제 속도도 빨라져서 긴장하고 들어야 한다. 문장의 의미가 무엇인지를 묻는 문제가 어렵게 출제되니 본 교재를 통해서 연습을 많이 해 두자! 예를 들어 대화에서 Well, that's a good question.이라는 말의 의미를 물어보는 질문이 나온다. 이때 해당 문장은 정말 질문을 잘했다는 의미가 아니라 He cannot provide the answer.(잘 몰라서 대답을 할 수 없다.)는 의미로 출제된다.
그래픽 문제는 생각보다 어렵게 출제되지 않고 있다.
Part 3가 리스닝의 점수를 좌우한다. 가장 많은 문제(39문제)가 출제되고 난이도도 높은 편이기 때문에 대비를 잘 해야 한다.

PART 4 핵심 전략

Part 4는 구토익과 비슷한 난이도를 유지하고 있다. Part 3, 4에서는 한 문장을 단서로 삼아 풀 수 있는 문제보다는 두서너 문장씩 잘 들어야 풀 수 있는 문제들이 출제되고 있다. Part 4의 그래픽 문제도 비교적 쉽게 출제되고 있다. Part 3, 4의 정답을 분석해 본 결과 같은 답이 세 번 연속해서 나오는 경우는 거의 없다. 다시 말해 AAA, BBB, CCC, DDD로 정답이 되는 경우가 거의 없다는 것이다. 잘못 들었을 경우에는 정답을 같은 것으로 찍기보다는 다양하게 고르는 것이 득점 확률이 높다는 사실도 팁으로 기억해 두자.

PART 5 핵심 전략

Part 5는 구토익보다 10문제 줄었고 난이도는 비슷하므로 평소에 하던 대로 풀어 나가면 된다. 그러나 쉽게 정답을 고르기 힘든 문제들이 간혹 출제된다. 예를 들어 be selective about ~라는 구문에서 selective(까다로운, 선별적인)가 정답인데 rigorous(엄격한)가 오답 함정으로 나와 혼동을 주는 경우이다. 이런 경우 문장에서 단어의 어울림을 관찰해야 한다. Part 5는 어느 달은 어렵고 어느 달은 쉽게 나온다. 비교적 어려운 문제 유형을 정리해 보자!

101. Tina is one of the most popular musical artists in the world, ------- only Mozart in record sales.
(A) except
(B) into
(C) from
(D) behind

정답 (D)

의미를 잘 따져야 풀 수 있는 문제이다. 티나가 세계적인 음악가이고 모짜르트에게만 서열상 뒤인 2등이라는 의미이다. 많은 수험생들이 틀리는 문제 유형이므로 잘 봐 두자.

해석 티나는 음반 판매에 있어서 모짜르트에게만 뒤지는 세계에서 가장 인기 있는 음악가이다.

102. This year's Kinglish Conference will be held in Seoul, though it has ------- alternated between Tokyo and San Fransisco.
(A) traditionally
(B) abruptly
(C) exactly
(D) necessarily

정답 (A)

선택지의 부사 중에서 알맞은 것을 고르는 문제이다. 이런 유형은 매번 출제되는데 보기보다 쉽지 않아 주의해야 한다.

해석 비록 전에는 도쿄와 샌프란시스코에서 교대로 열렸지만 올해 킹글리쉬 컨퍼런스는 서울에서 열릴 것이다.

103. As they had with the first, organizers of Kinglish Conference ------- managed to find an alternative speaker for the second canceled seminar.
(A) much
(B) excessively
(C) concurrently
(D) likewise

정답 (D)

선택지의 부사 중에서 알맞은 것을 고르는 문제이다.

해석 처음에도 그랬듯이 킹글리쉬 컨퍼런스의 조직위원들은 두 번째로 취소된 세미나 연사에 대해서도 첫 번째처럼 대체 연사를 이럭저럭 찾아냈다.

104. Please we should know that the terms are subject to change ------- when oil prices rise or fall.
(A) heavily
(B) quarterly
(C) still
(D) nearby

정답 (B)
문맥을 잘 파악해야 정답을 찾을 수 있다. 조건들이 분기별로 바뀔 수 있다는 문맥이다.
해석 기름 가격이 오르거나 내림에 따라 분기별로 조건이 바뀔 수 있다는 사실을 알아 두십시오.

105. ------- the world's tallest building was completed, HaJin and Tina Ltd. had already begun designing a taller one.
(A) By the time
(B) Whenever
(C) If
(D) Because

정답 (A)
과거완료 시제 문제이다. 과거완료, 미래완료 시제도 자주 출제되고 있다.
By the time + 주어 + 과거시제, 주어 + had p.p.
By the time + 주어 + 현재시제, 주어 + will have p.p.
해석 세계에서 가장 높은 빌딩이 완성될 즈음에 하진과 티나 유한책임회사는 이미 더 높은 건물을 디자인하기 시작했다.

PART 6 핵심 전략

Part 6에서 제일 어려운 문제는 빈칸에 들어갈 문장을 선택지(네 문장)에서 고르는 문제이다. 이 문제가 추가되어 문제를 푸는 데 시간도 많이 걸릴 뿐 아니라 평소에 문맥 잡기 훈련도 더 해야 한다. 이 문제 유형을 본서를 통해 철저히 분석하고 연습하자! Part 6의 난이도는 어느 달은 어렵다가 어느 달은 쉽다. 난이도가 일정하지 않으니 꾸준히 공부해야 한다.

PART 7 핵심 전략

요즘 들어 특히 Part 7의 어려움을 호소하는 경우가 많다. Part 7은 문항수가 늘어 총 54문항이 출제되므로 풀이 시간도 많이 걸리고 문제 자체도 쉽지 않다. 리스닝 점수가 Part 3로 좌우되듯이 리딩의 점수는 Part 7이 좌우한다. 그런데 구토익에서는 쉽게 풀고 넘어갈 수 있었던 단문 독해부터 어려워졌다. 더블 페시지(이중 지문)와 트리플 페시지(삼중 지문)도 서서히 어려워지는 경향이니 본서의 좋은 문제로 반복하여 연습하길 권한다.

또 수험자가 마지막 지문인 196~200번을 시간이 모자라 답을 찍을 경우에 대비하여 A, B, C, D 정답비중을 균등하게 하고 있으니 주의하자! 신토익 처음부터 이 책이 출간되는 최근까지 파트 7의 196-200번 정답을 분석해 본 결과 A가 정답인 경우가 18회, B가 정답인 경우 18회, C가 정답인 경우 18회, D가 정답인 경우 17회로 A, B, C, D의 정답 비중이 균등하다. 수험자가 Part 7 시간이 모자라 찍을 것을 예상하고 정답을 분산시킨 것이다. 최선을 다해 문제를 풀고 마지막 수단으로 활용하기 바란다.

또한 Part 7의 동의어 문제가 어려워지고 있는데, 보통 retain은 단어는 간직하다(to keep possession of)나 '계속 유지하다'의 의미로 많이 사용된다.
They insisted on retaining old customs. (그들은 오랜 관습을 유지해야 한다고 주장했다.)

그런데 retain은 계약을 통해 돈을 주고 누구를 '고용하다'의 의미로 쓰인다는 것을 알고 있는가? 예를 들어 'retain a lawyer'는 '변호사를 계약해서 고용하다'의 의미가 된다.
최근 토익 독해 문제에서 contract의 동의어로 retain이 출제되어 많은 수험생이 당황했다. 이 단어의 뜻은 영영 사전에서도 맨 뒤에 나오는 의미이다. 우리가 익숙한 단어를 공부할 때도 그 단어의 다른 의미가 없는지 주의하고 새로운 의미를 예문을 통해 배우는 태도가 중요하다!

The team failed to retain him, and he became a free agent.
그 팀은 그와 계약을 하는 데 실패했고 그는 자유계약자가 되었다.

They have decided to retain a firm to conduct a survey.
그들은 한 회사를 고용하여 설문조사를 실행하기로 결정했다.

You may need to retain an attorney.
당신은 변호사를 고용할 필요가 있을 것이다.

우선적으로는 본서의 토익 문제를 제대로 풀고 반복하되 예문들을 충분히 읽고 정리하는 습관이 중요하다!

본서 해설을 아프리카TV 방송을 통해서도 진행할 계획이니 김대균 토익킹 방송을 즐겨찾기 하는 것도 잊지 말자.

이 책의 구성과 학습 순서

토익킹의 완벽 재현 실전 문제

105. The new policies are designed to curb lateness and ------- employee accountability.
(A) promote
(B) declare
(C) obtain
(D) benefit

106. Most employees have cited the positive work ------- as the reason they have remained with the company.
(A) reconstruction
(B) environment
(C) employment
(D) position

107. Martin's Coffee ------- over 300 shops across Canada by next summer.
(A) will have
(B) has
(C) is having
(D) has had

110. Haverstock Telephone & Cable has built a ------- as a provider of prompt customer service.
(A) privilege
(B) character
(C) reputation
(D) consequence

111. The employee handbook ------- the proper procedure for handling customer complaints.
(A) outlining
(B) outlines
(C) to outline
(D) is outlined

112. Mr. Randal has decided to install new vending machines in the lounge ------- everyone to use.
(A) if
(B) to
(C) for
(D) until

실전 그대로 반영
신토익 경향을 완전 반영한 문제지를 푼다.

토익킹의 완벽 해설

1 스크립트 및 해석, 힌트 확인

해석해 보고 스크립트 또는 지문에 힌트가 나오는 위치를 확인한다.

2 신경향을 제대로 짚어 주는 해설

구토익과는 다른 신토익의 디테일한 변화까지 잡아낸 해설을 확인한다.

3 변형 표현 확인

토익에서 보기를 구성하는 기본 특징인 변형 표현을 확인한다.

4 추가/연계 정보

연계 문제로 출제 가능한 정보를 꼭 확인한다. 한 문제로 두세 문제를 한꺼번에 푸는 효과를 볼 수 있다.

ACTUAL TEST 1

a
100

b
200

c
300

d
400

e
500

f
600

READING TEST

In the Reading Test, you will read a variety of texts and answer several different types of reading comprehension questions. The entire Reading test will last 75 minutes. There are three parts, and directions are given for each part. You are encouraged to answer as many questions as possible within the time allowed.

You must mark your answers on the separate answer sheet. Do not write your answers in your test book.

PART 5

Directions: A word or phrase is missing in each of the sentences below. Four answer choices are given below each sentence. Select the best answer to complete the sentence. Then mark the letter (A), (B), (C), or (D) on your answer sheet.

101 All employees will receive ------- letters and severance pay upon termination of employment.
(A) recommends
(B) recommendation
(C) recommended
(D) recommending

102 Mr. Stevens picked up some new supplies for the office ------- Stationery and Paper World.
(A) but
(B) as
(C) at
(D) after

103 ------- needs to come and repair the photocopier as soon as possible.
(A) Someone
(B) Us
(C) They
(D) Any

104 The company's new software is designed to update to the most recent version -------.
(A) automate
(B) automatic
(C) automated
(D) automatically

105 The new policies are designed to curb lateness and ------- employee accountability.
(A) promote
(B) declare
(C) obtain
(D) benefit

106 Most employees have cited the positive work ------- as the reason they have remained with the company.
(A) reconstruction
(B) environment
(C) employment
(D) position

107 Martin's Coffee ------------ over 300 shops across Canada by next summer.
(A) will have
(B) has
(C) is having
(D) has had

108 This law was passed to protect citizens ------- own and operate small businesses.
(A) for
(B) who
(C) those
(D) as

109 The meeting with our new supplier has been rescheduled for ------- on Wednesday.
(A) hardly
(B) comfortably
(C) early
(D) eagerly

110 Haverstock Telephone & Cable has built a ------------ as a provider of prompt customer service.
(A) privilege
(B) character
(C) reputation
(D) consequence

111 The employee handbook ------- the proper procedure for handling customer complaints.
(A) outlining
(B) outlines
(C) to outline
(D) is outlined

112 Mr. Randal has decided to install new vending machines in the lounge ------- everyone to use.
(A) if
(B) to
(C) for
(D) until

113 Smith International Trading's department managers ------- conduct employee satisfaction surveys.
(A) lively
(B) harshly
(C) routinely
(D) vastly

114 The consulting firm ------- several procedural changes that would improve the shipping company's efficiency.
(A) proposing
(B) proposed
(C) proposal
(D) proposals

115 The main responsibility of the volunteers is to help visitors -------- their way around the exhibition hall.
(A) do
(B) find
(C) put
(D) ask

116 Please retain this e-mail as ------- that your payment information has been entered into our system.
(A) confirm
(B) confirmed
(C) confirmable
(D) confirmation

117 Ms. Derlago started working at this bank almost a decade ago and has -------- assumed the role of assistant manager.
(A) ever
(B) yet
(C) so
(D) since

118 Mr. Barns is attempting to collect several references ------- for gaining employment at the hospital.
(A) required
(B) requiring
(C) requires
(D) will require

119 The -------- for building within the city limits are all listed on the city's permit website.
(A) probabilities
(B) allowances
(C) regulations
(D) varieties

120 ------- at Austin Tech University is considered the most advanced in the country.
(A) Research
(B) Researchers
(C) Researched
(D) Researches

121 Covington Ice Cream attributes its recent surge in sales to the addition of its newest flavor --------- its advertising campaigns.
(A) as for
(B) even so
(C) rather than
(D) after all

122 The service at Wallace Limos improved ------- after the customer surveys were conducted.
(A) tightly
(B) markedly
(C) manageably
(D) separately

123 These computers are reserved for people searching --------- employment opportunities in downtown London.
(A) for
(B) up
(C) as
(D) to

124 Please ensure that you have written all your information -------, as an error could result in a long delay in the process.
(A) affordably
(B) precisely
(C) unitedly
(D) decisively

125 June Austin's article on THP Power's expansion plans was very unique due to her ------- as a former employee.
(A) detail
(B) prospect
(C) investment
(D) perspective

126 Human resources employees were able to solve the problem among ------- without intervention from the department manager.
(A) themselves
(B) theirs
(C) their
(D) they

127 Mr. Brown is ------- when it comes to international company policies, so we had better ask him.
(A) appropriate
(B) knowledgeable
(C) undeveloped
(D) triumphant

128 Car insurance claims must be made ------- policy owners receive bills for damages.
(A) as well as
(B) as soon as
(C) in regard to
(D) in addition to

129 With such a beautiful beach and huge assortment of art galleries, Adelaine Town is quite a --------- tourist spot.
(A) offering
(B) proposing
(C) promising
(D) identifying

130 The marketing department arranged to have weekly meetings to ensure a ------ effort is made on the new project.
(A) mundane
(B) transitional
(C) reduced
(D) concentrated

PART 6

Directions: Read the texts that follow. A word, phrase, or sentence is missing in parts of each text. Four answer choices for each question are given below the text. Select the best answer to complete the text. Then mark the letter (A), (B), (C), or (D) on your answer sheet.

Questions 131-134 refer to the following information.

Extended Vacations

Employees who have been with Star Packaging for at least two years may be __131__ to receive an additional five days of summer vacation. __132__ . Department managers will be responsible for reviewing the applications and those __133__ who qualify will have their names entered into a lottery system. Those who have been at the company for five years or longer will be given __134__, and up to fifteen names will be drawn from the lottery.

131 (A) prominent
(B) cooperative
(C) exclusive
(D) eligible

132 (A) Employees can fill out an application and return it to their manager.
(B) For example, all long-term employees will receive additional benefits packages.
(C) However, competitive salary raises will be given to a few deserving employees.
(D) Management is pleased to announce that new employees have been hired.

133 (A) candidates
(B) awardees
(C) suppliers
(D) occupants

134 (A) prefer
(B) preferred
(C) preference
(D) preferential

Questions 135-138 refer to the following notice.

Channel 8 News Turns 60!

On March 15, Channel 8 News, the city's number one news source, celebrates its sixtieth anniversary. That's six decades of studio and live ___135___. For well over half a century, we at Channel 8 News ___136___ our viewers breaking new coverage, insightful commentaries, and wonderful human-interest stories from across the city and region. We would like to invite you, our loyal viewers, to our celebration. On March 15, we will hold an open house from 4:30 P.M. to 6:00 P.M. at our studio on Kingsley Street. Take part in a studio tour and see first-hand what goes on behind the scenes and watch a demonstration of our state-of-the-art broadcasting equipment. ___137___. There is no charge to attend this event, but you do have to register. We hope to see you all at this ___138___ occasion.

135 (A) concerts
(B) discussions
(C) programming
(D) teaching

136 (A) offers
(B) offering
(C) will offer
(D) have offered

137 (A) The station will remain a vital part of this city for years to come.
(B) You will even have the chance to meet and talk with our news anchors.
(C) This celebration will be the third one to take place in March.
(D) Channel 8 News will be acquired by a national news network in a few months.

138 (A) special
(B) specialize
(C) especially
(D) specialization

Questions 139-142 refer to the following information.

This is just a reminder that residents of Archer Court are required to obtain a permit for any exterior home-improvement projects. Interior changes do not currently need a permit. __139__, all external jobs, large and small, must be authorized in advance.

In the past, some residents have assumed that their contractors are responsible for arranging permits. __140__ In truth, property owners must obtain the necessary permits themselves. Building inspectors may visit a site at any time, and if the property owner does not have a permit, fines may be issued.

__141__ permit laws is an important responsibility of building inspectors. The permit process ensures that all necessary safety standards __142__, which in turn protects the community from property damages and dangerous hazards.

To view a list of permits that might apply to your project, please visit renviewtown.com/permits.

139 (A) Namely
(B) Similarly
(C) Therefore
(D) However

140 (A) Contractors may charge extra for overtime.
(B) This commonly held belief is actually false.
(C) Most building inspectors also work as contractors.
(D) The cost of the project may increase seasonally.

141 (A) Questioning
(B) Eliminating
(C) Enforcing
(D) Reviewing

142 (A) are met
(B) to meet
(C) meeting
(D) have met

Questions 143-146 refer to the following webpage.

Star Credit Purchase Points

Star Credit would like to offer its credit card holders the ___143___ points program in the world. ___144___. Members can even double their points by shopping at any of the two hundred specially ___145___ stores. Points can be redeemed in exchange for gift cards at any of those two hundred stores. ___146___, points can be used on www.travelone.com to book flights and hotel rooms, and rent cars. To apply for Star Credit's points program, simply fill out the following form and click submit.

---

143 (A) comprehension
 (B) most comprehensive
 (C) comprehensive
 (D) most comprehensively

144 (A) With every purchase you make with your Star Credit Card, you can earn up to 100 points.
 (B) Points can only be used to lower your monthly interest rates on all credit card purchases.
 (C) Program members must not have applied for a Star Credit Card in the past.
 (D) Furthermore, program members can receive in-store discounts on all their purchases.

145 (A) select
 (B) selects
 (C) selected
 (D) selection

146 (A) Therefore
 (B) Regardless
 (C) In addition
 (D) For instance

GO ON TO THE NEXT PAGE

PART 7

Directions: In this part, you will read a selection of texts, such as magazine and newspaper articles, e-mail, and instant messages. Each text or set of texts is followed by several questions. Select the best answer for each question and mark the letter (A), (B), (C), or (D) on your answer sheet.

Questions 147-148 refer to the following website.

---

http://www.premiuminsurance.com

| Home | Policies | **My Account** | Sign Out |

Welcome back, Tom Schwarz! Now, you can easily access all your policy information with Premium Insurance's new website. Please take a moment to familiarize yourself with our website's features.

- Additional payment methods and online receipts of all payments
- Easy access to all your policy information in one place
- Upgraded security and timed log-outs to protect your sensitive information
- New customer service tools, such as an updated FAQ and a live chat function
- Simple online forms to update address and telephone information

---

147 Who most likely is Mr. Schwarz?

(A) An insurance salesman
(B) An insurance customer
(C) A web designer
(D) An insurance claims representative

148 What is NOT mentioned as a feature of the new website?

(A) Group insurance applications
(B) New customer service tools
(C) Consolidated information
(D) Improved Internet security

Questions 149-151 refer to the following information.

Affluence Pharmaceuticals

Manuel Rodriguez
Lead Researcher

A highly sought-after leader in today's pharmaceutical industry, Mr. Rodriquez had overseen all major research projects at Affluence Pharmaceuticals for the last five years. Mr. Rodriguez joined Affluence seven years ago and was quickly recognized for his great talent and vision. He was promoted to lead researcher and has since drastically improved employee productivity by more than 20%.

Mr. Rodriguez has been invited to speak at numerous conferences and was even honored at last year's Pharma Vision Conference as the keynote speaker. He also works as a consultant for Techtron University's medical department where he has contributed to numerous academic projects. Prior to joining Affluence, Mr. Rodriguez immigrated from Mexico and attended Stratford University where he graduated with honors.

149 What is the purpose of the information?

(A) To outline a university program
(B) To announce an employee promotion
(C) To introduce a company employee
(D) To celebrate an employee's retirement

150 What is NOT indicated about Mr. Rodriguez?

(A) He is employed as a university professor.
(B) He previously lived in Mexico.
(C) He has improved employee performance.
(D) He is an experienced public speaker.

151 What is suggested about Mr. Rodriguez's career?

(A) He often receives awards for his great work ethic.
(B) He completed two degrees before he applied for a job.
(C) He worked as an intern prior to being hired as lead researcher.
(D) He was not hired as lead researcher at first.

Questions 152-154 refer to the following article.

March 7 – the local mayor's office has just released the details of the Budding Futures Internship Program for Park County students. Led by the program director, Milly Andrews, the program is designed to give senior high school students a taste of what it's like working in a public office. ---[1]---

Mayor Steven Greenhorn announced the internship program last year. "I think it's important to include teenagers in public affairs," he said in an interview. "It may help them decide what course of study they want to pursue in college." ---[2]---

According to the newly released details, Milly Andrews will select fifteen students from fifteen schools across the county. Based on their areas of interest, the chosen students will be assigned various jobs in the mayor's downtown office. ---[3]--- The program will last eight weeks during the summer.

Applications for the program will be available on the mayor's website at the beginning of next week. ---[4]--- The selected interns will be announced in early May.

152 What is suggested about the Budding Futures Internship Program?
(A) It is available nationwide.
(B) It is a brand new program.
(C) It is for university students.
(D) It is led by Steven Greenhorn.

153 According to Mr. Greenhorn, what is the main goal of the internship program?
(A) Teaching students about elections
(B) Establishing a community of volunteers
(C) Providing students with well-paying jobs
(D) Guiding students in their future education

154 In which of the positions marked [1], [2], [3], and [4] does the following sentence best belong?

"Students are encouraged to collect at least one reference in advance."

(A) [1]
(B) [2]
(C) [3]
(D) [4]

Questions 155-156 refer to the following webpage.

ASPIRE UNLIMITED

As a client of our firm, you
- have access to around-the-clock surveillance
- pay a reasonable monthly fee with no additional costs
- can improve your office's security needs

We provide
- custom installations of CCTV equipment
- regular maintenance of all cameras and alarm systems
- 24-hour remote monitoring of your office
- fingerprint scanning technology for all entrances (additional charges will apply)
- access to Aspire's website for all your billing needs

---

155 What is one of the services offered by Aspire Unlimited?

(A) Office cleaning
(B) CCTV monitoring
(C) Website development
(D) Heating system maintenance

156 What is mentioned about fingerprint scanning technology?

(A) It is purchased on a weekly basis.
(B) It is one of Aspire's unique services.
(C) It can be purchased for an extra fee.
(D) It can be added to an account by phone.

Questions 157-158 refer to the following article.

ROUGE TOWNSHIP. March 3 – Rouge Township officials have recently announced a new development proposal for an amusement park that will be located on Rouge Lake's 4000-acre waterfront.

The new amusement park is expected to include numerous rollercoasters, an extensive aquarium, a waterpark, and a pavilion for live music. Several local businesses, such as Rotary Automobiles, Pancake House Restaurants, and Maverick Beverages have agreed to sponsor the park's development.

Following the release of the development proposal, several local activists have expressed concerns about effect the park will have on the waterfront's delicate ecosystem. "We can assure you that all precautions will be taken," Lead Developer, Jan Freedman, said in an interview yesterday. "The park will be located far enough away from the beach and the bike trails that it will have little effect on the surrounding wildlife."

Other Rouge Township residents have expressed excitement about the potential increase in business the new park will bring to the Rouge Lake area.

157 What is suggested about Rouge Township?

(A) It currently has a large tourism industry.
(B) It is home to a famous water park.
(C) Some of its residents disagree with the proposal.
(D) Much of the local wildlife is endangered.

158 What feature of the amusement park is NOT mentioned?

(A) Its large onsite aquarium
(B) Its location at the waterfront
(C) A place for live performances
(D) The gift shops and kiosks

Questions 159-161 refer to the following information.

Maintenance Services

The maintenance department of Fairsview Condos is available to make routine repairs to your condo and all shared spaces, most of which are available at no charge to residents. The following services are free of charge and must be booked two weeks in advance.

- Bathroom fixtures, such as showerheads, faucets, and toilet parts may be replaced once every two years. Free repairs of any broken components can be arranged once per year.
- Doors and windows, including window screens, will be repaired as needed at any time of the year.
- Fan filters above stoves and smoke detectors can be replaced every six months. Air conditioners are allotted one free cleaning service per year.
- For a full list of services, please visit our website. Reservations can be made by filling out a request form at www.fairsviewcondos.com/maintenance.

159 For whom is the information most likely intended?

(A) Real estate agents
(B) Employees at a building management company
(C) Landlords of a retirement home
(D) Residents at a complex

160 How often can bathroom fixtures be repaired at no cost?

(A) Once a month
(B) Every six months
(C) Once a year
(D) At any time

161 According to the information, how can readers arrange to have something repaired?

(A) By filling out an online form
(B) By calling a department
(C) By speaking to a landlord
(D) By signing up on a sheet

Questions 162-163 refer to the following text message chain.

Ron Parks [8:03]: Jim, can I get your input on the changes Jennifer asked me to make to tomorrow's presentation?

Jim Webber [8:05]: Sure. What do you need?

Ron Parks [8:07]: Can I e-mail you the new proposal? I've highlighted the changes in red, but I'm not sure if these reflect our full range of advertising services.

Jim Webber [8:08]: I'm afraid not. I'm just about to meet a client for dinner. How about I stop by your hotel room after?

Ron Parks [8:09]: That would be okay. Then I can show you the PowerPoint presentation I've made as well.

Jim Webber [8:10]: Okay, great. What room are you in?

Ron Parks [8:10]: Room 506. See you then!

---

162 Who most likely is Mr. Parks?

(A) An advertiser
(B) A hotel receptionist
(C) An art collector
(D) An IT specialist

163 At 8:08, what does Mr. Webber most likely mean when he writes "I'm afraid not"?

(A) He is worried about a presentation.
(B) He is unable to receive a document.
(C) He does not agree with some changes.
(D) He did not request the changes to be made.

Questions 164-167 refer to the following e-mail.

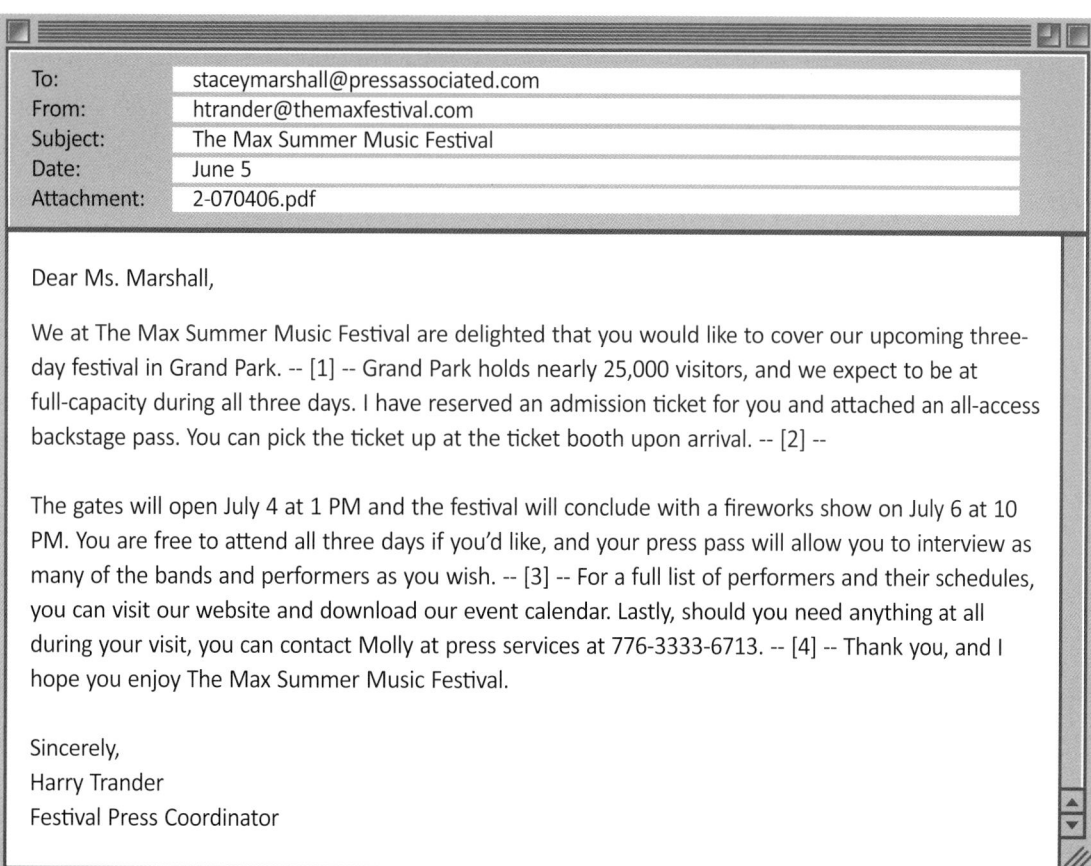

To: staceymarshall@pressassociated.com
From: htrander@themaxfestival.com
Subject: The Max Summer Music Festival
Date: June 5
Attachment: 2-070406.pdf

Dear Ms. Marshall,

We at The Max Summer Music Festival are delighted that you would like to cover our upcoming three-day festival in Grand Park. -- [1] -- Grand Park holds nearly 25,000 visitors, and we expect to be at full-capacity during all three days. I have reserved an admission ticket for you and attached an all-access backstage pass. You can pick the ticket up at the ticket booth upon arrival. -- [2] --

The gates will open July 4 at 1 PM and the festival will conclude with a fireworks show on July 6 at 10 PM. You are free to attend all three days if you'd like, and your press pass will allow you to interview as many of the bands and performers as you wish. -- [3] -- For a full list of performers and their schedules, you can visit our website and download our event calendar. Lastly, should you need anything at all during your visit, you can contact Molly at press services at 776-3333-6713. -- [4] -- Thank you, and I hope you enjoy The Max Summer Music Festival.

Sincerely,
Harry Trander
Festival Press Coordinator

164 Who most likely is Ms. Marshall?
(A) A customer
(B) A journalist
(C) A band manager
(D) A performer

165 What was sent with the e-mail?
(A) An admission ticket
(B) A parking voucher
(C) A schedule of performances
(D) A backstage press pass

166 According to the e-mail, what is a notable feature of the festival?
(A) It may accommodate more than 25,000 people.
(B) It will include jazz dance performances.
(C) It will end with a special fireworks display.
(D) It may include free camping services.

167 In which of the positions marked [1], [2], [3], and [4] does the following sentence best belong?

"It is our first festival and we have many bands lined up."

(A) [1]
(B) [2]
(C) [3]
(D) [4]

Questions 168-171 refer to the following online chat discussion.

Jessica Simon [10:32 A.M.] Marcus, do you have a minute? I'm trying to access our online store, but it's not loading. Does it load on your computer?

Marcus Adams [10:40 A.M.] It's the same for me. Was it like this yesterday?

Jessica Simon [10:42 A.M.] I don't think so. I have some orders that were placed online yesterday. But I got an e-mail from a repeat customer who said our site was down. Can you ask the IT department about it?

--Jeff Peters has been added to the chat--

Marcus Adams [10:44 A.M.] Jeff, something is wrong with our online store. It doesn't seem to be loading. Can you figure out what's wrong?

Jeff Peters [10:48 A.M.] This is strange. It looks like the hosting site is down.

Marcus Adams [10:50 A.M.] Do you have their telephone number?

Jeff Peters [10:55 A.M.] Yes, I just called them. They said they are having some technical difficulties, which should be fixed by tomorrow morning.

Jessica Simon [11:00 A.M.] Okay, I have a meeting with the sales manager shortly. I'll let him know about this problem.

---

168 What problem does Ms. Simon report?
  (A) Sales cannot be made online currently.
  (B) The online store includes wrong information.
  (C) A customer wants to return some items.
  (D) A product is no longer listed on the website.

169 From whom did Ms. Simon learn about the problem?
  (A) A department head
  (B) A customer
  (C) An IT manager
  (D) An assistant

170 At 10:50, what does Mr. Adams most likely mean when he writes, "Do you have their telephone number"?
  (A) He is requesting some information.
  (B) He wants Mr. Peters to call a company.
  (C) He would like a directory updated.
  (D) He is worried he will get lost.

171 What will Ms. Simon most likely do next?
  (A) Call some customers
  (B) Purchase items online
  (C) Attend a meeting
  (D) Contact a hosting site

Questions 172-175 refer to the following article.

Employment Weekly Column
Job Fairs

Job fairs are a quick and easy way to hire new employees. However, holding a job fair may be a costly event, especially if you're only hiring a few employees. Consider the following advice to determine if holding a job fair is right for your company.

How many employees are you hiring?
If your company is planning to hire a large group of employees, a job fair might be right for you. Job fairs can bring in a large number of applicants. However, if you're only interested in finding a few new workers, the number of applicants at a job fair may overwhelm human resources departments, making the hiring process even harder.

Is there a good location to hold the job fair?
High schools and universities are popular places to hold job fairs, but if your company is seeking more experienced candidates, schools are probably not the right place. It is critical to hold the job fair in a place where you can attract suitable employees, such as business conventions. Unfortunately, business conventions are only held at certain times of the year.

Can you hire employees another way?
Online job advertisement websites have changed the way people search for jobs. Prior to your company's hiring season, human resources staff members may be able to post job openings on numerous websites. This would garner a lot of attention and allow your company to list the experience requirements applicants must meet.

Is the cost worth it?
Before holding a job fair, consider the cost of the event. You may need to pay to rent a suitable space and would need to provide refreshments and application packages. If your hiring needs could be met by free online websites, a job fair may not be worth it.

172 What is the article about?
(A) Tips for increasing a worker's productivity
(B) Websites used to hire employees
(C) Methods of increasing the chances of being hired
(D) Strategies for efficient and economical recruitment

173 According to the article, what is a good reason to hold a job fair?
(A) To hire specialized workers
(B) To fill a large number of positions
(C) To provide employees with experience
(D) To promote the brand of a company

174 The word "critical" in paragraph 3, line 3, is closest in meaning to
(A) urgent
(B) essential
(C) creative
(D) negative

175 What is mentioned as an alternative way of finding job candidates?
(A) Advertising in local newspapers
(B) Using employment websites
(C) Holding job fairs at the office
(D) Sending out mass e-mails

Questions 176-180 refer to the following article and e-mail.

Publisher Instructs the Next Generation

January 10 -- Since his retirement last year, publisher and editor Jim Frank has run the Department of Publishing Studies at Western University. Frank is best known for his role at Maxwell Publishing House where he worked as a senior editor on numerous projects, including the publication of several successful series.

Jim Frank joined Western University as both a department head and a professor. He developed new courses such as E-publishing, Writing for the Web, and International Rights Management. Students who wish to work in the publishing industry as editors, book designers, or literary agents have benefited greatly from his wisdom.

As a result of Frank's hard work, Western University has also founded its first ever publishing internship. Students have been matched with editors, designers, and agents during three-week programs. Additionally, Frank has organized numerous events in which industry professionals have given presentations at the university on various topics. Because of Frank's innovation and connections, the publishing program at Western University has become one of the best in the country.

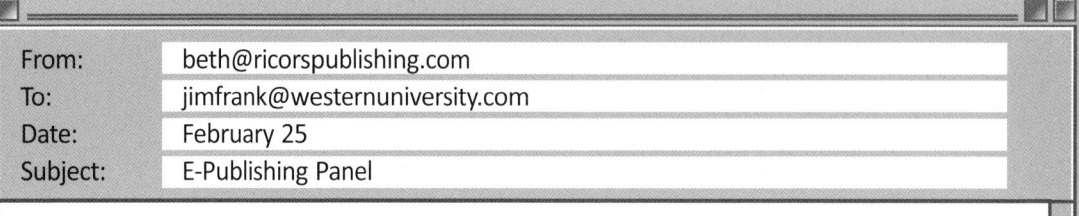

From:	beth@ricorspublishing.com
To:	jimfrank@westernuniversity.com
Date:	February 25
Subject:	E-Publishing Panel

Dear Mr. Frank,

Margaret Stevenson is currently doing her internship here at Ricors Publishing House. She mentioned that you're putting together another panel of guest speakers for your students next month. I'd love to join the panel if you still have any openings. As the director of e-publishing here at Ricors, I'm sure I'd be able to give some great information on working in this field.

I will be busy next week attending a conference overseas, but you can leave a message with my assistant and I'll get back to you the following week. My number is 443-223-0911 Ext. 3367.

I look forward to hearing from you.

Sincerely,
Beth Smith,
Director of E-Publishing,
Ricors Publishing House.

176 What does the article mainly discuss?
(A) A company's business practices
(B) An editor's career change
(C) A publisher's new series
(D) A student internship program

177 What is one contribution Jim Frank has made to the university?
(A) More courses have become available to students.
(B) A student employment website has been developed.
(C) A scholarship foundation has been established.
(D) A computer lab has recently opened.

178 Why did Ms. Smith send the e-mail?
(A) She is replying to a phone message.
(B) She would like to join a speaking event.
(C) She is looking for more interns.
(D) She wants to register in a course.

179 Who most likely is Ms. Stevenson?
(A) A director at Ricors Publishing House
(B) A student at Western University
(C) A guest speaker in a publishing course
(D) A former editor at Maxwell Publishing House

180 What does Ms. Smith say about her schedule?
(A) She can reschedule her meetings.
(B) She is not available for the panel in March.
(C) She can be reached only during the day.
(D) She will be away on business next week.

Questions 181-185 refer to the following memo and e-mail.

MEMO
Free Cloud Services

As you know, Roth Computer Sales has recently partnered with L&B Tech to improve our company's efficiency and file storage. In order to make saving and sharing files easier, we plan to install L&B's Cloud Software program on all our systems.

L&B's Cloud Software allows employees to store files of any size without taking up too much computer memory. Employees can easily send large files in seconds without worrying about slow upload speeds. Additionally, employees who bring their company laptops on business trips will be able to access their files remotely. Furthermore, L&B Cloud Software is extremely secure, so employees can rest assured that any sensitive files will be safe.

To use this new software, simply complete the setup, register with your company e-mail, and start storing and sending files. The service will be available on April 10th at 9 A.M. If you have any questions or concerns about setting up or using the new software, please contact Michael Brown in the IT Department at extension 3342 or by e-mail at michaelbrown@rothcomputers.com.

To:	michaelbrown@rothcomputers.com
From:	sandrabell@rothcomputers.com
Date:	April 12
Subject:	Cloud Software

Dear Mr. Brown,

I tried calling you on your extension, but you did not answer. I'm writing to request assistance with the new L&B Cloud Software. I set up my account on the first day the service was available, but today I was unable to access any of my files. It seems that all of the files I uploaded have been deleted, as my account is empty. Since these files include very important sales figures from last quarter, I really need to access them immediately. Can you give me an idea about how to recover these files? It would be great if you could stop by my office sometime today.

Sandra Bell

181 What is the purpose of the memo?
 (A) To announce a change in a policy
 (B) To remind employees to back-up computers
 (C) To give information about a new program
 (D) To explain a new set of rules

182 In the memo, the word "sensitive" in paragraph 2, line 5, is closest in meaning to
 (A) cautious
 (B) responsive
 (C) surprising
 (D) confidential

183 What is stated as a benefit of L&B Cloud Software?
 (A) It reduces cost.
 (B) It saves a company time.
 (C) It is free to install.
 (D) It scans documents for mistakes.

184 What problem is Ms. Bell having?
 (A) She has forgotten her password.
 (B) Her computer has crashed.
 (C) Some files have gone missing.
 (D) She cannot access a server.

185 When did Ms. Bell set up her account?
 (A) On April 10
 (B) On April 11
 (C) On April 12
 (D) On April 13

GO ON TO THE NEXT PAGE

Questions 186-190 refer to the following e-mails and form.

From:	oemerson@sommerfield.com
To:	mfernandez@rkdistribution.br
Subject:	demonstration
Date:	August 5

Dear Ms. Fernandez,

My plane landed in Sao Paulo and I am e-mailing you from a waiting room in the airport. Unfortunately, the large suitcase that I had checked has been misplaced. Even though I have printed summaries of all the items right here in my carry-on bag, the sample products for the demonstration are in the missing luggage. Airport staff informed me that they need at least three days to locate the bags and deliver them to where I am staying. That means, of course, that I will not have them in time for the demonstration scheduled for the day after tomorrow.

Once I reach my hotel, I will fax the summaries to your company. If it is not too much trouble, could we possibly postpone the demonstration for another two days? Please contact me about this as soon as possible.

Sincerely,
Oscar Emerson

Missing Baggage Claim Form

We would like to extend our deepest apologies for our mishandling of your belongings and any inconveniences it caused. The information you provide below will assist us greatly. Please provide a clear description of every piece of luggage as well as a list of the items inside each piece. This will definitely help expedite the entire process.

Claim No.:	341567S/3
Name of Passenger:	Oscar Emerson
E-mail:	oemerson@sommerfield.com

Permanent address:

409 Jackson Lane
Cleveland, OH, 44103
United States of America

Temporary address (Until August 12):

Piquiri Hotel
Av. Paulista 1209
Sao Paulo, Brazil
01310-060

Flight No.	Date	From	To
MTC971	August 3	Toledo	Buenos Aires
BTA302	August 5	Buenos Aires	Sao Paulo

Suitcase Type: Large leather bag, zipper, shoulder strap **Manufacturer:** Riggs **Color:** Brown

Contents (Please be as specific as possible)

Description	Number
Running shoes, tennis shoes, golf shoes, baseball shoes, high-top basketball sneakers	12 pairs
Top Guy brand Man's suits	2
Greyvalley brand digital camera with battery charger	1
Trousers, shorts, socks, etc.	6
South American pocket-sized travel guides	2

From:	airportlostfoundoffice@spinternat.com
To:	oemerson@sommerfield.com
Subject:	claim 341567S/3
Date:	August 6

Dear Mr. Emerson,

We are delighted to inform you that your missing suitcase has been located with all the items you listed. It will arrive at the temporary address you provided between 1:00 P.M. and 3:00 P.M. on August 7.
We truly appreciate your patience and understanding.

Regards
Sao Paulo International Lost and Found

186 What does Mr. Emerson indicate about the product summaries?
- (A) They will be sent by fax.
- (B) They are not ready yet.
- (C) They are longer than expected.
- (D) They need to be printed out.

187 What does Mr. Emerson ask Ms. Fernandez to do?
- (A) Deliver product samples
- (B) Submit an order form
- (C) Reschedule a meeting
- (D) Drive him to the hotel

188 What does Mr. Emerson want to demonstrate?
- (A) Bicycle tires
- (B) Athletic shoes
- (C) Image software
- (D) Coffee makers

189 In the form, the word "expedite" in paragraph 1, line 4, is closest in meaning to
- (A) discover
- (B) modify
- (C) elaborate
- (D) accelerate

190 Where will the delivery be sent?
- (A) To Cleveland
- (B) To Toledo
- (C) To Sao Paulo
- (D) To Buenos Aires

Questions 191-195 refer to the following e-mail, webpage, and article.

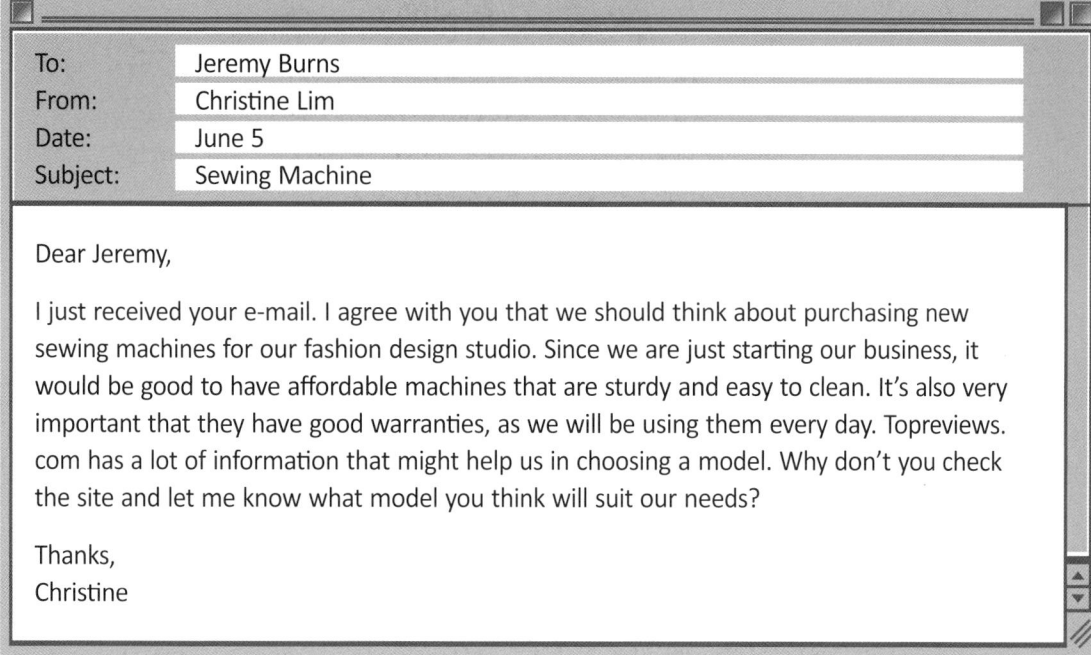

To:	Jeremy Burns
From:	Christine Lim
Date:	June 5
Subject:	Sewing Machine

Dear Jeremy,

I just received your e-mail. I agree with you that we should think about purchasing new sewing machines for our fashion design studio. Since we are just starting our business, it would be good to have affordable machines that are sturdy and easy to clean. It's also very important that they have good warranties, as we will be using them every day. Topreviews.com has a lot of information that might help us in choosing a model. Why don't you check the site and let me know what model you think will suit our needs?

Thanks,
Christine

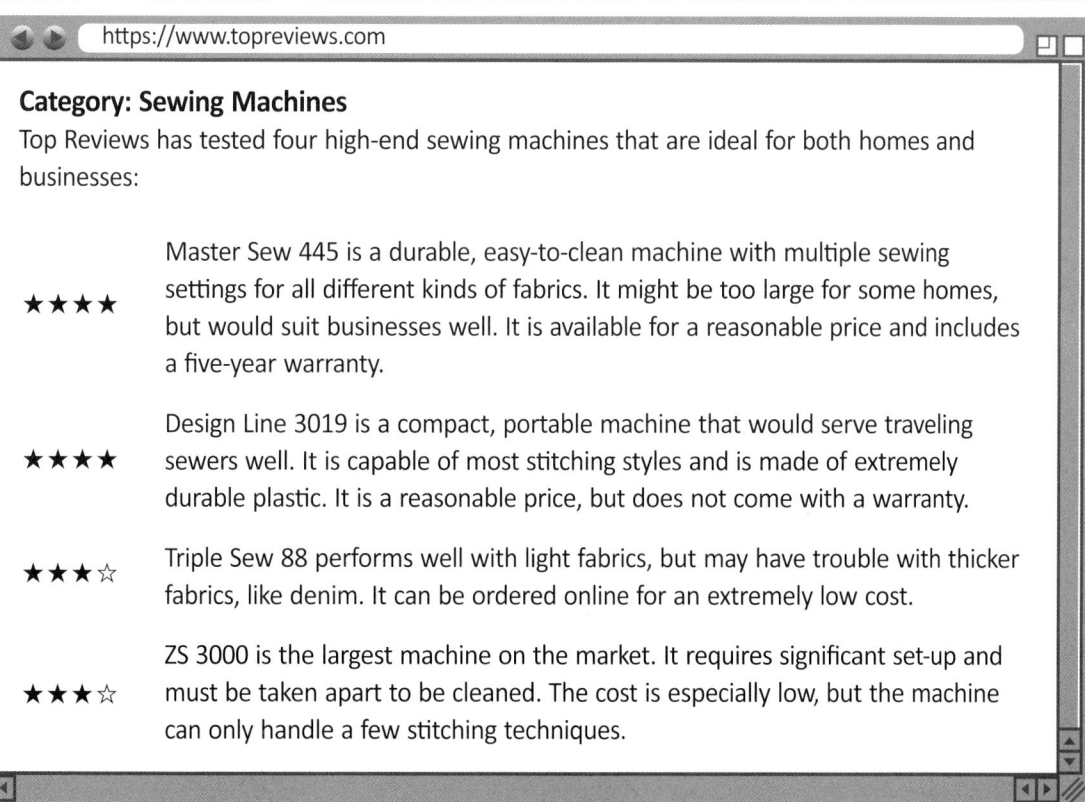

https://www.topreviews.com

Category: Sewing Machines

Top Reviews has tested four high-end sewing machines that are ideal for both homes and businesses:

★★★★ Master Sew 445 is a durable, easy-to-clean machine with multiple sewing settings for all different kinds of fabrics. It might be too large for some homes, but would suit businesses well. It is available for a reasonable price and includes a five-year warranty.

★★★★ Design Line 3019 is a compact, portable machine that would serve traveling sewers well. It is capable of most stitching styles and is made of extremely durable plastic. It is a reasonable price, but does not come with a warranty.

★★★☆ Triple Sew 88 performs well with light fabrics, but may have trouble with thicker fabrics, like denim. It can be ordered online for an extremely low cost.

★★★☆ ZS 3000 is the largest machine on the market. It requires significant set-up and must be taken apart to be cleaned. The cost is especially low, but the machine can only handle a few stitching techniques.

Fashion in Park Falls
By Zander Cornelli

December 20—Residents of Park Falls who monitor the latest trends in fashion were excited about attending the upscale fashion event held in the Park Falls Convention Center last week. Numerous companies that have made Park Falls the home of their growing businesses participated in the 10th Park Falls Fashion Festival. Over twenty fashion studios were showcased in the event, several of which are owned by local residents.

Rose Designs, which has been in the area for over twenty years, kicked off the festival with some incredible winter apparel. The show was followed by a presentation by Kim Miller, the owner of Accessories Forever. In-Style Fashions and Turnbull Jeans, which have been in business for six months and three years respectively, were newcomers to the festival. All items featured during the fashion shows are available for sale on company websites.

191 What is indicated about the ZS 3000?
(A) It is commonly used in homes.
(B) It has an extended warranty.
(C) It can be transported easily.
(D) It has limited functions.

192 What do all the machines mentioned on the webpage have in common?
(A) They are compact and portable.
(B) They are affordable prices.
(C) They come in various colors.
(D) They can be repaired easily.

193 What sewing machine did Mr. Burns most likely recommend to Ms. Lim?
(A) Master Sew 445
(B) Design Line 3019
(C) Triple Sew 88
(D) ZS 3000

194 In the article, in paragraph 1, line 1, the word "monitor" is closest in meaning to
(A) believe in
(B) observe
(C) supervise
(D) depend on

195 What company mentioned in the article do Ms. Lim and Mr. Burns most likely work for?
(A) Rose Designs
(B) Accessories Forever
(C) In-Style Fashions
(D) Turnbull Jeans

Questions 196-200 refer to the following webpage, online order form, and e-mail.

Http://www.martinmovers.com

| Home | Services | Estimates | Contact Us |

Martin Movers is ready to help you with all your moving needs. Our movers have a collective twenty years of experience tackling large and small jobs with the greatest care. Whether you are moving to a new home or you're looking to relocate your office to a new building, we can offer you the most competitive rates.

Our standard moving rates are as follows:

2 movers and 1 mid-sized truck = $75 per hour
4 movers and 1 full-sized truck = $150 per hour
Office moves (6 movers and 2 full-sized trucks) = $400 flat rate

Additional charges may apply to office moves should customers request to have our movers set up photocopiers, computers, printers, and projectors following the move. For each set up, a $5 charge may be added. To get a free estimate, just fill out our online form and we'll get back to you soon.

*New Year Special Promotion: Request an estimate by January 20th and receive $30 off the total cost of your move.

Martin Movers
Estimate Request Form

Date	January 10
Name	Connor Goldsmith
E-mail address	connor@goldsmithlegal.com
Telephone	409-333-2314
Moving from: Moving to:	54 First Avenue, New York City 889 Fallsview Lane, New York City
Moving date	February 23
Items to be moved	8 desks, 8 computers, 3 printers, 1 photocopier, 1 refrigerator, 1 conference table, 25 office chairs
Additional comments	My law office is moving to a new location. As we have our own IT employee, we will not require anyone to set up our equipment. Thus, I believe your standard flat rate will apply. Please contact me by e-mail to confirm the price and finalize the reservation.

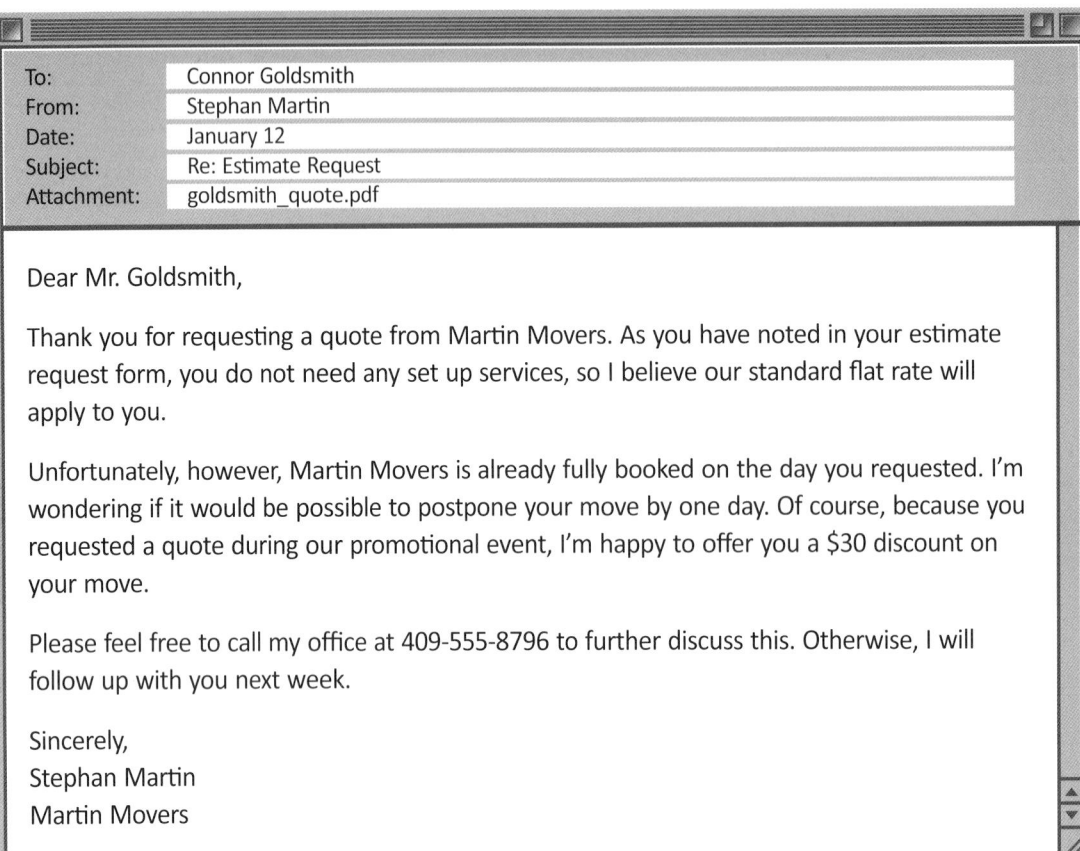

To: Connor Goldsmith
From: Stephan Martin
Date: January 12
Subject: Re: Estimate Request
Attachment: goldsmith_quote.pdf

Dear Mr. Goldsmith,

Thank you for requesting a quote from Martin Movers. As you have noted in your estimate request form, you do not need any set up services, so I believe our standard flat rate will apply to you.

Unfortunately, however, Martin Movers is already fully booked on the day you requested. I'm wondering if it would be possible to postpone your move by one day. Of course, because you requested a quote during our promotional event, I'm happy to offer you a $30 discount on your move.

Please feel free to call my office at 409-555-8796 to further discuss this. Otherwise, I will follow up with you next week.

Sincerely,
Stephan Martin
Martin Movers

196 In the webpage, the word "tackling" in paragraph 1, line 2, is closest in meaning to

(A) repairing
(B) handling
(C) considering
(D) entertaining

197 What is NOT mentioned about office moves?

(A) Six movers will be involved.
(B) More than one truck will be used.
(C) Estimates will be provided at no cost.
(D) It must be booked at least two weeks in advance.

198 What does Mr. Goldsmith mention about his company?

(A) It will discard several items.
(B) It will downsize its office space.
(C) It requires an additional mover.
(D) It employs an IT specialist.

199 If Mr. Goldsmith uses Martin Movers, how much will he be charged for his move?

(A) $75
(B) $150
(C) $370
(D) $400

200 What is suggested about Martin Movers?

(A) It is booked solid on February 23.
(B) It is located in New York City.
(C) It has five trucks in its fleet.
(D) It charges extra for work done on weekends.

This is the end of the test. You may review Part 5, 6, and 7 if you finish the test early.

ANSWERS

ACTUAL TEST 1

101. (B)	121. (C)	141. (C)	161. (A)	181. (C)
102. (C)	122. (B)	142. (A)	162. (A)	182. (D)
103. (A)	123. (A)	143. (B)	163. (B)	183. (B)
104. (D)	124. (B)	144. (A)	164. (B)	184. (C)
105. (A)	125. (D)	145. (C)	165. (D)	185. (A)
106. (B)	126. (A)	146. (C)	166. (C)	186. (A)
107. (A)	127. (B)	147. (B)	167. (A)	187. (C)
108. (B)	128. (B)	148. (A)	168. (A)	188. (B)
109. (C)	129. (C)	149. (C)	169. (B)	189. (D)
110. (C)	130. (D)	150. (A)	170. (B)	190. (C)
111. (B)	131. (D)	151. (D)	171. (C)	191. (D)
112. (C)	132. (A)	152. (B)	172. (D)	192. (B)
113. (C)	133. (A)	153. (D)	173. (B)	193. (A)
114. (B)	134. (C)	154. (D)	174. (B)	194. (B)
115. (B)	135. (C)	155. (B)	175. (B)	195. (C)
116. (D)	136. (D)	156. (C)	176. (B)	196. (B)
117. (D)	137. (B)	157. (C)	177. (A)	197. (D)
118. (A)	138. (A)	158. (D)	178. (B)	198. (D)
119. (C)	139. (D)	159. (D)	179. (B)	199. (C)
120. (A)	140. (B)	160. (C)	180. (D)	200. (A)

ACTUAL TEST 2

a **b** c
100 200 300

d e f
400 500 600

READING TEST

In the Reading Test, you will read a variety of texts and answer several different types of reading comprehension questions. The entire Reading test will last 75 minutes. There are three parts, and directions are given for each part. You are encouraged to answer as many questions as possible within the time allowed.

You must mark your answers on the separate answer sheet. Do not write your answers in your test book.

PART 5

Directions: A word or phrase is missing in each of the sentences below. Four answer choices are given below each sentence. Select the best answer to complete the sentence. Then mark the letter (A), (B), (C), or (D) on your answer sheet.

101. Ms. Parker plans to interview the applicants ------- because she understands the position better than anybody.
    (A) hers
    (B) herself
    (C) she
    (D) her

102. Tax rebates will be given to public servants ------- the State of California.
    (A) within
    (B) until
    (C) during
    (D) since

103. Interested parties can -------- register online for this weekend's seminar on real estate investing.
    (A) very
    (B) least
    (C) easily
    (D) more

104. The promotion will ------- employees with upgraded benefits, company cars, and more vacation days.
    (A) provide
    (B) earn
    (C) contrast
    (D) loan

105 Office staff at Morin Legal Services ---------- work four days a week, from Monday to Thursday.
(A) norm
(B) norms
(C) normal
(D) normally

106 Items can be exchanged ---------- they are returned within one week following the date of purchase.
(A) or
(B) if
(C) nor
(D) but

107 According to this newspaper article, earnings at BTR Electronics last quarter were ---------- than expected.
(A) lowest
(B) lowering
(C) lower
(D) low

108 Everyone ------- the store owner took a week-long vacation in the summertime last year.
(A) out of
(B) other
(C) except
(D) between

109 Even though all her landscape paintings are of actual places, Doris Clements puts a great deal of ---------- into her work.
(A) imagine
(B) imaginative
(C) imagination
(D) imaginary

110 The receptionist will provide the ------ client list to all sales personnel this afternoon.
(A) frequent
(B) updated
(C) certain
(D) monitored

111 The spring training course was developed to help sales employees think more -------.
(A) create
(B) creative
(C) creativity
(D) creatively

112 Before attempting to assemble this table, you should ---------- the instructions.
(A) direct
(B) review
(C) gather
(D) program

113 Ms. Jannel, the director of customer relations, ------- the poor reviews the company has received online at the staff meeting tomorrow.
(A) had been addressing
(B) is addressing
(C) will be addressed
(D) should be addressed

114 Larson Motors aims to improve its public image ------- the guidance of publicist Cynthia Morison of M&T Public Relations.
(A) under
(B) either
(C) among
(D) beyond

GO ON TO THE NEXT PAGE

115 When --------- to any new clients, don't forget to mention Beckingham's promotional event next week.
(A) spoken
(B) speaking
(C) spoke
(D) to speak

116 Tickets for Friday night's play at the Alexander Theater sold out quickly because the production --------- two famous actors from this area.
(A) feature
(B) features
(C) to feature
(D) featuring

117 The Thompson Art Gallery will extend its hours of operation ------- on August 1st.
(A) will begin
(B) has begun
(C) beginner
(D) beginning

118 Donald Mahoney is in charge of the supplies ------- to all plumbers working for Grady Pipe Repairs.
(A) distribute
(B) distribution
(C) distributes
(D) is distributed

119 The CEO is known for being ambitious as he expressed his ------- in an interview with Today Business Magazine last fall.
(A) interferences
(B) prevention
(C) views
(D) exchange

120 Anna Sanchez, founding editor of Financial Monthly, has quickly earned the respect of practically ---------- in the financial industry.
(A) everyone
(B) anything
(C) whatever
(D) each other

121 As stated in the reviews, the theater's new performance was ------- a big hit.
(A) clear
(B) clearly
(C) clearer
(D) clearing

122 ------- our hiring committee reads all the resumes, we will compile a list of 20 candidates to invite in for interviews.
(A) Compared to
(B) As soon as
(C) So that
(D) Not only

123 The concert was a huge success and drew a crowd of over 5,000 to Moose Park and Recreation Center, -------- the cold weather.
(A) while
(B) whereas
(C) notwithstanding
(D) moreover

124 The research staff at Pullford Pharmaceuticals will be using the conference room as its office ---------- the renovation period.
(A) opposite
(B) beside
(C) during
(D) with

125 As stated on the company's website, clients who wish to cancel their membership ------- it expires must pay a fee.

(A) before
(B) how
(C) why
(D) either

126 Although the job description is ------- to those at other firms, this job has a much higher salary.

(A) similar
(B) likable
(C) reflected
(D) considerate

127 Access to the research laboratory will be limited to senior employees to ensure ------- with all safety regulations.

(A) activation
(B) fulfillment
(C) compliance
(D) indication

128 If the window had been broken during installation, Riley's Building Supplies ----------- to replace it at no charge.

(A) would have offered
(B) has offered
(C) is being offered
(D) would have been offered

129 Prior to reviewing -----------, the town council agreed to three proposals in principle.

(A) specifics
(B) specify
(C) specific
(D) specifically

130 Administrators at the Ben Phillips Hospital maintain that ----------- to the facility will make many medical procedures more efficient.

(A) continuations
(B) increments
(C) deviations
(D) enhancements

PART 6

Directions: Read the texts that follow. A word, phrase, or sentence is missing in parts of each text. Four answer choices for each question are given below the text. Select the best answer to complete the text. Then mark the letter (A), (B), (C), or (D) on your answer sheet.

Questions 131-134 refer to the following article.

March 3--After nearly three years of planning, the largest stadium in Harpville will begin construction. The Expo Stadium will be located on Harpville's majestic waterfront and will have a capacity of up to ten thousand seats. ___131___. The project is expected to take three years to complete. It will be located amongst several other new developments currently ___132___ on the waterfront. According to Marshal Thomas, president of the Harpville Sports Association, the new stadium is a ___133___. "We're going to need a large stadium to accommodate our growing sports clubs," Mr. Thomas said. "___134___, we'll also be able to use the stadium for concerts and circus performances."

131 (A) Developers are unsure how long it will take to complete the project.
(B) The stadium will be moved from the waterfront to the outskirts of the city.
(C) It will also include over 100 press viewing rooms that hold up to ten people each.
(D) Delays occurred when the mayor refused to fund the city's development plans.

132 (A) to construct
(B) are constructing
(C) were constructed
(D) being constructed

133 (A) necessity
(B) nuisance
(C) risk
(D) bargain

134 (A) On the other hand
(B) In other words
(C) In the first place
(D) As a result

Questions 135-138 refer to the following press release.

Meredith Hobson, CEO and founder of Hobson Dining, Trenton's oldest family dining franchise, announced that she ___135___ $6,500 towards renovations to the Jasper Community Center in the city's downtown region. The funds were generated from ticket sales for a banquet held last Friday evening at her ___136___. Ms. Hobson will present the management staff of the center with a check at a special ceremony scheduled to take place tomorrow afternoon at 2:00. ___137___ the past 25 years, Ms. Hobson has organized a number of successful fund-raising events for community services and charities. ___138___.

135 (A) will donate
     (B) donated
     (C) might donate
     (D) donating

136 (A) gallery
     (B) hotel
     (C) academy
     (D) restaurant

137 (A) Despite
     (B) Over
     (C) Between
     (D) Beneath

138 (A) The Jasper Community Center has programs for both children and adults.
     (B) The opening ceremony at the center will be done by 2:30.
     (C) However, last Friday's event was, without a doubt, her most successful one.
     (D) Ms. Hobson plans to open a branch in uptown Trenton sometime next year.

Questions 139-142 refer to the following meeting summary.

Our monthly meeting commenced at 4:30 P.M. The meeting's purpose was to discuss the advantages and disadvantages of ___139___ LGQ International Shipping. Max Powel led the debate on the possible move by stressing the importance of furthering LGQ's current growth patterns. He explained that LGQ has grown to be one of the most successful ___140___ and that it ships the largest number of electronics in the country.

___141___. According to recent reports, the traveling distance from the closest harbor is becoming costly ___142___ LGQ begins to grow. Staff members discussed some possible solutions, but a final decision was not reached. Mr. Powel will do some more research and present his findings at the next meeting.

139 (A) acquiring
(B) joining
(C) promoting
(D) relocating

140 (A) distribute
(B) distributing
(C) distributors
(D) distributes

141 (A) Mr. Powel also outlined the challenges LGQ is experiencing as a result of its growth.
(B) The CEO then proceeded to discuss the advantages of the new facilities.
(C) Next, shareholders were invited to conduct a vote to decide the date.
(D) Mr. Powel directed employees to consider how operations would be conducted.

142 (A) now
(B) why
(C) just as
(D) ever since

Questions 143-146 refer to the following e-mail.

From: tina@lindcosmetics.com
To: mia@mymailnow.com
Date: September 8
Subject: Order 445009

Dear Ms. Kramar,

Thank you for writing to inquire about your order. According to our records, you ordered one tube of Lind SPF 50 Sunscreen, one bottle of Lind 500 Hand Cream, and two bottles of Lind Ultrashine Shampoo from our website on September 1st. Your products were scheduled to arrive on September 5th. I was surprised to hear that you have not received ___143___.

___144___. According to their schedule, your products will arrive on September 10th. If your order is not delivered by that day, feel free ___145___ us again.

I sincerely apologize for this inconvenience. Our shipping methods are usually fast and affordable. This situation is quite ___146___. I hope it will not discourage you from shopping at Lind Cosmetics.

Thank you.

Tina Speller
Lind Cosmetics

143 (A) it
    (B) one
    (C) them
    (D) some

144 (A) We would like to invite you to visit our store.
    (B) Please leave a review on our website.
    (C) We are currently sold out of that particular product.
    (D) I have contacted the shipping company on your behalf.

145 (A) contacted
    (B) to contact
    (C) contacting
    (D) contact

146 (A) similar
    (B) exciting
    (C) unusual
    (D) welcome

PART 7

Directions: In this part, you will read a selection of texts, such as magazine and newspaper articles, e-mail, and instant messages. Each text or set of texts is followed by several questions. Select the best answer for each question and mark the letter (A), (B), (C), or (D) on your answer sheet.

Questions 147-148 refer to the following advertisement.

Item for Sale	Price	Location
Model A7000 Flamesburg Barbecue	$450	Los Angeles, CA

Item Description:
Purchased new 3 years ago. Original cost was $700 and came with a 2-year warranty.
Grill pieces are charred. Buyer can purchase new ones on the Flamesburg website.
Exterior is in great condition. (Pictures available upon request)
Price is negotiable. Willing to deliver anywhere in the Los Angeles area.
E-mail rjohnson@mail.com if you have any questions.

147 What is NOT indicated about the barbecue?

(A) It comes in the original box.
(B) It needs new parts.
(C) Its price is not set.
(D) Its warranty has expired.

148 What is the seller willing to do?

(A) Reserve the item for up to a month
(B) Provide instructions on how to use the item
(C) Deliver anywhere in the country
(D) Send photographs to potential buyers

Questions 149-150 refer to the following notice.

We are delighted to announce that Cordelia Winters has joined IPM Talent as an associate agent. Ms. Winters is a graduate of Roden University's public relations program. While studying at Roden, she founded the university's first student-run magazine. Following graduation, she completed an internship at UV Media and Talent, a prestigious agency that represents a wide variety of musicians, authors, professional athletes, and actors. Ms. Winters has undergone exceptional training and will be a great asset to our growing team of agents. Please join us in conference room B tomorrow morning at 10:00 A.M. to welcome her to the team.

149 Where is the notice most likely posted?
- (A) In an advertising firm
- (B) In a university
- (C) In a music studio
- (D) In a talent agency

150 What are employees invited to do tomorrow?
- (A) Participate in a conference
- (B) Greet a new employee
- (C) Visit a competitor
- (D) Meet some new clients

Questions 151-152 refer to the following text message chain.

Tim Peterson [11:03 A.M.]
Hey, Amanda. Can you update me on the Sampson Lane job?

Amanda Ray [11:10]
We've cleared out the main floor and the garage. We're just starting on the second floor of the house now.

Tim Peterson [11:12]
Is that all? What time do you think you'll be done? We have a move scheduled for 3 P.M.

Amanda Ray [11:15]
We're behind schedule. When the estimate was done, it didn't take into account the old furniture in the garage.

Tim Peterson [11:20]
Really? Who did the estimate?

Amanda Rey [11:21]
Matthew did before he went on vacation.

Tim Peterson [11:23]
Okay. Contact me at 1:00 P.M. with a progress report. I'll decide then if I need to call in another crew for the afternoon job.

SEND

Type your message...

151 What type of business does Ms. Ray work for?
(A) A real estate agency
(B) A furniture store
(C) A moving company
(D) A truck rental service

152 At 11:12, what does Mr. Peterson mean when he says "Is that all"?
(A) He wants to know the address of a house.
(B) He thinks the employees are working slowly.
(C) He is surprised because the price is very cheap.
(D) He wants to confirm that everything is loaded on the truck.

Questions 153-154 refer to the following letter.

Rutherford Eye Clinic
54 Rutherford Avenue
Los Angeles, California

14 March

Katrina Serova
123 Colonel Lane
Los Angeles, California

Dear Ms. Serova,

It is important to us here at Rutherford Eye Clinic that all our customers receive advanced notice of changes to our policies. As of August 1st, all routine yearly eye exams will no longer be covered by most major insurance providers. To help offset the cost, we are reducing our fees by $15 per exam. Please see the enclosed list of affected insurance providers.

In some select cases, we are willing to provide eye exams to children free of charge should your family have a history of prior exams with us. Please contact our billing manager Maggie Wilson at 445-987-0023 to inquire about this service or if you have any questions.

Sincerely,
Nadia Fortuni
Dr. Nadia Fortuni

153 Why was the letter sent to Ms. Serova?
(A) To announce a billing change
(B) To advertise a new service
(C) To confirm an appointment
(D) To inform of a missed exam

154 What is indicated about Rutherford Eye Clinic?
(A) It wants to hire new staff members.
(B) It has extended its hours of operation.
(C) It caters to clients from all around the world.
(D) It will offer free exams to certain customers.

Questions 155-157 refer to the following article.

Westpoint Shopping Mall to Begin Construction

By Melanie Rosenberg, Staff Writer

March 23 -- Yesterday, in a press conference at Mayor Zanga's office downtown, the mayor announced the city's approval of development plans for a new shopping mall. According to the mayor, Westpoint Shopping Mall will be located at Park Road and Wilson Street. ----[1]----

The shopping mall is a joint project between the City of Forks and Windsor Partners, a private development corporation. The mall will include over 200 hundred new stores, 55 restaurants, and a department store. ----[2]---- Windsor Partners will be in charge of executing construction and overseeing initial operations.

"The City of Forks has never had a major shopping center," Mr. Johnson of Windsor Partners said in an interview. "By building this state of the art facility, the people of Forks will see an increase in jobs and tourism." ----[3]----

Many retailers have already signed contracts with Windsor Partners to reserve store space in the mall. However, some small business owners have expressed worry that they will lose business once the shopping mall opens. ----[4]---- "My store has been in business for two generations," Michelle Stevens of Shoe Blitz said. "My customers are loyal, but I won't be able to compete with shopping mall prices."

155 What does Windsor Partners hope to attract to Forks?
(A) Foreign students
(B) A supermarket
(C) More tourists
(D) New small businesses

156 Who most likely is Michelle Stevens?
(A) A newspaper reporter
(B) A retail store owner
(C) A city official
(D) A property developer

157 In which of the positions market [1], [2], [3], and [4] does the following sentence best belong?

"Last year, a fire consumed the auto factory located there, leaving the site open to new development."

(A) [1]
(B) [2]
(C) [3]
(D) [4]

Questions 158-160 refer to the following information.

Simone Decourte
Kites at Sunset
Mobile Installation, painted sheet metal and rods
1984

Kites at Sunset is one of the most popular mobile installations by Simone Decourte. Decourte revolutionized mobile art in the 1970s by including portable motors to create movement. *Kites at Sunset* is part of a larger series constructed by Decourte between 1970 to 1988. It has been featured in The Museum of Abstract Art in Milan, The Contemporary Art Gallery in New York City, and The New Art Movement Museum in London. Decourte originally donated the piece to the University of Montenegro. It remained there for ten years before being acquired by Maxwell George of the Wilson Fine Art Museum where it has remained as part of our permanent collection. Before her death, Decourte said *Kites at Sunset* was her "most vibrant piece ever created."

158 How does the information describe Simone Decourte?

(A) She was attentive to details.
(B) She created a lot of art work.
(C) She was an innovative artist.
(D) She worked for the poor.

159 Where is the information posted?

(A) At the Museum of Abstract Art
(B) At the Wilson Fine Art Museum
(C) At the Contemporary Art Gallery
(D) At the New Art Movement Museum

160 What is NOT stated about *Kites at Sunset*?

(A) The artist regarded it as one of her best works.
(B) It has traveled to several places.
(C) It was owned by a university.
(D) It took almost two decades to complete the piece.

Questions 161-163 refer to the following e-mail.

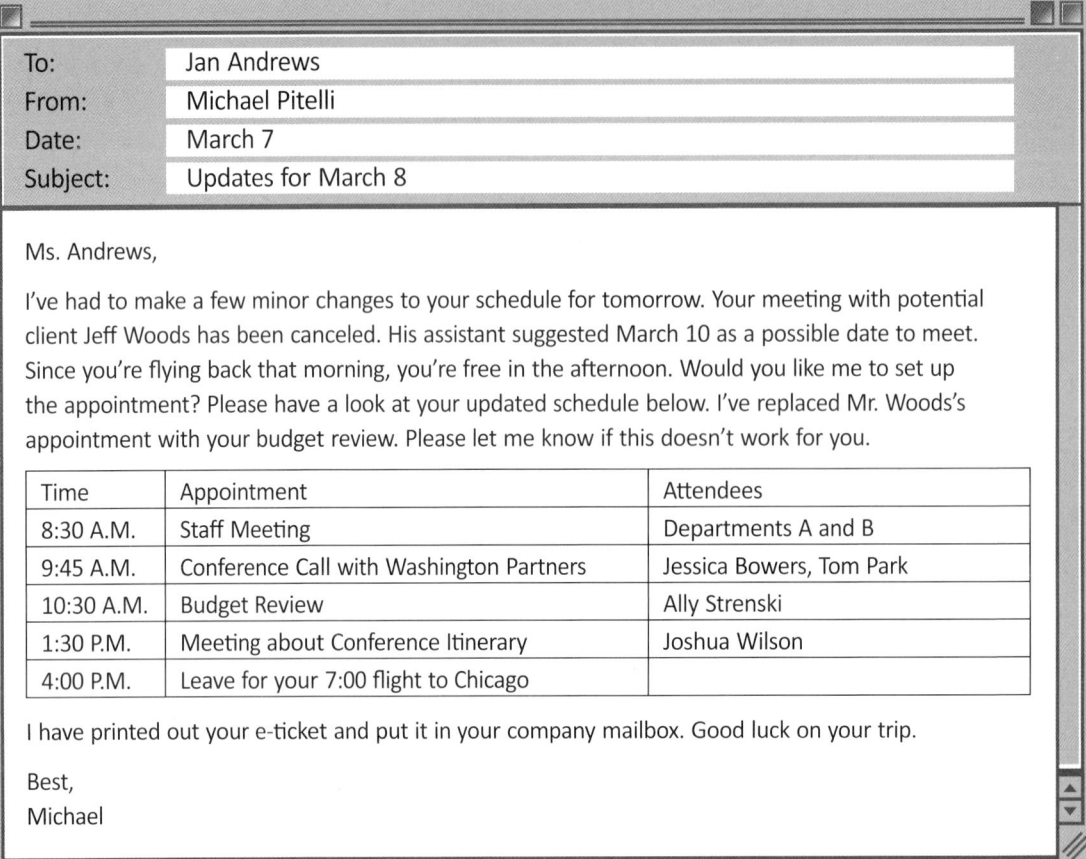

To: Jan Andrews
From: Michael Pitelli
Date: March 7
Subject: Updates for March 8

Ms. Andrews,

I've had to make a few minor changes to your schedule for tomorrow. Your meeting with potential client Jeff Woods has been canceled. His assistant suggested March 10 as a possible date to meet. Since you're flying back that morning, you're free in the afternoon. Would you like me to set up the appointment? Please have a look at your updated schedule below. I've replaced Mr. Woods's appointment with your budget review. Please let me know if this doesn't work for you.

Time	Appointment	Attendees
8:30 A.M.	Staff Meeting	Departments A and B
9:45 A.M.	Conference Call with Washington Partners	Jessica Bowers, Tom Park
10:30 A.M.	Budget Review	Ally Strenski
1:30 P.M.	Meeting about Conference Itinerary	Joshua Wilson
4:00 P.M.	Leave for your 7:00 flight to Chicago	

I have printed out your e-ticket and put it in your company mailbox. Good luck on your trip.

Best,
Michael

161 Why was the e-mail sent?
(A) To cancel an appointment next month
(B) To provide a travel itinerary
(C) To update a daily schedule
(D) To provide documents for a meeting

162 What will happen on March 10?
(A) Mr. Pitelli will fly to Washington.
(B) Ms. Andrews will attend a conference.
(C) Mr. Woods will hold a budget review.
(D) Ms. Andrews will return from Chicago.

163 At what time was Mr. Woods expected?
(A) 8:35 A.M.
(B) 9:45 A.M.
(C) 10:30 A.M.
(D) 1:30 P.M.

Questions 164-167 refer to the following e-mail.

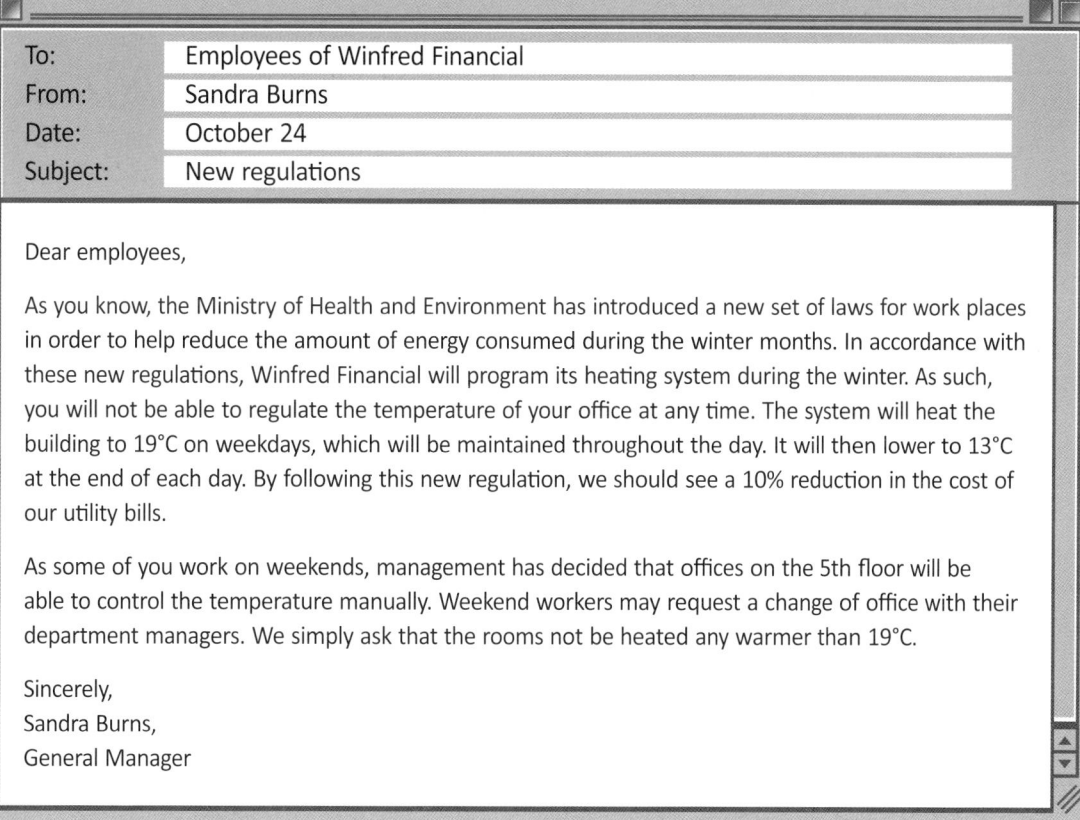

To: Employees of Winfred Financial
From: Sandra Burns
Date: October 24
Subject: New regulations

Dear employees,

As you know, the Ministry of Health and Environment has introduced a new set of laws for work places in order to help reduce the amount of energy consumed during the winter months. In accordance with these new regulations, Winfred Financial will program its heating system during the winter. As such, you will not be able to regulate the temperature of your office at any time. The system will heat the building to 19°C on weekdays, which will be maintained throughout the day. It will then lower to 13°C at the end of each day. By following this new regulation, we should see a 10% reduction in the cost of our utility bills.

As some of you work on weekends, management has decided that offices on the 5th floor will be able to control the temperature manually. Weekend workers may request a change of office with their department managers. We simply ask that the rooms not be heated any warmer than 19°C.

Sincerely,
Sandra Burns,
General Manager

164 What is the purpose of the e-mail?

(A) To announce an upcoming change in the workplace
(B) To inform employees of a scheduled inspection
(C) To encourage employees to choose new office furniture
(D) To offer managers the opportunity to get a promotion

165 The word "maintained" in paragraph 1, line 5, is closest in meaning to

(A) confirmed
(B) repaired
(C) taken
(D) kept

166 What is mentioned as a benefit of the new regulation?

(A) It will improve employee work efficiency.
(B) It can allow the company to hire more workers.
(C) It will help the company save money.
(D) It can be applied to public and private companies.

167 What are employees who work on weekends advised to do?

(A) E-mail Ms. Burns directly
(B) Request office changes
(C) Alter their work schedules
(D) Work at home on weekends

Questions 168-171 refer to the following online chat discussion.

Mary Renold	
Mary Renold (2:02 P.M.)	Hello, Ben. Can you spare a moment? I want to double check an inventory report with you.
Ben Jeffries (2:03 P.M.)	No problem.
Mary Renold (2:04 P.M.)	According to the report, we only have two A75 Canpro notebooks left. We've been selling a lot of that model lately. Should I order more?
Ben Jeffries (2:06 P.M.)	That's not necessary. The new A76 model has just come out, so we're going to carry that model instead. I ordered 50 of the new ones, but they haven't come in yet.
Mary Renold (2:10 P.M.)	Oh, okay. Thanks for explaining that.
Ben Jeffries (2:11 P.M.)	Next week, we'll start displaying them on the shelves, so make sure to print the product information for the displays.
Mary Renold (2:12 P.M.)	Sure. I'll get right on that.

168 At 2:03 P.M., what does Mr. Jeffries most likely mean when he writes, "No Problem"?
(A) He agrees with Ms. Renold's idea.
(B) He is available to answer Ms. Renold's question.
(C) He wants to set up a meeting with Ms. Renold.
(D) He did exactly as Ms. Renold requested.

169 What is mentioned about Mr. Jeffries?
(A) He already ordered some items.
(B) He downloaded some information.
(C) He set up some products today.
(D) He visited a supplier last week.

170 What type of business do Mr. Jeffries and Ms. Renold work for?
(A) A computer repair business
(B) A delivery company
(C) An electronics store
(D) A software developer

171 What will Mr. Jeffries and Ms. Renold do next week?
(A) Renovate a storefront
(B) Hold a sale for new products
(C) Return some obsolete items
(D) Set up some product displays

Questions 172-175 refer to the following article.

June 15 -- The Walter Horman Estate, the home of deceased millionaire Walter Horman, was recently purchased by the City of Rogerton. According to Malika Trenton, director of the Rogerton Historical Society, the estate will undergo light renovations and restorations before being turned into a local museum. --[1]-- According to Trenton, "The Horman family has included all of the original decorations and furnishings for visitors to enjoy."

Over the last several decades, the Walter Horman Estate has been unoccupied. Instead, the property was available for private party rentals and weddings. Some major film companies have even shot scenes at the estate. However, the cost of keeping the grounds in good condition proved to be too much for the family. --[2]-- Stephen Horman, grandson of the late Walter Horman, said, "It was a tough choice to make. The estate has been in our family for generations, but selling it was the best way to ensure its upkeep." The rest of the Horman family has expressed satisfaction that the estate will be turned into a museum. --[3]--

The Rogerton Historical Society intends to develop guided tours of the estate rooms, while still providing access to the gardens for private parties. Visitors to the estate can learn the history of the Horman family from its early immigrant beginning to its rise in society as the owner of one of the first food processing companies in the country. --[4]-- Tours are expected to begin next spring. Anyone interested in purchasing passes or learning about the estate's history can visit www.walterhormanestate.com/info.

172 What is suggested about the Walter Horman Estate?

(A) It was built by Walter Horman's father.
(B) It is expensive to reserve for parties.
(C) It will have its appliances upgraded.
(D) It includes the original furniture.

173 According to the article, what was difficult for the Horman family?

(A) Turning the property into a park
(B) Maintaining the estate
(C) Finding furniture for the rooms
(D) Locating a suitable buyer

174 According to the article, what will remain the same about the estate?

(A) It will be owned by the Horman family.
(B) Its exterior walls will be used for security.
(C) Its buildings will serve as guest houses.
(D) Its outdoor property will be available for rent.

175 In which of the positions marked [1],[2],[3], and [4] does the following sentence best belonging?

"They are pleased the memory of Walter Horman will be preserved."

(A) [1]   (B) [2]
(C) [3]   (D) [4]

Questions 176-180 refer to the following e-mails.

To:	samadams@adamsroofing.com
From:	ginachoi@homeimprovementmonthly.com
Date:	January 3
Subject:	Home Improvement Monthly

Dear Mr. Adams,

As a special New Year promotion, Home Improvement Monthly will be offering discounted prices for new advertisers in our magazine. Home Improvement Monthly has a readership of over 20,000 print subscriptions. Your advertisement will reach each subscriber in print as well as our many online subscribers. With our services, you can increase your business!

This offer is valid until March 1st. Our price packages are outlined below, and our designers are ready to create color advertisements according to your specifications. To purchase any of our packages, please reply by e-mail or visit us at www.homeimprovementmonthly.com/advertisments/orders.

Package	Advertisement Format	Monthly Price
1	One full-page print ad plus banner website ad	$300
2	One half-page print ad plus half-banner website ad	$275
3	One half-page print ad plus corner website ad	$250
4	One quarter-page print ad plus corner website ad	$225

Sincerely,
Gina Choi
Advertising Coordinator
Home Improvement Monthly

To:	ginachoi@homeimprovementmonthly.com
From:	samadams@adamsroofing.com
Date:	January 5
Subject: Re:	Home Improvement Monthly

Dear Ms. Choi,

Thank you for e-mailing me about your promotion. My business partner and I are interested in placing an ad in your magazine. However, I have some questions about your quarter-page print ad. I've purchased a copy of your magazine and looked at the advertisements. I noticed that some are in the front of the magazine and some are in the back. I'm wondering what determines the location of the ad? Do we need to pay additional fees to have our ad located in the front?

Thank you in advance for answering these questions.

Sincerely,
Sam Adams
Co-owner
Adams Roofing

176 Why did Ms. Choi e-mail Mr. Adams?

(A) To announce a new advertising opportunity
(B) To offer a promotional discount on subscriptions
(C) To encourage him to hire a marketing agency
(D) To inform him of a change in a contract

177 What is suggested about Home Improvement Monthly?

(A) Some of its issues were delivered late.
(B) Its advertisers do not pay for subscriptions.
(C) It will put out two issues every month starting next year.
(D) Some of its subscribers only pay for the website.

178 What is mentioned about Home Improvement Monthly's designers?

(A) They can provide custom work.
(B) They require additional fees.
(C) They also design the company website.
(D) They are unavailable until March.

179 In the second e-mail, the word "placing" in paragraph 1, line 2, is closest in meaning to

(A) hiring
(B) putting
(C) assigning
(D) calculating

180 What package does Mr. Adams most likely want?

(A) Package 1
(B) Package 2
(C) Package 3
(D) Package 4

Questions 181-185 refer to the following e-mails.

To:	mpordeski@mailme.com
From:	imranandal@pearsonmedicalresearch.com
Date:	April 12
Subject:	Pearson Medical Research Position
Attachment:	contract

Dear Ms. Pordeski,

I enjoyed speaking with you during your telephone interview, and I'm delighted to offer you a position on our team as a research assistant. As I'm sure you're aware, you will be working with the top medical researchers in the country using the most advanced equipment. Your education in both biology and engineering will be a great asset during your six-month contract.

As I mentioned to you, our company works jointly with Austin University. Thus, you will need to know your way around both our company headquarters and the laboratories at the university. As such, I would like to arrange an orientation for you and our other new researchers. You mentioned that you're finishing up your final year of your degree, so I'd like to arrange a time that does not interfere with your schedule. Please let me know which days in May you are available.

Please note, this position is an internship. Your wages will be $200 a week and the occasional work expenses will be reimbursed. However, following the six-month period, there will be permanent employment for our top interns. To finalize your acceptance of these terms, please sign and return the attached contract. Andrew Baxter, our human resources manager, will contact you if there are any problems.

Thank you, and I look forward to working with you!

Imran Andal
Lead Researcher
Pearson Medical Research

To:	Intern Group
From:	imranandal@pearsonmedicalresearch.com
Date:	April 24
Subject:	Orientation

Dear Research Interns,

Since most of you are not available at the same time, I'd like to hold two orientations, one on May 11 and the second on May 16. The May 16 orientation is scheduled on a weekend to accommodate the students in the group. However, if you're not a student, you will be expected to attend the May 11 orientation. Both orientations will start at 9 A.M. at our company headquarters. After a tour, we will have lunch at Buffy's Bistro and then make our way over to the university. Please bring photo ID in order to gain admittance to the university labs.

Thank you, and I'm looking forward to meeting you all!

Imran Andal,
Lead Researcher,
Pearson Medical Research

181 Why did Mr. Andal write to Ms. Pordeski?

(A) To negotiate a contract
(B) To invite her to apply for a job
(C) To provide medical assistance
(D) To offer her an internship

182 What document is Ms. Pordeski asked to return?

(A) An employer reference
(B) A signed contract
(C) A program application
(D) A university transcript

183 What is indicated about new staff at Pearson Medical Research?

(A) They may work from home.
(B) Their tax forms must be submitted online.
(C) They will not be paid for their work.
(D) Their performance will be evaluated.

184 Why might Andrew Baxter contact Ms. Pordeski?

(A) To review company regulations
(B) To resolve a contract issue
(C) To ask for additional references
(D) To explain payment procedures

185 When will Ms. Pordeski most likely attend the orientation?

(A) May 11
(B) May 15
(C) May 16
(D) May 19

Questions 186-190 refer to the following webpage and e-mails.

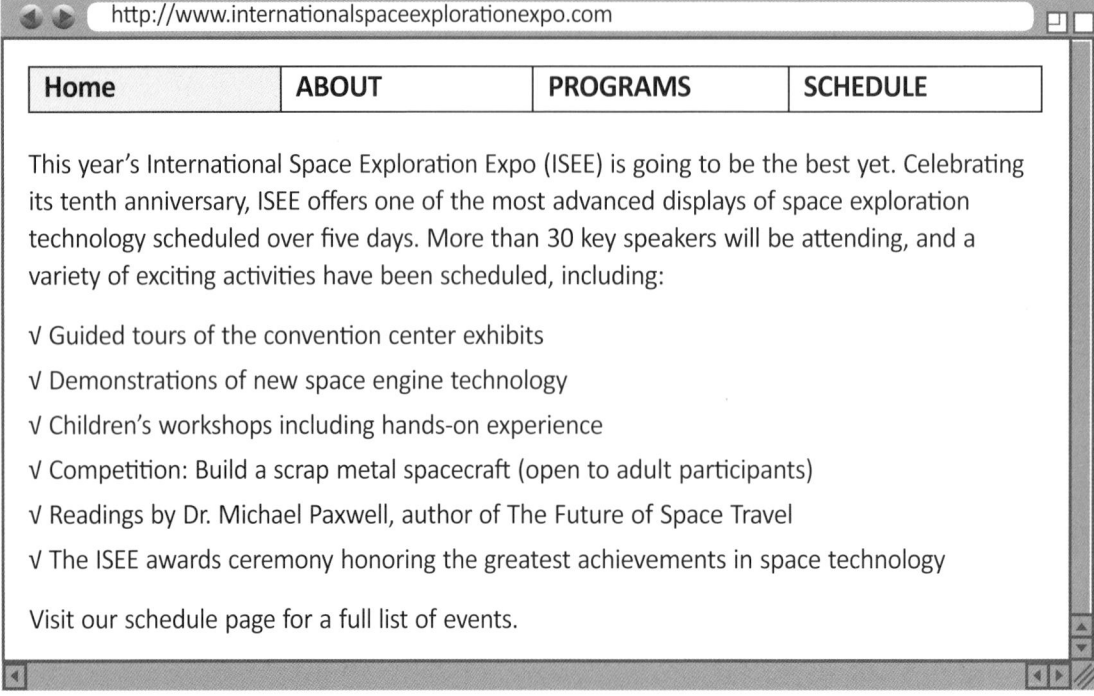

http://www.internationalspaceexplorationexpo.com

| Home | ABOUT | PROGRAMS | SCHEDULE |

This year's International Space Exploration Expo (ISEE) is going to be the best yet. Celebrating its tenth anniversary, ISEE offers one of the most advanced displays of space exploration technology scheduled over five days. More than 30 key speakers will be attending, and a variety of exciting activities have been scheduled, including:

√ Guided tours of the convention center exhibits
√ Demonstrations of new space engine technology
√ Children's workshops including hands-on experience
√ Competition: Build a scrap metal spacecraft (open to adult participants)
√ Readings by Dr. Michael Paxwell, author of The Future of Space Travel
√ The ISEE awards ceremony honoring the greatest achievements in space technology

Visit our schedule page for a full list of events.

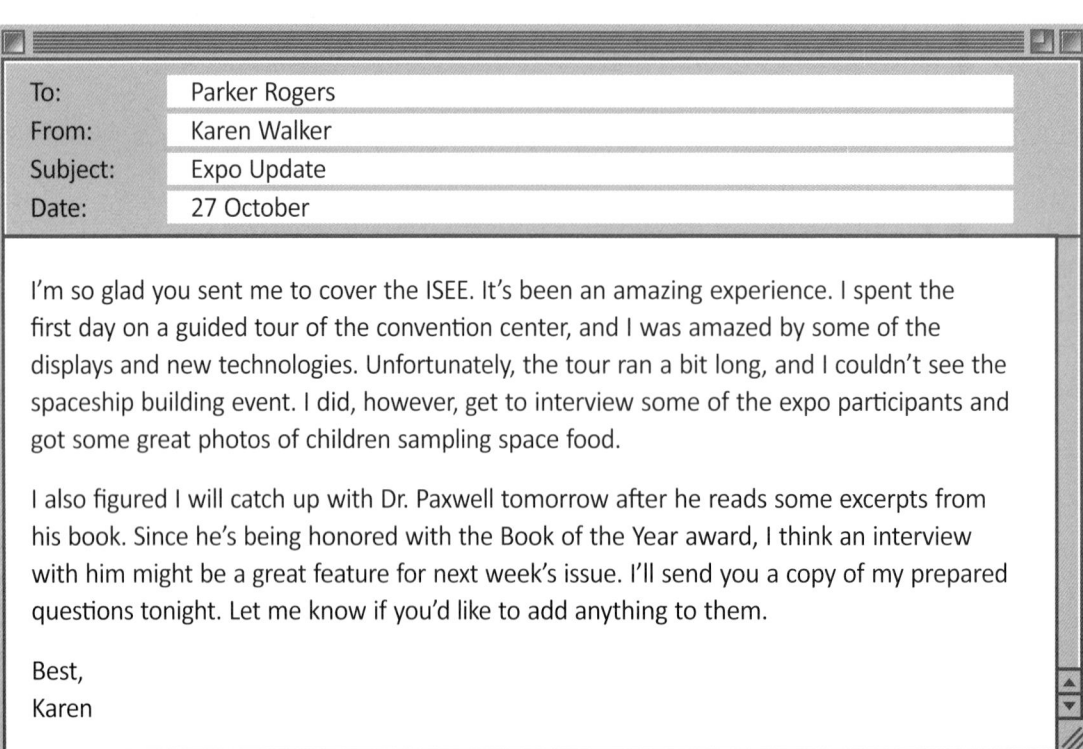

To:	Parker Rogers
From:	Karen Walker
Subject:	Expo Update
Date:	27 October

I'm so glad you sent me to cover the ISEE. It's been an amazing experience. I spent the first day on a guided tour of the convention center, and I was amazed by some of the displays and new technologies. Unfortunately, the tour ran a bit long, and I couldn't see the spaceship building event. I did, however, get to interview some of the expo participants and got some great photos of children sampling space food.

I also figured I will catch up with Dr. Paxwell tomorrow after he reads some excerpts from his book. Since he's being honored with the Book of the Year award, I think an interview with him might be a great feature for next week's issue. I'll send you a copy of my prepared questions tonight. Let me know if you'd like to add anything to them.

Best,
Karen

To: Michael Paxwell
From: Karen Walker
Subject: Follow Up Questions
Date: 29 October

Dear Dr. Paxwell,

It was wonderful to speak with you yesterday. I sent a copy of your interview to my editor. He loved your answers as well as the photos. However, he has a few more questions. I'd like to meet with you tomorrow after your reading. It shouldn't take more than ten or twenty minutes. Please let me know if that works for you.

Best,
Karen Walker

186 What is indicated about ISEE?
(A) It was originally designed for students.
(B) It is held multiple times per year.
(C) It has existed for several years.
(D) It has moved to a new venue.

187 Who most likely is Ms. Walker?
(A) A publisher
(B) An astronaut
(C) A scientist
(D) A journalist

188 According to Ms. Walker, what conference activity was she unable to attend?
(A) A demonstration
(B) A craft competition
(C) A guided tour
(D) A workshop

189 In the first e-mail, the word "figured" in paragraph 2, line 1, is closest in meaning to
(A) decided
(B) involved
(C) represented
(D) performed

190 What is suggested about Dr. Paxwell?
(A) He has won several awards this year.
(B) He will give multiple presentations at the expo.
(C) He is a well-known newspaper editor.
(D) He gives demonstrations every year.

Questions 191-195 refer to the following article, newspaper editorial, and e-mail.

BREDENBURY (June 11) --- Bredenbury town officials sat down today to discuss the fate of the Mossomin Bridge which has been in need of major repairs for years. Today's meeting was the first of several expected talks on the subject. Although an extensive restoration is one option, several complications may compel the town to demolish the structure.

"The cost to restore the bridge will be too great," said town planner Ilkay Tidsale. "The only financially feasible option I can see is replacing the structure."

According to Malcolm Vonda, a well-known structural engineer, traffic flow must also be taken into consideration. "Highway 209 will soon have two additional lanes; making it a four-lane highway. The Mossomin Bridge cannot accommodate such a huge increase in the number of vehicles," Vonda says. "I see no other alternative but to build a bigger, modern structure."

The town council would like input from residents on this issue as well. Anyone wishing to share their views can attend a public forum next Monday at 4:30 at Akber Square, in front of the town hall.

Letters to the Editor

June 12 – Yesterday's article concerning the future of the Mossomin Bridge prompted me to write this response. The bridge is more than just a bridge; it is an integral part of Bredenbury's culture. For this reason, the town must keep the structure intact. Plus, considering the high revenues generated annually by tourism industry, the short-term costs needed to restore this landmark will prove to be beneficial in the end.

--Pierre Atherton, founding member of the Bredenbury Preservation Society (BPS)

To:	members@bredenburypressoc.org
From:	isabellecharlebois@bredenburypressoc.org
Date:	June 23
Subject:	update on Mossomin Bridge

Dear BPS Members,

Congratulations! Thanks to our organization's undeniably strong presence at the town council event, combined with the countless e-mails, letters, and calls to the members of town council, it appears that the bridge is safe from demolition. According to an article in today's Bredenbury Herald, the town has decided to relocate Mossomin Bridge to the south end of the town where only pedestrians will be allowed to use it. The bridge will not be open to motorized vehicles.

All of you should feel proud for speaking out and expressing your concerns last Monday. Your actions definitely influenced the town's decision. Great work!

Thank you once again,

Isabelle Charlebois, President
Bredenbury Preservation Society

191 In the article, what is indicated about the town of Bredenbury?
(A) It will increase its yearly budget.
(B) It is going to upgrade a road.
(C) It is enforcing local parking laws.
(D) It will offer special tours to attract tourists.

192 What is NOT implied about Mr. Atherton?
(A) He works with Mr. Vonda.
(B) He disagrees with Ms. Tisdale.
(C) He read the June 11 newspaper article.
(D) He values a town landmark.

193 In the e-mail, the word "countless" in paragraph 1, line 2, is closest in meaning to
(A) unreported
(B) registered
(C) numerous
(D) ambiguous

194 Why does Ms. Charlebois congratulate BPS members?
(A) They helped influence a town decision.
(B) They elected a new vice-president.
(C) They were the subject of a front-page news story.
(D) They raised additional funds for town projects.

195 What is suggested about BPS members?
(A) They helped repair a structure.
(B) Many of them spoke out at Akber Square.
(C) Many of them reside in the south end.
(D) They meet on the first Monday of every month.

Questions 196-200 refer to the following webpage, receipt, and review.

http://www.grandcanyonexploreadventure.com

| Home | Tours | Reservations | Customer Service |

For over twenty years, our experienced pilots have been conducting spectacular, one of a kind sightseeing tours of the incredible Grand Canyon. Our trips are available for groups of up to six passengers and can be conducted in English, French, Spanish, and Chinese. Take a look at our trip itineraries below and then visit our reservations page for more information about pricing.

• Grand Canyon Helicopter Tour – Available every day from 14:30 P.M. – 15:30 P.M. Spend your afternoon flying over the magnificent Grand Canyon in a helicopter. You will see amazing views of the Hoover Dam, Lake Mead, and the surrounding desert.

• Grand Canyon Helicopter Tour & Lunch – Available every day from 11:30 A.M. – 15:00 P.M. See all the incredible aerial sights listed in the Grand Canyon Helicopter Tour. Following your flight, you will descend 4,000 feet to the canyon floor and enjoy a picnic lunch served on the shore of the Colorado River.

• Ultimate Grand Canyon Tour Package – Available every day from 11:30 A.M. – 18:00 P.M. Enjoy all the benefits of our other packages, including an aerial tour and a picnic lunch. Following lunch, you can explore the historical Native American lands before returning to your helicopter for a second flight to watch the beautiful sunset. Join us for a complimentary steak dinner at the Explore and Adventure Lodge.

---

http://www.grandcanyonexploreadventure.com/reservations/customerreceipt

Customer Reservation Receipt

Date of purchase:	August 3
Customer name:	June Thompson
Reference number:	877573999

Reservation Details	No. of Passengers	Payment Total
Ultimate Grand Canyon Tour Package (August 27 departure)	6 x $80	$480

Payment Method:	Credit Card
Card Number:	111222- 359229
Cardholder's Name:	June Thompson
Card Expiry Date:	07/20

Please retain a copy of this receipt for your records. We recommend that you print a copy and bring it with you on the day of your tour. Furthermore, we recommend that you arrive one hour in advance of your departure time in order to be briefed on all safety precautions.

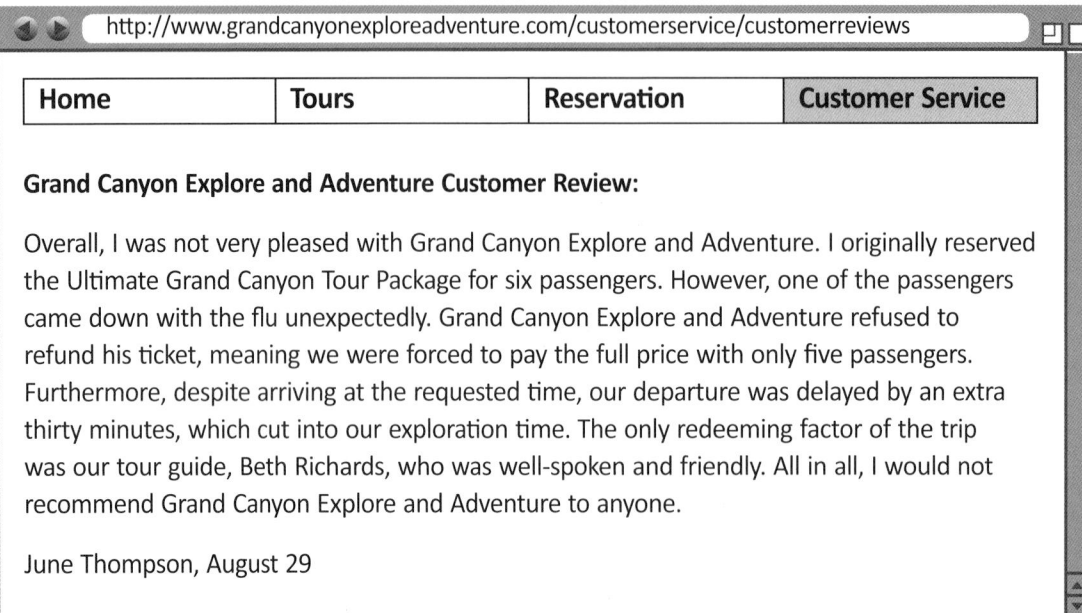

Grand Canyon Explore and Adventure Customer Review:

Overall, I was not very pleased with Grand Canyon Explore and Adventure. I originally reserved the Ultimate Grand Canyon Tour Package for six passengers. However, one of the passengers came down with the flu unexpectedly. Grand Canyon Explore and Adventure refused to refund his ticket, meaning we were forced to pay the full price with only five passengers. Furthermore, despite arriving at the requested time, our departure was delayed by an extra thirty minutes, which cut into our exploration time. The only redeeming factor of the trip was our tour guide, Beth Richards, who was well-spoken and friendly. All in all, I would not recommend Grand Canyon Explore and Adventure to anyone.

June Thompson, August 29

196 What is true about the Grand Canyon Helicopter Tour & Lunch Package?

(A) It is designed for large groups.
(B) It includes lunch in a restaurant.
(C) It is the most frequently purchased tour.
(D) It brings the guests over the Hoover Dam and Lake Mead.

197 What time and day must Ms. Thompson's group arrive for their tour?

(A) At 10:30 A.M. on August 3
(B) At 11:30 A.M. on August 3
(C) At 10:30 A.M. on August 27
(D) At 14:30 P.M. on August 27

198 What does Grand Canyon Explore and Adventure recommend Ms. Thompson to do?

(A) Write a review on their website
(B) Pay via bank transfer
(C) Bring some food with them
(D) Save a copy of her receipt

199 What is suggested about Ms. Thompson's tour?

(A) Ms. Thompson paid for it in cash.
(B) It featured a kayak tour along a river.
(C) The guide was rude and unprofessional.
(D) It concluded with a free meal.

200 According to Ms. Thompson, how much should her group have been charged?

(A) $80
(B) $350
(C) $400
(D) $450

This is the end of the test. You may review Part 5, 6, and 7 if you finish the test early.

ANSWERS

ACTUAL TEST 2

101. (B)	121. (B)	141. (A)	161. (C)	181. (D)
102. (A)	122. (B)	142. (C)	162. (D)	182. (B)
103. (C)	123. (C)	143. (C)	163. (C)	183. (D)
104. (A)	124. (C)	144. (D)	164. (A)	184. (B)
105. (D)	125. (A)	145. (B)	165. (D)	185. (C)
106. (B)	126. (A)	146. (C)	166. (C)	186. (C)
107. (C)	127. (C)	147. (A)	167. (B)	187. (D)
108. (C)	128. (A)	148. (D)	168. (B)	188. (B)
109. (C)	129. (A)	149. (D)	169. (A)	189. (A)
110. (B)	130. (D)	150. (B)	170. (C)	190. (B)
111. (D)	131. (C)	151. (C)	171. (D)	191. (B)
112. (B)	132. (D)	152. (B)	172. (D)	192. (A)
113. (B)	133. (A)	153. (A)	173. (B)	193. (C)
114. (A)	134. (A)	154. (D)	174. (D)	194. (A)
115. (B)	135. (A)	155. (C)	175. (C)	195. (B)
116. (B)	136. (D)	156. (B)	176. (A)	196. (D)
117. (D)	137. (B)	157. (A)	177. (D)	197. (C)
118. (B)	138. (C)	158. (C)	178. (A)	198. (D)
119. (C)	139. (D)	159. (B)	179. (B)	199. (D)
120. (A)	140. (C)	160. (D)	180. (D)	200. (C)

ACTUAL TEST 3

a b **c**
100 200 300

d e f
400 500 600

READING TEST

In the Reading Test, you will read a variety of texts and answer several different types of reading comprehension questions. The entire Reading test will last 75 minutes. There are three parts, and directions are given for each part. You are encouraged to answer as many questions as possible within the time allowed.

You must mark your answers on the separate answer sheet. Do not write your answers in your test book.

PART 5

Directions: A word or phrase is missing in each of the sentences below. Four answer choices are given below each sentence. Select the best answer to complete the sentence. Then mark the letter (A), (B), (C), or (D) on your answer sheet.

---

101 The ------- of additional city councilors will take place at the beginning of next year.

(A) appoint
(B) appoints
(C) appointed
(D) appointment

102 The president of Northern Star Footwear stated that ------ is drafting a proposal for a business merger.

(A) him
(B) he
(C) his
(D) himself

103 Ms. Wilson should update her itinerary before she ------- for her trip overseas.

(A) will leave
(B) leaves
(C) leaving
(D) left

104 According to the report, the recent ------ with the city mayor's office did not progress favorably.

(A) negotiator
(B) negotiations
(C) negotiated
(D) negotiates

105 Several of the candidates were given interviews, but only a few of ------- were chosen for the positions.
(A) we
(B) us
(C) our
(D) ourselves

106 The merger was successful because all the partners played a role in ------- planning the deal.
(A) strategy
(B) strategic
(C) strategized
(D) strategically

107 After completing his degree at an American university, Paul Bouchard ------- to Paris to teach at a local school.
(A) visited
(B) returned
(C) occurred
(D) related

108 Please ensure all deliveries are brought to the side ------- of the supermarket.
(A) entrant
(B) entered
(C) entering
(D) entrance

109 The urban planners met several times a week to discuss plans for the upcoming downtown development -------.
(A) statement
(B) permission
(C) project
(D) ability

110 The sales position will be open to new graduates, ------- means applicants must have completed a degree program.
(A) whoever
(B) who
(C) which
(D) whatever

111 Courses at the company ------- to both seasonal hires and long-term employees.
(A) are offered
(B) have offered
(C) an offer
(D) offering

112 The Benson Music School is situated just ---------- the Roland Dental Clinic on Boyd Avenue.
(A) into
(B) over
(C) among
(D) past

113 Following a mandatory probationary period, full-time employees are ------- to receive benefits.
(A) beneficial
(B) eligible
(C) convenient
(D) relevant

114 The Weston Grant ------- outstanding research conducted in the science and technology field.
(A) recognizes
(B) assumes
(C) reassures
(D) moderates

GO ON TO THE NEXT PAGE

115 Every staff member is given an employee handbook so they can ------- remind themselves of procedures.
(A) consecutively
(B) standardly
(C) namely
(D) easily

116 Sanford Shoes is the most popular outlet in the city because its products are always durable, ------- priced, and fashionable.
(A) reason
(B) reasoning
(C) reasonable
(D) reasonably

117 All staff at Brennan's are ------------ to discuss your home decorating needs either in person or over the phone.
(A) delighting
(B) delighted
(C) delights
(D) delight

118 Rose Textile Manufacturers uses the ------- latest manufacturing equipment and materials.
(A) so
(B) more
(C) very
(D) much

119 All Libby brand refrigerators come with a two-year guarantee -------- stated otherwise.
(A) whereas
(B) below
(C) neither
(D) unless

120 The community thanks you for your ------- in keeping Acorn Valley Apartments clean and safe.
(A) participant
(B) participation
(C) participate
(D) participated

121 The interest rates were a key ------- in the CEO's decision to switch to the Emerald Bank.
(A) factor
(B) position
(C) instructor
(D) composition

122 The health inspector will arrive at an unforeseen date ------- ensure the conditions of the inspection are fair.
(A) even if
(B) in order to
(C) after all
(D) given that

123 Peter Nugent's novel was made into an adventure movie two years ago after Winston Studios obtained -------- from Nugent's grandson.
(A) permission
(B) suggestion
(C) comparison
(D) registration

124 The mayor's office has issued a statement ------- the use of tax revenue to repair roads in the coming year.
(A) excluding
(B) during
(C) following
(D) regarding

125 The Delbert Condominium Tower is -------- located within walking distance of two subway stations.

(A) conveniently
(B) consistently
(C) continually
(D) commonly

126 Interns should ------- new applications if they wish to apply for any of the new full-time positions.

(A) reply
(B) submit
(C) vacate
(D) oppose

127 Ms. Houlahan's revised draft of Reynold Manufacturing's mission statement expresses the goals of the company --------.

(A) precise
(B) more precise
(C) preciseness
(D) precisely

128 ------- the park is open during the summer months, the public is restricted from accessing certain areas.

(A) While
(B) When
(C) For
(D) But

129 ------- the education level of Paul Rogers, it is no wonder that he is the highest-paid speaker at the convention.

(A) About
(B) Given
(C) Upon
(D) Since

130 Considering all the hot weather we're having, the number of people using public swimming pools is ---------- to increase.

(A) covered
(B) sought
(C) limited
(D) bound

PART 6

Directions: Read the texts that follow. A word, phrase, or sentence is missing in parts of each text. Four answer choices for each question are given below the text. Select the best answer to complete the text. Then mark the letter (A), (B), (C), or (D) on your answer sheet.

Questions 131-134 refer to the following information.

At Echo Stationery Supplies, we try to ship your orders as quickly as we can. If you have concerns that your shipment has been delayed, please ...**131**... our shipping policies. Our expected delivery times may range from 4 days up to 4 weeks, which depends on the method of shipping customers choose during checkout. ...**132**... We try to ensure our shipping estimates are accurate; however, some orders may take ...**133**... to arrive at your door. If you have found that your order is excessively ...**134**..., do not hesitate to contact us immediately. We promise to look into the problem and let you know the status of your shipment.

131 (A) note
(B) send
(C) prepare
(D) require

132 (A) Returned items will be eligible for exchanges only, not refunds.
(B) Contact our specialists to get an updated list of all of our new products.
(C) An approximate delivery date is indicated on your receipt.
(D) Visit our online feedback section and let us know how well we served you.

133 (A) length
(B) lengthy
(C) longer
(D) longest

134 (A) different
(B) delayed
(C) overpriced
(D) greater

Questions 135-138 refer to the following article.

April 24

After months of discussions, Nackawic Town Council has finally approved an agreement with DRTL Enterprises. Under the terms of the agreement, DRTL ...**135**... the 30-acre lot on the east end of Barrett Street. The detailed proposal calls for the building of both retail shops and offices in the area. Nackawic's mayor, Leona Hovey, is optimistic that the project will bring ...**136**... benefits to the town and surrounding areas. "It is expected to create 300 full-time jobs," says Hovey. "For a while, I felt the ongoing postponements would force us to cancel the project all together." ...**137**... DRTL spokesperson, Jeff Perkins believes the development will take three years to finish. At the same time, he cautions people that there may be more setbacks. "Of course, we provided the town council with our very best ...**138**..., but even so, we have no way of predicting everything that will happen," Perkins said.

135 (A) to develop
(B) will develop
(C) has developed
(D) could have developed

136 (A) economic
(B) unforeseen
(C) environmental
(D) frequent

137 (A) While the town is eager to get moving on this, delays are inevitable for major developments like this.
(B) Local residents, however, have approached us with legitimate concerns about the high noise levels construction will create.
(C) Members of town council are set to vote on four different proposals from well-known architects.
(D) Despite the town's promise to grant the developers a contract, they may now have to look at other options.

138 (A) argument
(B) background
(C) estimate
(D) combination

Questions 139-142 refer to the following article.

Roderick Opera House has announced that it will lengthen its run of Melanie Beck's new musical, The Birth of Jazz. Due to an increase in ...**139**... for tickets, the show will be playing nightly until the end of August. The announcement was unexpected, as the musical received ...**140**... criticism from renowned musical theatre critic Jeffrey O'pry. ...**141**... However, last week the show was sold out three nights in a row. According to representatives of the opera house, the show has been attracting an older crowd who may not normally attend musicals. The new attendees are ...**142**... excited about hearing the great jazz numbers reinvented by Beck.

139 (A) demand
(B) demanded
(C) demanding
(D) to demand

140 (A) brilliant
(B) deep
(C) harsh
(D) prompt

141 (A) Guests at the musical were mostly from out of town.
(B) The final show will be held on August 24th.
(C) Following the review, ticket sales dropped dramatically.
(D) Similarly, the theater has been suffering for years.

142 (A) apparent
(B) more apparent
(C) apparentness
(D) apparently

Questions 143-146 refer to the following e-mail.

From: Customer Care
To: Paul Kanagawa
Date: October 16
Subject: Welcome to Atlantic Music Trends
Attachment: Form

Dear Mr. Kanagawa,

Thank you very much for subscribing to Atlantic Music Trends! ...**143**... you will have detailed information about upcoming music classes, festivals, and concerts happening all over Canada's Atlantic coast. You can expect your first issue at your door by the 20th. ...**144**... After that, every issue will be sent out during the first week of the month. With this subscription, you will also have unlimited ...**145**... to online videos, song recordings, articles, schedules, and even ticketing information for concerts. All you have to do is log into our website using the user ID and eight-digit passwords listed ...**146**... the bottom line of the attached enrollment form.

Sincerely,
Veronica Van Zeyl
Customer Representative

143 (A) Now
(B) Afterward
(C) Then
(D) Meanwhile

144 (A) Please notify us if it does not arrive by that date.
(B) To subscribe, please phone during regular business hours.
(C) The next festival will take place in Moncton in mid November.
(D) We invite readers to submit reviews of concerts for publication.

145 (A) accessing
(B) accesses
(C) accessed
(D) access

146 (A) for
(B) about
(C) on
(D) at

PART 7

Directions: In this part, you will read a selection of texts, such as magazine and newspaper articles, e-mail, and instant messages. Each text or set of texts is followed by several questions. Select the best answer for each question and mark the letter (A), (B), (C), or (D) on your answer sheet.

Questions 147-148 refer to the following notice.

Jen's Salon and Spa

Holiday Information

- Spa hours will be extended from November 20 to January 20. (Monday – Saturday 10 A.M. to 10 P.M.)
- Please note, the spa will be closed from December 24 – 29.
- As always, cancelations must be made 24 hours in advance to avoid cancelation fees.

147 What is the purpose of the notice?
(A) To advertise a new service
(B) To explain a schedule
(C) To announce a sale
(D) To offer a refund

148 What is stated about cancelations?
(A) The spa requires advance notice of cancelations.
(B) Customers can cancel appointments online.
(C) A service fee is always applied to cancelations.
(D) Holiday appointments cannot be canceled.

Questions 149-150 refer to the following notice.

Notice for Eastpoint Community Residents

As of next month, our weekly community newsletter will be going paperless. In an effort to protect the environment and reduce the amount of paper we use, the newsletter will now be available online only.

Anyone who currently has a small business advertisement in the newsletter is encouraged to contact the newsletter editor for an updated contract at 900-555-3434. The first online newsletter is scheduled to be on www.eastpointcommunity.com/newsletter on November 1st. We hope you enjoy this new convenient way to receive your weekly newsletter.

Sincerely,

Eastpoint Community Newsletter Team

149 What change will be made to the newsletter?

(A) It will merge with another publication.
(B) It will be delivered faster.
(C) It will run less frequently.
(D) It will no longer be printed on paper.

150 According to the notice, why might advertisers contact the editor?

(A) To sign a new contract
(B) To receive a discount
(C) To upgrade a membership
(D) To change a listing

Questions 151-153 refer to the following agenda.

Unpaid Spring Training Session
9:30 A.M. to 4:30 P.M.

9:30 A.M.: Meet and Greet
Meet your managers as well as your fellow new employees. Enjoy coffee and donuts as you watch a short introduction video to the company.

10:30 A.M.: Rules and Procedures
Pick up your employee handbook and review the rules and procedures with the office manager. A short question and answer session will be included.

12:00 P.M.: Lunch Break
A light buffet lunch of sandwiches, salads, and desserts will be catered in the conference room. Vegetarian options will be provided for employees.

1:00 P.M.: Department Shadowing
Employees will visit their respective departments and receive hands-on training from an assigned veteran employee.

3:30 P.M.: Desk Assignments
Employees will be shown to their desks and given an opportunity to set up their company accounts and e-mails. IT will be available for any problems that may arise.

---

151 For whom is the session most likely intended?

(A) Company CEOs
(B) Computer technicians
(C) New office employees
(D) Department transfers

152 What portion of the session involves IT specialists?

(A) Meet and Greet
(B) Rules and Procedures
(C) Department Shadowing
(D) Desk Assignments

153 What is NOT indicated about the session?

(A) It is an unpaid event.
(B) It lasts for one work day.
(C) It is run by the HR director.
(D) It includes refreshments.

Questions 154-157 refer to the following report.

Rengrew Bedding

Weekly Status Report: September 5-9
Prepared by: Alexander Corbin, Project Coordinator

Accomplished this Week:

- Got in touch with four manufacturers in Mexico who currently produce bedding products. ---[1]--- E-mailed them design specifications along with questions about production pricing, turnaround time, fabric availability, and shipping costs.

- According to the replies, P&M Textiles appears to be the best candidate. ---[2]--- Additionally, Sammy Ruiz, a client services manager, e-mailed me promptly. Her responses to my questions were very detailed and professional. I believe she would ensure this transition is both smooth and efficient.

- The other three companies either did not have access to our preferred fabrics or they could not meet our supply demand. ---[3]--- As a result, we will no longer be able to consider them.

Plans for Next Week:

- Contact P&M Textiles to set up a conference call about payment and shipping terms. ---[4]---

- Review final designs for all products and request revisions if need be. Meet with the design team to discuss any changes.

---

154 What is suggested about Rengrew Bedding?

(A) It has just hired a new manager.
(B) It is a brand new company in Mexico.
(C) It has its own factories on site.
(D) It is getting ready to launch new products.

155 According to the report, what did Mr. Corbin do during the week of September 5?

(A) Finalized some design information
(B) Assessed potential business partners
(C) Visited a manufacturer in person
(D) Requested a payment be delayed

156 What is mentioned about Ms. Ruiz?

(A) She is new to P&M Textiles.
(B) She suggested some changes.
(C) She contacted some businesses.
(D) She is easy to work with.

157 In which of the positions marked [1], [2], [3], and [4] does the following sentence best belong?

"It is located further south than most companies, but it has the capacity to meet our supply needs."

(A) [1]
(B) [2]
(C) [3]
(D) [4]

Questions 158-159 refer to the following form.

Grand Avenue Hotel: Banquet Services

Thank you for choosing Grand Avenue Hotel for your banquet. Please fill out the information below. One of our guest services representatives will contact you to confirm your reservation and request payment information.

Reservation Name: _____   Event Date: _____
E-mail: _____   Business Phone: _____
Personal Phone: _____

Room Preference:
[ ] Diamond Room (up to 100 guests) [ ] Rose Room (up to 150 guests)
[ ] Starlight Room (up to 200 guests)

Requested Layout:
[ ] Dinner (round tables and chairs) [ ] Dinner and Dance (tables and a dance floor)
[ ] Dinner and Speech (tables and a stage) [ ] Other : _____

Food and Beverages:
[ ] Full-Service Buffet and Dessert Bar [ ] Three-Course Catered Dinner

AV Equipment Required: [ ] Yes [ ] No Explain: _____
Hotel Accommodation for Guests: [ ] Yes [ ] No Number of Rooms: _____

---

158 According to the form, what will Grand Avenue Hotel staff do?

(A) E-mail brochures with room photos
(B) Assist customers with set up and clean up
(C) Offer free accommodation vouchers to guests
(D) Contact customers about payment information

159 What is implied about Grand Avenue Hotel's banquet services?

(A) It requires payment for the use of audio-visual equipment.
(B) It will arrange the room to suit the event.
(C) It provides discounted hotel rooms to banquet guests.
(D) It offers free live music for dinner and dance events.

Questions 160-162 refer to the following job advertisement.

---

https://www.employmentfind.com

Find Employment Online

Build Your Career Today!

The real estate business can be hard when you're working alone. At Team Real Estate, you are not alone! Our large network of real estate agents makes showing and selling properties easy. By sharing information on potential buyers in our database, we sell more properties than any other agency in the country. Our shared commission rates encourage our team members to work together to get the job done.

Complete our new real estate training seminar and apply for your real estate license. If you're successful, you may be offered a full-time contract position with full benefits.

Education and experience will be considered before you are offered a contract. University degrees are a plus, but high school graduates may also apply. Applicants must have access to their own vehicle, as driving to and from local properties is a must.

To apply for this position, please click the button below. You'll need to input your e-mail address, phone number, and upload your resume. Only those selected for interviews will be contacted. Prior to interviews, we recommend that all candidates familiarize themselves with our company policies. Please visit www.teamrealestate.com/careers to learn more about this.

Apply Now

---

160 What duty is suggested as part of the job?

(A) Listing clients on a shared database
(B) Offering advice on upgrading properties
(C) Attracting clients through phone calls
(D) Coordinating a mentorship program

161 According to the advertisement, what is requested for a contract position?

(A) A college diploma
(B) A real estate license
(C) Marketing experience
(D) Employment references

162 According to the advertisement, why should applicants visit the Team Real Estate website?

(A) To learn about Team Real Estate's procedures
(B) To apply for a contract position with benefits
(C) To upload a resume and references
(D) To inquire about the time of a training session

Questions 163-166 refer to the following article.

50 Years of Community Service

March 27 -- Professor Abraham Drew is known in the local community not for his years as a teacher of psychology or for his numerous papers published in academic journals, but for his dedication to community outreach. Fifty years ago, Mr. Drew founded the first after-school program for local children, which has helped numerous children in the city. The program, which started as a baseball camp for troubled boys, has since grown into Homework Helpers for elementary school-aged children, Art on the Street for teenagers, and Give Back, a charity in which individuals and businesses organize food drives for the homeless. "I never thought my after-school program would develop into all these unique programs," Mr. Drew said, "but there was so much community interest. Everywhere, people were looking for a way to help out."

After fifty years of service, Mr. Drew will retire from both his job as a professor and as program coordinator. His grandson, Michael Drew, will retain control of the programs. "I'm very happy to continue what my grandfather started," Michael Drew said. "He's a great man, and the community needs the work he has done."

Mr. Drew's volunteers will host a retirement party to honor him next month at Wilfred Park. The party will include performances by local bands, food prepared by local restaurants, and a small fireworks show. The mayor will present Mr. Drew with a Lifetime Service Achievement Award as thanks for his years of giving back to the community. For details about this event, please visit www.wilfredpark.com/events/april.

163 Why most likely was the article written?
 (A) To celebrate the founding of a city
 (B) To encourage readers to donate to charity
 (C) To announce the closing of a community business
 (D) To highlight the achievements of a local figure

164 The word "retain" in paragraph 2, line 2, is closest in meaning to
 (A) contribute to
 (B) agree with
 (C) remember
 (D) keep

165 What is NOT suggested about Abraham Drew?
 (A) He started a baseball camp for boys.
 (B) He instructs students at a university.
 (C) He will open another school next year.
 (D) He inspired others to do charity work.

166 What is stated about the party at Wilfred Park?
 (A) Local comedy acts will perform.
 (B) The city will host the celebration.
 (C) Participants can attend for a small fee.
 (D) Mr. Drew will be honored with an award.

Questions 167-168 refer to the following text message chain.

Pedro Alando [11:00 A.M.]:
Ms. Wilson, please check your e-mail. I sent you an updated contract.

Tina Wilson [11:02 A.M.]:
Okay, thank you. Has the payment scale been updated as well?

Pedro Alando [11:03 A.M.]:
Certainly. Because you've been with us for longer than a year, you will now be paid $100 dollars for every color photo you take for our magazine instead of $80.

Tina Wilson [11:05 A.M.]:
Excellent. Thank you for clarifying that. I'll have a look at the contract, sign it, and send it back shortly.

Pedro Alando [11:08 A.M.]:
Fantastic. We are very pleased you have decided to work with us for another year.

SEND

---

167 At 11:03 A.M. what does Mr. Alando mean when he writes, "Certainly"?

(A) He will send an e-mail one more time.
(B) He is sure of the success of a plan.
(C) He is willing to share some information.
(D) He made a previously agreed-upon change.

168 Who most likely is Ms. Wilson?

(A) A contract lawyer
(B) A magazine editor
(C) A photographer
(D) A journalist

Questions 169-171 refer to the following e-mail.

To:	Janine Robertson <jrobertson@wetrainyou.com>
From:	Wendal Sparks <wbsparks@consumerconventioncenter.com>
Date:	4 January
Subject:	Annual Small Business Conference

Dear Ms. Robertson,

I was so glad to hear that you'll be participating in our third annual Small Business Conference on February 3. --[1]-- I know this was very last minute, so I really appreciate your enthusiasm about stepping in for Tim Brewers. Your experience heading a small business training company will really interest our participants. --[2]-- We'd especially love it if you could outline some of the first steps a new business must take toward training new employees.

If you would like to offer promotional pamphlets for your business, please send them at least a week prior to your speaking date. Also, please let me know what audio-visual equipment you'll need for your presentation. --[3]-- Additionally, may I use the biography you have on your website as material for our conference program? --[4]--

Thanks again for everything.

Sincerely,
Wendal Sparks
Conference Coordinator

169. Why did Mr. Sparks most likely send the e-mail?
(A) To propose an itinerary change
(B) To ask for an updated schedule
(C) To send a belated invitation
(D) To recognize an offer of acceptance

170. What is suggested about Mr. Brewers?
(A) He attends conferences every year.
(B) He is unable to speak at a conference.
(C) He works as an event coordinator.
(D) He started his own small business.

171. In which of the positions marked [1], [2], [3], and [4] does the following sentence best belong?

"If you'd prefer to use a different text, please e-mail it to me."

(A) [1]
(B) [2]
(C) [3]
(D) [4]

Questions 172-175 refer to the following text message chain.

Jan Swanson   4 September, 2:35
Jonathan, have you sent order #2256 out for delivery?
If not, we need to add another identical set of personalized pens and paper to it.

Jonathan Gruer   4 September, 2:37
The order is still in the storeroom, but it'll take at least two more days to produce the custom pens and paper.

Jan Swanson   4 September, 2:38
Is it possible to get it done sooner? The customer said it's urgent.

Jonathan Gruer   4 September, 2:40
Let's check with someone from manufacturing.

------Rowena MacArthur has been added to the chat-----

Jonathan Gruer   4 September, 2:41
Rowena, do you have time for a rush order? It's a duplicate of order #2256.

Rowena MacArthur   4 September, 2:43
I think I can get it done by tomorrow morning. Is that okay?

Jan Swanson   4 September, 2:44
Yes, that works. Thanks a lot!

---

172 What type of products does the company sell?
(A) Watches
(B) Stationery
(C) Furniture
(D) Electronics

173 Why does Mr. Gruer contact Ms. MacArthur?
(A) To pass on a customer complaint
(B) To find out where a staff meeting will be held
(C) To determine where an order has been shipped to
(D) To inquire about the timeframe for some work

174 What does the customer want to do?
(A) Double an order
(B) Cancel a delivery
(C) Return a damaged item
(D) Update payment information

175 At 2:44, what does Ms. Swanson most likely mean when she writes, "that works"?
(A) She can reschedule some appointments.
(B) She is impressed with a new product.
(C) A deadline will be acceptable for a customer.
(D) Some new items will be advertised online.

Questions 176-180 refer to the following e-mails.

To:	msimpson@tristarinternational.com
From:	bookings@stonewallhotel.com
Date:	May 17
Subject:	Booking CV1124

Dear Ms. Simpson,

Thank you for selecting Stonewall Hotel for your company's annual workshop. As you indicated on your online reservation, twelve king-sized ocean view suites have been booked for your group. Since the purpose of your visit is to conduct a business workshop, I have also reserved our executive lounge and conference room at no extra charge.

According to your online reservation, your check-in date will be August 5th and your check-out will be August 8th. A charge of $109 dollars for each room per night will be added to your final bill. Your reservation number is CV1124. Please ensure you record this number as you will need it should you request any changes to your reservation.

As you know, Stonewall Hotel includes many additional features and activities. If your group wish to take a complimentary surfing lesson, I suggest reserving a spot in advance. Furthermore, we offer complimentary breakfasts, room service packages, and have just opened up Stonewall Grill, a brand new steak restaurant located next to the lobby.

Thank you for choosing Stonewall Hotel. We look forward to serving you.

Booking Services, Stonewall Hotel

To:	bookings@stonewallhotel.com
From:	msimpson@tristarinternational.com
Date:	May 19
Subject: Re:	Booking CV1124

Dear booking services staff,

I am writing to let you know that there were a few errors with my reservation. My reservation number is CV1124. I indicated ten junior-sized suites when I reserved online, but your e-mail says something different. Additionally, I also paid for a catered lunch during my group's hiking trip on August 6th, but that was not mentioned in your e-mail. Please make sure this service has been booked in addition to updating the correct room size. I would appreciate it if you notified me about this issue as soon as possible.

Thank you for your assistance.

Sincerely,
Margo Simpson
Office of the CEO
Tristar International

176. What is the purpose of the first e-mail?
    (A) To confirm a group reservation
    (B) To inform of a new policy
    (C) To assist in making a reservation
    (D) To provide a free upgrade

177. What is suggested about Stonewall's surfing lessons?
    (A) They are available only in the mornings.
    (B) They are a new service.
    (C) They are being offered temporarily.
    (D) They are a popular feature.

178. What information in the hotel's records is missing?
    (A) The lounge has been reserved.
    (B) The group will arrive on August 5.
    (C) A catering service is booked.
    (D) The room bill has been prepaid.

179. What can be inferred about the group from Tristar International?
    (A) It consists of twelve members.
    (B) It will go hiking on the second day of the workshop.
    (C) It will have dinner at the Stonewall Grill.
    (D) It will arrive a day later than the reservation states.

180. In the second e-mail, the word "issue" in paragraph 2, line 6, is closest in meaning to
    (A) alteration
    (B) selection
    (C) price
    (D) problem

Questions 181-185 refer to the following notice and calendar.

Heber Birdwatching Club

April 2 -- The Northville Recreation Board recently announced the creation of the Heber Park Birdwatching Club at Heber Wildlife Park. The birdwatching club will meet from Friday through Sunday, from 1 P.M. until 3 P.M. The club meetings will run all summer long and will feature a number of lookout sites located on the Heber Trails. Each participant should dress appropriately for hiking on the trails and bring a supply of drinking water. Cameras are allowed for participants who want to photograph the numerous bird species located in Heber Wildlife Park. Up to ten members may join the club, and those interested can sign up with the club coordinator, Mindy Beckett (334-998-0034).

June Weekend Activities at Heber Wildlife Park

- **Friday**
  - 12:00 P.M. Children's Picnic (Camp and Recreation Park)
  - 2:00 P.M. Heber Birdwatching Club (Squirrel Trail)
  - 4:00 P.M. T&V Industries Weekly Baseball Game (Diamond)

- **Saturday**
  - 2:00 P.M. Heber Birdwatching Club (Squirrel Trail)
  - 4:00 P.M. Barbecue Madness (East Pavilion on June 10th and 24th only)

- **Sunday**
  - 10:00 A.M. Nature Watercolor Painting (Gallery Building, $15 per person)
  - 2:00 P.M. Heber Birdwatching Club (Squirrel Trail)
  - 4:00 P.M. Level A Soccer (Soccer field)
  - 6:00 P.M. Music at the Park (West Pavilion)

For more information on any of the above events, please visit www.heberwildlifepark.com or call 556-332-0989.

181 What is the purpose of the notice?

(A) To inform of a new activity at Heber Wildlife Park
(B) To announce a new coordinator for the Heber Birdwatching Club
(C) To apologize for the cancelation of an event at Heber Wildlife Park
(D) To advertise a new position at the Northville Recreation Board

182 In the notice, the word "run" in paragraph 1, line 3, is closest in meaning to

(A) jog
(B) continue
(C) roam
(D) grow

183 What is suggested about the birdwatching club in June?

(A) It has 12 members.
(B) It requires participants to bring cameras.
(C) Its meeting time has been changed.
(D) Its coordinator will be absent.

184 What activity will only occur twice in June?

(A) T&V Industries Baseball
(B) Barbecue Madness
(C) Nature Watercolor Painting
(D) Music at the Park

185 What is indicated about Heber Wildlife Park?

(A) Its pavilions have all been upgraded.
(B) Its campground is open all year round.
(C) It includes a lake and a water fountain.
(D) It has special programs for children.

Questions 186-190 refer to the following advertisement, e-mail, and website feedback.

Toronto Tours

★★★★★
Toronto, Ontario

To celebrate its first year of business, Toronto Tours is offering a special 20% discount on Culture of Toronto tours booked between April 5 and May 5. This is our most popular tour and is offered every Friday. The following is breakdown of our standard itinerary.

▶ The Royal Ontario Museum: Start at the famous Royal Ontario Museum. Enjoy some of the most beautiful art in the world in the ROM's many modern galleries. See the latest archeological discoveries on display and a number of large dinosaur species. April's special exhibit: 18th Century Maps.

▶ The Hockey Hall of Fame: Head over to the Hockey Hall of Fame and see Canada's greatest hockey legends remembered in numerous video exhibits. Learn the history of Canada's favorite sport, and view memorabilia that belonged to players of the past.

▶ The Danforth Festival: Conclude your tour at the Danforth Festival. Enjoy a taste of Greek culture at this energetic street party. Sample food from Toronto's many Greek restaurants while you enjoy live music and dancing. (Until April 20)

Note: The final portion of the tour will be subject to changes depending on which festivals are taking place downtown. Additionally, all entrance fees are covered in your package price, but food and beverages costs are extra.

From:	Susan Malek
To:	Samuel Park
Date:	April 10
Re:	Reservation Confirmation

Dear Mr. Park,

Thank you for booking your tour with Toronto Tours. Below is a summary of your tour information. Should you have any questions or concerns, please contact me at 416-888-3232.

Tour name: Culture of Toronto
Tour date: April 12
Starting Time: 9:00 A.M. at Toronto Union Station
Return to Union Station: 11:30 P.M.
Your credit card has been charged: $190.00

Thank you and enjoy your tour!

Best,
Susan Malek
Tour Coordinator

Customer Feedback:

This was my first time using Toronto Tours, and I found the tour to be much more impressive than the sightseeing bus tour I took the last time I visited Toronto. This company sure understands how to treat tourists' interest in the city's unique history and culture. Francis Weltz, our tour guide, was extremely helpful in getting us to and from locations as well as ensuring speedy entry to the listed stops. The only downside of the tour was the rainy weather, which made it hard to enjoy the final stop. As a result, I wish an alternate destination would've been available in the event of poor weather.

Posted by: Samuel Park

186 What is suggested about Toronto Tours?

(A) It operates several tour programs.
(B) It has been open for several years.
(C) It will stop offering summer tours.
(D) It has added a new sightseeing tour.

187 According to the advertisement, what does Toronto Tours offer clients?

(A) Vouchers for food and beverages
(B) Upgraded travel options
(C) Discounts on group packages
(D) Admission fees to museums

188 What is suggested about Mr. Park's tour?

(A) It included return airfare from Greece.
(B) It visited four main stops.
(C) It was purchased at a discount.
(D) It was originally developed for local artists.

189 In the website feedback, the word "treat" in paragraph 1, line 3, is closest in meaning to

(A) serve
(B) increase
(C) decide
(D) ignore

190 What portion of the tour was Mr. Park dissatisfied with?

(A) Seeing off at Union Station
(B) The Royal Ontario Museum
(C) The Hockey Hall of Fame
(D) The Danforth Festival

Questions 191-195 refer to the following schedule, e-mail, and review.

European Manufacturing Commission

4th Annual Convention
Rowensburg Conference Center
Berlin, Germany
Saturday, October 10

Tentative Schedule

Time	Location	
9:00 A.M. - 9:30 A.M.	Greetings and Opening Speech by EMC Chairman Alek Sorvenski in the Cranz Banquet Room	
	Strauss Room	Witman Room
10:00 A.M. - 11:30 A.M.	Textile Factory Management Techniques - Hans Tiskawet	Advanced Coloration and Bleaching Technologies - Michelle Perdeu
1:00 P.M. - 2:30 P.M.	Outsourcing and Overseas Management - Rowena Wentworth	Upgrading and Maintaining Equipment - Spencer Defiore
3:00 P.M. - 4:30 P.M.	Establishing Contacts with International Clothing Distributors - Anita Pitelli	International Shipping Strategies - Thao Lee

- Speakers must confirm their availability with Johanna Swartz (jswartz@emc.com) no later than August 28. Failure to report availability will result in an automatic change of speaker.

- Speakers will be given complimentary accommodation at the Deluxe Grand Hotel for one night. Please fill out the attached form and return it to Berta Joven by September 5. If you are traveling with a colleague or an assistant, you will need to book another room at an additional charge. Please indicate that on the form.

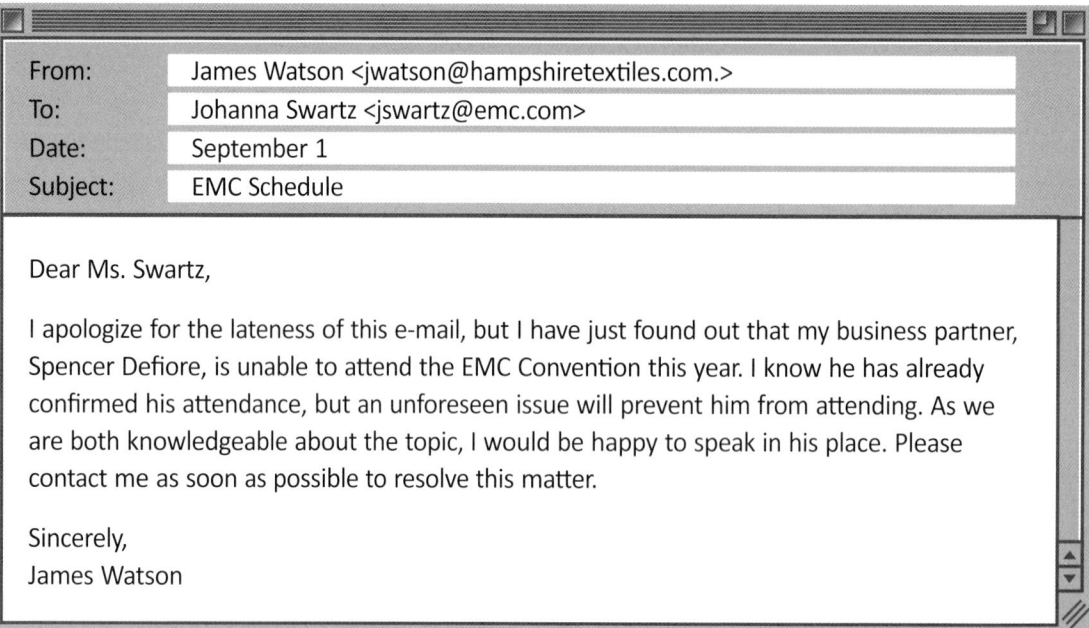

From: James Watson <jwatson@hampshiretextiles.com.>
To: Johanna Swartz <jswartz@emc.com>
Date: September 1
Subject: EMC Schedule

Dear Ms. Swartz,

I apologize for the lateness of this e-mail, but I have just found out that my business partner, Spencer Defiore, is unable to attend the EMC Convention this year. I know he has already confirmed his attendance, but an unforeseen issue will prevent him from attending. As we are both knowledgeable about the topic, I would be happy to speak in his place. Please contact me as soon as possible to resolve this matter.

Sincerely,
James Watson

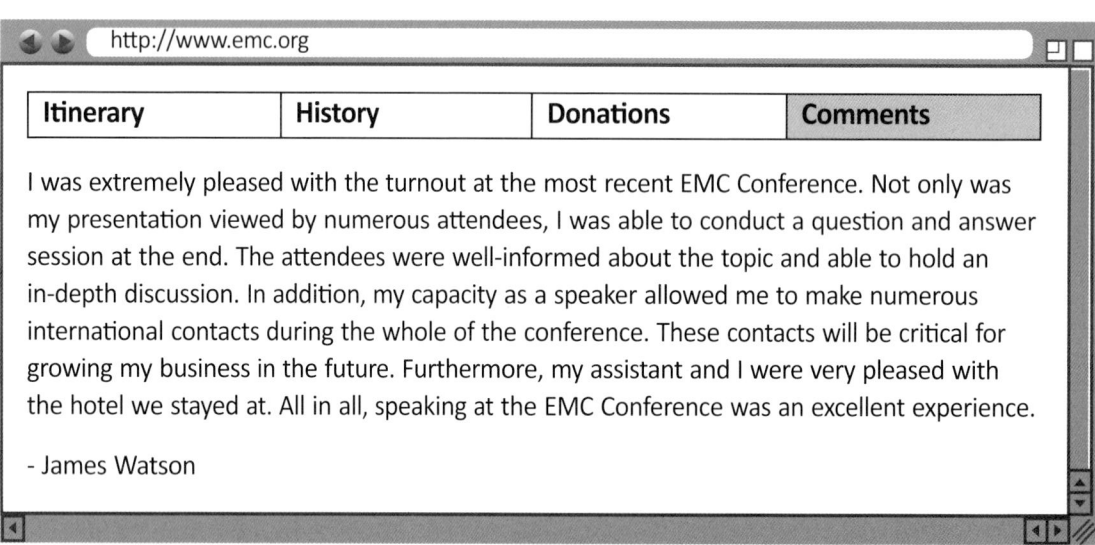

http://www.emc.org

| Itinerary | History | Donations | Comments |

I was extremely pleased with the turnout at the most recent EMC Conference. Not only was my presentation viewed by numerous attendees, I was able to conduct a question and answer session at the end. The attendees were well-informed about the topic and able to hold an in-depth discussion. In addition, my capacity as a speaker allowed me to make numerous international contacts during the whole of the conference. These contacts will be critical for growing my business in the future. Furthermore, my assistant and I were very pleased with the hotel we stayed at. All in all, speaking at the EMC Conference was an excellent experience.

- James Watson

191 What industry is the focus of the conference?
(A) Shipping
(B) Dairy
(C) Electronics
(D) Fabrics

192 According to the schedule, what are presenters expected to do?
(A) Pay for hotel accommodation
(B) Arrive in Berlin by October 8
(C) Ship some presentation materials
(D) Confirm their participation in an event

193 What topic will Mr. Watson most likely speak about?
(A) Textile Factory Management Techniques
(B) Outsourcing and Overseas Management
(C) Upgrading and Maintaining Equipment
(D) International Shipping Strategies

194 In the review, the word "capacity" in paragraph 1, line 4, is closest in meaning to
(A) role
(B) time
(C) perspective
(D) experience

195 What is probably true about Mr. Watson?
(A) He operates several manufacturing plants in Germany.
(B) He booked a second room at the Deluxe Grand Hotel.
(C) He attends the EMC conference every year.
(D) He changed his topic to a more difficult one.

Questions 196-200 refer to the following form, e-mail, and letter.

http://www.abi.org

Asia Business Insider

| This Issue | Contact Us | Subscriptions | FAQ |

Name: Calista Lao
E-mail Address: clao@rejuvenateproperties.com
City & Country: Ho Chi Minh City, Vietnam
Subject: Suggestion
Message: As you know, Asia Business Insider is only available as a quarterly print magazine. However, given that the printing takes place in Tokyo, some customers are not able to receive their magazines until weeks later. The delivery of my magazine is often delayed up to three weeks. This has caused my company, Rejuvenate Properties, to miss out on some of the key property sales advertised in Asia Business Insider. As a result, I think Asia Business Insider should provide customers with online subscriptions in the form of a downloadable e-book. This would help customers like me keep track of all current available deals.

Submit

To: ABI Editorial Staff
From: Akemi Nagata, Editorial Assistant
Date: Wednesday, 23 October
Subject: Meeting Summary

The following is a summary of the items discussed during the editorial meeting held on October 23rd with all members of the editorial staff.

Editorial director Hiroki Goto announced that Asia Business Insider will now include a downloadable e-book free of charge for all subscription holders. Furthermore, new subscribers may also choose to sign up for only the e-book issues at a lowered subscription price. The design company has hired two e-book designers to prepare each issue.

Editorial staff discussed which articles to include in ABI's next quarterly installment. Staff members agreed the issue will report on the merging of Haptrack International with Global Fund Partners as reported by Samuel Park. Articles on Surami Technologies in India and Triple Star Manufacturing in Taiwan will be prepared by Jan Dubey and Samuel Park respectively. Editorial staff member Aiko Yano is still waiting to receive articles from freelance writers regarding the development of the new World Conference Center in Beijing. If they cannot meet the deadline, the articles will be included in the next issue.

Asia Business Insider
January • Vol. 7 • Number 1

Letter from the Editor,

This issue celebrates the launch of Asia Business Insider's e-book series. Subscribers can now download fully designed e-books that include all aspects of our print versions. The January issue will cover numerous business deals taking place in Asia. It will also include the launch of our new Editor's Commentary section in which the editorial staff will respond to questions and comments placed online.

Make sure to keep an eye out for our next issue in which we cover all the pertinent details surrounding the plans for the World Conference Center in Beijing. Make sure to sign up on our website at that time for a chance to win free tickets to the center's grand opening business conference next year.

Hiroki Goto

196 What is true about Ms. Lao?
(A) She only buys property in Vietnam.
(B) Her ideas were implemented by ABI.
(C) She subscribes to several Japanese magazines.
(D) Her articles often appear in ABI.

197 Who will be discussing Surami Technologies?
(A) Hiroki Goto
(B) Samuel Park
(C) Jan Dubey
(D) Akemi Nagata

198 What is suggested about Aiko Yano?
(A) She joined ABI as an e-book designer.
(B) She did not receive some articles on time.
(C) She co-writes articles with Samuel Park.
(D) She was absent from the June 1 meeting.

199 What is indicated about Asia Business Insider?
(A) It has developed a new column.
(B) Its subscribers are mostly located in Vietnam.
(C) It will relocate to Beijing, China.
(D) It prints six issues per year.

200 What is mentioned about ABI's website?
(A) It is only for ABI subscribers.
(B) It will be upgraded next year.
(C) It is available in seven different languages.
(D) It will host a give-away for subscribers.

This is the end of the test. You may review Part 5, 6, and 7 if you finish the test early.

ANSWERS

ACTUAL TEST 3

101. (D)	121. (A)	141. (C)	161. (B)	181. (A)
102. (B)	122. (B)	142. (D)	162. (A)	182. (B)
103. (B)	123. (A)	143. (A)	163. (D)	183. (C)
104. (B)	124. (D)	144. (A)	164. (D)	184. (B)
105. (B)	125. (A)	145. (D)	165. (C)	185. (D)
106. (D)	126. (B)	146. (C)	166. (D)	186. (A)
107. (B)	127. (D)	147. (B)	167. (D)	187. (D)
108. (D)	128. (A)	148. (A)	168. (C)	188. (C)
109. (C)	129. (B)	149. (D)	169. (D)	189. (A)
110. (C)	130. (D)	150. (A)	170. (B)	190. (D)
111. (A)	131. (A)	151. (C)	171. (D)	191. (D)
112. (D)	132. (C)	152. (D)	172. (B)	192. (D)
113. (B)	133. (C)	153. (C)	173. (D)	193. (C)
114. (A)	134. (B)	154. (D)	174. (A)	194. (A)
115. (D)	135. (B)	155. (B)	175. (C)	195. (B)
116. (D)	136. (A)	156. (D)	176. (A)	196. (B)
117. (B)	137. (A)	157. (B)	177. (D)	197. (C)
118. (C)	138. (C)	158. (D)	178. (C)	198. (B)
119. (D)	139. (A)	159. (B)	179. (B)	199. (A)
120. (B)	140. (C)	160. (A)	180. (D)	200. (D)

ACTUAL TEST 4

a b c
100 200 300

d e f
400 500 600

READING TEST

In the Reading Test, you will read a variety of texts and answer several different types of reading comprehension questions. The entire Reading test will last 75 minutes. There are three parts, and directions are given for each part. You are encouraged to answer as many questions as possible within the time allowed.

You must mark your answers on the separate answer sheet. Do not write your answers in your test book.

PART 5

Directions: A word or phrase is missing in each of the sentences below. Four answer choices are given below each sentence. Select the best answer to complete the sentence. Then mark the letter (A), (B), (C), or (D) on your answer sheet.

101 Thanks to the ---------- recommendation from his previous employer, Derrick was immediately offered the managerial position.

(A) impress
(B) impression
(C) impressive
(D) impresses

102 Nemis Air is no longer ------- to transport freight to the northern regions.

(A) license
(B) licensed
(C) licenses
(D) licensing

103 Jereome tried to get tickets to tomorrow's game, but they are ------- sold out.

(A) complete
(B) completed
(C) completing
(D) completely

104 Nobody can enter this office ---------- proper authorization.

(A) without
(B) unless
(C) only
(D) although

105 The annual charity banquet hosted by the Fredericton Children Aid Society is ---------- to take place at the Grand Marian Hotel on December 7.
(A) given
(B) scheduled
(C) found
(D) considered

106 The owner's manual includes detailed ---------- on cleaning this microwave.
(A) instructions
(B) computers
(C) posters
(D) fixings

107 The city purchased the ---------- building on Balena Street to convert it into an elementary school.
(A) approaching
(B) adjustable
(C) vacant
(D) united

108 Customers must provide ---------- at the counter or prescriptions will not be filled.
(A) paid
(B) payers
(C) payment
(D) pays

109 The company will not reimburse staff for travel expenses unless original receipts are presented ------------ upon returning.
(A) mainly
(B) formerly
(C) nearly
(D) immediately

110 The Stickney Entertainment Guide is, without a doubt, the most reliable source ---------- finding the best places to eat in this region.
(A) around
(B) for
(C) as
(D) through

111 Mr. Tolliver, the head mechanic, started the repairs by ------------ this morning but two more staff were available to help him after lunch.
(A) he
(B) his
(C) him
(D) himself

112 For optimal results, the manufacturer ------------ applying this exterior paint when the weather is sunny.
(A) reminds
(B) recognizes
(C) recommends
(D) registers

113 Instructors at Darthmouth College have to submit their final student evaluations ------------ the last day of this month.
(A) in anticipation of
(B) already
(C) before
(D) so as to

114 The Fitzgerald Theater is being renovated so concert organizers for Roland Gagnon's band are --------- seeking another venue.
(A) actively
(B) activity
(C) active
(D) activate

115 Once the conveyor belt was fixed, the factory was ---------- to continue production.
(A) valuable
(B) responsible
(C) able
(D) possible

116 Someone should tell Mr. Sinopoli that ---------- car is parked in the section reserved for shopping center customers.
(A) he
(B) him
(C) his
(D) himself

117 Ratzenberg Motorcycles will benefit greatly --------- the proposed acquisition by Shefferville Auto.
(A) from
(B) to
(C) on
(D) about

118 The application forms we received yesterday ---------- have to be reviewed by one of the division heads.
(A) lately
(B) evenly
(C) ever
(D) still

119 If bad weather forces a cancellation of the baseball game, full refunds will be issued to ---------- who have purchased tickets.
(A) those
(B) which
(C) them
(D) whichever

120 Even though tourism revenue in this region usually ---------- during the cold winter months, it always recovers in the warm spring.
(A) declines
(B) delays
(C) impacts
(D) impedes

121 One important ---------- the new personnel manager is responsible for is meeting regularly with factory workers to discuss safety matters.
(A) initiative
(B) initiating
(C) initiation
(D) initiator

122 Ms. Gaitor is ---------- with implementing policies that led to a significant increase in the number of clients.
(A) credited
(B) scored
(C) agreed
(D) relied

123 Tickets to the gallery can be purchased online at a ---------- reduced price.
(A) slightest
(B) slighted
(C) slighting
(D) slightly

124 Our division ------------ last week's policy meeting, but there was a conflict with the schedule.
(A) can attend
(B) must have attended
(C) should attend
(D) would have attended

125 Mr. Gleason opted to lease office space on Queen Street instead of Morley Lane, ---------- a view of the lake.
(A) prefer
(B) preferring
(C) preferred
(D) preference

126 ---------- for next year's Grondin Literature Award must be received by the selection committee by the end of March.
(A) Subscriptions
(B) Nominations
(C) Supporters
(D) Venues

127 In an effort to make the team less ----------, the manager sent all the sales charts to everyone as e-mail attachments rather than printing out hardcopies.
(A) waste
(B) wasteful
(C) wastefully
(D) wasting

128 Ms. Wilson must contact the bank manager ------------- she needs a little more time for the payment.
(A) if
(B) soon
(C) only
(D) then

129 Besides speedy delivery, friendly service is something ---------- the management of Caron Courier will never sacrifice.
(A) where
(B) that
(C) when
(D) then

130 The editor of the sports section is more --------- about the articles she approves than the other editors.
(A) prominent
(B) punctual
(C) rigorous
(D) selective

PART 6

Directions: Read the texts that follow. A word, phrase, or sentence is missing in parts of each text. Four answer choices for each question are given below the text. Select the best answer to complete the text. Then mark the letter (A), (B), (C), or (D) on your answer sheet.

Questions 131-134 refer to the following article.

Bold Move by Popular Shop

CASTLEBAR – Flavor Fun, Castlebar's oldest and most popular yoghurt restaurant, has introduced a truly unanticipated change as the result of a growing number of ___131___. The restaurant's owner decided to introduce a policy that many find to be unusual. For the past two weeks, customers have not been permitted to work on laptops while eating in the restaurant. Flavor Fun is the first and only restaurant in the city to implement such a policy aimed at encouraging customers to leave the restaurant after eating. By making customers spend ___132___ time at a table, the restaurant has increased its daily sales by over 20 percent, and customers did not have to wait for a place to sit. ___133___ Now, some other popular eating spots throughout Castlebar ___134___ similar changes.

131 (A) staff
(B) prices
(C) complaints
(D) deliveries

132 (A) some
(B) less
(C) any
(D) much

133 (A) Customers will receive free coffee during the trial period.
(B) The new policy has already proven popular with customers.
(C) Flavor Fun also has an outdoor patio for dining.
(D) Owners believe new staff need more training before starting work.

134 (A) considers
(B) to consider
(C) being considered
(D) are considering

Questions 135-138 refer to the following letter.

Do You Use a Hearing Aid? Contact Knapton Technologies Today!

In August, Knapton Technologies will begin a detailed consumer study on behalf of Hearing 1000. For this huge undertaking, our team is ___135___ more than 300 individuals who wear hearing aids. All participants must have a doctor prescribed device that they began wearing no more than three years ago ___136___ the beginning of the study. ___137___ If you are interested, we ask that you visit us online at www.knaptontechnologies.com/hearingaidstudy and complete our short survey. One of our staff members will be contacting qualified applicants. Every participant ___138___ a gift voucher valued at $200 upon completing of this study.

135 (A) seeking
    (B) insuring
    (C) promoting
    (D) showing

136 (A) except for
    (B) as
    (C) because of
    (D) at

137 (A) A hard copy of the prescription must be presented for confirmation.
    (B) New batteries will be available for all participants.
    (C) We request that payment for your prescription is provided on the spot.
    (D) The prescription will be filled immediately after submission.

138 (A) will receive
    (B) had received
    (C) to receive
    (D) to be received

Questions 139-142 refer to the following press release.

Next month, the national headquarters of Zaki Ltd., Japan's top manufacturer of ___139___, will relocate to 117 Aoyagi Street, where a modern office building was recently renovated. Zaki will ___140___ the top seven floors of the Aoyagi Building. In this new location, the staff will enjoy over 90,000 square meters of beautiful office space and convenient amenities. ___141___ "That is the perfect place to display our latest high-tech refrigerators and ovens." said Kaori Akiba, spokesperson for Zaki. Ms. Akiba noted that the design and engineer divisions will remain in ___142___ original spot in the Ogawa Building.

139 (A) furniture
(B) apparel
(C) wallpaper
(D) appliances

140 (A) sell
(B) paint
(C) occupy
(D) photograph

141 (A) Zaki's products are known for their cutting-edge designs and energy efficiency.
(B) Zaki also plans to lease additional retail space on the first floor of the building.
(C) Zaki was listed in the Tokyo Times as one of the top 20 places to work in Asia.
(D) Zaki stock doubled in value immediately following the announcement.

142 (A) it
(B) their
(C) what
(D) any

Questions 143-146 refer to the following e-mail.

To: Kaori Sazaki <ssawaki601@e-mail.co.jp>
From: Customer Service <customerserv@elsworth.co.uk>
Date: Thursday, 16 October 8:56 P.M.
Subject: inquiry about website

Dear Ms. Sazaki:

We would like to thank you for leaving a comment in the feedback section of our website regarding the instruction booklet for the EW2500 digital camera. You indicated that the instructions on how to upload an image to a phone or mobile device is confusing and we completely agree with you __143__ that point. __144__ Our publications division has __145__ made some revisions to the section that details the specific software and cable needed to transfer an image from your particular camera. We have made the __146__ version of the instruction booklet available on our website. You can find it under the New Digital Camera section. If you prefer a print version, we will gladly send it by regular mail but delivery will take at least one week.

Sincerely,

Lirim Kilgore
Customer Service Agent
Elsworth Camera Company

143 (A) all
(B) on
(C) what
(D) of

144 (A) The EW2500 digital camera is currently our most popular item.
(B) We can send you the complete instructions via e-mail if you wish.
(C) Other customers have submitted feedback about the same issue.
(D) Most of our customers are based in the southern regions of Asia.

145 (A) instead
(B) likewise
(C) therefore
(D) nevertheless

146 (A) original
(B) updated
(C) absolute
(D) focused

PART 7

Directions: In this part, you will read a selection of texts, such as magazine and newspaper articles, e-mail, and instant messages. Each text or set of texts is followed by several questions. Select the best answer for each question and mark the letter (A), (B), (C), or (D) on your answer sheet.

Questions 147-148 refer to the following text message.

From: Ron Kapoor, 553-0304
To: Zelda Vincenti

Zelda, I left my schedule book in the office. I have to meet a client at 2:00, but I can't remember the exact location. I'm just about to leave Denny's Grill and had planned to go straight to the meeting. Can you check my book and send me the address?

147 Why did Mr. Kapoor send a text message to Ms. Vincenti?
(A) To ask if she found his briefcase
(B) To inquire about a canceled meeting
(C) To request that she send him an address
(D) To make a restaurant reservation

148 What will Mr. Kapoor probably do next?
(A) Leave a restaurant
(B) Go to his office
(C) Check a website
(D) Call a client

Questions 149-150 refer to the following advertisement.

The American chapter of Ancient Worlds Archaeological Foundation seeks two full-time interns to assist with our Archaeological dig near Siem Reap, Cambodia.

Candidates must have completed a 4-year degree in Archaeological studies or must be currently enrolled in their 4th year of an Archaeology program.

Research experience is a must, and candidates with hands-on field training will be given preference.

Applicants must be willing to travel to the dig site during the months of August through October. Accommodation and flights will be paid for by the foundation.

Interns will be paid a lump sum at the end of the trip. At the discretion of the project coordinator, interns may be hired as full-time employees following the dig's conclusion.

149 What is indicated about the American chapter of Ancient Worlds Archaeological Foundation?

(A) It wants to hire one part-time intern.
(B) It conducts digs in foreign countries.
(C) It does not pay its interns except for travel expenses.
(D) It was founded three years ago.

150 What is NOT a qualification for the position?

(A) University education
(B) Willingness to travel
(C) Field training
(D) Computer knowledge

Questions 151-153 refer to the following memo.

To: Timmons Medical Research Staff
From: Anderson Baxtor, Director of Employee Relations
Re: Presentation
Date: 5 April

Attention all staff members,

Next Thursday, 13 April, we will have a special presentation in auditorium 203. Maria Sergios is a senior researcher at the University of Westwood, where she has conducted research for the last five years. She headed the development of a new series of vaccines in addition to partnering with researchers in London, England to work on the development of several new treatments for cancer. Before joining the University of Westwood, Sergios made a name for herself at the Institute of Medical Research in Sydney, Australia. There, I had the chance to learn from her during several ground-breaking projects. Ms. Sergios will be here in Vancouver next week and has agreed to share her latest publication on laboratory techniques with us. All staff members are required to attend the presentation.

151 What does the memo discuss?
(A) Plans to found a new lab
(B) A new job opening
(C) A scientist's career
(D) Deadlines for a project

152 Where is Timmons Medical Research located?
(A) In London
(B) In Sydney
(C) In Westwood
(D) In Vancouver

153 What does Mr. Baxtor indicate about Ms. Sergios?
(A) She is his former mentor.
(B) She is moving to Vancouver.
(C) She will join his research team.
(D) She will open her own laboratory.

Questions 154-155 refer to the following text message chain.

Jamal Myers 10:30 A.M.

Hi, Ferguson. I'm still at Davis Printers waiting for our two banners. Could you go ahead and begin setting up? I put the key to the room in the top right drawer of my desk.

Ferguson Boyd 10:33 A.M.

Found it. I'm leaving now.

Jamal Myers 10:35 A.M.

Thanks a lot. I know the award ceremony doesn't start until 1:30, but we need to double check all the equipment.

Ferguson Boyd 10:40 A.M.

Just to make sure, we will be having the ceremony in the former city hall building on Elliot Street, right? Not the new one on Queen Street?

Jamal Myers 10:42 A.M.

Correct. Right after the ceremony, a photographer will take photos of the winners on the front lawn. That is why I ordered an additional banner to be used outside. I will catch up with you at the former city hall building as soon as I get the banners.

Ferguson Boyd 10:45 A.M.

Okay. See you in a little while!

---

154 At 10:33 A.M., what does Mr. Boyd most likely mean when he writes, "Found it"?

(A) He will pass on the information a client needs.
(B) He noticed Davis Printers while driving.
(C) He has the key to the venue in his hand.
(D) He is looking at a phone number in a directory.

155 Where most likely is Mr. Boyd going next?

(A) To the train station
(B) To company headquarters
(C) To a print shop
(D) To the old city hall

Questions 156-158 refer to the following letter.

Holt Golf and Country Club
34 Russet Drive
Edmonton, Alberta
www.holtgolf.ca

24 April

Mr. Henry MacArthur
220 Washington Avenue
Edmonton, Alberta

Dear Mr. MacArthur,

Thank you for purchasing a membership to Holt Golf and Country Club. --[1]-- From May 1st until September 30th, in addition to having your choice of tee-off time, you will have full access to our lounge, restaurant, and spa. Furthermore, carbonated beverages are complimentary in all our cafés. Simply show your membership card when you order. --[2]--

In addition to all these incredible services, Holt Golf and Country Club is announcing yet another service for its members. From now until the end of August, all members may invite guests for a round of golf on our extensive course. This feature is available from 8 A.M. until 4 P.M. only. Guest reservations must be made twenty-four hours in advance. --[3]--

If you have any questions or concerns, please contact our customer service hotline at 900-555-3344. --[4]--

Sincerely,
Mitchel Walker

---

156 What is true about Holt golf and Country Club?

(A) It offers its members free drinks.
(B) It only opens during the spring.
(C) It offers discount memberships.
(D) It hosts seasonal parties.

157 According to the letter, what will be different after August?

(A) Members cannot access the spa.
(B) Members may not bring guests.
(C) Golf times will be earlier.
(D) Golf lessons will be available.

158 In which of the positions marked [1], [2], [3], and [4] does the following sentence best belong?

"This year, you will be able to enjoy all our premium services."

(A) [1]
(B) [2]
(C) [3]
(D) [4]

Questions 159-162 refer to the following article.

Milan (July 14) – Roberto Pelini, lead designer at Marshenco Fashions, one of Europe's top design companies, has announced he will retire from his role at the company. --[1]--

Since first accepting the position ten years ago, Roberto Pelini has worked hard to make Marshenco Fashions one of the most-recognized names in the industry. Because of Pelini's passion and eye for design, Marshenco has become a favorite among celebrities and his designs can often be seen both on the runway and the red carpet. --[2]-- The company's success has even allowed for the founding of a sister company, Marshenco Accessories.

Irina Morova, former designer at Ruvera Design, will assume the position of lead designer at Marshenco. Morova has more than ten years of experience heading a major fashion company. Her work has been featured in numerous fashion festivals, magazines, and has clothed some of Europe's top singers and actors. --[3]--

Following his departure from Marshenco, Roberto Pelini will partner with Sophia Bertuski to found a new independent fashion house. Pelini is quoted as saying, "I look forward to working with Sophia. Her creative vision is similar to my own." --[4]--

159 What is the purpose of the article?
(A) To report on a company's closure
(B) To announce a change in a company's leadership
(C) To advertise a new job opening at a company
(D) To publicize a new line of products

160 What is indicated about Marshenco?
(A) It is based in North America.
(B) It was purchased by Pelini.
(C) It owns Ruvera Design.
(D) It founded a second company.

161 What is mentioned about Irina Morova?
(A) She will become Pelini's business partner.
(B) Her career at Ruvera Design was successful.
(C) She originally worked as a runway model.
(D) Her designs are for average consumers.

162 In which of the positions marked [1], [2], [3], and [4] does the following sentence best belong?

"There is no news as to when Pelini's new lines will be available to the public."

(A) [1]
(B) [2]
(C) [3]
(D) [4]

Questions 163-165 refer to the following advertisement.

The First Annual Waterfront Food Truck Festival!

Ajax Food and Beverage Association is pleased to announce the first ever Waterfront Food Truck Festival. From Monday August 8th through Sunday August 14th, the Ajax waterfront will host a number of local food trucks. Guests can enjoy live music, prizes, and children's entertainment between the hours of 11 A.M. and 6 P.M. Food truck items can be sampled for discount prices.

Famous Participating Food Trucks:

- ◆ Rio Tacos – Enjoy fresh appetizers and a variety of tacos and nachos
- ◆ Barbecue Madness – Marinated pork ribs, chicken wings, and pulled pork
- ◆ Benny's Fries – French fries topped with your choice of ingredients

Admission is free for all participants. Parking will be available on a limited basis, so make sure to get there early.

For a complete list of participating food trucks visit www.ajaxwaterfront.com/foodtruckfestival.

163 What is being advertised?
(A) A restaurant's grand opening
(B) A concert in the park
(C) An auto show
(D) A new community event

164 What is mentioned about the participating food trucks?
(A) They will travel to various cities.
(B) They will distribute free gifts.
(C) They will be open all day.
(D) They will sell food at reduced prices.

165 What are participants encouraged to do?
(A) Arrive at the site early
(B) Leave their cars at home
(C) Pay an admission fee
(D) Camp at the waterfront

Questions 166-169 refer to the following e-mail.

From:	Marcus Pentz
To:	Tamara Woods
Date:	October 10
Subject:	Information

Hi Tamara,

Thank you so much for covering for Samira while she's away visiting family. Prior to leaving for her trip abroad, she was working on advertisements for two local properties. According to her files, she has put together the following descriptions:

776 Marshall Avenue is a three-story home situated on Lake Scougog. It features four bedrooms, upgraded kitchen appliances, a fully furnished basement, and a wooden fireplace. It is situated in a quiet area, but is within walking distance of local schools.

9902 Fenton Street is a three-bedroom home with a large yard and an in-ground swimming pool. A garage was recently built on the property and can hold up to two cars. The home is located near all major shopping malls and the university.

I'm going to send over Samira's files, so you can update her descriptions and add any relevant information. These properties, along with photographs, must be submitted to Scougog Weekly's real estate editor by Friday. Please let me know if you have any questions or concerns.

Regards,
Marcus Pentz
Pentz Real Estate

166 Why was the e-mail sent?
 (A) To request some files
 (B) To give some job instructions
 (C) To provide payment information
 (D) To ask for some local contacts

167 What is suggested about Samira?
 (A) She often travels abroad.
 (B) She purchased a new home.
 (C) She works for a newspaper.
 (D) She has gone on vacation.

168 What is NOT mentioned about the property on Fenton Street?
 (A) It has a big yard and a swimming pool.
 (B) It was previously listed on a website.
 (C) It includes a newly built garage.
 (D) It is close to many important amenities.

169 According to the e-mail, what is indicated about Scougog Weekly?
 (A) It will feature the selections Ms. Woods must update.
 (B) It comes out every Friday.
 (C) It charges fees based on property prices.
 (D) It is distributed to local residents free of charge.

Questions 170-173 refer to the text message chain.

Blake Wyatt [3:23 P.M.]
Ms. Parker, I just found out there's going to be a parade on First Street. The area is going to be really crowded, so the repaving of your restaurant's parking lot will have to wait.

Janice Parker [3:26 P.M.]
So does that mean you won't be coming in at all?

Blake Wyatt [3:28 P.M.]
No, we'll still be there. We can help get the basement storage rooms finished.

Janice Parker [3:31 P.M.]
Okay, great. How long do you think it will take to get everything done down there?

Blake Wyatt [3:32 P.M.]
I'll check now.

--- *Tim Robins has been added to the conversation.* --

Blake Wyatt [3:35 P.M.]
Tim, how far have you gotten on the basement project?

Tim Robins [3:40 P.M.]
Well, things were running smoothly until we found some water damage in the southeast corner. It looks like a big clean up job.

Blake Wyatt [3:42 P.M.]
What if my crew gave you a hand tomorrow?

Tim Robins [3:44 P.M.]
That might get us back on schedule. We might even be able to install the new refrigerators.

Janice Parker [3:45 P.M.]
If you're moving the fridges, you'll need access to the service entrance behind the building. I think you still have the key, right?

Blake Wyatt [3:47 P.M.]
Yes, I've got it. Are there any spots behind the building where the guys can park for the day?

Janice Parker [3:50 P.M.]
There might not be any free if there's a parade. You should probably park in the empty lot on Fifth Avenue.

170 What does Mr. Wyatt suggest will interrupt tomorrow's work?
 (A) A public holiday
 (B) A street event
 (C) A lost delivery
 (D) A lack of equipment

171 At 3:40 P.M. what does Mr. Robins most likely mean when he writes, "It looks like a big clean up job"?
 (A) His crew usually does the cleaning.
 (B) Some damage was significant.
 (C) He does not like his current job.
 (D) His crew's project is too complicated.

172 Who most likely is Ms. Parker?
 (A) A restaurant owner
 (B) A construction worker
 (C) A parking attendant
 (D) An appliance manufacturer

173 What is one topic Mr. Wyatt asks about?
 (A) Directions to another entrance
 (B) The location of a building key
 (C) The time of a local event
 (D) The location of parking spaces

Questions 174-175 refer to the following webpage.

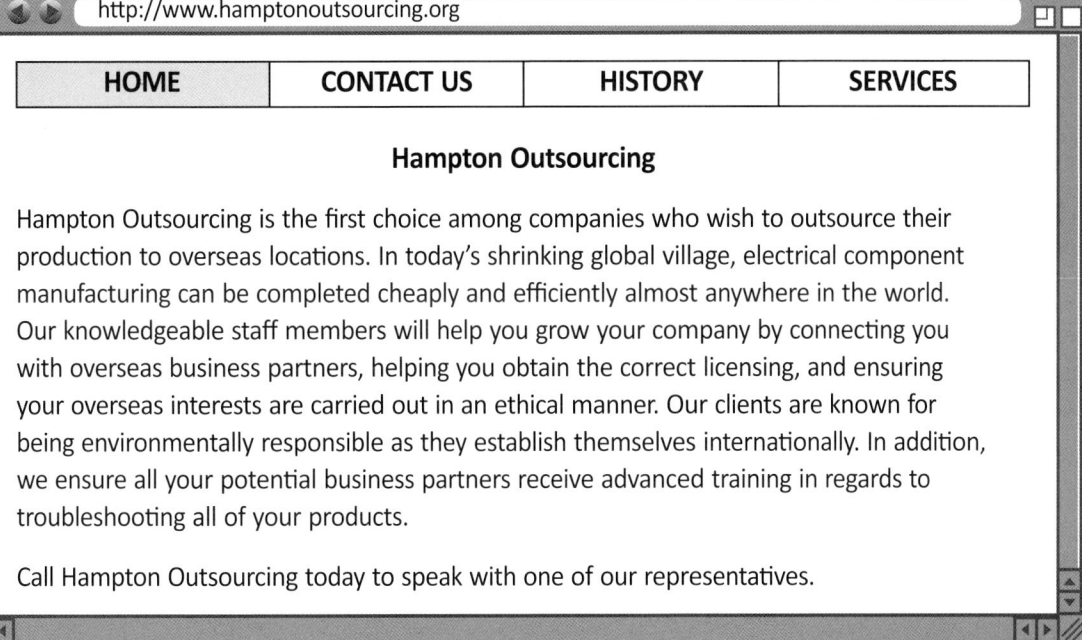

Hampton Outsourcing

Hampton Outsourcing is the first choice among companies who wish to outsource their production to overseas locations. In today's shrinking global village, electrical component manufacturing can be completed cheaply and efficiently almost anywhere in the world. Our knowledgeable staff members will help you grow your company by connecting you with overseas business partners, helping you obtain the correct licensing, and ensuring your overseas interests are carried out in an ethical manner. Our clients are known for being environmentally responsible as they establish themselves internationally. In addition, we ensure all your potential business partners receive advanced training in regards to troubleshooting all of your products.

Call Hampton Outsourcing today to speak with one of our representatives.

174 Who most likely will be a customer of Hampton Outsourcing?

(A) Call center workers
(B) Insurance brokers
(C) Environmental agencies
(D) Home appliance companies

175 What is NOT mentioned as a strength of Hampton Outsourcing?

(A) Superior employee training
(B) Knowledge of licensing
(C) Environmentally conscious procedures
(D) Familiarity with export taxes

Questions 176-180 refer to the following letter and voucher.

To:	Raphael Rosario <rosario@ebookmail.com>
From:	Janelle Parik <jparik@alliancepremiumairways.com>
Subject:	Your Flight
Date:	6 January
Attachment:	voucher

Dear Mr. Rosario,

Thank you for sharing your experience with Alliance Premium Airways Customer Service. I am sorry to learn about your negative experience on January 2. According to the online form you completed, you had reserved a business class seat on a third-party website but you were forced to fly economy class because your reservation had been lost.

I have contacted the website you used to book your flight. Apparently, there was a computer malfunction, which caused some prior bookings to be deleted. Unfortunately, this resulted in some seats being resold. I understand that you have already received a partial refund, but I'd like to offer you an additional coupon for your troubles. Please see the attachment for more information.

Sincerely,

Janelle Parik,
Customer Service Manager
Alliance Premium Airways

Alliance Premium Airways Voucher

$200 off your next flight

Details: Alliance Premium Airways would like to offer you $200 off your next flight. Please note, this coupon may only be used for international return flights. This coupon is good until December 31st of this year. You may use this coupon at any Alliance Premium Airways kiosk or online at www.alliancepremiumairways.com.

Voucher Number: YY7732999938   Date Issued: January 6

Issuing office: ___ Vancouver   ___ Edmonton   ___ Montreal   _X_ Toronto

176 Why did Ms. Parik send the e-mail?
(A) To reply to an online complaint
(B) To provide a job contract
(C) To cancel an airline ticket
(D) To inquire about a trip

177 What does Ms. Parik indicate happened on January 2?
(A) She solved a seating problem.
(B) A flight was unnecessarily delayed.
(C) Many business class seats were empty.
(D) Mr. Rosario got a seat in a lower class.

178 What is suggested about Mr. Rosario?
(A) He requested a last-minute flight change.
(B) He flew from Vancouver to Toronto.
(C) He paid for his flight in advance.
(D) He usually flies economy class.

179 In the voucher, the word "good" in paragraph 1, line 2, is closest in meaning to
(A) high quality
(B) lucky
(C) well behaved
(D) valid

180 Where most likely is Ms. Parik's office located?
(A) Vancouver
(B) Edmonton
(C) Montreal
(D) Toronto

Questions 181-185 refer to the following webpage and customer review.

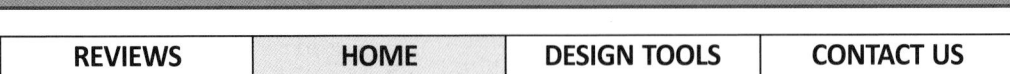

| REVIEWS | HOME | DESIGN TOOLS | CONTACT US |

Flyer Frenzy, the best online flyer generator for businesses large and small!

With Flyer Frenzy, you can create custom flyers for your business. Whether you are advertising the opening of your business or simply trying to generate awareness about your services, Flyer Frenzy has everything you need to design the perfect flyer.

Step 1: Design Your Flyer
Our online generator has numerous customizable templates. Browse through our categories and select the right template for you. All our fonts are easy to change with just the click of a mouse. If you want to accent your design with images, we have over 10,000 stock photos you can use at no extra cost. Furthermore, you can upload your own designs and logos to use along with any of our fonts.

Step 2: Select A Quantity
At Flyer Frenzy, we can print as few as 25 flyers for each order. However, the more flyers you order, the less you pay for each one.

Quantity	Price Per Item
25-300	20 cents
300-1,000	15 cents
1,001-1,500	10 cents
1,501 or more	5 cents

Step 3: Purchase A Digital Copy
For an extra flat fee of $50, you can download a digital copy of your design. This design is perfect for featuring on your business's website, as part of an e-mail newsletter, or as a printed advertisement.

Step 4: Finalize Your Order
Orders take five days to process; however, large orders may take longer to prepare. In the event that there are delays, you will be notified by e-mail.

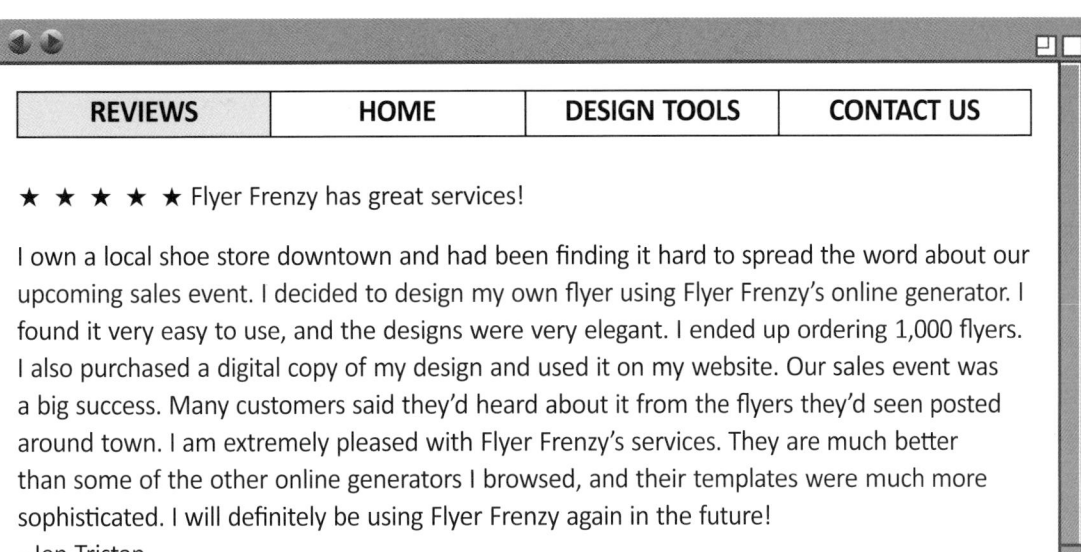

181 According to the webpage, what does the online generator allow users to do?
(A) Add images
(B) Include web links
(C) Select paper type
(D) Design a logo

182 What is mentioned on the webpage about Flyer Frenzy?
(A) It delivers products free of charge.
(B) It offers digital files for an extra fee.
(C) It allows users to see each other's designs.
(D) It only takes orders in person at a store.

183 What is indicated about Ms. Tristan?
(A) She received more flyers than she ordered.
(B) Her order was delayed by a few days.
(C) She received a fifty dollar discount.
(D) She paid fifteen cents per flyer.

184 What is suggested about Ms. Tristan's store?
(A) It advertises solely online.
(B) It put flyers up around town.
(C) It holds sales every month.
(D) It gives discounts for online orders.

185 According to the review, why does Ms. Tristan prefer Flyer Frenzy's services over other companies?
(A) They had faster delivery times.
(B) They had better design features.
(C) They used better quality paper.
(D) They were cheaper to use.

Questions 186-190 refer to following e-mails and log sheet.

From:	linda@mailmail.com
To:	billing@startelecom.com
Date:	April 23
Subject:	Bill Number 3788292

Dear Customer Service,

I am writing in regards to an unusually high cell phone bill I received in March. The amount listed on my phone bill was $155.33. Previously, my bill ranged between $80 and $90 per month.

I have already paid the bill to avoid any late fees, but I am interested in knowing why I was charged so much. My bill did not show any details to explain these charges. I know I recently upgraded my data usage, which would cost extra, but I also canceled the insurance policy I had for all my devices. These two costs should have balanced each other out if my request for cancelation was handled properly.

Please call me about this matter at 333-0967-5563. I am available to speak only in the afternoons after 3:30 P.M.

Sincerely,
Linda Albert

Customer Service Contact Log Sheet
Date: April 24

Representative Name	Account Number	Call Time	Resolved? Y/N
Michael Park	BG44532	9:33 A.M.	Yes
June Bartholdi	GH30993	10:42 A.M.	Yes
Nadia Kapoor	TZ33221	3:23 P.M.	No
Brooklyn Smith	GS17649	3:45 P.M.	No

To:	linda@mailmail.com
From:	tristan@startelecom.com
Date:	April 25
Subject:	Re: Bill Number 3788292

Dear Ms. Albert,

Thank you for e-mailing Star Telecom about your concerns. One of our representatives tried to call you at the time you specified yesterday, but there was no answer. I have looked into your problem personally and have found that your insurance cancelation never went through. Thus, your account registered charges for both the insurance policy and the upgraded data plan.

To correct this, I have canceled your insurance plan and credited your account with $63.98, which will be carried over to your next bill.

If you have any additional concerns or questions, please reply directly to this e-mail.

Sincerely,
Tristan Mathews
Star Telecom Customer Support

186 Why was the first e-mail sent?
- (A) To cancel a service
- (B) To request another bill
- (C) To ask about an invoice
- (D) To register for an account

187 What is suggested about Ms. Albert?
- (A) She previously worked for Star Telecom.
- (B) She called a Star Telecom customer service representative.
- (C) She correctly identified Star Telecom's mistake.
- (D) She wants to close her account with Star Telecom.

188 Who called Ms. Albert on April 24?
- (A) Michael Park
- (B) June Bartholdi
- (C) Nadia Kapoor
- (D) Brooklyn Smith

189 In the second e-mail, in paragraph 1, line 4 the word "registered" is closest in meaning to
- (A) enrolled
- (B) recorded
- (C) matched
- (D) allowed

190 What does Mr. Mathews indicate in his e-mail?
- (A) Some services will be offered for free.
- (B) Ms. Kapoor will call Ms. Albert tomorrow.
- (C) Ms. Albert's bill will decrease next month.
- (D) Customers will be charged for cancelations.

Questions 191-195 refer to the following e-mail, flyer, and text message.

To:	Graduate Students
From:	Ferdinand Montgomery
Subject:	Seminar Series
Date:	March 10

Dear Students,

I have great news! Mr. Philip Osan has agreed to give a presentation during our Careers in Fashion Seminar Series. As graduate students, your job will be to arrange his travel accommodations for June 1-2 as well as his transportation to and from campus. Also, please reserve a room for his presentation. I think the Belford Auditorium would be best. Mr. Osan's presentation will be very popular, so we might need the room with the largest capacity. However, if it's unavailable, please reserve another one.

Also, once Mr. Osan provides his information, I'll need you to design and print another flyer. I'm hoping you'll be able to divide these tasks up among the five of you without any major issues, but do let me know if you have any problems.

Ferdinand Montgomery,
Professor of Fashion Design

The College of Fashion and Design's
Careers in Fashion Seminar Series Presents:

Mr. Philip Osan
CEO and Lead Designer of Bath Fashion House

Fashion Design and Technology
June 1, 3:30 P.M.
Westmont Auditorium

Over the years, many fashion houses have switched from hand-drawn designs to fashion design software programs. As up-and-coming designers, you must be aware of all the newest innovations in fashion design software. How can you keep up to date on the newest software trends? One possible solution is to become fluent in each new program. However, that may be costly and time-consuming. There are several ways to predict which programs will be major players in the future of fashion design. I will share my insights regarding the technological trends in the fashion industry.

From: Robert Parker
To: Rosa Hernandez
Received: May 28

Rosa, I'm at the copy center in the Hurtz Building to print the flyers, but I noticed something is missing. It seems that Mr. Osan's photograph was deleted. Can you fix the flyer and e-mail me the new version as soon as possible? The copy center closes in less than an hour and Dr. Montgomery asked me to drop the flyers off at his office tonight.

191 What is suggested about the Westmont Auditorium?
(A) It is not available on June 1st.
(B) It is the location for all seminar presentations.
(C) It has fewer seats than the Belford Auditorium.
(D) It has a new projector system.

192 In the e-mail, the word "issues" in paragraph 2, line 3, is closest in meaning to
(A) conflicts
(B) periodicals
(C) distributions
(D) announcements

193 What is Mr. Osan's presentation about?
(A) New trends in design software
(B) Advancements in sewing machines
(C) Learning drawing techniques
(D) Characteristics of fashion houses

194 What problem does Mr. Parker mention?
(A) A location has been changed.
(B) The flyer is missing an image.
(C) A work history is incorrect.
(D) The time of an event is wrong.

195 Who most likely is Ms. Hernandez?
(A) Lead designer at Bath Fashion House
(B) A fashion design software developer
(C) A professor at The College of Fashion and Design
(D) A graduate student at The College of Fashion and Design

Questions 196-200 refer to the following advertisement, online form, and review.

Trenton Air Conditioning

Air Conditioning Units

Trenton Air Conditioning has been providing businesses with affordable air conditioning units for over fifteen years. We have provided numerous local cafés, restaurants, and supermarkets with reliable cooling solutions. All our units include cleaning services and repairs at your request, and should your unit be unsatisfactory in any way, we will replace it at no extra cost. Delivery to any location in the Sydney area and set up are both absolutely free of charge. A two-year contract must be signed by the business owner, and monthly payment plans are available.

Air Conditioning Unit Options:

Contract Option	Model	Type	Room size in square meters (m²)	Cost Per Month
Bronze	GP-A3000	Ceiling	9-25	$55.00
Silver	GP-A4000	Standing	26-55	$75.00
Gold	GP-A9999	Ceiling	55-100	$95.00
Platinum	GP-AR300	Ceiling	100-200	$115.00

Contact us for a free service quote today by visiting www.trentonaircon.com or calling one of our knowledgeable customer service agents at 1-800-444-2323.

Trenton Air Conditioning – Customer Service Quote Form

Name:	Medina Prias
Business:	Medina's Café
E-mail:	medina@mailme.com
Date:	23 April
Remarks:	I'm writing to inquire about your air conditioning units. The restaurant next to my café is currently using one of your units, and the owner, Mr. Smithe, highly recommends your services. Right now, the air conditioner in my café is nearly ten years old. Just keeping up with the repairs and cleaning is costing a fortune. I think it would be much cheaper to just rent from your company. Since my café is quite small with only 22 square meters, I think one of your cheaper packages would be suitable. However, I will rely on your recommendation about this. Also, can you make sure any unit you recommend comes with a remote control. Our current air conditioner does not have one. Thank you, and I look forward to hearing from you.

Customer Review

I have been a customer of Trenton Air Conditioning for a year, and I have to say that I am very pleased with their services. I was very surprised to receive a ten percent discount on my first year of service thanks to Trenton's referral program. Apparently, if you give the name of the person who connected you with Trenton, both parties will automatically receive a discount. Furthermore, I am very pleased with the contract conditions, which have allowed me to change my unit based on my business's needs. After my business went through an expansion, I called Trenton and the customer service representative agreed to upgrade my unit to a larger package. The new unit turned up only two days later and was installed free of charge even though the type changed from ceiling to standing. I highly recommend Trenton for their great business practices and customer service.

- Medina Prias, Owner of Medina's Café

196 What information about Trenton Air Conditioning is NOT included in the advertisement?
(A) The energy efficiency
(B) The monthly costs
(C) The room sizes
(D) The model numbers

197 What is probably true about Mr. Smithe?
(A) He can save on air conditioning for his restaurant.
(B) He purchased a café next to his restaurant.
(C) He received one year free from Trenton Air Conditioning.
(D) He will upgrade his air conditioning unit next year.

198 What is suggested about Medina's Café?
(A) It is owned by Mr. Smithe.
(B) It moved to a new location.
(C) It features nightly entertainment.
(D) It increased its size recently.

199 Which contract option is Ms. Prias currently using?
(A) Bronze
(B) Silver
(C) Gold
(D) Platinum

200 In the review, the phrase "turned up" in paragraph 1, line 8, is closest in meaning to
(A) removed
(B) considered
(C) designed
(D) arrived

This is the end of the test. You may review Part 5, 6, and 7 if you finish the test early.

ANSWERS

ACTUAL TEST 4

101. (C)	121. (A)	141. (B)	161. (B)	181. (A)
102. (B)	122. (A)	142. (B)	162. (D)	182. (B)
103. (D)	123. (D)	143. (B)	163. (D)	183. (D)
104. (A)	124. (D)	144. (C)	164. (D)	184. (B)
105. (B)	125. (B)	145. (C)	165. (A)	185. (B)
106. (A)	126. (B)	146. (B)	166. (B)	186. (C)
107. (C)	127. (B)	147. (C)	167. (D)	187. (C)
108. (C)	128. (A)	148. (A)	168. (B)	188. (D)
109. (D)	129. (B)	149. (B)	169. (A)	189. (B)
110. (B)	130. (D)	150. (D)	170. (B)	190. (C)
111. (D)	131. (C)	151. (C)	171. (B)	191. (C)
112. (C)	132. (B)	152. (D)	172. (A)	192. (A)
113. (C)	133. (B)	153. (A)	173. (D)	193. (A)
114. (A)	134. (D)	154. (C)	174. (D)	194. (B)
115. (C)	135. (A)	155. (D)	175. (D)	195. (D)
116. (C)	136. (D)	156. (A)	176. (A)	196. (A)
117. (A)	137. (A)	157. (B)	177. (D)	197. (A)
118. (D)	138. (A)	158. (A)	178. (C)	198. (D)
119. (A)	139. (D)	159. (B)	179. (D)	199. (B)
120. (A)	140. (C)	160. (D)	180. (D)	200. (D)

ACTUAL TEST 5

a b c
100 200 300

d e f
400 500 600

READING TEST

In the Reading Test, you will read a variety of texts and answer several different types of reading comprehension questions. The entire Reading test will last 75 minutes. There are three parts, and directions are given for each part. You are encouraged to answer as many questions as possible within the time allowed.

You must mark your answers on the separate answer sheet. Do not write your answers in your test book.

PART 5

Directions: A word or phrase is missing in each of the sentences below. Four answer choices are given below each sentence. Select the best answer to complete the sentence. Then mark the letter (A), (B), (C), or (D) on your answer sheet.

101 The colorful team uniforms were provided by Danchester Tires, --------- sister company.

(A) we
(B) our
(C) us
(D) ours

102 The family's visa will be processed as soon as all necessary travel --------- are received.

(A) document
(B) documents
(C) documented
(D) documenting

103 In his speech, the CEO of Grandstead Pharmaceuticals --------- mentioned the director of the research division as a contributor to the company's success.

(A) thoroughly
(B) utterly
(C) specifically
(D) densely

104 Joanne's managerial techniques are quite --------- from her predecessor's.

(A) different
(B) differently
(C) difference
(D) differences

105 Wearing a safety harness is not an option for roofers at Delbert Contractors but rather a --------.
(A) training
(B) fulfillment
(C) speculation
(D) requirement

106 One of our plumbers will ---------- how to replace a Malton DR sink drain quickly and easily.
(A) demonstrate
(B) respond
(C) inquire
(D) visit

107 Bramwell Carpets does not issue refunds of any kind so be sure to measure the floor space ------------ before purchasing.
(A) careful
(B) caring
(C) carefully
(D) cares

108 --------- annual profits are high or low, they still provide important economic information for business analysts.
(A) Whether
(B) Either
(C) Despite
(D) Even

109 The report provides a detailed ------- between the old Argo motorcycle design and the new Grandford one.
(A) comparable
(B) comparison
(C) compared
(D) comparative

110 ---------- speak to a customer service agent, please stay on the line.
(A) For
(B) Across
(C) With
(D) To

111 The storage space in the new warehouse is more than ----------- for three hundred bicycles.
(A) able
(B) great
(C) sure
(D) enough

112 Applying for a family visa in this country is a long and ----------- process.
(A) complicate
(B) complicated
(C) complication
(D) complicatedness

113 Leading automotive experts maintain that Woykin Oil filters deliver ---------- results.
(A) exceptionally
(B) exceptional
(C) exception
(D) exceptions

114 A credit card statement or phone bill can be --------- of residency.
(A) process
(B) analysis
(C) proof
(D) basis

115 Mr. Bolduc ---------- asked Gabriella to organize the workshop, but then assigned the task to Louise.
(A) initial
(B) initially
(C) initialize
(D) initialized

116 Job candidates need to submit three letters of recommendation ---------- the completed application.
(A) too
(B) in addition
(C) moreover
(D) along with

117 Even though Mr. Buono has never worked in refrigerator repair, his knowledge of refrigeration systems is ----------.
(A) extensive
(B) clever
(C) considered
(D) eager

118 The flowchart on page six describes the ------------ of duties among the different project managers.
(A) support
(B) attention
(C) division
(D) statement

119 These seeds will produce the biggest tomatoes but not ---------- the healthiest ones.
(A) expectedly
(B) necessarily
(C) preventively
(D) permanently

120 While the store does not issue refunds, customers can exchange any item for something ---------- in amount to the original sales price.
(A) equivalent
(B) profitable
(C) deliberate
(D) controlled

121 This newspaper photograph shows the mayor of Otterbury sitting ---------- the prime minister.
(A) from
(B) reverse
(C) opposite
(D) distant

122 The decision to launch a new line of footwear was ---------- the results of some market research.
(A) such as
(B) adjacent to
(C) except for
(D) based on

123 The Alderburn Employment Center is the only building on this block that is ---------- to people in wheelchairs.
(A) access
(B) accessibly
(C) accessible
(D) accessibility

124 Dr. Darius is striving ---------- the look of his office and is going to put a painting in the waiting room.
(A) to enhance
(B) enhances
(C) is enhancing
(D) enhanced

125 Players ---------- teams did not make it to the finals can watch the game for free.

(A) its
(B) which
(C) whose
(D) more

126 Local officials ------------ farmers that the pesticide sprayed on the potato crops was harmless to humans.

(A) assured
(B) arranged
(C) described
(D) committed

127 Factory laborers at Langford Manufacturing ----------- to working 30 minutes more each day to offset rising production costs.

(A) agreeing
(B) to agree
(C) agreement
(D) have agreed

128 ---------- Samuel's work experience in three continents, it was no surprise that the CEO put him in charge of the overseas project.

(A) Since
(B) Given
(C) Among
(D) Upon

129 A person who was not raised in this community may not understand the historical ---------- on the Steinhauer Street Bridge.

(A) signify
(B) significant
(C) significance
(D) significantly

130 Jennifer has more seniority than Bill at the company, ---------- she is much younger than him.

(A) as if
(B) so that
(C) in case
(D) even though

GO ON TO THE NEXT PAGE

PART 6

Directions: Read the texts that follow. A word, phrase, or sentence is missing in parts of each text. Four answer choices for each question are given below the text. Select the best answer to complete the text. Then mark the letter (A), (B), (C), or (D) on your answer sheet.

Questions 131-134 refer to the following e-mail.

To: <nina_haidara@kmail.net>
From: <duron_charette@wrnpharmaceuticals.com>
Date: September 7
Subject: Head of Research position

Dear Ms. Haidara,

WRN Pharmaceuticals is delighted to invite you to come in for a second interview next week. Since this is the second stage, our hiring committee will be speaking to only the top five applicants whom we feel are most ...**131**... for this challenging position. Our entire committee agrees that you posses almost all the ...**132**... we need. We trust that you are still interested in the position. ...**133**..., would you be available for an appointment next Wednesday at 2:30? Also, as part of the interview, we would like you to prepare a written research proposal related to one of the topics discussed at the first interview as well as a 10-minute presentation. ...**134**....

Best regards,

Duron Charette
WRN Pharmaceuticals
304-677-2426 ext. 18

---

131 (A) suiting (B) suitable
(C) suit (D) suits

132 (A) agreements (B) performances
(C) qualities (D) promotions

133 (A) Despite that (B) If so
(C) However (D) For example

134 (A) Our current research head will train you in your new duties.
(B) The CEO will be delighted to provide you with a letter of reference.
(C) You need to complete your current research project before Wednesday.
(D) We are looking forward to hearing your vision for a future project.

Questions 135-138 refer to the following the letter.

Chantal Youldon
302 Moline Street
Delavan, IL
61735

Dear Ms. Youldon,

We would like to remind you that the time for another eye examination is soon approaching. ___135___ Eye specialists ___136___ having your vision checked at least once a year. ___137___, eye problems can be detected early and the prescription for your eyeglasses can also be updated. Our number one ___138___ is providing our patients with the best vision possible. We will follow up this letter with a phone call in a few days. Please phone us at (309) 754-3231 if you would like to make an appointment. Thank you very much.

The Eye Care Team
Herrin Street Eye Clinic

135 (A) We recently expanded our waiting room to include a larger play are for children.
(B) Our records indicate that it has been eleven months since your last saw Dr. Hoban.
(C) Exercise and a healthy diet also have an impact on the condition of your eyes.
(D) Our office updated its website to include a convenient online appointment system.

136 (A) recommending
(B) had recommended
(C) recommend
(D) will recommend

137 (A) Nevertheless
(B) In this way
(C) For example
(D) Likewise

138 (A) manner
(B) opinion
(C) condition
(D) priority

Questions 139-142 refer to the following article.

Parrsboro Herald
Local News

(12 June) — On Tuesday afternoon, Parrsboro City Mayor Deborah Middleton announced city council's decision to implement a program of one-on-one training programs for aspiring city bus drivers. ___139___, she stated that 20 new drivers will be needed before the end of the year. Speaking at a press conference, she stressed that there is an urgent ___140___ for new drivers to replace those who are set to retire soon. The announcement ___141___ with approval by most city officials. Councilor Stephen Digby of Truro Region, however, continues to speak out against the city funding costly training programs when graduates of the Wolfville College of Vehicle Operations, just 50 km west of Parrsboro, are already qualified to fill the positions. ___142___

139
(A) Specifically
(B) Undoubtedly
(C) Regardless
(D) Besides

140
(A) settlement
(B) reduction
(C) demand
(D) difficulty

141
(A) will be meeting
(B) to meet
(C) had been meeting
(D) was met

142
(A) He believes the current buses can be improved to allow more seats.
(B) He wants the city to hire staff already skilled in the field.
(C) He feels the test to become a certified driver is too easy to pass.
(D) He expects the high fuel costs will lead to higher bus rates.

Questions 143-146 refer to the following letter.

To: Frans Vanek
From: Michelle Sekera
Date: 14 July
Subject: Good morning.

I learned of your upcoming ___143___ from a colleague. Even though the position of chief recruiter at our newly-opened office in Oslo officially ___144___ on August 2, I would like to take a moment now to wish you the very best in your new career. If you require any assistance, please do not hesitate to contact me. I am well aware that this type of transition, while exciting, is also extremely ___145___. Your work performance here in Paris at Chara Fashion as assistant hiring director has always been outstanding. ___146___ Congratulations and good luck!

Sincerely,

Michelle Sekera

143 (A) trip
(B) event
(C) award
(D) promotion

144 (A) begins
(B) began
(C) has begun
(D) could begin

145 (A) challenging
(B) challenge
(C) challenger
(D) challenges

146 (A) The Oslo office is a little smaller with a big parking lot.
(B) I'm still conducting interviews for all the new positions.
(C) You could ask about staff discounts at clothing shops.
(D) I am certain that your will be successful in your new position.

PART 7

Directions: In this part, you will read a selection of texts, such as magazine and newspaper articles, e-mail, and instant messages. Each text or set of texts is followed by several questions. Select the best answer for each question and mark the letter (A), (B), (C), or (D) on your answer sheet.

Questions 147-148 refer to the following receipt.

Park Home Outfitters
229 Park Road South
Edmonton, Alberta
(777) 223-4455

Date: May 12		Time: 10:37

- SALE -

3345	La Roux 4-Seat Sofa	$499.00
3348	La Roux Armchair	$199.00
3355	La Roux Footstool	$99.00
4489	D&F 6-drawer Dresser	
	4 $79.00/ea	$316.00
1223	Star Designs pillow	
	2 $19.00/ea	$38.00
Subtotal		$1151.00
Tax (5%)		$57.55
Total		$1208.55
Paid by credit card		$1208.55

Total number of items purchased: 9

Returns may be made for all non-sale items within 60 days of purchase. To view our return policy, please visit www.parkhomeoutfitters.ca/returns.
****

Sign up for a membership on our website and receive up to 50% off on select online purchases. Offer ends June 28.
****

Thank you for shopping at Park Home Outfitters.

147 What kind of store most likely is Park Home Outfitters?

(A) A furniture store
(B) A fabric outlet
(C) A construction company
(D) A clothing store

148 According to the receipt, how can customers get a discount?

(A) By applying for a membership
(B) By showing a coupon
(C) By completing a survey
(D) By purchasing two or more items

Questions 149-150 refer to the following e-mail.

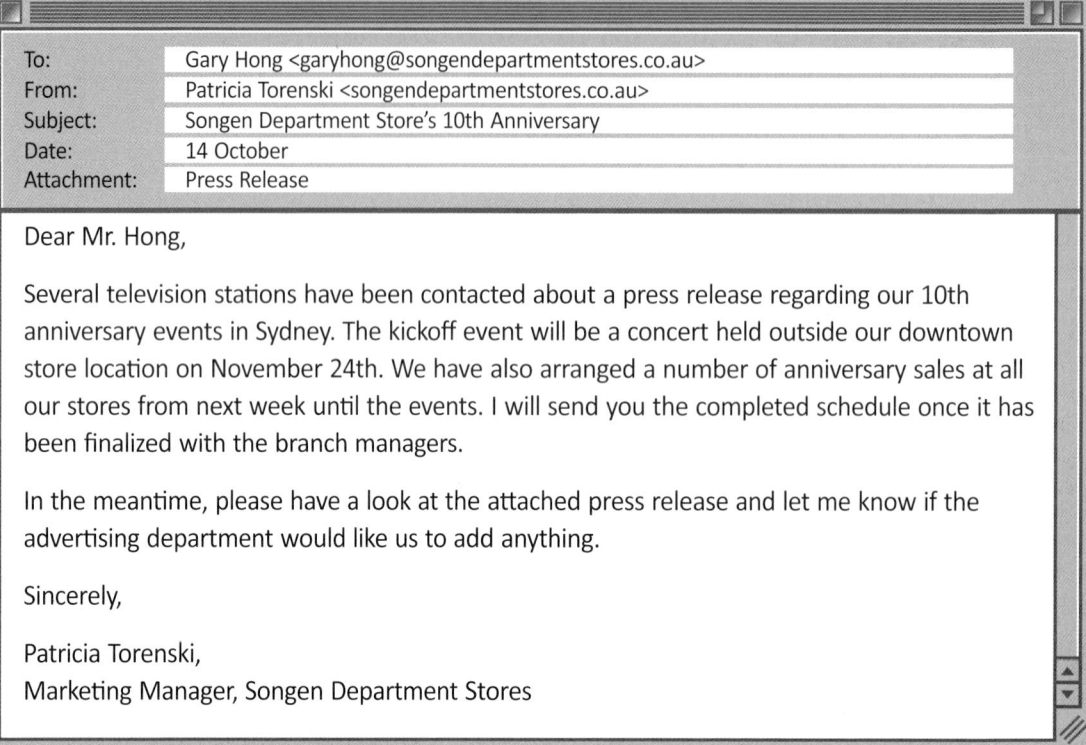

To: Gary Hong <garyhong@songendepartmentstores.co.au>
From: Patricia Torenski <songendepartmentstores.co.au>
Subject: Songen Department Store's 10th Anniversary
Date: 14 October
Attachment: Press Release

Dear Mr. Hong,

Several television stations have been contacted about a press release regarding our 10th anniversary events in Sydney. The kickoff event will be a concert held outside our downtown store location on November 24th. We have also arranged a number of anniversary sales at all our stores from next week until the events. I will send you the completed schedule once it has been finalized with the branch managers.

In the meantime, please have a look at the attached press release and let me know if the advertising department would like us to add anything.

Sincerely,

Patricia Torenski,
Marketing Manager, Songen Department Stores

149 What is the purpose of the e-mail?
 (A) To make a list of items for sale
 (B) To reschedule a live music event
 (C) To invite a coworker to attend an event
 (D) To give an update on a promotional plan

150 What does Ms. Torenski promise to send later?
 (A) A recent news article
 (B) A schedule of store discounts
 (C) A list of television stations
 (D) A revised press release

Questions 151-152 refer to the following article.

Around Town

Town Books owner Cynthia Purdel has announced her plans to open a second bookstore at 667 Brookside Avenue. The building, located across from Brookside Elementary School, was once the home of Smithton Bakery. Ms. Purdel's new bookstore, which has yet to be named, is scheduled to open in the spring of next year. The bookstore will include an extensive children's section, which Ms. Purdel hopes will attract numerous customers from Brookside Elementary School. Ms. Purdel's original bookstore, Town Books, is located on 5th Avenue and houses genres that are targeted to adult readers.

151 What is the purpose of the article?
(A) To discuss the closing of a business
(B) To profile a successful bakery owner
(C) To report on a store's relocation
(D) To announce the opening of a new business

152 What is indicated about the store on Brookside Avenue?
(A) It is located across from a popular bakery.
(B) It is scheduled to open this year.
(C) It is Ms. Purdel's first business venture.
(D) It is expected to receive business from students.

Questions 153-155 refer to the following notice.

St. Michael's Hospital Research Gala

St. Michael's Hospital will host a gala to benefit continued medical research. The gala will be held at the Grand Renaissance Hotel; however, the day has been changed due to a hotel booking error. Instead of September 20, the event will be held on October 5, from 5:00 P.M. until 8:00 P.M. Please note the following information before attending.

Directions to Grand Renaissance Hotel from Central Station:

Drive north on Parcelle Boulevard and turn right onto Meadow Drive. Turn left onto Bath Avenue and continue for five blocks before turning right onto Smithview Road. The Grand Renaissance Hotel is located across from the Mary Rose Theater. The gala will be held in Banquet Room 1A.

Parking Information:

Parking is available free of charge in the underground parking lot. Please ensure you have the parking pass that was issued along with your gala ticket. Otherwise, you will be responsible for paying for parking.

153 What has changed about the event?
  (A) The cost
  (B) The location
  (C) The sponsor
  (D) The date

154 Where is Central Station located?
  (A) Meadow Drive
  (B) Bath Avenue
  (C) Parcelle Boulevard
  (D) Smithview Road

155 What is indicated about the Grand Renaissance Hotel's parking?
  (A) Gala guests will have to pay for parking.
  (B) The parking lot is located across the street.
  (C) Parking is free with a guest pass.
  (D) The hotel has a shared parking garage.

Questions 156-157 refer to the following text message chain.

Steven Yoon 4:45 P.M.
Jennifer tried to call you about the meeting with the CEO tomorrow. She's wondering if you can call her back.

Roger Martinez 4:50 P.M.
I'm in the warehouse right now. Do you think she's worried the reports won't be finished in time?

Steven Yoon 4:52 P.M.
It's possible.

Roger Martinez 4:54 P.M.
Well, I'm checking the warehouse alarm system now. I got called away, because it seems to be acting up again.

Steven Yoon 4:57 P.M.
Do you want me to call the security company?

Roger Martinez 5:00 P.M.
I think I can fix it myself. Can you tell Jennifer to stop by my office at 5:30? I think we should discuss her concerns tonight before we go home.

Steven Yoon 5:01 P.M.
Okay. No problem.

---

156 At 4:50 P.M. what does Mr. Martinez most likely mean when he writes, "I'm in the warehouse right now"?

(A) He will not be in tomorrow.
(B) He has a delivery to make.
(C) He needs to speak with Mr. Yoon.
(D) He cannot call Jennifer.

157 What task is Mr. Yoon asked to do?

(A) Contact the CEO
(B) Set up a meeting
(C) Call a technician
(D) Leave the office

Questions 158-160 refer to the following letter.

October 10

Peter Stephenson
45 Ramsay Avenue
Cleveland, Ohio

Dear Mr. Stephenson:

Thank you very much for deciding to attend the very first International Magazine Festival that will take place in Paris, France. We received your registration. --[1]-- As requested, we billed your credit card to include both admission to the event as well as the extra fee needed to reserve a table for your display. Immediately upon arrival, we will show you to your table and also present you with a name badge that will allow you to receive discounts at any beverage and food vendors at the festival. --[2]--

We would like to remind you that accommodation is not included in the festival admission price. To reserve a room in the neighborhood, please visit www.parishotels.com. You may be able to book a room at 25% off the regular rate by providing proof that you are participating in our festival. --[3]--

Enclosed, please find a map of this particular area of Paris. This will allow you to acquaint yourself with the neighborhood. The map also includes the area's most popular restaurants and hotels. --[4]--

Again, thank you and we hope the International Magazine Festival turns out to be a rewarding experience for you.

Sincerely,

Nicole Desjardins,
Festival Coordinator

158 Why was the letter sent?
(A) To offer a partial refund
(B) To inform of an address change
(C) To explain a procedure
(D) To acknowledge registration

159 What is Mr. Stephenson advised to review ahead of time?
(A) A local map
(B) A meeting agenda
(C) Contract terms
(D) Flight times

160 n which of the positions marked [1], [2], [3], and [4] does the following sentence best belong?

"This letter is suitable verification so simply present it to the clerk when you check in."
(A) [1]
(B) [2]
(C) [3]
(D) [4]

Questions 161-164 refer to the following article.

Unforeseeable Delays for the Hammer Electronics 8000 Series

By Sophia Miachi

Last week, Hammer Electronics, the world's leading producer of smart phones, announced a delay in the launch of its new 8000 Series smart phone line. Industry professionals and customers alike were shocked by the news. Hammer Electronics enthusiasts took to social media to express their frustration with the cancelation of the much-anticipated 8000 Series.

According to Hammer representatives, the 8000 Series, which will consist of three individual models and various companion technologies, has been delayed due to unforeseeable problems with the company's new screen design. --[1]-- While the prototypes were initially approved, the first batch of devices were unable to pass safety tests. --[2]-- This may be due to a flaw in the glass used to construct the screens, which makes the internal components vulnerable to overheating.

In addition to not passing the inspections, Hammer's new line has proven to be less durable than the company intended. Because of the flawed materials, the 8000 Series has proven to be quite delicate. --[3]--

Hammer Electronics is now looking at alternative materials and plans to release the 8000 Series next year. --[4]-- However, the company may have already lost many of its eager customers.

161 What is indicated about Hammer Electronics?

(A) It is a top producer of smart phone technology.
(B) It will sell the 8000 Series at a discount.
(C) It is moving its headquarters to another country.
(D) It will continue producing a flawed design.

162 What is NOT mentioned as a problem with the 8000 Series design?

(A) The screens have flawed glass.
(B) The devices may overheat.
(C) The materials are too expensive.
(D) The devices are fragile.

163 Why will Hammer Electronics release the 8000 Series next year?

(A) They need to address a patent issue.
(B) Their inspections have been rescheduled.
(C) Some factories need to be upgraded.
(D) They need enough time to find new materials.

164 In which of the positions marked [1], [2], [3], and [4] does the following sentence best belong?

"For a company that prides itself on durable products, releasing this line of devices would be an embarrassment."

(A) [1]
(B) [2]
(C) [3]
(D) [4]

Questions 165-168 refer to the following text message chain.

Messages

Lester Gibbs [9:00]
Hi, Michelle. Are you at the office?

Michelle Chong [9:01]
Almost there. Why?

Lester Gibbs [9:03]
I'm working on a house here on Kensington Avenue, and just realized that I don't have enough red exterior paint left for the trim around the doors and windows. Do we have any cans of it left in our store? If not, I will just drive over to a store in Anders Park and pick up a can.

Michelle Chong [9:04]
Justin is at the office now. I'm including him right now. How many cans do you need?

--- Justin Whittaker has been added to the chat ---

Lester Gibbs [9:05]
I need two cans of red exterior paint. Can you please check the storage, Justin?

Justin Whittaker [9:07]
This must be your luck day.

Lester Gibbs [9:10]
Super! I have to finish painting the east side of the house and won't be starting the trim for at least an hour, so I will come by and pick them up after 10:00.

Michelle Chong [9:11]
Actually, I just backed my truck up to the loading dock and will get everything I need for a job on the corner of Nelson Avenue and Bicks Street. You're not far from that area so I can easily drop off the cans of red exterior first.

Lester Gibbs [9:15]
That would be great. Thanks a lot! Justin, please add my name and the current time to the stock record sheet. I will be sure to come by after lunch and sign the form.

Justin Whittaker [9:17]
No problem.

165 What type of business does Mr. Gibbs probably work for?
 (A) A home improvement contractor
 (B) A Internet provider
 (C) A plastics manufacturer
 (D) A fast food restaurant

166 Where does Ms. Chong say she will go next?
 (A) To Anders Park
 (B) To Kensington Avenue
 (C) To Bicks Street
 (D) To Nelson Avenue

167 At 9:07 A.M. what does Mr. Whittaker most likely mean when he writes, "This must be your lucky day"?
 (A) There is enough money for a new project.
 (B) The directions to the house are easy to follow.
 (C) The exact number of cans needed is in stock.
 (D) He will be able to help Mr. Gibbs in the evening.

168 What does Mr. Gibbs ask Mr. Whittaker to do?
 (A) Fill in the main details on a form
 (B) Place some items on a shelf
 (C) Set up a consultation with a client
 (D) Send an invoice to a local business

Questions 169-171 refer to the following advertisement.

BizNet
Networking at the click of a mouse!

BizNet is the latest development in online networking services. Quick, affordable, and easy-to-use, BizNet can connect you with industry professionals and help you land the job of your dreams. Our online services allow you to track trends in the job market as well as get up-to-date information on business conferences in your area.

In cooperation with our sister network, StudyNet, you get numerous advanced features, such as:
- A simple résumé builder that allows you to create a perfect résumé in minutes
- An extensive list of businesses and search tools for finding the right job opening
- A library of videos on everything from applying to interviewing for your dream job
- Weekly matching services that pair you up with new jobs based on your skills

For more information, visit www.biznet.com.

169 How would a customer most likely use BizNet?

(A) To shop for online services
(B) To find employment at a company
(C) To complete tax documents
(D) To advertise the services of a company

170 What is suggested about the company that developed BizNet?

(A) Its representatives can be contacted by telephone.
(B) It has a reputation for helping home businesses.
(C) It was founded by a large sales corporation.
(D) It has more than one networking website.

171 What is NOT mentioned as a feature of BizNet?

(A) A library of videos
(B) A résumé generator
(C) Tickets to conferences
(D) Employment search tools

Questions 172-175 refer to the following notice.

Lake Porticole Beach and Campground (LPBC)

Lake Porticole Beach and Campground will be open this spring & summer season beginning April 10 through to September 1. Please note, however, LPBC reserves the right to impose additional restrictions on campers. Due to the repeated occurrence of dry weather, campers may be prohibited from having open campfires at certain times. This does not apply to the use of camping stoves and barbecues for cooking, however. When fires are permitted, campers must purchase pre-cut wood from the park. Cutting down trees will not be permitted at any time.

Lake Porticole Beach may be accessed by non-campers for day visits for a small fee. Beach goers may arrive as early as 8 A.M. and stay until 5 P.M. Group tickets may be booked in advance for a discount. Additionally, the park offers guided tours of the Lake Porticole Museum, a historical estate originally owned by Sir William Marks. Tickets for the museum can be purchased at the front gate on the day of the tour.

Payment and Reservations
• For campsite reservations, call 888-341-0867. Campsites are $65.00 per night. A non-refundable deposit of $30.00 must be made at the time of reservation. This deposit goes toward the cost of your stay.
• Beach day passes for non-campers can be purchased upon arrival for $8.00 per person. Groups of more than fifteen can receive a 20% discount if reservations are made in advance.
• Lake Porticole Museum tickets are available for $7.00 per person. Tours are offered three times per day at 11 A.M., 1 P.M., and 3 P.M.

172 What is announced in the notice?
- (A) A new policy
- (B) A business's closing
- (C) An increase in fees
- (D) An operation schedule

173 What is indicated about visiting Lake Porticole's campground?
- (A) Campers can be fined for littering in the forest.
- (B) Campers might not be able to have campfires.
- (C) To see the museum, campers must be part of a group.
- (D) To access the beach, campers need to pay another fee.

174 What is mentioned about the Lake Porticole's non-camping services?
- (A) Museum tickets can be reserved.
- (B) Beach visitors can stay overnight on weekends.
- (C) Parasols are offered to beach visitors free of charge.
- (D) Groups can get a discount when visiting the beach.

175 What happens when a campsite reservation is canceled?
- (A) A reservation fee is lost.
- (B) A payment is refunded.
- (C) A bill will be sent.
- (D) A membership will be downgraded.

Questions 176-180 refer to the following letter and e-mail.

10 March

Ms. Kelly Norstram
Simpson Publishing
Human Resources Department
55 Center St.
Sydney, Australia

Dear Ms. Norstram,

I would like to take this opportunity to submit my application for the editorial director position at Simpson Publishing in its new Sydney office. As you can see from my enclosed résumé, I have extensive experience in the editorial field, including five years as head editor at Lush Magazine and three years as an editorial assistant at the Sydney Times newspaper.

Aside from this experience, I also have a Bachelor's degree in Journalism and a Master's degree in Publishing Studies. Furthermore, I believe I would add a new dimension to the editorial director position given that I am also a published author of seven children's books. I believe that my unique combination of experience will contribute greatly to the company.

Thank you very much for your time. I look forward to speaking with you.

Sincerely,
Adrian Perdu

To:	Simpson Publishing Editorial Staff
From:	Adrian Perdu
Date:	April 30
Subject:	Some Reminders

Editorial Staff Members,

It has been nearly a year since we first proposed our new line of educational children's books. I'd like to commend you all on your hard work on this series. With our publication date fast approaching, I'd just like to remind everyone of a few things.

First, please ensure you communicate with designers weekly regarding the overall design of our books. It is important that you give them your input and guidance in bringing our collective vision to fruition.

Second, some freelance proofreaders have fallen behind on their deadlines. Please make sure you keep in contact with them regularly and if need be, hire additional freelancers to complete the work.

Finally, as the release of our series will include a website launch, I'd like everyone to submit a biography for the "about us" section. A simple biography of about one hundred words will suffice.

Thank you all for your continued hard work, and I look forward to launch day!

Adrian

176 What is one purpose of the letter?
   (A) To inquire about a starting salary
   (B) To list some professional qualifications
   (C) To provide an employment reference
   (D) To ask about the location of a job

177 In the letter, the word "dimension" in paragraph 2, line 2, is closest in meaning to
   (A) demand
   (B) precedent
   (C) matter
   (D) characteristic

178 Why did Mr. Perdu write the e-mail?
   (A) To praise workers for getting tasks done
   (B) To stress the importance of some duties
   (C) To motivate employees to take on extra work
   (D) To inform new hires of special procedures

179 What is stated about Simpson Publishing?
   (A) It publishes primarily e-books.
   (B) It employs editors in seven countries.
   (C) It will discontinue some publications.
   (D) It will introduce its staff on its website.

180 What is suggested about Mr. Perdu?
   (A) He previously worked as a book designer.
   (B) He was hired by Simpson Publishing one year ago.
   (C) He moved to Sydney for a job opportunity.
   (D) He no longer writes books for children.

Questions 181-185 refer to the following e-mail and business plan.

To: Wanda Willis <willis@utcbankandloans.com>
From: Jeffrey Thomas <jthomas@mailmail.com>
Date: March 12
Re: Business Plan
Attachment: Revised Plan

Dear Ms. Willis,

Thank you so much for your quick reply. I am very happy you are able to help me secure financial backing for my new business venture. I have looked over all the feedback you sent and edited my business plan accordingly. As you advised, I have included a section that details our potential customers and attached the revised version.

I think this is all I need to complete the application package for my business loan. However, if there's anything else I need to fill out, please contact me.

I look forward to hearing from you.

Sincerely,
Jeffrey Thomas

Revised Business Plan: The Brim

Section 1. Purpose

Downtown Portside has become a bustling business district, filled with numerous office buildings, banks, and department stores. My business, The Brim, will be located near the prestigious court house, a busy area of the downtown core. We hope to offer a wide variety of international gourmet coffees at affordable prices, while also providing a relaxing atmosphere to enjoy our gourmet lunch items.

Section 2. Target Market

The Brim will serve business professionals working downtown. Because there are so many law offices and banks within walking distance, our customers are likely to visit our coffee house in the mornings, during break times, and at lunch. Furthermore, weekend customers will consist of shoppers who are visiting the nearby Portside Department Store.

Section 3. Timeline

The Brim is scheduled to open on June 1. We expect the following preparations to be completed by:

March 28	Sign the lease and apply for a business permit
April 10	Renovate the dining area and upgrade the kitchen
April 20	Hire staff and complete employee training
May 15	Finalize the menu, order inventory, and plan the grand opening

Section 4. Marketing Plan

Please see the attached spread sheet for our detailed marketing plans prior to opening and after.

181 What is the purpose of the e-mail?
(A) To review the guidelines of a permit
(B) To send feedback about some financial data
(C) To request advice on writing a business plan
(D) To respond to a requested revision

182 In the e-mail, the word "secure" in paragraph 1, line 1, is closest in meaning to
(A) guard
(B) obtain
(C) save
(D) fasten

183 What section of the business plan was added?
(A) Section 1
(B) Section 2
(C) Section 3
(D) Section 4

184 What type of business does Mr. Thomas plan to start?
(A) A loan company
(B) A department store
(C) A law office
(D) A gourmet cafe

185 According to the business plan, what information was submitted separately?
(A) A detailed estimate of expected profits
(B) Contact information for employment references
(C) A list of ways the business will advertise
(D) Recommendations for renovation companies

Questions 186-190 refer to the following webpage, e-mail, and form.

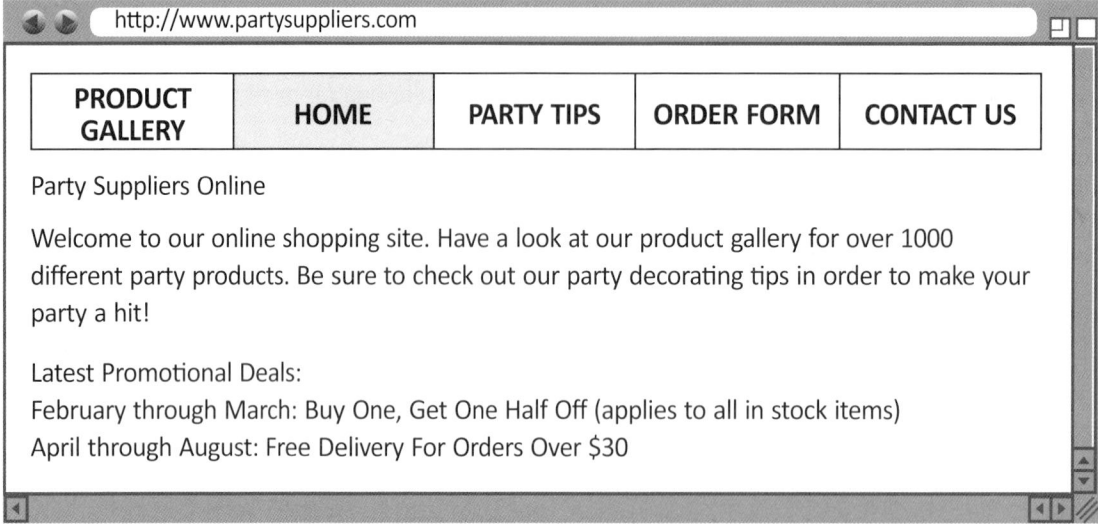

http://www.partysuppliers.com

| PRODUCT GALLERY | HOME | PARTY TIPS | ORDER FORM | CONTACT US |

Party Suppliers Online

Welcome to our online shopping site. Have a look at our product gallery for over 1000 different party products. Be sure to check out our party decorating tips in order to make your party a hit!

Latest Promotional Deals:
February through March: Buy One, Get One Half Off (applies to all in stock items)
April through August: Free Delivery For Orders Over $30

From:	Mathew Sparks [msparks@stantonautomotive.com]
To:	June Baxtor [juneb@stantonautomotive.com]
Date:	April 27
Subject:	Grand Opening Update

Hi June,

I've compared Party Suppliers Online with Cape Bernard Party Mart and chosen the former to get everything we need for the grand opening party on the 4th. They seem to provide a lot of great tips for setting up their products, so it shouldn't be much work to make the showroom look great.

I think we should order a custom banner for the showroom along with streamers and balloons. We can also get a larger banner made, which will hang in front of the door outside.

If you agree with me, I'd like to get our order in quickly. The workspace is still pretty messy, but the painters should finish up soon, which will give us just enough time to set up before the big day.

Let me know what you think when you get a chance.
Mathew

Order Number: 112233265
Contact Info: Mathew Sparks (444) 232-0916
Delivery To: Stanton Automotive Dealership, 14 Brooks Lane, Atlantic City
Delivery Window: 01-02 May, 09:00-13:00

Quantity	Product Code	Description
1	YZ0933	Custom Banner (3 feet long)
1	YZ0955	Custom Banner (6 feet long)
12	GH3345	Rainbow Balloons 12 per pack
2	BB3200	Streamers (white)
		Total: $104.50

Note: All our custom banners are printed at our manufacturing headquarters in Baltimore. Those items will be shipped into Atlantic City from Baltimore instead of our Port Edward store, which means you will have two separate shipments. Should you have any questions, do not hesitate to call us immediately.

186 What is indicated about Party Suppliers Online?
(A) It provides complimentary product samples.
(B) It offers decorating advice to customers.
(C) It recently opened up another store.
(D) It will expand its product line next year.

187 What is probably true about Stanton Automotive Dealership's order?
(A) It will be delivered for free.
(B) It includes foreign products.
(C) It includes half-price items.
(D) It will be refunded in May.

188 Why does Mr. Sparks probably prefer to schedule a delivery quickly?
(A) He needs time to purchase more items.
(B) He wants to take advantage of a promotion.
(C) He needs some workers to help clean up.
(D) He wants to have enough time to set up.

189 What product will most likely be placed outside Stanton Automotive Dealership?
(A) Custom Banner 3ft
(B) Custom Banner 6ft
(C) Rainbow Balloons
(D) Streamers

190 According to the form, where most likely will the balloons be shipped from?
(A) Baltimore
(B) Atlantic City
(C) Cape Bernard
(D) Port Edward

Questions 191-195 refer to the following e-mail, menu and comment card.

From:	Jimmy Pertelli <jperteilli@jimmysitalianrestaurant.com>
To:	Sue Hamilton <suehamilton@jimmysitalianrestaurant.com>
Date:	Monday, January 10
Subject:	Menu tasting event

Hello Sue,

It's hard to believe we're reopening in less than a month. Since we've yet to finalize a menu, let's take some time to think about the best dishes for Jimmy's Italian Restaurant. I think it would be a good idea to host a private tasting event for our friends and families next week on Saturday.

I have some ideas about what we could serve at the tasting. What about making a hearty deep-dish vegetarian pizza? This would really highlight our new vegetarian menu options. I think our baked lobster platter would be another great entrée choice. I'd also love to serve some of our new dessert options, but that all depends on whether or not construction on the pastry station is completed. In the event that it's not, how about serving some of our new organic ice cream flavors topped with your amazing chocolate sauce? I will leave it all up to you, though. As head chef, you have complete freedom.

Finally, I'd love to offer our guests an ice-cream making demonstration after the tasting. Let me know if you think that would be possible.

Thanks,
Jimmy

Jimmy's Italian Restaurant Tasting Menu
Saturday, January 15

Caprese Salad with mozzarella cheese and fresh basil
Coconut Shrimp
Baked Garlic Bread
Vegetarian Pasta with tomato sauce
Baked Lobster Platter smothered in melted butter
Ribeye Fire-Grilled Steak served with roasted potatoes
Jimmy's Famous Puff Pastries

Tasting Comment Card

Name: Fran Humphrey

Please comment on your tasting experience at Jimmy's Italian Restaurant.

I enjoyed the appetizers very much. The salad, however, had too much balsamic dressing for my taste. The vegetarian pasta dish was quite good, but I found the noodles to be a bit overcooked. The baked lobster, on the other hand, was the best I've ever tasted. I found the steak to be a bit rare, but the potatoes were seasoned very nicely. The dessert was perhaps too sweet for me, but I thought the pastry was cooked to perfection. I also enjoyed the ice cream making demonstration, though I wish we could've tasted some of the flavors.

---

191 What is the purpose of the menu tasting?
(A) To select dishes for a new menu
(B) To prepare for a restaurant inspection
(C) To audition new cooking staff
(D) To decide who will be head chef

192 In the e-mail, the word "hearty" in paragraph 2, line 1, is closest in meaning to
(A) sincere
(B) aromatic
(C) satisfying
(D) original

193 What is true about the tasting menu?
(A) It showcases only old menu items.
(B) It lists several new ice cream flavors.
(C) It is only available to customers on weekends.
(D) It includes an entrée suggested by Mr. Pertelli.

194 Which menu item was most likely Ms. Humphrey's favorite?
(A) The salad
(B) The pasta
(C) The lobster
(D) The steak

195 What is suggested about the pastry station?
(A) It was too large for the kitchen.
(B) It was moved to another location.
(C) It was damaged in a renovation.
(D) It was completed on time.

Questions 196-200 refer to the following advertisement, e-mail, and text message.

Hartford Opera House
45 Bellview Street
New York City
www.hartfordoperhouse.com

The Hartford Opera House is pleased to announce an exciting schedule of events that will take place this summer. We will be featuring everything from concerts to stage plays, so we are sure to have something for you. Tickets will be available on our website for each event, and seasonal passes may be purchased for a lump sum. Seasonal pass holders will be able to attend as many events as they wish and bring up to three guests at a time free of charge.

Schedule of Events:

June 23 - The Miller Brothers Classical Ensemble
July 3 - Stand-Up Comedy by Alan Brewer
July 4 - Into the Jungle, an award-winning musical featuring songs by Catrina Belford
July 10 - Women of Egypt, a stage play directed by Tommy Wilson

For a complete summer schedule, please visit www.hartfordoperahouse.com.

To:	Lila Sampson
From:	Roderick Kelly
Cc:	June Varek
Subject:	Your Trip to Meadworth Paper and Packaging
Date:	June 2

Dear Ms. Sampson,

We at Meadworth Paper and Packaging are looking forward to your visit to our company headquarters from July 2 to July 4. We are very pleased that your company has agreed to discuss the terms of a possible merger between our two businesses.

In addition to providing you with a tour of our factory and offices, we have an exciting schedule planned for you, which will include a lunch with our CEO, a trip to Westflower Golf Club, and an excursion at the Harbor Yacht Club. We have also scheduled an evening at our local opera house for some live entertainment on your last night. We hope you will enjoy your trip, and if you need anything else, please let me know.

Sincerely

Roderick Kelly
Meadworth Paper and Packaging

From: Varek

To: Kelly

The weather forecast predicts rain during our trip to the golf club with Ms. Sampson next week. I think it would be best if you switched the golf club visit with the opera house event. This will change the opera house event we'll attend, but there's no need to buy new tickets. I'm allowed to bring a few guests free of charge.

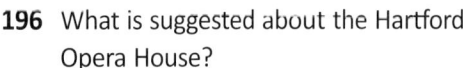

196 What is suggested about the Hartford Opera House?

(A) It is merging with another company.
(B) It gives away free seasonal passes.
(C) It is located next to a golf club.
(D) It schedules a variety of events.

197 What is Ms. Sampson scheduled to do during her visit?

(A) Discuss a new deal
(B) Review a contract
(C) Consult a lawyer
(D) Present a product

198 What opera house event was Ms. Sampson originally scheduled to attend?

(A) A classical music performance
(B) A live comedy performance
(C) A popular musical
(D) A stage play about Egypt

199 What does Mr. Kelly need to reschedule?

(A) A boat trip
(B) A game of golf
(C) A lunch meeting
(D) A factory tour

200 Why most likely does Ms. Varek not need to purchase tickets?

(A) The event they will attend is free for everyone.
(B) Ms. Sampson has not approved the schedule yet.
(C) Ms. Varek already has a seasonal pass for the opera house.
(D) Mr. Kelly must wait for some tickets to be refunded.

This is the end of the test. You may review Part 5, 6,
and 7 if you finish the test early.

ANSWERS

ACTUAL TEST 5

101. (B)	121. (C)	141. (D)	161. (A)	181. (D)
102. (B)	122. (D)	142. (B)	162. (C)	182. (B)
103. (C)	123. (C)	143. (D)	163. (D)	183. (B)
104. (A)	124. (A)	144. (A)	164. (C)	184. (D)
105. (D)	125. (C)	145. (A)	165. (A)	185. (C)
106. (A)	126. (A)	146. (D)	166. (B)	186. (B)
107. (C)	127. (D)	147. (A)	167. (C)	187. (A)
108. (A)	128. (B)	148. (A)	168. (A)	188. (D)
109. (B)	129. (C)	149. (D)	169. (B)	189. (B)
110. (D)	130. (D)	150. (B)	170. (D)	190. (D)
111. (D)	131. (B)	151. (D)	171. (C)	191. (A)
112. (B)	132. (C)	152. (D)	172. (D)	192. (C)
113. (B)	133. (B)	153. (D)	173. (B)	193. (D)
114. (C)	134. (D)	154. (C)	174. (D)	194. (C)
115. (B)	135. (B)	155. (C)	175. (A)	195. (D)
116. (D)	136. (C)	156. (D)	176. (B)	196. (D)
117. (A)	137. (B)	157. (B)	177. (D)	197. (A)
118. (C)	138. (D)	158. (D)	178. (B)	198. (C)
119. (B)	139. (A)	159. (A)	179. (D)	199. (B)
120. (A)	140. (C)	160. (C)	180. (B)	200. (C)

ACTUAL TEST 6

a b c
100 200 300

d e **f**
400 500 **600**

READING TEST

In the Reading Test, you will read a variety of texts and answer several different types of reading comprehension questions. The entire Reading test will last 75 minutes. There are three parts, and directions are given for each part. You are encouraged to answer as many questions as possible within the time allowed.

You must mark your answers on the separate answer sheet. Do not write your answers in your test book.

PART 5

Directions: A word or phrase is missing in each of the sentences below. Four answer choices are given below each sentence. Select the best answer to complete the sentence. Then mark the letter (A), (B), (C), or (D) on your answer sheet.

---

101 The shelves in the east warehouse must be ---------- stocked for the holiday season.

(A) full
(B) fully
(C) fuller
(D) fullest

102 ---------- to the swimming pool is reserved for guests staying in one of our deluxe suites.

(A) Access
(B) Accessed
(C) Accessing
(D) Accessible

103 Mr. Takashi admits that ---------- is expected to take on more managerial duties.

(A) he
(B) his
(C) him
(D) himself

104 At the end of the month, Davisville Incorporated is ------------ its Internet provider.

(A) changing
(B) attending
(C) holding
(D) turning

105 Better City Travel offers bicycle tours ---------- Skiff Lake at very reasonable rates.
(A) between
(B) along
(C) below
(D) apart

106 Of all snow tires, Marten's new MR-200 is, without a doubt, the most durable ----------.
(A) that
(B) any
(C) one
(D) either

107 As the amount of orders increased significantly, Lawford's Coffee Shop was able to ---------- new deals with its suppliers.
(A) negotiating
(B) negotiates
(C) negotiated
(D) negotiate

108 Pandora Hair Design offers employees ---------- opportunities to advance their careers.
(A) plenty
(B) each
(C) very
(D) many

109 Highway 56 between Greenville and Trenton has been blocked off ---------- fallen power poles.
(A) so that
(B) as a result
(C) in order to
(D) because of

110 It is impossible to rent an apartment in the Dorchester Building without a ------- from a current tenant.
(A) referring
(B) referred
(C) referral
(D) refer

111 A green sticker will be placed on the windshield ---------- after the inspection of the vehicle is complete.
(A) when
(B) only
(C) still
(D) most

112 Since two managers have opted for early retirement, it is --------- to find replacements by July 30.
(A) necessitating
(B) necessary
(C) necessarily
(D) necessities

113 The cargo elevator in the south end of the building will not be in operation ---------- further notice.
(A) until
(B) onto
(C) since
(D) all

114 The weight indicated on the outside of this package is ---------- accurate.
(A) fairness
(B) fairest
(C) fairly
(D) fair

115 David sent a link to a web site that has a ---------- of information on engine repair.
(A) wealth
(B) height
(C) labor
(D) fame

116 To find the easiest route to Simmons, Darthmouth, and nearby towns, be sure to look at an ---------- map.
(A) update
(B) updated
(C) updates
(D) updating

117 The hiring committee will start reviewing résumés --------- the application deadline has passed.
(A) how
(B) nor
(C) now that
(D) whether

118 On her television show, Gloria Van Cingel, the well-known art critic, --------- paintings from a variety of periods.
(A) analysis
(B) analyzer
(C) analyzes
(D) analyzing

119 The installation of several self-checkout kiosks in the Redford Supermarket is expected to create changes ---------- the number of employees.
(A) in
(B) again
(C) positions
(D) ultimately

120 Compared to everyone else, Donald prepared himself for the real estate license exam in a ---------- short period of time.
(A) surprised
(B) surprise
(C) surprisingly
(D) surprising

121 The production supervisor of Gleason Shoes is ---------- of all the factory's operations.
(A) aware
(B) current
(C) serious
(D) alert

122 The tourism --------- of Cape Breton Island has dramatically improved ever since the harbor was reopened last year.
(A) economical
(B) economic
(C) economize
(D) economy

123 Someone from Renforth Building Supplies asked us to -------- the type of lumber needed for the project.
(A) personify
(B) magnify
(C) specify
(D) testify

124 Fitzgerald Air offers flights to over 200 destinations ---------- northern Canada.
(A) toward
(B) throughout
(C) regarding
(D) aboard

125 The beginners' guitar class at the Lesterville Academy fills up quickly so we recommend filling out an online ---------- form.
(A) enrollment
(B) inventory
(C) complaint
(D) solicitation

126 On Friday, Lancaster Incorporated's newly -------- vice-president will address his staff for the first time.
(A) appoint
(B) appoints
(C) appointed
(D) appointing

127 The head of public relations must be continually in contact with the media so Randolph Industries ------------ someone with exceptional communication skills.
(A) seeking
(B) is seeking
(C) are sought
(D) have been sought

128 Ms. Laporte's approach to organizing a fundraising event is ------------ different from Ms. Halloway's.
(A) haltingly
(B) intimately
(C) permissibly
(D) markedly

129 Recently, Kingston has experienced a huge increase in the number of residents, ---------- are international students.
(A) inasmuch as
(B) the reason being
(C) because of them
(D) most of whom

130 To help the staff of the Carrington Inn make your stay more ------------ please fill out a guest feedback form and leave it at the front desk.
(A) knowledgeable
(B) considerable
(C) enjoyable
(D) available

PART 6

Directions: Read the texts that follow. A word, phrase, or sentence is missing in parts of each text. Four answer choices for each question are given below the text. Select the best answer to complete the text. Then mark the letter (A), (B), (C), or (D) on your answer sheet.

Questions 131-134 refer to the following e-mail.

To: sandrabae@gladstoneresearch.com.au
From: markjohnson@sydneyunienergy.au
Date: 15 May
Subject: Thank you!

Dear Dr. Bae,

Thank you very much for ...**131**... our main research center last Friday. Your expert advice, as always, ...**132**.... Our entire engineering team benefited greatly from your presentation on the exciting new advances in energy generation and consumption systems for industrial facilities. This fall, our department plans to hire five more engineering researchers. Would ...**133**... mind leading a training session on the topic you spoke of last week? ...**134**... We will look forward to your prompt response so that details can be discussed.

Sincerely,

Mark Johnson

131 (A) calling
(B) opening
(C) visiting
(D) staffing

132 (A) appreciates
(B) will be appreciated
(C) is appreciating
(D) was appreciated

133 (A) his
(B) yours
(C) you
(D) he

134 (A) All engineers must adhere to our center's strict regulations.
(B) A large number of candidates have impressive résumés.
(C) If you can, it would undoubtedly prove beneficial to the new staff.
(D) With your feedback, we will be able to build it quickly.

Questions 135-138 refer to the following article.

GEARY (April 5) - This morning, the National Transportation Authority announced that a $41 million grant has been awarded to Weston Valley Air Travel Network. Thanks to this ___135___, the dream of having two airports in Weston Valley will soon be realized. Many residents in the region welcome news of this expansion to the current air service. ___136___. Business owners throughout the Weston Valley are truly delighted. Jennifer Rossignol, a local business owner, expressed her delight with the grant earlier today. "This is fantastic news for someone like myself ___137___ has to travel to Toronto frequently on business," says Rossignol. "We have had no choice ___138___ years but to endure a four-hour bus ride into the city, but soon, I will be able to board a plane and be there in under an hour."

135 (A) funding
(B) policy
(C) design
(D) strategy

136 (A) Weston Valley Air Travel Network confirmed that the project must be delayed.
(B) Passengers will have access to more parking spaces at one of the airports.
(C) This development is expected to create over 500 jobs at both airports.
(D) Air fares for most regional flights, however, will most likely be raised.

137 (A) likewise
(B) another
(C) then
(D) who

138 (A) for
(B) with
(C) about
(D) on

Questions 139-142 refer to the following e-mail.

To: Arnold Mallory [amallory@channel6new.net]
From: Melinda Calhoun [mcalhoun@channel6news.net]
Re: Fantastic reviews
Date: March 21

Dear Arnold,

The managerial division here at Channel 6 News was positively excited to read sensational reviews of our program in both the Moncton Gazette and Uptown Entertainment. All of us agree that your work here has been nothing but ...**139**.... For this reason, Channel 6 News is truly delighted ...**140**... you a yearly bonus that will be added to your next monthly paycheck on March 30. ...**141**..., your current salary will be raised by 12% effective April 1. Since you took over as Head News Anchor last November, our number of regular viewers has tripled. ...**142**.... We could not have achieved any of this without your outstanding performance. On behalf of everyone at Channel 6 News, thank you for your hard work and dedication.

Melinda

139
(A) withdrawn
(B) matched
(C) affordable
(D) exceptiona

140
(A) to award
(B) an award
(C) it awarded
(D) that awards

141
(A) For example
(B) In addition
(C) Nevertheless
(D) On the other hand

142
(A) Channel 6 has also received fabulous reviews in national newspapers.
(B) An assistant news anchor will be hired sometime next month.
(C) Our team will meet next week to discuss changes to your show.
(D) You are one of two employees who are entitled to an annual bonus.

Questions 143-146 refer to the following article.

Electronics Trade Show
(25 August) The annual Global Electronics Trade Show came to Tokyo on Saturday, 23 August for the fifth consecutive year. ...143.... As was the case last year, China was the most ...144... represented nation. ...145..., organizers reported that the number of South American companies was significantly higher than previous years. Another noticeable change at this year's ...146... was the fact that the majority of companies showcased kitchen appliances rather than the usual entertainment electronics.

143 (A) Volunteers at the event were not required to pay the registration fee.
(B) Product demonstrations will be held in three different auditoriums.
(C) The event featured over 500 companies from every corner of the world.
(D) Recruiters collected résumés from university students in attendance.

144 (A) heavy
(B) heavily
(D) heavier
(D) heaviness

145 (A) Moreover
(B) Rather
(C) Instead
(D) Thus

146 (A) class
(B) demonstration
(C) event
(D) ceremony

PART 7

Directions: In this part, you will read a selection of texts, such as magazine and newspaper articles, e-mail, and instant messages. Each text or set of texts is followed by several questions. Select the best answer for each question and mark the letter (A), (B), (C), or (D) on your answer sheet.

Questions 147-148 refer to the following notice.

To our dear customers,

We are happy to announce that we will be hosting a weekly talent night starting in October. The event will be held every Wednesday from 6:00 P.M. until 8:00 P.M. and the stage will be set up on the first floor of our café.

Participants may sing, play instruments, or read poetry. Make sure to arrive early to sign up for a twenty-minute slot. All participants will be allowed free coffee or tea for the duration of the event.

For more information, please visit our website at www.cafemaria.com or call us at 777-4367.

147 Where would the notice most likely appear?
(A) In a subway station
(B) In a music book
(C) At a coffee house
(D) At a doctor's office

148 According to the notice, what will participants receive?
(A) Discount coupons
(B) A small payment
(C) A participation certificate
(D) Free beverages

Questions 149-150 refer to the following invoice.

Eastview Convention Center
55 Lakeview Road
Seattle, Washington

Date: April 12	**Bill To:**
Invoice number: 9800032	Trisha Baxter
	Pure Motorcycles
	90 Yamer Street
	Orlando, Florida

Invoice for the Eastview Convention Center's Annual Automotive Show from June 25 - June 27.

Item:	Rate:	Total:
Convention Booth (30 square feet)	$100.00/day	$300.00
Additional Services:		
3 display tables	$10.00/unit	$30.00
Storage	$30.00/unit	$120.00
Computer rental	$20.00/unit	$20.00
55-inch television rental	$30.00/unit	$30.00
Show passes	$20.00/person	$200.00
	Subtotal	$700.00
	Tax	$45.50
	Total	$745.50*

*Please visit your online account to arrange payment by April 20.

---

149 What is NOT included in the cost of the event?

(A) Passes to the show
(B) Display tables
(C) Television rental
(D) Set up and clean up

150 What is Ms. Baxter asked to do?

(A) Sign up for a membership
(B) Mail a check to the venue
(C) Settle an invoice
(D) Confirm the number of participants

Questions 151-152 refer to the following text message chain.

Jennifer Porter [11:23 A.M.]
Hi, Raphael. Were you able to stop by the Rickter Avenue property this weekend?

Raphael Morez [11:25 A.M.]
Yes, I went on Saturday. Since most of our photographers will be working at events every day, are you sure we need such a big place?

Jennifer Porter [11:27 A.M.]
The rooms are large, but as we expand, we'll need the space.

Raphael Morez [11:28 A.M.]
That might not happen for a few years, though.

Jennifer Porter [11:30 A.M.]
Yes, but we should be thinking about our long-term goals for the company. The Rickter Avenue property will give us a chance to finally develop an on-site studio.

Raphael Morez [11:32 A.M.]
You're right. We'll definitely need the extra space once we start offering portrait services.

151 At what kind of business do the people most likely work?
 (A) A photography company
 (B) A fashion design house
 (C) An event planning business
 (D) An art gallery

152 At 11:32 A.M., what does Mr. Morez most likely mean when he writes, "You're right"?
 (A) A location is too far from the city.
 (B) The building will help the company meet its goals.
 (C) Much interior design work is needed in the building.
 (D) The property has some significant flaws.

Questions 153-155 refer to the following e-mail.

To: Tristan Starr
From: Emilia Simpson
Date: June 2
Re: Walton Shopping Center contract

Hi Tristan,

I just got an e-mail from Marcus Pine about the budget proposal you sent him yesterday. Apparently, several of the figures are incorrect. It seems you included the initial figures we presented to him during our first advertising pitch on May 6 and not the figures we later agreed on during negotiations on May 20.

Mr. Pine was hoping to present the advertising plan to his superiors on June 5. He mentioned that there are several other agencies that have sent him proposals, and he will select one of them instead if we cannot get this paperwork done by June 3. Since I'm just about to fly to our Chicago office, I'm hoping you can handle this right away. Please send Mr. Pine the revised proposal and e-mail me when you get his response.

Sincerely,
Emilia

---

153 Why was the e-mail written?

(A) To request a vacation
(B) To introduce an applicant
(C) To announce a policy change
(D) To point out some mistakes

154 When was the proposal modified?

(A) On May 6th
(B) On May 20th
(C) On June 3rd
(D) On June 5th

155 What would Ms. Simpson like Mr. Starr to do?

(A) Make a phone call
(B) Issue a refund
(C) Send a document
(D) Speak with a manager

Questions 156-157 refer to the following article.

Restaurant sales are down in Plymouth County. According to a report in the Plymouth Journal, sales have dropped by more than fifteen percent this winter. The drop has shocked many restaurant owners, especially since the winter holidays usually increase restaurant business. Bob Fulton, owner of Little Italy Eatery, attributed the drop to an increase in wholesale prices as one factor of the drop. "With the prices of everything going up, we've had to increase our prices as well," Mr. Fulton said in an interview. "Most customers just don't want to pay that much for a meal." To encourage more business, many local restaurants have joined forces to develop membership programs. These programs provide customers with discounts at numerous restaurants in the county.

156 According to the article, why have restaurant sales dropped?

(A) The weather has become unpleasant.
(B) The costs have risen too high.
(C) Newer restaurants have been built.
(D) Many local jobs have been lost.

157 How are restaurant owners responding to the trend?

(A) By improving the quality of the food
(B) By decreasing the number of workers
(C) By working with other restaurants
(D) By launching television advertisements.

Questions 158-161 refer to the following online chat discussion.

Rita Frasier [2:23 P.M.]	Ms. Norton, do you have a minute? Thomas and I are unclear about our assignments. Last year, I was in charge of developing the seasonal training program, but Thomas was assigned the exact same job this year.
Patrina Norton [2:25 P.M.]	Yes, everyone needs a chance to work on developing their own programs for human resources.
Rita Frasier [2:26 P.M.]	So, we will no longer use the materials I developed last year?
Patrina Norton [2:28 P.M.]	That's right. Thomas is expected to develop new materials that will be used this year.
Thomas Woods [2:30 P.M.]	But what if I would like to use some of Rita's ideas?
Patrina Norton [2:33 P.M.]	Program development is part of the job.
Thomas Woods [2:35 P.M.]	Yes, but Rita's program was excellent last year. I would hate all her hard work to go to waste.
Patrina Norton [2:39 P.M.]	If Rita is okay with it, I think you could use some of her materials so long as you update them where appropriate. Let me review last year's materials first and get back to you.
Rita Frasier [2:41 P.M.]	What if Thomas and I worked together on the project?
Patrina Norton [2:44 P.M.]	I don't think that will be necessary.
Rita Frasier [2:45 P.M.]	Okay, I understand.
Thomas Woods [2:46 P.M.]	Let us know when you've decided. Thanks.

158 Who most likely is Ms. Norton?
- (A) A financial planner
- (B) A human resources manager
- (C) A company intern
- (D) An advertising consultant

159 What is suggested about Ms. Frasier?
- (A) She developed a successful training program last year.
- (B) She usually works with Mr. Woods on projects.
- (C) She is pleased with this year's assignment.
- (D) She will take over Ms. Norton's job next year.

160 At 2:33 P.M., what does Ms. Norton most likely mean when she writes, "Program development is part of the job"?
- (A) Her job duties include program development.
- (B) She believes Ms. Frasier is better suited for the job.
- (C) She disagrees with Mr. Woods's suggestion.
- (D) Her contract with the company needs revising.

161 What will most likely happen next?
- (A) Ms. Frasier will contact a supervisor.
- (B) Mr. Woods will begin working on a project.
- (C) Mr. Woods and Ms. Frasier will have a meeting.
- (D) Ms. Norton will look at some old materials.

Questions 162-165 refer to the following e-mail.

To: Tamika Keynes
From: Marcel Ventrue
Re: Information
Date: April 22

I'm writing in regards to the service quote you requested on our website. I'm delighted you're interested in Lawn and Garden Care's extensive range of services. --[1]-- I can assure you that we are the top landscaping company in the city. We service many local businesses, such as hotels and country clubs. --[2]-- We also maintain the extensive lawns at Memorial Stadium downtown.

I have attached the service quote you requested. --[3]-- The quote is based on weekly lawn maintenance services for The Renolds Gallery. However, in the event that you require additional services, such as garden planting or tree removal, you would be charged extra. --[4]-- Have a look at the quote and I will be in touch early next week to answer any questions you might have.

Sincerely,
Marcel Ventrue

162 What is the purpose of the e-mail?
(A) To change a schedule
(B) To respond to a request
(C) To send a blueprint
(D) To submit an application

163 For what kind of business does Ms. Keynes most likely work?
(A) An art gallery
(B) A stadium
(C) A country club
(D) A hotel

164 What is mentioned in the e-mail?
(A) Ms. Keynes is a new employee at Lawn and Garden Care.
(B) Lawn and Garden Care is a new business.
(C) Ms. Keynes will hear from Mr. Ventrue next week.
(D) Mr. Ventrue visited Ms. Keynes' business.

165 In which of the positions marked [1], [2], [3], and [4] does the following sentence best belong?

"However, all additional services will be discounted should you sign a two-year contract with us."

(A) [1]
(B) [2]
(C) [3]
(D) [4]

Questions 166-168 refer to the following article.

Parker Wallace to Join Adventure Software
By Amy Swanson, The Daily Chat

NEW YORK (24 February) - Parker Wallace has announced he will join the new start-up Adventure Software. Wallace, who has been developing software applications for five years now, is best known as the creator of Marble FM, a music sharing application. Marble FM accumulated over three million downloads in just two years, leading Wallace to become one of the most sought-after developers in the industry.

Despite turning down jobs at Liquid Apps and T&B Developers, Wallace has made the surprising move and accepted an offer to join a company that is less than two years old. "When I met Alan Pike of Adventure Software, I knew he and I shared the same goals," Wallace recently said at the launch of his latest app. "He and I are both passionate about music, and he had some great ideas for future projects. I am extremely confident that we'll be putting out hot new products in the next year."

Wallace's newest app, Marble Video, has already generated over 500,000 downloads in less than a month. The tech world will be expecting big things from the partnership between Wallace and Pike, starting with the rerelease of an upgraded version of Pike's Smart Symphony on March 30.

166 Who most likely is Mr. Pike?
(A) A film director
(B) A symphony composer
(C) A music video producer
(D) A software company owner

167 What most likely is true about Ms. Swanson?
(A) She was formerly employed at Liquid Apps.
(B) She attended the launch of Marble Video.
(C) She purchased a copy of Marble FM.
(D) She met with Mr. Pike at an event.

168 What is indicated about Smart Symphony?
(A) It is an already existing app.
(B) It was originally developed by T&B Developers.
(C) It will be limited to 500,000 copies.
(D) It will feature elements of Marble FM.

Questions 169-171 refer to the following brochure.

Energy Savers
Are you paying high utility bills during the summer or winter months? With Energy Savers, you can find the energy solutions that will save you money. Contact us for your free four-step consultation.

1. Determine your energy needs
Our qualified energy consultants will visit your home to determine what your energy needs are. You will be asked to complete a detailed survey regarding the number of hours you spend at home, your desired temperatures during each season, and your cooking and cleaning habits.

2. Home inspection
Once our consultants determine your needs, they will inspect the windows, walls, and doors of your home to ensure proper insulation. They will also test your heating, cooling, and lighting systems for weaknesses. Unlike other companies, Energy Savers will prepare a detailed report of flaws and make suggestions for improvements.

3. Choose your upgrades
Our consultants will discuss the recommended upgrades for your home while keeping your budget in mind. We can help you choose and install everything from double-paned glass for your windows to solar panels on your roof.

4. Installations
Our team will work around your schedule to install your upgrades. However, most installations take several days to complete. You will see instant savings on your utility bills and the best part is those savings never end. You will continue to save money for years to come. Should you have problems with your upgrades within the first year, Energy Savers will fix them free of charge.

169 What is the purpose of the brochure?

(A) To announce a new type of energy
(B) To compare two energy companies
(C) To advertise a company's services
(D) To discuss the benefits of insulation

170 What is NOT examined during the home consultation?

(A) The number of hours the home is occupied
(B) The home owner's preferred temperatures
(C) The efficiency of heating systems
(D) The current cost of monthly utilities

171 What does the brochure suggest is one disadvantage of the upgrades?

(A) The upgrades are costly to purchase.
(B) It takes time to install all the features.
(C) Home owners must be present during the installations.
(D) Monthly bills will not decrease for a year.

Questions 172-175 refer to the following article.

Newmont Technology Convention to Launch World Tour

March 5 - The Newmont Technology Convention (NTC) is scheduled to make the first stop on its world tour next month. The convention is one of the world's largest technology exhibitions and features everything from medical technology to aerospace engineering demonstrations. The NTC was founded in Sydney, Australia by Newmont Industries and its CEO, Barret Michaels. --[1]-- Every year, over 30,000 people visit the Sydney convention to see some of the most innovative technologies that have not yet reached the market.

The NTC commonly hosts scientists from all over the world, but this is the first year it will become an international traveling exhibition. --[2]-- Mr. Michaels stated in an interview, "We're very excited about this expansion. When we started the convention ten years ago, we had no idea it would grow to be the biggest technology event in the world. --[3]-- We're extremely happy to kick off our six-country tour in London, England next month. We're already expecting a huge crowd."

The U.S., Brazil, Japan, Germany, and South Africa will also host the NTC during its tour. Tickets to most of the tour dates are already sold out. --[4]-- "Industry professionals in both Canada and France have already reached out to us with proposals," Mr. Michaels said. "We're optimistic that other countries will make similar proposals."

172 What is true about Newmont Industries?

(A) It helped establish the Newmont Technology Convention.
(B) It has offices in England, Brazil, and Japan.
(C) It is the leading developer of medical technology.
(D) It buys and sells aerospace engineering equipment.

173 What is stated about the convention in Sydney?

(A) It took five years to become popular.
(B) It employs over 30,000 workers.
(C) It features technologies that cannot be purchased.
(D) It was the second location for the exhibition.

174 Where will the next Newmont Technology Convention be held?

(A) In France
(B) In England
(C) In Brazil
(D) In Japan

175 In which of the positions marked [1], [2], [3], and [4] does the following sentence best belong?

"If the NTC tour is successful, Mr. Michaels plans to add additional locations to next year's tour."

(A) [1]
(B) [2]
(C) [3]
(D) [4

Questions 176-180 refer to the following letter and survey.

Grand Palace Hotel
Koh Samui, Thailand

Bethanie Sparks
44 Brock Road,
Toronto, ON L1T 4W2

Dear Ms. Sparks,

Thank you for choosing the Grand Palace Hotel as your accommodation from October 12 to October 25. According to our records, you purchased your stay as part of our Vacation in Thailand package, which celebrated our hotel's 50th anniversary. We are conducting a short survey regarding this package. We would appreciate you completing the enclosed survey and returning it in the self-addressed envelope. If you respond by January 2, you will receive a 10% discount on your next trip as our thanks. However, should you send it back after that deadline, we would still like to enter you into a draw for a free night's stay in any of our hotels.

Sincerely,

Rita Lao
Grand Palace Hote

Grand Palace Hotel, Thailand
By participating in this survey, you can assist us in providing the best possible services to all our guests.

Name: Bethanie Sparks	**Date:** 28 November

1. May we call you to discuss your answers further?
• Yes, phone number_____   • NO

2. How would you rate the quality of our facilities and services?
• Poor   • Fair   • Average   • Good   • Excellent

Please explain your response: I found my room to be luxurious and clean. The food in the restaurant was also excellent. However, when I ordered room service, the food was always delivered quite late.

3. How would you rate our amenities?

• Poor   • Fair   • Average   • Good   • Excellent

Please explain your response: I enjoyed the variety of the activities you had to offer. During my stay, I was able to go scuba diving, cave exploring, attend a dance lesson, and even take a tour of the local markets. There were so many exciting things to do!

176 Why did Ms. Lao write to Ms. Sparks?

(A) To notify of a late payment
(B) To reschedule a hotel stay
(C) To request some customer feedback
(D) To respond to a complaint

177 What is indicated about the Grand Palace Hotel?

(A) Its head office is located in Thailand.
(B) It plans to build a hotel in Toronto.
(C) It wants to expand its recreational activities.
(D) It launched a promotion to celebrate an anniversary.

178 In the letter, the word "conducting" in paragraph 1 line 3 is closest in meaning to

(A) administering
(B) authorizing
(C) behaving
(D) transferring

179 What will Ms. Sparks most likely receive from the Grand Palace Hotel?

(A) A discount coupon
(B) Entrance into a contest
(C) Free scuba diving lessons
(D) A free night's stay

180 What does Ms. Sparks mention about the Grand Palace Hotel?

(A) Its staff did not help her solve a problem.
(B) It has a wide range of activities for guests.
(C) Its food was of poor quality.
(D) It has a great location in a large city.

Questions 181-185 refer to the following notice and form.

To:	Employees of Tombes Financial Monthly
From:	Tombes Publications Acquisition Board
Re:	Tombes-Parker Business and Finance
Date:	6 March

As you have been made aware, Tombes Financial Monthly plans to officially merge with Parker Business Magazine on April 27. This merger will be an exciting opportunity for both companies. Parker Business Magazine is one of the top three business publications and specializes in reporting on international business issues and trends. This merger will allow us to create the first-ever business and finance magazine, which we're sure will boost our publication to the number one spot. In addition, with our larger staff, we'll now be able to put out biweekly editions and generate more sales.

Department managers will meet during the week of April 2 to work out some of the details of the merger as well as the renovation of our brand-new office space downtown. If you have any concerns you'd like to raise during the meetings, please send an e-mail to the relevant department manager in advance.

Tombes Publications Acquisitions Board

Department	Date / Time	Department Managers
Editorial	Monday, April 2 9:00 A.M. – 1:00 P.M.	Joanne Steele, Editorial Director (Tombes Financial Monthly) / Tommy Renaldo, Editor-in-Chief (Parker Business Magazine)
Design	Tuesday, April 3 10:00 A.M. – 2:00 P.M.	Samuel Westford, Lead Designer (Tombes Financial Monthly) / Wendy Skeller, Head of Design (Parker Business Magazine)
Administrative	Wednesday, April 4 11:00 A.M. – 4:00 P.M.	Annabelle Cordel, Office Manager (Tombes Financial Monthly) / Steven Parinon, Office Manager (Parker Business Magazine)

| Public Relations | Thursday, April 5 09:30 A.M. – 12:00 P.M. | Laini Peterson, Lead Advertiser (Tombes Financial Monthly) / Sandy Baxter, Head of Advertising (Parker Business Magazine) |

*All meetings will take place at Tombes Financial Monthly in the relevant department.
*Steven Parinon will retire prior to the merger. Annabelle Cordel has been selected run the new office following the merger. All department managers are expected to attend the meeting on April 4, which will be in conference room A to accommodate the number of attendees.

181 What is one purpose of the memo?

(A) To remind of changes to a financial plan
(B) To explain why some employees were let go
(C) To announce the retirement of an office manager
(D) To note the benefits of an upcoming merger

182 According to the memo, what is Parker Business Magazine's area of expertise?

(A) Local finance
(B) Company mergers
(C) Government policies
(D) International business

183 What is suggested about the employees of Tombes-Parker Business and Finance?

(A) They have been asked to retire early.
(B) They will be able to apply for management positions.
(C) They will relocate to a new office building.
(D) They all need to attend the meeting on April 6.

184 What is indicated about Mr. Westford?

(A) He plans to take over the position of office manager.
(B) He will discuss some e-mailed questions at his meeting.
(C) He organized the merger between the two magazines.
(D) He chose the location for the new company headquarters.

185 What will happen at a meeting on April 4?

(A) A greater number of participants will be present.
(B) Mr. Parinon will be absent from the discussion.
(C) The CEO of Parker Business Magazine will give a presentation.
(D) Employees will be informed of their new job assignments.

GO ON TO THE NEXT PAGE

Questions 186-190 refer to the following announcement, instructions, and e-mail.

Individuals Needed for Mini Focus Groups

Dressler Marketing, the biggest market research company in Edmonton, is recruiting people between the ages of 21 and 70 for a study focused on travel. The event will take place in the conference center of the Sanderson Hotel, 48 Emery Avenue, during the second week of June. The study begins by viewing a series of short travel-related videos followed by small group discussions that are facilitated by our moderators. The entire session will last three hours and compensation will be provided for all who participate. Anyone interested can phone Dressler at 409-5321-8082. Be sure to mention study 73. To determine if a caller is eligible to take part in this study, he or she will be asked to remain on the line and respond to a few screening questions.

Roland,

Dressler Marketing really appreciates you taking time out from your busy work schedule to assist with our market research project for Pacific Adventures at the Sanderson Hotel. You will be facilitating four mini focus groups composed of five people each. Since the focus is travelling along Canada's west coast, our client insists that we locate individuals with extensive travel experience, either for business or leisure, in that region.

Schedule of Sessions from 3:00 to 6:00 P.M.
Age Range/Date
21-35 Tuesday, June 9
36-45 Wednesday, June 10
46-60 Thursday, June 11
61-70 Friday, June 12

Upon arrival, participants will be given yellow name tags. Make sure their name tags are clearly visible at all times during the study; especially when making the video recordings of the members' discussions. This will allow Dressler to refer to individuals by their names when submitting our findings and recommendations to Pacific Adventures.

Each of the four video clips centers on a different aspect of Pacific Adventures:

Video Clip 1: Group Discounts for Whale-watching tours
Video Clip 2: One-Day Kayaking Adventures
Video Clip 3: Popular Mountain Resorts
Video Clip 4: Hiking Adventures in Whistler Mountain

Nina Hernandez

To:	rothschild@pacificadventures.ca
From:	nhernandez@dressler.ca
Date:	28 June
Subject:	Study 73
Attachment:	Study 73 findings

Dear Mr. Rothschild

I am contacting to notify you that the research you requested last month for a specific target market has been completed. As the attached report indicates, one theme was the favorite of all focus groups. This theme represents an overview of the most popular places for travelers to stay. To ensure that we have covered all the key aspects in our findings, we would like to view the video with you and your representatives and have a lengthy discussion on it. Please inform us of a convenient time and date to meet.

Best regards,

Nina Hernandez
Head of Client Services, Dressler Marketing

186 What is NOT suggested about the participants of the mini focus groups?
(A) They will receive a payment.
(B) They need to answer questions when they call.
(C) They must be experienced travelers.
(D) They are hotel employees.

187 In the Instructions, paragraph 1, line 4, the word "locate" is the closest in meaning to
(A) remark
(B) believe
(C) find
(D) check

188 What is indicated about study 73?
(A) It will be held at Dressler's headquarters.
(B) It includes four groups of the same size.
(C) It centers solely on water leisure.
(D) It will be completed in two days.

189 According to the instructions, why were the participants provided with name tags?
(A) So that the marketing company can identify them easily.
(B) So that each registration number matches with the correct name.
(C) So that they would be able to find their seats quickly.
(D) So that they would be permitted to enter the conference center.

190 Based on the results of the study, what video clip was the most popular?
(A) Video Clip 1
(B) Video Clip 2
(C) Video Clip 3
(D) Video Clip 4

Questions 191-195 refer to the following schedule and two e-mails.

St. John Art Gallery
Upcoming Exhibitions

Dates	Title of Exhibition	Brief Description
11 April – 20 August	Recycled Materials as Sculptures	People usually see recycled materials as mere scrap piles. However, as this exhibition featuring the works of 10 artists throughout South America shows, any material can be transformed into breathtaking sculptures.
28 April – 3 October	The Portraits of Athletes	This watercolor collection features beautiful paintings of professional athletes by artists from every corner of the globe.
5 June – 29 November	More than Just Trees	This remarkable collection of photographs and paintings by artists throughout Africa and several Mediterranean nations captures the mesmerizing power of forests.
11 June – 14 July	The History of Food in Art	Through video recordings, sculptures, photographs, and paintings, this unique exhibition traces the history of food in the 15th to 19th century Europe.

Tickets can be purchased though our web site or by sending an e-mail to banderson@stjohnartgallery.org. To learn about our wonderful membership plans, simply go to our website and click on 'Become a St. John Art Gallery Member'! Members receive two free tickets to the exhibition of their choice.

From:	Chevon Jabar <CJabar@rogerstalent.ca>
To:	Belinda Anderson <banderson@stjohnartgallery.org>
Subject:	thank you
Date:	March 10

I am e-mailing to say thank you for the two free tickets to 'The History of Food in Art.' I also need another ticket for this event for my division head, Helena Lafleur. I assume the gallery has a record of my credit card details so please bill the same card and send the tickets to the same address.

I would like to thank your staff for providing such fantastic exhibitions.

Chevon Jabar

From:	Belinda Anderson <banderson@stjohnartgallery.org>
To:	Chevon Jabar <CJabar@rogerstalent.ca>
Subject:	a cancelled exhibition
Date:	March 14

Dear Mr. Jabar,

St. John Art Gallery would like to thank you for your patronage during the past seven years. We are truly sorry that the exhibition you and your colleague planned to see was cancelled due to circumstances beyond our control. However, we have already scheduled a replacement exhibition of black and white photographs. It is scheduled to run during the exact same dates (11 June- 14 July) and is called 'The Working Classes of Latin America'. I have already sent a new program guide in the mail to your office. Please let me know which exhibition you would like to see instead.

Thank you for your understanding in this matter.

Sincerely yours,

Belinda Anderson
St. John Art Gallery

191. According to the website, what do all of the exhibitions have in common?
    (A) They showcase works from various nations.
    (B) They showcase paintings from Mediterranean countries.
    (C) They include video presentations.
    (D) They include sculptures.

192. What is indicated about Mr. Jabar?
    (A) He donated a collection for an exhibition.
    (B) He is currently employed as an art instructor.
    (C) He has already seen three of the exhibits.
    (D) He is a paid member of the art gallery.

193. Which exhibition has been canceled?
    (A) Recycled Materials as Sculptures
    (B) The Portraits of Athletes
    (C) More Than Just Trees
    (D) The History of Food in Art

194. In the second e-mail, the word "run" in paragraph 1, line 4 is closest in meaning to
    (A) direct
    (B) remove
    (C) be shown
    (D) be announced

195. What did Ms. Anderson do for Mr. Jabar?
    (A) Bill his credit card
    (B) Mail an updated program guide
    (C) Upgrade his membership
    (D) Reschedule a social event

Questions 196-200 refer to the following e-mails and the attachment.

To:	Marcus Lount; Gabriella Sanchez; Daniel Wilkes
From:	Shelly Dorcas
Date:	July 16, 9:09 A.M.
Subject:	business space
Attachment:	available properties

Hi everyone,

I really enjoyed last Friday's lunch with you at the Davisville Grill. I am truly excited about opening our first Miami branch of Ebbet Construction Equipment Rentals. As Miami's housing market grows more and more each day, I am sure that we are all eager to attract our very first customers and start advising companies on the equipment that is most suitable for their projects and objectives.

I appreciate all the input you offered on the most appropriate business space. Using the budget and criteria you suggested, I searched for spaces at www.vanzylerealty.com. I found several possible spaces and compiled them into a list. That document is attached. Please have a look at it and get back to me with any comments you may have.

Shelly Dorcas, Ebbet Construction Equipment Rentals

13990 Gifford Way
Suburban two-story rental facility. Second floor office suites. Parking lot can accommodate up to 100 automobiles. Located across from Devon City's main bus terminal and near a large number of hotels used by business travelers. Half an hour from downtown Miami.
Monthly lease: $975

1389 Singleton Highway
Large retail space located in the heart of downtown Miami. Large sign on building makes it high visible to highway motorists. Building includes large storage facilities for parts and equipment. The newly installed air conditioning unit is guaranteed to keep you comfortable during the hot summers.
Monthly lease: $1,150

7643 Beckford Avenue
Third-floor retails and office space. Located uptown within Miami's main business district. Located on the same street as two major shopping centers. Facility includes state-of-the-art security alarm system. Printer/scanner/fax/color copier on-site for company use.
Monthly lease: $1,050

6094 Wilmot Drive
Single-story building. Comes with small office space. Land contract is also offered for property immediately behind facility. Located on the city's east side in lovely Ryerson Park, a prime Miami development site for condominium towers.
Monthly lease: $825

To:	Shelly Dorcas; Marcus Lount; Gabriella Sanchez
From:	Daniel Wilkes
Date:	July 20, 11:23 A.M.
Re:	business space

Hi everyone,

Thank you very much, Shelly, for all your work in narrowing our search to the options in the list you provided. I'm certain the strategy meeting held last Friday was quite productive. My apologies for not being there, but I was called to Boston all of a sudden on an urgent business matter. Also, I have to say thank all of you for being patient in waiting for my response to this important e-mail discussion.

Marcus, while I truly appreciate the need to save money on an inexpensive suburban facility, our company should not ignore the significance of having a facility conveniently located downtown as more and more homes are being built in that area.

I am also in agreement with Gabriella's idea that our company needs a booth at Miami's upcoming housing fair. Next week, I will be flying to Miami to visit relatives so I will look into the matter then. Also, while in Miami, I am scheduled to have lunch with a local realtor who worked for our company up until two years ago. Thank you, Shelly, for reminding me that Helen Richardson now resides in Miami. I'm sure she will have useful insights for us.

Daniel Wilkes, Ebbet Construction Equipment Rentals

196 Who most likely is Ms. Dorcas?
(A) A real estate expert
(B) An official in Miami Housing Bureau
(C) A construction equipment specialist
(D) A cook at Davisville Grill

197 What is one property feature mentioned in the attachment?
(A) An energy-efficient heating system
(B) A newly-installed carpet in the office
(C) A large cafeteria for employees
(D) A location close to housing development

198 What is suggested about Mr. Wilkes?
(A) He will fly to Miami tomorrow morning.
(B) He is renting some property in Boston.
(C) He did not make it to the Davisville Grill meeting.
(D) He plans to apply for a managerial position.

199 What is indicated about Ms. Sanchez?
(A) She suggested an idea to her colleagues by e-mail.
(B) She used to live in downtown Miami.
(C) She will meet a former colleague.
(D) She started her own equipment rental business.

200 Which property does Mr. Wilkes most likely favor?
(A) 13990 Gifford Way
(B) 1389 Singleton Highway
(C) 7643 Beckford Avenue
(D) 6094 Wilmot Drive

This is the end of the test. You may review Part 5, 6, and 7 if you finish the test early.

ANSWERS

ACTUAL TEST 6

101. (B)	121. (A)	141. (B)	161. (D)	181. (D)
102. (A)	122. (D)	142. (A)	162. (B)	182. (D)
103. (A)	123. (C)	143. (C)	163. (A)	183. (C)
104. (A)	124. (B)	144. (B)	164. (C)	184. (B)
105. (B)	125. (A)	145. (A)	165. (D)	185. (A)
106. (C)	126. (C)	146. (C)	166. (D)	186. (D)
107. (D)	127. (B)	147. (C)	167. (B)	187. (C)
108. (D)	128. (D)	148. (D)	168. (A)	188. (B)
109. (D)	129. (D)	149. (D)	169. (C)	189. (A)
110. (C)	130. (C)	150. (C)	170. (D)	190. (C)
111. (B)	131. (C)	151. (A)	171. (B)	191. (A)
112. (B)	132. (D)	152. (B)	172. (A)	192. (D)
113. (A)	133. (C)	153. (D)	173. (C)	193. (D)
114. (C)	134. (C)	154. (B)	174. (B)	194. (C)
115. (A)	135. (A)	155. (C)	175. (D)	195. (B)
116. (B)	136. (C)	156. (B)	176. (C)	196. (C)
117. (C)	137. (D)	157. (C)	177. (D)	197. (D)
118. (C)	138. (A)	158. (B)	178. (A)	198. (C)
119. (A)	139. (D)	159. (A)	179. (A)	199. (A)
120. (C)	140. (A)	160. (C)	180. (B)	200. (B)

RC 해설서
ACTUAL TEST 1

a
100

b
200

c
300

d
400

e
500

f
600

PART 5

모든 직원은 고용 종료 시 추천서와 퇴직금을 받을 것입니다.

어휘 receive 받다 severance pay 퇴직금 termination 종료 employment 고용

101 All employees will receive _____ letters and severance pay upon termination of employment.

(A) recommends (B) recommendation*
(C) recommended (D) recommending

타동사 receive의 목적어로서 letters와 함께 복합명사 '추천서'를 만들어 줄 명사 (B)가 정답이 된다. 명사 앞에 빈칸이 있으므로 형용사 역할을 할 수 있는 (C)와 (D)도 답으로 고려해 볼 수 있지만, 의미상 '추천된 편지' 또는 '추천하고 있는 편지'라는 어색한 어구가 되므로 오답이다. recommend 추천하다 recommendation 추천(장)

* 빈출 복합명사: travel document 여행 서류 account number 계좌 번호 construction delay 공사 지연 return policy 환불 정책 expiration date 만기일 product information 상품 정보 information distribution 정보 배포 retail sales 소매 판매 client satisfaction 고객 만족

정답 (B)

스티븐스 씨가 스테이셔너리 앤 페이퍼 월드에서 사무실용 새 비품을 구입해 왔습니다.

어휘 supplies 용품, 비품 stationery 문구류

102 Mr. Stevens picked up some new supplies for the office _____ Stationery and Paper World.

(A) but (B) as
(C) at* (D) after

적절한 전치사를 찾는 문제이다. 빈칸 이후는 비품을 구입한 장소(특정 업체: Stationery and Paper World)로 보는 것이 타당하므로 '~에서'를 뜻하는 (C)가 정답이다. 〈We at + 회사명〉이 주어로 시작되는 문장도 TOEIC에 종종 등장한다

정답 (C)

가능한 한 빨리 누군가 와서 복사기를 수리해야 합니다.

어휘 repair 수리하다, 수선하다

103 _____ needs to come and repair the photocopier as soon as possible.

(A) Someone* (B) Us
(C) They (D) Any

주어가 들어갈 자리이므로 (B)와 (D)는 바로 소거할 수 있다. 또한 빈칸 다음의 동사가 단수형이니 (C)도 부적절하다. 따라서 (A)가 정답이다. New TOEIC에서도 기본적인 수 일치 문제는 종종 출제된다.

정답 (A)

회사의 새 소프트웨어는 최근 버전으로 자동 업데이트하도록 설계되었습니다.

어휘 recent 최근의

104 The company's new software is designed to update to the most recent version _____.

(A) automate (B) automatic
(C) automated (D) automatically*

update라는 동사를 수식하기 위해 빈칸에는 부사 (D)가 들어갈 수 있다. automate 자동화하다 automatic 자동의 automatically 자동으로

정답 (D)

105

The new policies are designed to curb lateness and _____ employee accountability.

(A) promote* (B) declare
(C) obtain   (D) benefit

새 정책은 지각을 막고 직원들의 책임감을 고취시키기 위해 마련되었습니다.

어휘 policy 정책 curb 억제하다, 제한하다 lateness 늦음, 지각 accountability 책임

문맥상 '지각 방지'와 '책임감 장려'가 정책의 목적에 합당하므로 (A)가 정답이다. promote 촉진/장려/홍보하다, 승진시키다 declare 선언하다 obtain 얻다, 획득하다 benefit 유익하다, 유용하다

정답 (A)

106

Most employees have cited the positive work _____ as the reason they have remained with the company.

(A) reconstruction (B) environment*
(C) employment   (D) position

대다수 직원이 그들이 회사에 남는 이유로 긍정적인 근무 환경을 들었다.

어휘 cite A as B A를 B(이유, 예)로 들다 positive 긍정적인 reason 이유 remain 남다

'긍정적인 근무 환경'이 근속 이유로 타당하다. 따라서 work와 함께 복합명사를 이루어 자주 사용되는 (B)가 정답이다. reconstruction 복원, 재건 environment 환경 employment 고용, 채용 position 위치, 직책

* as의 '~로' 용례

work as ~로 일하다 regard A as B A를 B로 간주하다 treat A as B A를 B로 대하다, 취급하다 use A as B A를 B로 사용하다 come as a shock 충격으로 다가오다

정답 (B)

107

Martin's Coffee _____ over 300 shops across Canada by next summer.

(A) will have* (B) has
(C) is having (D) has had

마틴 커피는 내년 여름까지 캐나다 전역에 300여 개 매장을 두게 됩니다.

시간을 나타내는 부사구 next summer가 단서로 작용해 미래시제 (A)가 정답이 된다. 참고로, have는 소유를 의미할 때에는 진행형으로 쓰지 않는다.

* 진행형을 쓰지 않는 동사
소유를 나타내는 동사: have, own, possess
기호를 나타내는 동사: love, like, hate
인지를 나타내는 동사: know, recognize

정답 (A)

108

This law was passed to protect citizens _____ own and operate small businesses.

(A) for   (B) who*
(C) those (D) as

이 법은 소규모 업체를 소유 및 운영하는 시민들을 보호하기 위해 통과되었습니다.

어휘 law 법 pass 통과하다 protect 보호하다 own 소유하다 operate 운용/가동/경영하다

빈칸 앞에 '사람'을 나타내는 citizens가 선행사로 있으므로 주격 관계대명사 who가 들어갈 수 있다. 참고로, who는 여러 번 정답으로 출제되었다.

정답 (B)

새 공급 업체와의 미팅이 수요일 이른 시간으로 재조정되었습니다.

어휘 supplier 공급 업체 reschedule 일정을 다시 조정하다

109

The meeting with our new supplier has been rescheduled for _____ on Wednesday.

(A) hardly (B) comfortably
(C) early* (D) eagerly

문맥상 '수요일 일찍 미팅한다'는 요지를 완성해야 가장 자연스러우므로 적절한 부사는 시간과 관련된 (C)이다. hardly 거의 ~ 아니다 comfortably 편안하게, 수월하게 eagerly 열망하여, 간절히

정답 (C)

해버스톡 텔레폰 & 케이블은 즉각적인 고객 서비스 제공 업체로서 명성을 쌓았습니다.

어휘 provider 제공자, 제공 업체 prompt 즉각적인

110

Haverstock Telephone & Cable has built a _____ as a provider of prompt customer service.

(A) privilege (B) character
(C) reputation* (D) consequence

build의 목적어로 쓰일 만한 단어는 (B)와 (C)인데, '제공 업체로서 명성을 쌓았다'는 요지를 완성해야 가장 자연스러우므로 (C)가 정답이 된다. privilege 특혜, 특전 character 성격, 특징 reputation 평판, 명성 consequence 결과, 중요함
* have/earn/establish/build a reputation 평판(명성)을 가지다/얻다/확립하다/쌓다

정답 (C)

직원 편람에는 고객 불만을 다루기 위한 적절한 방법이 설명되어 있습니다.

어휘 handbook 편람, 안내서 proper 적절한 procedure 절차, 방법 handle 처리하다, 다루다 complaint 불평, 불만

111

The employee handbook _____ the proper procedure for handling customer complaints.

(A) outlining (B) outlines*
(C) to outline (D) is outlined

〈주어(The ~ handbook) + _____ + 목적어(the proper ~)〉의 구조이므로 목적어를 취할 수 있는 능동태 동사 (B)가 정답이다. outline 개요를 서술하다

정답 (B)

랜달 씨는 모두가 이용하도록 휴게실에 새 자판기들을 설치하기로 결정했습니다.

어휘 decide 결정하다 install 설치하다 vending machine 자판기

112

Mr. Randal has decided to install new vending machines in the lounge _____ everyone to use.

(A) if (B) to
(C) for* (D) until

맥락상 '모든 사람을 위해서'가 되어야 알맞다. 따라서 '~을 위하여'라는 의미의 전치사 (C)가 정답이다. 문법적으로는 to부정사(to use)의 의미상 주어를 나타내기 위해 〈for + 사람〉이 사용되었다. 가주어 문장에서도 It ~ for ~ to V의 구조로 for 다음에 의미상의 주어가 들어간다.

정답 (C)

113 Smith International Trading's department managers _____ conduct employee satisfaction surveys.

(A) lively
(B) harshly
(C) routinely*
(D) vastly

스미스 국제 무역사의 부서장들은 일상적으로 직원 만족 조사를 실시합니다.

어휘 department 부(서) satisfaction 만족 survey (설문)조사

'만족도 조사를 정기적으로 한다'는 요지의 문장이 되어야 가장 자연스러우므로 제시된 부사들 중 (C)가 적절하다. lively 활기 넘치는, 적극적인, 의욕적인 harshly 엄격히 routinely 일상적으로 vastly 대단히, 엄청나게

* 단순 현재시제는 일반적이고 지속적인 의미의 부사들과 잘 사용된다.
routinely, regularly, normally, always, usually, generally, often

정답 (C)

114 The consulting firm _____ several procedural changes that would improve the shipping company's efficiency.

(A) proposing
(B) proposed*
(C) proposal
(D) proposals

컨설팅 회사가 배송 회사의 효율을 개선할 만한 절차상의 몇 가지 변경 사항을 제안했습니다.

어휘 consulting 상담의, 자문의 firm 회사 procedural 절차의 change 변경 사항, 변화 improve 개선하다, 향상시키다 shipping 배송 efficiency 효율

빈칸은 전체 문장의 술어인 본동사 자리이다. 따라서 (B)가 들어갈 수 있다.
propose 제안하다 proposal 제안(서)

정답 (B)

115 The main responsibility of the volunteers is to help visitors _____ their way around the exhibition hall.

(A) do
(B) find*
(C) put
(D) ask

자원봉사자들의 주요 업무는 방문객들에게 전시장 곳곳의 길을 찾는 데 도움을 주는 것입니다.

responsibility 책임, 책무 find one's way around ~ 가는 길을 찾다, ~에 대한 사정이나 상태를 알게 되다

전시장 안에서 길을 '찾는' 데 도움을 주는 것이 임무라는 문맥을 완성해야 가장 자연스러우므로 (B)가 정답이 된다.

정답 (B)

116 Please retain this e-mail as _____ that your payment information has been entered into our system.

(A) confirm
(B) confirmed
(C) confirmable
(D) confirmation*

결제 정보를 우리 시스템에 입력했다는 확인으로서 이 이메일을 보관하시기 바랍니다.

어휘 retain 유지하다, 보유하다 payment 결제, 납부 enter 입력하다

전치사 as 다음에 추상명사 (D)가 들어가야 that절과 동격을 이룬다. 이처럼 쓰는 명사로 idea, suggestion 등이 있다. confirm 확실히 하다 confirmable 확인할 수 있는 confirmation 확인

정답 (D)

데라고 씨는 이 은행에서 약 10년 전에 일을 시작했으며 그때부터 쭉 부 매니저 직을 맡아 왔습니다.

어휘 decade 10년, 십년 assume (권력·책임을) 맡다

117

Ms. Derlago started working at this bank almost a decade ago and has _____ assumed the role of assistant manager.

(A) ever (B) yet
(C) so (D) since*

'과거의 특정 시점(a decade ago)부터 현재까지 지속적으로' 맡고 있는 역할에 대해 설명하는 현재완료 시제가 쓰였으므로 빈칸에 가장 적절한 부사는 (D)이다. since 그(때) 이후로, 그 후

* since의 다양한 용법
접속사: (S + V가 ~한) 이래로, ~이기 때문에
전치사: (명사)부터, 이후
부사: 그때 이후로, 그 후

정답 (D)

반즈 씨는 병원에 취업하는 데 필요한 추천서 몇 장을 모으려 하고 있습니다.

어휘 attempt 시도하다 collect 모으다 several 몇몇의 reference 추천서, 추천인 gain 얻다, 획득하다

118

Mr. Barns is attempting to collect several references _____ for gaining employment at the hospital.

(A) required* (B) requiring
(C) requires (D) will require

빈칸과 전치사 for가 '~하는 데 필요한'이라는 의미를 나타내야 하는데, 빈칸 앞에 which are가 생략된 것으로 보면 과거분사 (A)가 정답임을 알 수 있다. require는 타동사이므로 능동형인 (B) 뒤에는 바로 목적어가 따라 와야 한다. require 필요로 하다

정답 (A)

시 경계 내에 건물을 짓는 것에 대한 규정은 모두 시 허가 웹사이트에 올라 있습니다.

어휘 limit 한정, 경계 list 목록을 나열하다 permit 허가

119

The _____ for building within the city limits are all listed on the city's permit website.

(A) probabilities (B) allowances
(C) regulations* (D) varieties

후반부의 '허가(증)'를 뜻하는 permit과 가장 적절하게 어울릴 단어는 (C)이다. 참고로 (B) allowance는 TOEIC에서 종종 등장하는데, '용돈, 허용량(예: a baggage allowance of 20 kg)'이라는 뜻으로 잘 나온다. probability 개연성, 확률 allowance 용돈, 비용 regulation 규정, 규칙 variety 여러 가지

정답 (C)

오스틴 테크 대학에서 수행된 연구들은 국내에서 가장 앞서 나간 것으로 고려됩니다.

어휘 consider 고려하다 advanced 선진의, 고급의 상급의

120

_____ at Austin Tech University is considered the most advanced in the country.

(A) Research* (B) Researchers
(C) Researched (D) Researches

주어 자리이므로 명사인 (A)나 (B)를 답으로 고려할 수 있는데, 동사의 형태가 is considered이므로 단수 명사인 (A)가 정답이다. 참고로, research는 불가산명사라서 복수형을 쓰지 못한다. research 연구(하다) researcher 연구자

* 불가산명사
information, advice, progress, access, funding, correspondence, news, luggage/baggage, furniture, equipment, gear, clothing, merchandise, machinery, scenery, poetry, change(거스름돈), software, hardware, kitchenware, glassware, eyewear, footwear, sportswear

정답 (A)

121 Covington Ice Cream attributes its recent surge in sales to the addition of its newest flavor _____ its advertising campaigns.

(A) as for
(B) even so
(C) rather than*
(D) after all

코빙턴 아이스크림은 최근의 판매 증가를 광고보다는 최근 추가한 새로운 맛 때문이라고 봅니다.

어휘 attribute A to B A라는 결과를 B라는 원인에 돌리다 surge 급증, 급등 addition 추가(물) flavor 맛, 풍미

to 이하는 판매 증가의 원인이며, 빈칸 전후를 '비교'하는 맥락으로 볼 수 있으므로 (C)가 가장 적절하다. as for ~에 대해 말하자면 even so 그렇기는 하지만 rather than ~보다는 after all 결국에는

정답 (C)

---

122 The service at Wallace Limos improved _____ after the customer surveys were conducted.

(A) tightly
(B) markedly*
(C) manageably
(D) separately

월러스 리모의 서비스는 고객 설문 조사를 실시한 이래 두드러지게 개선됐습니다.

어휘 improve 개선되다, 향상시키다

'서비스가 설문 조사 후 (A) 단단히, 꽉 (B) 두드러지게 (C) 유순하게 (D) 별도로 개선됐다'에서 맥락상 가장 자연스러운 부사는 (B)이다. (B)의 동의어인 conspicuously(눈에 띄게, 두드러지게)도 함께 외워 두자.

정답 (B)

---

123 These computers are reserved for people searching _____ employment opportunities in downtown London.

(A) for*
(B) up
(C) as
(D) to

이 컴퓨터들은 런던 시내에서 고용 기회를 찾는 사람들을 위한 것입니다.

어휘 reserve 예약하다, (자리 등을) 따로 잡아두다 opportunity 기회

'~을 찾다'는 의미의 search for를 알면 쉽게 정답 (A)를 찾을 수 있다.

* search for = look for ~을 찾아보다
look up a word in a dictionary 사전에서 단어를 찾아보다
look up to 존경하다

정답 (A)

---

124 Please ensure that you have written all your information _____, as an error could result in a long delay in the process.

(A) affordably
(B) precisely*
(C) unitedly
(D) decisively

모든 정보를 정확히 작성해 주시기 바랍니다. 실수가 생기면 절차에 긴 지체가 발생할 수 있으니까요.

어휘 result in ~을 (결과로) 낳다, 야기하다 delay 지체, 지연 process 절차

콤마 이후가 '실수 발생 시 결과'이다. 따라서 '(실수가 생기지 않게) 정확히 써 달라'는 당부의 문맥이 완성되어야 타당하므로 (B)가 정답이 된다. affordably (가격이) 알맞게 precisely 정확히 unitedly 연합하여 decisively 단호히, 결정적으로

정답 (B)

THP 전력의 확장 계획에 대한 준 오스틴의 기사는 전 직원으로서의 그녀의 관점 때문에 매우 독특했습니다.

어휘 article 기사 expansion 확장, 확대 unique 독특한 former 이전의

125

June Austin's article on THP Power's expansion plans was very unique due to her _____ as a former employee.

(A) detail (B) prospect
(C) investment (D) perspective*

'직원이었던 기자는 자신의 (A) 세부 사항 (B) 가능성 (C) 투자 (D) 관점 덕에 독특한 기사를 쓸 수 있었다'는 의미를 담아야 하므로 가장 자연스러운 어휘는 (D)이다.

정답 (D)

인적 자원 부서 직원들은 부서 과장의 개입 없이 자신들의 힘으로 문제를 해결할 수 있었습니다.

어휘 human resources 인적 자원 solve 해결하다 intervention 개입, 간섭, 조정 department 부(서)

126

Human resources employees were able to solve the problem among _____ without intervention from the department manager.

(A) themselves* (B) theirs
(C) their (D) they

인칭대명사의 적절한 격을 찾는 문제로, 빈칸 앞의 전치사 among이 주요 단서가 된다. 목적격 (A)가 정답인데, 주어인 Human resources employees가 의미상 반복되는 상황이기 때문에 재귀대명사가 사용된 것이다.

정답 (A)

국제 회사 정책에 관한 한 브라운 씨가 아는 것이 많으니, 우리는 그에게 묻는 편이 낫습니다.

어휘 when it comes to ~에 관한 한 policy 정책

127

Mr. Brown is _____ when it comes to international company policies, so we had better ask him.

(A) appropriate (B) knowledgeable*
(C) undeveloped (D) triumphant

'그래서'라는 의미의 접속사 so로 두 절이 연결되어 있으므로, 콤마 앞 뒤의 근거가 되어야 한다. 따라서 '그에게 묻는 편이 낫다'는 결론이 도출되려면 '많이 알기 때문에'라는 맥락을 완성하는 (B)가 가장 적절하다. appropriate 적절한 knowledgeable 많이 아는 undeveloped 개발되지 않은 triumphant 크게 성공한, 의기양양한

정답 (B)

보험 계약자가 피해에 대한 청구서를 받자마자 자동차 보험금 지급 요청이 이루어져야 합니다.

어휘 insurance 보험 claims (보상금에 대한) 청구, 신청 policy owner 보험 계약자 bill 청구서 damage 손상, 피해

128

Car insurance claims must be made _____ policy owners receive bills for damages.

(A) as well as (B) as soon as*
(C) in regard to (D) in addition to

'청구서를 받자마자 지불 요청이 되어야 한다'는 요지를 완성해야 문맥상 가장 자연스러우므로 (B)가 정답이다. 참고로, (C)와 (D)는 to 다음에 명사가 와야 하니 〈주어 + 동사〉의 절이 연결된 빈칸에 들어갈 수 없다. as well as ~에 더하여, 게다가 as soon as ~하자마자 in regard to ~에 대하여 in addition to ~에 더하여, ~일 뿐 아니라

정답 (B)

129 With such a beautiful beach and huge assortment of art galleries, Adelaine Town is quite a _____ tourist spot.

(A) offering
(B) proposing
(C) promising*
(D) identifying

그토록 아름다운 해변과 엄청난 수의 미술 갤러리가 있으니, 아델레인 시는 상당히 유망한 관광지입니다.

어휘 huge 거대한, 막대한 assortment 모음 quite 상당히, 꽤 spot 장소

콤마 앞에 '관광 명소'로서의 특징이 되므로, tourist spot을 수식하기에 적절한 의미의 형용사는 '유망한'이란 뜻의 (C)이다. promising 유망한, 촉망되는 identify 확인하다

정답 (C)

130 The marketing department arranged to have weekly meetings to ensure a _____ effort is made on the new project.

(A) mundane
(B) transitional
(C) reduced
(D) concentrated*

새로운 프로젝트에 집중된 노력이 기울여질 수 있도록 하기 위해, 마케팅 부서는 주간 회의를 마련했습니다.

어휘 arrange 마련하다, 주선하다, 처리하다 weekly 매주의 ensure 반드시 ~하게 하다 effort 노력, 수고

'매주 회의하는 이유'는 '노력을 집중시키기 위해서'라고 보는 것이 타당하다. 따라서 (D)가 정답이 된다. (A) mundane은 매우 난이도가 높고 TOEIC에서 출제된 적이 없지만 최근에는 이런 단어도 출제되고 있다. mundane 재미없는, 일상적인 transitional 변천하는, 과도적인 reduced 줄인, 축소한 concentrated 집중된

* 명사 effort의 용례
make an effort 노력하다, 공을 들이다
in an effort to ~하기 위한 노력의 일환으로
a joint/group effort 공동의 작품
a concerted effort 합심한 노력

정답 (D)

PART 6

휴가 연장

스타 패키징에서 최소한 2년 동안 근무한 직원들은 여름 휴가를 5일 더 받을 자격이 될 수도 있습니다. ──── 부서 매니저들이 신청서를 검토할 것이며, 자격이 되는 신청자들은 추첨 시스템에 이름을 넣게 됩니다. 재직한 지 5년 이상 된 사람들에게 우선권이 주어지며, 열다섯 명까지 추첨될 것입니다.

어휘 extended 연장된 at least 적어도, 최소한 receive 받다 additional 추가의, 가외의 department 부(서) be responsible for ~을 맡다 application 신청(서) qualify 자격을 얻다 lottery 추첨 draw (제비를) 뽑다, 추첨하다

Questions 131-134 refer to the following information.

Extended Vacations

Employees who have been with Star Packaging for at least two years may be ---**131**--- to receive an additional five days of summer vacation. ---**132**---. Department managers will be responsible for reviewing the applications and those ---**133**--- who qualify will have their names entered into a lottery system. Those who have been at the company for five years or longer will be given ---**134**---, and up to fifteen names will be drawn from the lottery.

131
(A) prominent   (B) cooperative
(C) exclusive   (D) eligible*

빈칸 뒤의 to와 어울리며, 맥락상 '휴가를 받을 자격이 된다'는 요지를 완성해야 자연스러우므로 (D)가 정답이 된다. prominent 중요한, 유명한 cooperative 협력하는, 협동하는 exclusive 독점적인, 전용의 eligible (to V) ~할 자격이 되는

정답 (D)

(A) 직원들은 신청서를 작성해서 매니저에게 제출하면 됩니다.
(B) 예를 들어, 모든 장기 근속 직원들은 추가 혜택을 받게 됩니다.
(C) 하지만, 경쟁력 있는 임금 인상은 소수의 자격 있는 직원들에게 주어질 것입니다.
(D) 경영진은 신입 사원들이 고용됐음을 발표하게 되어 기쁩니다.

132
(A) Employees can fill out an application and return it to their manager.*
(B) For example, all long-term employees will receive additional benefits packages.
(C) However, competitive salary raises will be given to a few deserving employees.
(D) Management is pleased to announce that new employees have been hired.

이어지는 문장에서 '매니저들이 그 신청서들을 검토할 것'이라고 하므로 빈칸에는 '신청서'에 대한 내용이 언급된 (A)가 들어가야 전개가 자연스러워진다. fill out 기입하다, 작성하다 benefit 혜택, 이득 competitive 경쟁력 있는 raise 인상 deserving 받을 만한, 자격이 있는 management 경영(진) announce 발표하다 hire 고용하다

정답 (A)

133
(A) candidates*   (B) awardees
(C) suppliers   (D) occupants

'신청서를 낸 이들 중 자격이 되는 사람들'이라는 의미가 완성되어야 맥락상 타당하다. 따라서 제시된 어휘들 중 (A)가 알맞다. candidate 후보자 awardee 수상자 supplier 공급자 occupant 입주자, 사용자

정답 (A)

134

(A) prefer (B) preferred
(C) preference* (D) preferential

구조상 빈칸에는 '5년 이상 재직한 사람들에게 주어지는 것' 즉, 목적어로 사용되는 명사 (C)가 들어갈 수 있다. prefer 선호하다, 더 좋아하다 preferred 선취권이 있는, 우선의 preference 선호(도), 우선권 preferential 우선권을 주는, 특혜를 주는

정답(C)

채널 8 뉴스, 60주년을 맞이하다!

3월 15일이면, 우리 시 최고의 뉴스 소스인 채널 8 뉴스가 60주년을 맞이합니다. 스튜디오와 라이브 방송으로 60년이 흐른 것입니다. 반세기도 훨씬 넘는 동안, 저희 채널 8 뉴스는 시청자들에게 속보 방송, 통찰력 있는 실황 중계, 시청자들의 관심을 불러일으키는 시내 및 지역 곳곳의 근사한 이야기들을 제공해 왔습니다. 저희는 소중한 시청자들을 기념일에 초대하고 싶습니다. 3월 15일, 오후 4시 30분부터 저녁 6시까지 킹슬리 스트리트에 있는 저희 스튜디오를 오픈할 예정입니다. 스튜디오 견학에 참가하셔서 방송 화면 뒤에서 어떤 일이 진행되는지 직접 체험하시고 저희 최신식 장비의 시연을 보시기 바랍니다. ———. 이번 행사에 참가하기 위한 비용은 없습니다만, 등록을 하셔야 합니다. 이 특별 행사에서 시청자 여러분을 뵙기를 고대합니다.

어휘 celebrate 기념하다, 축하하다 anniversary 기념일 decade 10년 coverage 보도, 방송 insightful 통찰력 있는 commentary 실황 방송 human-interest 독자의 흥미/동정을 불러일으키는 invite 초대하다 celebration 기념 hold 열다 take part in ~에 참여하다 first-hand 직접 얻은, 경험한 demonstration 시연 state-of-the-art 최신식의 equipment 기기, 장비 charge 요금 attend 출석하다, 참석하다 register 등록하다 occasion 행사

Questions 135-138 refer to the following notice.

Channel 8 News Turns 60!

On March 15, Channel 8 News, the city's number one news source, celebrates its sixtieth anniversary. That's six decades of studio and live ---**135**---. For well over half a century, we at Channel 8 News ---**136**--- our viewers breaking new coverage, insightful commentaries, and wonderful human-interest stories from across the city and region. We would like to invite you, our loyal viewers, to our celebration. On March 15, we will hold an open house from 4:30 P.M. to 6:00 P.M. at our studio on Kingsley Street. Take part in a studio tour and see first-hand what goes on behind the scenes and watch a demonstration of our state-of-the-art broadcasting equipment. ---**137**---. There is no charge to attend this event, but you do have to register. We hope to see you all at this ---**138**--- occasion.

135

(A) concerts
(B) discussions
(C) programming*
(D) teaching

첫 문장에서 방송국임이 드러나므로(Channel 8 News, the city's number one news source) 빈칸에 적절한 어휘는 '방송, 프로그램과 관련된 (C)'이다. discussion 논의, 토론 programming (라디오, 텔레비전의) 방송 프로 편성

정답 (C)

136

(A) offers
(B) offering
(C) will offer
(D) have offered*

빈칸은 전체 문장의 술어이므로 (B)는 바로 소거할 수 있다. 과거의 한 시점(60년 전)부터 현재까지 계속해서 '제공해 온 상태'를 나타내야 하니 나머지 세 개 중 현재완료 (D)가 정답이 된다. offer 제공하다, 제안하다

정답 (D)

137

(A) The station will remain a vital part of this city for years to come.
(B) You will even have the chance to meet and talk with our news anchors.*
(C) This celebration will be the third one to take place in March.
(D) Channel 8 News will be acquired by a national news network in a few months.

(A) 방송국은 앞으로도 수년 간 이 도시의 주요 부분으로 남을 것입니다.
(B) 심지어 저희 뉴스 앵커들을 만나 이야기 나눌 기회도 있으십니다.
(C) 이 기념식은 3월에 세 번째로 열리는 것이 될 것입니다.
(D) 채널 8 뉴스는 몇 달 후에 국영 뉴스 방송국에 매입될 것입니다.

앞서 '스튜디오 견학 내용'이 언급되었으므로, 그 내용에 추가될 수 있는 (B)가 가장 적절하다. station 방송국, 프로 remain 계속 ~이다, 남다 vital 필수적인 chance 기회 acquire 얻다, 획득하다

정답 (B)

138

(A) special* (B) specialize
(C) especially (D) specialization

〈한정사(this) + _____ + 명사(occasion)〉의 빈칸에 들어갈 수 있는 것은 형용사 (A)뿐이다. special 특별한 specialize 전공하다, 전문으로 다루다 especially 특히 specialization 전문화, 전공 분야

정답 (A)

아처 코트 주민들에게 주택 외부 개조 프로젝트를 진행하기 위해서는 허가증을 받아야 함을 상기시켜 드리고자 합니다. 내부 변경은 현재 허가가 필요 없습니다. 하지만, 크건 작건 모든 외부 작업은 사전에 허가 받으셔야 합니다.

예전에, 일부 주민들은 허가증 준비는 공사 업체의 책임이라 생각했습니다. ──────── 사실, 부동산 소유주들은 필수 허가증을 직접 받아야 합니다. 건물 조사관이 아무 때나 공사 현장을 방문할 수 있는데, 부동산 소유주가 허가증을 갖고 있지 않으면, 벌금이 매겨질 수도 있습니다.

허가 법을 시행하는 것은 건물 조사관의 주요 책무입니다. 허가 절차는 모든 필수 안전 기준이 충족됐는지 확실히 하며, 이로써 부동산 피해 및 위험 요소로부터 주민들을 보호해 줍니다.

귀하의 프로젝트에 적용될 만한 허가증 목록을 보시려면, renviewtown.com/permits를 방문해 주십시오.

어휘 reminder 상기시키는 것 resident 주민 obtain 얻다, 획득하다 permit 허가(증) exterior 외부의 improvement 개선, 향상 change 변화, 변경 사항 currently 현재 external 외부의 authorize 인가하다, 허가하다 in advance 미리, 사전에 assume 추정하다, 상정하다 contractor 계약업체 responsible 책임이 있는 arrange 주선/마련하다 property 부동산, 재산 owner 소유주 necessary 필수적인 inspector 조사관 site 장소, 현장 fine 벌금 issue 발행하다, 발부하다 responsibility 책임 process 절차 ensure 확실히 하다 safety 보안, 안전 in turn 결국 protect 보호하다 damage 피해, 손상 hazard 위험 (요소) apply to ~에 적용되다

Questions 139-142 refer to the following information.

This is just a reminder that residents of Archer Court are required to obtain a permit for any exterior home-improvement projects. Interior changes do not currently need a permit. ---**139**---, all external jobs, large and small, must be authorized in advance.

In the past, some residents have assumed that their contractors are responsible for arranging permits. ---**140**---. In truth, property owners must obtain the necessary permits themselves. Building inspectors may visit a site at any time, and if the property owner does not have a permit, fines may be issued.

---**141**--- permit laws is an important responsibility of building inspectors. The permit process ensures that all necessary safety standards ---**142**---, which in turn protects the community from property damages and dangerous hazards.

To view a list of permits that might apply to your project, please visit renviewtown.com/permits.

139
(A) Namely (B) Similarly
(C) Therefore (D) However*

적절한 연결어를 찾는 문제이다. '내부 공사에는 불필요하다' 하지만 '외부 공사에는 꼭 있어야 한다'라는 흐름으로 전개되므로 역접을 나타내는 (D)가 정답이다. namely 즉, 다시 말해 similarly 비슷하게, 유사하게 therefore 따라서, 그러므로

정답 (D)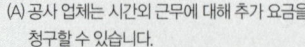

(A) 공사 업체는 시간외 근무에 대해 추가 요금을 청구할 수 있습니다.
(B) 흔히들 갖는 이 견해는 사실 틀린 것입니다.
(C) 대부분의 건물 조사관은 공사 업자로도 일합니다.
(D) 프로젝트 비용은 계절에 따라 늘어날 수 있습니다.

140
(A) Contractors may charge extra for overtime.
(B) This commonly held belief is actually false.*
(C) Most building inspectors also work as contractors.
(D) The cost of the project may increase seasonally.

전후 내용을 살펴보자. '예전에는 공사 업자가 허가증을 처리한다고 생각했다' 그런데 '사실 부동산 소유주가 직접 허가를 받아야 한다'며 앞의 생각이 잘못된 것임을 입증하는 맥락이다. 따라서 (B)가 가장 적절하다. charge 청구하다 overtime 시간외 근무 commonly 흔히 false 틀린, 사실이 아닌 cost 값, 비용 increase 늘다, 인상되다 seasonally 계절 따라, 정기적으로

정답 (B)

240 해설집

141

(A) Questioning (B) Eliminating
(C) Enforcing* (D) Reviewing

'법을 실행에 옮기는 것이 조사관의 책무'라는 요지를 완성해야 가장 타당하므로 (C)가 정답이다. question 질문하다, 심문하다 eliminate 제거하다, 삭제하다 enforce 강요하다, 집행하다, 실시하다 review 검토하다

정답 (C)

142

(A) are met* (B) to meet
(C) meeting (D) have met

빈칸이 that절의 서술부이니 동사가 아닌 (B)와 (C)는 바로 소거된다. 이 문장에서 meet은 타동사이므로, 목적어가 필요한 (D)도 들어갈 수 없다. 따라서 '기준이 충족됐는지'라는 의미의 수동태를 완성하는 (A)가 정답이다.

정답 (A)

스타 크레딧 구매 포인트

스타 크레딧은 신용 카드 소지자들께 세계에서 가장 포괄적인 포인트 프로그램을 제공합니다. ———. 회원들께서는 특별히 선택된 200개 매장 중에서 쇼핑함으로써 포인트를 두 배로 얻으실 수도 있습니다. 포인트를 그 200개 매장 어디에서나 상품권으로 교환하실 수 있습니다. 또한, 포인트는 www.travelone.com에서 항공권 및 호텔 객실을 예약하고 차를 빌리는 데 쓰실 수도 있습니다. 스타 크레딧 포인트 프로그램을 신청하시려면, 다음 서식을 작성하고 제출을 클릭하시기만 하면 됩니다.

어휘
purchase 구입(품) offer 제안하다, 제공하다 holder 소지자 redeem 현금(상품)으로 바꾸다 in exchange for ~ 대신의 교환으로 book 예약하다 flight 비행(편) rent 임대하다 apply for ~을 지원하다, 신청하다 fill out 기입하다, 작성하다 following 다음의 form 서식 submit 제출하다

Questions 143-146 refer to the following webpage.

Star Credit Purchase Points

Star Credit would like to offer its credit card holders the ---**143**--- points program in the world. ---**144**---. Members can even double their points by shopping at any of the two hundred specially ---**145**--- stores. Points can be redeemed in exchange for gift cards at any of those two hundred stores. ---**146**---, points can be used on www.travelone.com to book flights and hotel rooms, and rent cars. To apply for Star Credit's points program, simply fill out the following form and click submit.

143

(A) comprehension
(B) most comprehensive*
(C) comprehensive
(D) most comprehensively

〈정관사(the) + _____ + 명사(points program)〉의 빈칸에는 형용사가 들어갈 수 있는데, 문장 후반부에 in the world가 있으므로 '세상에서 가장 ~한'이란 의미를 완성시켜 줄 최상급 형용사 (B)가 들어가야 함을 알 수 있다. comprehension 이해력 comprehensive 포괄적인, 종합적인 comprehensively 완전히, 철저히

정답 (B)

(A) 스타 신용 카드로 구입하실 때마다, 100포인트까지 받으실 수 있습니다.
(B) 포인트는 모든 신용 카드 구입에 대해 월 이자를 낮추는 데만 쓸 수 있습니다.
(C) 프로그램 회원들은 과거에 스타 신용 카드를 신청한 적이 없어야 합니다.
(D) 더욱이, 프로그램 회원들은 모든 구입에 대해 매장 내 할인을 받을 수 있습니다.

144

(A) With every purchase you make with your Star Credit Card, you can earn up to 100 points.*
(B) Points can only be used to lower your monthly interest rates on all credit card purchases.
(C) Program members must not have applied for a Star Credit Card in the past.
(D) Furthermore, program members can receive in-store discounts on all their purchases.

프로그램에 대한 개괄적인 소개가 언급된 다음이며 '두 배의 특별 혜택'이 이어지므로 빈칸에는 '기본 혜택' (A)가 들어가야 흐름상 자연스럽다. (D)는 내용상으로는 연결이 가능하지만 furthermore로 이어져야 할 내용이 앞에서 언급되지 않았기 때문에 답이 될 수 없다. earn 얻다, 획득하다 lower 낮추다, 내리다 interest rate 금리, 이율 furthermore 더욱이 in-store 매장 내의

정답 (A)

145

(A) select
(B) selects
(C) selected*
(D) selection

빈칸은 뒤의 명사 stores를 수식하는 자리이다. 따라서 형용사 역할을 하는 (A)와 (C) 중에서 답을 골라야 하는데, 앞에 specially와 같은 부사가 붙었을 경우, 이 부사는 select하는 행위에 대한 묘사 성격이 강하기 때문에 동사에서 파생된 과거분사인 selected가 더 잘 어울린다. 〈부사 + select + 명사〉는 사용하지 않는다. 따라서 (C)가 정답이 된다. select 선택하다, 엄선된 selection 선택, 선정

정답 (C)

146

(A) Therefore
(B) Regardless
(C) In addition*
(D) For instance

포인트 받는 법, 사용법에 이어 '또 다른' 사용처를 언급한 문장이므로 '추가'를 나타내는 (C)가 가장 적절하다. therefore 그러므로, 그러니 regardless 상관하지 않고 in addition 게다가, 더욱이 for instance 이를테면, 예를 들어

정답 (C)

PART 7

http://www.premiuminsurance.com

다시 환영합니다. 톰 슈왈츠 씨! 이제, 147 고객님은 프리미엄 보험회사의 새 웹사이트에서 귀하의 모든 보험 계약 정보에 쉽게 접속하실 수 있습니다. 잠시 시간을 내서 저희 새 웹사이트의 특징들을 숙지하시기 바랍니다.

- 추가 결제 방법과 모든 결제에 대한 온라인 영수증
- 148 모든 보험 계약 정보를 한 곳에서 쉽게 접속
- 민감한 정보를 보호하기 위해 업그레이드된 보안 및 시한 로그아웃
- 갱신된 FAQ와 실시간 대화 기능 같은 새로운 고객 서비스 도구
- 주소 및 전화번호 정보를 업데이트하기 위한 간단한 온라인 서식

Questions 147-148 refer to the following website.

http://www.premiuminsurance.com

| Home | Policies | My Account | Sign Out |

Welcome back, Tom Schwarz! Now, ¹⁴⁷ you can easily access all your policy information with Premium Insurance's new website. Please take a moment to familiarize yourself with our website's features.

- Additional payment methods and online receipts of all payments
- ¹⁴⁸ ⁽ᶜ⁾ Easy access to all your policy information in one place
- ¹⁴⁸ ⁽ᴰ⁾ Upgraded security and timed log-outs to protect your sensitive information
- ¹⁴⁸ ⁽ᴮ⁾ New customer service tools, such as an updated FAQ and a live chat function
- Simple online forms to update address and telephone information

어휘 policy 정책, 보험 증권 account 계정, 계좌 access 접근하다, 접속하다 insurance 보험 familiarize 익숙하게 하다 feature 특징 additional 추가의, 가외의 payment 결제, 납부 method 방법 receipt 영수증 security 보안, 안전 timed 시한의 protect 보호하다 sensitive 고도의 신중을 요하는, 민감한 form 서식

슈왈츠 씨는 누구이겠는가?
(A) 보험 판매원
(B) 보험 고객
(C) 웹 디자이너
(D) 보험 청구 대리인

어휘 claim (보상금 등에 대한) 청구, 신청 representative 대리인

147

Who most likely is Mr. Schwarz?
(A) An insurance salesman
(B) An insurance customer*
(C) A web designer
(D) An insurance claims representative

핵심 인명이 언급된 바로 다음 문장 you can easily access all your policy information with Premium Insurance's new website를 통해 (B)가 정답임을 알 수 있다. policy는 '보험 증권'이란 의미로 insurance 관련 내용에서 매우 자주 등장하는 단어이다. 보험 상품, 보험 계약 등으로 해석할 수 있다.

정답 (B)

새 웹사이트 특징으로 언급되지 않은 것은?
(A) 단체 보험 신청
(B) 새로운 고객 서비스 도구
(C) 통합된 정보
(D) 개선된 인터넷 보안

어휘 application 신청(서) consolidated 정리된, 통합된 improved 개선된, 향상된

148

What is NOT mentioned as a feature of the new website?
(A) Group insurance applications*
(B) New customer service tools
(C) Consolidated information
(D) Improved Internet security

특징으로 언급된 부분을 찾아 각 선택지와 대조하면서 지문에서 언급된 사항을 소거해 나가는 식으로 문제를 해결한다. 둘째 항목 Easy access to all your policy information in one place에서 (C)를, 셋째 항목 Upgraded security에서 (D)를, 넷째 항목 New customer service tools에서 (B)를 확인할 수 있으므로 본 문제의 정답은 (A)가 된다.

정답 (A)

Questions 149-151 refer to the following information.

Affluence Pharmaceuticals

Manuel Rodriguez
Lead Researcher

A highly sought-after leader in today's pharmaceutical industry, Mr. Rodriquez had overseen all major research projects at Affluence Pharmaceuticals for the last five years. Mr. Rodriguez joined Affluence seven years ago and was quickly recognized for his great talent and vision. [151] He was promoted to lead researcher and [150 (C)] has since drastically improved employee productivity by more than 20%.

[149, 150 (D)] Mr. Rodriguez has been invited to speak at numerous conferences and was even honored at last year's Pharma Vision Conference as the keynote speaker. He also works as a consultant for Techtron University's medical department where he has contributed to numerous academic projects. Prior to joining Affluence, [150 (B)] Mr. Rodriguez immigrated from Mexico and attended Stratford University where he graduated with honors.

본 정보의 목적은 무엇인가?
(A) 대학 프로그램을 설명하기 위한 것이다.
(B) 직원 승진을 발표하기 위한 것이다.
(C) 회사 직원을 소개하기 위한 것이다.
(D) 직원의 은퇴를 기념하기 위한 것이다.

어휘 outline 개요를 말하다 announce 발표하다 promotion 승진 introduce 소개하다 celebrate 기념하다, 축하하다 retirement 은퇴

149

What is the purpose of the information?
(A) To outline a university program
(B) To announce an employee promotion
(C) To introduce a company employee*
(D) To celebrate an employee's retirement

첫째 문단에서는 한 개인의 업무 성과 위주로 설명하고 둘째 문단에서는 그의 경력을 간략히 설명하는 맥락이므로 (C)가 가장 적절하다. 대체로 글의 목적이 전반부에 드러나는 유형이 제시되나 이처럼 전체 맥락을 이해해야 해결할 수 있는 문제가 출제되기도 한다는 점을 유념하자.

정답 (C)

로드리게즈 씨에 대해 드러나지 않는 사항은?
(A) 대학 교수로 고용되어 있다.
(B) 이전에 멕시코에서 살았다.
(C) 직원들의 성과를 향상시켰다.
(D) 노련한 대중 연설가이다.

어휘 employ 고용하다 previously 이전에 performance 실적, 성과 experienced 노련한, 경험있는

150

What is NOT indicated about Mr. Rodriguez?
(A) He is employed as a university professor.*
(B) He previously lived in Mexico.
(C) He has improved employee performance.
(D) He is an experienced public speaker.

지문에 언급된 사항을 소거하는 식으로 해결한다. (B)는 마지막 부분의 Mr. Rodriguez immigrated from Mexico에서, (C)는 둘째 문단의 has since drastically improved employee productivity by more than 20%에서, (D)는 둘째 문단의 Mr. Rodriguez has been invited to speak at numerous conferences and was even honored at last year's Pharma Vision Conference as the keynote speaker.에서 유추할 수 있다. 따라서 (A)가 본 문제의 정답이 된다.

정답 (A)

로드리게즈 씨의 경력에 대해 드러나는 사항은?
(A) 우수한 직업 윤리 때문에 상을 자주 받았다.
(B) 일에 지원하기 전에 학위 두 개를 받았다.
(C) 수석 연구원으로 고용되기 전에 인턴으로 일했다.
(D) 처음에는 수석 연구원으로 고용되지 않았다.

어휘 receive 받다 award 상 ethic 윤리, 도덕 complete 완성하다 degree 학위 apply for ~에 지원하다, 신청하다 hire 고용하다

151

What is suggested about Mr. Rodriguez's career?
(A) He often receives awards for his great work ethic.
(B) He completed two degrees before he applied for a job.
(C) He worked as an intern prior to being hired as lead researcher.
(D) He was not hired as lead researcher at first.*

career에 집중해 지문을 살펴보자. 첫째 문단에서 입사한 지 7년이 됐고 수석 연구원으로 승진하면서(He was promoted to lead researcher) 생산성을 획기적으로 높였다고 하므로 (D)가 가장 적절하다.

정답 (D)

Questions 152-154 refer to the following article.

March 7 – the local mayor's office has just released the details of the Budding Futures Internship Program for Park County students. 152 (C), (D) Led by the program director, Milly Andrews, the program is designed to give senior high school students a taste of what it's like working in a public office. ---[1]---

152 (B) Mayor Steven Greenhorn announced the internship program last year. "I think it's important to include teenagers in public affairs," he said in an interview. 153 "It may help them decide what course of study they want to pursue in college." ---[2]---

152 (B) According to the newly released details, Milly Andrews will select fifteen students from fifteen schools across the county. Based on their areas of interest, the chosen students will be assigned various jobs in the mayor's downtown office. ---[3]--- The program will last eight weeks during the summer.

Applications for the program will be available on the mayor's website at the beginning of next week. ---[4]--- The selected interns will be announced in early May.

버딩 퓨처 인턴십 프로그램에 대해 드러나는 사항은?
(A) 전국적으로 진행된다.
(B) 새로운 프로그램이다.
(C) 대학생들을 대상으로 한다.
(D) 스티븐 그린혼이 이끈다.

어휘 nationwide 전국적인

152

What is suggested about the Budding Futures Internship Program?
(A) It is available nationwide.
(B) It is a brand new program.*
(C) It is for university students.
(D) It is led by Steven Greenhorn.

(C)와 (D)는 첫째 문단의 Led by the program director, Milly Andrews, the program is designed to give senior high school students a taste of what it's like working in a public office.에서, (A)는 셋째 문단 Milly Andrews will select fifteen students from fifteen schools across the county에서 오답임을 알 수 있다. 둘째 문단의 Mayor Steven Greenhorn announced the internship program last year.와 셋째 문단의 According to the newly released details를 통해 (B)가 정답임을 알 수 있다.

정답 (B)

그린혼 씨에 따르면, 인턴십 프로그램의 주요 목표는 무엇인가?
(A) 학생들에게 선거에 대해 가르치는 것
(B) 자원봉사 활동 공동체를 설립하는 것
(C) 학생들에게 보수가 좋은 일자리를 제공하는 것
(D) 학생들에게 장래 교육의 방향을 제시하는 것

어휘 election 선거 establish 수립하다

153

According to Mr. Greenhorn, what is the main goal of the internship program?
(A) Teaching students about elections
(B) Establishing a community of volunteers
(C) Providing students with well-paying jobs
(D) Guiding students in their future education*

둘째 문단에 인용된 Mr. Greenhorn의 인터뷰에서 It may help them decide what course of study they want to pursue in college.라며 대학 전공을 선택하는 데 도움을 줄 것이라 하므로 (D)가 가장 적절하다.

정답 (D)

---

[1], [2], [3], [4] 중 다음 문장이 들어가기에 가장 적합한 곳은?
"학생들은 최소한 추천서 한 통을 미리 받아 두기를 권한다."
(A) [1]
(B) [2]
(C) [3]
(D) [4]

어휘 encourage 격려하다, 고무하다 collect 모으다, 수집하다 at least 적어도, 최소한 reference 추천서 in advance 미리, 사전에

154

In which of the positions marked [1], [2], [3], and [4] does the following sentence best belong?

"Students are encouraged to collect at least one reference in advance."

(A) [1]   (B) [2]
(C) [3]   (D) [4]*

제시문이 '지원 서류'에 대한 정보에 해당되므로 지원 절차를 다룬 마지막 문단의 [4]가 가장 알맞다. 따라서 정답은 (D)이다.

정답 (D)

Questions 155-156 refer to the following webpage.

ASPIRE UNLIMITED

As a client of our firm, you
- have access to around-the-clock surveillance
- pay a reasonable monthly fee with no additional costs
- can improve your office's security needs

We provide
- [155] custom installations of CCTV equipment
- regular maintenance of all cameras and alarm systems
- [155] 24-hour remote monitoring of your office
- [156] fingerprint scanning technology for all entrances (additional charges will apply)
- access to Aspire's website for all your billing needs

어휘 aspire 열망하다, 염원하다 unlimited 무제한의 access 접근, 이용 around-the-clock 24시간의 surveillance 감시 pay 결제하다 reasonable 합리적인, (가격이) 적정한 fee 요금, 수수료 additional 추가의 cost 값, 비용 improve 개선하다, 향상시키다 security 보안, 안전 provide 제공하다 installation 설치 equipment 기기, 장비 maintenance 유지, 관리 remote 원격의 monitoring 감시, 관찰 fingerprint 지문 entrance 입구 charge 요금 apply 적용하다 billing 청구

---

155 What is one of the services offered by Aspire Unlimited?
(A) Office cleaning
(B) CCTV monitoring*
(C) Website development
(D) Heating system maintenance

둘째 문단의 '제공 서비스' 항목 중 첫 번째 custom installations of CCTV equipment 와 세 번째 24-hour remote monitoring of your office를 통해 정답 (B)를 확인할 수 있다.

정답 (B)

---

156 What is mentioned about fingerprint scanning technology?
(A) It is purchased on a weekly basis.
(B) It is one of Aspire's unique services.
(C) It can be purchased for an extra fee.*
(D) It can be added to an account by phone.

핵심 어구 fingerprint scanning technology에 유의해 지문을 살펴보면, 둘째 문단 네 번째 항목 fingerprint scanning technology for all entrances (additional charges will apply)에서 추가 요금이 발생할 것이라고 하므로 (C)가 정답이 된다. Part 7에서 ( ), *, Note는 답의 단서를 준다!

* paraphrasing: additional → extra, charge → fee

정답 (C)

Questions 157-158 refer to the following article.

ROUGE TOWNSHIP. March 3 – Rouge Township officials have recently announced a new development proposal for [158 (B)] an amusement park that will be located on Rouge Lake's 4000-acre waterfront.
   [158 (A), (C)] The new amusement park is expected to include numerous rollercoasters, an extensive aquarium, a waterpark, and a pavilion for live music. Several local businesses, such as Rotary Automobiles, Pancake House Restaurants, and Maverick Beverages have agreed to sponsor the park's development.
   [157] Following the release of the development proposal, several local activists have expressed concerns about effect the park will have on the waterfront's delicate ecosystem. "We can assure you that all precautions will be taken," Lead Developer, Jan Freedman, said in an interview yesterday. "The park will be located far enough away from the beach and the bike trails that it will have little effect on the surrounding wildlife."
   Other Rouge Township residents have expressed excitement about the potential increase in business the new park will bring to the Rouge Lake area.

어휘 recently 최근 proposal 제안(서) amusement park 놀이 공원 be located on ~에 있다 waterfront 물가, 부둣가 expect 기대하다, 예상하다 extensive 아주 넓은 aquarium 수족관 waterpark 수상 공원 automobile 자동차 beverage 음료 agree 동의하다 sponsor 후원하다, 지원하다 release 공개, 발표 concern 우려, 사항, 걱정 effect 효과, 결과 delicate 연약한, 민감한, 여린 ecosystem 생태계 assure 장담하다, 확인하다 precaution 예방책, 예방 조치 surrounding 주변의 wildlife 야생 동물 resident 주민 increase 증가, 인상의

157

What is suggested about Rouge Township?
(A) It currently has a large tourism industry.
(B) It is home to a famous waterpark.
(C) Some of its residents disagree with the proposal.*
(D) Much of the local wildlife is endangered.

셋째 문단에서 Following the release of the development proposal, several local activists have expressed concerns라며 일부 지역 활동가는 우려를 나타낸다고 했으므로 (C)가 가장 적절하다.
* paraphrasing: local activists → residents

정답 (C)

158

What feature of the amusement park is NOT mentioned?
(A) Its large onsite aquarium
(B) Its location at the waterfront
(C) A place for live performances
(D) The gift shops and kiosks*

지문에서 '놀이 공원의 특징'에 관련된 부분(첫째 문단, 둘째 문단)을 찾아 각 선택지와 대조하면서 지문에 언급된 사항을 소거하는 식으로 해결한다. (A)와 (C)는 둘째 문단의 The new amusement park is expected to include numerous rollercoasters, an extensive aquarium, a waterpark, and a pavilion for live music.에서, (B)는 첫째 문단의 an amusement park that will be located on Rouge Lake's 4000-acre waterfront에서 확인할 수 있다. 따라서 본 문제의 정답은 (D)가 된다.

정답 (D)

Questions 159-161 refer to the following information.

Maintenance Services

[159] The maintenance department of Fairsview Condos is available to make routine repairs to your condo and all shared spaces, most of which are available at no charge to residents. The following services are free of charge and must be booked two weeks in advance.

- Bathroom fixtures, such as showerheads, faucets, and toilet parts may be replaced once every two years. [160] Free repairs of any broken components can be arranged once per year.
- Doors and windows, including window screens, will be repaired as needed at any time of the year.
- Fan filters above stoves and smoke detectors can be replaced every six months. Air conditioners are allotted one free cleaning service per year.
- For a full list of services, please visit our website. [161] Reservations can be made by filling out a request form at www.fairsviewcondos.com/maintenance.

본 정보는 누구를 위한 것이겠는가?
(A) 부동산 중개인들
(B) 건물 관리 회사의 직원들
(C) 퇴직자 전용 주택 임대주들
(D) 복합 건물 주민들

어휘 real estate 부동산 management 관리 landlord 주인, 임대주 complex 복합 건물, (건물) 단지

159

For whom is the information most likely intended?
(A) Real estate agents
(B) Employees at a building management company
(C) Landlords of a retirement home
(D) Residents at a complex*

첫 문장 The maintenance department of Fairsview Condos is available to make routine repairs to your condo and all shared spaces, most of which are available at no charge to residents.를 통해 정답 (D)를 확인할 수 있다. condo란 단어는 우리나라의 아파트와 같은 개념으로 잘 쓰인다.

* paraphrasing: condo → complex

정답 (D)

욕실 붙박이 세간은 얼마나 자주 무료로 수리되는가?
(A) 한 달에 한 번
(B) 여섯 달마다
(C) 일 년에 한 번
(D) 언제든

160

How often can bathroom fixtures be repaired at no cost?
(A) Once a month
(B) Every six months
(C) Once a year*
(D) At any time

핵심 어구 bathroom fixtures에 유의해 지문을 살펴보면, 첫째 항목으로 다뤄지는데 '무료 수리 주기'에 대해서는 Free repairs of any broken components can be arranged once per year.를 통해 (C)가 정답임을 알 수 있다.

정답 (C)

본 정보에 따르면, 독자들은 어떻게 하면 수리를 예약할 수 있는가?
(A) 온라인 서식을 작성해서
(B) 부서에 전화해서
(C) 임대주에게 이야기해서
(D) 종이에 서명해서

161

According to the information, how can readers arrange to have something repaired?
(A) By filling out an online form*
(B) By calling a department
(C) By speaking to a landlord
(D) By signing up on a sheet

'수리 요청 절차'가 포인트임을 파악해야 한다. 마지막 항목에서 전체 서비스 목록은 웹사이트에 있으니 예약하려면 요청서를 작성하라(Reservations can be made by filling out a request form at www.fairsviewcondos.com/maintenance.)고 하므로 (A)가 정답이 된다.

정답 (A)

Questions 162-163 refer to the following text message chain.

Ron Parks [8:03]: Jim, can I get your input on the changes Jennifer asked me to make to tomorrow's presentation?
Jim Webber [8:05]: Sure. What do you need?
Ron Parks [8:07]: ¹⁶³ Can I e-mail you the new proposal? I've highlighted the changes in red, but ¹⁶² I'm not sure if these reflect our full range of advertising services.
Jim Webber [8:08]: I'm afraid not. ¹⁶³ I'm just about to meet a client for dinner. How about I stop by your hotel room after?
Ron Parks [8:09]: That would be okay. Then I can show you the PowerPoint presentation I've made as well.
Jim Webber [8:10]: Okay, great. What room are you in?
Ron Parks [8:10]: Room 506. See you then!

어휘 input 조언, 지식 change 변화, 변경 사항 highlight 강조하다 reflect 반영하다 stop by 들르다

162

Who most likely is Mr. Parks?

(A) An advertiser*
(B) A hotel receptionist
(C) An art collector
(D) An IT specialist

'직업'에 대한 질문임을 파악하고 관련 정보를 찾아보면, 파크스 씨가 8시 7분에 보낸 문자 중 I'm not sure if these reflect our full range of advertising services.를 통해 (A)가 정답임을 알 수 있다.

정답 (A)

163

At 8:08, what does Mr. Webber most likely mean when he writes "I'm afraid not"?

(A) He is worried about a presentation.
(B) He doesn't have time to review a document.*
(C) He does not agree with some changes.
(D) He did not request the changes to be made.

I'm afraid not은 특정 상황에 대해 No라는 대답을 정중하게 하는 표현이다. 한편, 앞서 파크스 씨가 Can I e-mail you the new proposal?이라며 이메일로 새 제안서를 보내도 되겠냐고 물은 데 대한 답변이며, '지금 어디를 가야 한다'고 말하므로 맥락상 (B)가 가장 적절하다.

정답 (B)

파크스 씨는 누구이겠는가?
(A) 광고 업자
(B) 호텔 접수계원
(C) 예술품 수집가
(D) IT 전문가

어휘 receptionist 접수 담당자

8시 8분에, 웨버 씨가 "미안하지만 안 되겠네요."라고 썼을 때 의미하는 바는?
(A) 발표에 대해 걱정하고 있다.
(B) 서류를 검토할 시간이 없다.
(C) 일부 변경 사항에 동의하지 않는다.
(D) 변경해 달라고 요청하지 않았다.

어휘 review 검토하다 request 요청하다

수신: staceymarshall@pressassociated.com
발신: htrander@themaxfestival.com
제목: 맥스 서머 뮤직 페스티벌
날짜: 6월 5일
첨부: 2-070406.pdf

마샬 씨 귀하,

164, 167 맥스 서머 뮤직 페스티벌은 귀하가 그랜드 파크에서 곧 열리게 될 3일짜리 페스티벌을 취재해 주신다니 기쁩니다. — [1] — 그랜드 파크는 약 25,000명의 방문객을 수용할 수 있으며, 3일 내내 가득 메워질 것으로 보입니다. 저는 귀하를 위해 입장권 한 장을 예약했고 **165** 모든 백스테이지에 들어가실 수 있는 통행권을 첨부해 드립니다. 입장권은 도착하시는 대로 매표소에서 받아 가시면 됩니다. — [2] —

입구는 7월 4일 오후 1시에 열릴 예정이며, **166** 축제는 7월 6일 밤 10시의 폭죽 쇼로 끝날 예정입니다. 원하시면 3일 전부 무료로 참석하실 수 있으며, 기자 통행권으로 원하시는 만큼 밴드 및 연주자들을 인터뷰하실 수 있습니다. — [3] — 연주자들과 일정의 전체 목록을 원하시면, 저희 웹사이트를 방문하셔서 행사 달력을 내려 받으시면 됩니다. 끝으로, 방문 중 필요하신 것이 있다면, 언론 서비스의 몰리에게 776-3333-6713로 연락하시면 됩니다. — [4] — 감사드리며, 맥스 서머 뮤직 페스티벌을 즐기시길 바랍니다.

그럼 이만,
해리 트랜더
축제 언론 코디네이터

Questions 164-167 refer to the following e-mail.

To: staceymarshall@pressassociated.com
From: htrander@themaxfestival.com
Subject: The Max Summer Music Festival
Date: June 5
Attachment: 2-070406.pdf

Dear Ms. Marshall,

164, 167 We at The Max Summer Music Festival are delighted that you would like to cover our upcoming three-day festival in Grand Park. -- [1] -- Grand Park holds nearly 25,000 visitors, and we expect to be at full-capacity during all three days. I have reserved an admission ticket for you and **165** attached an all-access backstage pass. You can pick the ticket up at the ticket booth upon arrival. -- [2] --

The gates will open July 4 at 1 P.M. and **166** the festival will conclude with a fireworks show on July 6 at 10 P.M. You are free to attend all three days if you'd like, and your press pass will allow you to interview as many of the bands and performers as you wish. -- [3] -- For a full list of performers and their schedules, you can visit our website and download our event calendar. Lastly, should you need anything at all during your visit, you can contact Molly at press services at 776-3333-6713. -- [4] -- Thank you, and I hope you enjoy The Max Summer Music Festival.

Sincerely,
Harry Trander
Festival Press Coordinator

어휘 attachment 첨부 cover 보도하다 upcoming 다가오는, 다음의 hold 열다 at full-capacity 전 능력을 기울이는 reserve 예약하다 admission 입장 attach 첨부하다 arrival 도착 conclude with ~로 마무리 짓다 firework 폭죽 allow 허용하다, 허락하다 performer 연주자 lastly 마지막으로 coordinator 진행자, 코디네이터

164

Who most likely is Ms. Marshall?

(A) A customer (B) A journalist*
(C) A band manager (D) A performer

'마샬 씨'는 본 이메일의 수신자(2인칭)인데 첫 문장에서 We at The Max Summer Music Festival are delighted that you would like to cover라며 '취재해 주신다니 기쁘다'고 하므로 (B)가 정답이 된다.

정답 (B)

마샬 씨는 누구이겠는가?
(A) 고객
(B) 기자
(C) 밴드 매니저
(D) 연주자
어휘 journalist 기자

165

What was sent with the e-mail?

(A) An admission ticket (B) A parking voucher
(C) A schedule of performances (D) A backstage press pass*

'동봉' 또는 '첨부'에 유념해 지문을 살펴보면, 첫째 문단의 attached an all-access backstage pass를 통해 정답 (D)를 확인할 수 있다.

정답 (D)

이메일과 함께 무엇이 발송됐는가?
(A) 입장권
(B) 주차권
(C) 공연 일정
(D) 백스테이지 기자 통행권
어휘 voucher 상품권, 할인권, 쿠폰

166

According to the e-mail, what is a notable feature of the festival?

(A) It may accommodate more than 25,000 people.
(B) It will include jazz dance performances.
(C) It will end with a special fireworks display.*
(D) It may include free camping services.

'행사의 특징'이 포인트임을 파악하고 지문을 살펴보면, 둘째 문단에서 the festival will conclude with a fireworks show라며 '폭죽 쇼로 마무리된다'고 하므로 (C)가 정답이다.
* paraphrasing: conclude → end, show → display

정답 (C)

본 이메일에 따르면, 축제의 눈에 띄는 특징은 무엇인가?
(A) 25,000명 이상 수용할 수 있다.
(B) 재즈 댄스 공연들을 포함할 것이다.
(C) 특별 폭죽 행사로 끝날 것이다.
(D) 무료 캠핑 서비스가 포함될 것이다.
어휘 notable 주목할 만한, 눈에 띄는
accommodate 공간을 제공하다, 수용하다

167

In which of the positions marked [1], [2], [3], and [4] does the following sentence best belong?

"It is our first festival and we have many bands lined up."

(A) [1]* (B) [2]
(C) [3] (D) [4]

대명사 It이 의미하는 단어가 앞 문장에 제시되는 곳을 찾아야 한다. [1]에 들어가면 It이 our upcoming three-day festival을 의미할 수 있으므로 가장 자연스럽다.

정답 (A)

[1], [2], [3], [4]로 표시된 곳 중 다음 문장이 들어가기에 가장 알맞은 곳은?
"이는 저희의 첫 번째 축제이며 많은 밴드가 준비돼 있습니다."
(A) [1]
(B) [2]
(C) [3]
(D) [4]

Questions 168-171 refer to the following online chat discussion.

Jessica Simon [10:32 A.M.] Marcus, do you have a minute? [168] I'm trying to access our online store, but it's not loading. Does it load on your computer?

Marcus Adams [10:40 A.M.] It's the same for me. Was it like this yesterday?

Jessica Simon [10:42 A.M.] I don't think so. I have some orders that were placed online yesterday. But [169] I got an e-mail from a repeat customer who said our site was down. Can you ask the IT department about it?

--Jeff Peters has been added to the chat--

Marcus Adams [10:44 A.M.] Jeff, something is wrong with our online store. It doesn't seem to be loading. Can you figure out what's wrong?

Jeff Peters [10:48 A.M.] This is strange. It looks like the hosting site is down.

Marcus Adams [10:50 A.M.] Do you have their telephone number?

Jeff Peters [10:55 A.M.] [170] Yes, I just called them. They said they are having some technical difficulties, which should be fixed by tomorrow morning.

Jessica Simon [11:00 A.M.] Okay, [171] I have a meeting with the sales manager shortly. I'll let him know about this problem.

어휘 access 접속하다, 접근하다 load (프로그램이나 데이터를) 로딩하다 order 주문 repeat customer 다시 찾는 고객 add 추가하다, 더하다 figure out 알아내다 fix 고치다

168

What problem does Ms. Simon report?

(A) Sales cannot be made online currently.*
(B) The online store includes wrong information.
(C) A customer wants to return some items.
(D) A product is no longer listed on the website.

Ms. Simon의 첫 번째 메시지 중 I'm trying to access our online store, but it's not loading.을 통해 (A)를 유추할 수 있다.

정답 (A)

사이먼 씨는 어떤 문제를 알리는가?
(A) 현재 온라인에서 판매가 되지 않는다.
(B) 온라인 매장에 잘못된 정보가 들어가 있다.
(C) 한 고객이 제품을 반품하고 싶어 한다.
(D) 한 제품이 웹사이트에 더는 올라 있지 않다.

어휘 item 물건, 제품 no longer 더는 ~ 않는

169

From whom did Ms. Simon learn about the problem?

(A) A department head   (B) A customer*
(C) An IT manager   (D) An assistant

Ms. Simon의 메시지에 집중해 지문을 살펴보면, 10시 42분 메시지에서 I got an e-mail from a repeat customer who said our site was down.이라며 고객이 이메일을 보냈다고 하므로 (B)가 정답이다.

정답 (B)

사이먼 씨는 누구를 통해 이 문제를 알았는가?
(A) 부장
(B) 고객
(C) IT 과장
(D) 비서

어휘 head 수석, 장 assistant 보조, 비서

170

At 10:50, what does Mr. Adams most likely mean when he writes, "Do you have their telephone number"?

(A) He is requesting some information.
(B) He wants Mr. Peters to call a company.*
(C) He would like a directory updated.
(D) He is worried he will get lost.

제시문 다음에 피터스 씨가 그렇다며 방금 전화했다(Yes, I just called them.)고 답한다. 따라서 (B)가 가장 적절하다.

정답 (B)

10시 50분에, 아담스 씨가 "거기 전화번호 있나요?"라고 쓴 의미하는 바는?
(A) 정보를 요청하고 있다.
(B) 피터스 씨가 한 회사에 전화하기를 원한다.
(C) 주소록을 갱신하고 싶어 한다.
(D) 길 잃을까 봐 걱정한다.

어휘 directory 주소록

171

What will Ms. Simon most likely do next?

(A) Call some customers
(B) Purchase items online
(C) Attend a meeting*
(D) Contact a hosting site

Ms. Simon의 메시지에 집중해 살펴보면, 마지막 메시지에서 I have a meeting with the sales manager shortly.라며 회의가 있다고 하므로 (C)가 정답이 된다.

정답 (C)

사이먼 씨는 다음에 무엇을 하겠는가?
(A) 몇몇 고객에게 전화할 것이다.
(B) 온라인으로 물건들을 살 것이다.
(C) 회의에 참석할 것이다.
(D) 호스팅 사이트에 연락할 것이다.

어휘 purchase 구입하다, 사다 contact 연락하다

Questions 172-175 refer to the following article.

Employment Weekly Column
Job Fairs

Job fairs are a quick and easy way to hire new employees. However, holding a job fair may be a costly event, especially if you're only hiring a few employees. ¹⁷² Consider the following advice to determine if holding a job fair is right for your company.

How many employees are you hiring?
¹⁷³ If your company is planning to hire a large group of employees, a job fair might be right for you. Job fairs can bring in a large number of applicants. However, if you're only interested in finding a few new workers, the number of applicants at a job fair may overwhelm human resources departments, making the hiring process even harder.

Is there a good location to hold the job fair?
High schools and universities are popular places to hold job fairs, but if your company is seeking more experienced candidates, schools are probably not the right place. It is critical to hold the job fair in a place where you can attract suitable employees, such as business conventions. Unfortunately, business conventions are only held at certain times of the year.

¹⁷⁵ Can you hire employees another way?
¹⁷⁵ Online job advertisement websites have changed the way people search for jobs. Prior to your company's hiring season, human resources staff members may be able to post job openings on numerous websites. This would garner a lot of attention and allow your company to list the experience requirements applicants must meet.

Is the cost worth it?
Before holding a job fair, consider the cost of the event. You may need to pay to rent a suitable space and would need to provide refreshments and application packages. If your hiring needs could be met by free online websites, a job fair may not be worth it.

172

What is the article about?

(A) Tips for increasing a worker's productivity
(B) Websites used to hire employees
(C) Methods of increasing the chances of being hired
(D) Strategies for efficient and economical recruitment*

제목에서 '채용'에 관련된 내용이 주로 전개되리라는 것을 알 수 있지만 관련성이 높은 선택지들이 제시되었으니 좀 더 살펴봐야 한다. 첫째 문단에서 Consider the following advice to determine if holding a job fair is right for your company.라고 하므로 (D)가 가장 적절하다.

* paraphrasing: advice → strategy

정답 (D)

본 기사는 무엇에 대한 것인가?
(A) 직원들의 생산성을 늘리기 위한 조언들
(B) 직원을 고용하는 데 이용되는 웹사이트들
(C) 채용될 기회를 늘리는 방법들
(D) 효율적이고 경제적인 채용 전략

어휘 increase 늘리다, 증가시키다 productivity 생산성 method 방법 strategy 전략 efficient 효율적인 economical 경제적인 recruitment 신규모집, 채용

173

According to the article, what is a good reason to hold a job fair?

(A) To hire specialized workers
(B) To fill a large number of positions*
(C) To provide employees with experience
(D) To promote the brand of a company

'채용 박람회의 효용성 또는 목적'이 포인트임을 파악하고 지문을 살펴보면, 둘째 문단의 If your company is planning to hire a large group of employees, a job fair might be right for you.를 통해 '많은 직원을 뽑을 때'에 적당하다는 것을 알 수 있다. 따라서 (B)가 가장 적절하다.

정답 (B)

본 기사에 따르면, 채용 박람회를 여는 이유로 좋은 것은?
(A) 전문화된 직원들을 고용하기 위해서
(B) 많은 자리를 채우기 위해서
(C) 직원들이 경험을 쌓게 하기 위해서
(D) 회사 브랜드를 홍보하기 위해서

어휘 position 직책 promote 홍보하다

174

The word "critical" in paragraph 3, line 3, is closest in meaning to

(A) urgent   (B) essential*
(C) creative   (D) negative

해당 부분은 '적당한 곳에서 채용 박람회를 여는 것이 중요하다'는 요지이다. 따라서 제시된 선택지들로 바꿨을 때 의미 전개가 가장 유사한 것은 (B)이다.

정답 (B)

셋째 문단 셋째 줄에 있는 "critical"과 의미상 가장 유사한 단어는?
(A) 긴급한
(B) 중요한
(C) 창의적인
(D) 부정적인

어휘 urgent 긴급한 essential 필수적인, 극히 중요한 creative 창조적인, 창의적인 negative 부정적인

175

What is mentioned as an alternative way of finding job candidates?

(A) Advertising in local newspapers
(B) Using employment websites*
(C) Holding job fairs at the office
(D) Sending out mass e-mails

다른 방법(Can you hire employees another way?)에 관련된 넷째 문단에서 웹사이트(Online job advertisement websites)를 다루므로 (B)가 정답이다.

정답 (B)

구직자를 찾기 위한 대안으로 언급된 것은?
(A) 지역 신문에 광고한다.
(B) 채용 웹사이트를 이용한다.
(C) 사무실에서 채용 박람회를 연다.
(D) 대량 이메일을 발송한다.

어휘 alternative 대체 가능한, 대안이 되는 mass 대량의, 대규모의

Questions 176-180 refer to the following article and e-mail.

176 Publisher Instructs the Next Generation

January 10 -- Since his retirement last year, publisher and editor Jim Frank has run the Department of Publishing Studies at Western University. Frank is best known for his role at Maxwell Publishing House where he worked as a senior editor on numerous projects, including the publication of several successful series.

Jim Frank joined Western University as both a department head and a professor. 177 He developed new courses such as E-publishing, Writing for the Web, and International Rights Management. Students who wish to work in the publishing industry as editors, book designers, or literary agents have benefited greatly from his wisdom.

As a result of Frank's hard work, Western University has also founded its first ever publishing internship. 179 Students have been matched with editors, designers, and agents during three-week programs. Additionally, Frank has organized numerous events in which industry professionals have given presentations at the university on various topics. Because of Frank's innovation and connections, the publishing program at Western University has become one of the best in the country.

From: beth@ricorspublishing.com
To: jimfrank@westernuniversity.com
Date: February 25
Subject: E-Publishing Panel

Dear Mr. Frank,

179 Margaret Stevenson is currently doing her internship here at Ricors Publishing House. She mentioned that you're putting together another panel of guest speakers for your students next month. 178 I'd love to join the panel if you still have any openings. As the director of e-publishing here at Ricors, I'm sure I'd be able to give some great information on working in this field.

180 I will be busy next week attending a conference overseas, but you can leave a message with my assistant and I'll get back to you the following week. My number is 443-223-0911 Ext. 3367.

I look forward to hearing from you.

Sincerely,
Beth Smith,
Director of E-Publishing,
Ricors Publishing House

어휘 panel 패널[특정 문제에 대해 조언하는 전문가 집단] put together 만들다, 준비하다 opening 공석, 빈자리 field 분야 Ext. 내선 번호 look forward to ~ing ~하기를 고대하다

176

What does the article mainly discuss?

(A) A company's business practices
(B) An editor's career change*
(C) A publisher's new series
(D) A student internship program

기사는 주로 무엇을 논의하는가?
(A) 한 회사의 사업 관행
(B) 한 편집자의 이력 변경
(C) 출판사의 새 시리즈물
(D) 학생 인턴십 프로그램
어휘 practice 실행, 관례

기사(지문 1) 제목이 글의 주제에 대한 결정적인 단서가 될 확률이 높다. Publisher Instructs the Next Generation이라는 제목을 통해 '편집자가 학생들을 가르친다'는 경력상 변화를 유추할 수 있으므로 (B)가 가장 적절하다.

정답 (B)

177

What is one contribution Jim Frank has made to the university?

(A) More courses have become available to students.*
(B) A student employment website has been developed.
(C) A scholarship foundation has been established.
(D) A computer lab has recently opened.

짐 프랭크가 대학에 기여한 한 가지는 무엇인가?
(A) 학생들을 위해 더 많은 코스가 열렸다.
(B) 학생 고용 웹사이트를 개발했다.
(C) 장학 재단을 설립했다.
(D) 컴퓨터 실험실을 최근 열었다
어휘 contribution 기여, 이바지 available 이용 가능한 employment 고용, 채용 scholarship 장학금 establish 설립하다 lab 실험실

Jim Frank의 경력 및 업적이 소재로 다뤄진 기사(지문 1)에서 둘째 문단의 He developed new courses를 통해 정답 (A)를 확인할 수 있다.

정답 (A)

178

Why did Ms. Smith send the e-mail?

(A) She is replying to a phone message.
(B) She would like to join a speaking event.*
(C) She is looking for more interns.
(D) She wants to register in a course.

스미스 씨는 이메일을 왜 보냈는가?
(A) 전화 메시지에 응하기 위해서
(B) 강연 행사에 합류하고 싶어서
(C) 인턴을 더 찾고 있어서
(D) 강좌에 등록하고 싶어서
어휘 reply to ~에 응하다, 대답하다 register 등록하다

이메일(지문 2)의 목적에 대한 문제이므로 전반부를 유념해서 살펴봐야 한다. 지문 2 첫째 문단에서 다음 달 초대 강사들을 모으는 중이라 들었다면서 공석이 있으면 자신도 함께하고 싶다(I'd love to join the panel if you still have any openings.)고 한다. 따라서 (B)가 정답이다.

정답 (B)

스티븐슨 씨는 누구이겠는가?
(A) 리코스 퍼블리싱 하우스의 디렉터
(B) 웨스턴 대학의 학생
(C) 출판 강좌의 초대 강사
(D) 맥스웰 퍼블리싱 하우스의 전 편집자

어휘 former 이전의

179

Who most likely is Ms. Stevenson?
(A) A director at Ricors Publishing House
(B) A student at Western University*
(C) A guest speaker in a publishing course
(D) A former editor at Maxwell Publishing House

Ms. Stevenson에 유념해 지문들을 살펴보면, 이메일(지문 2) 첫째 문단의 Margaret Stevenson is currently doing her internship here at Ricors Publishing House.를 통해 '인턴'임을 알 수 있다. 이와 관련해 기사(지문 1) 셋째 문단에서 웨스턴 대학에 설립된 인턴십 프로그램이 언급되는데 바로 이어 학생들이 이 프로그램을 통해 편집자, 디자이너, 대리인과 짝을 이룬다(Students have been matched with editors, designers, and agents during three-week programs.)고 하므로 (B)가 정답이 된다.

정답 (B)

스미스 씨는 일정에 대해 뭐라고 말하는가?
(A) 회의들의 일정을 조정할 수 있다.
(B) 3월에는 패널로 참여할 수 없다.
(C) 낮에만 연락할 수 있다.
(D) 다음 주에는 출장을 갈 예정이다.

어휘 reschedule 일정을 다시 조정하다 reach 연락하다

180

What does Ms. Smith say about her schedule?
(A) She can reschedule her meetings.
(B) She is not available for the panel in March.
(C) She can be reached only during the day.
(D) She will be away on business next week.*

Ms. Smith가 작성한 이메일(지문 2)을 살펴보면, schedule에 대한 둘째 문단의 I will be busy next week attending a conference overseas를 통해 정답 (D)를 확인할 수 있다.

정답 (D)

Questions 181-185 refer to the following memo and e-mail.

MEMO
Free Cloud Services

As you know, Roth Computer Sales has recently partnered with L&B Tech to improve our company's efficiency and file storage. 181 In order to make saving and sharing files easier, we plan to install L&B's Cloud Software program on all our systems.

L&B's Cloud Software allows employees to store files of any size without taking up too much computer memory. 183 Employees can easily send large files in seconds without worrying about slow upload speeds. Additionally, employees who bring their company laptops on business trips will be able to access their files remotely. Furthermore, L&B Cloud Software is extremely secure, so employees can rest assured that any sensitive files will be safe.

To use this new software, simply complete the setup, register with your company e-mail, and start storing and sending files. 185 The service will be available on April 10th at 9 A.M. If you have any questions or concerns about setting up or using the new software, please contact Michael Brown in the IT Department at extension 3342 or by e-mail at michaelbrown@rothcomputers.com.

To: michaelbrown@rothcomputers.com
From: sandrabell@rothcomputers.com
Date: April 12
Subject: Cloud Software

Dear Mr. Brown,

I tried calling you on your extension, but you did not answer. I'm writing to request assistance with the new L&B Cloud Software. 185 I set up my account on the first day the service was available, but today I was unable to find any of the files in my account. 184 It seems that all of the files I uploaded have been deleted, as my account is empty. Since these files include very important sales figures from last quarter, I really need to access them immediately. Can you give me an idea about how to recover these files? It would be great if you could stop by my office sometime today.

Sandra Bell

메모의 목적은 무엇인가?
(A) 정책의 변경 사항을 발표하기 위해서
(B) 직원들에게 컴퓨터 백업을 상기시키기 위해서
(C) 새 프로그램에 대한 정보를 주기 위해서
(D) 새로운 규칙들을 설명하기 위해서

어휘 announce 발표하다 remind 상기시키다

181

What is the purpose of the memo?
(A) To announce a change in a policy
(B) To remind employees to back-up computers
(C) To give information about a new program*
(D) To explain a new set of rules

첫째 문단에서 회사의 효율성을 개선하기 위해 기술 회사와 제휴했다며 새 프로그램을 설치할 계획(In order to make saving and sharing files easier, we plan to install L&B's Cloud Software program on all our systems.)이라고 덧붙이므로 (C)가 가장 적절하다. 글의 목적은 대체로 전반부에서 찾을 수 있다.

정답 (C)

메모에서, 둘째 문단 다섯째 줄에 있는 "sensitive"와 의미상 가장 유사한 단어는?
(A) 신중한
(B) 반응하는
(C) 놀라운
(D) 기밀의

어휘 cautious 조심스러운, 신중한 responsive (즉각) 반응하는 confidential 비밀의, 기밀의

182

In the memo, the word "sensitive" in paragraph 2, line 5, is closest in meaning to
(A) cautious
(B) responsive
(C) surprising
(D) confidential*

해당 부분은 '민감한' 파일의 보안 문제를 다룬다. 따라서 '비밀의, 기밀의'라는 뜻의 단어 (D)가 들어갔을 때 맥락상 가장 유사하게 전개된다. classified도 종종 유의어로 사용된다.

정답 (D)

L&B 클라우드 소프트웨어의 혜택으로 언급된 것은?
(A) 비용을 줄여 준다.
(B) 회사 시간을 아껴 준다.
(C) 설치비가 무료이다.
(D) 문서들에서 실수가 있는지 스캔한다.

어휘 benefit 혜택, 이득 reduce 줄이다, 축소하다 mistake 실수

183

What is stated as a benefit of L&B Cloud Software?
(A) It reduces cost.
(B) It saves a company time.*
(C) It is free to install.
(D) It scans documents for mistakes.

핵심 어구 L&B Cloud Software의 설치 절차 및 특징에 대한 메모(지문 1)를 살펴보면, 둘째 문단에서 여러 장점이 언급되는데, 특히 Employees can easily send large files in seconds without worrying about slow upload speed.를 통해 정답 (B)를 확인할 수 있다.

정답 (B)

184

What problem is Ms. Bell having?
(A) She has forgotten her password.
(B) Her computer has crashed.
(C) All files have gone missing.*
(D) She cannot access a server.

Ms. Bell이 작성한 이메일(지문 2)을 '문제'에 유념해 살펴보면, 중반부에서 파일들이 삭제된 듯하다(It seems that all of the files I uploaded have been deleted, as my account is empty.)고 하므로 (C)가 가장 적절하다.

정답 (C)

벨 씨는 어떤 문제를 겪고 있는가?
(A) 비밀번호를 잊었다.
(B) 컴퓨터가 다운됐다.
(C) 모든 파일들이 없어졌다.
(D) 서버에 접속할 수 없다.

185

When did Ms. Bell set up her account?
(A) On April 10*
(B) On April 11
(C) On April 12
(D) On April 13

벨 씨가 작성한 이메일(지문 2)부터 살펴보자. 전반부에서 I set up my account on the first day the service was available이라며 서비스가 시작된 첫 날 설치했다고 한다. '서비스 시행일'을 메모(지문 1)에서 찾아보면, 셋째 문단의 The service will be available on April 10th at 9 A.M.을 통해 (A)가 정답임을 알 수 있다.

정답 (A)

벨 씨는 언제 계정을 설치했는가?
(A) 4월 10일
(B) 4월 11일
(C) 4월 12일
(D) 4월 13일

발신: oemerson@sommerfield.com
수신: mfernandez@rkdistribution.br
제목: 시연
날짜: 8월 5일

페르난데즈 씨 귀하

제가 탄 비행기는 상파울루에 도착했고 공항 대기실에서 이메일 드립니다. 안타깝게도, 제가 수속한 대형 여행 가방을 잃어버렸습니다. 모든 제품들에 대한 요약 내용 인쇄본은 제 휴대용 가방에 갖고 있지만, 188 시연용 견본 제품들은 없어진 가방에 들어 있습니다. 공항 직원이 제게 가방을 찾아 제가 묵는 곳으로 보내는 데 최소 3일이 필요하답니다. 그 말은, 즉, 모레로 예정된 시연 일정에 맞춰 받지 못한다는 뜻입니다.

제가 호텔에 도착하면, 186 요약문을 귀사에 팩스로 보내겠습니다. 크게 문제되지 않는다면, 187 시연을 이틀 더 미룰 수 있을까요? 이에 대해 가능한 한 빨리 제게 연락 주시기 바랍니다.

그럼 이만,
오스카 에머슨

Questions 186-190 refer to the following e-mails and form.

From: oemerson@sommerfield.com
To: mfernandez@rkdistribution.br
Subject: demonstration
Date: August 5

Dear Ms. Fernandez,

My plane landed in Sao Paulo and I am e-mailing you from a waiting room in the airport. Unfortunately, the large suitcase that I had checked has been misplaced. Even though I have printed summaries of all the items right here in my carry-on bag, 188 the sample products for the demonstration are in the missing luggage. Airport staff informed me that they need at least three days to locate the bags and deliver them to where I am staying. That means, of course, that I will not have them in time for the demonstration scheduled for the day after tomorrow.

Once I reach my hotel, 186 I will fax the summaries to your company. If it is not too much trouble, 187 could we possibly postpone the demonstration for another two days? Please contact me about this as soon as possible.

Sincerely,
Oscar Emerson

어휘 demonstration 시연 land 도착하다, 상륙하다 unfortunately 안타깝게도, 공교롭게도 misplace 제자리에 두지 않다, 잃어버리다 even though 비록 ~일지라도 summary 요약, 개요 item 물건, 제품 carry-on 휴대용의 missing 사라진 luggage 짐, 수하물 inform 알리다 at least 적어도 locate (특정한 위치를) 찾다 deliver 배송하다, 배달하다 postpone 미루다, 연기하다

분실 수하물 청구 서식

고객님의 소지품을 잘못 처리하고 그로 인해 불편을 끼친 점에 대해 진심으로 사죄 드립니다. 아래 적어 주시는 정보가 대단히 도움이 될 것입니다. 모든 가방에 대한 묘사와 그 안에 든 물품의 목록을 정확히 적어 주시기 바랍니다. 이것은 분명 모든 과정이 더욱 빨리 진행될 수 있게 해 줄 것입니다.

청구 번호: 341567S/3
승객 이름: 오스카 에머슨
이메일: oemerson@sommerfield.com

거주지 주소:
409 잭슨 레인
클리블랜드, OH, 44103
미합중국

임시 주소 (8월 12일까지):
피쿠리 호텔
폴리스타 애비뉴 1209

Missing Baggage Claim Form

We would like to extend our deepest apologies for our mishandling of your belongings and any inconveniences it caused. The information you provide below will assist us greatly. Please provide a clear description of every piece of luggage as well as a list of the items inside each piece. This will definitely help expedite the entire process.

Claim No:	341567S/3
Name of Passenger:	Oscar Emerson
E-mail:	oemerson@sommerfield.com

Permanent address:
409 Jackson Lane
Cleveland, OH, 44103
United States of America

Temporary address (Until August 12):
Piquiri Hotel
Av. Paulista 1209

[190] Sao Paulo, Brazil
01310-060

Flight No.	Date	From	To
MTC971	August 3	Toledo	Buenos Aires
BTA302	August 5	Buenos Aires	Sao Paulo

Suitcase Type: Large leather bag, zipper, shoulder strap

Manufacturer: Riggs   Color: Brown

Contents (Please be as specific as possible)

Description	Number
[188] Running shoes, tennis shoes, golf shoes, baseball shoes, high-top basketball sneakers	12 pairs
Top Guy brand Man's suits	2
Greyvalley brand digital camera with battery charger	1
Trousers, shorts, socks, etc.	6
South American pocket-sized travel guides	2

From: airportlostfoundoffice@spinternat.com
To: oemerson@sommerfield.com
Subject: claim 341567S/3
Date: August 6

Dear Mr. Emerson,

We are delighted to inform you that your missing suitcase has been located with all the items you listed. [190] It will arrive at the temporary address you provided between 1:00 P.M. and 3:00 P.M. on August 7.
We truly appreciate your patience and understanding.

Regards
Sao Paulo International Lost and Found

에머슨 씨는 제품 요약문에 대해 뭐라고 하는가?
(A) 팩스로 보낼 것이다.
(B) 아직 준비되지 않았다.
(C) 예상보다 길다.
(D) 출력해야 한다.

어휘 indicate 가리키다, 나타내다
expect 기대하다, 예상하다

186 What does Mr. Emerson indicate about the product summaries?
(A) They will be sent by fax.*
(B) They are not ready yet.
(C) They are longer than expected.
(D) They need to be printed out.

핵심 어구 the product summaries에 유의해 에머슨 씨가 작성한 이메일(지문 1)을 살펴보면, 둘째 문단의 I will fax the summaries to your company를 통해 정답 (A)를 확인할 수 있다.

정답 (A)

에머슨 씨는 페르난데즈 씨에게 무엇을 요청하는가?
(A) 제품 견본을 배송해 달라.
(B) 주문서를 제출해 달라.
(C) 회의 일정을 조정해 달라.
(D) 호텔까지 태워 달라.

어휘 submit 제출하다

187 What does Mr. Emerson ask Ms. Fernandez to do?
(A) Deliver product samples
(B) Submit an order form
(C) Reschedule a meeting*
(D) Drive him to the hotel

에머슨이 작성자이며 페르난데즈가 수신자인 이메일(지문 1)에서 단서를 찾아야 한다. 둘째 문단에서 괜찮다면 이틀 더 미룰 수 있겠냐(could we possibly postpone the demonstration for another two days?)고 한 뒤 연락 달라고 하므로 (C)가 가장 적절하다.

* paraphrasing: postpone → reschedule

정답 (C)

에머슨 씨는 무엇을 시연하기를 원하는가?
(A) 자전거 타이어
(B) 운동화
(C) 이미지 소프트웨어
(D) 커피 메이커

어휘 athletic 육상의

188 What does Mr. Emerson want to demonstrate?
(A) Bicycle tires
(B) Athletic shoes*
(C) Image software
(D) Coffee makers

'시연 물품'이 포인트임을 파악하고 지문들을 살펴보면, 에머슨 씨가 작성한 이메일(지문 1) 첫째 문단에서 the sample products for the demonstration are in the missing luggage라고 하므로 '분실물'이 시연용 제품임이 드러난다. 분실물을 찾아 달라는 서식(지문 2) 내용물(Contents)에서 가장 눈에 띄는 것들은 Running shoes, tennis shoes, golf shoes, baseball shoes, high-top basketball sneakers이므로 이를 통칭하는 (B)가 정답이 된다.

정답 (B)

189 In the form, the word "expedite" in paragraph 1, line 4, is closest in meaning to

(A) discover
(B) modify
(C) elaborate
(D) accelerate*

'더 신속히 처리하다'라는 의미의 expedite를 대신해 쓸 수 있는 단어는 제시된 선택지들 중 (D)이다.

정답 (D)

서식에서, 첫째 문단 넷째 줄에 있는 "expedite"와 의미상 가장 유사한 단어는?
(A) 발견하다
(B) 수정하다
(C) 상술하다
(D) 가속화하다

어휘 discover 발견하다 modify 수정하다, 변경하다 elaborate 자세히 말하다, 상술하다 accelerate 가속화하다

190 Where will the delivery be sent?

(A) To Cleveland
(B) To Toledo
(C) To Sao Paulo*
(D) To Buenos Aires

공항 측이 작성한 메일(지문 3)의 It will arrive at the temporary address you provided를 통해 '임시 주소지'로 간다는 것을 알 수 있지만 제시된 선택지가 특정 지명이므로 이것들이 언급된 서식(지문 2)을 더 살펴봐야 한다. 지문 2의 Temporary address에 적힌 지명은 (C)이다.

정답 (C)

배송품은 어디로 가겠는가?
(A) 클리블랜드
(B) 톨레도
(C) 상파울루
(D) 부에노스아이레스

어휘 delivery 배송, 배달

수산: 제레미 번즈
발산: 크리스틴 림
날짜: 195 6월 5일
제목: 재봉틀

제레미 씨,

방금 당신 이메일을 받았어요. 우리 패션 디자인 스튜디오에 새 재봉틀들을 사야겠다는 당신 생각에 동의해요. 195 우리는 이제 막 창업했으니, 193 튼튼하고 청소하기 쉬운 적당한 가격의 재봉틀을 사 두는 게 좋을 것 같아요. 매일 사용할 테니까 보증 조건이 좋아야 한다는 것도 매우 중요하고요. Topreviews.com에 우리가 모델을 고를 때 도움이 될 만한 정보가 많아요. 그 사이트를 확인해 보시고 우리에게 어떤 모델이 적합할지 알려 주시겠어요?

고마워요,
크리스틴

범주: 재봉틀

탑 리뷰는 가정과 업체 모두에 이상적인 고급 재봉틀 네 종을 테스트했습니다:

★★★★ 마스터 소우 445는 193 오래 가고 청소하기 쉬우며, 모든 종류의 직물에 적합한 재봉 세팅을 갖췄습니다. 일부 가정에는 너무 클 수 있으나, 업체에는 최적일 것입니다. 192 적정한 가격에 구입하실 수 있으며 193 5년짜리 보증이 포함됩니다.

★★★★ 디자인 라인 3019는 소형이며 여행용으로도 쓸 수 있을 휴대용 재봉틀입니다. 대부분의 바느질에 사용 가능하며 아주 튼튼한 플라스틱으로 만들어져 있습니다. 193 가격은 적정한 지만, 보증서가 딸려 있지는 않습니다.

★★★☆ 트리플 소우 88은 얇은 천에 쓸 수 있지만, 데님 같은 두꺼운 천에는 힘들지도 모릅니다. 192 아주 저렴한 가격으로 온라인에서 주문하실 수 있습니다.

★★★☆ ZS 3000은 시장에서 가장 큰 재봉틀입니다. 세팅하는 데 상당한 주의가 필요하며 청소하려면 분해해야 합니다. 가격은 아주 저렴하지만, 191 이 재봉틀은 바느질 기술을 몇 가지만 처리할 수 있습니다.

Questions 191-195 refer to the following e-mail, webpage, and article.

To: Jeremy Burns
From: Christine Lim
Date: 195 June 5
Subject: Sewing Machine

Dear Jeremy,

I just received your e-mail. I agree with you that we should think about purchasing new sewing machines for our fashion design studio. 195 Since we are just starting our business, 193 it would be good to have affordable machines that are sturdy and easy to clean. It's also very important that they have good warranties, as we will be using them every day. Topreviews.com has a lot of information that might help us in choosing a model. Why don't you check the site and let me know what model you think will suit our needs?

Thanks,
Christine

어휘 sewing machine 재봉틀 agree 동의하다 purchase 구입하다, 사다 affordable (가격이) 알맞은, 감당할 수 있는 sturdy 튼튼한, 견고한 warranty 보증(서) choose 선택하다 check 확인하다 suit 맞다, 적합하다

---

https://www.topreviews.com

Category: Sewing Machines
Top Reviews has tested four high-end sewing machines that are ideal for both homes and businesses:

★★★★ Master Sew 445 is 193 a durable, easy-to-clean machine with multiple sewing settings for all different kinds of fabrics. It might be too large for some homes, but would suit businesses well. 192 It is available for a reasonable price and 193 includes a five-year warranty.

★★★★ Design Line 3019 is a compact, portable machine that would serve traveling sewers well. It is capable of most stitching styles and is made of extremely durable plastic. 193 It is a reasonable price, but does not come with a warranty.

★★★☆ Triple Sew 88 performs well with light fabrics, but may have trouble with thicker fabrics, like denim. It can be ordered online for 192 an extremely low cost.

★★★☆ ZS 3000 is the largest machine on the market. It requires significant set-up and must be taken apart to be cleaned. The cost is especially low, but 191 the machine can only handle a few stitching techniques.

어휘 high-end 고급의 durable 내구성이 있는, 오래 가는 multiple 많은, 다수의 fabric 천, 직물 reasonable (가격이) 적정한 compact 소형의 portable 휴대용의 capable of ~을 할 수 있는 stitching 꿰매기 extremely 극히 come with ~이 딸려 오다 triple 3개로 이뤄진 perform (수)행하다 cost 값, 비용 market 시장 require 필요로 하다 significant 중요한, 상당한 take ~ apart ~을 분해하다 especially 특히 handle 다루다, 처리하다

Fashion in Park Falls
By Zander Cornelli

195 December 20—Residents of Park Falls who monitor the latest trends in fashion were excited about attending the upscale fashion event held in the Park Falls Convention Center last week. Numerous companies that have made Park Falls the home of their growing businesses participated in the 10th Park Falls Fashion Festival. Over twenty fashion studios were showcased in the event, several of which are owned by local residents.

Rose Designs, which has been in the area for over twenty years, kicked off the festival with some incredible winter apparel. The show was followed by a presentation by Kim Miller, the owner of Accessories Forever. 195 In-Style Fashions and Turnbull Jeans, which have been in business for six months and three years respectively, were newcomers to the festival. All items featured during the fashion shows are available for sale on company websites.

어휘 resident 주민 monitor 감시하다, 관찰하다 trend 경향 upscale 평균 이상의 돈 많은 소비자의 마음에 드는 numerous 많은 participate in ~에 참여하다, 참가하다 showcase 전시하다, 진열하다, (신제품 등을) 소개하다 own 소유하다 kick off 경기를 시작하다 incredible 믿을 수 없는, 믿기 힘든 apparel 의류, 의복 be followed by ~이 이어지다, 계속되다 respectively 각자, 제각기 newcomer 신입

파크 폴스의 패션
잰더 코넬리 작성

195 12월 20일—패션의 신경향을 관찰하는 파크 폴스 주민들은 파크 폴스 컨벤션 센터에서 지난주에 열린 럭셔리 패션 행사에 참여하게 되어 흥분했다. 파크 폴스를 자신들의 성장 사업의 본거지로 삼은 수많은 업체가 제10회 파크 폴스 패션 페스티벌에 참가했다. 20여 개의 패션 스튜디오들이 행사에서 선보였는데 개중 일부는 지역 주민들이 소유한 곳이다.

이 지역에서 20년이 넘도록 영업해 온 로즈 디자인이 엄청난 겨울 의류로 페스티벌을 장악했다. 이 패션 쇼에 이어 액세서리 포에버 사장 킴 밀러가 프레젠테이션을 했다. 195 각각 6개월, 3년 동안 영업해 온 인스타일 패션, 턴불 진은 이번 페스티벌에 처음으로 참여했다. 패션 쇼에 등장한 전 제품을 회사 웹사이트들에서 구입할 수 있다.

191

What is indicated about the ZS 3000?

(A) It is commonly used in homes.
(B) It has an extended warranty.
(C) It can be transported easily.
(D) It has limited functions.*

ZS 3000에 대해 드러나는 사항은?
(A) 흔히 집에서 사용된다.
(B) 보증 기간이 길다.
(C) 쉽게 옮길 수 있다.
(D) 기능이 제한적이다.

어휘 commonly 흔히 extended 늘어난, 연장된 transport 수송하다, 옮기다 limited 제한된, 한정된 function 기능

핵심 어구 ZS 3000에 유의해 지문들을 살펴보면, 웹페이지(지문 2) 마지막 부분의 the machine can only handle a few stitching techniques를 통해 (D)가 정답임을 알 수 있다

* paraphrasing: a few → limited, technique → function

정답 (D)

웹페이지에서 언급된 모든 기계가 지닌 공통점은?
(A) 소형이고 휴대용이다.
(B) 가격이 저렴하다.
(C) 다양한 색상으로 출시된다.
(D) 쉽게 고칠 수 있다.

어휘 in common 공통으로 come in (상품 등이) 들어오다

192

What do all the machines mentioned on the webpage have in common?
(A) They are compact and portable.
(B) They are affordable prices.*
(C) They come in various colors.
(D) They can be repaired easily.

웹페이지(지문 2) 기계들 설명을 살펴보면, 각 설명의 후반부에 '저렴한 가격'(a reasonable price, an extremely low cost, The cost is especially low)을 확인할 수 있으므로 (B)가 정답이 된다.

정답 (B)

번즈 씨는 림 씨에게 어떤 재봉틀을 권했겠는가?
(A) 마스터 소우 445
(B) 디자인 라인 3019
(C) 트리플 소우 88
(D) ZS 3000

193

What sewing machine did Mr. Burns most likely recommend to Ms. Lim?
(A) Master Sew 445*   (B) Design Line 3019
(C) Triple Sew 88   (D) ZS 3000

핵심 인명들이 수신자와 발신자로 설정된 이메일(지문 1)부터 림 씨가 원하는 조건에 유념해 살펴보자. 중반부에서 it would be good to have affordable machines that are sturdy and easy to clean. It's also very important that they have good warranties, as we will be using them every day.라며 네 가지 조건을 제시한다. 이를 유념해 각 기계의 사양이 언급된 웹페이지(지문 2)를 보면, (A)에 대한 설명 중 durable, easy-to-clean machine, a reasonable price, includes a five-year warranty를 확인할 수 있다.

정답 (A)

기사에서, 첫째 문단 첫째 줄에 있는 "monitor"와 의미상 가장 유사한 단어는?
(A) 믿다
(B) 주시하다
(C) 감독하다
(D) 의존하다

어휘 observe 관찰/관측/주시하다 supervise 감독하다, 지도하다 depend on ~에 의존하다

194

In the article, in paragraph 1, line 1, the word "monitor" is closest in meaning to
(A) believe in   (B) observe*
(C) supervise   (D) depend on

해당 부분은 신경항에 '주목해 온' 주민들에 대한 내용이다. 따라서 제시된 선택지들 중 대신해 들어갔을 때 의미 전개가 가장 유사해지는 어휘는 (B)이다.

정답 (B)

기사에 언급된 회사들 중 림 씨와 번즈 씨가 일하는 곳은 어디이겠는가?
(A) 로즈 디자인
(B) 액세서리 포에버
(C) 인스타일 패션
(D) 턴불 진

195

What company mentioned in the article do Ms. Lim and Mr. Burns most likely work for?
(A) Rose Designs   (B) Accessories Forever
(C) In-Style Fashions*   (D) Turnbull Jeans

기사(지문 3)와 이메일(지문 1)을 연계해서 파악해야 하는 문제이다. 지문 1 전반부에서 Since we are just starting our business와 작성 날짜를 통해 6월에 창업했음이 드러나는데 이를 지문 3 둘째 문단의 In-Style Fashions and Turnbull Jeans, which have been in business for six months and three years respectively 및 작성 날짜와 대조해 보면 (C)가 정답임을 알 수 있다.

정답 (C)

Questions 196-200 refer to the following webpage, online order form, and e-mail.

Http://www.martinmovers.com

| Home | Services | Estimates | Contact Us |

Martin Movers is ready to help you with all your moving needs. Our movers have a collective twenty years of experience tackling large and small jobs with the greatest care. Whether you are moving to a new home or you're looking to relocate your office to a new building, we can offer you the most competitive rates.

Our standard moving rates are as follows:

2 movers and 1 mid-sized truck = $75 per hour
4 movers and 1 full-sized truck = $150 per hour
[197 (A),(B)] Office moves (6 movers and 2 full-sized trucks) = $400 flat rate

Additional charges may apply to office moves should customers request to have our movers set up photocopiers, computers, printers, and projectors following the move. For each set up, a $5 charge may be added. [197 (C)] To get a free estimate, just fill out our online form and we'll get back to you soon.

*New Year Special Promotion: Request an estimate by January 20th and receive $30 off the total cost of your move.

Martin Movers
Estimate Request Form

Date	January 10
Name	Connor Goldsmith
E-mail address	connor@goldsmithlegal.com
Telephone	409-333-2314
Moving from: Moving to:	54 First Avenue, New York City 889 Fallsview Lane, New York City
[200] Moving date	February 23
Items to be moved	8 desks, 8 computers, 3 printers, 1 photocopier, 1 refrigerator, 1 conference table, 25 office chairs
Additional comments	My law office is moving to a new location. As [198] we have our own IT employee, we will not require anyone to set up our equipment. Thus, [199] I believe your standard flat rate will apply. Please contact me by e-mail to confirm the price and finalize the reservation.

To: Connor Goldsmith
From: Stephan Martin
Date: January 12
Subject: Re: Estimate Request
Attachment: goldsmith_quote.pdf

Dear Mr. Goldsmith,

Thank you for requesting a quote from Martin Movers. As you have noted in your estimate request form, you do not need any set up services, so [199] I believe our standard flat rate will apply to you.

Unfortunately, however, [200] Martin Movers is already fully booked on the day you requested. I'm wondering if it would be possible to postpone your move by one day. Of course, because you requested a quote during our promotional event, [199] I'm happy to offer you a $30 discount on your move.

Please feel free to call my office at 409-555-8796 to further discuss this. Otherwise, I will follow up with you next week.

Sincerely,
Stephan Martin
Martin Movers

196 In the webpage, the word "tackling" in paragraph 1, line 2, is closest in meaning to

(A) repairing
(B) handling*
(C) considering
(D) entertaining

197

What is NOT mentioned about office moves?

(A) Six movers will be involved.
(B) More than one truck will be used.
(C) Estimates will be provided at no cost.
(D) It must be booked at least two weeks in advance.*

이삿짐 센터의 웹 페이지(지문 1)에서 office moves에 관련된 부분을 찾아 각 선택지들과 대조하면서 지문에 언급된 것을 소거하는 식으로 해결한다. Office moves (6 movers and 2 full-sized trucks)에서 (A)와 (B)를, 다음 문단의 To get a free estimate, just fill out our online form and we'll get back to you soon.에서는 공통된 사항 (C)를 확인할 수 있다. 따라서 본 문제의 정답은 (D)가 된다.

정답 (D)

사무실 이사에 대해 언급되지 않은 것은?
(A) 직원 여섯 명이 관여할 것이다.
(B) 트럭 한 대 이상이 쓰일 것이다.
(C) 견적은 무료로 제공될 것이다.
(D) 최소한 2주 전에 예약해야 한다.

어휘 involve 관련시키다, 연루시키다 provide 제공하다 at no cost 무료로 at least 적어도, 최소한 in advance 미리, 사전에

198

What does Mr. Goldsmith mention about his company?

(A) It will discard several items.
(B) It will downsize its office space.
(C) It requires an additional mover.
(D) It employs an IT specialist.*

Mr. Goldsmith가 작성한 요청서(지문 2) 마지막의 we have our own IT employee를 통해 (D)가 정답임을 알 수 있다.

정답 (D)

골드스미스 씨는 자신의 회사에 대해 뭐라고 언급하는가?
(A) 물건 몇 개를 버릴 것이다.
(B) 사무실 공간을 줄일 것이다.
(C) 이삿짐 직원 한 명이 더 필요하다.
(D) IT 전문가를 고용하고 있다.

어휘 discard 버리다, 폐기하다 several 몇몇의 downsize 줄이다, 축소하다 employ 고용하다

199

If Mr. Goldsmith uses Martin Movers, how much will he be charged for his move?

(A) $75   (B) $150
(C) $370*   (D) $400

우선, Mr. Goldsmith가 작성한 요청서(지문 2)에서 장비 설치는 안 해 줘도 된다고 한 뒤 I believe your standard flat rate will apply.라며 표준 정액 요금을 이야기한다. 지문 3 둘째 문단에서는 홍보 기간 중 요청했으니 30달러를 할인해 주겠다(I'm happy to offer you a $30 discount on your move.)는 말이 언급된다. '사무실 이사에 대한 표준 정액 요금'은 웹 페이지(지문 1)의 $400 flat rate에서 확인할 수 있으므로 여기에서 30달러를 뺀 (C)가 정답이다.

정답 (C)

골드스미스 씨가 마틴 이삿짐 센터를 이용한다면, 이사에 얼마가 청구되겠는가?
(A) 75달러
(B) 150달러
(C) 370달러
(D) 400달러

어휘 charge 청구하다

200

What is suggested about Martin Movers?

(A) It is booked solid on February 23.*
(B) It is located in New York City.
(C) It has five trucks in its fleet.
(D) It charges extra for work done on weekends.

지문 3 둘째 문단의 Martin Movers is already fully booked on the day you requested.를 통해 이메일 수신자가 요청한 날짜에 예약이 다 찼음을 알 수 있고, 요청서(지문 2)의 이사 날짜는 2월 23일로 확인되므로 (A)가 정답이다.

정답 (A)

마틴 이삿짐 센터에 대해 드러나는 사항은?
(A) 2월 23일에 예약이 다 찼다.
(B) 뉴욕 시에 있다.
(C) 트럭을 다섯 대 소유하고 있다.
(D) 주말 작업에 대해서는 추가 요금을 청구한다.

어휘 solid 견고한, 빈 데가 없는 be located in ~에 있다 fleet (한 기관이 소유한 비행기, 버스, 택시 등의) 무리

ACTUAL TEST 2

PART 5

파커 씨가 다른 누구보다 그 직책에 대해 잘 알고 있기 때문에 지원자들을 직접 면접할 계획입니다.

어휘 applicant 지원자 position 직(책)

101
Ms. Parker plans to interview the applicants _____ because she understands the position better than anybody.

(A) hers (B) herself*
(C) she (D) her

빈칸 앞까지 살펴보면, 〈주어(Ms. Parker) + 동사(plans) + 목적어(to interview the applicants)〉로 이루어진 완벽한 문장 구조이므로, 주격(she)이나 목적격(her) 대명사는 필요하지 않다. '직접'이라는 의미가 들어가 문장을 수식할 수 있으므로 재귀대명사 (B)가 들어갈 수 있다.

정답 (B)

세금 환급이 캘리포니아 주 내 공무원들에게 주어질 것입니다.

어휘 tax 세금 rebate 환불, 환급
public servant 공무원

102
Tax rebates will be given to public servants _____ the State of California.

(A) within* (B) until
(C) during (D) since

빈칸 다음에 특정 지역이 언급되었으므로 지리적 경계와 관련된 전치사 (A)가 가장 적절하다. with, within, without은 답이 잘 된다. within 이내에 until ~까지 during 동안 since 그 후로

정답 (A)

관심 있는 분들께서는 부동산 투자에 대한 이번 주말 세미나에 온라인으로 쉽게 등록할 수 있습니다.

어휘 party (소송, 계약 등의) 당사자 register 등록하다 real estate 부동산 investing 투자

103
Interested parties can _____ register online for this weekend's seminar on real estate investing.

(A) very (B) least
(C) easily* (D) more

〈조동사 + 동사〉 사이에 빈칸이 위치해 있어 동사 register를 수식할 부사가 필요한 상황이므로 '쉽게 등록할 수 있다'는 의미가 완성되어야 가장 자연스럽다. 따라서 (C)가 적절하다. least 가장 적게, 가장 덜

정답 (C)

승진은 직원들에게 업그레이드된 혜택, 회사 차량, 더 많은 휴가 일수를 가져다줄 것입니다.

어휘 promotion 승진 benefit 혜택, 이득

104
The promotion will _____ employees with upgraded benefits, company cars, and more vacation days.

(A) provide* (B) earn
(C) contrast (D) loan

승진이 직원들에게 여러 가지를 '가져다줄' 것이라는 맥락을 완성하는 데 가장 적절한 어휘는 (A)이다. 〈provide + 사물/혜택 + with + 사람〉의 형태로 사용된다는 것을 기억하자. provide 제공하다 earn 얻다, 획득하다 contrast 대조하다, 대비시키다 loan 대출하다, 융자하다

* 〈동사 + A + with + B〉
provide/supply/furnish/present A with B: A에게 B를 제공하다, 공급하다

정답 (A)

105

Office staff at Morin Legal Services _____ work four days a week, from Monday to Thursday.

(A) norm
(B) norms
(C) normal
(D) normally*

〈주어(Office ~ Services) + 자동사(work)〉의 완벽한 구조를 이룬 문장이며, 빈칸은 이 사이에 들어가 있으므로, 동사를 수식해 줄 부사 (D)가 정답이다. norm 표준, 기준 normal 보통의 normally 보통(때는)

* 집합체를 이루는 구성원들이 주어일 때, 현재시제 동사에 -s가 붙지 않는다.
staff, family, audience, committee, team, class, the police, the public, the press, the crowd

* 단순 현재시제는 일반적이고 지속적인 의미의 부사들과 잘 사용된다.
routinely, regularly, normally, always, usually, generally, often

정답 (D)

모린 법률 서비스의 사무 직원은 대체로 월요일부터 목요일까지 주4일 근무합니다.

어휘 legal 법률(상)의

106

Items can be exchanged _____ they are returned within one week following the date of purchase.

(A) or
(B) if*
(C) nor
(D) but

빈칸 이하는 교환이 가능한 '조건'에 해당된다. 따라서 (B)가 정답이다.

* 시간/조건 부사절: 미래에 일어나는 일이라도 조건절에 현재시제 사용!
시간을 나타내는 접속사 when, while, before, after, as soon as, until, once
조건을 나타내는 접속사 if, unless, as long as

정답 (B)

제품은 구입 날짜로부터 일주일 안에 반납하시면 교환 가능합니다.

어휘 item 물건, 제품 exchange 교환하다 return 반품하다 following ~에 이어 purchase 구입(품)

107

According to this newspaper article, earnings at BTR Electronics last quarter were _____ than expected.

(A) lowest
(B) lowering
(C) lower*
(D) low

비교의 대상을 나타내는 전치사 than이 뒤따르므로 빈칸에는 비교급 (C)가 들어갈 수 있다. lowering 저하시키는, 하락시키는 low 낮은

정답 (C)

이 신문 기사에 따르면, 지난 분기 BTR 일렉트로닉스의 수입은 예상보다 더 낮았습니다.

어휘 earnings 소득, 수입 electronics 전자 제품 quarter 분기 expect 기대하다, 예상하다

108

Everyone _____ the store owner took a week-long vacation in the summertime last year.

(A) out of
(B) other
(C) except*
(D) between

'사장만 빼고 전부 휴가를 다녀왔다'는 요지를 완성해 줄 수 있는 전치사 (C)가 가장 적절하다. except ~을 제외하고는

정답 (C)

매장 소유주를 제외하고 모두가 작년 여름에 일주일간 휴가를 다녀왔습니다.

어휘 owner 소유주

도리스 클레멘츠의 모든 풍경화는 실제 장소에 대한 것이지만, 그녀는 자신의 작품에 엄청난 상상력을 쏟아 붓습니다.

어휘 even though 비록 ~일지라도 actual 실제의 a great deal of 다량의, 많은

109

Even though all her landscape paintings are of actual places, Doris Clements puts a great deal of _____ into her work.

(A) imagine (B) imaginative
(C) imagination* (D) imaginary

적절한 성분을 찾는 문제이다. 빈칸은 전치사 of의 목적어가 되므로 명사 (C)만 들어갈 수 있다. imagine 상상하다 imaginative 상상력이 풍부한, 창의적인 imagination 상상(력) imaginary 상상에만 존재하는, 가상적인

* '많은'을 표현하는 다양한 방법
√ a large amount of, a great deal of + 불가산명사 → 단수 동사 (= much)
√ a number of + 가산명사 → 복수 동사 (= many)

정답 (C)

접수계원이 오늘 오후에 모든 판매 직원들에게 갱신된 고객 목록을 제공할 것입니다.

어휘 provide 제공하다 personnel 인사(부의)

110

The receptionist will provide the _____ client list to all sales personnel this afternoon.

(A) frequent (B) updated*
(C) certain (D) monitored

판매 직원들에게 줄 목록의 성격은 '새롭게 추가 또는 수정된(갱신된)' 것이어야 가장 적절하므로 (B)가 정답이다. certain은 명사 앞에서 '어떤, 무슨'이란 의미로 사용될 수 있는데, 의미상 정관사 the(the는 특정한 명사를 지칭할 때 사용)와는 어울리지 않으므로 (C)는 답이 될 수 없다. frequent 잦은, 빈번한 certain 어떤, 무슨 monitored 관찰된, 감시된

정답 (B)

봄 교육 강좌는 판매부 직원들이 더욱 창의적으로 생각하도록 돕기 위해 개발되었습니다.

어휘 training 교육, 훈련 course 강의, 강좌

111

The spring training course was developed to help sales employees think more _____.

(A) create (B) creative
(C) creativity (D) creatively*

〈준사역동사(help) + 목적어(sales employees) + 목적격 보어(think)〉의 5형식 구조를 완벽히 갖추었으므로 목적격 보어를 수식해 줄 수 있는 부사구를 완성해야 한다. 따라서 (D)가 정답이다. create 창조하다, 창작하다 creative 창조적인, 창의적인 creativity 창조적임, 창조성 creatively 창조적으로

*〈동사 + 목적어(사람) + to부정사〉의 구조로 쓰이는 동사
enable 가능하게 하다 allow 허용하다 permit 허락하다 advise 조언하다 instruct 지시하다 schedule ~하도록 일정을 잡다 encourage 격려하다 remind 상기시키다 convince 설득하다 invite 초대하다 require 요구하다 request 요청하다 urge 촉구하다 order 명령하다 persuade 설득시키다

정답 (D)

이 탁자를 조립하려고 시도하기 전에, 설명서를 검토하셔야 합니다.

어휘 attempt 시도하다 assemble 조립하다 instruction 설명, 지시

112

Before attempting to assemble this table, you should _____ the instructions.

(A) direct (B) review*
(C) gather (D) program

'조립하기 전에 설명서를 참조하라'는 요지의 문장이 되어야 가장 자연스럽다. 따라서 (B)가 적절하다. direct 향하다, 지휘하다, 총괄하다 review 검토하다 gather 모으다 program 프로그램을 짜다

정답 (B)

113

Ms. Jannel, the director of customer relations, _____ the poor reviews the company has received online at the staff meeting tomorrow.

(A) had been addressing (B) is addressing*
(C) will be addressed   (D) should be addressed

선택지를 통해 태와 시제를 결정하는 문제임을 알 수 있다. address는 '~에 대해 말하다, (문제점을) 다루다'는 의미로 사용되는데, 빈칸 뒤에 목적어가 있으므로 (A)와 (B) 중에서 답을 찾아야 한다. 문장 맨 끝에 tomorrow라는 미래를 나타내는 부사가 있으므로 미래시제를 표현할 수 있는 (B)가 정답이다. be going to와 be ~ing, 단순현재 시제 모두 미래를 표현할 수 있다는 점에 유의하자. address 연설하다, (문제 등에 대해) 다루다, 언급하다

정답 (B)

고객 관계 부장 자넬 씨는 회사가 온라인으로 받은 나쁜 평들에 대해 내일 열릴 직원 회의에서 언급할 것입니다.

어휘 receive 받다

114

Larson Motors aims to improve its public image _____ the guidance of publicist Cynthia Morison of M&T Public Relations.

(A) under*   (B) either
(C) among   (D) beyond

'~의 지도 하에'라는 의미의 under the guidance of라는 표현을 알면 쉽게 해결할 수 있는 문제이다.

* 〈under + 명사〉 용례
under + the direction/name/pressure/warranty/new management of ~의 지도/명의/압박/보증/새로운 경영진 하에

정답 (A)

라슨 모터스는 M&T 홍보 회사의 홍보 전문가인 신시아 모리슨의 지도 하에 대중 이미지를 개선하는 것을 목표로 하고 있습니다.

어휘 aim to ~하는 것을 목적으로 하다 guidance 지도, 안내 publicist 홍보 담당자 public relations 홍보, 선전

115

When _____ to any new clients, don't forget to mention Beckingham's promotional event next week.

(A) spoken   (B) speaking*
(C) spoke   (D) to speak

〈When + 주어 + 동사 ~〉에서 주어를 생략하고 동사를 분사로 바꾼 분사 구문이다. 따라서 정답은 (B)이다. 〈before/after/when/while/since/though + ~ing〉 구문은 자주 출제된다!

정답 (B)

신규 고객과 이야기를 나눌 때는, 베킹험의 다음 주 판촉 행사를 꼭 언급하세요.

어휘 promotional 홍보의, 판촉의

116

Tickets for Friday night's play at the Alexander Theater sold out quickly because the production _____ two famous actors from this area.

(A) feature   (B) features*
(C) to feature   (D) featuring

접속사 because 이하의 절에서 빈칸이 서술부에 해당되므로 (C)와 (D)는 바로 소거할 수 있다. 또한 주어가 3인칭 단수(the production)이니 (B)가 답이 된다. feature 특징, 특색, 특징으로 삼다

정답 (B)

알렉산더 극장의 금요일 밤 연극 표가 금세 매진됐습니다. 이 지역 출신의 유명 배우 두 명이 이 작품에 등장하기 때문이지요.

어휘 play 연극 sell out 다 팔리다 production 제작, 작품 actor 배우

톰슨 아트 갤러리는 8월 1일부터 운영 시간을 연장할 예정입니다.

어휘 extend 늘리다, 연장하다 operation 영업, 운용

117

The Thompson Art Gallery will extend its hours of operation _____ on August 1st.

(A) will begin (B) has begun
(C) beginner (D) beginning*

특정 날짜를 기점으로 시작되는 상황을 나타낼 때 사용되는 것은 (D)이다. starting, effective도 같은 용법을 갖고 있다. beginner 초보자

정답 (D)

도널드 마호니는 그레이디 배관 수리 회사에서 일하는 모든 배관공에게 비품을 배급하는 일을 맡고 있습니다.

어휘 be in charge of ~을 담당하다 supplies 비품, 용품 plumber 배관공

118

Donald Mahoney is in charge of the supplies _____ to all plumbers working for Grady Pipe Repairs.

(A) distribute (B) distribution*
(C) distributes (D) is distributed

의미상 the supplies _____ 은 '~의 책임을 맡다'는 뜻의 be in charge of의 목적어에 해당된다. 따라서 복합명사를 완성할 명사 (B)가 정답이다. distribute 나눠 주다, 분배하다 distribution 분배, 배급

* 고난이도 빈출 복합명사
attendance record 출석률, 참가자 수 budget constraints 예산 제한 building modification 건축 변경 사항 business correspondence 상업 통신 consumer awareness 소비자 인식 contingency plan 비상 대책 earnings growth 수익 증가 installment payment 할부 납부 maternity leave 출산 휴가 media coverage 언론 보도 power failure 정전 savings plan 예금 상품 utility bill 전기, 가스, 수도 요금

정답 (B)

CEO는 지난 가을 투데이 비즈니스 매거진과의 인터뷰에서 자신의 견해를 밝혀 야심가로 유명합니다.

어휘 be known for ~로 유명하다 ambitious 야심 있는

119

The CEO is known for being ambitious as he expressed his _____ in an interview with Today Business Magazine last fall.

(A) interferences (B) prevention
(C) views* (D) exchange

제시된 명사들 중 '견해를 표명하다'라는 의미를 적절히 완성하는 것은 (C)이다. interference 간섭, 방해 prevention 예방 view 견해, 관점 exchange 교환

* express와 함께 잘 사용되는 명사
express concern about ~에 대한 우려를 표하다
express fears/doubts/reservations 두려움/의구심/망설임을 나타내다
express interest/surprise/regret 흥미/놀라움/후회를 나타내다

정답 (C)

파이낸셜 먼슬리의 설립 멤버이자 편집자인 안나 산체스는 사실상 금융 분야의 모든 사람들로부터 금세 존경을 얻었습니다.

어휘 found 설립하다 financial 재정의, 금융의 earn 얻다, 획득하다 respect 존경 practically 사실상, 거의

120

Anna Sanchez, founding editor of Financial Monthly, has quickly earned the respect of practically _____ in the financial industry.

(A) everyone* (B) anything
(C) whatever (D) each other

전치사 of의 목적어가 될 수 있는 대명사 (A)나 (B)가 가능한데 문맥상 '모든 이의 존경을 받다'는 요지를 완성해야 타당하다. 따라서 (A)가 정답이다. whatever ~한 모든 each other 서로

정답 (A)

121

As stated in the reviews, the theater's new performance was _____ a big hit.

(A) clear
(B) clearly*
(C) clearer
(D) clearing

〈주어(the ~ performance) + be동사(was) + 주격 보어(a big hit)〉의 완벽한 2형식 문장이다. 따라서 빈칸에는 동사 was를 수식할 수 있는 부사 (B)가 들어갈 수 있다. It is predominantly through ~라는 be동사 수식 부사 문제가 예전에도 출제된 바 있다. clear 분명한 clearly 분명히

정답 (B)

평론에 언급된 대로, 그 극장의 새 공연은 분명히 대성공이었습니다.

어휘 performance 공연

122

_____ our hiring committee reads all the resumes, we will compile a list of 20 candidates to invite in for interviews.

(A) Compared to
(B) As soon as*
(C) So that
(D) Not only

면접 명단 작성은 이력서 검토 이후여야 순서상 적절하다. 따라서 (B)가 가장 알맞은 연결 어구이다. 참고로 (D)는 '~뿐 아니라 ~도'라는 의미의 not only ~ (but) also 구문으로 쓰인다. compared to ~와 비교하여 as soon as ~하는 대로 so that ~하도록

정답 (B)

저희 고용 위원회가 모든 이력서를 읽는 대로, 면접에 부를 지원자 20명의 목록을 만들 것입니다.

어휘 hiring 고용 committee 위원회 resume 이력서 compile 엮다, 편찬하다, 편집하다 candidate 지원자, 후보자 invite 초대하다, 권하다

123

The concert was a huge success and drew a crowd of over 5,000 to Moose Park and Recreation Center, _____ the cold weather.

(A) while
(B) whereas
(C) notwithstanding*
(D) moreover

'콘서트는 성공적이었다' → '추운 날씨였지만'이라는 흐름이 되어야 가장 자연스러우므로 (A), (B), (C)를 생각할 수 있는데, (A)와 (B)는 〈주어 + 동사〉로 이루어진 절을 이끄는 접속사이므로 전치사로 사용될 수 있는 (C)가 정답이 된다. while 반면 whereas 반면 notwithstanding ~에도 불구하고 moreover 게다가, 더욱이

* 고난이도 전치사
excluding ~을 제외하고 regarding ~에 관하여(= about, concerning) following ~에 뒤이어 barring ~이 없으면, ~을 제외하고는 considering ~을 고려할 때 prior to ~ 전에(= before) according to ~에 따르면 based on ~에 근거하여, ~에 따라 in terms of ~의 점(각도)에서 보면 in/with regard to ~에 관해서 regardless of ~에 상관없이

정답 (C)

추운 날씨에도 불구하고, 콘서트는 막대한 성공을 거두어 5천 명 이상의 사람들을 무스 파크 & 레크리에이션 센터로 이끌었습니다.

어휘 huge 막대한, 거대한 draw 끌다 crowd 군중

124

The research staff at Pullford Pharmaceuticals will be using the conference room as its office _____ the renovation period.

(A) opposite
(B) beside
(C) during*
(D) with

'기간'을 나타내는 period가 주요 단서로 작용한다. 개조하는 '동안' 회의실을 쓸 것이라는 맥락이 완성되어야 타당하므로 (C)가 정답이다. during 다음에는 기간을 나타내는 명사가, for 다음에는 〈숫자 + 단위를 나타내는 명사〉가 나온다는 점을 반드시 기억하자. opposite 건너편에, 맞은편에 beside ~옆에, ~에 비해

* 전치사로 기간을 나타내는 방법
for + 숫자 (예: for three years)
during + 명사 (예: during the vacation)
since + 시점 (예: since 1998)

정답 (C)

풀포드 제약회사 연구원들은 개조 기간 동안 회의실을 사무실로 이용할 것입니다.

어휘 research 연구, 조사 pharmaceuticals 제약회사 renovation 개조 period 기간

회사 웹사이트에 적힌 대로, 멤버십을 취소하고자 하는 고객들은 만료되기 전에 수수료를 내야 합니다.

어휘 state 진술하다, 말하다 cancel 취소하다 expire 만료되다 pay 결제하다, 지불하다 fee 요금, 수수료

125

As stated on the company's website, clients who wish to cancel their membership _____ it expires must pay a fee.

(A) before* (B) how
(C) why (D) either

who부터 expires까지가 하나의 관계대명사절로 clients를 수식하는 구조인데, 빈칸 다음에 〈주어(it) + 동사(expires)〉가 있으니 절을 이끄는 접속사 (A)가 들어가야 한다. either (둘 중) 어느 하나의

정답 (A)

이 업무 내용은 다른 회사들에서의 업무와 비슷하지만, 이 일은 월급을 훨씬 많이 받습니다.

어휘 description 설명, 묘사 salary 급여, 월급

126

Although the job description is _____ to those at other firms, this job has a much higher salary.

(A) similar* (B) likable
(C) reflected (D) considerate

'~과 비슷한'이라는 의미의 similar to 구문을 알면 쉽게 해결할 수 있는 문제이다. similar 비슷한 likable 마음에 드는 reflected 반사되는 considerate 배려하는

* be동사 + 형용사 + to + 명사
be accessible to + 사람 ~에게 접근/이용 가능하다 be adjacent to ~에 가까이 있다 be attractive to + 사람 ~에게 매력적이다 be available to + 사람 ~에게 이용 가능하다 be close to ~에 가까이 있다, 근접하다 be committed to = be dedicated to = be devoted to ~에 헌신하다, 전념하다 be equivalent to ~와 동등하다, 필적하다 be identical to ~와 동일하다, 매우 흡사하다 be native to + 지역 ~에 기원을 두다, ~지역 산이다 be subject to (laws/rules) (법/규칙) 등을 준수해야 한다 be subject to approval 승인/찬성을 받아야 한다.

정답 (A)

모든 안전 규정을 철저히 준수하기 위해 선임 직원들에게만 연구실 출입이 허가될 것입니다.

어휘 access 접근, 이용 research 연구, 조사 laboratory 실험실 limit 제한하다, 한정하다 senior 선임의 ensure 보장하다, 반드시 ~하게 하다 safety 보안, 안전 regulation 규정, 규제

127

Access to the research laboratory will be limited to senior employees to ensure _____ with all safety regulations.

(A) activation (B) fulfillment
(C) compliance* (D) indication

'규정, 규제'를 의미하는 regulations가 단서이다. '규정, 준수'를 뜻하는 명사 (C)가 정답이 된다. '~을 준수하다, ~에 순응하다'라는 의미의 다른 표현들 be in compliance with, be compliant with, comply with도 참고로 익혀 두자. activation 활동적으로 하기, 활성화 fulfillment 이행, 수행 compliance 준수, 따름 indication 말, 암시

정답 (C)

창문이 설치 중에 깨졌더라면, 릴리 건자재 회사가 무료로 그것을 교체해 드렸을 것입니다.

어휘 broken 깨진, 고장 난 installation 설치 replace 대체하다, 교체하다 at no charge 무료로

128

If the window had been broken during installation, Riley's Building Supplies _____ to replace it at no charge.

(A) would have offered* (B) has offered
(C) is being offered (D) would have been offered

가정법 과거완료 〈If + 주어 + had p.p., 주어 + would/should/could + have p.p.〉가 완성되어야 하므로 빈칸에는 (A)나 (D)가 들어갈 수 있는데 Riley's Building Supplies가 (교체)해 주는 '주체'이므로 능동태 (A)가 정답이 된다.

* 가정법 과거: 현재 사실에 반대
〈If + 주어 + 동사 과거형, 주어 + would/should/could + 동사원형〉

* 가정법 과거완료: 과거 사실에 반대
〈If + 주어 + had p.p., 주어 + would/should/could + have p.p.〉

정답 (A)

129

Prior to reviewing _____, the town council agreed to three proposals in principle.

(A) specifics*
(B) specify
(C) specific
(D) specifically

빈칸은 타동사 review의 목적어 자리이므로 명사 (A)가 들어갈 수 있다. specifics 세부 사항 specify 명시하다 specific 명확한, 구체적인 specifically 명확하게

정답 (A)

세부 사항을 검토하기 전에, 시 의회는 세 가지 제안에 원칙적으로 동의했습니다.

어휘 prior to ~ 이전에 council 의회 agree 동의하다 principle 원칙

130

Administrators at the Ben Phillips Hospital maintain that _____ to the facility will make many medical procedures more efficient.

(A) continuations
(B) increments
(C) deviations
(D) enhancements*

'효율성 증가'의 원인으로 타당한 것은 '시설에 대한 개선'이므로 빈칸에는 (D)가 들어가야 그에 상응하는 의미를 완성한다. continuation 계속, 지속 increment 증가, 임금 인상 deviation 일탈, 탈선 enhancement 향상, 증대

* 전치사 to와 자주 쓰이는 명사들
solution/exposure/response/trip/answer/visit/approach/access + to + 명사

정답 (D)

벤 필립스 병원 경영진은 시설 개선으로 인해 많은 의료 절차가 더욱 효율적으로 될 것이라고 주장합니다.

어휘 administrator 관리자, 행정인 maintain 주장하다 facility 시설 medical 의료의 procedure 절차, 순서 efficient 능률적인, 효율적인

PART 6

3월 3일 — 근 3년의 기획 단계를 거친 하프빌의 최대 스포츠 경기장이 착공될 예정이다. 엑스포 스타디움은 하프빌의 드넓은 해안가에 들어설 것이며 최대 만 개의 좌석이 들어갈 것이다. ―――. 이 프로젝트가 완성되는 데 3년이 걸릴 것으로 예상된다. 현재 해안가에 건설 중인 여러 다른 신개발 가운데 진행될 것이다. 하프빌 스포츠 협회장 마샬 토마스에 따르면, 이 새 경기장은 꼭 필요한 것이다. "우리 시의 늘어나는 스포츠 클럽들을 수용하려면 대규모 경기장이 필요합니다." 토마스 씨가 말했다. "한편으로는, 이 경기장을 콘서트나 서커스 공연에도 사용할 수 있을 겁니다."

어휘 nearly 거의 construction 건설, 공사 be located on ~에 있다 majestic 장엄한 waterfront 해안가, 물가 capacity 용량, 수용력 up to ~까지 expect 기대하다, 예상하다 complete 완성하다, 완료하다 several 몇몇의 currently 현재 association 협회 accommodate 수용하다 performance 공연

(A) 개발자들은 프로젝트를 완성하는 데 얼마나 오래 걸릴지 모른다.
(B) 경기장은 해안가에서 시외로 옮겨질 것이다.
(C) 각기 10명까지 들어갈 수 있는 언론 관람실 100여 개도 포함될 것이다.
(D) 시장이 도시 개발 계획에 자금을 대기를 거부했을 때 지체됐다.

Questions 131-134 refer to the following article.

March 3 -- After nearly three years of planning, the largest stadium in Harpville will begin construction. The Expo Stadium will be located on Harpville's majestic waterfront and will have a capacity of up to ten thousand seats. ---**131**---. The project is expected to take three years to complete. It will be located amongst several other new developments currently ---**132**--- on the waterfront. According to Marshal Thomas, president of the Harpville Sports Association, the new stadium is a ---**133**---. "We're going to need a large stadium to accommodate our growing sports clubs," Mr. Thomas said. "---**134**---, we'll also be able to use the stadium for concerts and circus performances."

131
(A) Developers are unsure how long it will take to complete the project.
(B) The stadium will be moved from the waterfront to the outskirts of the city.
(C) It will also include over 100 press viewing rooms that hold up to ten people each.*
(D) Delays occurred when the mayor refused to fund the city's development plans.

공사 규모 및 시설(ten thousand seats)과 공사 기간(three years to complete) 사이에 들어가기에 가장 적절한 문장은 '시설에 대한 추가 설명'인 (C)이다. unsure 확신하지 못하는 outskirts 변두리, 교외 include 포함하다 press 신문, 언론 hold (사람, 사물을) 수용하다 delay 지체, 지연 occur 발생하다, 일어나다 mayor 시장 refuse 거절하다 fund 자금을 대다

정답 (C)

132
(A) to construct   (B) are constructing
(C) were constructed   (D) being constructed*

문장 전체의 서술부가 will be located로 이미 나와 있으므로 동사인 (B)와 (C)는 소거할 수 있다. 빈칸은 developments를 후치 수식하는 구조가 되어야 하는데, developments는 '건설되는' 것이니 (D)가 정답이 된다. developments that are being constructed에서 that are가 생략된 구조이다. construct 건설하다

정답 (D)

133

(A) necessity* (B) nuisance
(C) risk (D) bargain

바로 이어 '필요해질 것(We're going to need)'이라고 하는 데서 정답 (A)를 유추할 수 있다. necessity 필요, 불가피한 일 nuisance 성가신 사람/것 risk 위험 (요소) bargain 싸게 파는 물건, 합의

정답 (A)

134

(A) On the other hand* (B) In other words
(C) In the first place (D) As a result

문맥상 경기장이 필요한 주된 이유를 빈칸 앞에, '부수적인' 이유를 빈칸 다음에 기술하고 있다. 따라서 '한편'이라는 의미의 (A)가 가장 적절하다. on the other hand 다른 한편으로는 in other words 다시 말해서 in the first place 우선, 첫째로 as a result 결과적으로

정답 (A)

트렌턴에서 가장 오래된 패밀리 식당 체인점인 홉슨 다이닝의 CEO이자 창립자인 메레디스 홉슨이 시내 지역의 재스퍼 커뮤니티 센터 개조에 6,500달러를 기부하겠다고 발표했다. 이 기금은 지난주 금요일 저녁 그녀의 식당에서 열린 연회의 티켓 판매로 마련됐다. 홉슨 씨는 내일 오후 2시에 진행될 특별 행사에서 센터 경영진에게 수표를 증정할 예정이다. 지난 25년간, 홉슨 씨는 지역 서비스 및 자선 단체를 위해 성공적인 모금 행사를 무수히 열어 왔다. ──────.

어휘 founder 설립자 announce 발표하다 renovation 개조 region 지역 fund 자금, 기금 generate 발생시키다, 만들어 내다 banquet 연회 management 경영, 운영 check 수표 ceremony (의식) take place 개최되다 organize 준비하다, 조직하다 fund-raising 모금 charity 자선 (단체)

Questions 135-138 refer to the following press release.

Meredith Hobson, CEO and founder of Hobson Dining, Trenton's oldest family dining franchise, announced that she ---**135**--- $6,500 towards renovations to the Jasper Community Center in the city's downtown region. The funds were generated from ticket sales for a banquet held last Friday evening at her ---**136**---. Ms. Hobson will present the management staff of the center with a check at a special ceremony scheduled to take place tomorrow afternoon at 2:00. ---**137**--- the past 25 years, Ms. Hobson has organized a number of successful fund-raising events for community services and charities. ---**138**---.

135

(A) will donate* (B) donated
(C) might donate (D) donating

빈칸은 술어에 해당되므로 (D)는 들어갈 수 없다. 중반부의 Ms. Hobson will present the management staff of the center with a check ~에서 '앞으로' 진행될 일에 대한 설명임을 알 수 있으니 미래시제 (A)가 정답이 된다. donate 기부하다, 기증하다

정답 (A)

136

(A) gallery (B) hotel
(C) academy (D) restaurant*

첫 문장에 언급된 업체명(Meredith Hobson, CEO and founder of Hobson Dining)과 업체 성격(Trenton's oldest family dining franchise)을 통해 (D)가 정답임을 알 수 있다.

정답 (D)

137

(A) Despite (B) Over*
(C) Between (D) Beneath

지난 25년 '동안'의 행적을 나타낸 문장이므로 '(기간) ~에 걸쳐서'라는 의미를 나타내는 전치사 (B)가 빈칸에 가장 적절하다. despite ~에도 불구하고 beneath 아래에, ~보다 못한

정답 (B)

138

(A) The Jasper Community Center has programs for both children and adults.
(B) The opening ceremony at the center will be done by 2:30.
(C) However, last Friday's event was, without a doubt, her most successful one.*
(D) Ms. Hobson plans to open a branch in uptown Trenton sometime next year.

바로 앞 문장에서 '성공적인 모금 행사들'에 대해 언급되었다. 따라서 '모금 행사'를 대명사 one으로 받으면서 '가장 성공적인 행사였다'고 부연하는 (C)가 문맥상 가장 적절하다.
without a doubt 의심할 여지없이 branch 지점, 지사

정답 (C)

(A) 재스퍼 커뮤니티 센터는 아동과 성인 모두를 위한 프로그램을 갖고 있습니다.
(B) 센터 개업식은 2시 30분에 끝날 것입니다.
(C) 하지만, 지난주 금요일 행사는, 의심할 여지없이, 가장 성공적이었습니다.
(D) 홉슨 씨는 내년 중으로 트렌턴 주택 지구에 지점을 하나 열 계획입니다.

Questions 139-142 refer to the following meeting summary.

Our monthly meeting commenced at 4:30 P.M. The meeting's purpose was to discuss the advantages and disadvantages of ---**139**--- LGQ International Shipping. Max Powel led the debate on the possible move by stressing the importance of furthering LGQ's current growth patterns. He explained that LGQ has grown to be one of the most successful ---**140**--- and that it ships the largest number of electronics in the country.

---**141**---. According to recent reports, the traveling distance from the closest harbor is becoming costly ---**142**--- LGQ begins to grow. Staff members discussed some possible solutions, but a final decision was not reached. Mr. Powel will do some more research and present his findings at the next meeting.

139

(A) acquiring (B) joining
(C) promoting (D) relocating*

바로 이어지는 문장에서 '이전 가능성(possible move)'에 대해 논의를 이끌었다'고 하므로 맥락상 '이전에 대한 장단점'이라는 요지가 완성되어야 알맞다. 따라서 (D)가 정답이다. acquire 습득하다, 얻다 promote 승진시키다, 홍보하다 relocate 이전하다, 옮기다

정답 (D)

140

(A) distribute (B) distributing
(C) distributors* (D) distributes

형용사 successful의 수식을 받는 자리이므로 명사 (C)만 들어갈 수 있다. distribute 나눠 주다 distributing 분배의, 배급의 distributor 배급 업자, 유통 업자

정답 (C)

141

(A) Mr. Powel also outlined the challenges LGQ is experiencing as a result of its growth.*
(B) The CEO then proceeded to discuss the advantages of the new facilities.
(C) Next, shareholders were invited to conduct a vote to decide the date.
(D) Mr. Powel directed employees to consider how operations would be conducted.

(A) 파웰 씨는 LGQ가 성장의 결과로 인해 겪고 있는 난제들에 대해서도 설명했습니다.
(B) 그 다음, CEO가 이어서 새 시설의 장점들을 논의했습니다.
(C) 다음에는, 주주들이 와서 날짜를 결정하는 투표를 했습니다.
(D) 파웰 씨는 직원들에게 일이 어떻게 진행될지 숙고해 보라고 지시했습니다.

빈칸 앞 부분의 '성장 현황'과 빈칸 뒤 부분의 '성장에 따른 비용 문제'를 이어 주는 데 적절한 것은 (A)이다. outline 개요를 말하다 challenge 난제, 도전 experience 경험하다 as a result of ~의 결과로서 proceed 계속 ~하다 facility 시설 shareholder 주주 invite 초대하다, 권하다 conduct (특정한 일을) 하다 vote 투표 direct 지휘하다 consider 고려하다, 숙고하다 operation 작전, 활동, 사업

정답 (A)

142

(A) now
(B) why
(C) just as*
(D) ever since

'성장세에 더불어 비용이 많이 들기 시작했다'는 요지의 문장을 완성해야 하므로 동시 상황을 나타내는 (C)가 정답이 된다. 참고로, '~이래로 줄곧'이라는 의미의 ever since가 들어가려면 뒤의 시제가 과거형이어야 한다.

정답 (C)

발신: tina@lindcosmetics.com
수신: mia@mymailnow.com
날짜: 9월 8일
제목: 주문 445009

크라마 씨 귀하,

고객님의 주문에 대해 문의해 주셔서 고맙습니다. 저희 기록에 따르면, 고객님은 린드 SPF 50 선스크린 하나, 린드 500 핸드 크림 한 병, 린드 울트라샤인 샴푸 두 병을 9월 1일에 저희 웹사이트에서 주문하셨습니다. 제품들은 9월 5일에 도착할 예정이었고요. 그것들을 못 받으셨다니 놀랐습니다.

----------. 그들 일정에 따르면, 고객님 제품은 9월 10일에 도착할 예정입니다. 그날까지 주문품이 배송되지 않는다면, 언제든 저희에게 다시 연락 주시기 바랍니다.

이렇게 불편을 끼쳐 드려 정말 죄송합니다. 저희 배송 방법은 대체로 빠르고 저렴합니다. 이런 상황은 극히 드물고요. 이 일로 인해 린드 화장품에서 구입하기를 꺼리시게 되지 않았으면 합니다.

감사합니다.

티나 스펠러
린드 화장품

어휘 order 주문, 주문하다 inquire 문의하다 be scheduled to ~할 예정이다 arrive 도착하다 deliver 배송하다, 배달하다 feel free to 언제든 ~하다 sincerely 진심으로 apologize for ~에 대해 사죄하다 inconvenience 불편 shipping 배송 method 방법 affordable (가격이) 알맞은 situation 상황 quite 상당히, 꽤 discourage 막다, 의욕을 꺾다 cosmetics 화장품

Questions 143-146 refer to the following e-mail.

From: tina@lindcosmetics.com
To: mia@mymailnow.com
Date: September 8
Subject: Order 445009

Dear Ms. Kramar,

Thank you for writing to inquire about your order. According to our records, you ordered one tube of Lind SPF 50 Sunscreen, one bottle of Lind 500 Hand Cream, and two bottles of Lind Ultrashine Shampoo from our website on September 1st. Your products were scheduled to arrive on September 5th. I was surprised to hear that you have not received ---**143**---.

---**144**---. According to their schedule, your products will arrive on September 10th. If your order is not delivered by that day, feel free ---**145**--- us again.

I sincerely apologize for this inconvenience. Our shipping methods are usually fast and affordable. This situation is quite ---**146**---. I hope it will not discourage you from shopping at Lind Cosmetics.

Thank you.

Tina Speller
Lind Cosmetics

143
(A) it (B) one
(C) them* (D) some

지시대명사가 가리키는 것이 앞 문장에서 무엇인지 찾아보면 복수형 products(여러 화장품들)임을 알 수 있으므로 (C)가 정답이다.

정답 (C)

144

(A) We would like to invite you to visit our store.
(B) Please leave a review on our website.
(C) We are currently sold out of that particular product.
(D) I have contacted the shipping company on your behalf.*

빈칸 다음에는 '알아본 일정(their schedule)'이 이어진다. 따라서 their에 해당하는 the shipping company가 언급된 (D)가 들어가야 맥락상 자연스럽게 전개된다. invite 초대하다, 권하다 leave 남기다 contact 연락하다 on behalf 대신해서

정답 (D)

145

(A) contacted   (B) to contact*
(C) contacting   (D) contact

'거리낌 없이 ~하다, 언제든 ~하다'라는 의미의 관용 어구 〈feel free to + 동사원형〉을 알면 정답 (B)를 쉽게 찾을 수 있다. 이러한 상황에서 〈don't hesitate to + 동사원형〉도 쓰인다는 점을 참고로 알아 두자.

정답 (B)

146

(A) similar   (B) exciting
(C) unusual*   (D) welcome

배송 지연에 대한 사과의 이메일이며 바로 앞 문장은 '대체로(usually) 빠르다'는 요지이므로 이와 대구를 이룰 만한 (C)가 정답이 된다. similar 유사한, 비슷한 unusual 특이한, 흔치 않은

정답 (C)

PART 7

판매 물건	가격	위치
모델 A7000 플레임버그 바비큐	450달러	로스앤젤레스, CA

제품 설명:

147 (D) 3년 전 신형 구입. 원래 가격은 700달러였고 2년짜리 보증서가 들어 있었음. 그릴 부분이 탔음. 147 (B) 구입자는 플레임버그 웹사이트에서 새것을 살 수 있음. 외부는 상태가 아주 좋음. (148 요청 시 사진 보여 줌) 147 (C) 가격은 협상 가능함. 로스앤젤레스 내라면 어디든 배달 가능함. 궁금한 점이 있으면 rjohnson@mail.com으로 이메일 바람.

Questions 147-148 refer to the following advertisement.

Item for Sale   **Price**   **Location**
Model A7000 $450   Los Angeles, CA
Flamesburg Barbecue

Item Description:

147 (D) Purchased new 3 years ago. Original cost was $700 and came with a 2-year warranty. Grill pieces are charred. 147 (B) Buyer can purchase new ones on the Flamesburg website. Exterior is in great condition. (148 Pictures available upon request) 147 (C) Price is negotiable. Willing to deliver anywhere in the Los Angeles area. E-mail rjohnson@mail.com if you have any questions.

어휘 item 물건, 제품 location 위치, 소재지 description 설명, 묘사 purchase 구입하다, 사다 cost 값, 비용 come with ~이 딸려 있다 warranty 보증(서) char 까맣게 태우다 exterior 외부 condition 상태 available 입수할 수 있는, 이용할 수 있는 request 요청 negotiable 협상의 여지가 있는, 절충 가능한 deliver 배송하다, 배달하다

바비큐에 대해 드러나지 않는 사항은?
(A) 원래 포장 박스에 들어 있다.
(B) 새 부품이 필요하다.
(C) 가격은 확정되지 않았다.
(D) 보증 기간은 만료됐다.

어휘 part 부품 expire 만료되다, 만기되다

147

What is NOT indicated about the barbecue?
(A) It comes in the original box.*
(B) It needs new parts.
(C) Its price is not set.
(D) Its warranty has expired.

barbecue를 구체적으로 설명한 부분(Item Description)과 각 선택지를 대조해 지문에서 언급된 사항을 소거하는 식으로 해결한다. 전반부의 Purchased new 3 years ago. Original cost was $700 and came with a 2-year warranty.를 통해 (D)를, Buyer can purchase new ones on the Flamesburg website.를 통해 (B)를, Price is negotiable.을 통해 (C)를 확인할 수 있다. 따라서 본 문제의 정답은 (A)이다.

* paraphrasing: negotiable → not set

정답 (A)

판매자는 기꺼이 어떻게 할 것인가?
(A) 물건을 한 달까지 맡아줄 것이다.
(B) 물건 사용법에 관한 설명을 해 줄 것이다.
(C) 국내 어디든 배송해 줄 것이다.
(D) 잠재 구매자에게 사진을 보내 줄 것이다.

어휘 reserve 예약하다, 유보하다 provide 제공하다 instructions 설명, 지시 potential 잠재적인

148

What is the seller willing to do?
(A) Reserve the item for up to a month
(B) Provide instructions on how to use the item
(C) Deliver anywhere in the country
(D) Send photographs to potential buyers*

'판매자의 의향'에 유념해 지문을 살펴보면, Pictures available upon request라며 요청할 경우 사진을 보여 주겠다고 하므로 (D)가 가장 적절하다.

정답 (D)

Questions 149-150 refer to the following notice.

¹⁴⁹ **We are delighted to announce that Cordelia Winters has joined IPM Talent as an associate agent.** Ms. Winters is a graduate of Roden University's public relations program. While studying at Roden, she founded the university's first student-run magazine. Following graduation, she completed an internship at UV Media and Talent, a prestigious agency that represents a wide variety of musicians, authors, professional athletes, and actors. Ms. Winters has undergone exceptional training and will be a great asset to our growing team of agents. ¹⁵⁰ Please join us in conference room B tomorrow morning at 10:00 A.M. to welcome her to the team.

어휘 associate 동료 graduate 졸업자 public relations 홍보, 선전 found 설립하다 following ~에 이어 graduation 졸업 complete 완료하다, 완성하다 prestigious 명망 있는 represent 대표하다 a wide variety of 매우 다양한 author 작가 athlete (육상) 선수 undergo 겪다 exceptional 이례적일 정도로 우수한 asset 자산, 재산

149 코델리아 윈터스가 동료 에이전트로 IPM 탤런트에 입사하게 됐음을 기쁜 마음으로 발표합니다. 윈터스 씨는 로덴 대학 홍보 학부 졸업생입니다. 그녀는 로덴에서 공부하면서, 학교 최초로 학생이 운영하는 잡지를 창간했습니다. 졸업 후, 다양한 음악가, 작가, 프로 선수, 배우들을 대리하는 UV 미디어 앤 탤런트에서 인턴십을 마쳤습니다. 윈터스 씨는 아주 훌륭한 훈련을 거쳤고, 성장세의 우리 팀에 훌륭한 자산이 될 것입니다. 150 모두 내일 오전 10시 회의실 B로 와서 그녀를 환영해 주시기 바랍니다.

149

Where is the notice most likely posted?

(A) In an advertising firm
(B) In a university
(C) In a music studio
(D) In a talent agency*

본 공지는 어디에 올라가겠는가?
(A) 광고 회사에
(B) 대학에
(C) 음악 스튜디오에
(D) 연예 기획사에

어휘 talent agency 연예 기획사

첫 문장 We are delighted to announce that Cordelia Winters has joined IPM Talent as an associate agent.를 통해 (D)가 정답임을 알 수 있다.

정답 (D)

150

What are employees invited to do tomorrow?

(A) Participate in a conference
(B) Greet a new employee*
(C) Visit a competitor
(D) Meet some new clients

직원들에게 내일 무엇을 해 달라고 권하는가?
(A) 회의에 참가하라.
(B) 신입 사원을 맞이하라.
(C) 경쟁 업체를 방문하라.
(D) 몇몇 신규 고객들을 만나라.

어휘 participate in ~에 참가하다, 참여하다 greet 맞이하다, 환영하다 competitor 경쟁자, 경쟁 업체

키워드 tomorrow에 유념해 보면, 마지막 문장에서 내일 회의실에서 함께 환영해 달라(Please join us in conference room B tomorrow morning at 10:00 A.M. to welcome her to the team.)고 하므로 (B)가 정답이 된다.
* paraphrasing: welcome → greet

정답 (B)

팀 피터슨 [오전 11:03]
안녕하세요, 아만다. 샘슨 레인 일에 대해 현재 상황을 알려 주시겠어요?

아만다 레이 [11:10]
1층과 차고는 끝냈어요. 이제 집 2층을 시작하려던 참이에요.

팀 피터슨 [11:12]
그게 다인가요? 152 몇 시쯤 다 될 것 같아요? 151 오후 3시에 이사 일정이 또 있어요.

아만다 레이 [11:15]
일정이 늦어지고 있어요. 견적 낼 때, 차고의 낡은 가구를 고려하지 않았나 봐요.

팀 피터슨 [11:20]
정말요? 누가 견적을 냈죠?

아만다 레이 [11:21]
매튜가 휴가 가기 전에요.

팀 피터슨 [11:23]
좋아요. 제게 오후 1시에 경과 보고를 해 주세요. 오후 일에 다른 팀을 불러야 할지 그때 결정할게요.

발송

메시지를 입력하세요…

레이 씨는 어떤 업체에서 일하는가?
(A) 부동산 중개소
(B) 가구 매장
(C) 이삿짐 회사
(D) 트럭 임대 서비스

어휘 real estate 부동산 rental 임대

11시 12분에 피터슨 씨가 "그게 다인가요?"라고 말할 때 의미하는 바는?
(A) 집 주소를 알고 싶어 한다.
(B) 직원들이 일을 느리게 하고 있다고 생각한다.
(C) 가격이 매우 싸서 놀랐다.
(D) 모든 것이 트럭에 실렸는지 확인하고 싶어 한다.

어휘 load (짐을) 싣다

Questions 151-152 refer to the following text message chain.

Tim Peterson [11:03 A.M.]
Hey, Amanda. Can you update me on the Sampson Lane job?

Amanda Ray [11:10]
We've cleared out the main floor and the garage. We're just starting on the second floor of the house now.

Tim Peterson [11:12]
Is that all? 152 What time do you think you'll be done? 151 We have a move scheduled for 3 P.M.

Amanda Ray [11:15]
We're behind schedule. When the estimate was done, it didn't take into account the old furniture in the garage.

Tim Peterson [11:20]
Really? Who did the estimate?

Amanda Rey [11:21]
Matthew did before he went on vacation.

Tim Peterson [11:23]
Okay. Contact me at 1:00 P.M. with a progress report. I'll decide then if I need to call in another crew for the afternoon job.

SEND

Type your message...

어휘 garage 차고, 주차장 behind schedule 일정이 뒤처진 estimate 견적(서) take into account ~을 고려하다 decide 결정하다 crew 작업 팀

151

What type of business does Ms. Ray work for?
(A) A real estate agency   (B) A furniture store
(C) A moving company*   (D) A truck rental service

오전 11시 12분 팀 피터슨의 메시지 중 We have a move scheduled for 3 P.M.을 통해 '이사와 관련된 업체에서 일하는 사람들끼리의 문자임을 유추할 수 있으므로 (C)가 정답이 된다.

정답 (C)

152

At 11:12, what does Mr. Peterson mean when he says "Is that all"?
(A) He wants to know the address of a house.
(B) He thinks the employees are working slowly.*
(C) He is surprised because the price is very cheap.
(D) He wants to confirm that everything is loaded on the truck.

이어지는 문장에서 몇 시쯤 다 되겠냐(What time do you think you'll be done?)고 재촉하는 맥락으로 볼 때 (B)가 가장 적절하다.

정답 (B)

Questions 153-154 refer to the following letter.

Rutherford Eye Clinic
54 Rutherford Avenue
Los Angeles, California

14 March

Katrina Serova
123 Colonel Lane
Los Angeles, California

Dear Ms. Serova,

[153] It is important to us here at Rutherford Eye Clinic that all our customers receive advanced notice of changes to our policies. As of August 1st, all routine yearly eye exams will no longer be covered by most major insurance providers. To help offset the cost, we are reducing our fees by $15 per exam. Please see the enclosed list of affected insurance providers.

[154] In some select cases, we are willing to provide eye exams to children free of charge should your family have a history of prior exams with us. Please contact our billing manager Maggie Wilson at 445-987-0023 to inquire about this service or if you have any questions.

Sincerely,
Nadia Fortuni
Dr. Nadia Fortuni

본 편지는 세로바 씨에게 왜 발송되었는가?
(A) 청구 변경 사항을 안내하기 위해서
(B) 새로운 서비스를 광고하기 위해서
(C) 예약을 확인하기 위해서
(D) 놓친 검진을 알리기 위해서

어휘 announce 발표하다 appointment 예약, 약속 inform 알리다

153

Why was the letter sent to Ms. Serova?
(A) To announce a billing change*
(B) To advertise a new service
(C) To confirm an appointment
(D) To inform of a missed exam

첫째 문단의 It is important to us here at Rutherford Eye Clinic that all our customers receive advanced notice of changes to our policies.를 통해 정책 변경에 대한 내용이 주로 전개되리라는 것을 유추할 수 있는데, 보험 적용 대상이 달라져서 비용이 청구되며, 이에 도움을 주고자 요금을 할인하겠다는 내용이 첫째 문단 전반에서 설명되므로 (A)가 정답이다.

정답 (A)

루더포드 안과에 대해 드러나는 사항은?
(A) 신입 사원들을 고용하기를 원한다.
(B) 영업 시간을 연장했다.
(C) 전 세계 고객들을 상대로 한다.
(D) 특정 고객들에게 무료 검진을 제공할 것이다.

어휘 hire 고용하다 extend 확대하다, 확장하다 operation 운영, 영업 cater to 사람 ~의 구미에 맞추다, ~에 영합하다 certain 어떤, 무슨

154

What is indicated about Rutherford Eye Clinic?
(A) It wants to hire new staff members.
(B) It has extended its hours of operation.
(C) It caters to clients from all around the world.
(D) It will offer free exams to certain customers.*

특정 경우에 한해, 이전에 검진 받은 적이 있다면 자녀에게 무료로 검진해 줄 것(In some select cases, we are willing to provide eye exams to children free of charge should your family have a history of prior exams with us.)이라고 둘째 문단에서 말한다. 따라서 (D)가 가장 적절하다.

* paraphrasing: provide → offer, free of charge → free

정답 (D)

Questions 155-157 refer to the following article.

Westpoint Shopping Mall to Begin Construction

By Melanie Rosenberg, Staff Writer

March 23 -- Yesterday, in a press conference at Mayor Zanga's office downtown, the mayor announced the city's approval of development plans for a new shopping mall. According to the mayor, 157 Westpoint Shopping Mall will be located at Park Road and Wilson Street. ----[1]----

The shopping mall is a joint project between the City of Forks and Windsor Partners, a private development corporation. The mall will include over 200 hundred new stores, 55 restaurants, and a department store. ----[2]---- Windsor Partners will be in charge of executing construction and overseeing initial operations.

"The City of Forks has never had a major shopping center," Mr. Johnson of Windsor Partners said in an interview. "By building this state of the art facility, 155 the people of Forks will see an increase in jobs and tourism." ----[3]----

Many retailers have already signed contracts with Windsor Partners to reserve store space in the mall. 156 However, some small business owners have expressed worry that they will lose business once the shopping mall opens. ----[4]---- "My store has been in business for two generations," Michelle Stevens of Shoe Blitz said. "My customers are loyal, but I won't be able to compete with shopping mall prices."

어휘 construction 공사, 건설 press conference 기자 회견 mayor 시장 approval 승인 corporation 법인 include 포함하다 department store 백화점 be in charge of ~을 책임지다 execute 실행하다, 수행하다 oversee 감독하다 관리하다 initial 초기의 state of the art 최첨단의, 최신식의 facility 시설 increase 증가, 인상 tourism 관광업 retailer 소매상, 소매업자 contract 계약(서) reserve 예약하다 owner 소유주 generation 세대 compete 경쟁하다

윈저 파트너는 포크스에 무엇을 유치하기를 바라는가?
(A) 외국 학생들
(B) 슈퍼마켓
(C) 더 많은 관광객
(D) 새로운 소규모 업체들

어휘 attract 끌어모으다, 유치하다

155

What does Windsor Partners hope to attract to Forks?
(A) Foreign students
(B) A supermarket
(C) More tourists*
(D) New small businesses

핵심 어구 Windsor Partners의 바람이 직접적으로 드러난 인터뷰가 둘째 문단에 나온다. 이 내용 중 the people of Forks will see an increase in jobs and tourism을 통해 정답 (C)를 확인할 수 있다.

정답 (C)

미셸 스티븐스는 누구이겠는가?
(A) 신문 기자
(B) 소매 매장 소유주
(C) 시 공무원
(D) 부동산 개발 업자

어휘 property 부동산, 재산

156

Who most likely is Michelle Stevens?
(A) A newspaper reporter
(B) A retail store owner*
(C) A city official
(D) A property developer

핵심 인명 Michelle Stevens에 유의해 지문을 살펴보면, 넷째 문단에서 우려하는 소규모 매장 업주들(However, some small business owners have expressed worry that they will lose business once the shopping mall opens.)을 언급한 다음 인터뷰 대상자로 나오므로 (B)가 정답이다.

정답 (B)

다음 문장은 [1], [2], [3], [4] 중 어느 곳에 들어가야 가장 적절한가?

"작년, 화재로 인해 거기에 있던 자동차 공장이 전소되었고, 그 부지는 새로운 개발을 기다리고 있었다."
(A) [1]
(B) [2]
(C) [3]
(D) [4]

어휘 consume (불이) 전소시키다 auto 자동차 factory 공장 leave 남기다

157

In which of the positions market [1], [2], [3], and [4] does the following sentence best belong?

"Last year, a fire consumed the auto factory located there, leaving the site open to new development."
(A) [1]*   (B) [2]
(C) [3]   (D) [4]

맥락상 '공사 부지 선정 이유'를 나타내는 문장이다. 따라서 첫째 문단에서 공사 부지 위치를 설명한 문장 Westpoint Shopping Mall will be located at Park Road and Wilson Street 다음 자리가 알맞다.

정답 (A)

Questions 158-160 refer to the following information.

Simone Decourte
Kites at Sunset
Mobile Installation, painted sheet metal and rods
1984

Kites at Sunset is one of the most popular mobile installations by Simone Decourte. [158] Decourte revolutionized mobile art in the 1970s by including portable motors to create movement. *Kites at Sunset* is part of a larger series constructed by Decourte between 1970 to 1988. [160 (B)] It has been featured in The Museum of Abstract Art in Milan, The Contemporary Art Gallery in New York City, and The New Art Movement Museum in London. [160 (C)] Decourte originally donated the piece to the University of Montenegro. [159] It remained there for ten years before being acquired by Maxwell George of the Wilson Fine Art Museum where it has remained as part of our permanent collection. Before her death, [160 (A)] Decourte said *Kites at Sunset* was her "most vibrant piece ever created."

본 정보는 시몬 드코트를 어떻게 묘사하는가?
(A) 세부 사항에 주의를 기울였다.
(B) 많은 예술품을 만들었다.
(C) 획기적인 예술가였다.
(D) 가난한 사람들을 위해 작업했다.

어휘 describe 설명하다, 묘사하다 attentive 주의를 기울이는 details 세부 사항 innovative 획기적인

158

How does the information describe Simone Decourte?

(A) She was attentive to details.
(B) She created a lot of art work.
(C) She was an innovative artist.*
(D) She worked for the poor.

전반부에서 Decourte revolutionized mobile art in the 1970s라며 1970년대 미술계에 대변혁을 일으켰다고 하므로 (C)가 가장 적절하다.

정답 (C)

본 정보는 어디에 게재돼 있는가?
(A) 추상 미술 박물관에
(B) 윌슨 파인 아트 박물관에
(C) 현대 미술 갤러리에
(D) 뉴 아트 무브먼트 박물관에

159

Where is the information posted?

(A) At the Museum of Abstract Art
(B) At the Wilson Fine Art Museum*
(C) At the Contemporary Art Gallery
(D) At the New Art Movement Museum

행간을 읽을 수 있어야 풀 수 있는 문제이다. 후반부에서 몬테네그로 대학에 기증되어 10년간 있다가 윌슨 파인 아트 박물관에서 매입했다(It remained there for ten years before being acquired by Maxwell George of the Wilson Fine Art Museum)고 한 후, 우리의(our → Wilson Fine Art Museum) 영구 소장품이라고(where it has remained as part of our permanent collection) 한다. 따라서 (B)가 정답이 된다.

정답 (B)

'해질녘 연'에 대해 언급되지 않는 사항은?
(A) 예술가가 자신의 최고 작품 중 하나로 간주했다.
(B) 여러 곳을 옮겨 다녔다.
(C) 대학에서 소유했었다.
(D) 작품을 완성하는 데 20년 가까이 걸렸다.

어휘 regard 여기다, 간주하다 several 몇몇의 own 소유하다 decade 10년 complete 완성하다

160

What is NOT stated about *Kites at Sunset*?

(A) The artist regarded it as one of her best works.
(B) It has traveled to several places.
(C) It was owned by a university.
(D) It took almost two decades to complete the piece.*

각 선택지를 지문과 대조하면서 언급된 사항을 소거하는 식으로 문제를 해결한다. (A)는 마지막 문장의 Decourte said Kites at Sunset was her "most vibrant piece ever created."에서, (B)와 (C)는 중반부의 It has been featured in The Museum of Abstract Art in Milan, The Contemporary Art Gallery in New York City, and The New Art Movement Museum in London.과 Decourte originally donated the piece to the University of Montenegro.에서 확인할 수 있다. 따라서 본 문제의 정답은 (D)가 된다.

정답 (D)

Questions 161-163 refer to the following e-mail.

To: Jan Andrews
From: Michael Pitelli
Date: March 7
[161] Subject: Updates for March 8

Ms. Andrews,

I've had to make a few minor changes to your schedule for tomorrow. Your meeting with potential client Jeff Woods has been canceled. [162] His assistant suggested March 10 as a possible date to meet. [162] Since you're flying back that morning, you're free in the afternoon. Would you like me to set up the appointment? Please have a look at your updated schedule below. [163] I've replaced Mr. Woods's appointment with your budget review. Please let me know if this doesn't work for you.

Time	Appointment	Attendees
8:30 A.M.	Staff Meeting	Departments A and B
9:45 A.M.	Conference Call with Washington Partners	Jessica Bowers, Tom Park
[163] 10:30 A.M.	Budget Review	Ally Strenski
1:30 P.M.	Meeting about Conference Itinerary	Joshua Wilson
4:00 P.M.	Leave for your 7:00 [162] flight to Chicago	

I have printed out your e-ticket and put it in your company mailbox. Good luck on your trip.

Best,
Michael

본 이메일은 왜 발송됐는가?
(A) 다음 달 약속을 취소하기 위해서
(B) 여행 일정표를 제공하기 위해서
(C) 일일 일정표를 업데이트하기 위해서
(D) 회의를 위해 서류를 제공하기 위해서

어휘 provide 제공하다

161

Why was the e-mail sent?
(A) To cancel an appointment next month
(B) To provide a travel itinerary
(C) To update a daily schedule*
(D) To provide documents for a meeting

이메일 제목이 목적에 대한 결정적인 단서가 될 확률이 높다. Subject: Updates for March 8를 통해 (C)가 정답임을 알 수 있다.

정답 (C)

3월 10일에 어떤 일이 있을 예정인가?
(A) 피텔리 씨가 워싱턴으로 갈 것이다.
(B) 앤드류스 씨가 회의에 참석할 것이다.
(C) 우즈 씨가 예산 검토를 할 것이다.
(D) 앤드류스 씨가 시카고에서 돌아올 것이다.

어휘 attend 참석하다, 출석하다 hold 열다, 진행하다

162

What will happen on March 10?
(A) Mr. Pitelli will fly to Washington.
(B) Ms. Andrews will attend a conference.
(C) Mr. Woods will hold a budget review.
(D) Ms. Andrews will return from Chicago.*

핵심 어구 March 10에 유념해 지문을 살펴보면 첫째 문단에서 His assistant suggested March 10 as a possible date to meet.라며 3월 10일에 미팅이 가능하다고 한 다음 바로 그날 아침 당신(이메일 수신자: 앤드류스 씨)이 돌아온다(Since you're flying back that morning)고 덧붙인다. 또한, 일정에서 시카고행(flight to Chicago)이라고 하므로 (D)가 정답이 된다.

정답 (D)

우즈 씨는 몇 시에 올 예정이었는가?
(A) 오전 8:35
(B) 오전 9:45
(C) 오전 10:30
(D) 오후 1:30

어휘 expect 기대하다, 예상하다

163

At what time was Mr. Woods expected?
(A) 8:35 A.M.
(B) 9:45 A.M.
(C) 10:30 A.M.*
(D) 1:30 P.M.

'애초 미팅 시간'이 포인트임을 파악해야 한다. 첫째 문단에서 I've replaced Mr. Woods's appointment with your budget review.라며 예산 검토 시간과 맞바꾸었다고 하므로 표의 10:30 A.M. Budget Review를 통해 원래 오기로 했던 시간은 (C)임을 알 수 있다.

정답 (C)

Questions 164-167 refer to the following e-mail.

To: Employees of Winfred Financial
From: Sandra Burns
Date: October 24
Subject: New regulations

Dear employees,

As you know, the Ministry of Health and Environment has introduced a new set of laws for work places in order to help reduce the amount of energy consumed during the winter months. **164** In accordance with these new regulations, Winfred Financial will program its heating system during the winter. As such, you will not be able to regulate the temperature of your office at any time. The system will heat the building to 19°C on weekdays, which will be maintained throughout the day. It will then lower to 13°C at the end of each day. **166** By following this new regulation, we should see a 10% reduction in the cost of our utility bills.

As some of you work on weekends, management has decided that offices on the 5th floor will be able to control the temperature manually. **167** Weekend workers may request a change of office with their department managers. We simply ask that the rooms not be heated any warmer than 19°C.

Sincerely,
Sandra Burns,
General Manager

164

What is the purpose of the e-mail?

(A) To announce an upcoming change in the workplace*
(B) To inform employees of a scheduled inspection
(C) To encourage employees to choose new office furniture
(D) To offer managers the opportunity to get a promotion

첫째 문단 다섯째 줄에 있는 "maintained"와 의미상 가장 유사한 단어는?
(A) 확인되다
(B) 수리되다
(C) 소지되다
(D) 유지되다

어휘 confirm 확실히 하다 repair 수리하다, 수선하다

165

The word "maintained" in paragraph 1, line 5, is closest in meaning to
(A) confirmed
(B) repaired
(C) taken
(D) kept*

해당 문장은 온도가 종일 '유지된다'는 요지이다. 따라서 '유지되다, 계속되다'라는 의미의 (D)가 정답이 된다.

정답 (D)

무엇이 새 규정의 이점으로 언급되는가?
(A) 직원들에게 업무 효율을 개선시켜 줄 것이다.
(B) 회사가 직원을 더 고용할 수 있게 할 것이다.
(C) 회사가 돈을 아끼게 해 줄 것이다.
(D) 국영 및 민영 회사들에 적용될 것이다.

어휘 benefit 혜택, 이득 improve 개선하다 efficiency 효율 allow 허용하다, 허락하다 hire 고용하다 save 아끼다 apply to ~에 적용하다

166

What is mentioned as a benefit of the new regulation?
(A) It will improve employee work efficiency.
(B) It can allow the company to hire more workers.
(C) It will help the company save money.*
(D) It can be applied to public and private companies.

첫째 문단에서 By following this new regulation, we should see a 10% reduction in the cost of our utility bills.라며 '새 규정을 따르면 공과금을 줄일 것'이라고 하므로 (C)가 정답이다.

* paraphrasing: cost → money

정답 (C)

주말에 일하는 직원들은 어떻게 하라는 조언을 받는가?
(A) 번즈 씨에게로 이메일을 직접 보내라.
(B) 사무실 변경을 요청하라.
(C) 근무 일정을 변경하라.
(D) 주말에는 집에서 일하라.

어휘 alter 바꾸다

167

What are employees who work on weekends advised to do?
(A) E-mail Ms. Burns directly
(B) Request office changes*
(C) Alter their work schedules
(D) Work at home on weekends

키워드 weekends에 유념해 지문을 살펴보면, 둘째 문단에서 주말 근무자에게 적용되는 예외 사항이 언급된다. 이를 이용하려면 부서 과장에게 사무실을 바꿔 달라고 요청하라(Weekend workers may request a change of office with their department managers.)고 한다. 따라서 (B)가 정답이 된다.

정답 (B)

Questions 168-171 refer to the following online chat discussion.

Mary Renold

Mary Renold (2:02 P.M.)	Hello, Ben. 168 Can you spare a moment? I want to double check an inventory report with you.
Ben Jeffries (2:03 P.M.)	No problem.
Mary Renold (2:04 P.M.)	According to the report, 170 we only have two A75 Canpro notebooks left. We've been selling a lot of that model lately. Should I order more?
Ben Jeffries (2:06 P.M.)	That's not necessary. The new A76 model has just come out, so we're going to carry that model instead. 169 I ordered 50 of the new ones, but they haven't come in yet.
Mary Renold (2:10 P.M.)	Oh, okay. Thanks for explaining that.
Ben Jeffries (2:11 P.M.)	171 Next week, we'll start displaying them on the shelves, so make sure to print the product information for the displays.
Mary Renold (2:12 P.M.)	Sure. I'll get right on that.

168 At 2:03 P.M., what does Mr. Jeffries most likely mean when he writes, "No Problem"?

(A) He agrees with Ms. Renold's idea.
(B) He is available to answer Ms. Renold's question.*
(C) He wants to set up a meeting with Ms. Renold.
(D) He did exactly as Ms. Renold requested.

제프리스 씨에 대해 뭐라고 언급되는가?
(A) 몇 가지 물품을 이미 주문했다.
(B) 정보를 다운로드했다.
(C) 오늘 몇 가지 제품을 준비했다.
(D) 지난주에 공급 업체를 방문했다.

어휘 supplier 공급 업체, 공급 업자

169

What is mentioned about Mr. Jeffries?
(A) He already ordered some items.*
(B) He downloaded some information.
(C) He set up some products today.
(D) He visited a supplier last week.

'제프리스 씨의 행적'에 유념해 지문을 살펴보면, 2시 6분에 적은 내용 중 I ordered 50 of the new ones를 통해 (A)가 정답임을 알 수 있다.

정답 (A)

제프리스 씨와 레놀드 씨는 어떤 업체에서 일하는가?
(A) 컴퓨터 수리 업체
(B) 배송 회사
(C) 전자 제품 매장
(D) 소프트웨어 개발 업체

어휘 delivery 배송, 배달 electronics 전자 제품

170

What type of business do Mr. Jeffries and Ms. Renold work for?
(A) A computer repair business
(B) A delivery company
(C) An electronics store*
(D) A software developer

전반부에서 레놀드 씨가 재고 보고서를 언급하며 특정 노트북이 겨우 두 개 남았다(we only have two A75 Canpro notebooks left)고 하므로 (C)가 가장 적절하다.

정답 (C)

제프리스 씨와 레놀드 씨는 다음 주에 무엇을 할 예정인가?
(A) 가게 앞을 개조할 것이다.
(B) 신제품 할인 행사를 할 것이다.
(C) 일부 구형 물건을 반품할 것이다.
(D) 일부 제품 진열을 할 것이다.

어휘 renovate 개조하다 storefront 가게 앞에 딸린 공간 obsolete 더 이상 쓸모가 없는, 한물간, 구식의

171

What will Mr. Jeffries and Ms. Renold do next week?
(A) Renovate a storefront
(B) Hold a sale for new products
(C) Return some obsolete items
(D) Set up some product displays*

핵심 어구 next week에 유의해 지문을 살펴보면, 2시 11분의 문자 중 Next week, we'll start displaying them on the shelves에서 (D)가 정답임을 알 수 있다.

정답 (D)

Questions 172-175 refer to the following article.

June 15 -- The Walter Horman Estate, the home of deceased millionaire Walter Horman, was recently purchased by the City of Rogerton. According to Malika Trenton, director of the Rogerton Historical Society, the estate will undergo light renovations and restorations before being turned into a local museum. --[1]-- According to Trenton, 172 "The Horman family has included all of the original decorations and furnishings for visitors to enjoy."

Over the last several decades, the Walter Horman Estate has been unoccupied. Instead, the property was available for private party rentals and weddings. Some major film companies have even shot scenes at the estate. 173 However, the cost of keeping the grounds in good condition proved to be too much for the family. --[2]-- Stephen Horman, grandson of the late Walter Horman, said, "It was a tough choice to make. The estate has been in our family for generations, but selling it was the best way to ensure its upkeep." 175 The rest of the Horman family has expressed satisfaction that the estate will be turned into a museum. --[3]--

174 The Rogerton Historical Society intends to develop guided tours of the estate rooms, while still providing access to the gardens for private parties. Visitors to the estate can learn the history of the Horman family from its early immigrant beginning to its rise in society as the owner of one of the first food processing companies in the country. --[4]-- Tours are expected to begin next spring. Anyone interested in purchasing passes or learning about the estate's history can visit www.walterhormanestate.com/info.

어휘 estate 사유지, 토지 deceased 사망한 millionaire 백만장자 purchase 구입하다, 사다 renovation 개조 restoration 복원, 복구 decade 10년 unoccupied 비어 있는 instead 대신에 property 부동산 rental 임대(료) shoot (영화/사진을) 촬영하다 cost 값, 비용 condition 상태 prove to ~임이 판명되다, 드러나다 late 사망한 make a choice 선택하다 generation 세대 ensure 반드시 ~하게 하다, 보장하다 upkeep 유지(비) rest 나머지 express 표현하다 satisfaction 만족 intend 의도하다, 작정하다 access 접근, 이용 immigrant 이민자, 이주민 rise 성공, 출세 owner 소유주 processing 처리, 가공 expect 기대하다, 예상하다

6월 15일 -- 고인이 된 백만장자 월터 호만의 저택인 월터 호만 에스테이트를 최근 로저턴 시에서 매입했다. 로저턴 역사 협회장 마리카 트렌턴에 따르면, 그 저택을 약간 개조 및 복원해서 지역 박물관으로 바꿀 예정이다. —[1]— 트렌턴이 말하길, 172 "호만 가는 원래 장식과 가구를 전부 보존해서 방문객들이 감상할 수 있게 할 것이다."

지난 수십 년간, 월터 호만 에스테이트는 빈 집이었다. 대신, 그 저택은 개인 파티 및 결혼식용으로 임대해 쓸 수 있었다. 몇몇 큰 영화사들은 그곳에서 장면들을 촬영하기도 했다. 173 하지만, 부지를 계속 좋은 상태로 유지하는 데 드는 비용이 가족으로서는 많이 부담스러웠다. —[2]— 고 월터 호만의 손자인 스티븐 호만은 이렇게 말했다. "어려운 선택이었습니다. 그 저택은 몇 세대를 거치면서 우리와 함께했지만, 매각하는 것이 그것을 유지하는 데 최선의 방법이었어요." 175 나머지 호만 가족들은 저택이 박물관으로 바뀐다는 것에 만족을 표했다. —[3]—

174 로저턴 역사 협회는 저택의 여러 방들에 대한 가이드 관광을 개발할 계획이지만, 정원은 계속 개인 파티용으로 제공할 수 있게 할 작정이다. 이곳 방문객은 초기 이주 시기 때부터 국내 최초의 식품 가공 회사 소유주로 사회적으로 성공하기까지 호만 일가의 역사를 배울 수 있다. —[4]— 투어는 내년 봄에 시작될 전망이다. 입장권을 사거나 저택의 역사를 알고 싶은 사람은 www.walterhormanestate.com/info을 방문할 수 있다.

172

What is suggested about the Walter Horman Estate?

(A) It was built by Walter Horman's father.
(B) It is expensive to reserve for parties.
(C) It will have its appliances upgraded.
(D) It includes the original furniture.*

첫째 문단에서 원래 장식 및 가구를 포함시켰다(The Horman family has included all of the original decorations and furnishings for visitors to enjoy)고 하므로 (D)가 가장 적절하다.

정답 (D)

월터 호만 에스테이트에 대해 드러나는 사항은?
(A) 월터 호만의 아버지가 지었다.
(B) 파티용으로 예약하는 데 돈이 많이 든다.
(C) 가전제품을 업그레이드할 것이다.
(D) 원래의 가구가 포함된다.

어휘 expensive 돈이 많이 드는 reserve 예약하다 appliance 기기, 가전제품

본 기사에 따르면, 호만 일가는 어떤 어려움을 겪었는가?
(A) 부지를 공원으로 바꾸는 것
(B) 저택을 유지하는 것
(C) 방들을 위한 가구를 찾는 것
(D) 적절한 구매자를 찾는 것

어휘 maintain 유지하다 locate (특정한 위치를) 찾다 suitable 적절한

173

According to the article, what was difficult for the Horman family?
(A) Turning the property into a park
(B) Maintaining the estate*
(C) Finding furniture for the rooms
(D) Locating a suitable buyer

키워드 difficult에 유념해 보면, 둘째 문단의 However, the cost of keeping the grounds in good condition proved to be too much for the family.를 통해 정답 (B)를 확인할 수 있다.

* paraphrasing: keep ~ in good condition → maintain

정답 (B)

본 기사에 따르면, 집에 대한 무엇이 그대로일 것인가?
(A) 호만 일가가 소유할 것이다.
(B) 외부 벽들은 보안용으로 이용될 것이다.
(C) 건물들은 게스트 하우스로 제공될 것이다.
(D) 야외 부지는 임대용으로 쓸 것이다.

어휘 own 소유하다 security 보안, 안전

174

According to the article, what will remain the same about the estate?
(A) It will be owned by the Horman family.
(B) Its exterior walls will be used for security.
(C) Its buildings will serve as guest houses.
(D) Its outdoor property will be available for rent.*

'현상 유지 부분'이 포인트임을 파악해야 한다. 마지막 문단에서 정원은 파티용으로 계속 이용할 수 있게 한다(The Rogerton Historical Society intends to develop guided tours of the estate rooms, while still providing access to the gardens for private parties.)고 하므로 (D)가 가장 적절하다.

* paraphrasing: garden → outdoor property

정답 (D)

다음 문장은 [1], [2], [3], [4] 중 어느 곳에 들어가야 가장 적절한가?
"그들은 월터 호만에 대한 기억이 보존될 것이라며 기뻐했다."
(A) [1]
(B) [2]
(C) [3]
(D) [4]

어휘 preserve 지키다, 보호하다

175

In which of the positions marked [1], [2], [3], and [4] does the following sentence best belonging?

"They are pleased the memory of Walter Horman will be preserved."

(A) [1]   (B) [2]
(C) [3]*   (D) [4]

인칭대명사 they가 가리킬 만한 단어가 앞서 나와야 하는데, 둘째 문단의 The rest of the Horman family has expressed satisfaction that the estate will be turned into a museum.에서 The rest of the Horman family를 they로 지칭하기에 알맞다. 또한 has expressed satisfaction과 be pleased라는 감정이 자연스럽게 연결되므로 (C)가 가장 알맞다.

정답 (C)

Questions 176-180 refer to the following e-mails.

To: samadams@adamsroofing.com
From: ginachoi@homeimprovementmonthly.com
Date: January 3
Subject: Home Improvement Monthly

Dear Mr. Adams,

¹⁷⁶ As a special New Year promotion, Home Improvement Monthly will be offering discounted prices for new advertisers in our magazine. Home Improvement Monthly has a readership of over 20,000 print subscriptions. ¹⁷⁷ Your advertisement will reach each subscriber in print as well as our many online subscribers. With our services, you can increase your business!

This offer is valid until March 1st. Our price packages are outlined below, and ¹⁷⁸ our designers are ready to create color advertisements according to your specifications. To purchase any of our packages, please reply by e-mail or visit us at www.homeimprovementmonthly.com/advertisements/orders.

Package	Advertisement Format	Monthly Price
1	One full-page print ad plus banner website ad	$300
2	One half-page print ad plus half-banner website ad	$275
3	One half-page print ad plus corner website ad	$250
4	¹⁸⁰ One quarter-page print ad plus corner website ad	$225

Sincerely,
Gina Choi
Advertising Coordinator
Home Improvement Monthly

To: ginachoi@homeimprovementmonthly.com
From: samadams@adamsroofing.com
Date: January 5
Subject: Re: Home Improvement Monthly

Dear Ms. Choi,

Thank you for e-mailing me about your promotion. My business partner and I are interested in placing an ad in your magazine. However, I have some questions about ¹⁸⁰ your quarter-page print ad. I've purchased a copy of your magazine and looked at the advertisements. I noticed that some are in the front of the magazine and some are in the back. I'm wondering what determines the location of the ad. Do we need to pay additional fees to have our ad located in the front?

Thank you in advance for answering these questions.

Sincerely,
Sam Adams
Co-owner
Adams Roofing

최 씨는 아담스 씨에게 왜 이메일을 썼는가?
(A) 새 광고 기회를 안내하기 위해서
(B) 구독료에 대한 판촉 할인을 제공하기 위해서
(C) 마케팅 회사를 고용하라고 권하기 위해서
(D) 계약상의 변경 사항을 알리기 위해서

어휘 opportunity 기회 promotional 홍보의, 판촉의 encourage 고무하다, 격려하다, 장려하다 hire 고용하다 inform 알리다

176

Why did Ms. Choi e-mail Mr. Adams?
(A) To announce a new advertising opportunity*
(B) To offer a promotional discount on subscriptions
(C) To encourage him to hire a marketing agency
(D) To inform him of a change in a contract

첫 번째 이메일(지문 1)의 목적에 관련된 문제이다. 첫 문장 As a special New Year promotion, Home Improvement Monthly will be offering discounted prices for new advertisers in our magazine.을 통해 '신년맞이 광고 할인'에 대한 내용이 주로 전개되리라는 것을 알 수 있으므로 (A)가 정답이 된다.

정답 (A)

홈 임프루브먼트 먼슬리에 대해 드러나는 사항은?
(A) 몇 호는 늦게 배송됐다.
(B) 광고주는 구독료를 내지 않는다.
(C) 내년부터는 매달 두 번 발행할 것이다.
(D) 구독자 일부는 웹사이트만 결제한다.

177

What is suggested about Home Improvement Monthly?
(A) Some of its issues were delivered late.
(B) Its advertisers do not pay for subscriptions.
(C) It will put out two issues every month starting next year.
(D) Some of its subscribers only pay for the website.*

Home Improvement Monthly 측이 작성한 첫 번째 이메일(지문 1)을 각 선택지와 대조해 보자. 지문 1 첫째 문단에서 인쇄물 구독자와 온라인 구독자에게 광고가 전달될 것(Your advertisement will reach each subscriber in print as well as our many online subscribers.)이라고 하므로 (D)를 유추할 수 있다.

정답 (D)

홈 임프루브먼트 먼슬리의 디자이너에 대해 뭐라고 언급되는가?
(A) 맞춤형 작업을 제공할 수 있다.
(B) 추가 요금을 받는다.
(C) 회사 웹사이트도 디자인한다.
(D) 3월까지는 시간이 나지 않는다.

어휘 custom 주문 제작된 require 필요로 하다 unavailable 입수할 수 없는, 이용할 수 없는

178

What is mentioned about Home Improvement Monthly's designers?
(A) They can provide custom work.*
(B) They require additional fees.
(C) They also design the company website.
(D) They are unavailable until March.

지문 1을 키워드 designer에 유의해 살펴보면, 둘째 문단에서 our designers are ready to create color advertisements according to your specifications라며 지시에 따라 컬러 광고를 제작한다고 하므로 (A)가 정답이 된다.

정답 (A)

179

In the second e-mail, the word "placing" in paragraph 1, line 2, is closest in meaning to

(A) hiring
(B) putting*
(C) assigning
(D) calculating

해당 부분을 찾아보면, '광고하다(place an ad)'는 요지이다. 따라서 '어떠한 장소, 위치에 두다'라는 의미의 put이 가장 유사한 단어이다.

정답 (B)

두 번째 이메일에서, 첫째 문단 둘째 줄에 있는 "placing"과 의미상 가장 유사한 단어는?
(A) 고용하다
(B) 넣다
(C) 맡기다
(D) 계산하다

어휘 assign 맡기다, 배정하다 calculate 계산하다

180

What package does Mr. Adams most likely want?

(A) Package 1
(B) Package 2
(C) Package 3
(D) Package 4*

Mr. Adams가 작성한 두 번째 이메일(지문 2)의 your quarter-page print ad를 유념해 패키지들이 소개된 첫 번째 이메일(지문 1)을 연계해서 파악하면 마지막 항목의 One quarter-page print ad plus corner website ad를 통해 정답 (D)를 확인할 수 있다

정답 (D)

아담스 씨는 어떤 상품을 원하는가?
(A) 패키지 1
(B) 패키지 2
(C) 패키지 3
(D) 패키지 4

Questions 181-185 refer to the following e-mails.

To: mpordeski@mailme.com
From: imranandal@pearsonmedicalresearch.com
Date: April 12
[181] Subject: Pearson Medical Research Position
Attachment: contract

Dear Ms. Pordeski,

I enjoyed speaking with you during your telephone interview, and I'm delighted to offer you a position on our team as a research assistant. As I'm sure you're aware, you will be working with the top medical researchers in the country using the most advanced equipment. Your education in both biology and engineering will be a great asset during your six-month contract.

As I mentioned to you, our company works jointly with Austin University. Thus, you will need to know your way around both our company headquarters and the laboratories at the university. As such, I would like to arrange an orientation for you and our other new researchers. [185] You mentioned that you're finishing up your final year of your degree, so I'd like to arrange a time that does not interfere with your schedule. Please let me know which days in May you are available.

[181] Please note, this position is an internship. Your wages will be $200 a week and the occasional work expenses will be reimbursed. However, [183] following the six-month period, there will be permanent employment for our top interns. [182] To finalize your acceptance of these terms, please sign and return the attached contract. [184] Andrew Baxter, our human resources manager, will contact you if there are any problems.

Thank you, and I look forward to working with you!

Imran Andal
Lead Researcher
Pearson Medical Research

To: Intern Group
From: imranandal@pearsonmedicalresearch.com
Date: April 24
[181] Subject: Orientation

Dear Research Interns,

Since most of you are not available at the same time, I'd like to hold two orientations, one on May 11 and the second on May 16. ¹⁸⁵ The May 16 orientation is scheduled on a weekend to accommodate the students in the group. However, if you're not a student, you will be expected to attend the May 11 orientation. Both orientations will start at 9 A.M. at our company headquarters. After a tour, we will have lunch at Buffy's Bistro and then make our way over to the university. Please bring photo ID in order to gain admittance to the university labs.

Thank you, and I'm looking forward to meeting you all!

Imran Andal,
Lead Researcher,
Pearson Medical Research

어휘 accommodate 수용하다 in order to ~하기 위해 gain 얻다, 획득하다 admittance 입장

181
Why did Mr. Andal write to Ms. Pordeski?

(A) To negotiate a contract
(B) To invite her to apply for a job
(C) To provide medical assistance
(D) To offer her an internship*

안달 씨는 왜 포데스키 씨에게 이메일을 썼는가?
(A) 계약을 협상하기 위해서
(B) 일에 지원하라고 권하기 위해서
(C) 의료 지원을 해 주기 위해서
(D) 인턴을 제안하기 위해서

어휘 negotiate 협상하다 apply for ~에 지원하다, 신청하다 assistance 도움, 지원

첫 번째 이메일(지문 1)의 목적을 묻는 문제이다. Subject: Pearson Medical Research Position이라는 제목을 통해 '일자리(position)'에 대한 내용이 주로 전개되리라는 것을 유추할 수 있는데, 셋째 문단의 Please note, this position is an internship.에서 인턴 직임이 드러나므로 (D)가 정답이 된다.

정답 (D)

182
What document is Ms. Pordeski asked to return?

(A) An employer reference
(B) A signed contract*
(C) A program application
(D) A university transcript

포데스키 씨는 어떤 서류를 반송하라는 요청을 받는가?
(A) 고용주 추천서
(B) 서명된 계약서
(C) 프로그램 지원서
(D) 대학 성적 증명서

어휘 reference 추천(서) application 지원(서) transcript 성적 증명서

Ms. Pordeski가 수신자인 첫 번째 이메일(지문 1)에서 발신자의 요청 사항을 찾아보자. 셋째 문단에서 To finalize your acceptance of these terms, please sign and return the attached contract.라며 첨부된 계약서에 서명하고 반송하라고 하므로 (B)가 정답이다.

정답 (B)

피어슨 의료 연구의 신입 사원들에 대해 드러나는 사항은?
(A) 집에서 일할 것이다.
(B) 세금 서식은 온라인으로 제출되어야 한다.
(C) 일에 대해 돈을 받지 못할 것이다.
(D) 성과가 평가될 것이다.

어휘 tax 세금 performance 실적, 성과 evaluate 평가하다, 감정하다

183

What is indicated about new staff at Pearson Medical Research?
(A) They may work from home.
(B) Their tax forms must be submitted online.
(C) They will not be paid for their work.
(D) Their performance will be evaluated.*

Pearson Medical Research 측에서 인턴 제의를 위해 작성한 첫 번째 이메일(지문 1) 셋째 문단에서 인턴십이 끝나면 최고 인턴을 정식 고용할 것(following the six-month period, there will be permanent employment for our top interns)이라고 하므로 (D)를 유추할 수 있다.

정답 (D)

앤드류 백스터는 왜 포데스키 씨에게 연락하겠는가?
(A) 회사 규정을 검토하기 위해서
(B) 계약상의 문제를 해결하기 위해서
(C) 추가 추천서를 요청하기 위해서
(D) 결제 절차를 설명하기 위해서

어휘 regulation 규정, 규칙 resolve 해결하다 issue 문제, 사안 explain 설명하다 procedure 절차, 방법

184

Why might Andrew Baxter contact Ms. Pordeski?
(A) To review company regulations
(B) To resolve a contract issue*
(C) To ask for additional references
(D) To explain payment procedures

핵심 인명 Andrew Baxter에 유의해 지문들을 살펴보면, 첫 번째 이메일(지문 1) 셋째 문단에서 Andrew Baxter, our human resources manager, will contact you if there are any problems.라며 (서명된 계약서 송부 후) 문제가 있으면 연락할 것이라고 한다. 따라서 (B)가 정답이 된다.
* paraphrasing: problem → issue

정답 (B)

포데스키 씨는 언제 오리엔테이션에 참석하겠는가?
(A) 5월 11일
(B) 5월 15일
(C) 5월 16일
(D) 5월 19일

185

When will Ms. Pordeski most likely attend the orientation?
(A) May 11
(B) May 15
(C) May 16*
(D) May 19

'오리엔테이션 날짜'에 유념해 지문들을 살펴보면, 전체 인턴에게 발송된 두 번째 이메일(지문 2) 첫째 문단에서 (A)와 (C)를 언급한 후 학생들 오리엔테이션은 (C)라고 덧붙인다(The May 16 orientation is scheduled on a weekend to accommodate the students in the group.). 첫 번째 이메일(지문 1) 둘째 문단의 You mentioned that you're finishing up your final year of your degree에서 포데스키 씨가 아직 학생 신분이라고 했으므로 (C)가 정답이다.

정답 (C)

Question 186-190 refer to the following webpage and e-mails.

http://www.internationalspaceexplorationexpo.com

| HOME | ABOUT | PROGRAMS | SCHEDULE |

This year's International Space Exploration Expo (ISEE) is going to be the best yet. [186] Celebrating its tenth anniversary, ISEE offers one of the most advanced displays of space exploration technology scheduled over five days. More than 30 key speakers will be attending, and a variety of exciting activities have been scheduled, including:

√ Guided tours of the convention center exhibits
√ Demonstrations of new space engine technology
√ Children's workshops including hands-on experience
√ [188] Competition: Build a scrap metal spacecraft (open to adult participants)
√ [190] Readings by Dr. Michael Paxwell, author of The Future of Space Travel
√ The ISEE awards ceremony honoring the greatest achievements in space technology

Visit our schedule page for a full list of events.

To: Parker Rogers
From: Karen Walker
Subject: Expo Update
Date: 27 October

[187] I'm so glad you sent me to cover the ISEE. It's been an amazing experience. I spent the first day on a guided tour of the convention center, and I was amazed by some of the displays and new technologies. [188] Unfortunately, the tour ran a bit long, and I couldn't see the spaceship building event. I did, however, get to interview some of the expo participants and got some great photos of children sampling space food.

I also figured [190] I will catch up with Dr. Paxwell tomorrow after he reads some excerpts from his book. Since he's being honored with the Book of the Year award, I think an interview with him might be a great feature for next week's issue. I'll send you a copy of my prepared questions tonight. Let me know if you'd like to add anything to them.

Best,
Karen

수신: 마이클 팩스웰
발신: 캐런 워커
제목: 추가 질문
날짜: 10월 29일

팩스웰 박사 귀하,

어제 박사님과 이야기 나눠 근사했습니다. 인터뷰 사본을 편집자에게 보냈어요. 그는 박사님 말씀과 사진을 좋아했습니다. 다만, 질문 몇 가지가 더 있답니다. 190 내일 낭독 후에 뵈었으면 하는데요. 10분에서 20분 이상은 걸리지 않을 거예요. 괜찮으신지 알려 주시기 바랍니다.

그럼 이만,
캐런 워커

To: Michael Paxwell
From: Karen Walker
Subject: Follow Up Questions
Date: 29 October

Dear Dr. Paxwell,

It was wonderful to speak with you yesterday. I sent a copy of your interview to my editor. He loved your answers as well as the photos. However, he has a few more questions. 190 I'd like to meet with you tomorrow after your reading. It shouldn't take more than ten or twenty minutes. Please let me know if that works for you.

Best,
Karen Walker

어휘 follow up 후속 조치

ISEE에 대해 드러나는 사항은?
(A) 원래 학생들을 대상으로 만들어졌다.
(B) 1년에 여러 번 열린다.
(C) 몇 년째 이어져 왔다.
(D) 새로운 곳으로 옮겼다.

어휘 originally 원래 be held 열리다 multiple 많은, 다수의, 복수의 exist 존재하다, 실재하다 venue 현장, 장소

186

What is indicated about ISEE?
(A) It was originally designed for students.
(B) It is held multiple times per year.
(C) It has existed for several years.*
(D) It has moved to a new venue.

키워드 ISEE에 대해 설명된 웹페이지(지문 1) 첫째 문단의 Celebrating its tenth anniversary, ISEE offers one of the most advanced displays of space exploration technology scheduled over five days.를 통해 정답 (C)를 유추할 수 있다.

정답 (C)

워커 씨는 누구이겠는가?
(A) 출판업자
(B) 우주 비행사
(C) 과학자
(D) 기자

어휘 astronaut 우주 비행사

187

Who most likely is Ms. Walker?
(A) A publisher
(B) An astronaut
(C) A scientist
(D) A journalist*

Ms. Walker가 작성한 이메일들 중 첫 번째(지문 2) 이메일의 첫 문장 I'm so glad you sent me to cover the ISEE.에서 ISEE를 '취재하러' 온 상황임이 드러나므로 (D)가 정답이 된다.

정답 (D)

188

According to Ms. Walker, what conference activity was she unable to attend?

(A) A demonstration
(B) A craft competition*
(C) A guided tour
(D) A workshop

Ms. Walker의 첫 번째 이메일(지문 2)부터 살펴보면, 첫째 문단의 Unfortunately, the tour ran a bit long, and I couldn't see the spaceship building event.를 통해 '만들기' 행사를 놓쳤다는 것을 알 수 있다. 행사 관련 웹페이지(지문 1)의 Competition: Build a scrap metal spacecraft와 연계해 보면, (B)가 정답이 된다.

* paraphrasing: event → activity, building → craft

정답 (B)

워커 씨에 따르면, 그녀는 어떤 행사 활동에 참석하지 못했는가?
(A) 시연
(B) 만들기 대회
(C) 가이드 투어
(D) 워크숍

어휘 craft 공예

189

In the first e-mail, the word "figured" in paragraph 2, line 1, is closest in meaning to

(A) decided*
(B) involved
(C) represented
(D) performed

해당 문장은 그와 인터뷰를 '하기로 했다'는 요지이므로 제시된 선택지들 중 대신 들어갔을 때 맥락이 가장 유사하게 전개되는 어휘는 (A)이다.

정답 (A)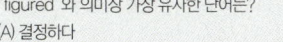

첫 번째 이메일에서, 둘째 문단 첫째 줄에 있는 "figured"와 의미상 가장 유사한 단어는?
(A) 결정하다
(B) 포함하다
(C) 대표하다
(D) 수행하다

어휘 decide 결정하다 involve 포함하다, 관련시키다 represent 대표하다, 대신하다 perform 수행하다, 실시하다

190

What is suggested about Dr. Paxwell?

(A) He has won several awards this year.
(B) He will give multiple presentations at the expo.*
(C) He is a well-known newspaper editor.
(D) He gives demonstrations every year.

지문 2의 I will catch up with Dr. Paxwell tomorrow after he reads some excerpts from his book.에서 내일(10월 28일) '낭독(지문 1: Readings by Dr. Michael Paxwell)'이 있을 것임을 알 수 있다. 지문 3 첫째 문단에서는 I'd like to meet with you tomorrow after your reading.을 통해 내일(10월 30일) 또 낭독이 있다는 것을 알 수 있다. 따라서 이들 정보를 연계했을 때 (B)가 정답이다.

정답 (B)

팩스웰 씨에 대해 드러나는 사항은?
(A) 올해 상을 여러 번 받았다.
(B) 박람회에서 발표를 여러 번 할 것이다.
(C) 유명 신문 편집자이다.
(D) 매년 시연회를 한다.

어휘 well-known 유명한

Questions 191-195 refer to the following article, newspaper editorial, and e-mail.

BREDENBURY (June 11) --- Bredenbury town officials sat down today to discuss the fate of the Mossomin Bridge which has been in need of major repairs for years. Today's meeting was the first of several expected talks on the subject. Although an extensive restoration is one option, several complications may compel the town to demolish the structure.

192 (B) "The cost to restore the bridge will be too great," said town planner Ilkay Tidsale. "The only financially feasible option I can see is replacing the structure."

According to Malcolm Vonda, a well-known structural engineer, traffic flow must also be taken into consideration. "191 Highway 209 will soon have two additional lanes; making it a four-lane highway. The Mossomin Bridge cannot accommodate such a huge increase in the number of vehicles," Vonda says. "I see no other alternative but to build a bigger, modern structure."

The town council would like input from residents on this issue as well. 195 Anyone wishing to share their views can attend a public forum next Monday at 4:30 at Akber Square, in front of the town hall.

어휘 fate 운명 in need of ~을 필요로 하는 extensive 대규모의 restoration 복원, 복구 complication 문제 compel 강요하다, 강제하다, (어떤 반응을) 불러오다 demolish 철거하다 structure 구조(물) restore 복원하다, 복구하다 great 엄청난 financially 재정상, 재정적으로 feasible 실현 가능한 replace 교체하다 traffic flow 교통 흐름 take into consideration ~을 고려하다 lane 길, 차선 accommodate 수용하다 alternative 대안 input 조언 resident 주민 in front of ~의 앞에

Letters to the Editor

192 (C) June 12 – Yesterday's article concerning the future of the Mossomin Bridge prompted me to write this response. The bridge is more than just a bridge; 192 (D) it is an integral part of Bredenbury's culture. For this reason, the town must keep the structure intact. Plus, considering the high revenues generated annually by tourism industry, 192 (B) the short-term costs needed to restore this landmark will prove to be beneficial in the end.

--Pierre Atherton, founding member of the Bredenbury Preservation Society (BPS)

어휘 concerning ~에 대해서 prompt (~하도록) 하다, 촉발하다 response 대답, 답장 integral 필수적인 intact 온전한 considering ~을 고려하면 revenue 수익, 수입 generate 만들어 내다 prove to ~로 판명되다 beneficial 유익한 in the end 마침내, 결국 founding 창립, 설립 preservation 보존

To: members@bredenburypressoc.org
From: isabellecharlebois@bredenburypressoc.org
Date: June 23
Subject: update on Mossomin Bridge

Dear BPS Members,

Congratulations! Thanks to our organization's undeniably strong presence at the town council event, combined with the countless e-mails, letters, and calls to the members of town council, it appears that the bridge is safe from demolition. According to an article in today's Bredenbury Herald, the town has decided to relocate Mossomin Bridge to the south end of the town where only pedestrians will be allowed to use it. The bridge will not be open to motorized vehicles.

195 All of you should feel proud for speaking out and expressing your concerns last Monday. 194 Your actions definitely influenced the town's decision. Great work!

Thank you once again,

Isabelle Charlebois, President
Bredenbury Preservation Society

---

191. In the article, what is indicated about the town of Bredenbury?
(A) It will increase its yearly budget.
(B) It is going to upgrade a road.*
(C) It is enforcing local parking laws.
(D) It will offer special tours to attract tourists.

애서턴 씨에 대해 유추할 수 없는 사항은?
(A) 본다 씨와 함께 일한다.
(B) 티스데일 씨에게 동의하지 않는다.
(C) 6월 11일 신문 기사를 읽었다.
(D) 도시 랜드마크를 소중하게 여긴다.

어휘 disagree 동의하지 않다 value 소중하게 생각하다

192
What is NOT implied about Mr. Atherton?
(A) He works with Mr. Vonda.*
(B) He disagrees with Ms. Tisdale.
(C) He read the June 11 newspaper article.
(D) He values a town landmark.

Mr. Atherton이 작성한 글(지문 2)부터 살펴보자. June 12 – Yesterday's article concerning the future of the Mossomin Bridge prompted me to write this response.에서 (C)를, it is an integral part of Bredenbury's culture에서 (D)를 유추할 수 있다. 한편, 기사(지문 1) 둘째 문단의 The cost to restore the bridge will be too great," said town planner Ilkay Tidsale.과 지문 2 후반부의 the short-term costs needed to restore this landmark will prove to be beneficial in the end를 연계해 (B)를 유추할 수 있다. 따라서 본 문제의 정답은 (A)가 된다.

정답 (A)

이메일에서, 첫째 문단 2번째 줄에 있는 "countless"와 의미상 가장 유사한 단어는?
(A) 알려지지 않은
(B) 등록한
(C) 무수한
(D) 애매모호한

어휘 unreported 알려지지 않은 registered 등록한, 기명의 ambiguous 애매모호한

193
In the e-mail, the word "countless" in paragraph 1, line 2, is closest in meaning to
(A) unreported
(B) registered
(C) numerous*
(D) ambiguous

'무수한, 셀 수 없이 많은'이란 의미의 countless를 대신하기에 가장 적절한 단어는 (C)이다.

정답 (C)

샤를르브 씨는 왜 BPS 회원들을 축하하는가?
(A) 도시의 결정에 영향력을 끼쳐서
(B) 새 부회장을 뽑아서
(C) 뉴스의 1면 주제가 되어서
(D) 도시 프로젝트들을 위한 추가 자금을 모아서

어휘 elect 선출하다 raise (자금, 사람 등을) 모으다 fund 자금, 기금

194
Why does Ms. Charlebois congratulate BPS members?
(A) They helped influence a town decision.*
(B) They elected a new vice-president.
(C) They were the subject of a front-page news story.
(D) They raised additional funds for town projects.

Ms. Charlebois가 BPS members에게 쓴 이메일(지문 3)의 목적에 관련된 문제이다. 첫째 문단에서 상황의 추이를 이야기한 뒤 둘째 문단에서 '여러분이 시의 결정에 영향력을 행사했다(Your actions definitely influenced the town's decision.)'고 하므로 (A)가 가장 적절하다.

정답 (A)

BPS 회원들에 대해 드러나는 사항은?
(A) 구조물 수리를 도왔다.
(B) 많은 회원들이 아크버 광장에서 발언했다.
(C) 많은 회원들이 남단에 살고 있다.
(D) 그들은 매달 첫 주 월요일에 만난다.

어휘 reside in ~에 살다, 거주하다

195
What is suggested about BPS members?
(A) They helped repair a structure.
(B) Many of them spoke out at Akber Square.*
(C) Many of them reside in the south end.
(D) They meet on the first Monday of every month.

BPS members가 수신자인 이메일(지문 3)부터 살펴보면, 마지막 문단에서 All of your should feel proud for speaking out and expressing your concerns last Monday. 라고 하는데, Monday에 대한 내용은 기사(지문 1) 마지막 문장 Anyone wishing to share their views can attend a public forum next Monday at 4:30 at Akber Square, in front of the town hall.에서 확인되므로 (B)가 정답임을 알 수 있다.

정답 (B)

Questions 196-200 refer to the following webpage, receipt, and review.

http://www.grandcanyonexploreadventure.com

| Home | Tours | Reservations | Customer Service |

For over twenty years, our experienced pilots have been conducting spectacular, one of a kind sightseeing tours of the incredible Grand Canyon. Our trips are available for groups of up to six passengers and can be conducted in English, French, Spanish, and Chinese. Take a look at our trip itineraries below and then visit our reservations page for more information about pricing.

- Grand Canyon Helicopter Tour – Available every day from 14:30 P.M. – 15:30 P.M. Spend your afternoon flying over the magnificent Grand Canyon in a helicopter. [196] You will see amazing views of the Hoover Dam, Lake Mead, and the surrounding desert.
- Grand Canyon Helicopter Tour & Lunch – Available every day from 11:30 A.M. – 15:00 P.M. [196] See all the incredible aerial sights listed in the Grand Canyon Helicopter Tour. Following your flight, you will descend 4,000 feet to the canyon floor and enjoy a picnic lunch served on the shore of the Colorado River.
- [197] Ultimate Grand Canyon Tour Package – Available every day from 11:30 A.M. – 18:00 P.M. Enjoy all the benefits of our other packages, including an aerial tour and a picnic lunch. Following lunch, you can explore the historical Native American lands before returning to your helicopter for a second flight to watch the beautiful sunset. [199] Join us for a complimentary steak dinner at the Explore and Adventure Lodge.

어휘 experienced 경험 있는, 노련한 pilot 조종사 conduct (특정한 일을) 하다 spectacular 장관을 이루는 one of a kind 독특한 sightseeing 관광 incredible 믿을 수 없는 available 이용/입수할 수 있는 itinerary (여행) 일정 magnificent 웅장한 aerial 공중의, 대기의 flight 비행(편) descend 내려가다 shore 해안, 호숫가 ultimate 궁극의, 최고의 benefit 혜택, 이득 lodge 오두막, 산장

http://www.grandcanyonexploreadventure.com/reservations/customerreceipt

Customer Reservation Receipt

Date of purchase:	August 3
Customer name:	June Thompson
Reference number:	877573999

Reservation Details	No. of Passengers	Payment Total
[197, 200] Ultimate Grand Canyon Tour Package (August 27 departure)	6 x $80	$480

[199] Payment Method:	Credit Card
Card Number:	111222- 359229
Cardholder's Name:	June Thompson
Card Expiry Date:	07/20

[198] Please retain a copy of this receipt for your records. We recommend that you print a copy and bring it with you on the day of your tour. Furthermore, [197] we recommend that you arrive one hour in advance of your departure time in order to be briefed on all safety precautions.

어휘 receipt 영수증 purchase 구입(품) reference 참고 payment 결제, 납부 departure 출발 expiry 만료, 만기 retain 유지하다, 보유하다 recommend 추천하다 in advance 미리 in order to ~하기 위해 brief 알려 주다, 보고하다 safety 안전, 보안 precaution 예방책, 예방 조치

http://www.grandcanyonexploreadventure.com/customerservice/customerreviews

| Home | Tours | Reservation | Customer Service |

Grand Canyon Explore and Adventure Customer Review:

Overall, I was not very pleased with Grand Canyon Explore and Adventure. I originally reserved the Ultimate Grand Canyon Tour Package for six passengers. However, one of the passengers came down with the flu unexpectedly. [200] Grand Canyon Explore and Adventure refused to refund his ticket, meaning we were forced to pay the full price with only five passengers. Furthermore, despite arriving at the requested time, our departure was delayed by an extra thirty minutes, which cut into our exploration time. The only redeeming factor of the trip was our tour guide, Beth Richards, who was well-spoken and friendly. All in all, I would not recommend Grand Canyon Explore and Adventure to anyone.

June Thompson, August 29

어휘 overall 전반적으로 reserve 예약하다 come down with (병이) 걸리다 flu 독감 unexpectedly 뜻밖에 refuse 거절하다 refund 환불하다 pay 결제하다 despite ~에도 불구하고 extra 추가의, 가외의 cut into (이익, 가치 등을) 줄이다 exploration 탐험 redeeming (결점 등을) 보충하는, 벌충하는 factor 요소 all in all 대체로

196

What is true about the Grand Canyon Helicopter Tour & Lunch Package?

(A) It is designed for large groups.
(B) It includes lunch in a restaurant.
(C) It is the most frequently purchased tour.
(D) It brings the guests over the Hoover Dam and Lake Mead.*

핵심 어구 Grand Canyon Helicopter Tour & Lunch뿐 아니라 여러 여행 상품이 설명된 웹 페이지(지문 1)를 보면, See all the incredible aerial sights listed in the Grand Canyon Helicopter Tour.와 '그랜드 캐니언 헬리콥터 투어' 설명의 You will see amazing views of the Hoover Dam, Lake Mead, and the surrounding desert.를 연계해 (D)가 정답임을 알 수 있다.

정답 (D)

197

What time and day must Ms. Thompson's group arrive for their tour?

(A) At 10:30 A.M. on August 3
(B) At 11:30 A.M. on August 3
(C) At 10:30 A.M. on August 27 *
(D) At 14:30 P.M. on August 27

Ms. Thompson의 영수증(지문 2)에서 Ultimate Grand Canyon Tour Package, August 27 departure를 통해 (C)나 (D)를 추려낼 수 있다. 한편, 후반부 주의 사항에서 we recommend that you arrive one hour in advance of your departure time in order to be briefed on all safety precautions라며 출발 시각보다 한 시간 미리 와 달라고 당부한다. 앞서 언급된 여행 상품을 웹 페이지(지문 1)에서 찾아보면, Ultimate Grand Canyon Tour Package – Available every day from 11:30 A.M. – 18:00 P.M.이므로 (C)가 정답이 된다.

정답 (C)

198 What does Grand Canyon Explore and Adventure recommend Ms. Thompson to do?

(A) Write a review on their website
(B) Pay via bank transfer
(C) Bring some food with them
(D) Save a copy of her receipt*

---

199 What is suggested about Ms. Thompson's tour?

(A) Ms. Thompson paid for it in cash.
(B) It featured a kayak tour along a river.
(C) The guide was rude and unprofessional.
(D) It concluded with a free meal.*

---

200 According to Ms. Thompson, how much should her group have been charged?

(A) $80
(C) $400*
(B) $350
(D) $450

ACTUAL TEST 3

a b **c**
100 200 300

d e f
400 500 600

PART 5

추가로 뽑힌 시의원들의 임명은 내년 초에 진행될 것입니다.

어휘 additional 추가의 councilor (시의회 등의) 의원 take place 개최되다

101
The _____ of additional city councilors will take place at the beginning of next year.

(A) appoint
(B) appoints
(C) appointed
(D) appointment*

〈정관사(The) + _____ + 전치사(of)〉의 빈칸에 적합한 성분은 명사 (D)뿐이다. appoint 임명하다, 지명하다 appointment 약속, 임명

정답 (D)

노던 스타 풋웨어 사장은 사업 합병 제안서를 쓰고 있다고 말했습니다.

어휘 footwear 신발 state 진술하다, 말하다 draft 초안/원고를 작성하다 proposal 제안(서)

102
The president of Northern Star Footwear stated that _____ is drafting a proposal for a business merger.

(A) him
(B) he*
(C) his
(D) himself

적절한 인칭대명사의 격을 찾는 문제이다. 빈칸은 that 절의 주어 자리이므로 (B)가 정답이 된다.

정답 (B)

윌슨 씨는 해외 여행을 떠나기 전에 자신의 일정을 업데이트해야 합니다.

어휘 itinerary (여행) 일정 overseas 해외로

103
Ms. Wilson should update her itinerary before she _____ for her trip overseas.

(A) will leave
(B) leaves*
(C) leaving
(D) left

시간/조건을 나타내는 종속절에서는 미래의 일이라도 현재시제를 써야 한다. 따라서 (B)가 정답이다. leave 떠나다

* 시간/조건 부사절: 미래에 일어나는 일이라도 조건절에는 현재시제 사용!
시간을 나타내는 접속사 when, while, before, after, as soon as, until, once
조건을 나타내는 접속사 if, unless, as long as

정답 (B)

보고서에 따르면, 최근 시장 사무실과의 협상이 호의적으로 진행되지 않았습니다.

어휘 according to ~에 따르면 mayor 시장 progress 진행되다 favorably 호의적으로

104
According to the report, the recent _____ with the city mayor's office did not progress favorably.

(A) negotiator
(B) negotiations*
(C) negotiated
(D) negotiates

〈정관사(the) + 형용사(recent) + _____〉의 빈칸에는 명사 (A)나 (B)가 들어갈 수 있는데 의미상 '최근의 협상'이 타당하므로 (B)가 정답이다. negotiator 협상자, 교섭자 negotiation 협상, 교섭 negotiate 협상하다, 교섭하다

정답 (B)

105

Several of the candidates were given interviews, but only a few of _____ were chosen for the positions.

(A) we
(B) us*
(C) our
(D) ourselves

지원자들 중 몇 명이 면접 기회를 얻었지만, 우리 중 소수만이 그 직책에 뽑혔습니다.

어휘 candidate 지원자, 후보자 choose 선택하다 position 직(책)

전치사 of의 목적어가 필요하므로 목적격인 (B)가 들어갈 수 있다.

정답 (B)

106

The merger was successful because all the partners played a role in _____ planning the deal.

(A) strategy
(B) strategic
(C) strategized
(D) strategically*

모든 파트너가 계약을 전략적으로 계획하는 데 제 역할을 했기 때문에 합병은 성공적이었다.

어휘 merger 합병 play a role 역할을 하다 deal 거래, 합의

품사 문제가 제시되면 문장 구조를 파악해야 한다. 전치사 in의 목적어로 동명사 planning이 제시되어 있고, 빈칸은 동명사를 수식하는 자리이므로 부사 (D)가 정답이 된다. strategy 전략 strategic 전략적인, 전략상 중요한 strategize 전략을 짜다 strategically 전략적으로

정답 (D)

107

After completing his degree at an American university, Paul Bouchard _____ to Paris to teach at a local school.

(A) visited
(B) returned*
(C) occurred
(D) related

미국 대학에서 학위를 수료한 후, 폴 부차드는 마을 학교에서 가르치기 위해 파리로 돌아왔습니다.

어휘 complete 완성하다, 완료하다 degree 학위

빈칸 다음에 방향 및 목적지를 나타내는 전치사 to가 쓰였으므로, 장소를 나타내는 목적어가 바로 뒤따라 와야 하는 (A)는 소거할 수 있으며, (C)와 (D)는 맥락상 어울리지 않는다. 〈occur to + 사람〉은 '~에게 생각이 떠오르다'란 뜻이고 relate A to B는 'A를 B에 결부시키다'는 뜻이다. 따라서 (B)가 정답이 된다. visit 방문하다 return 되돌아 오다 occur to 떠오르다, 생각나다 be related to ~와 관계가 있다

정답 (B)

108

Please ensure all deliveries are brought to the side _____ of the supermarket.

(A) entrant
(B) entered
(C) entering
(D) entrance*

모든 배송품은 슈퍼마켓 옆 문으로 들어오게 해 주십시오.

어휘 ensure 반드시 ~하게 하다, 보장하다 delivery 배송, 배달

〈정관사(the) + 형용사(side) + _____〉의 빈칸에는 명사 (A)나 (D)가 들어갈 수 있는데 의미상 '옆 문'이 적절하므로 (D)가 정답이다. entrant 갓 들어온 사람, 출전자, 참가자 enter 들어가다 entrance 문

정답 (D)

도시 계획가들은 일주일에 몇 번씩 모여 다음 도시 개발 프로젝트에 대한 계획을 논의했습니다.

어휘 discuss 논의하다, 토론하다 upcoming 다음의, 다가오는 development 개발

109

The urban planners met several times a week to discuss plans for the upcoming downtown development _____.

(A) statement
(B) permission
(C) project*
(D) ability

문맥상 '도시 계획가들의 논의 주제'로 '개발 프로젝트'가 자연스럽다. 따라서 (C)가 정답이다. statement 진술, 성명 permission 허락, 허가 ability 능력, 재능

정답 (C)

그 판매 직은 대학을 갓 졸업한 사람들에게 열릴 것입니다. 즉, 지원자들은 학위 프로그램을 수료한 분이어야 한다는 뜻입니다.

어휘 graduate (대학) 졸업자 mean 뜻하다, 의미하다 complete 완수하다, 완성하다 degree 학위

110

The sales position will be open to new graduates, _____ means applicants must have completed a degree program.

(A) whoever
(B) who
(C) which*
(D) whatever

콤마로 연결된 두 절의 관계를 고려할 때, 빈칸 뒤의 동사 means(의미하다)의 주어가 되는 것은 앞 문장 전체를 의미한다. 즉, 앞뒤 절을 접속사와 주어로 연결한다면 and it(이때 it은 앞 문장 전체를 의미)이 될 수 있다. 따라서 이러한 경우에 사용할 수 있는 관계사는 (C)뿐이다. whoever 누구든 whatever 무엇이든

정답 (C)

회사에 개설된 강좌들은 단기 임시직 및 정규 직원들 모두에게 제공됩니다.

어휘 course 강의, 강좌 seasonal 계절적인, 계절에 따른 hire 고용(인), 신입 사원

111

Courses at the company _____ to both seasonal hires and long-term employees.

(A) are offered*
(B) have offered
(C) an offer
(D) offering

빈칸은 서술부에 해당되므로 (A)나 (B)를 우선 고려할 수 있는데 강좌는 직원들에게 '제공되는' 것이므로 수동태를 나타내는 (A)가 정답이다. offer 제안하다, 제공하다, 제안, 제공, (단기) 할인

* 4형식 동사가 3형식 문장으로 쓰일 때 필요한 전치사
give, tell, teach, show, lend, pass, offer + 직접목적어 + to + 간접목적어
buy, make, find, get + 직접목적어 + for + 간접목적어

정답 (A)

벤슨 뮤직 스쿨은 보이드 애비뉴의 롤랜드 치과를 지나자마자 있습니다.

어휘 situate 위치시키다 dental 치과의 clinic 진료소

112

The Benson Music School is situated just _____ the Roland Dental Clinic on Boyd Avenue.

(A) into
(B) over
(C) among
(D) past*

'학원은 병원을 지나자마자 있다'는 요지가 완성되어야 가장 자연스러운 문장이다. 따라서 (D)가 정답이 된다. past (위치상으로 ~을) 지나서

정답 (D)

113

Following a mandatory probationary period, full-time employees are _____ to receive benefits.

(A) beneficial
(B) eligible*
(C) convenient
(D) relevant

의무 수습 기간 후에, 상근 직원은 직원 혜택을 받을 수 있게 됩니다.

어휘 following ~에 이어 mandatory 의무적인 probationary 시험적인, 수습의, 견습의 period 기간 benefit 혜택, 이득

'~할 자격이 있다'는 의미의 be eligible to 구문을 알면 쉽게 해결할 수 있는 문제이다. 같은 의미의 〈be eligible for + 명사〉 구문도 참고로 알아 두자. beneficial 유익한, 이로운 eligible ~을 가질 수 있는 convenient 편리한 relevant 관련 있는, 적절한

* 〈be동사 + 형용사 + to부정사〉 용례
be able to ~할 수 있다   be anxious to ~하기를 갈망하다   be due to ~할 예정이다
be willing to 기꺼이 ~하다   be afraid to ~하기를 꺼리다   be liable to ~하기 쉽다
be reluctant to 마지못해 ~하다

정답 (B)

114

The Weston Grant _____ outstanding research conducted in the science and technology field.

(A) recognizes*
(B) assumes
(C) reassures
(D) moderates

웨스턴 기금은 과학 기술 분야에서 수행된 뛰어난 연구에 수여됩니다.

어휘 grant 보조금, 기금 outstanding 뛰어난, 걸출한 research 연구, 조사 conduct (특정한 일을) 하다 field 분야

'뛰어난 연구에 기금을 준다'는 요지의 문장이 완성되어야 가장 자연스럽다. 따라서 '공로를 인정하다 (그래서 상을 주다)'라는 뜻의 (A)가 정답이 된다. recognize 인정하다, 표창하다 assume 추정하다, 상정하다, (책임을) 맡다 reassure 안심시키다 moderate 누그러지다, 누그러뜨리다

정답 (A)

115

Every staff member is given an employee handbook so they can _____ remind themselves of procedures.

(A) consecutively
(B) standardly
(C) namely
(D) easily*

모든 직원들이 스스로 업무 절차를 쉽게 상기할 수 있도록 각 직원들에게 직원 편람을 주었습니다.

어휘 handbook 편람, 안내서 remind 상기시키다 procedure 절차, 방법

조동사(can)와 본동사(remind) 사이에 들어가 적절하게 꾸며 줄 부사를 찾는 문제로, 문맥상 '(곁에 두고) 쉽게 참고할 수 있도록'이라는 요지를 완성해야 한다. 따라서 (D)가 정답이 된다. 참고로, (A)는 'for three consecutive days(3일 연속하여)'와 같은 형태로 자주 쓰이며, (C)는 ', or'로 paraphrasing할 수 있다. consecutively 연속하여 standardly 표준적으로 namely 즉, 다시 말해

정답 (D)

116

Sanford Shoes is the most popular outlet in the city because its products are always durable, _____ priced, and fashionable.

(A) reason
(B) reasoning
(C) reasonable
(D) reasonably*

샌포드 슈즈는 제품이 항상 튼튼하고, 가격이 적정하며, 패셔너블하므로 시내에서 가장 인기 있는 매장입니다.

어휘 outlet 직판점, 전문 매장 product 제품, 생산품 durable 내구성이 있는, 오래 가는 priced 값이 붙은

빈칸이 뒤의 형용사 priced(가격이 매겨진)를 수식하는 자리이니 부사 (D)가 정답이다. reasoning 추리, 추론 reasonable 타당한, (가격이) 적정한 reasonably 타당하게, 적정하게

정답 (D)

브레난의 전 직원은 고객님의 주택 장식 사안에 대해 직접 가서든 전화 통화로든 기꺼이 논의합니다.

어휘 in person 직접, 몸소

117

All staff at Brennan's are _____ to discuss your home decorating needs either in person or over the phone.

(A) delighting (B) delighted* (C) delights (D) delight

빈칸은 be 동사와 서술부를 이룬다. 따라서 (C)나 (D)는 바로 소거할 수 있다. 나머지에서 to 이하를 '기쁨으로 여기는 상황'을 나타낼 수 있는 것은 (B)이다. 〈사람 + be delighted/pleased/happy to + 동사원형〉을 '~해서 기쁘다, 기꺼이 ~하다'라는 의미의 관용 어구로 익혀 두자. delighting 기쁘게 하는 delighted 기뻐하는 delight 기쁨을 주다, 기쁨을 주는 것

정답 (B)

로즈 직물 제조 업체는 최고 최신 생산 장비와 자재를 사용합니다.

어휘 textile 직물, 옷감 manufacturer 제조 업체 manufacturing 제조(업)의 equipment 기기, 장비 material 재료, 자재

118

Rose Textile Manufacturers uses the _____ latest manufacturing equipment and materials.

(A) so (B) more (C) very* (D) much

형용사의 최상급인 latest 앞에 빈칸이 제시되어 있는데, 최상급 앞에서 강조의 뜻을 나타내는 (C)가 정답이다. 참고로, very는 동사를 수식하지 못한다는 점을 유념하자(I very thank you처럼 쓸 수 없다). very가 명사 앞에 놓여 the very man과 같이 쓰인다면 '바로 그 ~'를 의미한다.

* 최상급 수식

quite/by far the ~est, the ~est ever/possible, the single/very ~est

정답 (C)

리비 브랜드의 모든 냉장고에는 다른 언급이 없는 한 2년짜리 보증서가 딸려 있습니다.

어휘 refrigerator 냉장고 come with ~이 딸려오다 otherwise 다르게, 달리, 그렇지 않으면

119

All Libby brand refrigerators come with a two-year guarantee _____ stated otherwise.

(A) whereas (B) below (C) neither (D) unless*

'별다른 말이 없다면 전부 2년짜리 보증이 된다'는 요지를 완성해야 가장 자연스럽다. 따라서 (D)가 정답이다. whereas 반면 unless ~하지 않는 한

* unless 사용 용례

unless otherwise indicated 별도의 표시가 없으면
unless otherwise agreed 별도 합의된 사항이 없으면
unless otherwise noted 별도 언급이 없으면
unless I'm mistaken 착각한 것이 아니라면
unless you have further questions 더 이상 질문이 없다면

정답 (D)

애콘 밸리 아파트를 깨끗하고 안전하게 유지하는 데 참여해 주셔서 지역 사회는 당신께 감사드립니다.

120

The community thanks you for your _____ in keeping Acorn Valley Apartments clean and safe.

(A) participant (B) participation*
(C) participate (D) participated

〈소유격 인칭대명사(your) + _____ + 전치사(in)〉의 빈칸에 들어갈 수 있는 것은 명사 (A)나 (B)인데 문맥상 당신의 '참여에 감사하다는 의미가 자연스러우므로 (B)가 정답이 된다. participant 참가자 participation 참가 participate 참가하다

* in과 함께 자주 쓰이는 명사

change in ~에 있어서의 변화 experience in ~에 있어서의 경험 rise/increase in ~에 있어서의 증가 decrease/fall/reduction in ~에 있어서의 감소/하락 delay in ~에 있어서의 지체 difficulty/interest/pleasure in ~에 있어서의 어려움/흥미/기쁨

정답 (B)

121 The interest rates were a key _____ in the CEO's decision to switch to the Emerald Bank.

(A) factor*
(B) position
(C) instructor
(D) composition

CEO가 에메랄드 뱅크로 바꾸기로 결정한 것의 주요 원인은 금리였습니다.

어휘 interest rate 금리, 이율 decision 결정 switch 전환하다, 바꾸다

'금리가 거래처 변경에 결정적인 요인이었다'는 요지를 완성해야 가장 적절하므로 (A)가 알맞다. factor 요인, 요소 position 직(책) instructor 강사 composition 구성 (요소)

정답 (A)

122 The health inspector will arrive at an unforeseen date _____ ensure the conditions of the inspection are fair.

(A) even if
(B) in order to*
(C) after all
(D) given that

위생 조사관은 검사 조건이 공정하도록 하기 위해서 예상치 못한 날짜에 올 것입니다.

어휘 inspector 조사관, 감독관 arrive 도착하다 unforeseen 예측하지 못한, 뜻밖의 condition 조건 inspection 조사, 점검 fair 공정한

빈칸 이하는 '조사관이 불시에 찾아오는 목적'이 되어야 맥락상 타당하다. 따라서 (B)가 정답이다. even if ~라 할지라도 in order to ~하기 위해서 after all 결국 given that ~으로 보건대, ~을 고려하면

정답 (B)

123 Peter Nugent's novel was made into an adventure movie two years ago after Winston Studios obtained _____ from Nugent's grandson.

(A) permission*
(B) suggestion
(C) comparison
(D) registration

피터 뉴젠트의 소설은 윈스턴 스튜디오가 뉴젠트의 손자로부터 허가를 얻은 후, 2년 전에 모험 영화로 만들어졌습니다.

어휘 obtain 얻다, 획득하다 grandson 손자

소설이 영화로 만들어지려면 저작권자의 '허가'가 필요하다. 따라서 (A)가 정답이다. permission 허락, 허가 suggestion 제안 comparison 비교 registration 등록, 신고

* obtain과 함께 자주 쓰이는 명사
obtain advice/information 충고/정보를 얻다
obtain approval 승인을 얻다
obtain admission to ~에 들어갈 수 있는 허가를 받다
obtain a patent 특허를 따다
obtain (secure) employment (확실한) 일자리를 얻다
obtain a copy of the report 보고서 한 부를 입수하다

정답 (A)

124 The mayor's office has issued a statement _____ the use of tax revenue to repair roads in the coming year.

(A) excluding
(B) during
(C) following
(D) regarding*

시장 사무실에서 내년에 도로를 수리하는 데 세수를 이용하겠다는 내용에 대하여 성명서를 발표했습니다.

어휘 mayor 시장 issue 발행하다, 발부하다 statement 성명(서) tax revenue 세수(입) repair 수리하다, 수선하다

빈칸 이하가 성명서(statement)의 주제이므로 '~에 대하여'라는 의미의 (D)가 정답이 된다. 유사 표현 concerning/about/as to/pertaining to ~도 익혀 두자. excluding ~을 제외하고 following ~에 이어 regarding ~에 관하여

정답 (D)

델버트 콘도미니엄 타워는 지하철역 두 곳에서 도보 거리인 편리한 위치에 입지해 있습니다.

어휘 condominium 아파트, 공동 주택 locate (특정 위치에) 두다 walking distance 도보 거리

125
The Delbert Condominium Tower is _____ located within walking distance of two subway stations.
(A) conveniently* (B) consistently
(C) continually (D) commonly

문맥상 '입지 조건'에 해당되므로 빈칸에 들어가기에 가장 적절한 어휘는 (A)이다. '편리한 위치에 있다'는 뜻의 be conveniently located는 매우 자주 사용되는 collocation(연어)이다. conveniently 편리하게 consistently 지속적으로 continually 계속적으로 commonly 흔히, 보통

정답 (A)

인턴들은 새 상근직에 지원하고 싶다면 지원서를 새로 제출해야 합니다.

어휘 application 신청(서) apply for 신청하다

126
Interns should _____ new applications if they wish to apply for any of the new full-time positions.
(A) reply (B) submit*
(C) vacate (D) oppose

문맥상 '지원서를 제출하라'는 요지를 완성해야 하므로 (B)가 정답이다. 참고로, apply 다음에 목적어가 바로 오면 '바르다, 칠하다'라는 의미이고 전치사 for 대신 to가 오면 (apply to) '~에 적용하다'라는 의미를 나타낸다. reply 대답하다 submit 제출하다 vacate 비우다, 떠나다 oppose 반대하다, 겨루다

정답 (B)

레이놀드 제조사의 기업 강령에 대한 홀라한 씨의 수정된 원고는 그 회사의 목표를 정확히 드러냅니다.

어휘 revise 변경하다, 수정하다 draft 초고, 원고 manufacturing 제조(업) mission statement 성명, 진술 express 나타내다, 표현하다 goal 목표

127
Ms. Houlahan's revised draft of Reynold Manufacturing's mission statement expresses the goals of the company _____.
(A) precise (B) more precise
(C) preciseness (D) precisely*

구조상 〈주어(Ms. Houlahan's ~ statement) + 타동사(expresses) + 목적어(the ~ company)〉의 완벽한 3형식 문장이므로 빈칸은 생략되어도 무방하다. 따라서 문장 끝에서 수식의 역할을 할 수 있는 부사 (D)만 들어갈 수 있다. precise 정확한, 정밀한 preciseness 정확성 precisely 정확히

정답 (D)

하절기 동안 공원이 개방되지만, 특정 구역은 대중이 접근할 수 없습니다.

어휘 restrict 제한하다, 한정하다 access 접근하다, 이용하다

128
_____ the park is open during the summer months, the public is restricted from accessing certain areas.
(A) While* (B) When
(C) For (D) But

콤마 전후로 상반된 내용(open ↔ restricted)이 연결되므로 '역접'을 나타내는 접속사 (A)가 가장 적절하다. (D)도 의미상 '역접'을 나타내지만 본 문장과 같이 두 절이 나란히 배치될 때에는 문두에 쓸 수 없다.

정답 (A)

129

_____ the education level of Paul Rogers, it is no wonder that he is the highest-paid speaker at the convention.

(A) About
(B) Given*
(C) Upon
(D) Since

빈칸부터 콤마 앞까지의 내용이 '돈을 가장 많이 받는 근거'가 되어야 흐름상 가장 자연스러우므로 '~을 고려하면'이라는 의미의 (B) Given이 정답이다. 이때 given은 전치사로 사용되었으며 considering과 유의어이다.

정답 (B)

폴 로저스의 교육 수준을 고려하면, 그가 컨벤션에서 돈을 가장 많이 받는 강연자인 것이 놀랍지 않습니다.

어휘 education 교육 it is no wonder that ~인 것은 놀랄 일이 아니다

130

Considering all the hot weather we're having, the number of people using public swimming pools is _____ to increase.

(A) covered
(B) sought
(C) limited
(D) bound*

'틀림없이 ~할 것이다'라는 의미의 관용구 be bound to를 알면 쉽게 정답 (D)를 찾을 수 있다. be sure to도 함께 익혀 두자. cover 가리다, 포함하다 seek 찾다, 구하다 limit 제한하다

* be bound to = be sure to, be certain to
* a bus/train bound for ~행 버스/기차

정답 (D)

이렇게 더운 날씨를 겪고 있음을 고려하면, 공공 수영장을 이용하는 사람들 수가 분명 늘 것입니다.

어휘 considering ~을 고려하면, ~을 감안하면 increase 증가하다

PART 6

에코 문구 용품사는 고객님의 주문품을 최대한 빨리 보내 드리기 위해 애쓰고 있습니다. 배송이 지체되는 것 같아 걱정되신다면, 저희 배송 정책을 유념해 주십시오. 예상 배송 시간은 고객님께서 결제 중에 선택한 배송 방법에 따라, 4일에서 4주까지 걸릴 수 있습니다. ─────── 저희는 배송 예상일을 정확하게 예측하려 노력하지만, 어떤 주문품은 고객님 댁에 도착하기까지 더 오랜 시간이 걸릴 수도 있습니다. 주문품이 너무 지체된다 싶으시면, 저희에게 바로 연락 주십시오. 문제를 살펴보고 고객님의 배송품 상태를 알려 드리겠습니다.

어휘 stationery 문구류, 문방구 supply 용품, 비품 ship 배송하다 order 주문하다, 주문 concern 우려 사항, 걱정 shipment 선적(물) delay 지체시키다, 지연시키다 policy 정책 expected 예상되는 delivery 배송, 배달 range from A up to B 범위가 A에서 B에 이르다 depend on ~에 따라 다르다 method 방법 choose 선택하다 ensure 보장하다, 반드시 ~하게 하다 estimate 견적(서) accurate 정확한, 정밀한 arrive 도착하다 excessively 지나치게, 매우 hesitate 망설이다, 주저하다 contact 연락하다 immediately 즉시 status 상태

Questions 131-134 refer to the following information.

At Echo Stationery Supplies, we try to ship your orders as quickly as we can. If you have concerns that your shipment has been delayed, please ---**131**--- our shipping policies. Our expected delivery times may range from 4 days up to 4 weeks, which depends on the method of shipping customers choose during checkout. ---**132**--- We try to ensure our shipping estimates are accurate; however, some orders may take ---**133**--- to arrive at your door. If you have found that your order is excessively ---**134**---, do not hesitate to contact us immediately. We promise to look into the problem and let you know the status of your shipment.

131

(A) note*
(B) send
(C) prepare
(D) require

'지체가 우려될 경우 배송 정책을 확인해 보라'는 요지의 문장이 완성되어야 맥락상 가장 적절하다. 따라서 빈칸에 어울리는 어휘는 '유념하다, 주의해서 보다'라는 뜻의 (A)이다. note 유념하다 prepare 준비하다 require 요청하다

정답 (A)

132

(A) Returned items will be eligible for exchanges only, not refunds.
(B) Contact our specialists to get an updated list of all of our new products.
(C) An approximate delivery date is indicated on your receipt.*
(D) Visit our online feedback section and let us know how well we served you.

(A) 반품된 제품은 환불은 안 되고 교환만 가능합니다.
(B) 모든 신제품이 나열된 갱신된 목록을 얻으시려면 저희 전문가들에게 연락하십시오.
(C) 대략적인 배송 날짜는 고객님 영수증에 나와 있습니다.
(D) 온라인 피드백 섹션을 방문해서 저희 서비스가 어땠는지 알려 주십시오.

빈칸 앞에서는 주문품 결제 시에 선택한 방법에 따라 배송 기간이 달라진다고 말하고 있는데, 빈칸 뒤에서는 배송 예상 날짜(shipping estimate)가 언급되고 있다. 따라서 이 두 내용의 중간 단계로 어울리는 것은 (C)이다. item 물건, 제품 eligible ~을 할 수 있는, 자격이 되는 exchange 교환 refund 환불 product 제품, 생산품 approximate 거의 비슷한, 근사치인 indicate 가리키다, 나타내다 receipt 영수증

정답 (C)

336 해설집

133
(A) length (B) lengthy
(C) longer* (D) longest

'시간이 걸리다'는 표현은 It takes long. 또는 It takes a long time.으로 나타낼 수 있다. 선택지들 중 long은 없으므로, long의 비교급인 longer를 넣을 수 있다. length 길이, 시간 lengthy 너무 긴, 장황한

정답 (C)

134
(A) different (B) delayed*
(C) overpriced (D) greater

전체 맥락상 '배송'에 대한 안내이므로 작성자 측에 연락할 경우는 배송이 너무 (B) '지체될' 때라는 의미가 되어야 자연스럽다. overpriced 너무 비싼

정답 (B)

4월 24일

몇 달간의 논의 끝에, 나카윅 시의회가 마침내 DRTL 엔터프라이즈와의 계약을 승인했다. 계약 조항에 의거, DRTL은 배렛 스트리트 동단의 30에이커짜리 부지를 개발할 것이다. 세부 제안서에는 그 지역의 소매점 및 사무 건물들의 건설 필요성도 담고 있다. 나카윅 시장 레오나 호베이는 이 프로젝트가 시와 주변 지역에 경제적인 혜택을 가져다줄 것이라며 낙관적으로 본다. 호베이 시장은 이렇게 말했다. "그 프로젝트는 상근직 300개를 만들 것이라 예상됩니다. 한동안, 계속된 지체로 인해 프로젝트를 전부 취소할 수밖에 없을 것이라 여겼죠." ————. DRTL 대변인 제프 퍼킨스는 이 개발이 마무리되는 데 3년이 걸릴 것이라 본다. 동시에, 그는 차질이 더 있을 수도 있다고 사람들에게 주의를 준다. "물론, 저희가 시의회에 최선의 추정을 제공했지만, 그렇다 하더라도, 일어날 모든 일에 대해서 예측할 방법은 없습니다."라고 퍼킨스는 말했다.

어휘 council 의회 approve 승인하다 agreement 합의, 계약 term 조항 lot 지역, 부지 proposal 제안(서) call for ~을 필요로 하다 retail 소매 mayor 시장 optimistic 낙관적인 benefit 혜택, 이득 ongoing 진행 중인 postponement 연기, 미루기 all together 다 함께, 동시에 spokesperson 대변인 caution 주의를 주다, 경고하다 setback 차질 provide 제공하다 predict 예측하다, 예견하다

Questions 135-138 refer to the following article.

April 24
After months of discussions, Nackawic Town Council has finally approved an agreement with DRTL Enterprises. Under the terms of the agreement, DRTL ---**135**--- the 30-acre lot on the east end of Barrett Street. The detailed proposal calls for the building of both retail shops and offices in the area. Nackawic's mayor, Leona Hovey, is optimistic that the project will bring ---**136**--- benefits to the town and surrounding areas. "It is expected to create 300 full-time jobs," says Hovey. "For a while, I felt the ongoing postponements would force us to cancel the project all together." ---**137**---. DRTL spokesperson, Jeff Perkins believes the development will take three years to finish. At the same time, he cautions people that there may be more setbacks. "Of course, we provided the town council with our very best ---**138**---, but even so, we have no way of predicting everything that will happen," Perkins said.

135
(A) to develop (B) will develop*
(C) has developed (D) could have developed

빈칸이 전체 문장의 술어이므로 (A)는 바로 소거할 수 있다. 첫 문장에서 approved an agreement라고 했으므로 부지 개발은 이제 시행될 예정임을 알 수 있다. 따라서 미래시제 (B)가 정답이다. develop 개발하다

정답 (B)

136
(A) economic* (B) unforeseen
(C) environmental (D) frequent

'개발 프로젝트가 지역에 가져다줄 혜택'을 설명하는 데 가장 적절한 형용사는 (A)이다. economic 경제의, 실리적인 unforeseen 예측하지 못한, 뜻밖의 environmental 환경의, 환경과 관련된 frequent 잦은, 빈번한

정답 (A)

137

(A) While the town is eager to get moving on this, delays are inevitable for major developments like this.*
(B) Local residents, however, have approached us with legitimate concerns about the high noise levels construction will create.
(C) Members of town council are set to vote on four different proposals from well-known architects.
(D) Despite the town's promise to grant the developers a contract, they may now have to look at other options.

(A) 시에서 이것을 간절히 진전시키고자 하더라도, 이렇게 큰 개발 프로젝트에는 지체가 불가피하게 발생한다.
(B) 하지만 지역 주민들은 공사가 만들어 낼 강도 높은 소음에 대해 정당한 우려 사항을 우리에게 이야기했다.
(C) 시의회 의원들은 유명한 건축가들이 낸 다른 제안서 네 가지에 투표를 할 예정이다.
(D) 개발 업체들에게 계약을 승인하겠다는 시의 약속에도 불구하고, 이제 그들은 다른 선택 사항을 찾아야 할 수도 있다.

'프로젝트 지체로 인한 우려와 실망감'을 나타내는 문장에 이어진 것이므로 이를 뒷받침해 줄 (A)가 가장 적절하다. eager 열렬한, 간절히 바라는 delay 지체, 지연 inevitable 불가피한, 필연적인 resident 주민 approach (말하기 위해) 접촉하다, 접근하다 legitimate 정당한, 타당한 concern 우려 사항, 걱정 construction 공사, 건설 be set to ~할 예정이다 vote 투표하다 architect 건축가 grant 승인하다, 허락하다 contract 계약(서) option 선택(권)

정답 (A)

138

(A) argument
(B) background
(C) estimate*
(D) combination

문맥상 '프로젝트 일정에 대한 가장 최선의 추정을 냈지만, 변수는 늘 있게 마련이다'라는 요지가 완성되어야 가장 타당하다. 따라서 (C)가 정답이 된다. argument 논쟁, 언쟁 background 배경 estimate 추정, 견적(서) combination 조합, 결합

정답 (C)

로데릭 오페라 하우스는 멜라니 벡의 새 뮤지컬, '재즈의 탄생' 공연을 연장할 것이라고 발표했다. 티켓 수요가 증가했기 때문에, 쇼는 8월 말까지 매일 밤 공연될 예정이다. 이 뮤지컬은 유명 뮤지컬 극장 비평가 제프리 오프라이의 혹평을 받았기에, 이 발표는 뜻밖이었다. ──────── 하지만, 지난주에 3일 밤 연속으로 쇼가 매진됐다. 오페라 하우스 직원들에 따르면, 쇼는 보통 때 뮤지컬을 잘 보러 오지 않는 노년층을 끌었다. 이 새로운 관객들은 벡이 새롭게 해석한 재즈 명곡들을 듣는 데 흥분한 듯하다.

어휘 announce 발표하다 lengthen 연장하다, 늘이다 due to ~때문에 increase 증가 nightly 밤마다 하는 announcement 발표 unexpected 뜻밖의 receive 받다 criticism 비판 renowned 유명한 critic 비평가 sold out 표가 매진된 in a row 잇달아, 연이어 according to ~에 따르면 representative 직원 attract 끌어모으다, 유치하다 crowd 군중 normally 보통 (때는) attend 참석하다, 출석하다 attendee 참석자 number (공연에서 여러 개 중의 한) 노래 reinvent 다른 모습을 보여 주다, 개혁하다

Questions 139-142 refer to the following article.

Roderick Opera House has announced that it will lengthen its run of Melanie Beck's new musical, The Birth of Jazz. Due to an increase in ---**139**--- for tickets, the show will be playing nightly until the end of August. The announcement was unexpected, as the musical received ---**140**--- criticism from renowned musical theatre critic Jeffrey O'pry. ---**141**--- However, last week the show was sold out three nights in a row. According to representatives of the opera house, the show has been attracting an older crowd who may not normally attend musicals. The new attendees are ---**142**--- excited about hearing the great jazz numbers reinvented by Beck.

139
(A) demand*   (B) demanded
(C) demanding   (D) to demand

전치사 in 다음에 목적어가 필요하므로 명사인 (A)가 정답이다. 동명사로 볼 수 있는 (C)도 문법적으로 고려할 수 있지만, 의미에 맞맞은 명사가 존재하는 경우 동명사를 대신 쓰지 않는다. demand 수요, 요구하다 demanding 부담이 큰, 요구가 많은

정답 (A)

140
(A) brilliant   (B) deep
(C) harsh*   (D) prompt

공연 연장 발표가 '의외의 소식'이 되려면 공연에 대한 반응이 나빴다는 의미가 완성되어야 전개상 타당하다. 따라서 '혹평'을 나타낼 (C)가 가장 적절하다. brilliant 훌륭한, 멋진 deep 깊은 harsh 가혹한, 냉혹한 prompt 즉각적인

정답 (C)

141

(A) Guests at the musical were mostly from out of town.
(B) The final show will be held on August 24th.
(C) Following the review, ticket sales dropped dramatically.*
(D) Similarly, the theater has been suffering for years.

(A) 뮤지컬 손님들은 대체로 시외에서 왔다.
(B) 마지막 쇼는 8월 24일에 진행될 예정이다.
(C) 그 평가 후, 티켓 판매가 극적으로 떨어졌다.
(D) 유사하게, 극장은 수년째 고초를 겪고 있다.

앞서 언급된 '유명 비평가의 평가(criticism from renowned musical theatre critic)'가 가져 온 결과가 빈칸에 적절하게 들어갈 수 있는데, 다음 문장에서는 However를 통해 역접하며 '매진 상황(the show was sold out)'을 언급하므로 '표 판매가 급락했다'는 내용의 (C)가 정답이 된다. mostly 주로, 일반적으로 be held 열리다 following ~에 이어 drop 떨어지다, 하락하다 dramatically 극적으로 similarly 비슷하게, 유사하게 suffer 고통 받다, 시달리다

정답 (C)

142

(A) apparent
(B) more apparent
(C) apparentness
(D) apparently*

적절한 문장 성분을 찾는 문제이다. 빈칸이 들어간 문장은 이미 구조상 완벽하므로 서술부를 수식하며 생략 가능한 부사 (D)가 정답이다. be와 p.p. 사이의 빈칸에는 부사가 정답이라는 공식을 외워 두자. apparent 분명한 apparentness 명백함 apparently 듣자 하니, 보아 하니

정답 (D)

발신: 고객 관리
수신: 폴 카나가와
날짜: 10월 16일
제목: 애틀랜틱 뮤직 트렌드에 오신 것을 환영합니다
첨부: 서식

카나가와 씨 귀하,

애틀랜틱 뮤직 트렌드를 구독해 주셔서 대단히 감사합니다! 이제 고객님은 캐나다의 대서양 인접 지역 전역에서 앞으로 진행될 음악 강좌, 페스티벌, 콘서트에 관한 상세한 정보를 받게 됩니다. 첫 번째 잡지는 20일까지 댁에 도착할 것입니다. ――― 그 다음부터, 매달 첫째 주에 각 호가 발송될 예정입니다. 이 구독으로, 고객님은 온라인 비디오, 노래 녹음, 기사, 일정, 콘서트 티켓 정보까지도 무제한으로 이용하시게 됩니다. 첨부된 등록서 맨 아래 적힌 사용자 ID와 여덟 자리 비밀번호를 이용해 저희 웹사이트에 로그인만 하시면 됩니다.

그럼 이만,
베로니카 반 제일
고객 담당자

어휘 Atlantic 대서양의 attachment 첨부 subscribe (예약) 구독하다 upcoming 다가오는 coast 연안 issue (잡지 등의) 호 subscription 구독 unlimited 무제한의 digit 숫자, 자리 수 bottom 맨 아래 attached 첨부된 enrollment 등록 representative 직원

Questions 143-146 refer to the following e-mail.

From: Customer Care
To: Paul Kanagawa
Date: October 16
Subject: Welcome to Atlantic Music Trends
Attachment: Form

Dear Mr. Kanagawa,

Thank you very much for subscribing to Atlantic Music Trends! ---**143**--- you will have detailed information about upcoming music classes, festivals, and concerts happening all over Canada's Atlantic coast. You can expect your first issue at your door by the 20th. ---**144**--- After that, every issue will be sent out during the first week of the month. With this subscription, you will also have unlimited ---**145**--- to online videos, song recordings, articles, schedules, and even ticketing information for concerts. All you have to do is log into our web site using the user ID and eight-digit passwords listed ---**146**--- the bottom line of the attached enrollment form.

Sincerely,
Veronica Van Zeyl
Customer Representative

143

(A) Now*
(B) Afterward
(C) Then
(D) Meanwhile

문맥상 구독 신청했으니 '이제부터' 이용할 수 있는 권한에 대한 내용이 주로 전개된다고 보는 것이 타당하므로 (A)가 가장 적절하다. afterward 후에, 나중에 meanwhile 그 동안에

정답 (A)

144

(A) 그 날짜까지 도착하지 않으면 저희에게 알려주시기 바랍니다.
(B) 구독하시려면, 정기 업무 시간에 전화 주시기 바랍니다.
(C) 다음 페스티벌은 11월 중순에 몽크턴에서 개최될 예정입니다.
(D) 출판을 위해서 콘서트 평가를 제출해 주실 것을 독자분들께 권합니다.

(A) Please notify us if it does not arrive by that date.*
(B) To subscribe, please phone during regular business hours.
(C) The next festival will take place in Moncton in mid November.
(D) We invite readers to submit reviews of concerts for publication.

'첫 번째 잡지의 배송 날짜'가 앞서 언급되었다. 따라서 '그 날짜(that date)까지 배송되지 않을 경우에 대한 당부'(A)가 이어져야 흐름상 자연스럽다. notify 알리다 submit 제출하다 publication 출판(물)

정답 (A)

145

(A) accessing (B) accesses
(C) accessed (D) access*

〈타동사(have) + 형용사(unlimited) + _____〉의 빈칸에 들어갈 수 있는 것은 동사의 목적어 역할을 할 명사 (D)뿐이다. 〈access + (명사) + to ~〉는 '~에 대한 이용, 접근'이란 의미이다. access가 동사로 사용될 경우에는 전치사(to) 없이 바로 목적어가 뒤따른다. access 접근(하다), 접속(하다)

정답 (D)

146

(A) for (B) about
(C) on* (D) at

적절한 전치사를 찾는 문제로, 'line 위'를 표현할 때 사용되는 (C)가 정답이다. 참고로 전치사 across/along/over도 line과 함께 자주 사용된다.

정답 (C)

PART 7

Questions 147-148 refer to the following notice.

Jen's Salon and Spa

Holiday Information

- Spa hours will be extended from November 20 to January 20. (Monday – Saturday 10 A.M. to 10 P.M.).
- Please note, the spa will be closed from December 24 – 29.
- As always, ¹⁴⁸ cancelations must be made 24 hours in advance to avoid cancelation fees.

어휘 extend 연장하다 note 유념하다 cancelation 취소, 말소 avoid 피하다 fee 수수료, 요금

젠 살롱 앤 스파

시즌 정보

● 스파 시간이 11월 20일부터 1월 20일까지 연장될 예정입니다.
(월요일-토요일 오전 10시부터 밤 10시까지)
● 스파는 12월 24일부터 29일까지 휴무임을 유념해 주십시오.
● 언제나처럼, 148 취소는 24시간 전에 하셔야 취소 수수료를 물지 않습니다.

147

What is the purpose of the notice?

(A) To advertise a new service
(B) To explain a schedule*
(C) To announce a sale
(D) To offer a refund

본 공지의 목적은 무엇인가?
(A) 새 서비스를 광고하기 위해서
(B) 일정을 설명하기 위해서
(C) 할인 판매를 발표하기 위해서
(D) 환불을 제공하기 위해서

어휘 advertise 광고하다 offer 제안하다, 제공하다 refund 환불

첫째 항목은 '영업 기간 연장'이고, 둘째 항목은 '휴무 기간 안내'이므로, 이를 종합하는 (B)가 가장 적절하다.

정답 (B)

148

What is stated about cancelations?

(A) The spa requires advance notice of cancelations.*
(B) Customers can cancel appointments online.
(C) A service fee is always applied to cancelations.
(D) Holiday appointments cannot be canceled.

취소에 대해 뭐라고 언급하는가?
(A) 스파는 사전 취소 공지가 필요하다.
(B) 고객들은 온라인으로 예약을 취소할 수 있다.
(C) 서비스 요금이 취소에 항상 적용된다.
(D) 휴가철 예약은 취소할 수 없다.

어휘 require 필요로 하다 advance 사전의 cancel 취소하다 appointment 예약, 약속 apply to ~에 적용되다

cancelations에 관련된 셋째 항목에서 24시간 전에는 취소해야 수수료가 붙지 않는다 (cancelations must be made 24 hours in advance to avoid cancelation fees)고 하므로 (A)가 정답이다.

정답 (A)

Questions 149-150 refer to the following notice.

Notice for Eastpoint Community Residents

149 As of next month, our weekly community newsletter will be going paperless. In an effort to protect the environment and reduce the amount of paper we use, the newsletter will now be available online only.

150 Anyone who currently has a small business advertisement in the newsletter is encouraged to contact the newsletter editor for an updated contract at 900-555-3434. The first online newsletter is scheduled to be on www.eastpointcommunity.com/newsletter on November 1st. We hope you enjoy this new convenient way to receive your weekly newsletter.

Sincerely,
Eastpoint Community Newsletter Team

149

What change will be made to the newsletter?

(A) It will merge with another publication.
(B) It will be delivered faster.
(C) It will run less frequently.
(D) It will no longer be printed on paper.*

150

According to the notice, why might advertisers contact the editor?

(A) To sign a new contract*
(B) To receive a discount
(C) To upgrade a membership
(D) To change a listing

153 (A), (B) 무보수 봄 교육 세션
오전 9:30 – 오후 4:30

오전 9:30: 만남 및 인사
151 매니저들과 동료 신입 사원들을 만납니다. 회사 소개용 짧은 비디오를 보는 동안 커피와 도넛을 드세요.

오전 10:30: 규칙 및 절차
직원 편람을 받으시고 부서 매니저와 함께 규칙 및 절차를 검토하세요. 잠시 동안의 질의 응답 시간이 포함됩니다.

오후 12:00: 153 (D) 점심 휴식
회의실에 샌드위치, 샐러드, 후식으로 된 가벼운 뷔페식 점심이 마련됩니다. 채식주의자들을 위한 메뉴도 제공될 것입니다.

오후 1:00: 부서 방문
직원들은 각자 부서를 방문해서 배정된 선배 직원으로부터 현장 교육을 받을 것입니다.

오후 3:30: 자리 배정
직원들 각자에게 책상을 안내하고 회사 계정 및 이메일을 설정할 시간을 줄 것입니다. 152 문제 발생 시를 대비해 IT 부서가 대기할 것입니다.

Questions 151-153 refer to the following agenda.

153 (A), (B) Unpaid Spring Training Session
9:30 A.M. to 4:30 P.M.

9:30 A.M.: Meet and Greet
151 Meet your managers as well as your fellow new employees. Enjoy coffee and donuts as you watch a short introduction video to the company.

10:30 A.M.: Rules and Procedures
Pick up your employee handbook and review the rules and procedures with the office manager. A short question and answer session will be included.

12:00 P.M.: 153 (D) Lunch Break
A light buffet lunch of sandwiches, salads, and desserts will be catered in the conference room. Vegetarian options will be provided for employees.

1:00 P.M.: Department Shadowing
Employees will visit their respective departments and receive hands-on training from an assigned veteran employee.

3:30 P.M.: Desk Assignments
Employees will be shown to their desks and given an opportunity to set up their company accounts and e-mails. 152 IT will be available for any problems that may arise.

어휘 unpaid 무보수의, 미불의 fellow 동료 procedure 절차, 방법 include 포함하다 cater 음식을 조달하다 vegetarian 채식주의자 option 선택(권) provide 제공하다 department 부(서) shadow (누군가로부터 무엇을 배우기 위해) 함께하다 respective 각자의 hands-on 직접 해 보는, 실천하는 assigned 할당된 veteran 노련한, 오랜 경험을 쌓은 assignment 배정, 할당 opportunity 기회 account 계정, 계좌 arise 생기다, 발생하다

본 세션은 누구를 위한 것이겠는가?
(A) 회사 CEO들
(B) 컴퓨터 기술자들
(C) 신입 사원들
(D) 부서 발령자들

어휘 technician 기술자 transfer 이동

151 For whom is the session most likely intended?
(A) Company CEOs
(B) Computer technicians
(C) New office employees*
(D) Department transfers

첫 번째 순서 중 특히 Meet your managers as well as your fellow new employees.를 통해 정답 (C)를 확인할 수 있다. 이 문장에서 fellow는 '동료, 동년배'를 의미하므로 you 또한 new employee가 된다.

정답 (C)

152

What portion of the session involves IT specialists?

(A) Meet and Greet
(B) Rules and Procedures
(C) Department Shadowing
(D) Desk Assignments*

키워드 IT에 유념해 지문을 살펴보면, 마지막 순서 (D)에 대한 설명에서 IT will be available for any problems that may arise.를 확인할 수 있다.

정답 (D)

세션의 어느 순서에서 IT 전문가들이 관여하는가?
(A) 만남 및 인사
(B) 규칙 및 절차
(C) 부서 방문
(D) 자리 배정

어휘 portion 부분 involve 관련시키다, 연루시키다

153

What is NOT indicated about the session?

(A) It is an unpaid event.
(B) It lasts for one work day.
(C) It is run by the HR director.*
(D) It includes refreshments.

지문과 각 선택지를 대조하면서 지문에 언급된 사항을 소거하는 식으로 문제를 해결한다. (A)는 제목 Unpaid Spring Training Session에서, (B)는 9:30 A.M. to 4:30 P.M.에서, (D)는 Lunch Break 설명에서 확인할 수 있다. 따라서 본 문제의 정답은 (C)가 된다.

정답 (C)

본 세션에 대해 드러나지 않는 사항은?
(A) 무보수 행사이다.
(B) 하루의 근무 시간 동안 진행된다.
(C) 인사부 부장이 이끈다.
(D) 가벼운 식사가 포함된다.

어휘 last 지속하다 refreshment 다과, 가벼운 식사

렝그루 침구

주간 상황 보고: 9월 5-9일
담당자: 알렉산더 코빈, 프로젝트 코디네이터

155, 157 이번 주 성과:

- 현재 침구 제품을 생산 중인 멕시코 내의 제조업체 네 군데에 연락했습니다. ──[1]── 154 새로운 침구 세트의 디자인 사양과 함께 제품 가격, 회전 시간, 직물 입수 가능성, 배송 비용에 대한 질문을 그들에게 이메일로 보냈습니다.
- 답장에 따르면, 157 P&M 텍스타일이 최적의 후보자인 듯합니다. ──[2]── 게다가, 고객 서비스 매니저인 새미 루이즈는 즉시 제게 이메일을 보냈습니다. 156 제 질문에 대한 그녀의 답변은 매우 자세하고 전문적이었습니다. 그녀가 이 이행 과정을 매끄럽고도 효율적으로 처리할 것이라 봅니다.
- 나머지 세 회사는 우리가 선호하는 직물을 입수할 수 없거나 우리의 공급 수요를 맞추지 못할 것입니다. ──[3]── 따라서, 그들은 더 고려할 수 없습니다.

다음 주 계획:

- P&M 텍스타일에 연락해 결제 및 배송 조건에 대한 전화 회의를 마련할 것입니다. ──[4]──
- 전 제품의 최종 디자인을 검토하고 필요하다면 수정을 요청할 것입니다. 디자인 팀을 만나 변경 사항을 논의할 것입니다.

Questions 154-157 refer to the following report.

Rengrew Bedding

Weekly Status Report: September 5-9
Prepared by: Alexander Corbin, Project Coordinator

155, 157 Accomplished this Week:

- Got in touch with four manufacturers in Mexico who currently produce bedding products. ---[1]--- 154 E-mailed them design specifications for our new bedding sets along with questions about production pricing, turnaround time, fabric availability, and shipping costs.
- According to the replies, 157 P&M Textiles appears to be the best candidate. ---[2]--- Additionally, Sammy Ruiz, a client services manager, e-mailed me promptly. 156 Her responses to my questions were very detailed and professional. I believe she would ensure this transition is both smooth and efficient.
- The other three companies either did not have access to our preferred fabrics or they could not meet our supply demand. ---[3]--- As a result, we will no longer be able to consider them.

Plans for Next Week:

- Contact P&M Textiles to set up a conference call about payment and shipping terms. ---[4]---
- Review final designs for all products and request revisions if need be. Meet with the design team to discuss any changes.

어휘 bedding 침구 status 상황 prepare 준비하다 coordinator 기획자 accomplish 완수하다, 성취하다 get in touch with ~와 접촉하다, 연락하다 manufacturer 제조 업체 currently 현재 produce 생산하다 specification 설명서, 사양 along with ~와 함께 production 생산(량) pricing 가격 책정 turnaround 한 가지 일을 끝내는 시간 fabric 직물, 천 availability 유용성, 입수성 shipping 배송 reply 대답, 답장 textile 직물, 옷감 appear ~인 것 같다 candidate 후보자, 지원자 additionally 게다가 promptly 즉시 response 대답, 응답 ensure 반드시 ~하게 하다, 보장하다 transition 이행, 과도 efficient 유능한, 효율적인 access 접근, 이용 preferred 선호하는 meet 충족시키다, 만나다 supply 공급 demand 수요, 요구 as a result 결과적으로 consider 고려하다 payment 결제, 납부 term 조건, 조항 revision 수정, 정정 discuss 논의하다, 토론하다

렝그루 침구에 대해 드러나는 사항은?
(A) 새 매니저를 이제 막 고용했다.
(B) 멕시코에 새로 생긴 회사이다.
(C) 현지에 자체 공장들이 있다.
(D) 신제품 출시를 준비 중이다.

어휘 own 자체의 factory 공장 launch 출시하다, 발표하다

154

What is suggested about Rengrew Bedding?

(A) It has just hired a new manager.
(B) It is a brand new company in Mexico.
(C) It has its own factories on site.
(D) It is getting ready to launch new products.*

이번 주 첫 번째 성과에서 E-mailed them design specifications for our new bedding sets along with questions about production pricing, turnaround time, fabric availability, and shipping costs.라며 새로운 침구 세트의 디자인부터 배송까지를 언급하므로 (D)가 가장 적절하다.

정답 (D)

155

According to the report, what did Mr. Corbin do during the week of September 5?

(A) Finalized some design information
(B) Assessed potential business partners*
(C) Visited a manufacturer in person
(D) Requested a payment be delayed

'이번 주 성과(Accomplished this Week)'를 묻는 질문임을 파악해야 한다. 지문에 언급된 세 가지를 종합하면 (B)가 정답임을 알 수 있다.

정답 (B)

본 보고서에 따르면, 코빈 씨는 9월 5일이 있는 주에 무엇을 했는가?
(A) 몇몇 디자인 정보를 마무리했다.
(B) 잠재적인 사업 파트너들을 평가했다.
(C) 제조 업체를 직접 방문했다.
(D) 결제를 미뤄 달라고 요청했다.

어휘 finalize 마무리 짓다, 완결하다 assess 재다, 평가하다, 사정하다 in person 직접 delay 지체시키다, 지연시키다

156

What is mentioned about Ms. Ruiz?

(A) She is new to P&M Textiles.
(B) She suggested some changes.
(C) She contacted some businesses.
(D) She is easy to work with.*

핵심 인명 Ms. Ruiz에 유의해 지문을 살펴보면, P&M 텍스타일 답변을 언급한 두 번째 사항에서 그녀가 답변을 빨리 보냈는데 답변이 상세하고 전문적(Her responses to my questions were very detailed and professional.)이니 이번 일을 매끄럽고 효율적으로 처리할 것(she would ensure this transition is both smooth and efficient)이라고 하므로 (D)가 가장 적절하다.

정답 (D)

루이즈 씨에 대해 뭐라고 언급되는가?
(A) P&M 텍스타일 신입 사원이다.
(B) 몇 가지 변경 사항을 제안했다.
(C) 몇몇 업체들에 연락했다.
(D) 함께 일하기에 편하다.

어휘 be easy to ~하기 쉽다

157

In which of the positions marked [1], [2], [3], and [4] does the following sentence best belong?

"It is located further south than most companies, but it has the capacity to meet our supply needs."

(A) [1]
(B) [2]*
(C) [3]
(D) [4]

'특정 업체에 대한 (위치, 생산성) 평가'이므로 '이번 주 성과(Accomplished this Week)'에 맥락상 어울린다. 특히 대명사 It이 가리키는 대상이 앞 문장에 언급되어야 하는데, [2] 앞에는 P&M Textiles라는 회사명이 언급되고 있다. 따라서 정답은 (B)이다.

정답 (B)

다음 문장은 [1], [2], [3], [4]로 표시된 곳 중 어디에 가장 적합한가?
"대부분 회사보다 훨씬 남쪽으로 떨어져 있지만, 우리 공급 수요를 충족시킬 능력이 있습니다."
(A) [1]
(B) [2]
(C) [3]
(D) [4]

어휘 capacity (생산) 능력

그랜드 애비뉴 호텔: 연회 서비스

연회를 위해 그랜드 애비뉴 호텔을 선택해 주셔서 감사합니다. 아래 정보를 작성해 주시기 바랍니다. 158 저희 고객 서비스 직원이 귀하께 연락해 예약을 확인하고 결제 정보를 요청할 것입니다.

예약 성함: _____ 행사 날짜: _____
이메일: _____ 회사 전화: _____
개인 전화: _____

선호 객실:
[ ] 다이아몬드 룸 (100명까지) [ ] 로즈 룸 (150명까지)
[ ] 스타라이트 룸 (200명까지)

159 원하는 배치:
[ ] 만찬 (원형 테이블 및 의자) [ ] 만찬 및 무도회 (테이블 및 무도회장)
[ ] 만찬 및 연설 (테이블 및 무대) [ ] 기타: _____

식사 및 음료:
[ ] 풀서비스 뷔페 및 후식 바 [ ] 3 코스로 준비되는 만찬

시청각 장비 필요: [ ] 네 [ ] 아니오 설명: _____

하객을 위한 호텔 숙소: [ ] 네 [ ] 아니오 객실 수: _____

서식에 따르면, 그랜드 애비뉴 호텔 직원은 무엇을 할 것인가?
(A) 객실 사진이 담긴 브로셔를 이메일로 보낼 것이다.
(B) 고객을 도와 설치하고 청소할 것이다.
(C) 고객들에게 무료 숙박권을 제공할 것이다.
(D) 결제 정보에 대해 고객에게 연락할 것이다.

어휘 assist 돕다, 지원하다 set up 설치, 준비 offer 제안하다, 제공하다 free 무료의 voucher 상품권, 할인권

그랜드 애비뉴 호텔 연회 서비스에 대해 유추되는 사항은?
(A) 시청각 장비를 이용하려면 결제가 필요하다.
(B) 행사에 맞게 방을 준비할 것이다.
(C) 연회 손님들에게 호텔 객실을 할인해 준다.
(D) 만찬 및 무도회 행사에 무료로 라이브 뮤직을 제공한다.

어휘 arrange 배열하다, 정돈하다 suit ~에 맞추다

Questions 158-159 refer to the following form.

Grand Avenue Hotel: Banquet Services

Thank you for choosing Grand Avenue Hotel for your banquet. Please fill out the information below. 158 One of our guest services representatives will contact you to confirm your reservation and request payment information.

Reservation Name: _____ Event Date: _____
E-mail: _____ Business Phone: _____
Personal Phone: _____

Room Preference:
[ ] Diamond Room (up to 100 guests) [ ] Rose Room (up to 150 guests)
[ ] Starlight Room (up to 200 guests)

159 Requested Layout:
[ ] Dinner (round tables and chairs) [ ] Dinner and Dance (tables and a dance floor)
[ ] Dinner and Speech (tables and a stage) [ ] Other : _____

Food and Beverages:
[ ] Full-Service Buffet and Dessert Bar [ ] Three-Course Catered Dinner

AV Equipment Required: [ ] Yes [ ] No Explain: _____
Hotel Accommodation for Guests: [ ] Yes [ ] No Number of Rooms: _____

어휘 banquet 연회 choose 선택하다 fill out 기입하다, 작성하다 below 아래 representative 직원 contact 연락하다 confirm 확실히 하다 reservation 예약 request 요청하다 event 행사 preference 선호(도) layout 배치 beverage 음료 equipment 기기, 장비 accommodation 숙소

---

158 According to the form, what will Grand Avenue Hotel staff do?
(A) E-mail brochures with room photos
(B) Assist customers with set up and clean up
(C) Offer free accommodation vouchers to guests
(D) Contact customers about payment information*

'직원 일정'에 유념해 지문을 살펴보면, 첫째 문단에서 One of our guest services representatives will contact you to confirm your reservation and request payment information.이라며 연락해서 예약 확인 및 결제 정보를 요청할 것이라고 하므로 (D)가 정답이다.

* paraphrasing: representative → staff

정답 (D)

---

159 What is implied about Grand Avenue Hotel's banquet services?
(A) It requires payment for the use of audio-visual equipment.
(B) It will arrange the room to suit the event.*
(C) It provides discounted hotel rooms to banquet guests.
(D) It offers free live music for dinner and dance events.

Requested Layout을 보면 식사만 하는 행사, 식사와 무도가 포함된 행사, 식사와 연설이 포함된 행사 및 기타 옵션이 들어 있다. 따라서 행사의 성격에 맞추어 실내 가구들을 배열한다는 것을 알 수 있으므로 (B)가 정답이 된다.

정답 (B)

Questions 160-162 refer to the following job advertisement.

https://www.employmentfind.com

Find Employment Online

Build Your Career Today!

The real estate business can be hard when you're working alone. At Team Real Estate, you are not alone! Our large network of real estate agents makes showing and selling properties easy. 160 By sharing information on potential buyers in our database, we sell more properties than any other agency in the country. Our shared commission rates encourage our team members to work together to get the job done.

161 Complete our new real estate training seminar and apply for your real estate license. If you're successful, you may be offered a full-time contract position with full benefits.

Education and experience will be considered before you are offered a contract. University degrees are a plus, but high school graduates may also apply. Applicants must have access to their own vehicle, as driving to and from local properties is a must.

To apply for this position, please click the button below. You'll need to input your e-mail address, phone number, and upload your resume. Only those selected for interviews will be contacted. Prior to interviews, we recommend that all candidates familiarize themselves with our company policies. 162 Please visit www.teamrealestate.com/careers to learn more about this.

Apply Now

어떤 직무가 일의 일환인가?
(A) 공동 데이터베이스에 고객 목록 올리기
(B) 부동산 개조에 대해 조언하기
(C) 전화로 고객들을 유치하기
(D) 멘토링 프로그램 관리하기

어휘 attract 끌어모으다, 유치하다

160

What duty is suggested as part of the job?
(A) Listing clients on a shared database*
(B) Offering advice on upgrading properties
(C) Attracting clients through phone calls
(D) Coordinating a mentorship program

'일의 내용'에 유념해 지문을 살펴보면, 첫째 문단에서 By sharing information on potential buyers in our database, we sell more properties than any other agency in the country.라며 데이터베이스에서의 정보 공유를 언급하므로 (A)가 가장 적절하다.

정답 (A)

본 광고에 따르면, 계약직에 무엇이 필요한가?
(A) 대학 학위
(B) 부동산 면허
(C) 마케팅 경력
(D) 고용 추천서

어휘 diploma 졸업장, 수료증 reference 추천서, 추천인

161

According to the advertisement, what is requested for a contract position?
(A) A college diploma
(B) A real estate license*
(C) Marketing experience
(D) Employment references

둘째 문단에서 교육 세미나를 받고 면허를 신청하라(Complete our new real estate training seminar and apply for your real estate license.)고 한 뒤 성공하면 풀타임 직책에 지원할 수 있다고 한다. 따라서 (B)가 정답이 된다.

정답 (B)

본 광고에 따르면, 지원자들은 왜 팀 부동산 웹사이트를 방문하겠는가?
(A) 팀 부동산의 절차에 대해 알기 위해서
(B) 근로 혜택이 포함되는 계약직에 지원하기 위해서
(C) 이력서와 추천서를 등록하기 위해서
(D) 교육 세션 시간에 대해 문의하기 위해서

어휘 procedure 절차, 방법 inquire 문의하다

162

According to the advertisement, why should applicants visit the Team Real Estate website?
(A) To learn about Team Real Estate's procedures*
(B) To apply for a contract position with benefits
(C) To upload a resume and references
(D) To inquire about the time of a training session

키워드 website에 유념해 지문을 살펴보면, 마지막 문단에서 Please visit www.teamrealestate.com/careers to learn more about this.라고 하는데, this는 앞 문장에서 말한 company policy를 숙지하는 것을 의미하므로 (A)가 가장 적절하다.

정답 (A)

Questions 163-166 refer to the following article.

163 50 Years of Community Service

March 27 -- 163, 165 (B) Professor Abraham Drew is known in the local community not for his years as a teacher of psychology or for his numerous papers published in academic journals, but for his dedication to community outreach. Fifty years ago, Mr. Drew founded the first after-school program for local children, which has helped numerous children in the city. 165 (A) The program, which started as a baseball camp for troubled boys, has since grown into Homework Helpers for elementary school-aged children, Art on the Street for teenagers, and Give Back, a charity in which individuals and businesses organize food drives for the homeless. "I never thought my after-school program would develop into all these unique programs," Mr. Drew said, "but 165 (D) there was so much community interest. Everywhere, people were looking for a way to help out."

After fifty years of service, Mr. Drew will retire from both his job as a professor and as program coordinator. His grandson, Michael Drew, will retain control of the programs. "I'm very happy to continue what my grandfather started," Michael Drew said. "He's a great man, and the community needs the work he has done."

165 (D) Mr. Drew's volunteers will host a retirement party to honor him next month at Wilfred Park. The party will include performances by local bands, food prepared by local restaurants, and a small fireworks show. 166 The mayor will present Mr. Drew with a Lifetime Service Achievement Award as thanks for his years of giving back to the community. For details about this event, please visit www.wilfredpark.com/events/april.

163

Why most likely was the article written?
(A) To celebrate the founding of a city
(B) To encourage readers to donate to charity
(C) To announce the closing of a community business
(D) To highlight the achievements of a local figure*

둘째 문단 둘째 줄에 있는 "retain"과 의미상 가장 유사한 단어는?
(A) 기여하다
(B) 동의하다
(C) 기억하다
(D) 유지하다

어휘 contribute 기여/이바지/기부/기증하다 agree 동의하다

164

The word "retain" in paragraph 2, line 2, is closest in meaning to
(A) contribute to
(B) agree with
(C) remember
(D) keep*

해당 부분은 손자가 '계속' 관리해 나간다는 요지의 문장이다. 따라서 이를 완성하는 데 가장 적절한 어휘는 (D)이다.

정답 (D)

아브라함 드루에 대해 드러난 사항이 아닌 것은?
(A) 남자 아이들을 위한 야구 캠프를 시작했다.
(B) 대학에서 학생들을 가르친다.
(C) 내년에 다른 학교를 개교할 예정이다.
(D) 다른 사람들이 자선 활동을 하도록 고무했다.

어휘 instruct 가르치다 inspire 고무하다, 격려하다

165

What is NOT suggested about Abraham Drew?
(A) He started a baseball camp for boys.
(B) He instructs students at a university.
(C) He will open another school next year.*
(D) He inspired others to do charity work.

핵심 인명 Abraham Drew의 경력이 자세히 다뤄진 첫째 문단 내용과 각 선택지를 대조해 지문에 언급된 사항을 소거하는 식으로 해결한다. (A)는 The program, which started as a baseball camp for troubled boys에서, (B)는 Professor Abraham Drew is known in the local community not for his years as a teacher of psychology.에서 확인할 수 있으며, (D)는 there was so much community interest. Everywhere, people were looking for a way to help out와 마지막 문단의 Mr. Drew's volunteers에서 유추할 수 있다. 따라서 본 문제의 정답은 (C)가 된다.

정답 (C)

윌프레드 파크에서의 파티에 대해 뭐라고 하는가?
(A) 지역 코미디 배우들이 공연할 것이다.
(B) 시에서 기념식을 열 것이다.
(C) 참가자들은 소정의 요금을 내고 참석할 수 있다.
(D) 드루 씨가 상을 받을 것이다.

어휘 perform 공연하다, 연주하다 celebration 기념, 축하 participant 참가자 attend 참석하다, 출석하다

166

What is stated about the party at Wilfred Park?
(A) Local comedy acts will perform.
(B) The city will host the celebration.
(C) Participants can attend for a small fee.
(D) Mr. Drew will be honored with an award.*

핵심 어구 Wilfred Park에 유념해 지문을 살펴보면, 마지막 문단에서 파티에 대한 내용이 언급되는데 특히 The mayor will present Mr. Drew with a Lifetime Service Achievement Award as thanks for his years of giving back to the community.를 통해 정답 (D)를 확인할 수 있다.

정답 (D)

Questions 167-168 refer to the following text message chain.

Pedro Alando [11:00 A.M.]:
Ms. Wilson, please check your e-mail. I sent you an updated contract.

Tina Wilson [11:02 A.M.]:
Okay, thank you. ¹⁶⁷ Has the payment scale been updated as well?

Pedro Alando [11:03 A.M.]:
¹⁶⁷ Certainly. Because you've been with us for longer than a year, ¹⁶⁸ you will now be paid $100 dollars for every color photo you take for our magazine instead of $80.

Tina Wilson [11:05 A.M.]:
Excellent. Thank you for clarifying that. I'll have a look at the contract, sign it, and send it back shortly.

Pedro Alando [11:08 A.M.]:
Fantastic. We are very pleased you have decided to work with us for another year.

SEND

167 At 11:03 A.M. what does Mr. Alando mean when he writes, "Certainly"?
(A) He will send an e-mail one more time.
(B) He is sure of the success of a plan.
(C) He is willing to share some information.
(D) He made a previously agreed-upon change.*

168 Who most likely is Ms. Wilson?
(A) A contract lawyer
(B) A magazine editor
(C) A photographer*
(D) A journalist

수신: 재닌 로버트슨 〈jrobertson@wetrainyou.com〉
발신: 웬달 스파크스 〈wbsparks@consumerconventioncenter.com〉
날짜: 1월 4일
제목: 연례 소상공인 컨퍼런스

로버트슨 씨 귀하,

169 2월 3일에 열릴 제3회 연례 소상공인 컨퍼런스에 참여하시겠다니 정말 기쁩니다. ㅡ[1]ㅡ 170 이것이 너무 갑작스러운 요청이었음을 알기에, 팀 브루어스를 대신해 주시는 열의에 정말 감사 드립니다. 소기업 교육 전문 회사를 이끄셨던 귀하의 경험이 우리 참가자들에게 정말 흥미를 불러일으킬 것입니다. ㅡ[2]ㅡ 새내기 사업가가 신입 사원을 교육하는 데 꼭 필요한 몇 가지 기본 과정들을 설명해 주신다면 특히 기쁘겠습니다.

귀사의 홍보용 팸플릿을 제공하시겠다면, 발표날보다 최소한 일주일 먼저 보내 주시기 바랍니다. 또한, 발표하실 때 어떤 시청각 장비가 필요하실지 알려 주십시오. ㅡ[3]ㅡ 그리고, 171 귀사 홈페이지에 있는 귀하의 약력을 컨퍼런스 프로그램에 써도 괜찮을지요? ㅡ[4]ㅡ

모든 것에 대해 다시 한번 감사 드립니다.

그럼 이만,
웬달 스파크스
컨퍼런스 기획자

Questions 169-171 refer to the following e-mail.

To: Janine Robertson <jrobertson@wetrainyou.com>
From: Wendal Sparks <wbsparks@consumerconventioncenter.com>
Date: 4 January
Subject: Annual Small Business Conference

Dear Ms. Robertson,

169 I was so glad to hear that you'll be participating in our third annual Small Business Conference on February 3. --[1]-- 170 I know this was very last minute, so I really appreciate your enthusiasm about stepping in for Tim Brewers. Your experience heading a small business training company will really interest our participants. --[2]-- We'd especially love it if you could outline some of the first steps a new business must take toward training new employees.

If you would like to offer promotional pamphlets for your business, please send them at least a week prior to your speaking date. Also, please let me know what audio-visual equipment you'll need for your presentation. --[3]-- Additionally, 171 may I use the biography you have on your website as material for our conference program? --[4]--

Thanks again for everything.

Sincerely,
Wendal Sparks
Conference Coordinator

어휘 annual 연례의 participate in ~에 참여하다 appreciate 감사하다 enthusiasm 열정, 열의 head 이끌다 participant 참가자 especially 특히 outline 개요를 말하다 promotional 홍보의, 판촉의 at least 적어도, 최소한 prior to ~에 앞서 additionally 게다가 biography 전기 material 재료, 자재

스파크스 씨는 본 이메일을 왜 보냈는가?
(A) 일정 변경을 제안하기 위해서
(B) 갱신된 일정에 대해 문의하기 위해서
(C) 뒤늦은 초대장을 보내기 위해서
(D) 제안 수락을 감사하기 위해서

어휘 propose 제안하다 itinerary (여행) 일정 belated 뒤늦은 invitation 초대 recognize 인정하다, 인사하다 acceptance 수락

169

Why did Mr. Sparks most likely send the e-mail?
(A) To propose an itinerary change
(B) To ask for an updated schedule
(C) To send a belated invitation
(D) To recognize an offer of acceptance*

첫 문장 I was so glad to hear that you'll be participating in our third annual Small Business Conference on February 3.을 통해 '참여 의사 표시에 대한 감사'가 주요 목적임을 알 수 있다. 따라서 (D)가 가장 적절하다.

정답 (D)

170

What is suggested about Mr. Brewers?
(A) He attends conferences every year.
(B) He is unable to speak at a conference.*
(C) He works as an event coordinator.
(D) He started his own small business.

브루어스 씨에 대해 드러나는 사항은?
(A) 컨퍼런스에 매년 참가한다.
(B) 컨퍼런스에서 강연하지 못한다.
(C) 행사 기획자로 일한다.
(D) 소규모 업체를 창업했다.

핵심 인명 Mr. Brewers에 유의해 지문을 살펴보면, 첫째 문단에서 촉박한 연락에도 불구하고 팀 브루어스 순서를 대신 맡아 주겠다는 열의가 정말 고맙다(I know this was very last minute, so I really appreciate your enthusiasm about stepping in for Tim Brewers.)고 하므로 (B)가 가장 적절하다.

정답 (B)

171

In which of the positions marked [1], [2], [3], and [4] does the following sentence best belong?

"If you'd prefer to use a different text, please e-mail it to me."

(A) [1]
(B) [2]
(C) [3]
(D) [4]*

다음 문장은 [1], [2], [3], [4] 중 어느 곳에 들어가야 가장 적절한가?
"다른 텍스트를 사용하고 싶으시다면, 제게 이메일을 주시기 바랍니다."
(A) [1]
(B) [2]
(C) [3]
(D) [4]

어휘 prefer 선호하다. 더 좋아하다

앞서 '텍스트 사용'에 관련된 내용이 언급되어야 흐름상 자연스럽다. 따라서 홈페이지의 약력을 써도 될지 묻는 may I use the biography you have on your website as material for our conference program? 다음의 (D)가 정답이 된다.

정답 (D)

잔 스완슨　　9월 4일, 2:35
조나단, 주문 #2256 배송 보냈나요?
아니라면, 172, 174 똑같은 맞춤형 펜과 종이 세트를 그 주문에 추가해야 해요.

조나단 그루어　　9월 4일, 2:37
주문품은 아직 보관실에 있지만, 맞춤형 펜과 종이를 생산하는 데 최소한 이틀은 더 걸려요.

잔 스완슨　　9월 4일, 2:38
더 빨리 하는 게 가능할까요? 고객이 급하다고 하셨어요.

조나단 그루어　　9월 4일, 2:40
제조 부서 사람에게 확인해 보죠.

―로웨나 맥아더가 대화에 추가됐습니다―

조나단 그루어　　9월 4일, 2:41
173 로웨나, 급한 주문 하나 처리할 시간 되나요? 174 주문 #2256을 더블로 해야 돼요.

로웨나 맥아더　　9월 4일, 2:43
175 내일 오전까지는 할 수 있을 것 같아요. 그럼 되나요?

잔 스완슨　　9월 4일, 2:44
네, 175 그러면 돼요. 고마워요!

이 회사는 어떤 제품을 파는가?
(A) 시계
(B) 문구
(C) 가구
(D) 전자 제품

어휘 stationery 문구류 electronics 전자 제품

Questions 172-175 refer to the following text message chain.

Jan Swanson　　4 September, 2:35
Jonathan, have you sent order #2256 out for delivery?
If not, 172, 174 we need to add another identical set of personalized pens and paper to it.

Jonathan Gruer　　4 September, 2:37
The order is still in the storeroom, but it'll take at least two more days to produce the custom pens and paper.

Jan Swanson　　4 September, 2:38
Is it possible to get it done sooner? The customer said it's urgent.

Jonathan Gruer　　4 September, 2:40
Let's check with someone from manufacturing.

------Rowena MacArthur has been added to the chat-----

Jonathan Gruer　　4 September, 2:41
173 Rowena, do you have time for a rush order? 174 It's a duplicate of order #2256.

Rowena MacArthur　　4 September, 2:43
175 I think I can get it done by tomorrow morning. Is that okay?

Jan Swanson　　4 September, 2:44
Yes, 175 that works. Thanks a lot!

어휘 order 주문 delivery 배송, 배달 add 추가하다. 더하다 identical 동일한. 똑같은 personalized 개인이 원하는 대로 할 수 있는 storeroom 저장실, 보관실 at least 적어도, 최소한 produce 생산하다 custom 주문 제작한 urgent 긴급한, 시급한 check 확인하다 manufacturing 제조(업) rush 급한, 바쁜 rush order 긴급 주문 duplicate 사본 work (원하는) 효과가 나다

172

What type of products does the company sell?
(A) Watches
(B) Stationery*
(C) Furniture
(D) Electronics

첫 번째 메시지 중 we need to add another identical set of personalized pens and paper to it에 언급된 펜과 종이가 주요 단서이다. 정답은 (B)이다.

정답 (B)

173 Why does Mr. Gruer contact Ms. MacArthur?

(A) To pass on a customer complaint
(B) To find out where a staff meeting will be held
(C) To determine where an order has been shipped to
(D) To inquire about the timeframe for some work*

Mr. Gruer의 2시 41분 메시지에서 Rowena, do you have time for a rush order?라며 급한 주문 건을 처리할 시간이 되느냐고 묻는다. 따라서 (D)가 가장 적절하다.

정답 (D)

그루어 씨는 왜 맥아더 씨에게 연락하는가?
(A) 고객의 불만을 전달하기 위해서
(B) 직원 회의가 어디에서 열릴지 알아내기 위해서
(C) 주문이 어디로 배송됐는지 알아내기 위해서
(D) 작업에 걸리는 시간을 문의하기 위해서

어휘 complaint 불평, 불만 find out 알아내다 be held 열리다 determine 밝히다, 결정하다 ship 배송하다 inquire 문의하다 timeframe 시간, 기간

174 What does the customer want to do?

(A) Double an order*
(B) Cancel a delivery
(C) Return a damaged item
(D) Update payment information

2시 35분 메시지에서 another identical set(똑같은 세트 하나 더), 2시 41분 메시지에서 a duplicate of order(더블 주문)을 보고 (A)를 답으로 찾을 수 있다.
* paraphrasing: duplicate → double

정답 (A)

고객은 무엇을 하고 싶어 하는가?
(A) 주문을 두 배로 하고 싶어 한다.
(B) 배송을 취소하고 싶어 한다.
(C) 손상된 제품을 반납하고 싶어 한다.
(D) 결제 정보를 갱신하고 싶어 한다.

어휘 damaged 손상을 입은 item 물건, 제품

175 At 2:44, what does Ms. Swanson most likely mean when she writes, "that works"?

(A) She can reschedule some appointments.
(B) She is impressed with a new product.
(C) A deadline will be acceptable for a customer.*
(D) Some new items will be advertised online.

맥락을 살펴보면, 급한 주문이 내일 오전까지는 해결된다며, 그 일정이 괜찮겠냐고 묻는 상황에 나온 반응이다. 따라서 (C)가 가장 적절하다.

정답 (C)

2시 44분에, 스완슨 씨가 "그러면 돼요"라고 쓸 때 의미하는 바는?
(A) 약속 일정을 조정할 수 있다.
(B) 신제품이 인상적이다.
(C) 마감을 고객이 받아들일 것이다.
(D) 일부 신제품이 온라인에서 광고될 것이다.

어휘 reschedule 일정을 다시 정하다 be impressed with ~에 감동하다 deadline 마감 acceptable 용인되는, 받아들여지는

수신: msimpson@tristarinternational.com
발신: bookings@stonewallhotel.com
날짜: 5월 17일
176 제목: CV1124 예약

심슨 씨 귀하,

스톤월 호텔을 귀사 연례 워크숍에 선택해 주셔서 고맙습니다. 176 귀하가 온라인 예약 신청서에 적으신 대로, 킹사이즈 바다 전망 객실 12개가 귀 단체에 예약됐습니다. 귀하의 방문 목적이 비즈니스 워크숍이므로, VIP 휴게실과 회의실도 무료로 예약해 드렸습니다.

귀하의 온라인 예약에 따르면, 179 체크인 날짜는 8월 5일이고 체크아웃 날짜는 8월 8일입니다. 객실마다 하룻밤당 요금 109달러가 최종 청구서에 추가될 것입니다. 귀하의 예약 번호는 CV1124입니다. 예약에 무엇이든 변경을 요청하시려면 필요할 테니 이 번호를 꼭 기록해 두시기 바랍니다.

아시다시피, 스톤월 호텔은 그밖에 여러 특징과 프로그램이 있습니다. 177 귀하의 단체가 무료 서핑 강좌를 원하시면, 자리를 미리 예약하실 것을 권합니다. 더욱이, 무료 조찬과 룸 서비스 패키지를 제공하며, 최근에는 로비 옆에 스테이크 식당인 스톤월 그릴도 새로 열었습니다.

스톤월 호텔을 선택해 주셔서 고맙습니다. 귀하를 모시기를 고대합니다.

예약 서비스, 스톤월 호텔

수신: bookings@stonewallhotel.com
발신: msimpson@tristarinternational.com
날짜: 5월 19일
제목: 회신: CV1124 예약

예약 서비스 담당자 귀하,

제 예약에 몇 가지 오류가 있어서 알려 드리고자 메일 씁니다. 제 예약 번호는 CV1124입니다. 179 저는 온라인으로 예약할 때 주니어사이즈 객실 열 개라 했는데, 귀하의 이메일에는 다른 것이 적혀 있더군요. 게다가, 178, 179 8월 6일 저희 그룹이 하이킹을 하는 동안 현장에서 제공된 점심 식사에 대해서도 결제했는데, 귀하의 이메일에 언급되지 않았습니다. 제대로 된 객실 사이즈로 업데이트해 주시고, 이 서비스가 예약되었는지도 확인해 주시기 바랍니다. 이 사안에 대해 가능한 한 빨리 알려 주시면 고맙겠습니다.

Questions 176-180 refer to the following e-mails.

To: msimpson@tristarinternational.com
From: bookings@stonewallhotel.com
Date: May 17
176 Subject: Booking CV1124

Dear Ms. Simpson,

Thank you for selecting Stonewall Hotel for your company's annual workshop. 176 As you indicated on your online reservation, twelve king-sized ocean view suites have been booked for your group. Since the purpose of your visit is to conduct a business workshop, I have also reserved our executive lounge and conference room at no extra charge.

According to your online reservation, 179 your check-in date will be August 5th and your check-out will be August 8th. A charge of $109 dollars for each room per night will be added to your final bill. Your reservation number is CV1124. Please ensure you record this number as you will need it should you request any changes to your reservation.

As you know, Stonewall Hotel includes many additional features and activities. 177 If your group wish to take a complimentary surfing lesson, I suggest reserving a spot in advance. Furthermore, we offer complimentary breakfasts, room service packages, and have just opened up Stonewall Grill, a brand new steak restaurant located next to the lobby.

Thank you for choosing Stonewall Hotel. We look forward to serving you.

Booking Services, Stonewall Hotel

어휘 book 예약하다 select 선택하다 annual 연례의 indicate 가리키다, 나타내다 reservation 예약 suite 객실 purpose 목적 conduct (특정한 일을) 하다 reserve 예약하다 executive 고급의 at no extra charge 추가 요금 없이 charge 요금 bill 청구서 ensure 확실히 하다 include 포함하다 additional 추가의, 가외의 activity 활동 complimentary 무료의 suggest 제안하다 spot 장소 in advance 미리 furthermore 더욱이 offer 제안하다, 제공하다 choose 선택하다 look forward to -ing ~하기를 고대하다

To: bookings@stonewallhotel.com
From: msimpson@tristarinternational.com
Date: May 19
Subject: Re: Booking CV1124

Dear booking services staff,

I am writing to let you know that there were a few errors with my reservation. My reservation number is CV1124. 179 I indicated ten junior-sized suites when I reserved online, but your e-mail says something different. Additionally, 178 I also paid for a catered lunch during 179 my group's hiking trip on August 6th, but that was not mentioned in your e-mail. Please make sure this service has been booked in addition to updating the correct room size. I would appreciate it if you notified me about this issue as soon as possible.

Thank you for your assistance.

Sincerely,
Margo Simpson
Office of the CEO
Tristar International

어휘 error 오류 indicate 나타내다 additionally 게다가 cater (행사에) 음식을 공급하다 make sure ~을 확실히 하다 in addition to ~에 더해 appreciate 감사하다 notify 알리다 issue 문제, 사안 assistance 도움, 지원

176

What is the purpose of the first e-mail?

(A) To confirm a group reservation*
(B) To inform of a new policy
(C) To assist in making a reservation
(D) To provide a free upgrade

제목 Subject: Booking CV1124를 통해 '예약'에 관련된 내용이 주로 전개되리라는 것을 알 수 있는데, 첫째 문단의 As you indicated on your online reservation, twelve king-sized ocean view suites have been booked for your group.에서 (A)가 정답임을 알 수 있다.

정답 (A)

첫 번째 이메일의 목적은 무엇인가?
(A) 단체 예약을 확인하기 위해서
(B) 새로운 정책을 알리기 위해서
(C) 예약하는 것을 돕기 위해서
(D) 무료 업그레이드를 제공하기 위해서

어휘 confirm 확실히 하다 inform 알리다 policy 정책 assist 돕다, 지원하다 make a reservation 예약하다

177

What is suggested about Stonewall's surfing lessons?

(A) They are available only in the mornings.
(B) They are a new service.
(C) They are being offered temporarily.
(D) They are a popular feature.*

핵심 어구 surfing lessons에 유념해 지문들을 살펴보면, 첫 번째 이메일(지문 1) 셋째 문단에서 스톤월 호텔에는 그밖에 여러 특징 및 프로그램이 있다며 무료 서핑 강좌를 바로 예시하는데(If your group wish to take a complimentary surfing lesson) 미리 예약을 해야 한다(I suggest reserving a spot in advance)는 것은 인기가 많아 자리가 없을 수 있다는 뜻으로 볼 수 있다. 따라서 (D)가 가장 적절하다.

정답 (D)

스톤월 서핑 강좌에 대해 암시되는 것은?
(A) 오전에만 이용할 수 있다.
(B) 새로운 서비스이다.
(C) 임시로 제공되고 있다.
(D) 인기 있는 것이다.

어휘 available 입수/이용할 수 있는 temporarily 일시적으로

178

What information in the hotel's records is missing?

(A) The lounge has been reserved.
(B) The group will arrive on August 5.
(C) A catering service is booked.*
(D) The room bill has been prepaid.

'누락 정보'에 유념해 지문들을 살펴보면, 두 번째 이메일(지문 2) 중반부에서 I also paid for a catered lunch during my group's hiking trip on August 6th, but that was not mentioned in your e-mail이라며 점심 식사에 관련된 내용이 언급되지 않았다고 하므로 (C)가 정답이 된다.

정답 (C)

호텔 기록에서 어떤 정보가 빠졌는가?
(A) 휴게실이 예약됐다.
(B) 단체는 8월 5일에 도착할 것이다.
(C) 음식 출장 서비스가 예약됐다.
(D) 객실 청구서는 미리 결제되었다.

어휘 arrive 도착하다 prepay 선불하다

트리스타 인터내셔널에서 오는 단체에 대해 유추할 수 있는 것은?
(A) 열두 명으로 구성된다.
(B) 워크숍 둘째 날 하이킹을 갈 예정이다.
(C) 스톤월 그릴에서 만찬을 열 것이다.
(D) 예약 날짜보다 하루 늦게 도착할 것이다.

어휘 consist of ~로 구성되다 state 진술하다, 말하다

179

What can be inferred about the group from Tristar International?
(A) It consists of twelve members.
(B) It will go hiking on the second day of the workshop.*
(C) It will have dinner at the Stonewall Grill.
(D) It will arrive a day later than the reservation states.

핵심 어구 Tristar International 측이 작성한 두 번째 이메일(지문 2)부터 살펴보면, 전반부의 I indicated ten junior-sized suites when I reserved online을 통해 (A)를 바로 소거할 수 있다. 지문 2 중반부의 my group's hiking trip on August 6th와 지문 1 둘째 문단의 your check-in date will be August 5th and your check-out will be August 8th를 연계해 (B)가 정답임을 알 수 있다.

정답 (B)

두 번째 이메일에서, 첫째 문단 여섯째 줄에 있는 "issue"와 의미상 가장 유사한 단어는?
(A) 변경
(B) 선택
(C) 가격
(D) 문제

어휘 alteration 개조, 변경 selection 선택, 선정

180

In the second e-mail, the word "issue" in paragraph 1, line 6, is closest in meaning to
(A) alteration
(B) selection
(C) price
(D) problem*

해당 부분을 찾아 요지를 파악하자. 선택지들 중 이 '문제'에 대해 빨리 알려 달라는 맥락을 완성하는 데 가장 적절한 어휘는 (D)이다.

정답 (D)

Questions 181-185 refer to the following notice and calendar.

Heber Birdwatching Club

April 2 -- [181] The Northville Recreation Board recently announced the creation of the Heber Park Birdwatching Club at Heber Wildlife Park. [183] The birdwatching club will meet from Friday through Sunday, from 1 P.M. until 3 P.M. The club meetings will run all summer long and will feature a number of lookout sites located on the Heber Trails. Each participant should dress appropriately for hiking on the trails and bring a supply of drinking water. Cameras are allowed for participants who want to photograph the numerous bird species located in Heber Wildlife Park. Up to ten members may join the club, and those interested can sign up with the club coordinator, Mindy Beckett (334-998-0034).

어휘 birdwatching 들새 관찰, 탐조 recreation 오락 board 이사회, 위원회 creation 창조, 창작 wildlife 야생동물 a number of 다수의 lookout 파수꾼, 망루 trail 오솔길 participant 참가자 dress 옷을 입다 appropriately 적당하게, 알맞게 supply 용품, 비품 species 종 up to ~까지 interested 관심 있는

June Weekend Activities at Heber Wildlife Park

- **Friday**
  - 12:00 P.M. Children's Picnic (Camp and Recreation Park)
  - [183]2:00 P.M. Heber Birdwatching Club (Squirrel Trail)
  - 4:00 P.M. T&V Industries Weekly Baseball Game (Diamond)

- **Saturday**
  - [183]2:00 P.M. Heber Birdwatching Club (Squirrel Trail)
  - 4:00 P.M. Barbecue Madness (East Pavilion on June 10th and 24th only)

- **Sunday**
  - 10:00 A.M. Nature Watercolor Painting (Gallery Building, $15 per person)
  - [183]2:00 P.M. Heber Birdwatching Club (Squirrel Trail)
  - 4:00 P.M. Level A Soccer (Soccer field)
  - 6:00 P.M. Music at the Park (West Pavilion)

For more information on any of the above events, please visit www.heberwildlifepark.com or call 556-332-0989.

어휘 activities 활동 squirrel 다람쥐 field 들판, ~장 above 위의

공지의 목적은 무엇인가?
(A) 헤버 야생동물 공원의 새로운 활동을 알리기 위해서
(B) 헤버 탐조 클럽의 새 기획자를 발표하기 위해서
(C) 헤버 야생동물 공원의 행사 취소에 대해 사과하기 위해서
(D) 노스빌 레크리에이션 위원회의 새로운 자리를 광고하기 위해서

어휘 apologize 사과하다 cancelation 취소 position 직(책)

181

What is the purpose of the notice?
(A) To inform of a new activity at Heber Wildlife Park*
(B) To announce a new coordinator for the Heber Birdwatching Club
(C) To apologize for the cancelation of an event at Heber Wildlife Park
(D) To advertise a new position at the Northville Recreation Board

공지(지문 1) 첫째 문단의 The Northville Recreation Board recently announced the creation of the Heber Park Birdwatching Club at Heber Wildlife Park.를 통해 (A)가 정답임을 알 수 있다. 글의 주제에 대한 결정적인 단서는 대체로 전반부에 언급된다.

정답 (A)

공지에서, 첫째 문단 셋째 줄에 있는 "run"과 의미상 가장 유사한 단어는?
(A) 조깅하다
(B) 계속하다
(C) 배회하다
(D) 성장하다

어휘 jog 조깅하다 continue 계속하다 roam 배회하다, 방랑하다 grow 자라다, 크다

182

In the notice, the word "run" in paragraph 1, line 3, is closest in meaning to
(A) jog
(B) continue*
(C) roam
(D) grow

해당 문장은 여름 내내 '계속 운영된다'는 요지이므로 선택지들 중 맥락상 가장 유사해질 수 있는 어휘는 (B)이다.

정답 (B)

6월 탐조 클럽에 대해 드러나는 사항은?
(A) 회원이 12명이다.
(B) 참가자들은 카메라를 가지고 와야 한다.
(C) 만나는 시간이 바뀌었다.
(D) 기획자가 자리를 비울 것이다.

어휘 absent 결석한, 결근한

183

What is suggested about the birdwatching club in June?
(A) It has 12 members.
(B) It requires participants to bring cameras.
(C) Its meeting time has been changed.*
(D) Its coordinator will be absent.

June 일정표(지문 2)와 the birdwatching club 시행에 관한 공지(지문 1)를 연계해서 파악해야 해결할 수 있는 문제이다. 지문 1 첫째 문단의 The birdwatching club will meet from Friday through Sunday, from 1 P.M. until 3 P.M.과 지문 2의 시간 2:00 P.M.을 통해 정답 (C)를 확인할 수 있다.

정답 (C)

184 What activity will only occur twice in June?

(A) T&V Industries Baseball
(B) Barbecue Madness*
(C) Nature Watercolor Painting
(D) Music at the Park

일정표(지문 2)에서 '2회 행사'를 찾아보면, 토요일 설명에서 Barbecue Madness (East Pavilion on June 10th and 24th only)라고 하므로 (B)가 정답이다.

정답 (B)

6월에 어떤 활동이 두 번만 있을 예정인가?
(A) T&V 인더스트리즈 야구
(B) 바비큐 매드니스
(C) 자연 수채화
(D) 공원 음악회

어휘 occur 발생하다, 일어나다

185 What is indicated about Heber Wildlife Park?

(A) Its pavilions have all been upgraded.
(B) Its campground is open all year round.
(C) It includes a lake and a water fountain.
(D) It has special programs for children.*

핵심 어구 Heber Wildlife Park 측이 작성한 일정표(지문 2)에서 금요일 행사 중 Children's Picnic을 통해 정답 (D)를 유추할 수 있다.

정답 (D)

헤버 야생동물 공원에 대해 드러나는 사항은?
(A) 모든 파빌리온이 업그레이드됐다.
(B) 야영지는 일년 내내 운영된다.
(C) 호수와 분수가 있다.
(D) 아이들을 위한 특별 프로그램이 있다.

어휘 campground 야영지 all year round 일년 내내 lake 호수 water fountain 분수

Questions 186-190 refer to the following advertisement, e-mail, and website feedback.

Toronto Tours

★★★★★
Toronto, Ontario

¹⁸⁶ To celebrate its first year of business, ¹⁸⁸ Toronto Tours is offering a special 20% discount on Culture of Toronto tours booked between April 5 and May 5. ¹⁸⁶ This is our most popular tour and is offered every Friday. The following is breakdown of our standard itinerary.

▶ The Royal Ontario Museum: Start at the famous Royal Ontario Museum. Enjoy some of the most beautiful art in the world in the ROM's many modern galleries. See the latest archeological discoveries on display and a number of large dinosaur species. April's special exhibit: 18th Century Maps.

▶ The Hockey Hall of Fame: Head over to the Hockey Hall of Fame and see Canada's greatest hockey legends remembered in numerous video exhibits. Learn the history of Canada's favorite sport, and view memorabilia that belonged to players of the past.

▶¹⁹⁰ The Danforth Festival: Conclude your tour at the Danforth Festival. Enjoy a taste of Greek culture at this energetic street party. Sample food from Toronto's many Greek restaurants while you enjoy live music and dancing. (Until April 20)

Note: The final portion of the tour will be subject to changes depending on which festivals are taking place downtown. Additionally, ¹⁸⁷ all entrance fees are covered in your package price, but food and beverages costs are extra.

From: Susan Malek
To: Samuel Park
¹⁸⁸ Date: April 10
Re: Reservation Confirmation

Dear Mr. Park,

Thank you for booking your tour with Toronto Tours. Below is a summary of your tour information. Should you have any questions or concerns, please contact me at 416-888-3232.

Tour name: Culture of Toronto
Tour date: April 12
Starting Time: 9:00 A.M. at Toronto Union Station
Return to Union Station: 11:30 P.M.
Your credit card has been charged: $190.00

Thank you and enjoy your tour!

Best,
Susan Malek
Tour Coordinator

어휘 reservation 예약 confirmation 확인 summary 요약 concern 우려 사항, 걱정 charge 청구하다

Customer Feedback:

This was my first time using Toronto Tours, and I found the tour to be much more impressive than the sightseeing bus tour I took the last time I visited Toronto. This company sure understands how to treat tourists' interest in the city's unique history and culture. Francis Weltz, our tour guide, was extremely helpful in getting us to and from locations as well as ensuring speedy entry to the listed stops. [190] The only downside of the tour was the rainy weather, which made it hard to enjoy the final stop. As a result, I wish an alternate destination would've been available in the event of poor weather.

Posted by: Samuel Park

어휘 impressive 인상적인 sightseeing 관광 treat 대하다, 다루다 interest 관심, 흥미 extremely 극히 location 위치, 소재지 ensure 보장하다, 확실히 하다 downside 불리한 면, 덜 긍정적인 면 as a result 결과적으로 alternate 교체의, 교대의, 대안의 destination 목적지

토론토 투어에 대해 드러나는 사항은?
(A) 투어 프로그램을 여러 개 운영한다.
(B) 영업한 지 몇 년 되었다.
(C) 여름 투어를 중단할 것이다.
(D) 새로운 관광 투어를 추가했다.

어휘 operate 운용하다, 영업하다, 가동하다

186

What is suggested about Toronto Tours?
(A) It operates several tour programs.*
(B) It has been open for several years.
(C) It will stop offering summer tours.
(D) It has added a new sightseeing tour.

핵심 어구 Toronto Tours 측에서 작성한 광고(지문 1)를 주의해서 살펴보자. 첫째 문단의 This is our most popular tour에서 '가장 인기 있는 상품'이라고 했으므로 이는 여러 개의 다른 상품도 있음을 의미한다. 따라서 (A)가 정답이 된다. 참고로, (B)는 첫 문장의 To celebrate its first year of business를 통해 오답임을 알 수 있다

정답 (A)

광고에 따르면, 토론토 투어는 고객들에게 무엇을 제공하는가?
(A) 식사 및 음료 상품권
(B) 업그레이드된 여행 선택권
(C) 단체 여행 할인
(D) 박물관 입장료

어휘 voucher 상품권, 할인권

187

According to the advertisement, what does Toronto Tours offer clients?
(A) Vouchers for food and beverages
(B) Upgraded travel options
(C) Discounts on group packages
(D) Admission fees to museums*

여행사가 '기본적으로' 제공하는 것을 파악해야 한다. 광고(지문 1) 마지막 문단에서 all entrance fees are covered in your package price, but food and beverages costs are extra라며 입장료는 패키지에 포함되나 식사 및 음료는 따로 계산한다고 하므로 (D)가 가장 적절하다.

* paraphrasing: entrance → admission

정답 (D)

박 씨의 투어에 대해 드러나는 사항은?
(A) 그리스 왕복 비행기삯이 포함되어 있다.
(B) 네 군데를 방문했다.
(C) 할인가에 구입했다.
(D) 원래는 지역 예술가들을 위해 개발되었다.

어휘 return (티켓) 왕복권 airfare 항공 요금 originally 원래

188

What is suggested about Mr. Park's tour?
(A) It included return airfare from Greece.
(B) It visited four main stops.
(C) It was purchased at a discount.*
(D) It was originally developed for local artists.

두 지문을 연계해서 파악해야 해결할 수 있는 문제이다. 지문 1 첫째 문단의 Toronto Tours is offering a special 20% discount on Culture of Toronto tours booked between April 5 and May 5와 지문 2 작성 날짜 Date: April 10을 통해 정답 (C)를 찾을 수 있다.

정답 (C)

189

In the website feedback, the word "treat" in paragraph 1, line 3, is closest in meaning to

(A) serve*
(B) increase
(C) decide
(D) ignore

해당 부분의 문맥은 '관광객들의 관심사를 헤아려 그에 알맞게 처리하다(서비스를 제공하다)'는 요지이므로 제시된 선택지들 중 맥락상 가장 유사하게 전개되는 어휘는 (A)이다.

정답 (A)

웹사이트 피드백에서, 첫째 문단 셋째 줄에 있는 "treat"와 의미상 가장 유사한 단어는?
(A) 돕다
(B) 늘리다
(C) 결정하다
(D) 무시하다

어휘 serve 제공하다, 기여하다, 시중을 들다, (구매를) 돕다 ignore 무시하다

190

What portion of the tour was Mr. Park dissatisfied with?

(A) Seeing off at Union Station
(B) The Royal Ontario Museum
(C) The Hockey Hall of Fame
(D) The Danforth Festival*

Mr. Park의 평가가 담긴 피드백(지문 3)과 각 선택지가 여행 상품으로 소개된 광고(지문 1)를 연계해서 해결할 수 있는 문제이다. 지문 3 후반부에서 The only downside of the tour was the rainy weather, which made it hard to enjoy the final stop이라며 '마지막 차례' 때 날씨 때문에 안 좋았던 것이 유일한 단점이라고 하는데, 지문 1에서 투어의 마지막 순서(destination)를 찾아보면 (D)가 정답임을 알 수 있다.

정답 (D)

박 씨는 투어의 어느 부분이 불만족스러웠는가?
(A) 유니언 역에서의 배웅
(B) 로얄 온타리오 박물관
(C) 하키 명예의 전당
(D) 댄포쓰 페스티벌

어휘 dissatisfied 불만스러워 하는 see ~ off ~을 전송하다, 배웅하다

Questions 191-195 refer to the following schedule, e-mail, and review.

European Manufacturing Commission

4th Annual Convention
Rowensburg Conference Center
Berlin, Germany
Saturday, October 10

Tentative Schedule

Time	Location	
9:00 A.M. - 9:30 A.M.	Greetings and Opening Speech by EMC Chairman Alek Sorvenski in the Cranz Banquet Room	
	Strauss Room	Witman Room
10:00 A.M. - 11:30 A.M.	[191] Textile Factory Management Techniques - Hans Tiskawet	Advanced [191] Coloration and Bleaching Technologies - Michelle Perdeu
1:00 P.M. - 2:30 P.M.	Outsourcing and Overseas Management - Rowena Wentworth	[193] Upgrading and Maintaining Equipment - Spencer Defiore
3:00 P.M. - 4:30 P.M.	Establishing Contacts with International Clothing Distributors - Anita Pitelli	International Shipping Strategies - Thao Lee

- [192] Speakers must confirm their availability with Johanna Swartz (jswartz@emc.com) no later than August 28. Failure to report availability will result in an automatic change of speaker.
- Speakers will be given complimentary accommodation at the [195] Deluxe Grand Hotel for one night. Please fill out the attached form and return it to Berta Joven by September 5. [195] If you are traveling with a colleague or an assistant, you will need to book another room at an additional charge. Please indicate that on the form.

From: James Watson <jwatson@hampshiretextiles.com.>
To: Johanna Swartz <jswartz@emc.com>
Date: September 1
Subject: EMC Schedule

Dear Ms. Swartz,

I apologize for the lateness of this e-mail, but I have just found out that my business partner, Spencer Defiore, is unable to attend the EMC Convention this year. I know he has already confirmed his attendance, but an unforeseen issue will prevent him from attending. ¹⁹³ As we are both knowledgeable about the topic, I would be happy to speak in his place. Please contact me as soon as possible to resolve this matter.

Sincerely,
James Watson

---

http://www.emc.org

| Itinerary | History | Donations | **Comments** |

I was extremely pleased with the turnout at the most recent EMC Conference. Not only was my presentation viewed by numerous attendees, I was able to conduct a question and answer session at the end. The attendees were well-informed about the topic and able to hold an in-depth discussion. In addition, my capacity as a speaker allowed me to make numerous international contacts during the whole of the conference. These contacts will be critical for growing my business in the future. Furthermore, ¹⁹⁵ my assistant and I were very pleased with the hotel we stayed at. All in all, speaking at the EMC Conference was an excellent experience.

- James Watson

---

191 What industry is the focus of the conference?

(A) Shipping
(B) Dairy
(C) Electronics
(D) Fabrics*

일정에 따르면, 발표자들은 무엇을 해야 되는가?
(A) 호텔 숙박비를 낸다.
(B) 10월 8일까지 베를린에 도착한다.
(C) 발표 자료를 보낸다.
(D) 행사 참석 여부를 확정한다.

어휘 ship 선적하다, 배송하다 participation 참가, 참여

192

According to the schedule, what are presenters expected to do?
(A) Pay for hotel accommodation
(B) Arrive in Berlin by October 8
(C) Ship some presentation materials
(D) Confirm their participation in an event*

일정(지문 1) 후반부에서 Speakers must confirm their availability with Johanna Swartz (jswartz@emc.com) no later than August 28.라며 참석 여부를 알려 달라고 하므로 (D)가 정답이 된다.

* paraphrasing: availability → participation

정답 (D)

왓슨 씨는 무엇에 대해 이야기하겠는가?
(A) 직물 공장 관리 기술
(B) 외주 및 해외 경영
(C) 기기 업그레이드 및 유지
(D) 해외 배송 전략

193

What topic will Mr. Watson most likely speak about?
(A) Textile Factory Management Techniques
(B) Outsourcing and Overseas Management
(C) Upgrading and Maintaining Equipment*
(D) International Shipping Strategies

각 선택지가 적힌 일정(지문 1)과 앞으로 있을 컨퍼런스에 대해 참석 의사를 밝힌 Mr. Watson의 이메일(지문 2)을 연계해서 파악해야 한다. '강연 주제'에 유념해 지문 2부터 살펴보면, 불가피하게 스펜서 드피오레가 빠지게 됐다며 그 대신 자신이 강연하겠다(As we are both knowledgeable about the topic, I would be happy to speak in his place.)고 한다. 지문 1에서 '스펜서 드피오레'의 강연을 찾아 보면 정답은 (C)임을 알 수 있다.

정답 (C)

리뷰에서, 첫째 문단 넷째 줄에 있는 "capacity"와 의미상 가장 유사한 단어는?
(A) 역할
(B) 시간
(C) 관점
(D) 경험

어휘 role 역할 perspective 관점, 시각

194

In the review, the word "capacity" in paragraph 1, line 4, is closest in meaning to
(A) role*
(B) time
(C) perspective
(D) experience

capacity는 '능력, 용량'이라는 뜻도 있지만 '(공식적인) 지위, 역할'이라는 뜻으로도 사용된다. 강사로서의 '지위' 덕에 인맥을 쌓았다는 요지이므로 선택지들 중 대신 들어갈 수 있는 단어는 (A)이다.

정답 (A)

왓슨 씨에 대해 무엇이 사실이겠는가?
(A) 독일에서 제조 공장 몇 개를 운영한다.
(B) 디럭스 그랜드 호텔 객실을 하나 더 예약했다.
(C) EMC 컨퍼런스에 매년 참석한다.
(D) 더 어려운 것으로 주제를 바꿨다.

어휘 operate 운영하다 plant 공장

195

What is probably true about Mr. Watson?
(A) He operates several manufacturing plants in Germany.
(B) He booked a second room at the Deluxe Grand Hotel.*
(C) He attends the EMC conference every year.
(D) He changed his topic to a more difficult one.

Mr. Watson이 작성한 이메일(지문 2) 및 리뷰(지문 3)를 살펴보면, 지문 3 후반부의 my assistant and I were very pleased with the hotel we stayed at이라고 하는데, '숙박에 관련된 부분을 일정(지문 1) 마지막 If you are traveling with a colleague or an assistant, you will need to book another room at an additional charge.에서 확인할 수 있다. 이에 앞서 언급된 호텔 이름이 Deluxe Grand Hotel이므로 (B)가 정답이다.

정답 (B)

Questions 196-200 refer to the following form, e-mail, and letter.

http://www.abi.org

Asia Business Insider

| This Issue | Contact Us | Subscriptions | FAQ |

Name:	Calista Lao
E-mail Address:	clao@rejuvenateproperties.com
City & Country:	Ho Chi Minh City, Vietnam
Subject:	Suggestion
Message:	As you know, Asia Business Insider is only available as a quarterly print magazine. However, given that the printing takes place in Tokyo, some customers are not able to receive their magazines until weeks later. The delivery of my magazine is often delayed up to three weeks. This has caused my company, Rejuvenate Properties, to miss out on some of the key property sales advertised in Asia Business Insider. 196 As a result, I think Asia Business Insider should provide customers with online subscriptions in the form of a downloadable e-book. This would help customers like me keep track of all current available deals.

Submit

To: ABI Editorial Staff
From: Akemi Nagata, Editorial Assistant
Date: Wednesday, 23 October
Subject: Meeting Summary

The following is a summary of the items discussed during the editorial meeting held on October 23rd with all members of the editorial staff.

196 Editorial director Hiroki Goto announced that Asia Business Insider will now include a downloadable e-book free of charge for all subscription holders. Furthermore, new subscribers may also choose to sign up for only the e-book issues at a lowered subscription price. The design company has hired two e-book designers to prepare each issue.

Editorial staff discussed which articles to include in ABI's next quarterly installment. Staff members agreed the issue will report on the merging of Haptrack International with Global Fund Partners as reported by Samuel Park. Articles on 197 Surami Technologies in India and Triple Star Manufacturing in Taiwan will be prepared by Jan Dubey and Samuel Park respectively. Editorial staff member Aiko Yano is still waiting to receive articles from freelance writers regarding the development of the new World Conference Center in Beijing.

¹⁹⁸ If they cannot meet the deadline, the articles will be included in the next issue.

어휘 editorial 편집의, 편집과 관련된 summary 요약, 개요 free of charge 무료로 furthermore 더욱이 subscriber 구독자 sign up for ~을 신청하다 installment 1회분, 한 권 merging 합병 manufacturing 제조(업) prepare 준비하다 respectively 각각 regarding ~에 관해 development 개발 meet 충족시키다 deadline 마감

Asia Business Insider
January · Vol. 7 · Number 1

Letter from the Editor,

This issue celebrates the launch of Asia Business Insider's e-book series. Subscribers can now download fully designed e-books that include all aspects of our print versions. The January issue will cover numerous business deals taking place in Asia. ¹⁹⁹ It will also include the launch of our new Editor's Commentary section in which the editorial staff will respond to questions and comments placed online.

¹⁹⁸ Make sure to keep an eye out for our next issue in which we cover all the pertinent details surrounding the plans for the World Conference Center in Beijing. ²⁰⁰ Make sure to sign up on our website at that time for a chance to win free tickets to the center's grand opening business conference next year.

Hiroki Goto

어휘 editor 편집자 launch 출시, 발표 aspect (국)면 cover 보도하다, 취재하다 commentary 해설, 논평 respond to ~에 응하다 comment 논평 make sure ~을 확실히 하다 keep an eye out for ~을 경계하다, 감시하다, 지켜보다 pertinent 적절한, 관련 있는

---

196 What is true about Ms. Lao?
(A) She only buys property in Vietnam.
(B) Her ideas were implemented by ABI.*
(C) She subscribes to several Japanese magazines.
(D) Her articles often appear in ABI.

Ms. Lao가 작성한 서식(지문 1)부터 살펴보면, 후반부의 I think Asia Business Insider should provide customers with online subscriptions in the form of a downloadable e-book에서 e북 제작을 제안한다. ABI 측이 작성한 이메일(지문 2) 둘째 문단에서도 e북 제작에 대한 내용이 언급(Editorial director Hiroki Goto announced that Asia Business Insider will now include a downloadable e-book free of charge for all subscription holders)되므로 이들 내용을 연계했을 때 (B)가 정답이 된다.

정답 (B)

197

Who will be discussing Surami Technologies?

(A) Hiroki Goto   (B) Samuel Park
(C) Jan Dubey*   (D) Akemi Nagata

Surami Technologies에 유념해 지문들을 살펴보면, 이메일(지문 2) 셋째 문단의 Surami Technologies in India and Triple Star Manufacturing in Taiwan will be prepared by Jan Dubey and Samuel Park respectively를 통해 정답 (C)를 확인할 수 있다. respectively는 두 가지 이상의 명사가 나열되고 그 각각에 대한 설명이 뒤따를 때, '(말한) 순서대로'라는 의미를 더해 문장을 명확하게 만드는 부사이다.

정답 (C)

수라미 테크놀로지에 대해 누가 논의할 것인가?
(A) 히로키 고토
(B) 사무엘 박
(C) 잔 두베이
(D) 아케미 나가타

198

What is suggested about Aiko Yano?

(A) She joined ABI as an e-book designer.
(B) She did not receive some articles on time.*
(C) She co-writes articles with Samuel Park.
(D) She was absent from the June 1 meeting.

Aiko Yano에 유념해 지문을 살펴보자. 지문 2 셋째 문단에서 베이징의 신개발 프로젝트에 대한 기사를 아직 기다리고 있다며 마감에 못 맞추면 다음 호에 실을 예정(If they cannot meet the deadline, the articles will be included in the next issue.)이라고 한다. 이와 관련된 선택지는 (B)인데 내용을 확실히 하기 위해 다른 지문들도 살펴보면, 지문 3 둘째 문단에 언급된 다음 호 예고(Make sure to keep an eye out for our next issue in which we cover all the pertinent details surrounding the plans for the World Conference Center in Beijing.)로 확인할 수 있다.

정답 (B)

아이코 야노에 대해 드러나는 사항은?
(A) e북 디자이너로서 ABI에 입사했다.
(B) 일부 기사를 제때 받지 못했다.
(C) 사무엘 박과 함께 기사를 쓴다.
(D) 6월 1일 회의에 불참했다.

어휘 absent 결석한, 결근한

199

What is indicated about Asia Business Insider?

(A) It has developed a new column.*
(B) Its subscribers are mostly located in Vietnam.
(C) It will relocate to Beijing, China.
(D) It prints six issues per year.

지문 3 첫째 문단에서 It will also include the launch of our new Editor's Commentary section in which the editorial staff will respond to questions and comments placed online.이라며 편집자 논평 섹션을 새로 만들었다고 한다. 따라서 (A)가 가장 적절하다.

* paraphrasing: section → column

정답 (A)

아시아 비즈니스 인사이더에 대해 드러나는 사항은?
(A) 새로운 칼럼을 개발했다.
(B) 구독자 대부분이 베트남에 있다.
(C) 중국 베이징으로 이전할 것이다.
(D) 1년에 여섯 호를 낸다.

어휘 relocate 이전하다, 옮기다

200

What is mentioned about ABI's website?

(A) It is only for ABI subscribers.
(B) It will be upgraded next year.
(C) It is available in seven different languages.
(D) It will host a give-away for subscribers.*

ABI's website에 유념해 지문들을 살펴보면, 지문 3 후반부에서 Make sure to sign up on our website at that time for a chance to win free tickets라며 무료 티켓을 받을 기회를 놓치지 말라고 강조한다. 따라서 (D)가 정답이 된다.

* paraphrasing: free ticket → give-away

정답 (D)

ABI 웹사이트에 대해 뭐라고 언급되는가?
(A) ABI 구독자들 전용이다.
(B) 내년에 업그레이드될 것이다.
(C) 7개 국어로 이용할 수 있다.
(D) 구독자들을 위한 경품 행사를 열 것이다.

어휘 give-away 증정품, 경품

ACTUAL TEST 4

a 100
b 200
c 300
d 400
e 500
f 600

PART 5

전 고용주의 인상적인 추천서 덕분에, 데릭은 관리직을 즉시 제안 받았습니다.

어휘 thanks to ~덕분에 recommendation 추천(서) previous 이전의 employer 고용주 immediately 즉시 offer 제안하다, 제공하다 managerial 경영의, 관리의

101

Thanks to the _____ recommendation from his previous employer, Derrick was immediately offered the managerial position.

(A) impress (B) impression
(C) impressive* (D) impresses

〈정관사(the) + _____ + 명사(recommendation)〉의 빈칸에 들어갈 수 있는 것은 명사를 수식하는 형용사 (C)뿐이다. 선택지 중에는 없지만 impressing도 문법적으로는 가능하다. 그러나 impressive라는 형용사가 이미 존재하기 때문에 이러한 경우에는 impressive를 사용한다. impress 깊은 인상을 주다, 감동을 주다 impression 인상, 감동 impressive 인상적인, 인상 깊은

* 감정과 관련된 현재분사/과거분사

- exciting - excited 흥분시키는 – 흥분한
- boring - bored 지루하게 하는 – 지루한
- interesting - interested 흥미로운 – 흥미를 느낀
- confusing - confused 혼란스럽게 하는 – 혼란스러운
- satisfying - satisfied 만족할 만한 – 만족스러운
- embarrassing - embarrassed 난처하게 하는 – 난처한
- surprising - surprised 놀라운 – 놀란
- disappointing - disappointed 실망스러운 – 실망한
- pleasing - pleased 기쁨을 주는 – 기쁨을 느끼는
- frustrating - frustrated 좌절감을 주는 – 좌절한
- tiring - tired 피로감을 주는 – 피로한
- depressing - depressed 우울함을 주는 – 우울함을 느끼는
- troubling - troubled 당황하게 하는 – 당황한
- worrying - worried 우려를 끼치는 – 우려를 느끼는

정답 (C)

네미스 에어는 더 이상 북쪽 지역들로 화물을 수송하지 못합니다.

어휘 no longer 더 이상 ~않는 transport 수송하다 freight 화물 region 지역

102

Nemis Air is no longer _____ to transport freight to the northern regions.

(A) license (B) licensed*
(C) licenses (D) licensing

be동사와 함께 동사구를 완성해야 하므로 (B)와 (D) 중에서 답을 찾을 수 있는데, 항공사는 화물 운송의 허가를 '내주는' 주체가 아니라 '받는' 대상이므로 수동태를 나타내는 과거분사 (B)가 정답이 된다. 또 능동태로 쓰였을 경우 license 다음에는 목적어가 바로 와야 하는데 빈칸 뒤에는 to가 있으므로 (D)는 오답임을 확인할 수 있다. license 면허(증), 허가하다 licensing 주류 판매를 허용하는

정답 (B)

제롬이 내일 경기 티켓을 구하려 했는데, 완전히 매진되었어요.

어휘 sell out 다 팔리다, 매진되다

103

Jereome tried to get tickets to tomorrow's game, but they are _____ sold out.

(A) complete (B) completed
(C) completing (D) completely*

<be + p.p.> 사이에 빈칸이 있으니 부사 (D)만 들어갈 수 있다. complete 완벽한, 완료하다, 완성하다 completely 완전히, 전적으로

정답 (D)

104

Nobody can enter this office _____ proper authorization.

(A) without* (B) unless
(C) only   (D) although

적절한 허가증 없이는 이 사무실에 아무도 들어갈 수 없습니다.

어휘 proper 적절한, 제대로 된 authorization 허가(증), 인가

'허가가 없으면 들어가지 못한다'는 요지를 완성해야 가장 자연스럽다. 따라서 (A)가 정답이 된다. without은 정답으로 매우 자주 출제된다. without ~없이 unless ~하지 않는 한 although ~이긴 하지만

정답 (A)

105

The annual charity banquet hosted by the Fredericton Children Aid Society is _____ to take place at the Grand Marian Hotel on December 7.

(A) given   (B) scheduled*
(C) found   (D) considered

프레더릭턴 아동 지원 협회가 주최하는 연례 자선 연회가 그랜드 마리안 호텔에서 12월 7일에 개최될 예정입니다.

어휘 annual 연례의 charity 자선 (단체) banquet 연회 aid 원조, 지원 take place 개최되다

행사 일정을 나타내는 문장이므로 (B)가 들어가 '~할 예정이다'라는 의미의 be scheduled to를 완성해야 한다. consider 고려하다

* 빈출 〈be p.p. to〉 문형
be advised to + 동사원형: ~하라고 조언을 듣다
be allowed to + 동사원형: ~하기로 허락되다
be asked to + 동사원형: ~하라고 요청을 받다
be expected to + 동사원형: ~하리라고 예상되다, ~할 예정이다
be invited to + 동사원형: ~하라고 부탁 받다, ~하도록 초청되다
be reminded to + 동사원형: ~하라고 상기되다
be required to + 동사원형: ~하도록 요구 받다

정답 (B)

106

The owner's manual includes detailed _____ on cleaning this microwave.

(A) instructions* (B) computers
(C) posters   (D) fixings

사용자 설명서에 이 전자레인지 청소에 관한 상세한 설명이 들어 있습니다.

어휘 manual 설명서 detailed 상세한 microwave 전자레인지

문맥상 청소하는 법에 대한 '설명'이라는 요지를 완성해야 가장 자연스럽다. 따라서 (A)가 정답이다. 이와 같은 문맥에서는 복수형인 instructions로 사용되며 전치사 on이 뒤따른다는 점을 익혀 두자. instruction 설명, 지시 fixing 고정, 설치, 설비

* 빈출 〈명사 + on〉 용례
ban on ~에 대한 금지
advice on ~에 대한 조언
reliance on ~에 대한 의존
focus on ~에 대한 집중/주목
opinion/view on ~에 대한 의견/견해
report/news/information on ~에 대한 보도/뉴스/정보
conference/workshop on ~에 대한 컨퍼런스/워크숍
effect/influence on ~에 대한 효과/영향력

정답 (A)

시 당국은 발레나 스트리트에 있는 빈 건물을 초등학교로 개조하기 위해 매입했습니다.

어휘 convert 전환시키다, 개조하다
elementary school 초등학교

107

The city purchased the _____ building on Balena Street to convert it into an elementary school.

(A) approaching (B) adjustable
(C) vacant*   (D) united

빈칸에는 building을 수식하기에 적합한 형용사가 들어가야 한다. 따라서 '비어 있는'이란 뜻의 (C)가 정답이다. approaching 다가오는 adjustable 조절 가능한 vacant 빈 united 연합한, 통합된

정답 (C)

고객들은 계산대에서 결제해야 합니다. 그렇지 않으면 처방전대로 조제되지 않을 것입니다.

어휘 provide 제공하다 counter 계산대, 판매대 prescription 처방(전) fill (처방전대로) 조제하다, (주문대로) 이행하다

108

Customers must provide _____ at the counter or prescriptions will not be filled.

(A) paid   (B) payers
(C) payment*   (D) pays

〈조동사(must) + 타동사(provide) + _____〉의 빈칸에는 목적어가 될 수 있는 명사 (B)나 (C)가 들어갈 수 있다. 그런데 문맥상 고객들이 '돈을 내야 한다'는 요지가 완성되어야 자연스러우므로 (C)가 정답이 된다. paid 유급의, 보수가 주어지는 payer 지급인, 납부자 payment 결제, 납부 pay 결제하다, 납부하다

정답 (C)

돌아오는 즉시 원본 영수증을 제시하지 않으면 회사는 직원에게 출장 비용을 변제하지 않을 것입니다.

어휘 reimburse 배상하다, 변제하다 expense 돈, 비용 unless ~하지 않는 한 original 원본의 present 제출하다 receipt 영수증

109

The company will not reimburse staff for travel expenses unless original receipts are presented _____ upon returning.

(A) mainly   (B) formerly
(C) nearly   (D) immediately*

'비용을 돌려 받으려면 돌아오는 대로 영수증을 제출하라'는 요지의 문장을 완성해야 가장 타당하다. 따라서 (D)가 정답이 된다. mainly 주로, 대부분 formerly 이전에 nearly 거의 immediately 즉시, 바로

정답 (D)

스틱크니 엔터테인먼트 가이드는 이 지역에서 식사하기 제일 좋은 곳을 찾기 위한 분명 가장 믿을 만한 출처입니다.

어휘 without a doubt 의심할 여지 없이, 틀림없이 reliable 믿을 수 있는, 신뢰할 수 있는 source 원천, 출처 region 지역

110

The Stickney Entertainment Guide is, without a doubt, the most reliable source _____ finding the best places to eat in this region.

(A) around   (B) for*
(C) as   (D) through

빈칸 이하가 믿을 만한 출처의 '목적' 또는 '근거'를 나타낸다. 따라서 전치사 (B)가 알맞다. around 둘레에, 주위에 as ~로서, ~처럼 through ~을 통해, ~사이로

정답 (B)

111

Mr. Tolliver, the head mechanic, started the repairs by _____ this morning but two more staff were available to help him after lunch.

(A) he
(B) his
(C) him
(D) himself*

빈칸은 전치사의 목적어 자리이므로 (A)와 (B)는 바로 소거할 수 있다. but 이하와 상반되는 상황을 만들려면 '혼자서, 다른 사람 없이'라는 의미의 (all) by oneself를 완성하는 (D)가 들어가야 알맞다.

정답 (D)

112

For optimal results, the manufacturer _____ applying this exterior paint when the weather is sunny.

(A) reminds
(B) recognizes
(C) recommends*
(D) registers

빈칸 뒤에 동명사가 있으니, 먼저 선택지 중에서 동명사를 목적어로 취하는 동사를 찾아보자. (C)가 문법상 적절한데, 문맥을 살펴보면 빈칸 이하는 최상의 결과를 위한 '권장' 사항이므로 정답임을 확인할 수 있다. remind 상기시키다 recognize 알아보다, 인정하다 recommend 추천하다, 권하다 register 등록하다

* 동명사를 목적어로 취하는 동사: enjoy, keep, finish, delay, postpone, mind, avoid, deny, give up, admit, consider, suggest

정답 (C)

113

Instructors at Darthmouth College have to submit their final student evaluations _____ the last day of this month.

(A) in anticipation of
(B) already
(C) before*
(D) so as to

빈칸 이하가 '특정일'을 가리키므로 '~전에'라는 의미의 전치사 (C)가 가장 적절하다. in anticipation of ~을 예상하고 so as to ~하기 위해서

정답 (C)

114

The Fitzgerald Theater is being renovated so concert organizers for Roland Gagnon's band are _____ seeking another venue.

(A) actively*
(B) activity
(C) active
(D) activate

진행형 동사구인 〈be동사 + -ing〉 사이에 빈칸이 있으므로 서술부를 수식해 줄 부사 (A)가 정답이다. actively 활발히, 활동적으로 activity 활기, 활동 active 활동적인, 적극적인 activate 작동시키다, 활성화시키다

정답 (A)

컨베이어 벨트가 수리되자, 공장은 생산을 계속할 수 있었습니다.

어휘 fix 고치다 continue 계속하다 production 생산(량)

115

Once the conveyor belt was fixed, the factory was _____ to continue production.

(A) valuable (B) responsible
(C) able*   (D) possible

'~할 수 있다'라는 의미의 be able to(= can)를 알면 쉽게 해결되는 문제이다. possible은 be able to처럼 '~을 할 수 있는 능력이 있음'을 의미하는 것이 아니라, 어떤 일이 일어날 '가능성이 있음'을 의미하며, It is possible to ~의 형태로 주로 사용된다. valuable 소중한, 귀중한 responsible 책임지고 있는, 책임이 있는 able ~할 수 있는 possible 가능한

정답 (C)

누군가 시모폴리 씨에게 그의 차가 쇼핑 센터 고객 전용 구획에 주차되어 있다고 말해야 해요.

어휘 park 주차하다 section 부분, 구획 reserve 예약하다, (자리 등을) 따로 남겨 두다

116

Someone should tell Mr. Sinopoli that _____ car is parked in the section reserved for shopping center customers.

(A) he   (B) him
(C) his* (D) himself

적절한 인칭대명사의 격을 찾는 문제이다. that절의 주어인 car를 한정하는 데 적절한 것은 소유격 (C)이다. 대명사의 격을 묻는 문제에서는 소유격이 자주 답으로 출제된다.

정답 (C)

라첸버그 모토사이클은 셰퍼빌 오토의 인수 제안으로 인해 상당한 이득을 누릴 것입니다.

어휘 benefit from ~에서 득을 보다 proposed 제안된 acquisition 습득, (기업) 인수

117

Ratzenberg Motorcycles will benefit greatly _____ the proposed acquisition by Shefferville Auto.

(A) from* (B) to
(C) on   (D) about

benefit이 자동사로서 전치사 from과 함께 쓰일 경우 '~에서 득을 보다'라는 의미를 나타낸다. 정답은 (A)이다.

정답 (A)

우리가 어제 받은 지원서들을 부장님들 중 한 분이 아직 검토해야 합니다.

어휘 application 지원(서), 신청(서) form 서식 division 부(서)

118

The application forms we received yesterday _____ have to be reviewed by one of the division heads.

(A) lately (B) evenly
(C) ever   (D) still*

적절한 부사를 찾는 문제이다. 지원서 검토가 '아직' 끝나지 않았다는 요지를 완성하는 데 알맞은 것은 (D)이다. 참고로, ever는 부정문이나 의문문 또는 if가 쓰인 문장에서 사용된다. lately 최근에, 얼마 전에 evenly 고르게, 균등하게, 대등하게 ever 언제나, 언제든 still 아직

정답 (D)

119

If bad weather forces a cancellation of the baseball game, full refunds will be issued to _____ who have purchased tickets.

(A) those* (B) which
(C) them (D) whichever

who 관계사절의 수식을 받을 수 있는 것은 (A)이다. '~한 사람들'이란 뜻의 those who를 통째로 외워 두자. whichever 어느 쪽이든, 무엇이든 ~한 것

정답 (A)

악천후로 야구 경기가 취소되면, 티켓을 구입한 분들께 전액 환불해 드릴 것입니다.

어휘 force 강요하다, 어쩔 수 없이 ~하게 하다 cancellation 취소 refund 환불 issue 발행하다, 발부하다 purchase 구입하다, 사다

120

Even though tourism revenue in this region usually _____ during the cold winter months, it always recovers in the warm spring.

(A) declines* (B) delays
(C) impacts (D) impedes

상반된 의미를 연결하는 even though가 문맥 연결에 대한 단서가 된다. 콤마 이하의 따뜻한 봄에는 '회복된다'와 대응되게 하려면 추운 겨울에는 '감소한다'는 뜻을 완성할 (A)가 알맞다. decline 줄어들다, 감소하다 delay 미루다, 연기하다 impact 영향을 주다, 충격을 주다 impede 지연시키다, 방해하다

정답 (A)

이 지역의 관광 수입이 추운 겨울에는 대체로 쇠퇴하지만, 따뜻한 봄이 되면 늘 회복됩니다.

어휘 even though ~일지라도 tourism 관광(업) revenue 수익, 수입 recover 회복되다

121

One important _____ the new personnel manager is responsible for is meeting regularly with factory workers to discuss safety matters.

(A) initiative* (B) initiating
(C) initiation (D) initiator

빈칸에는 is responsible for의 목적어가 되는 명사가 들어가야 하는데 문맥상 work, project 등과 의미가 유사한 단어가 필요하다는 것을 알 수 있다. 이때 사용하는 명사가 바로 (A)이다. initiative 계획, 진취성 initiating 기폭약 initiation 가입, 개시 initiator 개시, 발기인

* -ive로 끝나는 명사
alternative 대안 directive 지시 사항 executive 중역 initiative 솔선, 계획, 캠페인 objective 목적 relative 친척 representative 대표자, 대리인 adhesive 접착제 additive 첨가제

정답 (A)

신임 인사 과장이 맡고 있는 한 가지 주요 계획은 공장 인부들을 정기적으로 만나 안전 문제를 논의하는 것입니다.

어휘 personnel 인사(부)의 be responsible for ~에 책임이 있다, ~을 담당하다 regularly 정기적으로 discuss 논의하다, 토론하다 safety 보안, 안전 matter 문제, 사안

122

Ms. Gaitor is _____ with implementing policies that led to a significant increase in the number of clients.

(A) credited* (B) scored
(C) agreed (D) relied

'B를 A의 공으로 믿다, 공이라고 말하다'는 의미이며 대개 수동태로 표현되는 credit A with B(= A is credited with B)를 알면 해결할 수 있는 문제이다. score 득점하다, 채점하다 agree 동의하다 rely 의지하다, 신뢰하다, 믿다

정답 (A)

게이터 씨는 고객 수의 상당한 증가를 가져오게 한 정책들을 시행한 공이 있다고 여겨진다.

어휘 implement 시행하다 policy 정책 lead to (결과적으로) ~을 낳다 significant 중요한, 상당한 increase 증가, 인상

갤러리 티켓은 온라인에서 약간 할인된 가격에 구입하실 수 있습니다.

어휘 reduced 감소한, 할인한

123 Tickets to the gallery can be purchased online at a _____ reduced price.

(A) slightest (B) slighted (C) slighting (D) slightly*

〈부정관사(a) + _____ + 형용사(reduced) + 명사(price)〉의 빈칸에 들어갈 수 있는 단어를 찾아야 한다. 빈칸은 형용사를 수식하는 자리로 정답은 '약간 할인된'이란 뜻을 완성하는 부사인 (D)이다. slightest 최소의 slight 약간의, ~을 무시하다 slighting 깔보는, 경멸하는, 무시하는 slightly 약간, 조금

정답 (D)

지난 주 정책 회의에 우리 부서가 참석하려고 했는데, 일정상 상충되는 부분이 있었습니다.

어휘 division 부(서) conflict 갈등, 충돌

124 Our division _____ last week's policy meeting, but there was a conflict with the schedule.

(A) can attend (B) must have attended
(C) should attend (D) would have attended*

역접을 나타내는 but이 단서가 된다. 실제로는 일정이 상충되어 참석하지 못했다는 뉘앙스이므로 '~하려고 했었다'는 의미의 would have p.p.인 (D)가 적절하다. attend 참석하다, 출석하다

* 조동사 + have p.p.
would have p.p. ~하려고 (계획, 의도)했었다 (그런데 하지 않았다)
should have p.p. ~했어야 했다 (그런데 하지 않았다)
must have p.p. ~했음이 틀림없다   might have p.p. ~했을 것 같다
could have p.p. ~할 수도 있었다 (그런데 하지 않았다)
cannot have p.p. ~였을 리가 없다

정답 (D)

글리슨 씨는 호수 경관이 마음에 들어서 몰리 레인 대신 퀸 스트리트에 있는 사무 공간을 임대하기로 결정했습니다.

어휘 opt 택하다 lease 임대하다, 대여하다 instead of ~대신에

125 Mr. Gleason opted to lease office space on Queen Street instead of Morley Lane, _____ a view of the lake.

(A) prefer (B) preferring* (C) preferred (D) preference

빈칸 이하가 '이유'를 나타내고 있는데, 글리슨 씨가 '선호하는' 것이므로 능동을 나타내는 현재분사 (B)가 수동을 나타내는 과거분사 (C)보다 알맞다. because he preferred a view of the lake에서 접속사와 주어를 생략하고 동사를 현재분사로 만든 구문으로 볼 수 있다. prefer 선호하다, 더 좋아하다 preference 선호(도)

정답 (B)

내년 그롱댕 문학상 추천서들은 3월 말까지 선정 위원회에 제출돼야 합니다.

어휘 literature 문학 selection 선발, 선정 committee 위원회

126 _____ for next year's Grondin Literature Award must be received by the selection committee by the end of March.

(A) Subscriptions (B) Nominations*
(C) Supporters (D) Venues

'문학상 선정 위원회'가 수령할 대상으로 문맥상 적절한 것은 (B)이다. subscription (예약) 구독 nomination 지명, 추천 supporter 지지자, 후원자 venue 현장, 장소

* 빈출 〈명사 + for〉 용례
hope/desire for ~을 향한 희망/바람   demand/need for ~에 대한 요구/필요성
preference for ~에 대한 선호   admiration/respect for ~에 대한 존경
advertisement for ~에 대한 광고   reputation for ~에 대한 명성
reason/motivation for ~에 대한 이유/동기

정답 (B)

127

In an effort to make the team less _____, the manager sent all the sales charts to everyone as e-mail attachments rather than printing out hardcopies.

(A) waste (B) wasteful*
(C) wastefully (D) wasting

사역동사 make를 이용해 〈make + 목적어(명사) + 목적격 보어(형용사, 명사, 동사원형)〉의 문장을 만들 수 있는데, 빈칸 앞에 열등 비교를 나타내는 less가 있으므로 형용사가 들어가야 한다. 따라서 (B)가 정답이다. waste 낭비하다, 낭비, 쓰레기 wasteful 낭비하는 wastefully 낭비되게

정답 (B)

부서가 자원을 덜 낭비하게 하려는 노력으로, 매니저는 모든 판매 도표들을 출력하는 대신 모두에게 이메일 첨부 파일로 보냈습니다.

어휘 in an effort to ~해 보려는 노력으로 attachment 첨부 rather than ~보다는, ~하지 않고 hardcopy 출력/인쇄된 자료

128

Ms. Wilson must contact the bank manager _____ she needs a little more time for the payment.

(A) if* (B) soon
(C) only (D) then

빈칸 전후로 두 개의 절이 있으므로 빈칸에는 접속사가 들어가야 한다. 선택지 중 접속사는 (A)뿐이다. 문맥을 살펴보면 '연락해야 한다' 만약 '시간이 더 필요하다면'이라는 '경우, 조건'에 해당되므로 (A)가 정답임을 한번 더 확인할 수 있다.

정답 (A)

윌슨 씨는 납부에 시간이 더 필요하다면 은행 매니저에게 연락해야 합니다.

어휘 payment 결제, 납부

129

Besides speedy delivery, friendly service is something _____ the management of Caron Courier will never sacrifice.

(A) where (B) that*
(C) when (D) then

선행사 something에 대한 설명이 빈칸 이하이므로 목적격 관계대명사로 쓰일 수 있는 (B)가 들어가야 적합하다.

정답 (B)

신속한 배달 외에, 친절한 서비스도 캐론 택배 회사의 경영진이 절대 소홀히 하지 않을 사항입니다.

어휘 besides ~외에, 게다가 speedy 빠른 delivery 배송, 배달 management 경영(진) courier 택배 회사 sacrifice 희생하다

130

The editor of the sports section is more _____ about the articles she approves than the other editors.

(A) prominent (B) punctual
(C) rigorous (D) selective*

문맥상 '기사에 대해 훨씬 까다롭다'는 요지를 완성해야 가장 자연스럽다. 따라서 (D)가 정답이 된다. prominent 중요한, 눈에 잘 띄는 punctual 시간을 엄수하는 rigorous 철저한, 엄격한 selective 선택적인, 조심해서 고르는, 까다로운

정답 (D)

스포츠 섹션 편집자는 본인이 승인해야 하는 기사들에 대해 다른 편집자들보다 더 까다롭습니다.

어휘 editor 편집자 article 기사 approve 승인하다, 괜찮다고 생각하다

PART 6

인기 매장의 과감한 조치

캐슬바 — 캐슬바에서 가장 오래되고 제일 유명한 요거트 식당인 플래버 펀이 점차 늘어나는 불만에 대응해 실로 뜻밖의 변화를 도입했다. 식당 소유주는 많은 이들이 이례적이라고 느끼는 정책을 도입하기로 결정했다. 지난 2주간, 고객들은 식당에서 식사하는 동안 노트북으로 업무를 보는 일이 허용되지 않았다. 플래버 펀은 고객들이 식사 후 식당에서 자리를 뜨도록 장려하기 위한 정책을 이 도시에서 최초로 그리고 유일하게 시행한 식당이다. 고객들이 테이블에서 더 적은 시간을 머무르게 함으로써, 식당은 일일 매출을 20% 이상 늘렸으며, 고객들은 자리가 날 때까지 기다릴 필요가 없었다. ——133—— 이제, 캐슬바 곳곳의 몇몇 다른 유명 식당들도 비슷한 변화를 고려하고 있다.

어휘 bold move 과감한 조치 introduce 도입하다 unanticipated 예상하지 않은 result 결과 policy 정책 unusual 특이한 permit 허락하다, 허가하다 implement 시행하다 aim 목표하다 encourage 고무/격려/장려하다 throughout 전역의 similar 비슷한

Questions 131-134 refer to the following article.

Bold Move by Popular Shop

CASTLEBAR — Flavor Fun, Castlebar's oldest and most popular yoghurt restaurant, has introduced a truly unanticipated change as the result of a growing number of ---**131**---. The restaurant's owner decided to introduce a policy that many find to be unusual. For the past two weeks, customers have not been permitted to work on laptops while eating in the restaurant. Flavor Fun is the first and only restaurant in the city to implement such a policy aimed at encouraging customers to leave the restaurant after eating. By making customers spend ---**132**--- time at a table, the restaurant has increased its daily sales by over 20 percent, and customers did not have to wait for a place to sit. ---**133**--- Now, some other popular eating spots throughout Castlebar ---**134**--- similar changes.

131
(A) staff (B) prices
(C) complaints* (D) deliveries

무엇 때문에 변화가 도입되었는지 문맥을 살펴서 해결해야 한다. 식당 손님들이 테이블에서 오래 머물지 않도록 노트북 사용을 금지시킴으로 다른 손님들이 기다리는 일이 없어졌다는 내용이 뒤따르고 있으므로, 대기 시간에 대한 '불만'을 시정하기 위한 변화로 짐작할 수 있다. 따라서 정답은 (C)이다. complaint 불평, 불만 delivery 배송, 배달

정답 (C)

132
(A) some (B) less*
(C) any (D) much

노트북 사용을 허가하지 않음으로써, '자리에서 더 적은 시간 머물게 한다'는 요지의 문맥을 형성해야 가장 자연스럽다. 따라서 (B)가 정답이 된다. 참고로, any는 부정문과 의문문 또는 if/whether절에 쓰인다. less 더 적은

정답 (B)

133

(A) Customers will receive free coffee during the trial period.
(B) The new policy has already proven popular with customers.*
(C) Flavor Fun also has an outdoor patio for dining.
(D) Owners believe new staff need more training before starting work.

(A) 고객들은 시험 기간 동안 무료 커피를 받을 것이다.
(B) 새 정책이 고객들에게 인기 있음이 이미 입증되었다.
(C) 플래버 펀은 야외 식사용 파티오도 있다.
(D) 소유주들은 신입 사원들이 일을 시작하기 전에 더 훈련해야 한다고 생각한다.

전후 맥락을 살펴보면, '대기 시간이 줄었으며, 다른 곳들도 비슷한 변화를 도모한다'고 전개되므로 (B)가 가장 적절하다. trial 시험 삼아 해 보는, 시험적인 prove 입증하다, 증명하다 dine 식사를 하다

정답 (B)

134

(A) considers
(B) to consider
(C) being considered
(D) are considering*

빈칸은 문장의 술어에 해당되므로 (B)와 (C)는 바로 소거된다. 주어가 some other popular eating spots로 복수이니 (D)가 정답이다. consider 고려하다

정답 (D)

보청기를 쓰십니까? 냅턴 테크놀로지에 오늘 연락하세요!

8월에, 냅턴 테크놀로지는 히어링 1000에 대한 상세한 소비자 연구를 시작할 예정입니다. 이 엄청난 작업을 위해, 저희 팀은 300명 이상의 보청기 사용자를 찾고 있습니다. 참가자는 의사의 처방을 받은 보청기를 연구 시작일로부터 3년 이내에 사용하기 시작하신 분이어야 합니다. ──137── 관심 있으시면, 저희 웹사이트 www.knaptontechnologies.com/hearingaidstudy에 방문하셔서 간단한 설문에 응해 주시기 바랍니다. 저희 직원이 자격이 있는 지원자들께 연락할 것입니다. 모든 참가자는 이 연구가 끝날 때 200달러짜리 상품권을 받게 됩니다.

어휘 hearing aid 보청기 consumer 소비자 on behalf of ~을 대신해 huge 막대한, 거대한 undertaking (힘든, 중요한) 일 individual 개인 participant 참가자 prescribe 처방하다 complete 완성하다, 작성하다 survey (설문)조사 qualified 자격이 있는 voucher 상품권, 할인권 value (가치/가격을) 평가하다

Questions 135-138 refer to the following letter.

Do You Use a Hearing Aid? Contact Knapton Technologies Today!

In August, Knapton Technologies will begin a detailed consumer study on behalf of Hearing 1000. For this huge undertaking, our team is ----**135**---- more than 300 individuals who wear hearing aids. All participants must have a doctor prescribed device that they began wearing no more than three years ago ---**136**--- the beginning of the study. ---**137**--- If you are interested, we ask that you visit us online at www.knaptontechnologies.com/hearingaidstudy and complete our short survey. One of our staff members will be contacting qualified applicants. Every participant ---**138**--- a gift voucher valued at $200 upon completing of this study.

135
(A) seeking*   (B) insuring
(C) promoting (D) showing

제목 및 첫 번째 문장을 볼 때 '보청기 사용자를 모집'하는 글임을 알 수 있다. 따라서 해당 문장의 빈칸에는 (A)가 알맞다. seek 찾다, (추)구하다 insure 보험에 들다 promote 승진하다, 홍보하다

정답 (A)

136
(A) except for   (B) as
(C) because of   (D) at*

'연구 시작일을 기점으로 3년 전부터 보청기를 썼어야 한다'는 요지를 완성해야 문맥상 자연스러우므로 '특정 상태 또는 시점'을 나타내는 데 적절한 전치사 (D)가 정답이 된다. at the beginning of = at the start of ~의 초반에서 except for ~이 없으면, ~을 제외하고는

정답 (D)

137

(A) A hard copy of the prescription must be presented for confirmation.*
(B) New batteries will be available for all participants.
(C) We request that payment for your prescription is provided on the spot.
(D) The prescription will be filled immediately after submission.

(A) 처방전 사본을 확인용으로 내셔야 합니다.
(B) 새 배터리가 모든 참가자에게 주어질 것입니다.
(C) 처방전에 대한 결제는 그곳에서 해 주시기를 요청합니다.
(D) 처방전 제출 직후 조제가 될 것입니다.

'보청기를 처방 받은 사람만 참여 가능하다'는 요건 설명에 이어지는 자리이다. 따라서 '처방전을 받았음을 증빙하는 방법'에 대한 (A)가 가장 적절하다. prescription 처방전 present 제출하다 confirmation 확인 payment 결제, 납부 fill 충족시키다, (어떤 일을) 하다 immediately after 직후 submission 제출

정답 (A)

138

(A) will receive*   (B) had received
(C) to receive   (D) to be received

빈칸은 문장의 술어에 해당되므로 (C)와 (D)는 바로 소거할 수 있다. 한편, 연구가 끝나고 상품권을 받는 것은 '앞으로 있을 일'에 대한 설명이니 미래시제 (A)가 정답이다.

정답 (A)

다음 달에, 일본 최고의 가전제품 제조사인 자키 주식회사의 본사가 현대식 사무 건물이 최근 개조된 아오가이 스트리트 117번지로 이전할 예정입니다. 자키는 아오가이 건물 최상부의 7개 층을 쓸 것입니다. 이 새로운 곳에서, 직원들은 근사한 사무 공간과 편리한 편의 시설로 이루어진 약 90,000평방미터를 사용할 것입니다. —141— "우리의 최신 하이테크 냉장고와 오븐들을 전시하기에 최적인 장소입니다."라고 자키 대변인 카오리 아키바 씨가 말했습니다. 아키바 씨는 디자인 및 기술 부서들은 원래 장소인 오가와 건물에 남을 것이라고도 말했습니다.

어휘 headquarters 본사 manufacturer 제조업체 relocate 이전하다 renovate 개조하다 square meter 평방미터 convenient 편리한 amenities 편의 시설, 오락 시설 refrigerator 냉장고 spokesperson 대변인 note 주목하다, 언급하다 remain 남다 original 원래의 spot 장소, 곳

Questions 139-142 refer to the following press release.

Next month, the national headquarters of Zaki Ltd., Japan's top manufacturer of ---**139**---, will relocate to 117 Aoyagi Street, where a modern office building was recently renovated. Zaki will ---**140**--- the top seven floors of the Aoyagi Building. In this new location, the staff will enjoy over 90,000 square meters of beautiful office space and convenient amenities. ---**141**--- "That is the perfect place to display our latest high-tech refrigerators and ovens." said Kaori Akiba, spokesperson for Zaki. Ms. Akiba noted that the design and engineer divisions will remain in ---**142**--- original spot in the Ogawa Building.

139

(A) furniture (B) apparel
(C) wallpaper (D) appliances*

업체 성격을 나타내는 적절한 어휘를 골라야 한다. 후반부에서 냉장고와 오븐이 언급되므로(high-tech refrigerators and ovens) 이를 통칭할 수 있는 (D)가 정답이 된다. apparel 의류 wallpaper 벽지 appliances 가전제품

정답 (D)

140

(A) sell (B) paint
(C) occupy* (D) photograph

건물의 특정 층을 '쓸' 것이라는 맥락이 완성되어야 가장 타당하다. 따라서 (C)가 정답이다. occupy 차지하다, 사용하다 photograph 사진을 찍다

정답 (C)

141

(A) Zaki's products are known for their cutting-edge designs and energy efficiency.
(B) Zaki also plans to lease additional retail space on the first floor of the building.*
(C) Zaki was listed in the Tokyo Times as one of the top 20 places to work in Asia.
(D) Zaki stock doubled in value immediately following the announcement.

(A) 자키의 제품들은 최첨단 디자인과 에너지 효율로 유명합니다.
(B) 자키는 건물 1층에 판매 공간도 추가로 임대할 계획입니다.
(C) 자키는 아시아에서 가장 일하기 좋은 곳 20 군데 중 한 곳으로 도쿄 타임즈에 실렸습니다.
(D) 자키 주식은 발표 직후 가치가 두 배로 올랐습니다.

앞서 '층 사용'에 대해 언급되었으므로 (B)처럼 '공간 임대'에 대한 내용이 전개되어야 가장 자연스럽다. 또 빈칸 뒤의 문장도 제품 전시를 위한 공간에 대해 언급하고 있으므로 (B)가 정답임을 한번 더 확인할 수 있다. cutting-edge 최첨단의 energy efficiency 에너지 효율 lease 임대하다 retail 소매(상) stock 주식 자본 immediately following 직후

정답 (B)

142

(A) it   (B) their*
(C) what   (D) any

〈형용사 + 명사〉 앞에 들어가야 하므로 소유격 대명사 (B)나 한정사 (D)가 들어갈 수 있는데 문맥상 '두 부서'(design and engineer divisions)의 위치에 대한 설명이므로 (B)가 정답이다.

정답 (B)

Questions 143-146 refer to the following e-mail.

To: Kaori Sazaki <ssawaki601@e-mail.co.jp>
From: Customer Service <customerserv@elsworth.co.uk>
Date: Thursday, 16 October 8:56 P.M.
Subject: inquiry about website

Dear Ms. Sazaki:

We would like to thank you for leaving a comment in the feedback section of our website regarding the instruction booklet for the EW2500 digital camera. You indicated that the instructions on how to upload an image to a phone or mobile device is confusing and we completely agree with you ----**143**---- that point. ---**144**--- Our publications division has ---**145**--- made some revisions to the section that details the specific software and cable needed to transfer an image from your particular camera. We have made the ----**146**---- version of the instruction booklet available on our website. You can find it under the New Digital Camera section. If you prefer a print version, we will gladly send it by regular mail but delivery will take at least one week.

Sincerely,

Lirim Kilgore
Customer Service Agent
Elsworth Camera Company

143

(A) all (B) on*
(C) what (D) of

그 점에 '대해' 동의한다는 요지의 문맥이므로 '~에 관하여'라는 의미를 나타낼 전치사 (B)가 빈칸에 가장 적절하다.

정답 (B)

144

(A) The EW2500 digital camera is currently our most popular item.
(B) We can send you the complete instructions via e-mail if you wish.
(C) Other customers have submitted feedback about the same issue.*
(D) Most of our customers are based in the southern regions of Asia.

빈칸 앞에서는 고객이 제기한 문제의 내용이, 빈칸 뒤에서는 수정 사항이 언급된다. 그러니 동일한 문제가 여러 번 발생 또는 제기되었다는 내용인 (C)가 들어가야 흐름상 타당하다. item 물건, 제품 complete 완전한 submit 제출하다 issue 문제, 사안 be based in ~에 근거지를 두다

정답 (C)

145

(A) instead (B) likewise
(C) therefore* (D) nevertheless

〈문제 제기 → 해결 방안〉이라는 흐름이므로 '인과관계'를 나타내는 (C)가 가장 적절하다.
instead 대신에 likewise 똑같이 therefore 따라서 nevertheless 그런데도

정답 (C)

146

(A) original (B) updated*
(C) absolute (D) focused

앞서 made some revisions이라며 안내 책자를 수정했다고 한다. 따라서 '수정판'이라는 의미를 드러내는 데 적절한 형용사는 (B)이다. original 원래의 updated 개정된 absolute 완전한 focused 집중한, 집중적인

정답 (B)

수신: 론 카푸어, 553-0304
발신: 젤다 빈센티

젤다 씨, 제 스케줄북을 사무실에 두었어요. 2시에 고객을 만나야 하는데 정확한 장소가 기억 나지 않아요. 148 막 데니스 그릴을 나서 회의로 바로 가려던 참이었어요. 147 제 스케줄북을 확인해서 주소 좀 보내 주시겠어요?

PART 7

Questions 147-148 refer to the following text message.

From: Ron Kapoor, 553-0304
To: Zelda Vincenti

Zelda, I left my schedule book in the office. I have to meet a client at 2:00, but I can't remember the exact location. 148 I'm just about to leave Denny's Grill and had planned to go straight to the meeting. 147 Can you check my book and send me the address?

어휘 leave 남기다, 떠나다 exact 정확한 location 위치, 소재지 check 확인하다

카푸어 씨는 빈센티 씨에게 왜 문자를 보냈는가?
(A) 그의 서류 가방을 찾았는지 물어보기 위해서
(B) 취소된 회의에 대해 문의하기 위해서
(C) 주소를 보내 달라고 요청하기 위해서
(D) 식당을 예약하기 위해서

어휘 briefcase 서류 가방 inquire 문의하다 request 요청하다 make a reservation 예약하다

147

Why did Mr. Kapoor send a text message to Ms. Vincenti?
(A) To ask if she found his briefcase
(B) To inquire about a canceled meeting
(C) To request that she send him an address*
(D) To make a restaurant reservation

사무실에 수첩을 놓고 나왔다며 확인하고 미팅 주소를 보내 달라(Can you check my book and send me the address?)고 부탁하는 맥락으로 볼 때 (C)가 가장 적절하다. 짧은 지문에서는 이처럼 전체 맥락을 이해해야 해결할 수 있는 문제가 종종 출제된다.

정답 (C)

카푸어 씨는 아마도 다음에 무엇을 하겠는가?
(A) 식당을 나갈 것이다.
(B) 사무실로 갈 것이다.
(C) 웹사이트를 확인할 것이다.
(D) 고객에게 전화할 것이다.

148

What will Mr. Kapoor probably do next?
(A) Leave a restaurant*
(B) Go to his office
(C) Check a website
(D) Call a client

I'm just about to leave Denny's Grill and had planned to go straight to the meeting.이라며 이제 식당(Denny's Grill)을 나가려는 참이라고 했으므로 (A)가 정답이 된다.

정답 (A)

Questions 149-150 refer to the following advertisement.

[149] The American chapter of Ancient Worlds Archaeological Foundation seeks two full-time interns to assist with our Archaeological dig near Siem Reap, Cambodia.

[150 (A)] Candidates must have completed a 4-year degree in Archaeological studies or must be currently enrolled in their 4th year of an Archaeology program.

Research experience is a must, and [150 (C)] candidates with hands-on field training will be given preference.

[150 (B)] Applicants must be willing to travel to the dig site during the months of August through October. Accommodation and flights will be paid for by the foundation.

Interns will be paid a lump sum at the end of the trip. At the discretion of the project coordinator, interns may be hired as full-time employees following the dig's conclusion.

---

149 What is indicated about the American chapter of Ancient Worlds Archaeological Foundation?

(A) It wants to hire one part-time intern.
(B) It conducts digs in foreign countries.*
(C) It does not pay its interns except for travel expenses.
(D) It was founded three years ago.

150 What is NOT a qualification for the position?

(A) University education
(B) Willingness to travel
(C) Field training
(D) Computer knowledge*

수신: 티몬스 의료 연구소 직원들
발신: 앤더슨 백스터, 노무 부서장
제목: 발표
날짜: 4월 5일

전 직원에게 알립니다.

다음 주 목요일, 4월 13일에, 203호 강당에서 특별 발표회가 있을 예정입니다. **151 마리아 세르지오는 웨스트우드 대학의 수석 연구원으로**, 지난 5년간 그곳에서 연구를 해 왔습니다. 그녀는 새로운 백신 개발 프로젝트를 이끌었으며 몇 가지 새로운 암 치료법을 개발하기 위해 영국 런던의 연구원들과 협력해 왔습니다. 웨스트우드 대학에 합류하기 전에, 세르지오는 호주 시드니의 의료 연구 협회에서 명성을 떨쳤습니다. 그곳에서, **153 저는 몇몇 획기적인 프로젝트들을 수행하는 가운데 그녀에게서 배울 기회가 있었습니다. 152 세르지오 씨는 다음 주에 이곳 밴쿠버로 와서** 실험 기법들에 관한 자신의 신간에 대해 이야기해 주기로 했습니다. 그 발표에 전 직원이 참석하시기 바랍니다.

Questions 151-153 refer to the following memo.

To: Timmons Medical Research Staff
From: Anderson Baxtor, Director of Employee Relations
Re: Presentation
Date: 5 April

Attention all staff members,

Next Thursday, 13 April, we will have a special presentation in auditorium 203. **151 Maria Sergios is a senior researcher** at the University of Westwood, where she has conducted research for the last five years. She headed the development of a new series of vaccines in addition to partnering with researchers in London, England to work on the development of several new treatments for cancer. Before joining the University of Westwood, Sergios made a name for herself at the Institute of Medical Research in Sydney, Australia. There, **153 I had the chance to learn from her during several ground-breaking projects. 152 Ms. Sergios will be here in Vancouver next week** and has agreed to share her latest publication on laboratory techniques with us. All staff members are required to attend the presentation.

어휘 relation 관계 auditorium 객석, 강당 senior 선임의 conduct (특정한 일을) 하다 head 이끌다, 책임지다 development 개발 in addition to ~에 더하여 several 몇몇의 treatment 치료(법) make a name for oneself 이름을 떨치다, 유명해지다 institute 기관, 협회 ground-breaking 신기원을 이룬, 획기적인 agree 동의하다 share 공유하다 publication 출판(물) laboratory 실험실 attend 참석하다, 출석하다

본 메모는 무엇을 논의하는가?
(A) 새로운 실험실을 설립하기 위한 계획
(B) 새로운 일자리
(C) 한 과학자의 경력
(D) 프로젝트 마감일들

어휘 found 설립하다 deadline 마감

151

What does the memo discuss?
(A) Plans to found a new lab
(B) A new job opening
(C) A scientist's career*
(D) Deadlines for a project

다음 주로 예정된 발표회에서 강연할 연구원(Maria Sergios is a senior researcher)에 대한 소개가 전반적으로 다뤄진다. 따라서 (C)가 가장 적절하다.

* paraphrasing: researcher → scientist

정답 (C)

152

Where is Timmons Medical Research located?

(A) In London
(B) In Sydney
(C) In Westwood
(D) In Vancouver*

Timmons Medical Research가 본 메모 작성자 및 수신자의 직장임을 파악하고 특정 지명에 유의해 지문을 살펴보면, 후반부의 Ms. Sergios will be here in Vancouver next week의 here를 통해 정답 (D)를 찾을 수 있다.

정답 (D)

티몬스 의료 연구소는 어디에 있는가?
(A) 런던에
(B) 시드니에
(C) 웨스트우드에
(D) 밴쿠버에

153

What does Mr. Baxtor indicate about Ms. Sergios?

(A) She is his former mentor.*
(B) She is moving to Vancouver.
(C) She will join his research team.
(D) She will open her own laboratory.

Mr. Baxter가 작성자(1인칭)임을 유념하고 살펴보면, 후반부에서 프로젝트들을 수행하는 가운데 그녀에게서 배웠다(I had the chance to learn from her during several ground-breaking projects.)고 하는 데서 (A)가 정답임을 알 수 있다.

정답 (A)

백스터 씨는 세르지오 씨에 대해 뭐라고 하는가?
(A) 그녀는 자신의 멘토였다.
(B) 그녀는 밴쿠버로 이사할 것이다.
(C) 그녀는 자신의 연구 팀에 들어올 것이다.
(D) 그녀는 실험실을 열 것이다.

어휘 former 이전의

자말 마이어스 오전 10:30
안녕하세요, 퍼거슨. 전 아직 데이비스 프린터스에서 현수막 두 개를 기다리고 있어요. 먼저 가서 설치를 시작하시겠어요? 154 제 책상 맨 위 오른쪽 서랍에 행사장 열쇠를 두었어요.

퍼거슨 보이드 오전 10:33
찾았어요. 지금 출발할게요.

자말 마이어스 오전 10:35
정말 고마워요. 시상식이 1시 30분에야 시작하지만, 모든 장비를 재확인해야 해요.

퍼거슨 보이드 오전 10:40
확실히 하기 위해 그러는데요, 155 시상식을 엘리엇 스트리트에 있는 구 시청 건물에서 하죠, 맞죠? 퀸 스트리트에 있는 새 건물이 아니죠?

자말 마이어스 오전 10:42
155 맞아요. 시상식 직후에는, 사진사가 앞 잔디밭에서 수상자들 사진을 찍을 거예요. 그래서 제가 야외에서 쓸 현수막을 하나 더 주문했어요. 현수막을 받는 대로 구 시청 건물로 갈게요.

퍼거슨 보이드 오전 10:45
좋아요, 이따 봬요!

Questions 154-155 refer to the following text message chain.

Jamal Myers 10:30 A.M.
Hi, Ferguson. I'm still at Davis Printers waiting for our two banners. Could you go ahead and begin setting up? 154 I put the key to the room in the top right drawer of my desk.

Ferguson Boyd 10:33 A.M.
Found it. I'm leaving now.

Jamal Myers 10:35 A.M.
Thanks a lot. I know the award ceremony doesn't start until 1:30, but we need to double check all the equipment.

Ferguson Boyd 10:40 A.M.
Just to make sure, 155 we will be having the ceremony in the former city hall building on Elliot Street, right? Not the new one on Queen Street?

Jamal Myers 10:42 A.M.
155 Correct. Right after the ceremony, a photographer will take photos of the winners on the front lawn. That is why I ordered an additional banner to be used outside. I will catch up with you at the former city hall building as soon as I get the banners.

Ferguson Boyd 10:45 A.M.
Okay. See you in a little while!

어휘 go ahead 시작하다, 진행하다 set up 설치하다 drawer 서랍 leave 떠나다 equipment 기기, 장비 make sure 확실히 하다 former 이전의 lawn 잔디(밭) catch up (먼저 간 사람을) 따라잡다

오전 10시 33분에, 보이드 씨가 "찾았어요."라고 쓸 때 의미하는 바는?
(A) 고객이 필요로 하는 정보를 전달하겠다.
(B) 운전 중에 데이비스 프린터스를 발견했다.
(C) 현장 열쇠를 손에 넣었다.
(D) 주소록에서 전화번호를 보고 있다.

어휘 notice 알아채다 venue 현장 directory 주소록

154
At 10:33 A.M., what does Mr. Boyd most likely mean when he writes, "Found it"?
(A) He will pass on the information a client needs.
(B) He noticed Davis Printers while driving.
(C) He has the key to the venue in his hand.*
(D) He is looking at a phone number in a directory.

바로 앞 문장에서 I put the key to the room in the top right drawer of my desk.라며 행사장 열쇠가 있는 장소가 언급되었으므로 (C)가 가장 적절하다.
* paraphrasing: room → venue

정답 (C)

보이드 씨는 다음에 어디로 가겠는가?
(A) 기차역으로
(B) 회사 본사로
(C) 인쇄소로
(D) 구 시청으로

어휘 headquarters 본사

155
Where most likely is Mr. Boyd going next?
(A) To the train station
(B) To company headquarters
(C) To a print shop
(D) To the old city hall*

'목적지'에 유념해 지문을 살펴보면, 보이드 씨의 오전 10시 40분 메시지 중 we will be having the ceremony in the former city hall building on Elliot Street, right?와 그에 대한 대답인 Correct.(맞아요.)를 통해 정답 (D)를 확인할 수 있다.
* paraphrasing: former → old

정답 (D)

Questions 156-158 refer to the following letter.

Holt Golf and Country Club
34 Russet Drive
Edmonton, Alberta
www.holtgolf.ca

24 April

Mr. Henry MacArthur
220 Washington Avenue
Edmonton, Alberta

Dear Mr. MacArthur,

Thank you for purchasing a membership to Holt Golf and Country Club. --[1]-- From May 1st until September 30th, in addition to having your choice of tee-off time, you will have full access to our lounge, restaurant, and spa. Furthermore, [156] carbonated beverages are complimentary in all our cafés. Simply show your membership card when you order. --[2]--

In addition to all these incredible services, Holt Golf and Country Club is announcing yet another service for its members. [157] From now until the end of August, all members may invite guests for a round of golf on our extensive course. This feature is available from 8 A.M. until 4 P.M. only. Guest reservations must be made twenty-four hours in advance. --[3]--

If you have any questions or concerns, please contact our customer service hotline at 900-555-3344. --[4]--

Sincerely,
Mitchel Walker

어휘 purchase 구입하다, 사다 in addition to ~에 더해 tee-off 티에서 공을 치는, 티샷을 치는 access 접근, 이용 furthermore 더욱이 carbonated 탄산이 든 beverage 음료 complimentary 무료의 order 주문하다 incredible 믿을 수 없는 extensive 아주 넓은, 대규모의 feature 특색, 특징 in advance 미리, 사전에

156

What is true about Holt golf and Country Club?
(A) It offers its members free drinks.*
(B) It only opens during the spring.
(C) It offers discount memberships.
(D) It hosts seasonal parties.

회원들의 기본 혜택에 대해 언급한 첫째 문단에서 carbonated beverages are complimentary in all our cafés. Simply show your membership card when you order.라며 회원증을 보여 주면 카페의 탄산 음료가 무료라고 하므로 (A)가 정답이다.

* paraphrasing: beverage → drink, complimentary → free

정답 (A)

본 편지에 따르면, 8월 이후 무엇이 달라질 예정인가?
(A) 회원들이 스파를 이용하지 못한다.
(B) 회원들이 손님들을 데려오지 못한다.
(C) 골프 시간이 더 빨라질 것이다.
(D) 골프 강좌를 이용할 수 있다.

어휘 access 접근하다, 이용하다
bring 가져오다/가다, 데려오다/가다

157

According to the letter, what will be different after August?
(A) Members cannot access the spa.
(B) Members may not bring guests.*
(C) Golf times will be earlier.
(D) Golf lessons will be available.

키워드 August에 유념해 살펴보면, 둘째 문단에서 From now until the end of August, all members may invite guests for a round of golf on our extensive course.라며 지금부터 8월까지 손님을 동반할 수 있다고 하므로 이후에는 불가능하다는 (B)가 정답이 된다.

정답 (B)

다음 문장은 [1], [2], [3], [4] 중 어느 곳에 가장 적절한가?
"올해, 고객님께서는 저희의 모든 프리미엄 서비스를 누리실 수 있습니다."
(A) [1]
(B) [2]
(C) [3]
(D) [4]

158

In which of the positions marked [1], [2], [3], and [4] does the following sentence best belong?
"This year, you will be able to enjoy all our premium services."
(A) [1]*
(B) [2]
(C) [3]
(D) [4]

[1] 이후부터 여러 가지 회원 혜택이 나열되고 있다. 따라서 all our premium services 라는 말로 상세 내용이 기술될 것임을 예고하는 본 문장은 [1]에 가장 적절하다.

정답 (A)

Questions 159-162 refer to the following article.

Milan (July 14) – [159] Roberto Pelini, lead designer at Marshenco Fashions, one of Europe's top design companies, has announced he will retire from his role at the company. --[1]--

Since first accepting the position ten years ago, Roberto Pelini has worked hard to make Marshenco Fashions one of the most-recognized names in the industry. Because of Pelini's passion and eye for design, Marshenco has become a favorite among celebrities and his designs can often be seen both on the runway and the red carpet. --[2]-- [160] The company's success has even allowed for the founding of a sister company, Marshenco Accessories.

Irina Morova, former designer at Ruvera Design, will assume the position of lead designer at Marshenco. Morova has more than ten years of experience heading a major fashion company. [161] Her work has been featured in numerous fashion festivals, magazines, and has clothed some of Europe's top singers and actors. --[3]--

Following his departure from Marshenco, [162] Roberto Pelini will partner with Sophia Bertuski to found a new independent fashion house. Pelini is quoted as saying, [162] "I look forward to working with Sophia. Her creative vision is similar to my own." --[4]--

어휘 retire 은퇴하다 role 역할 accept 받다, 수락하다 position 직(책) recognized 인정된, 알려진 industry 산업 passion 열정 celebrity 유명 인사 allow 허용하다, 허락하다 founding 설립 assume 맡다 head 이끌다, 책임지다 numerous 무수한 clothe 옷을 입히다 following ~에 이어 departure 떠남, 출발 found 설립하다 quote 인용하다 look forward to -ing ~하기를 고대하다 similar 비슷한

159 What is the purpose of the article?
(A) To report on a company's closure
(B) To announce a change in a company's leadership*
(C) To advertise a new job opening at a company
(D) To publicize a new line of products

첫 문장 Roberto Pelini, lead designer at Marshenco Fashions, one of Europe's top design companies, has announced he will retire from his role at the company.를 통해 특정 회사의 인사 이동이 주제가 되리라는 것을 짐작할 수 있으므로 (B)가 가장 적절하다.

정답 (B)

마셴코에 대해 드러나는 사항은?
(A) 북미에 본사가 있다.
(B) 펠리니가 매입했다.
(C) 루베라 디자인을 소유한다.
(D) 두 번째 회사를 창립했다.

160 What is indicated about Marshenco?
(A) It is based in North America.
(B) It was purchased by Pelini.
(C) It owns Ruvera Design.
(D) It founded a second company.*

둘째 문단에서 The company's success has even allowed for the founding of a sister company, Marshenco Accessories.라며 성공에 힘입어 자회사를 설립하기까지 했다고 한다. 따라서 (D)가 정답이다.
* paraphrasing: sister company → second company

정답 (D)

이리나 모로바에 대해 뭐라고 언급하는가?
(A) 펠리니의 동업자가 될 것이다.
(B) 루베라 디자인에서의 활동은 성공적이었다.
(C) 원래 런웨이 모델로 일했다.
(D) 그녀의 디자인은 일반 소비자들을 위한 것이다.

어휘 originally 원래 average 평균의, 보통의, 일반적인 consumer 소비자

161 What is mentioned about Irina Morova?
(A) She will become Pelini's business partner.
(B) Her career at Ruvera Design was successful.*
(C) She originally worked as a runway model.
(D) Her designs are for average consumers.

핵심 인명 Irina Morova에 유념해 지문을 살펴보면, 셋째 문단에서 후임자로 언급된다. 이어 다뤄진 짤막한 경력과 성과(Her work has been featured in numerous fashion festivals, magazines, and has clothed some of Europe's top singers and actors.)를 통해 정답 (B)를 확인할 수 있다.

정답 (B)

다음 문장은 [1], [2], [3], [4] 중 어디로 들어가야 가장 적절한가?
"펠리니의 새로운 작품이 대중에게 언제 공개될지에 대해서는 소식이 없습니다."
(A) [1]
(B) [2]
(C) [3]
(D) [4]

어휘 as to ~에 관해

162 In which of the positions marked [1], [2], [3], and [4] does the following sentence best belong?
"There is no news as to when Pelini's new lines will be available to the public."
(A) [1]   (B) [2]
(C) [3]   (D) [4]*

'펠리니의 새 작품'은 마지막 문단의 향후 계획(새로운 패션 업체 창립)과 관련성이 높으므로 (D)가 가장 적절하다.

정답 (D)

Questions 163-165 refer to the following advertisement.

163 The First Annual Waterfront Food Truck Festival!

Ajax Food and Beverage Association is pleased to announce the first ever Waterfront Food Truck Festival. From Monday August 8th through Sunday August 14th, the Ajax waterfront will host a number of local food trucks. Guests can enjoy live music, prizes, and children's entertainment between the hours of 11 A.M. and 6 P.M. 164 Food truck items can be sampled for discount prices.

Famous Participating Food Trucks:

- ◆ Rio Tacos – Enjoy fresh appetizers and a variety of tacos and nachos
- ◆ Barbecue Madness – Marinated pork ribs, chicken wings, and pulled pork
- ◆ Benny's Fries – French fries topped with your choice of ingredients

Admission is free for all participants. 165 Parking will be available on a limited basis, so make sure to get there early.

For a complete list of participating food trucks visit www.ajaxwaterfront.com/foodtruckfestival.

어휘 annual 연례의 waterfront 물가 beverage 음료 association 협회 host 주최하다 a number of 다수의 participating 참가하는 appetizer 전채 a variety of 온갖 marinate 양념장에 재워 두다 pork rib 돼지 갈비 top with 표면을 덮다. 위를 덮다 ingredient 재료, 구성 요소 admission 입장 participant 참가자 limited 제한된 make sure ~을 확실히 하다 complete 완전한

---

163 제1회 연례 워터프런트 푸드 트럭 페스티벌!

아작스 음식 음료 협회가 제1회 워터프런트 푸드 트럭 페스티벌을 개최합니다. 8월 8일 월요일부터 8월 14일 일요일까지, 아작스 워터프런트에 우리 지역의 많은 푸드 트럭이 모일 예정입니다. 손님들은 라이브 음악, 상품, 어린이 프로그램을 오전 11시부터 저녁 6시까지 즐기실 수 있습니다. 164 푸드 트럭 음식들은 할인가에 시식하실 수 있습니다.

참가하는 유명 푸드 트럭은 다음과 같습니다:

- ◆ 리오 타코 – 신선한 전채 요리와 온갖 타코 및 나초를 즐기세요
- ◆ 바비큐 매드니스 – 돼지 양념 갈비, 닭 날개, 풀드 포크
- ◆ 베니 프라이즈 – 원하는 토핑을 얹은 프렌치 프라이

입장은 모든 참가자에게 무료입니다. 165 주차 공간이 부족하니, 일찍 도착하십시오.

참가하는 푸드 트럭 전체 목록을 확인하시려면 www.ajaxwaterfront.com/foodtruckfestival을 방문하시기 바랍니다.

163

What is being advertised?

(A) A restaurant's grand opening
(B) A concert in the park
(C) An auto show
(D) A new community event*

제목 The First Annual Waterfront Food Truck Festival!을 통해 (D)가 가장 적절하다는 것을 알 수 있다.

* paraphrasing: first → new, festival → event

정답 (D)

무엇이 광고되고 있는가?
(A) 식당의 개점
(B) 공원에서의 콘서트
(C) 자동차 박람회
(D) 지역의 새로운 행사

참가하는 푸드 트럭에 대해 뭐라고 언급되는가?
(A) 다양한 도시들로 여행할 것이다.
(B) 무료 선물을 나눠 줄 것이다.
(C) 종일 영업할 것이다.
(D) 할인된 가격에 음식을 팔 것이다.

어휘 distribute 나눠 주다, 유통하다 reduced 할인된

164

What is mentioned about the participating food trucks?
(A) They will travel to various cities.
(B) They will distribute free gifts.
(C) They will be open all day.
(D) They will sell food at reduced prices.*

첫째 문단에서 Food truck items can be sampled for discount prices.라며 할인가에 시식할 수 있다고 하므로 (D)가 정답이 된다.

* paraphrasing: item → food, discount → reduced

정답 (D)

참가자들에게 어떻게 하라고 권하는가?
(A) 현장에 일찍 도착하라.
(B) 차는 집에 두고 오라.
(C) 입장료를 내라.
(D) 물가에서 야영하라.

어휘 encourage 격려/장려/고무하다 arrive 도착하다 leave 남겨 두다 camp 야영하다

165

What are participants encouraged to do?
(A) Arrive at the site early*
(B) Leave their cars at home
(C) Pay an admission fee
(D) Camp at the waterfront

권고 사항은 대체로 후반부에 나온다. 주차 공간이 제한적이니 일찍 오라(Parking will be available on a limited basis, so make sure to get there early.)는 당부를 하므로 (A)가 정답임을 알 수 있다.

* paraphrasing: get → arrive

정답 (A)

Questions 166-169 refer to the following e-mail.

From: Marcus Pentz
To: Tamara Woods
Date: October 10
¹⁶⁶ Subject: Information

Hi Tamara,

¹⁶⁷ Thank you so much for covering for Samira while she's away visiting family. Prior to leaving for her trip abroad, she was working on advertisements for two local properties. According to her files, she has put together the following descriptions:

776 Marshall Avenue is a three-story home situated on Lake Scougog. It features four bedrooms, upgraded kitchen appliances, a fully furnished basement, and a wooden fireplace. It is situated in a quiet area, but is within walking distance of local schools.

9902 Fenton Street is a three-bedroom home with ¹⁶⁸ ⁽ᴬ⁾ a large yard and an in-ground swimming pool. ¹⁶⁸ ⁽ᶜ⁾ A garage was recently built on the property and can hold up to two cars. ¹⁶⁸ ⁽ᴰ⁾ The home is located near all major shopping malls and the university.

I'm going to send over Samira's files, so you can update her descriptions and add any relevant information. ¹⁶⁹ These properties, along with photographs, must be submitted to Scougog Weekly's real estate editor by Friday. Please let me know if you have any questions or concerns.

Regards,
Marcus Pentz
Pentz Real Estate

---

166 Why was the e-mail sent?

(A) To request some files
(B) To give some job instructions*
(C) To provide payment information
(D) To ask for some local contacts

사미라에 대해 드러나는 사항은?
(A) 해외 여행을 자주 한다.
(B) 새 집을 구입했다.
(C) 신문사에서 일한다.
(D) 휴가를 떠났다.

167

What is suggested about Samira?
(A) She often travels abroad.
(B) She purchased a new home.
(C) She works for a newspaper.
(D) She has gone on vacation.*

Samira에 유념해 지문을 살펴보면, 첫째 문장 Thank you so much for covering for Samira while she's away visiting family.를 통해 (D)가 가장 적절함을 알 수 있다.

정답 (D)

펜턴 스트리트에 있는 주택에 대해 언급되지 않은 것은?
(A) 큰 뜰과 수영장이 있다.
(B) 이전에 웹사이트에 올랐었다.
(C) 새로 건축된 차고를 포함한다.
(D) 많은 주요 편의 시설과 가깝다.

어휘 amenities 편의 시설, 오락 시설

168

What is NOT mentioned about the property on Fenton Street?
(A) It has a big yard and a swimming pool.
(B) It was previously listed on a website.*
(C) It includes a newly built garage.
(D) It is close to many important amenities.

핵심 어구 Fenton Street가 언급된 셋째 문단과 각 선택지를 대조하면서 지문에 언급된 사항을 소거하는 식으로 문제를 해결한다. (A)는 첫째 문장의 a large yard and an in-ground swimming pool에서, (C)는 바로 이어지는 문장의 A garage was recently built on the property에서, (D)는 다음 문장 The home is located near all major shopping malls and the university.에서 확인할 수 있다. 따라서 본 문제의 정답은 (B)가 된다.

정답 (B)

본 이메일에 따르면, 스쿠고그 위클리에 대해 드러나는 사항은?
(A) 우즈 씨가 업데이트해야 하는 선정물들을 특집으로 다룰 것이다.
(B) 금요일마다 나온다.
(C) 부동산 가격에 따라 수수료를 청구한다.
(D) 지역 주민들에게 무료로 배포된다.

어휘 selection 선택, 선정(물) charge 청구하다 based on ~에 근거해 resident 주민 free of charge 무료로

169

According to the e-mail, what is indicated about Scougog Weekly?
(A) It will feature the selections Ms. Woods must update.*
(B) It comes out every Friday.
(C) It charges fees based on property prices.
(D) It is distributed to local residents free of charge.

핵심 어구 Scougog Weekly가 언급된 넷째 문단의 These properties, along with photographs, must be submitted to Scougog Weekly's real estate editor by Friday.를 통해 정답 (A)를 확인할 수 있다.

정답 (A)

Questions 170-173 refer to the text message chain.

Blake Wyatt [3:23 P.M.]
Ms. Parker, 170 I just found out there's going to be a parade on First Street. The area is going to be really crowded, so 172 the repaving of your restaurant's parking lot will have to wait.

Janice Parker [3:26 P.M.]
So does that mean you won't be coming in at all?

Blake Wyatt [3:28 P.M.]
No, we'll still be there. We can help get the basement storage rooms finished.

Janice Parker [3:31 P.M.]
Okay, great. How long do you think it will take to get everything done down there?

Blake Wyatt [3:32 P.M.]
I'll check now.

– Tim Robins has been added to the conversation. –

Blake Wyatt [3:35 P.M.]
Tim, how far have you gotten on the basement project?

Tim Robins [3:40 P.M.]
Well, 171 things were running smoothly until we found some water damage in the southeast corner. It looks like a big clean up job.

Blake Wyatt [3:42 P.M.]
What if my crew gave you a hand tomorrow?

Tim Robins [3:44 P.M.]
That might get us back on schedule. We might even be able to install the new refrigerators.

Janice Parker [3:45 P.M.]
If you're moving the fridges, you'll need access to the service entrance behind the building. I think you still have the key, right?

Blake Wyatt [3:47 P.M.]
Yes, I've got it. 173 Are there any spots behind the building where the guys can park for the day?

Janice Parker [3:50 P.M.]
There might not be any free if there's a parade. You should probably park in the empty lot on Fifth Avenue.

어휘 crowded 붐비는, 복잡한 repaving 재포장 parking lot 주차장 mean 뜻하다 basement 지하 storage 보관, 저장 check 확인하다 smoothly 부드럽게, 순조롭게 damage 피해, 손상 crew 작업반 give a hand 돕다 install 설치하다 refrigerator 냉장고 fridge 냉장고(= refrigerator) access 접근, 이용 entrance 입구 spot 장소 empty 빈

와이어트 씨는 무엇이 내일 작업을 방해할 것이라고 하는가?
(A) 공휴일
(B) 거리 행사
(C) 분실된 배송품
(D) 장비 부족

어휘 interrupt 방해하다, 중단시키다 event 행사 lack 부족

170

What does Mr. Wyatt suggest will interrupt tomorrow's work?
(A) A public holiday   (B) A street event*
(C) A lost delivery   (D) A lack of equipment

Mr. Wyatt의 메시지를 유념해 살펴보면, 3시 23분 내용에서 퍼레이드가 열린다(I just found out there's going to be a parade on First Street.)며 기다려야 할 것이라고 덧붙인다. 따라서 (B)가 정답이 된다.

* paraphrasing: parade → street event

정답 (B)

오후 3시 40분에, 로빈스 씨가 "대청소가 될 듯해요"라고 쓸 때 의미하는 바는?
(A) 보통 그의 작업반이 청소한다.
(B) 피해가 엄청났다.
(C) 현재 일을 좋아하지 않는다.
(D) 그의 작업반이 맡은 프로젝트는 너무 복잡하다.

어휘 significant 상당한 complicated 복잡한

171

At 3:40 P.M., what does Mr. Robins most likely mean when he writes, "It looks like a big clean up job"?
(A) His crew usually does the cleaning.
(B) Some damage was significant.*
(C) He does not like his current job.
(D) His crew's project is too complicated.

제시문 앞에 things were running smoothly until we found some water damage in the southeast corner라며 누수 문제를 발견할 때까지는 일이 순조로웠다고 하므로 문제가 심각하다는 뉘앙스로 보아야 적절하다. 따라서 (B)가 정답이다.

정답 (B)

파커 씨는 누구이겠는가?
(A) 식당 소유주
(B) 공사 인부
(C) 주차장 직원
(D) 가전제품 제조자

어휘 owner 소유주 attendant (공공장소) 수행원, 안내원 appliance (가정용) 기기 manufacturer 제조자, 제조 업체

172

Who most likely is Ms. Parker?
(A) A restaurant owner*   (B) A construction worker
(C) A parking attendant   (D) An appliance manufacturer

핵심 인명 Ms. Parker에게 이야기를 시작하는 첫 번째 문장에서 the repaving of your restaurant's parking lot will have to wait를 통해 정답 (A)를 확인할 수 있다.

정답 (A)

와이어트 씨의 질문 사항 한 가지는 무엇인가?
(A) 다른 입구로 가는 길
(B) 건물 열쇠가 있는 장소
(C) 지역 행사 시간
(D) 주차 공간 위치

어휘 directions 길 안내

173

What is one topic Mr. Wyatt asks about?
(A) Directions to another entrance
(B) The location of a building key
(C) The time of a local event
(D) The location of parking spaces*

Mr. Wyatt의 메시지를 집중해 살펴보자. 그의 메시지 중 의문문이 몇 개 나오는데 그 중에서 주차 공간을 문의(Are there any spots behind the building where the guys can park for the day?)하는 (D)가 이 문제의 정답이 된다.

정답 (D)

Questions 174-175 refer to the following webpage.

http://www.hamptonoutsourcing.org

HOME   CONTACT US   HISTORY   SERVICES

Hampton Outsourcing

Hampton Outsourcing is the first choice among companies who wish to outsource their production to overseas locations. In today's shrinking global village, [174] electrical component manufacturing can be completed cheaply and efficiently almost anywhere in the world. Our knowledgeable staff members will help you grow your company by connecting you with overseas business partners, [175 (B)] helping you obtain the correct licensing, and ensuring your overseas interests are carried out in an ethical manner. [175 (C)] Our clients are known for being environmentally responsible as they establish themselves internationally. In addition, [175 (A)] we ensure all your potential business partners receive advanced training in regards to troubleshooting all of your products.

Call Hampton Outsourcing today to speak with one of our representatives.

어휘 outsource 외부 위탁하다 overseas 해외의 location 위치, 소재지 shrinking 움츠리는 global village 지구촌 electrical 전기의, 전기를 이용하는 component 요소, 부품 manufacturing 제조업 complete 완료하다, 완성하다 knowledgeable 많이 아는 connect 연결하다 obtain 얻다, 획득하다 correct 정확한 license 허가하다 ensure 보장하다, 반드시 ~하게 하다 interests 이익, 이해관계 carry out ~을 수행하다, 이행하다 ethical 윤리적인 manner 방식 environmentally 환경(보호)적으로 responsible 책임지는 establish 설립하다, 수립하다 in addition 게다가, 더욱이 potential 잠재적인 advanced 고급의 in regards to ~에 관해서 troubleshoot 고장 수리원의 역할을 하다, 분쟁을 조정하다 representative 직원

---

174 Who most likely will be a customer of Hampton Outsourcing?
(A) Call center workers
(B) Insurance brokers
(C) Environmental agencies
(D) Home appliance companies*

첫째 문단의 electrical component manufacturing can be completed cheaply and efficiently almost anywhere in the world를 통해 '전기 부품 제조'와 관련된 업체가 고객이 될 수 있음을 알 수 있다. 따라서 (D)가 정답이다.

정답 (D)

175 What is NOT mentioned as a strength of Hampton Outsourcing?
(A) Superior employee training
(B) Knowledge of licensing
(C) Environmentally conscious procedures
(D) Familiarity with export taxes*

각 선택지와 지문을 전체적으로 대조하면서 지문에 언급된 내용을 소거하는 식으로 문제를 해결한다. (A)는 첫째 문단 마지막의 we ensure all your potential business partners receive advanced training in regards to troubleshooting all of your products에서, (B)는 helping you obtain the correct licensing에서, (C)는 Our clients are known for being environmentally responsible as they establish themselves internationally.에서 확인할 수 있다. 따라서 (D)가 정답이 된다.

정답 (D)

Questions 176-180 refer to the following letter and voucher.

To: Raphael Rosario <rosario@ebookmail.com>
From: Janelle Parik <jparik@alliancepremiumairways.com>
Subject: Your Flight
[180] Date: 6 January
[180] Attachment: voucher

Dear Mr. Rosario,

[176] Thank you for sharing your experience with Alliance Premium Airways Customer Service. [176, 177] I am sorry to learn about your negative experience on January 2. [177] According to the online form you completed, you had reserved a business class seat on a third-party website but you were forced to fly economy class because your reservation had been lost.

I have contacted the website you used to book your flight. Apparently, there was a computer malfunction, which caused some prior bookings to be deleted. Unfortunately, this resulted in some seats being resold. [178] I understand that you have already received a partial refund, but I'd like to offer you an additional coupon for your troubles. Please see the attachment for more information.

Sincerely,

Janelle Parik,
Customer Service Manager
Alliance Premium Airways

Alliance Premium Airways Voucher

$200 off your next flight

Details: Alliance Premium Airways would like to offer you $200 off your next flight. Please note, this coupon may only be used for international return flights. This coupon is [179] good until December 31st of this year. You may use this coupon at any Alliance Premium Airways kiosk or online at www.alliancepremiumairways.com.

Voucher Number: YY7732999938   Date Issued: January 6

[180] Issuing office :   ___ Vancouver   ___ Edmonton   ___ Montreal   [180] X Toronto

176

Why did Ms. Parik send the e-mail?

(A) To reply to an online complaint*
(B) To provide a job contract
(C) To cancel an airline ticket
(D) To inquire about a trip

이메일(지문 1)의 목적에 대한 결정적인 단서는 대체로 전반부에서 확인할 수 있다. 첫째 문단에서 경험담을 공유해 줘서 고맙다(Thank you for sharing your experience with Alliance Premium Airways Customer Service.)고 한 뒤 불쾌한 경험을 당하게 해 미안하다고 사죄(I am sorry to learn about your negative experience on January 2.)를 덧붙인다. 따라서 (A)가 정답이 된다.

정답 (A)

파리크 씨는 왜 이메일을 보냈는가?
(A) 온라인 불평에 대해 답장하기 위해서
(B) 채용 계약서를 제공하기 위해서
(C) 항공권을 취소하기 위해서
(D) 여행에 대해 문의하기 위해서

어휘 reply 응답하다, 대답하다 complaint 불평, 불만

177

What does Ms. Parik indicate happened on January 2?

(A) She solved a seating problem.
(B) A flight was unnecessarily delayed.
(C) Many business class seats were empty.
(D) Mr. Rosario got a seat in a lower class.*

Ms. Parik가 작성한 이메일(지문 1)에서 January 2에 관련된 부분을 찾아보자. 첫째 문단에서 1월 2일에 겪은 불쾌한 경험(According to the online form you completed, you had reserved a business class seat on a third-party website but you were forced to fly economy class because your reservation had been lost.)이 상술되므로 정답 (D)를 확인할 수 있다.

정답 (D)

파리크 씨는 1월 2일에 어떤 일이 생겼다고 말하는가?
(A) 자신이 좌석 문제를 해결했다.
(B) 비행기가 불필요하게 지체되었다.
(C) 비즈니스석이 많이 비었다.
(D) 로사리오 씨가 등급이 낮은 좌석을 받았다.

어휘 solve 해결하다 unnecessarily 불필요하게 delay 지체시키다, 지연시키다

178

What is suggested about Mr. Rosario?

(A) He requested a last-minute flight change.
(B) He flew from Vancouver to Toronto.
(C) He paid for his flight in advance.*
(D) He usually flies economy class.

Mr. Rosario가 수신자인 이메일(지문 1) 둘째 문단에서 I understand that you have already received a partial refund라며 '일부 환불을 받았다'고 하는데, 이는 이미 항공료를 냈음을 의미한다. 따라서 (C)가 가장 적절하다.

정답 (C)

로사리오 씨에 대해 드러나는 사항은?
(A) 막바지에 항공권 변경을 요청했다.
(B) 밴쿠버에서 토론토로 갔다.
(C) 항공료를 미리 냈다.
(D) 대체로 일반석을 이용한다.

어휘 last-minute 막바지의 in advance 미리, 사전에

상품권에서, 첫째 문단 둘째 줄에 있는 "good"과 의미상 가장 유사한 단어는?
(A) 양질의
(B) 운이 좋은
(C) 예의 바른
(D) 유효한

어휘 well behaved 예의 바른 valid 유효한, 정당한

179

In the voucher, the word "good" in paragraph 1, line 2, is closest in meaning to
(A) high quality
(B) lucky
(C) well behaved
(D) valid*

해당 부분을 찾아보고 제시된 보기들로 바꿨을 때 가장 유사한 맥락으로 전개되는 어휘를 정답으로 택해야 한다. '12월 31일까지 쓸 수 있다'는 요지의 문장을 완성하는 데 가장 적절한 단어는 (D)이다.

정답 (D)

파리크 씨의 사무실은 어디에 있겠는가?
(A) 밴쿠버
(B) 에드먼턴
(C) 몬트리올
(D) 토론토

180

Where most likely is Ms. Parik's office located?
(A) Vancouver
(B) Edmonton
(C) Montreal
(D) Toronto*

Ms. Parik가 작성한 이메일(지문 1)과 첨부 파일인 상품권(지문 2)을 연계해서 파악해야 해결할 수 있는 문제이다. 이 상품권은 1월 6일 Ms. Parik가 발행한 것인데 발행 지점(Issuing office)이 토론토에 표시되어 있으므로 정답은 (D)이다.

정답 (D)

Questions 181-185 refer to the following webpage and customer review.

REVIEWS   HOME   DESIGN TOOLS   CONTACT US

Flyer Frenzy, the best online flyer generator for businesses large and small!

With Flyer Frenzy, you can create custom flyers for your business. Whether you are advertising the opening of your business or simply trying to generate awareness about your services, Flyer Frenzy has everything you need to design the perfect flyer.

Step 1: Design Your Flyer

Our online generator has numerous customizable templates. Browse through our categories and select the right template for you. All our fonts are easy to change with just the click of a mouse. 181 If you want to accent your design with images, we have over 10,000 stock photos you can use at no extra cost. Furthermore, you can upload your own designs and logos to use along with any of our fonts.

Step 2: Select A Quantity

At Flyer Frenzy, we can print as few as 25 flyers for each order. However, the more flyers you order, the less you pay for each one.

Quantity	Price Per Item
25-300	20 cents
183 300-1,000	15 cents
1,001-1,500	10 cents
1,501 or more	5 cents

Step 3: Purchase A Digital Copy

182 For an extra flat fee of $50, you can download a digital copy of your design. This design is perfect for featuring on your business's website, as part of an e-mail newsletter, or as a printed advertisement.

Step 4: Finalize Your Order

Orders take five days to process; however, large orders may take longer to prepare. In the event that there are delays, you will be notified by e-mail.

REVIEWS   HOME   DESIGN TOOLS   CONTACT US

★ ★ ★ ★ ★ Flyer Frenzy has great services!

I own a local shoe store downtown and had been finding it hard to spread the word about our upcoming sales event. I decided to design my own flyer using Flyer Frenzy's online generator. I found it very easy to use, and the designs

을 1천 장 주문하게 되었어요. 제 디자인의 디지털 카피도 사서 웹사이트에 이용했습니다. 할인 행사는 대성공이었어요. 184 많은 고객이 시내 곳곳에 붙인 전단을 보고 행사에 대해 알았다고 하시더군요. 플라이어 프렌지 서비스가 무척 마음에 듭니다. 185 제가 둘러 본 여느 온라인 생성기들보다 훨씬 나아요. 그리고 템플릿은 훨씬 세련되고요. 다음에도 꼭 플라이어 프렌지를 이용할 겁니다!
— 젠 트리스탄

were very elegant. 183 **I ended up ordering 1,000 flyers.** I also purchased a digital copy of my design and used it on my website. Our sales event was a big success. 184 **Many customers said they'd heard about it from the flyers they'd seen posted around town.** I am extremely pleased with Flyer Frenzy's services. 185 **They are much better than some of the other online generators I browsed, and their templates were much more sophisticated.** I will definitely be using Flyer Frenzy again in the future!

- Jen Tristan

어휘 own 소유하다 spread 퍼뜨리다 upcoming 다음의, 다가오는 event 행사 elegant 우아한 end up -ing 결국 ~하게 되다 extremely 아주 be pleased with ~에 만족하다 sophisticated 세련된 definitely 확실히

웹페이지에 따르면, 온라인 생성기는 사용자들에게 무엇을 허용하는가?
(A) 이미지를 더할 수 있다.
(B) 웹 링크를 넣을 수 있다.
(C) 종이를 선택할 수 있다.
(D) 로고를 디자인할 수 있다.

181

According to the webpage, what does the online generator allow users to do?

(A) Add images*
(B) Include web links
(C) Select paper type
(D) Design a logo

'온라인 생성기' 이용법을 제시한 첫 번째 지문 단계 1에서 If you want to accent your design with images, we have over 10,000 stock photos you can use at no extra cost. 라며 이미지를 무료로 이용해 넣을 수 있다고 하므로 (A)가 정답이다.

정답 (A)

플라이어 프렌지에 대해 웹페이지에서 뭐라고 언급되는가?
(A) 제품을 무료 배송한다.
(B) 추가 요금을 내면 디지털 파일을 준다.
(C) 사용자들이 서로 디자인을 볼 수 있게 한다.
(D) 주문은 직접 매장에서만 받는다.

어휘 deliver 배송하다, 배달하다 free of charge 무료로 in person 직접, 몸소

182

What is mentioned on the webpage about Flyer Frenzy?

(A) It delivers products free of charge.
(B) It offers digital files for an extra fee.*
(C) It allows users to see each other's designs.
(D) It only takes orders in person at a store.

지문 1의 단계 3에서 일정 금액을 내면 디지털 카피를 받을 수 있다(For an extra flat fee of $50, you can download a digital copy of your design.)고 한다. 따라서 (B)가 정답이 된다.

* paraphrasing: copy → file

정답 (B)

183

What is indicated about Ms. Tristan?

(A) She received more flyers than she ordered.
(B) Her order was delayed by a few days.
(C) She received a fifty dollar discount.
(D) She paid fifteen cents per flyer.*

Ms. Tristan이 작성한 평가(지문 2)부터 '주문 내역'에 집중해 살펴보면, 중반부에서 I ended up ordering 1,000 flyers.라고 한다. 이 수량에 관련된 부분을 웹페이지(지문 1)에서 찾아보면 (D)가 정답임을 알 수 있다.

정답 (D)

트리스탄 씨에 대해 드러나는 사항은?
(A) 전단을 주문한 것보다 많이 받았다.
(B) 주문이 며칠 늦었다.
(C) 50달러를 할인 받았다.
(D) 전단 1장당 15센트를 냈다.

어휘 order 주문(품), 주문하다 delay 지체시키다, 지연시키다 pay 결제하다

184

What is suggested about Ms. Tristan's store?

(A) It advertises solely online.
(B) It put flyers up around town.*
(C) It holds sales every month.
(D) It gives discounts for online orders.

Ms. Tristan이 작성한 평가(지문 2)에서 Many customers said they'd heard about it from the flyers they'd seen posted around town.이라며 시내에 붙은 전단을 보고 왔다는 고객들의 말을 전하므로 (B)가 가장 적절하다.

정답 (B)

트리스탄 씨의 매장에 대해 드러나는 사항은?
(A) 온라인으로만 광고한다.
(B) 전단을 시내 곳곳에 붙였다.
(C) 매달 세일한다.
(D) 온라인 주문에 할인해 준다.

어휘 solely 오로지

185

According to the review, why does Ms. Tristan prefer Flyer Frenzy's services over other companies?

(A) They had faster delivery times.
(B) They had better design features.*
(C) They used better quality paper.
(D) They were cheaper to use.

평가(지문 2) 후반부에서 둘러 본 여러 곳보다 낫다며 템플릿이 훨씬 세련되었다(They are much better than some of the other online generators I browsed, and their templates were much more sophisticated.)고 덧붙인다. 따라서 (B)가 정답이 된다.

정답 (B)

평가에 따르면, 트리스탄 씨는 플라이어 프렌지 서비스를 왜 다른 회사들보다 좋아하는가?
(A) 배송 시간이 빨라서
(B) 디자인이 나아서
(C) 더 좋은 종이를 써서
(D) 사용하기에 더 저렴해서

어휘 cheap 싼, 저렴한

발신: linda@mailmail.com
수신: billing@startelecom.com
날짜: 4월 23일
제목: 청구서 번호 3788292

고객 서비스 담당자에게,

제가 3월에 받은, 유독 높게 부과된 휴대 전화 청구서에 관해 씁니다. 전화 청구서에 적힌 총액은 155.33달러였습니다. 이전에, 제 청구서는 매달 80달러에서 90달러 사이였고요.

연체료를 내지 않으려고 청구서를 이미 지불했습니다만, 186 왜 그렇게 많이 청구되었는지 이유를 알고 싶습니다. 제 청구서에는 이 요금을 설명하는 세부 사항이 없더군요. 최근 저는 데이터 사용을 업그레이드했었고, 그래서 추가 요금이 발생했을 수 있지만, 모든 장비에 대해 들어 두었던 보험을 취소하기도 했습니다. 187 제 취소 요청이 제대로 처리되었다면 이 두 가지 비용이 서로 상쇄됐을 겁니다.

이 문제에 대해 제게 333-0967-5563로 전화 주시기 바랍니다. 188 저는 오후 3시 30분 이후에만 통화 가능합니다.

그럼 이만,
린다 앨버트

Questions 186-190 refer to the following e-mails and log sheet.

From: linda@mailmail.com
To: billing@startelecom.com
Date: April 23
Subject: Bill Number 3788292

Dear Customer Service,

I am writing in regards to an unusually high cell phone bill I received in March. The amount listed on my phone bill was $155.33. Previously, my bill ranged between $80 and $90 per month.

I have already paid the bill to avoid any late fees, but [186] I am interested in knowing why I was charged so much. My bill did not show any details to explain these charges. I know I recently upgraded my data usage, which would cost extra, but I also canceled the insurance policy I had for all my devices. [187] These two costs should have balanced each other out if my request for cancelation was handled properly.

Please call me about this matter at 333-0967-5563. [188] I am available to speak only in the afternoons after 3:30 P.M.

Sincerely,
Linda Albert

어휘 bill 청구서, 고지서 in regards to ~에 관해서 unusually 대단히, 평소와 달리 amount 총액, 총계 previously 이전에 range 범위가 ~에서 ~ 사이이다 avoid 피하다 fee 수수료, 요금 charge 청구, 청구하다 usage 사용 cost 값, 비용, 값이 ~들다 insurance 보험 policy 정책 device 장치 balance (out) 상쇄되다 cancelation 취소 handle 처리하다 properly 제대로, 적절히 matter 문제, 사안

고객 서비스 연락 기록 시트
날짜: 4월 24일

직원 이름	계정 번호	전화 시간	해결 여부 예/아니오
마이클 박	BG44532	오전 9:33	예
준 바솔디	GH30993	오전 10:42	예
나디아 카푸어	TZ33221	오후 3:23	아니오
188 브루클린 스미스	GS17649	오후 3:45	아니오

Customer Service Contact Log Sheet
Date: April 24

Representative Name	Account Number	Call Time	Resolved? Y/N
Michael Park	BG44532	9:33 A.M.	Yes
June Bartholdi	GH30993	10:42 A.M.	Yes
Nadia Kapoor	TZ33221	3:23 P.M.	No
[188] Brooklyn Smith	GS17649	3:45 P.M.	No

어휘 log 일지, 기록 representative 직원 account 계좌, 계정 resolve 해결하다

To: linda@mailmail.com
From: tristan@startelecom.com
Date: April 25
Subject: Re: Bill Number 3788292

Dear Ms. Albert,

Thank you for e-mailing Star Telecom about your concerns. One of our representatives tried to call you at the time you specified yesterday, but there was no answer. I have looked into your problem personally and have found that your insurance cancelation never went through. Thus, [187] your account [189] registered charges for both the insurance policy and the upgraded data plan.

To correct this, [190] I have canceled your insurance plan and credited your account with $63.98, which will be carried over to your next bill.

If you have any additional concerns or questions, please reply directly to this e-mail.

Sincerely,
Tristan Mathews
Star Telecom Customer Support

---

186 Why was the first e-mail sent?
(A) To cancel a service
(B) To request another bill
(C) To ask about an invoice*
(D) To register for an account

187 What is suggested about Ms. Albert?
(A) She previously worked for Star Telecom.
(B) She called a Star Telecom customer service representative.
(C) She correctly identified Star Telecom's mistake.*
(D) She wants to close her account with Star Telecom.

4월 24일에 누가 앨버트 씨에게 전화했는가?
(A) 마이클 박
(B) 준 바솔디
(C) 나디아 카푸어
(D) 브루클린 스미스

188

Who called Ms. Albert on April 24?
(A) Michael Park
(B) June Bartholdi
(C) Nadia Kapoor
(D) Brooklyn Smith*

Ms. Albert가 작성한 이메일(지문 1)과 직원들의 업무 기록(지문 2)을 연계해서 파악해야 하는 문제이다. 지문 1 셋째 문단의 I am available to speak only in the afternoons after 3:30 P.M.을 통해 확인할 수 있는 통화 가능한 시간대(3시 30분 이후)를 염두에 두고 지문 2를 살펴보면, (D)가 정답임이 드러난다.

정답 (D)

두 번째 이메일에서, 첫째 문단 넷째 줄에 있는 "registered"와 의미상 가장 유사한 단어는?
(A) 등록하다
(B) 기록하다
(C) 어울리다
(D) 허용하다

어휘 enroll 등록하다 match 맞다, 어울리다, 필적하다, 대등하다

189

In the second e-mail, in paragraph 1, line 4 the word "registered" is closest in meaning to
(A) enrolled
(B) recorded*
(C) matched
(D) allowed

이 문장에서 register는 '(계기가 특정한 양을) 기록하다'라는 의미로 사용되었다. 따라서 (B)와 가장 유사한 의미이다.

정답 (B)

매튜스 씨는 이메일에서 뭐라고 하는가?
(A) 일부 서비스가 무료로 제공될 것이다.
(B) 카푸어 씨가 앨버트 씨에게 내일 전화할 예정이다.
(C) 앨버트 씨의 청구 금액이 다음 달에는 줄어들 것이다.
(D) 고객들은 해지 비용을 청구 받을 것이다.

어휘 indicate 가리키다, 나타내다 decrease 줄다, 감소하다

190

What does Mr. Mathews indicate in his e-mail?
(A) Some services will be offered for free.
(B) Ms. Kapoor will call Ms. Albert tomorrow.
(C) Ms. Albert's bill will decrease next month.*
(D) Customers will be charged for cancelations.

Mr. Mathews가 작성한 이메일(지문 3) 둘째 문단에서 차액을 계좌로 환급 조치했으니 다음 달에는 그만큼 적용될 것(I have canceled your insurance plan and credited your account with $63.98, which will be carried over to your next bill.)이라고 하므로 (C)가 가장 적절하다.

정답 (C)

Questions 191-195 refer to the following e-mail, flyer, and text message.

To: Graduate Students
From: Ferdinand Montgomery
Subject: Seminar Series
Date: March 10

Dear Students,

I have great news! Mr. Philip Osan has agreed to give a presentation during our Careers in Fashion Seminar Series. As graduate students, your job will be to arrange his travel accommodations for June 1-2 as well as his transportation to and from campus. Also, please reserve a room for his presentation. [191] I think the Belford Auditorium would be best. Mr. Osan's presentation will be very popular, so we might need the room with the largest capacity. However, if it's unavailable, please reserve another one.

Also, once Mr. Osan provides his information, I'll need you to design and print another flyer. I'm hoping you'll be able to divide these tasks up among the five of you without any major [192] issues, but do let me know if you have any problems.

Ferdinand Montgomery,
Professor of Fashion Design

The College of Fashion and Design's
Careers in Fashion Seminar Series Presents:

Mr. Philip Osan
CEO and Lead Designer of Bath Fashion House

[193] *Fashion Design and Technology*
June 1, 3:30 P.M.
[191] Westmont Auditorium

Over the years, many fashion houses have switched from hand-drawn designs to fashion design software programs. As up-and-coming designers, you must be aware of all [193] the newest innovations in fashion design software. How can you keep up to date on [193] the newest software trends? One possible solution is to become fluent in each new program. However, that may be costly and time-consuming. There are several ways to predict which programs will be major players in the future of fashion design. I will share my insights regarding the technological trends in the fashion industry.

발신: 로버트 파커
수신: 로사 헤르난데즈
받음: 5월 28일

로사, 전단을 출력하려고 허츠 건물 복사실에 와서 보니, 뭔가 빠졌네요. 194 오산 씨의 사진이 삭제된 것 같아요. 195 전단을 수정해서 가능한 한 빨리 이메일로 보내 주시겠어요? 복사실이 한 시간 안에 닫는데 몽고메리 선생님이 오늘밤까지 연구실에 전단을 가져다 놓으라고 하셨거든요.

From: Robert Parker
To: Rosa Hernandez
Received: May 28

Rosa, I'm at the copy center in the Hurtz Building to print the flyers, but I noticed something is missing. 194 It seems that Mr. Osan's photograph was deleted. 195 Can you fix the flyer and e-mail me the new version as soon as possible? The copy center closes in less than an hour and Dr. Montgomery asked me to drop the flyers off at his office tonight.

어휘 notice 알아채다 missing 사라진 delete 삭제하다 fix 고치다

웨스트몽 강당에 대해 드러나는 사항은?
(A) 6월 1일에는 쓸 수 없다.
(B) 모든 세미나 강연이 진행되는 곳이다.
(C) 벨포드 강당보다 좌석이 적다.
(D) 새 영사기 시스템이 있다.

191 What is suggested about the Westmont Auditorium?
(A) It is not available on June 1st.
(B) It is the location for all seminar presentations.
(C) It has fewer seats than the Belford Auditorium.*
(D) It has a new projector system.

'강연 장소'에 유념해 지문들을 살펴보면, 이메일(지문 1) 첫째 문단에서 벨포드가 가장 크니 적당할 테지만(I think the Belford Auditorium would be best.) 그곳이 안 된다면 다른 곳을 예약하라(if it's unavailable, please reserve another one)고 한다. 그러나 강연을 알리는 전단(지문 2)에서 웨스트몽 강당이 확정된 장소로 언급된 것으로 미루어 보건대 (C)가 정답이다.

정답 (C)

이메일에서, 둘째 문단 셋째 줄에 있는 "issues"와 의미상 가장 유사한 단어는?
(A) 갈등
(B) 학술지
(C) 분배
(D) 발표

어휘 conflict 갈등, 충돌 periodical 정기 간행물, 학술지 distribution 분배, 유통 announcement 발표

192 In the e-mail, the word "issues" in paragraph 2, line 3, is closest in meaning to
(A) conflicts*
(B) periodicals
(C) distributions
(D) announcements

해당 부분은 '문제 없이 일을 처리하리라 믿는다'는 요지의 문장이다. 따라서 (A)가 들어갔을 때 의미 전개가 가장 유사해진다.

정답 (A)

193

What is Mr. Osan's presentation about?

(A) New trends in design software*
(B) Advancements in sewing machines
(C) Learning drawing techniques
(D) Characteristics of fashion houses

전단(지문 2)에 명시된 세미나 제목이 디자인과 기술(Fashion Design and Technology)인데, 본문에서 언급되는 the newest innovations in fashion design software, the newest software trends 등을 통해 (A)가 정답임을 알 수 있다.

정답 (A)

오산 씨의 발표 주제는 무엇인가?
(A) 디자인 소프트웨어의 신경향
(B) 재봉틀의 발전
(C) 그리는 기술 습득
(D) 패션 업체들의 특징

어휘 advancement 발전, 진보 sewing machine 재봉틀 characteristic 특징

194

What problem does Mr. Parker mention?

(A) A location has been changed.
(B) The flyer is missing an image.*
(C) A work history is incorrect.
(D) The time of an event is wrong.

Mr. Parker가 작성한 문자 메시지(지문 3)를 살펴보면, 전단에 뭔가 빠졌다며 사진이 삭제된 듯하다(It seems that Mr. Osan's photograph was deleted.)고 설명한다. 따라서 (B)가 정답이 된다.

* paraphrasing: photograph → image

정답 (B)

파커 씨는 어떤 문제를 언급하는가?
(A) 장소가 바뀌었다.
(B) 전단에 사진이 없다.
(C) 작업 내역이 부정확하다.
(D) 행사 시간이 틀렸다.

어휘 change 바꾸다 incorrect 부정확한

195

Who most likely is Ms. Hernandez?

(A) Lead designer at Bath Fashion House
(B) A fashion design software developer
(C) A professor at The College of Fashion and Design
(D) A graduate student at The College of Fashion and Design*

Ms. Hernandez가 언급된 문자 메시지(지문 3)부터 살펴보면, 전단을 공동 작업하는 상황임을 Can you fix the flyer and e-mail me the new version as soon as possible?에서 유추할 수 있다. '전단 작업'에 유념해 나머지 지문들을 보면, 작업을 지시한 교수의 이메일(지문 1) 수신자가 Graduate Students이므로 (D)가 정답이다.

정답 (D)

헤르난데즈 씨는 누구이겠는가?
(A) 바스 패션 하우스의 수석 디자이너
(B) 패션 디자인 소프트웨어 개발자
(C) 패션 디자인 대학 교수
(D) 패션 디자인 대학 대학원생

Questions 196-200 refer to the following advertisement, online form, and review.

Trenton Air Conditioning
Air Conditioning Units

Trenton Air Conditioning has been providing businesses with affordable air conditioning units for over fifteen years. We have provided numerous local cafés, restaurants, and supermarkets with reliable cooling solutions. All our units include cleaning services and repairs at your request, and should your unit be unsatisfactory in any way, we will replace it at no extra cost. Delivery to any location in the Sydney area and set up are both absolutely free of charge. A two-year contract must be signed by the business owner, and monthly payment plans are available.

Air Conditioning Unit Options:

Contract Option	196(D) Model	Type	196(C) Room size in square meters (m²)	196(B) Cost Per Month
Bronze	GP-A3000	Ceiling	9-25	$55.00
199 Silver	GP-A4000	Standing	26-55	$75.00
Gold	GP-A9999	Ceiling	55-100	$95.00
Platinum	GP-AR300	Ceiling	100-200	$115.00

Contact us for a free service quote today by visiting www.trentonaircon.com or calling one of our knowledgeable customer service agents at 1-800-444-2323.

Trenton Air Conditioning – Customer Service Quote Form

Name: Medina Prias
Business: Medina's Café
E-mail: medina@mailme.com
Date: 23 April
Remarks: I'm writing to inquire about your air conditioning units. The restaurant next to my café is currently using one of your units, and 197 the owner, Mr. Smithe, highly recommends your services.
Right now, the air conditioner in my café is nearly ten years old. Just keeping up with the repairs and cleaning is costing a fortune. I think it would be much cheaper to just rent from your company. Since my café is quite small with only 22 square meters, I think one of your cheaper packages would be suitable. However, I will rely on your recommendation about this. Also, can you make sure any unit you recommend comes with a remote control. Our current air conditioner does not have one. Thank you, and I look forward to hearing from you.

Customer Review

I have been a customer of Trenton Air Conditioning for a year, and I have to say that I am very pleased with their services. I was very surprised to receive a ten percent discount on my first year of service thanks to Trenton's referral program. Apparently, [197] if you give the name of the person who connected you with Trenton, both parties will automatically receive a discount. Furthermore, I am very pleased with the contract conditions, which have allowed me to change my unit based on my business's needs. [198] After my business went through an expansion, I called Trenton and the customer service representative agreed to upgrade my unit to a larger package. The new unit [200] turned up only two days later and [199] was installed free of charge even though the type changed from ceiling to standing. I highly recommend Trenton for their great business practices and customer service.

- Medina Prias, Owner of Medina's Café

어휘 be pleased with ~에 만족하다 thanks to ~덕분에 referral 소개, 위탁 apparently 아무래도 ~같은 party (계약 등의) 당사자 automatically 자동으로 furthermore 더욱이 condition 상황, (요구) 조건 allow 허용하다 based on ~에 근거해 expansion 확장 turn up 나타나다 install 설치하다 even though (비록) ~일지라도 practice 관행, 업무

고객 평가

저는 한해 동안 트렌턴 에어 컨디셔닝을 이용했습니다. 이곳 서비스에 무척 만족한다고 말해야겠어요. 트렌턴 사의 소개 프로그램 덕분에 첫해 서비스를 10% 할인 받아서 무척 놀랐습니다. 197 트렌턴에 연결해 준 사람 이름을 알려 주면, 양쪽 다 자동으로 할인 받는 듯합니다. 게다가, 계약 조건도 매우 마음에 들어요. 제 업체의 요건에 맞춰 설비를 변경할 수 있었거든요. 198 저희 매장을 확장한 후에, 트렌턴에 전화했더니 고객 서비스 직원이 더 큰 상품으로 업그레이드해 주기로 동의했습니다. 새 설비는 단 이틀 후에 200 왔고 199 천장에서 입식으로 타입이 바뀌었는데도 무료로 설치되었어요. 트렌턴의 훌륭한 사업 처리와 고객 서비스 때문에 적극 추천합니다.

– 메디나 프리아스, 메디나 카페 소유주

196

What information about Trenton Air Conditioning is NOT included in the advertisement?

(A) The energy efficiency*
(B) The monthly costs
(C) The room sizes
(D) The model numbers

광고(지문 1)와 선택지를 대조하면서 지문에 언급된 사항을 소거하는 식으로 해결한다. Cost Per Month로 (B)를, Room size in square meters (m²)로 (C)를, Model로 (D)를 확인할 수 있다. 따라서 본 문제의 정답은 (A)이다.

정답 (A)

트렌턴 에어 컨디셔닝에 대한 어떤 정보가 광고에 포함되지 않았는가?
(A) 에너지 효율성
(B) 월 요금
(C) 방 크기
(D) 모델 번호

197

What is probably true about Mr. Smithe?

(A) He can save on air conditioning for his restaurant.*
(B) He purchased a café next to his restaurant.
(C) He received one year free from Trenton Air Conditioning.
(D) He will upgrade his air conditioning unit next year.

Mr. Smithe에 유념해 지문들을 살펴보면, 서식(지문 2)의 the owner, Mr. Smithe, highly recommends your services에서 '추천자'로 언급되는데, 평가(지문 3) 중반부에서 if you give the name of the person who connected you with Trenton, both parties will automatically receive a discount라며 추천자의 이름을 대면 둘 다 자동으로 할인 받는다고 하므로 (A)가 가장 적절하다.

정답 (A)

스미드 씨에 대해 아마도 사실인 것은?
(A) 자신의 식당 에어컨에 돈을 아꼈다.
(B) 식당 옆 카페를 매입했다.
(C) 트렌턴 에어 컨디셔닝에서 1년을 무상으로 받았다.
(D) 내년에 에어컨을 업그레이드할 것이다.

메디나 카페에 대해 드러나는 사항은?
(A) 스미드 씨가 소유하고 있다.
(B) 새로운 곳으로 옮겼다.
(C) 야간에 공연을 제공한다.
(D) 최근 규모를 늘렸다.

어휘 increase 늘리다, 증가시키다, 인상시키다

198

What is suggested about Medina's Café?
(A) It is owned by Mr. Smithe.
(B) It moved to a new location.
(C) It features nightly entertainment.
(D) It increased its size recently.*

카페 소유주의 평가(지문 3) 중반부의 After my business went through an expansion을 통해 정답 (D)를 유추할 수 있다.
* paraphrasing: went through an expansion → increased its size

정답 (D)

프리아스 씨는 현재 어떤 계약 옵션을 이용하는가?
(A) 브론즈
(B) 실버
(C) 골드
(D) 플래티넘

199

Which contract option is Ms. Prias currently using?
(A) Bronze
(B) Silver*
(C) Gold
(D) Platinum

Ms. Prias가 작성한 지문들과 선택지들이 언급된 광고(지문 1)를 연계해서 파악해야 한다. 평가(지문 3) 후반부에서 '입식으로' 바꿨는데도 무료였다(was installed free of charge even though the type changed from ceiling to standing)고 한다. 이를 유념해 지문 1을 살펴보면, (B)가 정답임을 알 수 있다.

정답 (B)

평가에서, 첫째 문단 여덟 번째 줄에 있는 구 "turned up"과 의미상 가장 유사한 단어는?
(A) 제거하다
(B) 고려하다
(C) 설계하다
(D) 도착하다

어휘 remove 없애다, 제거하다

200

In the review, the phrase "turned up" in paragraph 1, line 8, is closest in meaning to
(A) removed
(B) considered
(C) designed
(D) arrived*

해당 부분은 겨우 이틀 만에 '나타났다'는 요지이므로 (D)가 들어갔을 때 가장 적절한 의미가 완성된다.

정답 (D)

ACTUAL TEST 5

PART 5

그 화려한 팀 유니폼은 우리 자회사인 댄체스터 타이어즈가 제공했습니다.

어휘 sister company 자매 회사

101 The colorful team uniforms were provided by Danchester Tires, _____ sister company.

(A) we (B) our*
(C) us (D) ours

인칭대명사의 적절한 격을 찾는 문제로, 복합 명사 sister company를 한정할 수 있는 소유격 (B)가 정답이 된다. 대명사 문제에서 소유격은 답이 잘 된다.

정답 (B)

모든 필수 여행 서류들을 받는 대로 가족 비자가 처리될 것입니다.

어휘 process 처리하다 necessary 필수의 receive 받다

102 The family's visa will be processed as soon as all necessary travel _____ are received.

(A) document (B) documents*
(C) documented (D) documenting

형용사 necessary의 수식을 받는 복합명사를 완성해야 하므로 (A)나 (B)가 들어갈 수 있는데 복수 명사와 함께 쓰는 한정사 all이 앞에 있으니 (B)가 정답이 된다. document 서류, 문서, 기록하다

* 빈출 복합명사: account number 계좌 번호 construction delay 공사 지연 return policy 반환 정책 expiration date 만기일 product information 상품 정보 information distribution 정보 배포 retail sales 소매 판매 client satisfaction 고객 만족 recommendation letter 추천서

정답 (B)

연설 중에, 그랜드스테드 제약 회사 CEO는 연구부 부장을 회사 성공의 기여자로 특별히 언급했습니다.

어휘 pharmaceuticals 제약 회사 mention 언급하다 research 연구, 조사 division 부(서) contributor 기부자, 공헌자

103 In his speech, the CEO of Grandstead Pharmaceuticals _____ mentioned the director of the research division as a contributor to the company's success.

(A) thoroughly (B) utterly
(C) specifically* (D) densely

연설 중에 (특정인을) '특별히' 언급했다는 요지가 완성되어야 적절하므로 (C)가 정답이다. thoroughly 완전히, 철저히 utterly 완전히, 순전히 specifically 분명히, 특별히 densely 밀집하여, 빽빽이

정답 (C)

조앤의 관리 기술은 전임자와 상당히 다릅니다.

어휘 managerial 경영/관리/운영의 quite 상당히, 꽤 predecessor 전임자

104 Joanne's managerial techniques are quite _____ from her predecessor's.

(A) different* (B) differently
(C) difference (D) differences

〈주어(Joanne's ~ techniques) + be동사(are) + _____ 〉의 2형식 구조상 빈칸은 주격 보어인 데다 부사 quite의 수식을 받는 자리이므로 형용사 (A)만 들어갈 수 있다. different 다른 differently 다르게 difference 다름, 차이

* 〈be동사 + 형용사 + 전치사〉 숙어:
be full of ~으로 가득하다 be similar to ~와 비슷하다 be responsible for ~을 맡고 있다, ~에 책임이 있다 be familiar to ~에 잘 알려지다 be packed with ~으로 가득 차 있다 be resistant to ~에 강하다, 내성이 있다 be content with ~에 만족하다

정답 (A)

426 해설집

105
Wearing a safety harness is not an option for roofers at Delbert Contractors but rather a _____.

(A) training
(B) fulfillment
(C) speculation
(D) requirement*

안전 벨트 장치를 착용하는 것은 델버트 건설 회사의 지붕 기술자들에게 선택 사항이 아닌 필수 사항입니다.

어휘 safety 보안, 안전 harness 벨트, 마구 option 선택(권) roofer 지붕 이는 사람, 수리하는 사람 contractor 계약자, 도급 업자 rather 오히려

역접을 나타내는 등위접속사 but 앞에 '선택 사항'을 뜻하는 option이 쓰였으므로 이에 상반되는 (D)가 가장 적절하다. training 교육, 훈련 fulfillment 이행, 수행 speculation 추측, 짐작 requirement 필요 조건, 요건

정답 (D)

106
One of our plumbers will _____ how to replace a Malton DR sink drain quickly and easily.

(A) demonstrate*
(B) respond
(C) inquire
(D) visit

저희 배관공들 중 한 명이 말턴 DR 싱크대 배수관을 빠르고 쉽게 교체하는 법을 보여 드릴 것입니다.

어휘 plumber 배관공 replace 교체하다, 대체하다 sink 싱크대 drain 배수관

문맥상 '배관공이 배수관 교체법을 (직접) 보여 준다'는 요지를 완성해야 가장 적절하므로 (A)가 정답이다. (B)는 전치사 to와, (C)는 전치사 about과 함께 사용된다. demonstrate 시연하다 respond 대답하다 inquire 문의하다

정답 (A)

107
Bramwell Carpets does not issue refunds of any kind so be sure to measure the floor space _____ before purchasing.

(A) careful
(B) caring
(C) carefully*
(D) cares

브램웰 카펫은 어떤 유형의 환불도 제공하지 않으니 구입 전에 바닥 공간을 신중하게 측정하시기 바랍니다.

어휘 issue 발부하다, 발행하다 refund 환불 measure 측정하다 purchase 구입하다, 사다

빈칸이 생략되어도 구조상 완벽한 문장이므로 동사 measure를 수식해 의미를 강조해 줄 수 있는 부사 (C)가 가장 적절하다. careful 신중한, 세심한, 주의 깊은 caring 배려하는, 보살피는 carefully 신중하게 care 조심, 주의, 상관하다, 관심을 가지다

정답 (C)

108
_____ annual profits are high or low, they still provide important economic information for business analysts.

(A) Whether*
(B) Either
(C) Despite
(D) Even

연 수익이 높든 낮든 간에, 그것들은 경제 분석가들에게 여전히 중요한 경제 정보를 제공합니다.

어휘 profit 이익, 수익 economic 경제의, 경제성이 있는 analyst 분석가

두 개의 절이 콤마를 사이에 두고 이어진 문장이므로 빈칸에는 접속사가 필요하다. '~이든 ~이든 간에'라는 의미를 만들어 주는 접속사 (A) Whether가 정답이 된다. 참고로, either A or B는 'A나 B 둘 중에 어느 하나'라는 의미의 상관접속사로 종종 출제된다. despite ~에도 불구하고 even 심지어 ~도, ~조차

정답 (A)

그 기사는 구형 아르고 모토사이클 디자인과 신형 그랜드포드 간의 상세한 비교를 제시합니다.

어휘 provide 제공하다 detailed 상세한

109

The report provides a detailed _____ between the old Argo motorcycle design and the new Grandford one.

(A) comparable (B) comparison*
(C) compared (D) comparative

〈부정관사(a) + 형용사(detailed) + _____〉의 빈칸에 들어갈 수 있는 것은 명사 (B)뿐이다. comparable 비슷한, 비교할 만한 comparison 비교, 비유 compare 비교하다, 필적하다 comparative 비교를 통한, 비교의

* 〈detailed + 명사〉의 빈출 표현
detailed information 상세 정보 detailed description 상세 묘사 detailed assessment 상세 평가 detailed forecast 상세 예보 detailed analysis 상세 분석

정답 (B)

고객 서비스 직원에게 말씀하시려면, 수화기를 들고 기다려 주시기 바랍니다.

어휘 stay on the line 수화기를 들고 기다리다

110

_____ speak to a customer service agent, please stay on the line.

(A) For (B) Across
(C) With (D) To*

문맥상 콤마 앞이 통화 대기를 해야 하는 '목적' 또는 '이유'에 해당된다. 따라서 to부정사를 완성할 (D)가 정답이다.

정답 (D)

새 창고의 저장 공간은 자전거 300대가 들어가기에 충분하고도 남습니다.

어휘 storage 저장, 보관 warehouse 창고

111

The storage space in the new warehouse is more than _____ for three hundred bicycles.

(A) able (B) great
(C) sure (D) enough*

'~하기에 족한, 모자라지 않는, ~할 만큼의'라는 의미의 enough for/to부정사를 알면 해결할 수 있는 문제이다. able ~할 수 있는 great 큰, 엄청난 sure 확신하는 enough 충분한

정답 (D)

이 나라에서 가족 비자를 신청하는 것은 길고 복잡한 과정입니다.

어휘 apply for ~에 지원하다, 신청하다 process 과정, 절차

112

Applying for a family visa in this country is a long and _____ process.

(A) complicate (B) complicated*
(C) complication (D) complicatedness

등위접속사 and 앞뒤로는 동일한 성분이 온다. 따라서 형용사 long과 짝을 이루어 명사 process를 수식할 (B)가 정답이 된다. (A)를 형용사로 착각한 수험생이 많았는데, 비슷한 철자의 complete는 동사/형용사(완료하다/완전한)로 사용되지만 complicate는 동사로만 사용된다는 점을 알아 두자. complicate 복잡하게 만들다 complicated 복잡한 complication 문제, 합병증 complicatedness 복잡성

정답 (B)

113 Leading automotive experts maintain that Woykin Oil filters deliver _____ results.

(A) exceptionally
(B) exceptional*
(C) exception
(D) exceptions

deliver의 목적어인 명사 results를 수식하는 자리에 적절한 것은 형용사 (B)뿐이다. exceptionally 유난히, 특별히, 예외적으로 exceptional 이례일 정도로 우수한 exception 예외, 이례

정답 (B)

선두적인 자동차 전문가들은 워이킨 오일 필터가 뛰어난 결과를 낳는다고 주장합니다.

어휘 leading 가장 중요한, 선두적인 automotive 자동차의 expert 전문가 maintain 주장하다 deliver (결과를) 내놓다, 산출하다

---

114 A credit card statement or phone bill can be _____ of residency.

(A) process
(B) analysis
(C) proof*
(D) basis

문맥상 '거주 증빙 자료'라는 요지를 완성해야 가장 타당하므로 (C)가 정답이 된다. process 과정, 절차 analysis 분석 proof 증거 basis 이유, 기준 (단위)

정답 (C)

신용 카드 내역이나 전화 청구서가 거주 증거가 될 수 있습니다.

어휘 statement (입출금) 내역서 bill 청구서 residency 거주

---

115 Mr. Bolduc _____ asked Gabriella to organize the workshop, but then assigned the task to Louise.

(A) initial
(B) initially*
(C) initialize
(D) initialized

〈주어 + 동사〉 사이에 빈칸이 있으므로 부사 (B)가 들어가야 구조상 알맞다. initial 처음의, 초기의 initially 처음에 initialize 초기 내용을 설정하다 initialized 초기화된

정답 (B)

볼덕 씨가 처음에는 가브리엘라에게 워크숍 준비를 요청했으나, 나중에는 그 일을 루이스에게 맡겼습니다.

어휘 organize (회의 등을) 준비하다, 조직하다 assign 맡기다, 배정하다 task 일, 업무

---

116 Job candidates need to submit three letters of recommendation _____ the completed application.

(A) too
(B) in addition
(C) moreover
(D) along with*

빈칸 뒤의 application을 목적어로 취할 전치사가 필요하므로 (D)가 정답이다. 문맥을 살펴보면, '추천서와 지원서를 함께 내라'는 요지를 완성하므로 (D)가 정답임을 다시 한번 확인할 수 있다. (B)는 in addition to로 썼을 때만 전치사로 사용될 수 있다. in addition 게다가(부사) moreover 게다가, 더욱이(부사) along with ~와 함께(전치사)

정답 (D)

구직자들은 완성된 지원서와 함께 추천서 세 통을 제출해야 합니다.

어휘 candidate 지원자, 후보자 submit 제출하다 recommendation 추천(서) application 지원(서)

부오노 씨는 냉장고 수리 부서에서 일한 적은 없지만, 냉장 시스템에 대한 해박한 지식을 갖고 있습니다.

어휘 even though ~일지라도 refrigerator 냉장고 repair 수리, 수선 refrigeration 냉장, 냉동

117

Even though Mr. Buono has never worked in refrigerator repair, his knowledge of refrigeration systems is _____.

(A) extensive*   (B) clever   (C) considered   (D) eager

빈칸에는 knowledge를 서술할 형용사가 들어가야 한다. (B)와 (D)는 knowledge와 같은 추상 명사와는 어울리지 않고 (C)는 뒤에 to be ~ 등과 같은 추가 설명이 덧붙어야 자연스럽다. 따라서 '지식이 해박함'을 의미하는 (A)가 정답이다. extensive 광범위한, 폭넓은 clever 영리한, 똑똑한 considered 깊이 생각한 eager 열렬한, 간절히 바라는

정답 (A)

6쪽에 있는 업무 흐름도는 여러 프로젝트 매니저들 사이의 역할 분담을 나타냅니다.

어휘 flowchart 플로 차트, 업무 흐름도 describe 설명하다, 묘사하다 duty 임무

118

The flowchart on page six describes the _____ of duties among the different project managers.

(A) support   (B) attention   (C) division*   (D) statement

'일의 분담'에 대한 요지를 완성해야 문맥상 자연스럽다. 따라서 제시된 명사들 중 (C)가 정답이 된다. support 지지, 후원 attention 주목, 관심 division 분할, 분배 statement 성명, 진술

정답 (C)

이 씨앗들은 가장 큰 토마토들을 산출시킬 것이지만, 그것들이 최상품 토마토라고까지는 할 수 없습니다.

어휘 seed 씨, 씨앗 produce 생산하다

119

These seeds will produce the biggest tomatoes but not _____ the healthiest ones.

(A) expectedly   (B) necessarily*
(C) preventively   (D) permanently

역접을 나타내는 등위접속사 but에 주목하자. '크기는 가장 큰데 상태가 가장 좋다고 하기는 힘들다'는 의미를 완성해야 자연스럽다. 따라서 빈칸 앞의 not과 함께 쓰여 '반드시/꼭 ~은 아닌'이라는 의미를 나타내는 (B)가 가장 적절하다. expectedly 예상한 바와 같이 necessarily 어쩔 수 없이, 필연적으로 preventively 예방용으로 permanently 영구히, 불변으로

정답 (B)

저희 매장은 환불을 해 주지 않지만, 고객들은 원래 판매가의 총액에 해당되는 제품으로 교환하실 수 있습니다.

어휘 exchange 교환하다 item 물건, 제품 amount 총액, 총계

120

While the store does not issue refunds, customers can exchange any item for something _____ in amount to the original sales price.

(A) equivalent*   (B) profitable   (C) deliberate   (D) controlled

문맥상 '동일한' 가격의 제품으로 교환할 수 있다는 요지가 완성되어야 가장 자연스럽다. 따라서 (A)가 정답이 된다. equivalent 동등한, 맞먹는 profitable 수익성이 있는 deliberate 고의의, 의도적인, 계획적인 controlled 아주 조심스러운, (법으로) 제어 받는

* 후치 수식이 사용되는 경우
1) thing, body, one, where 형태로 끝나는 명사를 수식할 때
  • something small
2) 형용사가 겹쳐서 명사를 한정할 때
  • a friend kind, caring and funny
3) 분사형용사(현재분사, 과거분사)가 수식어를 수반할 때
  • a wall painted in yellow
4) 최상급이 수식하는 명사를 다시 수식할 때
  • the best actress alive

정답 (A)

121

This newspaper photograph shows the mayor of Otterbury sitting _____ the prime minister.

(A) from
(B) reverse
(C) opposite*
(D) distant

이 신문 사진은 오터버리 시장이 수상 맞은편에 앉아 있는 것을 보여 줍니다.
어휘 mayor 시장 prime minister 수상

위치를 나타내는 전치사가 필요한 문맥이므로 '맞은편에 앉아 있다'는 요지를 완성할 (C)가 정답이 된다. reverse 거꾸로 opposite 맞은편에 distant 떨어진

정답 (C)

122

The decision to launch a new line of footwear was _____ the results of some market research.

(A) such as
(B) adjacent to
(C) except for
(D) based on*

신발 신제품을 출시하려는 결정은 시장 조사 결과에 근거한 것이었습니다.
어휘 decision 결정, 판단 launch 출시하다 footwear 신발 result 결과

빈칸 이하가 '결정의 근거'에 해당되므로 (D)가 가장 적절하다. such as 예를 들어, ~와 같은 adjacent to ~에 인접한 except for ~이 없으면, ~을 제외하고는 based on ~에 근거하여

정답 (D)

123

The Alderburn Employment Center is the only building on this block that is _____ to people in wheelchairs.

(A) access
(B) accessibly
(C) accessible*
(D) accessibility

이 블록에서는 앨더번 고용 센터가 휠체어를 타는 사람들이 접근하기 쉬운 유일한 건물입니다.
어휘 employment 고용, 채용

빈칸은 that절의 주격 보어에 해당되므로 형용사 또는 명사가 들어갈 수 있는데, 명사가 들어가면 '건물은 접근이다'라는 의미가 되어 이상하다. 따라서 형용사 (C)가 들어가 '건물에 접근할 수 있다'는 문맥을 완성해야 한다. access 접근, 접근하다 accessibly 접근 가능하게 accessible 접근 가능한 accessibility 접근 가능성, 접근하기 쉬움

* access(동사) + 장소: ~에 들어가다 (이때는 to를 쓰지 않는다.)
  access(명사) + to + 장소: ~에 들어갈 수 있음(~에 들어갈/접근할 수 있는 권한)
  accessible + to + 사람: ~가 들어갈 수 있는

정답 (C)

124

Dr. Darius is striving _____ the look of his office and is going to put a painting in the waiting room.

(A) to enhance*
(B) enhances
(C) is enhancing
(D) enhanced

다리우스 박사는 사무실 외관을 향상시키기 위해 애쓰고 있는데 대기실에 회화 작품을 들이려고 합니다.
어휘 strive 분투하다

'~하기 위해 분투하다, ~하느라 애쓰다'라는 의미의 〈strive to + 동사원형〉의 표현을 알면 쉽게 해결할 수 있는 문제이다. enhance 높이다, 향상시키다

* to부정사를 목적어로 취하는 동사:
  want, hope, plan, decide, expect, wish, promise, afford, agree, pretend, fail, refuse

정답 (A)

결승에 이르지 못한 팀 선수들은 경기를 무료로 볼 수 있습니다.

어휘 make it to ~에 이르다, 도착하다
final 결승전

125

Players _____ teams did not make it to the finals can watch the game for free.

(A) its (B) which
(C) whose* (D) more

빈칸에서 finals까지는 players를 수식하는 구조이므로 관계사절을 완성시킬 단어가 빈칸에 필요하다. players와 teams의 관계를 생각해 보면 their(= players') teams로 정의할 수 있으므로 소유격 관계대명사 (C)가 빈칸에 들어갈 수 있다.

정답 (C)

시 공무원들은 감자 농작물에 뿌려진 농약이 인체에 무해하다고 농부들에게 장담했습니다.

어휘 farmer 농부, 농장주 pesticide 농약, 살충제 crop 작물 harmless 무해한

126

Local officials _____ farmers that the pesticide sprayed on the potato crops was harmless to humans.

(A) assured* (B) arranged
(C) described (D) committed

that 이하의 내용을 농부들에게 '말하다'는 요지의 의미를 완성해야 가장 타당하므로 (A)가 문맥상 알맞다. assure 장담하다, 확언하다 arrange 주선하다, 마련하다 commit (범죄를) 저지르다

* 〈주어 + 동사 + 사람 + that ~〉의 형태를 취하는 동사:
advise, tell, inform, notify, convince, instruct, remind

정답 (A)

랭포드 제조 회사 공장 인부들은 급증하는 생산비를 상쇄하기 위해 날마다 30분 추가 근무하는 데 동의했습니다.

어휘 laborer 노동자, 인부 manufacturing 제조(업) offset 상쇄하다, 벌충하다 rising 올라가는 cost 값, 비용

127

Factory laborers at Langford Manufacturing _____ to working 30 minutes more each day to offset rising production costs.

(A) agreeing (B) to agree
(C) agreement (D) have agreed*

〈주어(Factory laborers at Langford Manufacturing) + 동사(_____)〉 구조를 완성해야 하는데, 선택지 중 서술어로 사용될 수 있는 것은 (D)뿐이다. agreeing 동의하는 agree 동의하다 agreement 동의, 합의

정답 (D)

사무엘이 3개 대륙에서 일한 경력으로 볼 때, CEO가 그를 해외 프로젝트 담당자로 택한 것은 당연합니다.

어휘 continent (유럽) 대륙 in charge of ~을 담당해서 overseas 해외의

128

_____ Samuel's work experience in three continents, it was no surprise that the CEO put him in charge of the overseas project.

(A) Since (B) Given*
(C) Among (D) Upon

문맥상 콤마 앞이 해외 프로젝트 담당자가 된 '근거'에 해당된다. 따라서 전치사로서 '~을 고려해 볼 때'라는 의미를 나타내는 (B)가 정답이 된다.

정답 (B)

129

A person who was not raised in this community may not understand the historical _____ on the Steinhauer Street Bridge.

(A) signify
(B) significant
(C) significance*
(D) significantly

〈정관사(the) + 형용사(historical) + _____〉의 빈칸에 들어갈 수 있는 것은 명사 (C) 뿐이다. the significance on ~은 '~의 의의, 중요성'을 뜻한다. signify 의미하다, 뜻하다 significant 중요한, 의미 있는 significance 중요성, 의의 significantly 중요하게, 상당히

정답 (C)

이 지역 사회에서 자라지 않은 사람은 스타이너 스트리트 교각의 역사적 의의를 이해하지 못할 수 있습니다.

어휘 raise 키우다, 기르다 historical 역사적인

130

Jennifer has more seniority than Bill at the company, _____ she is much younger than him.

(A) as if
(B) so that
(C) in case
(D) even though*

빈칸 전후의 절 내용을 파악하고 어떤 관계로 이어져야 가장 적절할지 살펴보자. '근속 연수가 더 길다' 그런데 '훨씬 어리다'는 상반된 의미로 연결되는 것이 타당하므로 양보 접속사 (D)가 정답이 된다. as if 마치 ~인 듯 so that ~하도록 in case ~할 경우에 대비해서

정답 (D)

회사에서 제니퍼는 빌보다 훨씬 어리지만 근속 연수가 더 됩니다.

어휘 seniority 선임, (근무 햇수에 따른) 연공서열

PART 6

수신: <nina_haidara@kmail.net>
발신: <duron_charette@wrnpharmaceuticals.com>
날짜: 9월 7일
제목: 수석 연구원 직

하이다라 씨 귀하,

WRN 제약 회사는 귀하께서 다음 주에 두 번째 면접을 보러 오셨으면 합니다. 이는 두 번째 단계이니, 저희 채용 위원회는 이 도전적인 직책에 적임자로 여겨지는 지원자 다섯 분하고만 이야기 나눌 것입니다. 귀하께서 우리가 필요로 하는 모든 자격을 갖추고 있다는 데 저희 위원 모두 동의하고 있습니다. 이 직책에 귀하께서 여전히 관심 있으리라 여깁니다. 그렇다면, 다음 주 수요일 2시 30분에 시간이 되시겠습니까? 또, 면접의 일환으로, 첫 번째 면접 때 논의된 주제들 중 하나에 관해 서면 연구 제안서와 10분 간의 발표를 준비해 주셨으면 합니다. ——134——.

그럼 이만,
두롱 샤렛
WRN 제약 회사
304-677-2426 내선 18

어휘 head 수석, 장 position 직(책) pharmaceuticals 제약 회사 hiring 고용(의) committee 위원회 applicant 지원자 challenging 도전적인 entire 전체의 posses 소유/소지/보유하다 appointment 예약, 약속 prepare 준비하다 proposal 제안(서) related to ~에 관련된 discuss 토론하다, 논의하다

Questions 131-134 refer to the following e-mail.

To: <nina_haidara@kmail.net>
From: <duron_charette@wrnpharmaceuticals.com>
Date: September 7
Subject: Head of Research Position

Dear Ms. Haidara,

WRN Pharmaceuticals is delighted to invite you to come in for a second interview next week. Since this is the second stage, our hiring committee will be speaking to only the top five applicants whom we feel are most ---**131**--- for this challenging position. Our entire committee agrees that you posses almost all the ---**132**--- we need. We trust that you are still interested in the position. ---**133**---, would you be available for an appointment next Wednesday at 2:30? Also, as part of the interview, we would like you to prepare a written research proposal related to one of the topics discussed at the first interview as well as a 10-minute presentation. ---**134**---.

Best regards,

Duron Charette
WRN Pharmaceuticals
304-677-2426 ext. 18

131
(A) suiting
(B) suitable*
(C) suit
(D) suits

빈칸은 be동사(are)의 주격 보어 자리이므로 형용사 (B)가 들어갈 수 있다. suiting 양복감 suitable 적절한, 알맞은 suit 정장, ~에 맞다, 어울리다

정답 (B)

132
(A) agreements
(B) performances
(C) qualities*
(D) promotions

동사 posses의 목적어가 될 적절한 명사를 찾는 문제이다. 해당 문장이 '채용 위원회의 평가를 나타낸다는 점으로 보건대 후보자가 어떤 '자질'을 갖고 있다는 내용이 되어야 한다. 따라서 (C)가 정답이 된다. agreement 합의, 동의 performance 공연, 성과 quality 자질, 특성 promotion 홍보, 승진

정답 (C)

133

(A) Despite that (B) If so*
(C) However (D) For example

'당신이 아직 이 직책에 관심 있다고 본다' 그러니 '그렇다면 면접을 치르자'는 흐름으로 보는 것이 가장 타당하다. 따라서 정답은 (B)이다. despite ~에도 불구하고 if so 그렇다면 however 그러나 for example 예를 들면

정답 (B)

134

(A) Our current research head will train you in your new duties.
(B) The CEO will be delighted to provide you with a letter of reference.
(C) You need to complete your current research project before Wednesday.
(D) We are looking forward to hearing your vision for a future project.*

(A) 현 수석 연구원이 새로운 일들을 가르쳐 줄 것입니다.
(B) CEO가 추천서를 기꺼이 써 주실 것입니다.
(C) 귀하는 수요일 전에 현재 작업 중인 연구 프로젝트를 완성하셔야 합니다.
(D) 향후 프로젝트에 대한 귀하의 의견을 듣게 될 때를 고대합니다.

첫 번째 면접 때 얘기 나눈 주제들 중 하나를 선정해 제안서 및 발표 자료를 준비하라고 요청한 데 이어지는 문장이므로 (D)가 가장 적절하다. train 교육하다, 훈련하다 provide 제공하다 a letter of reference 추천서 look forward to -ing ~하기를 고대하다

정답 (D)

찬탈 율던
302 몰린 스트리트
델라번, IL
61735

율던 씨 귀하,

또 한 번 시력 검진 받을 때가 임박했음을 상기시켜 드립니다. ---135--- 안과 전문가들은 최소 1년에 한 번은 시력을 검사 받을 것을 권합니다. 이로써, 시력 문제를 초기에 발견할 수 있으며 안경 처방도 업데이트할 수 있습니다. 저희 최우선 과제는 환자들에게 가능한 한 최상의 시력을 제공하는 것입니다. 이 편지에 대한 후속 조처로서 며칠 후에 전화를 드릴 예정입니다. 예약하시려면 (309) 754-3231로 저희에게 전화 주시기 바랍니다. 대단히 감사합니다.

시력 케어 부서
헤린 스트리트 안과

어휘 remind 상기시키다 examination 조사, 검사 approach 다가오다 vision 시력, 눈 detect 발견하다, 감지하다 prescription 처방(전) follow up 후속 조처를 취하다 make an appointment 예약하다

(A) 최근 대기실을 확장해 어린이들을 위한 더 큰 놀이 공간을 마련했습니다.
(B) 저희 기록에 따르면 귀하가 마지막으로 호반 박사를 만난 지 열한 달이 지났습니다.
(C) 운동과 건강에 좋은 식사도 눈 상태에 영향을 줍니다.
(D) 저희 사무실은 편리한 온라인 예약 시스템이 들어가도록 웹사이트를 갱신했습니다.

Questions 135-138 refer to the following the letter.

Chantal Youldon
302 Moline Street
Delavan, IL
61735

Dear Ms. Youldon,

We would like to remind you that the time for another eye examination is soon approaching. ---135--- Eye specialists ---136--- having your vision checked at least once a year. ---137---, eye problems can be detected early and the prescription for your eyeglasses can also be updated. Our number one ---138--- is providing our patients with the best vision possible. We will follow up this letter with a phone call in a few days. Please phone us at (309) 754-3231 if you would like to make an appointment. Thank you very much.

The Eye Care Team
Herrin Street Eye Clinic

135
(A) We recently expanded our waiting room to include a larger play are for children.
(B) Our records indicate that it has been eleven months since your last saw Dr. Hoban.*
(C) Exercise and a healthy diet also have an impact on the condition of your eyes.
(D) Our office updated its website to include a convenient online appointment system.

이어서 '검진 주기'에 대한 의료 정보를 덧붙이므로 (B)가 가장 적절하다. expand 확장하다 indicate 가리키다, 나타내다 exercise 운동 healthy 건강한, 건강에 좋은 diet 식사 have an impact on ~에 영향을 주다 condition 상태 convenient 편리한, 간편한

정답 (B)

136
(A) recommending (B) had recommended
(C) recommend*   (D) will recommend

문장의 술어에 해당되며 '일반적인 사실'을 나타내고 있으므로 단순 현재시제인 (C)가 정답이다. recommend 추천하다, 권하다

정답 (C)

137

(A) Nevertheless (B) In this way*
(C) For example (D) Likewise

1년에 한 번 이상 검진하는 '방법을 통해' 문제를 초기에 발견하고 안경을 업데이트할 수 있다는 맥락이다. 따라서 '이러한 방법으로'를 의미하는 (B)가 정답이다. nevertheless 그럼에도 불구하고 in this way 이렇게 하여 likewise 또한

정답 (B)

138

(A) manner (B) opinion
(C) condition (D) priority*

'고객에게 최상의 눈 상태를 제공하는 것'이 이 업체가 '1순위에 두는 것, 제일 중요시 하는 것'이라는 맥락이 바람직하므로 (D)가 정답이 된다. manner 방식, 태도 opinion 선택(권) priority 우선 (사항)

정답 (D)

Questions 139-142 refer to the following article.

Parrsboro Herald
Local News

(12 June) — On Tuesday afternoon, Parrsboro City Mayor Deborah Middleton announced city council's decision to implement a program of one-on-one training programs for aspiring city bus drivers. ---**139**---, she stated that 20 new drivers will be needed before the end of the year. Speaking at a press conference, she stressed that there is an urgent ---**140**--- for new drivers to replace those who are set to retire soon. The announcement ---**141**--- with approval by most city officials. Councilor Stephen Digby of Truro Region, however, continues to speak out against the city funding costly training programs when graduates of the Wolfville College of Vehicle Operations, just 50 km west of Parrsboro, are already qualified to fill the positions. ---**142**---

139

(A) Specifically*
(B) Undoubtedly
(C) Regardless
(D) Besides

빈칸 전후로 기자 회견장에서 말한 내용이 있는데, 뒷문장에서는 앞서 말한 내용을 좀 더 구체적으로 (앞으로 버스 기사가 될 사람들 → 연말까지 20명의 새 기사) 설명한다. 따라서 빈칸에 적절한 부사는 (A)이다. specifically 특히, 분명히 undoubtedly 확실히, 의심할 여지없이 regardless 상관하지 않고 besides ~외에, 게다가

정답 (A)

140

(A) settlement
(B) reduction
(C) demand*
(D) difficulty

빈칸 뒤의 for와 어울리는 단어는 '~을 위한 요구, 필요, 수요'를 의미하는 (C)이다. settlement of ~에 대한 합의, 해결 reduction in ~의 축소, 할인 demand for ~에 대한 수요, 요구 difficulty in ~하는 데 어려움, 곤경

정답 (C)

141

(A) will be meeting (B) to meet
(C) had been meeting (D) was met*

(B)는 술어 자리에 들어갈 수 없다. 나머지 선택지 중에서 문맥상 적절한 시제는 '과거'로, (C)나 (D)인데, '동의를 얻다'는 be met with approval로 표현하므로 수동태 (D)가 알맞다.

정답 (D)

142

(A) He believes the current buses can be improved to allow more seats.
(B) He wants the city to hire staff already skilled in the field.*
(C) He feels the test to become a certified driver is too easy to pass.
(D) He expects the high fuel costs will lead to higher bus rates.

(A) 그는 현재 버스들이 좌석을 더 늘려 개선될 수 있다고 여긴다.
(B) 그는 시가 이미 업무 능력을 갖춘 직원들을 고용하기를 바란다.
(C) 그는 기사 자격 시험이 통과하기 너무 쉽다고 생각한다.
(D) 그는 비싼 연료비 때문에 버스 운임도 비싸지리라 예상한다.

앞 문장을 살펴보면, '전문 실력을 갖춘 졸업생들'이 있는데 새로 훈련시킨다면 돈 낭비라는 맥락이다. 따라서 (B)가 들어가야 흐름상 자연스럽다. improve 개선하다, 향상시키다 field 분야 certified 보증된, 증명된 cost 값, 비용 lead to (결과적으로) ~을 낳다 rate 운임, 요금

정답 (B)

수신: 프란스 바넥
발신: 미셸 세케라
날짜: 7월 14일
제목: 안녕하세요.

동료로부터 당신의 다가오는 승진에 대해 알게 됐어요. 오슬로에 새로 연 지사의 수석 리크루터 직이 8월 2일에나 공식적으로 시작되기는 하지만, 당신의 새로운 경력에 지금 행운을 빌어 주고 싶어요. 도움이 필요하시면, 언제든 제게 연락하세요. 저는 이런 유형의 변화가 흥미진진함과 동시에 전혀 녹록하지 않다는 것을 잘 알고 있으니까요. 차라 패션 파리 지사에서 당신의 부고용 디렉터로서의 근무 실적은 늘 뛰어났어요. ——146—— 축하하고 행운을 빌어요!

그럼 이만,

미셸 세케라

어휘 upcoming 다가오는, 다음의 colleague 동료 even though (비록) ~일지라도 recruiter 모집자 officially 공식적으로 require 필요하다 assistance 도움, 지원 hesitate 망설이다, 주저하다 transition 이행, 과도 extremely 극히 performance 실적 outstanding 뛰어난, 걸출한

Questions 143-146 refer to the following letter.

To: Frans Vanek
From: Michelle Sekera
Date: 14 July
Subject: Good morning.

I learned of your upcoming ---143--- from a colleague. Even though the position of chief recruiter at our newly-opened office in Oslo officially ---144--- on August 2, I would like to take a moment now to wish you the very best in your new career. If you require any assistance, please do not hesitate to contact me. I am well aware that this type of transition, while exciting, is also extremely ---145---. Your work performance here in Paris at Chara Fashion as assistant hiring director has always been outstanding. ---146--- Congratulations and good luck!

Sincerely,
Michelle Sekera

143
(A) trip   (B) event
(C) award   (D) promotion*

assistant hiring director에서 chief recruiter로 직책이 바뀌는 사람에게 축하 인사를 전하는 메일이므로 '승진'을 뜻하는 (D)가 가장 적절하다. award 상 promotion 승진

정답 (D)

144
(A) begins*   (B) began
(C) has begun   (D) could begin

현재의 날짜는 7월 14일인데, 8월 2일에 '시작될' 자리를 설명하는 문맥이므로 '미래'를 나타내는 단순 현재시제 (A)가 정답이 된다. 조건절에서는 미래에 벌어질 일이라 하더라도 현재시제를 사용해야 한다는 규칙도 함께 익혀 두자.

정답 (A)

145

(A) challenging*
(B) challenge
(C) challenger
(D) challenges

빈칸은 is의 보어가 되며 앞의 부사 extremely의 수식을 받는 자리이다. 따라서 형용사 (A)만 들어갈 수 있다. challenging 도전적인, 도전 의식을 북돋우는 challenge 도전, 도전하다 challenger 도전자

정답 (A)

146

(A) The Oslo office is a little smaller with a big parking lot.
(B) I'm still conducting interviews for all the new positions.
(C) You could ask about staff discounts at clothing shops.
(D) I am certain that your will be successful in your new position.*

앞서 '현재의 직책에서 늘 일을 잘해냈다'는 요지가 언급되었으므로 빈칸에 들어가기에 가장 적절한 내용은 (D)이다. parking lot 주차장 conduct (특정한 일을) 하다

정답 (D)

(A) 오슬로 지사는 더 작지만 주차장이 커요.
(B) 저는 모든 새로운 직책들을 위해 아직도 면접하고 있어요.
(C) 의류 매장에서 직원 할인에 대해 요청할 수 있어요.
(D) 당신이 새 자리에서도 성공적으로 해내리라 확신해요.

PART 7

Questions 147-148 refer to the following receipt.

Park Home Outfitters
229 Park Road South
Edmonton, Alberta
(777) 223-4455

Date: May 12   Time: 10:37
- SALE -

3345	[147] La Roux 4-Seat Sofa	$499.00
3348	La Roux Armchair	$199.00
3355	La Roux Footstool	$99.00
4489	D&F 6-drawer Dresser	
	4 $79.00/ea	$316.00
1223	Star Designs pillow	
	2 $19.00/ea	$38.00
Subtotal		$1151.00
Tax (5%)		$57.55
Total		$1208.55
Paid by credit card		$1208.55

Total number of items purchased: 9

Returns may be made for all non-sale items within 60 days of purchase. To view our return policy, please visit www.parkhomeoutfitters.ca/returns.

****

[148] Sign up for a membership on our website and receive up to 50% off on select online purchases. Offer ends June 28.

****

Thank you for shopping at Park Home Outfitters.

---

147 What kind of store most likely is Park Home Outfitters?

(A) A furniture store*
(B) A fabric outlet
(C) A construction company
(D) A clothing store

---

148 According to the receipt, how can customers get a discount?

(A) By applying for a membership*
(B) By showing a coupon
(C) By completing a survey
(D) By purchasing two or more items

Questions 149-150 refer to the following e-mail.

To: Gary Hong <garyhong@songendepartmentstores.co.au>
From: Patricia Torenski <songendepartmentstores.co.au>
Subject: Songen Department Store's 10th Anniversary
Date: 14 October
Attachment: Press Release

Dear Mr. Hong,

Several television stations have been contacted about a press release regarding our 10th anniversary events in Sydney. The kickoff event will be a concert held outside our downtown store location on November 24th. ^{149, 150} We have also arranged a number of anniversary sales at all our stores from next week until the events. I will send you the completed schedule once it has been finalized with the branch managers.

In the meantime, please have a look at the attached press release and let me know if the advertising department would like us to add anything.

Sincerely,

Patricia Torenski,
Marketing Manager, Songen Department Stores

---

149 What is the purpose of the e-mail?

(A) To make a list of items for sale
(B) To reschedule a live music event
(C) To invite a coworker to attend an event
(D) To give an update on a promotional plan*

150 What does Ms. Torenski promise to send later?

(A) A recent news article
(B) A schedule of store discounts*
(C) A list of television stations
(D) A revised press release

어라운드 타운

151 타운 북스 소유주 신시아 푸델은 브룩사이드 애비뉴 667번지에 두 번째 서점을 열 계획을 발표했다. 브룩사이드 초등학교 맞은편에 있는 이 건물은 이전에는 스미슨 베이커리였다. 이름이 아직 정해지지 않은 푸델 씨의 새 서점은 내년 봄에 열 예정이다. 이 서점은 폭넓은 아동 도서 섹션을 포함할 것이며, **152** 푸델 씨는 브룩사이드 초등학교로부터 많은 고객들을 유치하기를 바란다. 푸델 씨의 1호 서점인 타운 북스는 5번 애비뉴에 있으며 성인 독자들을 대상으로 한 장르들을 다룬다.

본 기사의 목적은 무엇인가?
(A) 업체 폐업을 논의하기 위해서
(B) 성공적인 제과점 소유주를 소개하기 위해서
(C) 매장 이전을 보도하기 위해서
(D) 새 업체 개업을 발표하기 위해서

어휘 discuss 토론하다, 논의하다 profile 개요, 프로필, 개요를 알려 주다/작성하다 relocation 이전

Questions 151-152 refer to the following article.

Around Town

151 Town Books owner Cynthia Purdel has announced her plans to open a second bookstore at 667 Brookside Avenue. The building, located across from Brookside Elementary School, was once the home of Smithton Bakery. Ms. Purdel's new bookstore, which has yet to be named, is scheduled to open in the spring of next year. The bookstore will include an extensive children's section, which **152** Ms. Purdel hopes will attract numerous customers from Brookside Elementary School. Ms. Purdel's original bookstore, Town Books, is located on 5th Avenue and houses genres that are targeted to adult readers.

어휘 owner 소유주 announce 발표하다 elementary school 초등학교 name 이름을 짓다 extensive 광범위한, 폭넓은 attract 끌어모으다, 유치하다 numerous 수많은 house 보관/수용/저장하다 target ~을 대상으로 삼다

151

What is the purpose of the article?
(A) To discuss the closing of a business
(B) To profile a successful bakery owner
(C) To report on a store's relocation
(D) To announce the opening of a new business*

첫 문장 Town Books owner Cynthia Purdel has announced her plans to open a second bookstore at 667 Brookside Avenue.를 통해 정답 (D)를 확인할 수 있다. 기존 store를 이전하는 것이 아니라 또 하나의 store(= business)를 개업하는 것이니 (C)는 잘못된 설명이다.

* paraphrasing: a second bookstore → a new business

정답 (D)

브룩사이드 애비뉴의 매장에 대해 드러나는 사항은?
(A) 유명한 제과점 맞은편에 있다.
(B) 올해 문을 열 예정이다.
(C) 푸델 씨의 첫 번째 사업체이다.
(D) 학생들을 대상으로 한 영업이 예상된다.

어휘 venture 모험, 사업 business (회사 등의) 사업, 영업, 실적

152

What is indicated about the store on Brookside Avenue?
(A) It is located across from a popular bakery.
(B) It is scheduled to open this year.
(C) It is Ms. Purdel's first business venture.
(D) It is expected to receive business from students.*

bookstore에 대한 문제임을 파악하고 지문을 살펴보면, 후반부에서 Ms. Purdel hopes will attract numerous customers from Brookside Elementary School.이라며 초등학교에서 많은 고객이 오기를 바란다고 하므로 (D)가 가장 적절하다.

정답 (D)

Questions 153-155 refer to the following notice.

St. Michael's Hospital Research Gala

St. Michael's Hospital will host a gala to benefit continued medical research. The gala will be held at the Grand Renaissance Hotel; however, [153] the day has been changed due to a hotel booking error. Instead of September 20, the event will be held on October 5, from 5:00 P.M. until 8:00 P.M. Please note the following information before attending.

[154] Directions to Grand Renaissance Hotel from Central Station:

[154] Drive north on Parcelle Boulevard and turn right onto Meadow Drive. Turn left onto Bath Avenue and continue for five blocks before turning right onto Smithview Road. The Grand Renaissance Hotel is located across from the Mary Rose Theater. The gala will be held in Banquet Room 1A.

Parking Information:

[155] Parking is available free of charge in the underground parking lot. Please ensure you have the parking pass that was issued along with your gala ticket. Otherwise, you will be responsible for paying for parking.

어휘 gala 경축, 축제 host 주최하다 benefit ~에게 도움이 되다 continued 지속적인 medical 의료의 be held 열리다 due to ~때문에 booking 예약 instead of ~대신에 note 유념하다 attend 참여하다, 출석하다 boulevard 대로 banquet 연회 free of charge 무료로 parking lot 주차장 ensure 확실히 하다 issue 발행하다, 발부하다 along with ~와 함께 otherwise 그렇지 않으면 be responsible for ~을 책임지다

153

What has changed about the event?

(A) The cost
(B) The location
(C) The sponsor
(D) The date*

첫째 문단에서 the day has been changed due to a hotel booking error라며 오류로 인해 날짜가 변경됐다고 하므로 (D)가 정답이다.

* paraphrasing: day → date

정답 (D)

154

Where is Central Station located?

(A) Meadow Drive
(B) Bath Avenue
(C) Parcelle Boulevard*
(D) Smithview Road

중앙역에서 행사장까지 가는 방법(Directions to Grand Renaissance Hotel from Central Station:)에서 처음 언급(Drive north on Parcelle Boulevard)된 도로는 (C)이다.

정답 (C)

성 미카엘 병원 연구를 위한 연회

성 미카엘 병원이 지속적인 의료 연구를 지원하기 위한 연회를 엽니다. 연회는 그랜드 르네상스 호텔에서 열립니다만, 153 날짜는 호텔의 예약 오류 때문에 변경됐습니다. 행사는 9월 20일이 아니라 10월 5일 오후 5시부터 저녁 8시까지 진행됩니다. 참석하시기 전에 다음 정보를 숙지해 주십시오.

154 중앙역에서 그랜드 르네상스 호텔까지 가는 방법:

154 파셀 불러바드에서 북쪽으로 운전하다가 메도 드라이브로 우회전하십시오. 바스 애비뉴로 좌회전한 다음 다섯 블록을 직진하시다가 스미스뷰 로드로 우회전하십시오. 그랜드 르네상스 호텔은 메리 로즈 씨어터 맞은편에 있습니다. 연회는 1A 연회장에서 열립니다.

주차 정보:

155 주차는 지하 주차장에 무료로 하실 수 있습니다. 연회 티켓과 함께 발부된 주차권을 꼭 가져오십시오. 그렇지 않으면, 주차비를 내셔야 합니다.

행사에 대해 무엇이 변경됐는가?
(A) 비용
(B) 장소
(C) 후원 업체
(D) 날짜

어휘 cost 값, 비용 sponsor 후원자, 후원 업체

중앙역은 어디에 있는가?
(A) 메도 드라이브
(B) 바스 애비뉴
(C) 파셀 불러바드
(D) 스미스뷰 로드

그랜드 르네상스 호텔의 주차에 대해 드러나는 사항은?
(A) 연회 참석자들은 주차비를 내야 할 것이다.
(B) 주차장은 길 건너에 있다.
(C) 주차는 패스가 있으면 무료이다.
(D) 호텔은 주차장을 다른 곳과 공유한다.

어휘 shared 공유의 garage 차고, 주차장

155

What is indicated about the Grand Renaissance Hotel's parking?
(A) Gala guests will have to pay for parking.
(B) The parking lot is located across the street.
(C) Parking is free with a guest pass.*
(D) The hotel has a shared parking garage.

parking에 관련된 부분을 찾아보자. 후반부의 주차 정보에서 무료로 주차할 수 있다며 주차권을 가져오라고 당부(Please ensure you have the parking pass that was issued along with your gala ticket.)한다. 따라서 (C)가 가장 적절하다.

정답 (C)

Questions 156-157 refer to the following text message chain.

Steven Yoon 4:45 P.M.
Jennifer tried to call you about the meeting with the CEO tomorrow. ^156 She's wondering if you can call her back.

Roger Martinez 4:50 P.M.
I'm in the warehouse right now. Do you think she's worried the reports won't be finished in time?

Steven Yoon 4:52 P.M.
It's possible.

Roger Martinez 4:54 P.M.
Well, I'm checking the warehouse alarm system now. I got called away, because it seems to be acting up again.

Steven Yoon 4:57 P.M.
Do you want me to call the security company?

Roger Martinez 5:00 P.M.
I think I can fix it myself. ^157 Can you tell Jennifer to stop by my office at 5:30? I think we should discuss her concerns tonight before we go home.

Steven Yoon 5:01 P.M.
Okay. No problem.

어휘 warehouse 창고, 도매점 call away ~을 불러내다 act up 제멋대로 행동하다 security 보안, 안전 fix 고치다 stop by 잠시 들르다 concern 우려 사항, 걱정

오후 4시 50분에, 마르티네즈 씨가 "제가 지금은 창고에 있어요"라고 쓸 때 의미하는 바는?
(A) 내일 회사에 없을 것이다.
(B) 배송할 것이 있다.
(C) 윤 씨와 이야기해야 한다.
(D) 제니퍼에게 전화할 수 없다.

어휘 delivery 배송, 배달

156

At 4:50 P.M. what does Mr. Martinez most likely mean when he writes, "I'm in the warehouse right now"?
(A) He will not be in tomorrow.
(B) He has a delivery to make.
(C) He needs to speak with Mr. Yoon.
(D) He cannot call Jennifer.*

앞서 제니퍼가 전화했었다며 회신을 줄 수 있냐(She's wondering if you can call her back.)고 물은 데 대한 반응이므로 (D)가 가장 적절하다.

정답 (D)

윤 씨는 무엇을 해 달라는 부탁을 받는가?
(A) CEO에게 연락하라.
(B) 회의를 잡아 달라.
(C) 기술자에게 연락하라.
(D) 사무실에서 나가라.

어휘 task 일, 업무

157

What task is Mr. Yoon asked to do?
(A) Contact the CEO
(B) Set up a meeting*
(C) Call a technician
(D) Leave the office

'Mr. Martinez가 부탁한 내용'이 포인트임을 파악하고 마르티네즈 씨의 문자를 집중적으로 살펴보면, 오후 5시 내용에서 Can you tell Jennifer to stop by my office at 5:30?라며 제니퍼에게 들르라고 전해 달라 한 뒤 퇴근 전에 이야기를 나눠야겠다고 덧붙인다. 따라서 이를 meeting이라는 단어로 요약한 (B)가 가장 적절하다.

정답 (B)

Questions 158-160 refer to the following letter.

October 10

Peter Stephenson
45 Ramsay Avenue
Cleveland, Ohio

Dear Mr. Stephenson:

Thank you very much for deciding to attend the very first International Magazine Festival that will take place in Paris, France. [158] We received your registration. --[1]-- As requested, we billed your credit card to include both admission to the event as well as the extra fee needed to reserve a table for your display. Immediately upon arrival, we will show you to your table and also present you with a name badge that will allow you to receive discounts at any beverage and food vendors at the festival. --[2]--

We would like to remind you that accommodation is not included in the festival admission price. To reserve a room in the neighborhood, please visit www.parishotels.com. [160] You may be able to book a room at 25% off the regular rate by providing proof that you are participating in our festival. --[3]--

[159] Enclosed, please find a map of this particular area of Paris. This will allow you to acquaint yourself with the neighborhood. The map also includes the area's most popular restaurants and hotels. --[4]--

Again, thank you and we hope the International Magazine Festival turns out to be a rewarding experience for you.

Sincerely,

Nicole Desjardins,
Festival Coordinator

본 편지는 왜 발송됐는가?
(A) 부분 환불을 제안하기 위해서
(B) 주소 변경을 알리기 위해서
(C) 절차를 설명하기 위해서
(D) 등록되었음을 알리기 위해서

어휘 offer 제공하다, 제안하다 partial 부분적인
refund 환불 inform 알리다 procedure 절차,
방법 acknowledge 인정하다, (편지 등을)
받았음을 알리다

158

Why was the letter sent?
(A) To offer a partial refund
(B) To inform of an address change
(C) To explain a procedure
(D) To acknowledge registration*

글의 목적에 대한 결정적인 단서는 대체로 전반부에 나온다. 첫 문장에서 페스티벌 참여 결정을 고마워한 다음 등록 서류를 받았다(We received your registration.)고 덧붙이므로 (D)가 정답이다.

정답 (D)

스티븐슨 씨는 무엇을 미리 검토할 것을 조언 받는가?
(A) 지역 지도
(B) 회의 안건
(C) 계약 조항
(D) 비행 시간

어휘 agenda 안건 contract 계약(서) term
조항 flight 비행(편)

159

What is Mr. Stephenson advised to review ahead of time?
(A) A local map*
(B) A meeting agenda
(C) Contract terms
(D) Flight times

셋째 문단에서 Enclosed, please find a map of this particular area of Paris.라며 지도를 동봉했다고 한 뒤 지역을 익히는 데 도움이 될 것이라고 설명하므로 (A)가 정답이다.

정답 (A)

다음 문장은 [1], [2], [3], [4] 중 어디에 가장 적절한가?
"이 편지가 적합한 확인증이니 체크인하실 때 직원에게 보여 주시면 됩니다."
(A) [1]
(B) [2]
(C) [3]
(D) [4]

어휘 suitable 적합한, 적절한 verification
확인, 조회

160

In which of the positions marked [1], [2], [3], and [4] does the following sentence best belong?
"This letter is suitable verification so simply present it to the clerk when you check in."
(A) [1]
(B) [2]
(C) [3]*
(D) [4]

'투숙' 수속을 밟을 때 쓰는 표현 check in이 주요 단서가 된다. 따라서 숙소를 예약할 때 할인 받는 방법이 언급된 문장 다음인 (C)가 가장 적절하다.

정답 (C)

Questions 161-164 refer to the following article.

Unforeseeable Delays for the Hammer Electronics 8000 Series

By Sophia Miachi

Last week, [161] Hammer Electronics, the world's leading producer of smart phones, announced a delay in the launch of its new 8000 Series smart phone line. Industry professionals and customers alike were shocked by the news. Hammer Electronics enthusiasts took to social media to express their frustration with the cancelation of the much-anticipated 8000 Series.

According to Hammer representatives, the 8000 Series, which will consist of three individual models and various companion technologies, has been delayed due to unforeseeable problems with the company's new screen design. --[1]-- While the prototypes were initially approved, the first batch of devices were unable to pass safety tests. --[2]-- [162 (A), (B)] This may be due to a flaw in the glass used to construct the screens, which makes the internal components vulnerable to overheating.

In addition to not passing the inspections, [164] Hammer's new line has proven to be less durable than the company intended. [162 (D)] Because of the flawed materials, the 8000 Series has proven to be quite delicate. --[3]--

[163] Hammer Electronics is now looking at alternative materials and plans to release the 8000 Series next year. --[4]-- However, the company may have already lost many of its eager customers.

어휘 **unforeseeable** 예견할 수 없는 **delay** 지체, 지연, 지체시키다, 지연시키다 **electronics** 전자 제품 **launch** 출시, 발표 **alike** 둘 다, 똑같이 **shock** 충격을 주다, 경악하게 하다 **enthusiast** 열광적인 팬, 열렬한 지지자 **take to** ~에 호소하다 **frustration** 불만, 좌절감 **cancelation** 취소 **anticipate** 기대하다, 예상하다 **representative** 직원, 대리인 **consist of** ~로 구성되다 **individual** 각각의, 개개의 **companion** 동행, 짝 **due to** ~때문에 **prototype** 원형 **initially** 처음에 **approve** 찬성/승인/허가하다 **batch** 묶음, 다발 **device** 기기, 장비 **pass** 통과하다 **safety** 보안, 안전 **flaw** 결함, 망가지다 **construct** 건설하다, 구성하다 **internal** 내부의 **component** 요소, 부품 **vulnerable** 취약한, 연약한 **overheating** 과열 **in addition to** ~에 더해 **inspection** 점검, 조사 **prove to** ~임이 드러나다, 판명되다 **durable** 내구성이 있는, 오래가는 **intend** 의도하다, 작정하다 **material** 재료, 자재 **quite** 꽤, 상당히 **delicate** 연약한, 여린 **alternative** 대체 가능한, 대안이 되는 **release** 공개하다, 발표하다 **eager** 열렬한

161

What is indicated about Hammer Electronics?
(A) It is a top producer of smart phone technology.*
(B) It will sell the 8000 Series at a discount.
(C) It is moving its headquarters to another country.
(D) It will continue producing a flawed design.

첫째 문단의 Hammer Electronics, the world's leading producer of smart phones를 통해 (A)가 정답임을 알 수 있다.

* paraphrasing: leading → top

정답 (A)

8000 시리즈의 디자인 문제로 언급되지 않은 것은?
(A) 스크린 유리에 문제가 있다.
(B) 기기가 과열될 우려가 있다.
(C) 자재가 너무 비싸다.
(D) 기기가 약하다.

어휘 overheat 과열되다 expensive 돈이 많이 드는 fragile 손상되기 쉬운, 취약한

162

What is NOT mentioned as a problem with the 8000 Series design?

(A) The screens have flawed glass.
(B) The devices may overheat.
(C) The materials are too expensive.*
(D) The devices are fragile.

각 선택지를 지문과 대조하면서 언급된 '문제점'을 소거하는 식으로 해결한다. (A)와 (B)는 둘째 문단의 This may be due to a flaw in the glass used to construct the screens, which makes the internal components vulnerable to overheating.에서, (D)는 셋째 문단의 Because of the flawed materials, the 8000 Series has proven to be quite delicate.에서 확인할 수 있다. 따라서 본 문제의 정답은 (C)가 된다.

정답 (C)

해머 일렉트로닉스는 8000 시리즈를 왜 내년에 출시할 예정인가?
(A) 특허 문제를 처리해야 해서
(B) 점검 일정이 다시 잡혀서
(C) 일부 공장을 개선해야 해서
(D) 새 자재를 찾을 시간이 필요해서

어휘 address (문제를) 다루다 patent 특허(권) issue 문제, 사안

163

Why will Hammer Electronics release the 8000 Series next year?

(A) They need to address a patent issue.
(B) Their inspections have been rescheduled.
(C) Some factories need to be upgraded.
(D) They need enough time to find new materials.*

핵심 어구 next year에 유념해 지문을 살펴보면, 마지막 문단에서 Hammer Electronics is now looking at alternative materials and plans to release the 8000 Series next year.라며 지금은 대체 자재를 찾는 중이고 내년에 출시할 계획이라고 하므로 (D)가 가장 적절하다.

* paraphrasing: alternative → new

정답 (D)

---

[1], [2], [3], [4] 중 다음 문장이 들어가기에 가장 적절한 곳은?
"오래가는 제품을 자랑으로 삼는 회사이므로, 이번 제품들을 출시하는 것은 부끄러운 일이 될 것이다."
(A) [1]
(B) [2]
(C) [3]
(D) [4]

어휘 embarrassment 쑥스러움, 곤란한 상황

164

In which of the positions marked [1], [2], [3], and [4] does the following sentence best belong?

"For a company that prides itself on durable products, releasing this line of devices would be an embarrassment."

(A) [1]
(B) [2]
(C) [3]*
(D) [4]

'제품의 내구성'이 포인트인 제시문의 요지로 볼 때, 회사의 예상보다 내구성이 부족한 제품으로 드러났다(less durable than the company intended)는 셋째 문단의 맥락에 가장 적절하다. 따라서 (C)가 정답이 된다.

정답 (C)

Questions 165-168 refer to the following text message chain.

| Messages | | Edit |

Lester Gibbs [9:00]
Hi, Michelle. Are you at the office?

Michelle Chong [9:01]
Almost there. Why?

Lester Gibbs [9:03]
165, 166 I'm working on a house here on Kensington Avenue, and just realized that I don't have enough red exterior paint left for the trim around the doors and windows. Do we have any cans of it left in our store? If not, I will just drive over to a store in Anders Park and pick up a can.

Michelle Chong [9:04]
Justin is at the office now. I'm including him right now. How many cans do you need?

— Justin Whittaker has been added to the chat —

Lester Gibbs [9:05]
167 I need two cans of red exterior paint. Can you please check the storage, Justin?

Justin Whittaker [9:07]
This must be your luck day.

Lester Gibbs [9:10]
Super! I have to finish painting the east side of the house and won't be starting the trim for at least an hour, so I will come by and pick them up after 10:00.

Michelle Chong [9:11]
Actually, I just backed my truck up to the loading dock and will get everything I need for a job on the corner of Nelson Avenue and Bicks Street. 166 You're not far from that area so I can easily drop off the cans of red exterior first.

Lester Gibbs [9:15]
That would be great. Thanks a lot! 168 Justin, please add my name and the current time to the stock record sheet. I will be sure to come by after lunch and sign the form.

Justin Whittaker [9:17]
No problem.

깁스 씨는 어떤 업체에서 일하겠는가?
(A) 주택 개조 공사 업체
(B) 인터넷 제공 업체
(C) 플라스틱 제조 업체
(D) 패스트푸드 레스토랑

어휘 improvement 개선, 향상 contractor 계약자, 도급 업자

165

What type of business does Mr. Gibbs probably work for?

(A) A home improvement contractor*
(B) A Internet provider
(C) A plastics manufacturer
(D) A fast food restaurant

깁스 씨의 9시 3분 메시지 중에서 I'm working on a house here on Kensington Avenue, and just realized that I don't have enough red exterior paint left for the trim around the doors and windows.를 통해 (A)가 가장 적절함을 알 수 있다.

정답 (A)

청 씨는 다음에 어디로 갈 것이라고 말하는가?
(A) 앤더스 파크로
(B) 켄싱턴 애비뉴로
(C) 빅스 스트리트로
(D) 넬슨 애비뉴로

166

Where does Ms. Chong say she will go next?

(A) To Anders Park   (B) To Kensington Avenue*
(C) To Bicks Street   (D) To Nelson Avenue

Ms. Chong의 메시지를 주목해 보면, 9시 11분 내용에서 당신(Mr. Gibbs)이 있는 곳부터 들르겠다(You're not far from that area so I can easily drop off the cans of red exterior first.)고 한다. 깁스 씨의 현재 장소를 찾아보자면, 9시 3분 메시지 중 I'm working on a house here on Kensington Avenue에서 정답 (B)를 확인할 수 있다.

정답 (B)

오전 9시 7분에, 휘태커 씨가 "오늘 운 좋으시네요"라고 쓸 때 의미하는 바는?
(A) 새 프로젝트를 위한 자금이 충분하다.
(B) 그 집까지 가는 길을 찾기 쉽다.
(C) 딱 필요한 만큼 재고가 있다.
(D) 저녁에 깁스 씨를 도울 수 있을 것이다.

어휘 in stock 재고가 있는

167

At 9:07 A.M. what does Mr. Whittaker most likely mean when he writes, "This must be your lucky day"?

(A) There is enough money for a new project.
(B) The directions to the house are easy to follow.
(C) The exact number of cans needed is in stock.*
(D) He will be able to help Mr. Gibbs in the evening.

해당 메시지의 전후 맥락을 살펴봐야 한다. 앞서 깁스 씨가 페인트 두 통이 필요하다(I need two cans of red exterior paint.)며 확인을 요청했으므로 운 좋다는 말은 (C)를 의미한다.

정답 (C)

깁스 씨는 휘태커 씨에게 무엇을 해 달라고 부탁하는가?
(A) 서식에 주요 사항들을 적어 달라.
(B) 선반에 물건들을 둬 달라.
(C) 고객과 상담 약속을 잡아 달라.
(D) 지역 업체에 송장을 보내 달라.

어휘 fill in 기입하다, 섬하다 shelf 선반 consultation 상담, 상의 invoice 송장, 인보이스

168

What does Mr. Gibbs ask Mr. Whittaker to do?

(A) Fill in the main details on a form*
(B) Place some items on a shelf
(C) Set up a consultation with a client
(D) Send an invoice to a local business

Mr. Whittaker를 향한 메시지를 집중해서 찾아보자. 9시 15분에 깁스 씨가 쓴 메시지에서 Justin, please add my name and the current time to the stock record sheet.라며 이름과 현재 시각을 추가해 달라고 부탁한다. 따라서 (A)가 가장 적절하다.

* paraphrasing: add → fill in, name and the current time → main details, stock record sheet → form

정답 (A)

454 해설집

Questions 169-171 refer to the following advertisement.

BizNet
Networking at the click of a mouse!

BizNet is the latest development in online networking services. Quick, affordable, and easy-to-use, ¹⁶⁹ BizNet can connect you with industry professionals and help you land the job of your dreams. Our online services allow you to track trends in the job market as well as get up-to-date information on business conferences in your area.

In cooperation with ¹⁷⁰ our sister network, StudyNet, you get numerous advanced features, such as:
- ¹⁷¹ ⁽ᴮ⁾ A simple résumé builder that allows you to create a perfect résumé in minutes
- An extensive list of businesses and ¹⁷¹ ⁽ᴰ⁾ search tools for finding the right job opening
- ¹⁷¹ ⁽ᴬ⁾ A library of videos on everything from applying to interviewing for your dream job
- Weekly matching services that pair you up with new jobs based on your skills

For more information, visit www.biznet.com.

어휘 latest 최신의 affordable (가격이) 알맞은 land (많은 사람이 원하는 직장 등을) 차지하다 track 추적하다 trend 경향 up-to-date 최신의 in cooperation with ~와 협력하여, 협동하여 numerous 무수한 advanced 고급의, 상급의 résumé 이력서 extensive 광범위한, 폭넓은 apply for ~에 지원하다 pair 짝을 짓다 based on ~에 근거해

169

How would a customer most likely use BizNet?

(A) To shop for online services
(B) To find employment at a company*
(C) To complete tax documents
(D) To advertise the services of a company

BizNet이 하는 일의 성격을 묻는 문제이다. 첫째 문단에서 BizNet can connect you with industry professionals and help you land the job of your dreams라며 '취직'을 언급하므로 (B)가 정답이다.

정답 (B)

비즈넷
마우스 클릭 한 번으로 네트워킹!

비즈넷은 최근에 개발된 온라인 네트워킹 서비스입니다. 169 신속하고, 저렴하며, 사용하기 쉬운 비즈넷이 여러분을 업계 전문가들과 이어주고 꿈의 직장을 차지하도록 돕습니다. 저희 온라인 서비스로 여러분은 채용 시장의 최신 트렌드를 추적하고 가까운 지역의 비즈니스 컨퍼런스에 관한 최신 정보를 얻으실 수 있습니다.

170 자매 회사인 스터디넷과 협력해, 여러분께 다음과 같은 다양한 고급 혜택을 제공합니다:
- 몇 분 내에 완벽한 이력서를 작성할 수 있는 171 (B) 간단한 이력서 제작 툴
- 무수한 업체 목록과 171 (D) 적절한 일자리를 찾는 데 유용한 검색툴
- 꿈의 직장에 지원해서 면접을 보기까지 모든 것에 대한 171 (A) 비디오 자료관
- 귀하의 기술에 근거해 새로운 일과 연결하는 주간 매칭 서비스

더 많은 정보를 원하시면, www.biznet.com을 방문하십시오.

고객은 비즈넷을 어떤 식으로 이용하겠는가?
(A) 온라인 서비스를 구매하기 위해서
(B) 한 회사에서 일자리를 찾기 위해서
(C) 세금 서류를 작성하기 위해서
(D) 회사 서비스를 광고하기 위해서

어휘 employment 채용, 고용 complete 완성하다, 작성하다 tax 세금

비즈넷을 개발한 회사에 대해 드러나는 사항은?
(A) 그곳 직원들에게 전화로 연락할 수 있다.
(B) 재택 사업을 돕는 것으로 유명하다.
(C) 판매 대기업이 설립했다.
(D) 네트워킹 웹사이트가 한 개 이상 있다.

어휘 representative 직원 reputation 평판, 명성 found 설립하다 corporation 법인, 회사

170

What is suggested about the company that developed BizNet?
(A) Its representatives can be contacted by telephone.
(B) It has a reputation for helping home businesses.
(C) It was founded by a large sales corporation.
(D) It has more than one networking website.*

둘째 문단의 our sister network, StudyNet을 통해 (D)가 가장 적절한 설명임을 알 수 있다.

정답 (D)

비즈넷의 특징으로 언급되지 않은 것은?
(A) 비디오 자료관
(B) 이력서 생성 프로그램
(C) 컨퍼런스 티켓
(D) 채용 검색 툴

어휘 generator 발생기, 생성 프로그램

171

What is NOT mentioned as a feature of BizNet?
(A) A library of videos
(B) A résumé generator
(C) Tickets to conferences*
(D) Employment search tools

지문에서 feature에 관련된 부분(마지막 문단)을 찾아 각 선택지와 대조하면서 지문에 언급된 것을 소거하는 식으로 해결한다. 첫째 항목 A simple résumé builder에서 (B)를, 둘째 항목 search tools for finding the right job opening에서 (D)를, 셋째 항목 A library of videos에서 (A)를 확인할 수 있다. 따라서 본 문제의 정답은 (C)이다.

정답 (C)

Questions 172-175 refer to the following notice.

Lake Porticole Beach and Campground (LPBC)

[172] Lake Porticole Beach and Campground will be open this spring & summer season beginning April 10 through to September 1. Please note, however, LPBC reserves the right to impose additional restrictions on campers. [173] Due to the repeated occurrence of dry weather, campers may be prohibited from having open campfires at certain times. This does not apply to the use of camping stoves and barbecues for cooking, however. When fires are permitted, campers must purchase pre-cut wood from the park. Cutting down trees will not be permitted at any time.

Lake Porticole Beach may be accessed by non-campers for day visits for a small fee. Beach goers may arrive as early as 8 A.M. and stay until 5 P.M. [174] Group tickets may be booked in advance for a discount. Additionally, the park offers guided tours of the Lake Porticole Museum, a historical estate originally owned by Sir William Marks. Tickets for the museum can be purchased at the front gate on the day of the tour.

Payment and Reservations
• For campsite reservations, call 888-341-0867. Campsites are $65.00 per night. [175] A non-refundable deposit of $30.00 must be made at the time of reservation. This deposit goes toward the cost of your stay.
• Beach day passes for non-campers can be purchased upon arrival for $8.00 per person. Groups of more than fifteen can receive a 20% discount if reservations are made in advance.
• Lake Porticole Museum tickets are available for $7.00 per person. Tours are offered three times per day at 11 A.M., 1 P.M., and 3 P.M.

172 What is announced in the notice?
(A) A new policy
(B) A business's closing
(C) An increase in fees
(D) An operation schedule*

레이크 포티콜의 야영장을 방문하는 것에 대해 드러나는 사항은?
(A) 캠핑하는 사람들은 숲에 쓰레기를 버릴 경우 벌금을 물 수 있다.
(B) 캠핑하는 사람들은 캠프 파이어를 하지 못할 수 있다.
(C) 박물관을 보려면, 캠핑하는 사람들은 단체여야 한다.
(D) 해변에 들어가 가려면, 캠핑하는 사람들은 추가 요금을 내야 한다.

어휘 indicate 가리키다, 나타내다 fine 벌금을 부과하다 litter 어지럽히다, 쓰레기를 버리다 forest 숲 pay 결제하다, 지불하다

173

What is indicated about visiting Lake Porticole's campground?
(A) Campers can be fined for littering in the forest.
(B) Campers might not be able to have campfires. *
(C) To see the museum, campers must be part of a group.
(D) To access the beach, campers need to pay another fee.

'야영장 이용 시 주의 사항'이 포인트이다. 첫째 문단에서 추가적인 규제가 있을 수 있다며 특정 기간에는 캠프 파이어가 불가능하다(Due to the repeated occurrence of dry weather, campers may be prohibited from having open campfires at certain times.)고 설명한다. 따라서 (B)가 정답이 된다.

정답 (B)

레이크 포티콜의 캠핑 이외의 서비스에 대해 언급된 것은?
(A) 박물관 티켓은 예약할 수 있다.
(B) 해변 방문자들은 주말에는 밤새 머물 수 있다.
(C) 해변 방문자들에게 파라솔이 무료로 제공된다.
(D) 단체는 해변에 방문할 때 할인 받을 수 있다.

어휘 reserve 예약하다 overnight 하룻밤 동안 free of charge 무료로

174

What is mentioned about the Lake Porticole's non-camping services?
(A) Museum tickets can be reserved.
(B) Beach visitors can stay overnight on weekends.
(C) Parasols are offered to beach visitors free of charge.
(D) Groups can get a discount when visiting the beach. *

'캠핑하지 않는 사람들'에 관련된 둘째 문단에서 Group tickets may be booked in advance for a discount.라며 '사전 예약 시 단체 티켓은 할인된다'고 하므로 (D)가 정답이다.

정답 (D)

야영장 예약이 취소될 때 어떤 일이 생기는가?
(A) 예약금을 잃는다.
(B) 결제가 환불된다.
(C) 청구서가 발송된다.
(D) 회원 등급이 낮아진다.

어휘 lose 잃다 refund 환불하다 bill 청구서

175

What happens when a campsite reservation is canceled?
(A) A reservation fee is lost. *
(B) A payment is refunded.
(C) A bill will be sent.
(D) A membership will be downgraded.

'예약'에 유의해 지문을 살펴보면, Payment and Reservations의 첫 번째 항목에서 '환불 불가능한 보증금(A non-refundable deposit of $30.00 must be made at the time of reservation.)'이 언급된다. 따라서 (A)가 가장 적절하다.

정답 (A)

Questions 176-180 refer to following letter and e-mail.

10 March

Ms. Kelly Norstram
Simpson Publishing
Human Resources Department
55 Center St.
Sydney, Australia

Dear Ms. Norstram,

I would like to take this opportunity to submit my application for the editorial director position at Simpson Publishing in its new Sydney office. [176] As you can see from my enclosed résumé, I have extensive experience in the editorial field, including five years as head editor at Lush Magazine and three years as an editorial assistant at the Sydney Times newspaper.

[176] Aside from this experience, I also have a Bachelor's degree in Journalism and a Master's degree in Publishing Studies. Furthermore, I believe I would add a new [177] dimension to the editorial director position given that I am also a published author of seven children's books. I believe that my unique combination of experience will contribute greatly to the company.

Thank you very much for your time. I look forward to speaking with you.

Sincerely,
Adrian Perdu

To: Simpson Publishing Editorial Staff
From: Adrian Perdu
Date: April 30
Subject: [178] Some Reminders

Editorial Staff Members,

[180] It has been nearly a year since we first proposed our new line of educational children's books. I'd like to commend you all on your hard work on this series. With our publication date fast approaching, [178] I'd just like to remind everyone of a few things.

First, please ensure you communicate with designers weekly regarding the overall design of our books. It is important that you give them your input and guidance in bringing our collective vision to fruition.

Second, some freelance proofreaders have fallen behind on their deadlines. Please make sure you keep in contact with them regularly and if need be, hire additional freelancers to complete the work.

끝으로, 179 우리 시리즈 발간에 웹사이트 출시가 포함되니, "회사 소개" 섹션에 들어갈 약력을 모두 제출하셨으면 합니다. 1백 단어 정도의 약력이면 충분할 것입니다.

계속 애써 주셔서 모두 고맙습니다. 발행일을 고대합니다!

아드리안

Finally, [179] as the release of our series will include a website launch, I'd like everyone to submit a biography for the "about us" section. A simple biography of about one hundred words will suffice.

Thank you all for your continued hard work, and I look forward to launch day!

Adrian

어휘 reminder 상기시키는 것 propose 제안하다 commend 칭찬하다, 추천하다 publication 출판 approach 다가오다 remind 상기시키다 regarding ~에 관해 overall 전반적인, 종합적인 input 조언 guidance 지도, 안내 collective 집단의, 단체의 fruition 성과, 결실 proofreader 교정자 fall behind ~에 뒤지다 keep in contact with ~와 접촉/연락을 유지하다 regularly 정기적으로, 규칙적으로 additional 추가적인 complete 완성하다 release 발표, 공개, 발간 launch 출시 submit 제출하다 biography 전기, 인물 소개 suffice 충분하다

편지의 한 가지 목적은 무엇인가?
(A) 초봉에 대해 문의하기 위해서
(B) 전문적인 자질들을 열거하기 위해서
(C) 고용 추천서를 제공하기 위해서
(D) 일자리 위치를 묻기 위해서

어휘 salary 급여, 봉급 qualification 자격(증), 자질 reference 추천(서)

176

What is one purpose of the letter?
(A) To inquire about a starting salary
(B) To list some professional qualifications*
(C) To provide an employment reference
(D) To ask about the location of a job

편지(지문 1) 첫째 문단과 둘째 문단에 경력 및 학력이 소개된다. 따라서 (B)가 가장 적절하다.

정답 (B)

편지에서, 둘째 문단 둘째 줄에 있는 "dimension"과 의미상 가장 유사한 단어는?
(A) 수요
(B) 선례
(C) 문제
(D) 특징

어휘 demand 수요, 요구 precedent 선례, 판례 matter 문제, 사안 characteristic 특징, 특질

177

In the letter, the word "dimension" in paragraph 2, line 2, is closest in meaning to
(A) demand
(B) precedent
(C) matter
(D) characteristic*

편집 부장 직에 새로운 '차원, 관점'을 더하다라는 의미와 가장 유사하게 쓰일 수 있는 어휘는 (D)이다.

정답 (D)

페두 씨는 왜 이메일을 썼는가?
(A) 직원들의 과제 완수를 칭찬하기 위해서
(B) 몇몇 업무의 중요성을 강조하기 위해서
(C) 직원들이 추가 근무를 하도록 동기 부여하기 위해서
(D) 특별 절차에 대해 신입 직원들에게 알리기 위해서

어휘 praise 칭찬하다 task 과제 stress 강조하다 motivate 동기를 부여하다 inform 알리다

178

Why did Mr. Perdu write the e-mail?
(A) To praise workers for getting tasks done
(B) To stress the importance of some duties*
(C) To motivate employees to take on extra work
(D) To inform new hires of special procedures

이메일(지문 2)의 제목 Some Reminders를 통해서 '상기 사항 몇 가지'가 주로 전개되리라는 것이 드러나는데, 주제문(I'd just like to remind everyone of a few things) 다음의 세 문단을 통해 필요한 각 업무에 대해 지시하고 있으므로 (B)가 가장 적절하다.

정답 (B)

179 What is stated about Simpson Publishing?
(A) It publishes primarily e-books.
(B) It employs editors in seven countries.
(C) It will discontinue some publications.
(D) It will introduce its staff on its website.*

심슨 퍼블리싱에 대해 뭐라고 언급되는가?
(A) 주로 전자책을 출간한다.
(B) 7개국에서 편집자들을 고용한다.
(C) 일부 출간을 중단할 것이다.
(D) 웹사이트에 직원들을 소개할 것이다.

어휘 primarily 주로 employ 고용하다 discontinue 중단하다

Simpson Publishing 직원들을 대상으로 한 이메일(지문 2) 넷째 문단에서 '새로운 웹사이트'를 언급하며 각 직원의 소개문을 제출하라(as the release of our series will include a website launch, I'd like everyone to submit a biography for the "about us" section)고 한다. 따라서 (D)가 정답이 된다.

정답 (D)

180 What is suggested about Mr. Perdu?
(A) He previously worked as a book designer.
(B) He was hired by Simpson Publishing one year ago.*
(C) He moved to Sydney for a job opportunity.
(D) He no longer writes books for children.

페두 씨에 대해 드러나는 사항은?
(A) 이전에는 북 디자이너로 일했다.
(B) 1년 전에 심슨 퍼블리싱에 고용되었다.
(C) 채용 기회 때문에 시드니로 이사했다.
(D) 아동 도서는 더 이상 쓰지 않는다.

어휘 previously 이전에

편지(지문 1)는 Mr. Perdu가 Simpson Publishing의 새로운 지점의 편집 부장 직에 지원하는 내용이고 이메일(지문 2)은 Mr. Perdu가 Simpson Publishing 편집부에 지시하는 내용이다. 또, 지문 2 첫째 문단의 It has been nearly a year since we first proposed our new line of educational children's books.를 통해 (입사 후) 새로운 프로젝트를 시작한 지 1년 가까이 흘렀음을 알 수 있으므로 (B)가 정답이다.

정답 (B)

Questions 181-185 refer to the following e-mail and business plan.

To: Wanda Willis <willis@utcbankandloans.com>
From: Jeffrey Thomas <jthomas@mailmail.com>
Date: March 12
Re: Business Plan
Attachment: Revised Plan

Dear Ms. Willis,

Thank you so much for your quick reply. I am very happy you are able to help me [182] secure financial backing for my new business venture. [181] I have looked over all the feedback you sent and edited my business plan accordingly. As you advised, [183] I have included a section that details our potential customers and attached the revised version.

I think this is all I need to complete the application package for my business loan. However, if there's anything else I need to fill out, please contact me.

I look forward to hearing from you.

Sincerely,
Jeffrey Thomas

Business Plan: The Brim

Section 1. Purpose
Downtown Portside has become a bustling business district, filled with numerous office buildings, banks, and department stores. My business, The Brim, will be located near the prestigious court house, a busy area of the downtown core. [184] We hope to offer a wide variety of international gourmet coffees at affordable prices, while also providing a relaxing atmosphere to enjoy our gourmet lunch items.

[183] Section 2. Target Market
The Brim will serve business professionals working downtown. Because there are so many law offices and banks within walking distance, our customers are likely to visit our coffee house in the mornings, during break times, and at lunch. Furthermore, weekend customers will consist of shoppers who are visiting the nearby Portside Department Store.

Section 3. Timeline
The Brim is scheduled to open on June 1. We expect the following preparations to be completed by:

March 28   Sign the lease and apply for a business permit
April 10   Renovate the dining area and upgrade the kitchen
April 20   Hire staff and complete employee training
May 15   Finalize the menu, order inventory, and plan the grand opening

Section 4. Marketing Plan
185 Please see the attached spread sheet for our detailed marketing plans prior to opening and after.

어휘 purpose 목적 bustling 부산한 district 구역 prestigious 명망 높은 court house 법원 a wide variety of 아주 다양한 gourmet 미식가, 식도락가 affordable (가격이) 알맞은 relaxing 마음을 느긋하게 해 주는 atmosphere 분위기 consist of ~로 구성되다 department store 백화점 preparation 준비 lease 계약 permit 허가 renovate 개조하다 inventory 재고 prior to ~이전에

181

What is the purpose of the e-mail?

(A) To review the guidelines of a permit
(B) To send feedback about some financial data
(C) To request advice on writing a business plan
(D) To respond to a requested revision*

이메일(지문 1) 첫째 문단의 I have looked over all the feedback you sent and edited my business plan accordingly.를 통해 (D)가 가장 적절함을 알 수 있다. 글의 목적은 대체로 전반부에서 확인할 수 있다.

정답 (D)

이메일의 목적은 무엇인가?
(A) 허가 안내를 검토하기 위해서
(B) 재정 데이터에 대해 피드백을 보내기 위해서
(C) 사업 계획을 작성하는 데 조언을 요청하기 위해서
(D) 요청된 수정에 답변하기 위해서

어휘 respond 응답하다, 대답하다 revision 수정

182

In the e-mail, the word "secure" in paragraph 1, line 1, is closest in meaning to

(A) guard   (B) obtain*
(C) save   (D) fasten

해당 부분의 요지를 살펴보면, 재정 지원을 '받게' 도와줘서 고맙다는 내용이다. 따라서 제시된 선택지들 중 이를 대신할 수 있는 동사는 (B)이다.

정답 (B)

이메일에서, 첫째 문단 첫째 줄에 있는 "secure"와 의미상 가장 유사한 단어는?
(A) 보호하다
(B) 획득하다
(C) 구하다
(D) 매다

어휘 guard 지키다, 보호하다 obtain 얻다, 획득하다 save 구하다 fasten 매다, 채우다

사업 계획 중 어느 섹션이 추가되었는가?
(A) 섹션 1
(B) 섹션 2
(C) 섹션 3
(D) 섹션 4

183
What section of the business plan was added?
(A) Section 1   (B) Section 2*
(C) Section 3   (D) Section 4

Jeffrey Thomas가 작성한 첫 번째 이메일(지문 1) '추가 부분'에 유의해 '수정안'이 첨부된 이메일(지문 1)부터 살펴보면, 첫째 문단의 I have included a section that details our potential customers and attached the revised version.에서 '잠재 고객'에 관련된 내용이 언급된다. 이를 토대로 계획안(지문 2)을 대조해 보면 고객층에 대한 내용이라고 볼 수 있는 (B) Section 2. Target Market을 확인할 수 있다.

정답 (B)

토마스 씨는 어떤 업체를 시작하려고 하는가?
(A) 대출 회사
(B) 백화점
(C) 법률 회사
(D) 구오메이 카페

184
What type of business does Mr. Thomas plan to start?
(A) A loan company   (B) A department store
(C) A law office   (D) A gourmet cafe*

'업체 성격'에 관련된 문제이므로 사업 계획안(지문 2)을 집중적으로 살펴봐야 한다. 지문 2 첫째 문단의 We hope to offer a wide variety of international gourmet coffees at affordable prices, while also providing a relaxing atmosphere to enjoy our gourmet lunch items.에서 (D)가 정답임을 알 수 있다. gourmet는 '미식가'라는 뜻으로 음식, 와인 앞에 붙여졌을 때 그것이 '고급'임을 의미한다.

정답 (D)

사업 계획에 따르면, 어떤 정보가 별도로 제출되었는가?
(A) 예상 수익에 대한 상세 견적
(B) 고용 추천을 위한 연락처
(C) 업체 광고 방법에 대한 목록
(D) 개조 회사 추천

어휘 submit 제출하다 separately 별도로 estimate 견적(서) profit 수익 reference 추천(서) recommendation 권고, 추천

185
According to the business plan, what information was submitted separately?
(A) A detailed estimate of expected profits
(B) Contact information for employment references
(C) A list of ways the business will advertise*
(D) Recommendations for renovation companies

사업 계획(지문 2)에서 '별도 제출물'에 관련된 부분을 찾아보자. 마지막 문단에서 개업 전후의 마케팅 계획은 첨부된 스프레드시트(엑셀 파일 등)를 참고해 달라(Please see the attached spread sheet for our detailed marketing plans prior to opening and after.)고 한다. 따라서 (C)가 정답이다.

정답 (C)

Questions 186-190 refer to the following webpage, e-mail, and form.

http://www.partysuppliers.com

| PRODUCT GALLERY | HOME | PARTY TIPS | ORDER FORM | CONTACT US |

Party Suppliers Online

Welcome to our online shopping site. Have a look at our product gallery for over 1000 different party products. [186] Be sure to check out our party decorating tips in order to make your party a hit!

Latest Promotional Deals:
February through March: Buy One, Get One Half Off (applies to all in stock items)
[187] April through August: Free Delivery For Orders Over $30

From: Mathew Sparks [msparks@stantonautomotive.com]
To: June Baxtor [juneb@stantonautomotive.com]
Date: April 27
Subject: Grand Opening Update

Hi June,

I've compared Party Suppliers Online with Cape Bernard Party Mart and chosen the former to get everything we need for the grand opening party on the 4th. They seem to provide a lot of great tips for setting up their products, so it shouldn't be much work to make the showroom look great.

I think we should order a custom banner for the showroom along with streamers and balloons. [189] We can also get a larger banner made, which will hang in front of the door outside.

If you agree with me, I'd like to get our order in quickly. The workspace is still pretty messy, but [188] the painters should finish up soon, which will give us just enough time to set up before the big day.

Let me know what you think when you get a chance.
Mathew

Order Number: 112233265
Contact Info: Mathew Sparks (444) 232-0916
Delivery To: Stanton Automotive Dealership, 14 Brooks Lane, Atlantic City
Delivery Window: 01-02 May, 09:00-13:00

Quantity	Product Code	Description
1	YZ0933	Custom Banner (3 feet long)
1	YZ0955	[189] Custom Banner (6 feet long)
12	GH3345	Rainbow Balloons 12 per pack
2	BB3200	Streamers (white)
		[187] Total: $104.50

Note: [190] All our custom banners are printed at our manufacturing headquarters in Baltimore. Those items will be shipped into Atlantic City from Baltimore instead of our Port Edward store, which means you will have two separate shipments. Should you have any questions, do not hesitate to call us immediately.

186

What is indicated about Party Suppliers Online?

(A) It provides complimentary product samples.
(B) It offers decorating advice to customers.*
(C) It recently opened up another store.
(D) It will expand its product line next year.

핵심 어구 Party Suppliers Online 측의 웹페이지(지문 1) 첫째 문단에서 Be sure to check out our party decorating tips in order to make your party a hit!를 통해 (B)가 정답임을 알 수 있다.

* paraphrasing: tip → advice

정답 (B)

187

What is probably true about Stanton Automotive Dealership's order?

(A) It will be delivered for free.*
(B) It includes foreign products.
(C) It includes half-price items.
(D) It will be refunded in May.

지문 3의 주문 내역에서 총계가 $104.50임을 알 수 있다. 또한 주문 및 배송이 4월 말에서 5월 초 사이에 이루어지고 있음을 지문 2, 3을 통해서 알 수 있다. 주문을 받는 업체의 웹페이지(지문 1) 하단에서 April through August: Free Delivery For Orders Over $30라고 하므로 이 내용을 연계했을 때 (A)가 정답이 된다.

정답 (A)

188 Why does Mr. Sparks probably prefer to schedule a delivery quickly?

(A) He needs time to purchase more items.
(B) He wants to take advantage of a promotion.
(C) He needs some workers to help clean up.
(D) He wants to have enough time to set up.*

Mr. Sparks가 작성한 이메일(지문 2) 셋째 문단에서 빨리 주문하고 싶다며 페인트 칠하는 사람들이 곧 끝내면 설치할 시간이 충분할 것(the painters should finish up soon, which will give us just enough time to set up before the big day)이라고 덧붙인다. 따라서 (D)가 정답이 된다.

정답 (D)

스파크스 씨는 왜 빨리 배송 일정을 정하고 싶겠는가?
(A) 더 많은 제품을 구입할 시간이 필요해서
(B) 프로모션을 이용하고 싶어서
(C) 청소를 도와줄 직원들이 필요해서
(D) 설치할 시간을 충분히 두고 싶어 해서

어휘 prefer 선호하다, 더 좋아하다 purchase 구입하다, 사다 take advantage of ~을 이용하다 promotion 홍보, 판촉

189 What product will most likely be placed outside Stanton Automotive Dealership?

(A) Custom Banner 3ft   (B) Custom Banner 6ft*
(C) Rainbow Balloons   (D) Streamers

이메일(지문 2) 둘째 문단의 We can also get a larger banner made, which will hang in front of the door outside.에서 더 큰 현수막을 야외에 설치하리라는 것을 알 수 있다. 서식(지문 3)에서 현수막 중에 큰 것에 해당하는 Custom Banner (6 feet long)를 보고 정답 (B)를 확인할 수 있다.

정답 (B)

어떤 제품이 스탠턴 자동차 대리점 밖에 설치되겠는가?
(A) 맞춤 현수막 3피트짜리
(B) 맞춤 현수막 6피트짜리
(C) 레인보우 풍선
(D) 띠

190 According to the form, where most likely will the balloons be shipped from?

(A) Baltimore   (B) Atlantic City
(C) Cape Bernard   (D) Port Edward*

'배송 출발지'에 유념해 서식(지문 3)을 살펴보자. 마지막 주의 사항(Note)에서 현수막은 제조 본사가 있는 볼티모어에서 나머지 제품은 포트 에드워드에서 출발하므로 배송품이 두 개가 된다(Those items will be shipped into Atlantic City from Baltimore instead of our Port Edward store, which means you will have two separate shipments.)고 한다. 따라서 현수막이 아닌 풍선은 포트 에드워드에서 배송된다는 의미이므로 (D)가 가장 적절하다.

정답 (D)

서식에 따르면, 풍선은 어디에서 배송되겠는가?
(A) 볼티모어
(B) 애틀랜틱 시티
(C) 케이프 버나드
(D) 포트 에드워드

Questions 191-195 refer to the following e-mail, menu and comment card.

From: Jimmy Pertelli <jperteilli@jimmysitalianrestaurant.com>
To: Sue Hamilton <suehamilton@jimmysitalianrestaurant.com>
Date: Monday, January 10
Subject: Menu tasting event

Hello Sue,

It's hard to believe we're reopening in less than a month. ¹⁹¹ Since we've yet to finalize a menu, let's take some time to think about the best dishes for Jimmy's Italian Restaurant. I think it would be a good idea to host a private tasting event for our friends and families next week on Saturday.

I have some ideas about what we could serve at the tasting. What about making a ¹⁹² hearty deep-dish vegetarian pizza? This would really highlight our new vegetarian menu options. ¹⁹³ I think our baked lobster platter would be another great entrée choice. ¹⁹⁵ I'd also love to serve some of our new dessert options, but that all depends on whether or not construction on the pastry station is completed. In the event that it's not, how about serving some of our new organic ice cream flavors topped with your amazing chocolate sauce? I will leave it all up to you, though. As head chef, you have complete freedom.

Finally, I'd love to offer our guests an ice-cream making demonstration after the tasting. Let me know if you think that would be possible.

Thanks,
Jimmy

Jimmy's Italian Restaurant Tasting Menu
Saturday, January 15

Caprese Salad with mozzarella cheese and fresh basil
Coconut Shrimp
Baked Garlic Bread
Vegetarian Pasta with tomato sauce
¹⁹³ Baked Lobster Platter smothered in melted butter
Ribeye Fire-Grilled Steak served with roasted potatoes
¹⁹⁵ Jimmy's Famous Puff Pastries

Tasting Comment Card

Name: Fran Humphrey

Please comment on your tasting experience at Jimmy's Italian Restaurant.

I enjoyed the appetizers very much. The salad, however, had too much balsamic dressing for my taste. The vegetarian pasta dish was quite good, but I found the noodles to be a bit overcooked. [194] The baked lobster, on the other hand, was the best I've ever tasted. I found the steak to be a bit rare, but the potatoes were seasoned very nicely. The dessert was perhaps too sweet for me, but I thought the pastry was cooked to perfection. I also enjoyed the ice cream making demonstration, though I wish we could've tasted some of the flavors.

---

191 What is the purpose of the menu tasting?

(A) To select dishes for a new menu*
(B) To prepare for a restaurant inspection
(C) To audition new cooking staff
(D) To decide who will be head chef

---

192 In the e-mail, the word "hearty" in paragraph 2, line 1, is closest in meaning to

(A) sincere   (B) aromatic
(C) satisfying*   (D) original

시식 메뉴에 대해 사실인 것은?
(A) 옛날 메뉴들만 소개한다.
(B) 새로운 아이스크림 맛을 몇 개 넣었다.
(C) 고객들이 주말에만 이용할 수 있다.
(D) 퍼텔리 씨가 제안한 주요리가 들어가 있다

어휘 showcases 전시하다, 소개하다 several 몇몇 available 이용할 수 있는, 입수할 수 있는

193

What is true about the tasting menu?
(A) It showcases only old menu items.
(B) It lists several new ice cream flavors.
(C) It is only available to customers on weekends.
(D) It includes an entrée suggested by Mr. Pertelli.*

확정된 메뉴(지문 2)와 시식 메뉴를 제안한 이메일(지문 1)을 연계해서 파악해야 해결할 수 있는 문제이다. 지문 1 둘째 문단의 I think our baked lobster platter would be another great entrée choice.와 지문 2의 Baked Lobster Platter를 통해 정답 (D)를 확인할 수 있다.

정답 (D)

험프리 씨가 제일 좋아한 메뉴는 무엇이겠는가?
(A) 샐러드
(B) 파스타
(C) 바닷가재
(D) 스테이크

194

Which menu item was most likely Ms. Humphrey's favorite?
(A) The salad
(B) The pasta
(C) The lobster*
(D) The steak

Ms. Humphrey가 작성한 카드(지문 3) 중반부에서 The baked lobster, on the other hand, was the best I've ever tasted.라며 (C)가 이제까지 먹어 본 중 최고였다고 한다.

정답 (C)

패스트리 구역에 대해 드러나는 사항은?
(A) 부엌에 비해 너무 컸다.
(B) 다른 곳으로 옮겨졌다.
(C) 개조 중에 망가졌다.
(D) 시간 안에 완공되었다.

어휘 location 위치, 소재지 damage 손상을 입히다 renovation 개조

195

What is suggested about the pastry station?
(A) It was too large for the kitchen.
(B) It was moved to another location.
(C) It was damaged in a renovation.
(D) It was completed on time.*

핵심 어구 the pastry station에 유념해 살펴보면, 이메일(지문 1) 둘째 문단의 I'd also love to serve some of our new dessert options, but that all depends on whether or not construction on the pastry station is completed.를 통해서 공사가 끝나야 새로운 후식(패스트리)이 가능하다고 하는데, 메뉴(지문 2)에 적힌 후식이 Jimmy's Famous Puff Pastries이므로 제때 공사가 끝났다는 것을 유추할 수 있다. 따라서 (D)가 정답이 된다.

정답 (D)

Questions 196-200 refer to the following advertisement, e-mail, and text message.

Hartford Opera House
45 Bellview Street
New York City
www.hartfordoperhouse.com

The Hartford Opera House is pleased to announce an exciting schedule of events that will take place this summer. ¹⁹⁶ We will be featuring everything from concerts to stage plays, so we are sure to have something for you. Tickets will be available on our website for each event, and seasonal passes may be purchased for a lump sum. ²⁰⁰ Seasonal pass holders will be able to attend as many events as they wish and bring up to three guests at a time free of charge.

Schedule of Events:

June 23 - The Miller Brothers Classical Ensemble
July 3 - Stand-Up Comedy by Alan Brewer
¹⁹⁸ July 4 - Into the Jungle, an award-winning musical featuring songs by Catrina Belford
July 10 - Women of Egypt, a stage play directed by Tommy Wilson

For a complete summer schedule, please visit www.hartfordoperahouse.com.

To: Lila Sampson
From: Roderick Kelly
Cc: June Varek
Subject: Your Trip to Meadworth Paper and Packaging
Date: June 2

Dear Ms. Sampson,

We at Meadworth Paper and Packaging are looking forward to your visit to our company headquarters from July 2 to ¹⁹⁸ July 4. ¹⁹⁷ We are very pleased that your company has agreed to discuss the terms of a possible merger between our two businesses.

In addition to providing you with a tour of our factory and offices, we have an exciting schedule planned for you, which will include a lunch with our CEO, a trip to Westflower Golf Club, and an excursion at the Harbor Yacht Club. ¹⁹⁸ We have also scheduled an evening at our local opera house for some live entertainment on your last night. We hope you will enjoy your trip, and if you need anything else, please let me know.

Sincerely

Roderick Kelly
Meadworth Paper and Packaging

발신: 바렉

수신: 켈리

일기 예보를 보니 다음 주 샘슨 씨와 골프 클럽에 가는 날 비가 온다고 하네요. 199 오페라 하우스 행사와 골프 클럽을 바꾸는 편이 나을 것 같아요. 이러면 우리가 가는 오페라 하우스 행사가 바뀔 테지만, 표를 새로 살 필요는 없어요. 200 제가 손님 몇 명을 무료로 모실 수 있거든요.

From: Varek

To: Kelly

The weather forecast predicts rain during our trip to the golf club with Ms. Sampson next week. 199 I think it would be best if you switched the golf club visit with the opera house event. This will change the opera house event we'll attend, but there's no need to buy new tickets. 200 I'm allowed to bring a few guests free of charge.

어휘 forecast 예측, 예보 switch 바꾸다 attend 참석하다

핫포드 오페라 하우스에 대해 드러나는 사항은?
(A) 다른 회사와 합병할 것이다.
(B) 무료 정기권을 나눠 준다.
(C) 골프 클럽 옆에 있다.
(D) 다양한 행사 일정이 있다.

어휘 merge with ~와 합병되다 a variety of 온갖

196

What is suggested about the Hartford Opera House?
(A) It is merging with another company.
(B) It gives away free seasonal passes.
(C) It is located next to a golf club.
(D) It schedules a variety of events.*

핵심 어구 the Hartford Opera House 측의 광고(지문 1) 첫째 문단의 We will be featuring everything from concerts to stage plays, so we are sure to have something for you.를 통해 (D)가 정답임을 알 수 있다.

정답 (D)

샘슨 씨는 방문 중에 무엇을 할 예정인가?
(A) 새로운 계약을 논의할 것이다.
(B) 계약서를 검토할 것이다.
(C) 변호사와 상담할 것이다.
(D) 제품을 발표할 것이다.

어휘 deal 거래, (사업상의) 합의 lawyer 변호사

197

What is Ms. Sampson scheduled to do during her visit?
(A) Discuss a new deal*   (B) Review a contract
(C) Consult a lawyer   (D) Present a product

'방문 목적'에 유념해 Ms. Sampson이 수신자인 이메일(지문 2)를 살펴보면, 첫째 문단에서 합병 조항을 논의하기로 해줘서 고맙다(We are very pleased that your company has agreed to discuss the terms of a possible merger between our two businesses.)고 하므로 (A)가 가장 적절하다.

정답 (A)

198 What opera house event was Ms. Sampson originally scheduled to attend?

(A) A classical music performance
(B) A live comedy performance
(C) A popular musical*
(D) A stage play about Egypt

Ms. Sampson이 받는 이메일(지문 2)와 Opera House의 광고(지문 1)를 연계해서 파악해야 한다. 지문 2 둘째 문단의 We have also scheduled an evening at our local opera house for some live entertainment on your last night.와 첫째 문단의 July 4에서 날짜를 확인하고 지문 1의 일정을 살펴보면, July 4 - Into the Jungle, an award-winning musical featuring songs by Catrina Belford이므로 (C)가 정답이 된다.

정답 (C)

샘슨 씨는 오페라 하우스의 어떤 행사에 원래 참석할 예정이었는가?
(A) 클래식 음악 공연
(B) 라이브 코미디 공연
(C) 인기 뮤지컬
(D) 이집트에 대한 연극

어휘 performance 공연, 연주

199 What does Mr. Kelly need to reschedule?

(A) A boat trip
(B) A game of golf*
(C) A lunch meeting
(D) A factory tour

Mr. Kelly가 수신자인 메시지(지문 3)를 '일정 변경'에 유념해 살펴보면, 골프 클럽 일정과 오페라 하우스 행사 일정을 바꿔야 한다(I think it would be best if you switched the golf club visit with the opera house event.)는 데서 정답 (B)를 확인할 수 있다.

정답 (B)

켈리 씨는 어떤 일정을 바꿔야 하는가?
(A) 보트 여행
(B) 골프 경기
(C) 오찬 회의
(D) 공장 방문

200 Why most likely does Ms. Varek not need to purchase tickets?

(A) The event they will attend is free for everyone.
(B) Ms. Sampson has not approved the schedule yet.
(C) Ms. Varek already has a seasonal pass for the opera house.*
(D) Mr. Kelly must wait for some tickets to be refunded.

Ms. Varek이 작성한 메시지(지문 3)에서 티켓 구입과 관련된 부분을 찾아보면, 후반부에서 손님 몇 명을 무료로 데려갈 수 있다(I'm allowed to bring a few guests free of charge.)고 한다. 이를 유념해 '티켓'을 판매하는 측의 광고(지문 1)를 살펴보면, 첫째 문단의 Seasonal pass holders will be able to attend as many events as they wish and bring up to three guests at a time free of charge.를 통해 (C)를 유추할 수 있다.

정답 (C)

바렉 씨는 왜 티켓을 살 필요가 없겠는가?
(A) 참석할 행사가 모두에게 무료라서
(B) 샘슨 씨가 일정을 아직 승인하지 않아서
(C) 바렉 씨가 이미 오페라 하우스의 정기권을 가지고 있어서
(D) 켈리 씨가 티켓을 환불 받기 위해 기다려야 해서

어휘 approve 승인하다, 허가하다 refund 환불하다

ACTUAL TEST 6

a b c
100 200 300

d e **f**
400 500 **600**

PART 5

휴가 시즌을 맞이해 동쪽 창고 선반들을 가득 채워야 합니다.

어휘 shelf 선반 warehouse 창고 stock (재고를) 채우다. 갖추다

101
The shelves in the east warehouse must be _____ stocked for the holiday season.

(A) full
(B) fully*
(C) fuller
(D) fullest

수동태 동사구인 be p.p. 사이에 빈칸이 있으므로 빈칸은 술어를 수식하는 부사 (B)가 들어갈 수 있다. full 완전한, 가득한 fully 완전히, 가득히

정답 (B)

수영장 입장은 디럭스 객실에 묵는 손님들에게만 허용됩니다.

어휘 reserve 예약하다, (자리 등을) 따로 잡아두다 stay 머물다, 체류하다 deluxe 고급의 suit 객실

102
_____ to the swimming pool is reserved for guests staying in one of our deluxe suites.

(A) Access*
(B) Accessed
(C) Accessing
(D) Accessible

빈칸은 문장의 주어로 to 이하의 후치 수식을 받는 자리이다. 따라서 명사 (A)가 들어갈 수 있다. access는 명사로 쓰일 때는 〈access to + 장소 명사〉의 형태가 되지만, 동사로 쓰일 때는 〈access + 장소 명사〉로 to 없이 사용된다. access 접근, 입장, 접근하다, 입장하다 accessible 접근 가능한, 입장 가능한

* 전치사 to와 자주 쓰이는 명사들
solution/exposure/response/trip/answer/visit/approach/access + to + 명사

정답 (A)

타카시 씨는 관리 임무를 더 많이 맡아야 한다고 인정합니다.

어휘 admit 인정하다, 시인하다 expect 기대하다, 예상하다 managerial 경영의, 관리의 duty 임무

103
Mr. Takashi admits that _____ is expected to take on more managerial duties.

(A) he*
(B) his
(C) him
(D) himself

적절한 인칭대명사의 격을 찾는 문제로, that절의 주어가 필요하다. 따라서 주격 (A)가 정답이다.

정답 (A)

이달 말에, 데이비스빌 주식회사는 인터넷 공급 업체를 변경할 예정입니다.

어휘 incorporated 주식회사 provider 제공 업체

104
At the end of the month, Davisville Incorporated is _____ its Internet provider.

(A) changing*
(B) attending
(C) holding
(D) turning

'인터넷 공급 업체를 ~하다'라는 문맥상 적절한 타동사를 찾아야 하므로 (A)가 가장 적절하다. 현재진행형으로 미래에 예정된 일을 나타낼 수 있다는 것을 알아 두자. change 변경하다, 바꾸다 attend 참석하다, 출석하다 hold 열다 turn 돌리다

정답 (A)

105

Better City Travel offers bicycle tours _____ Skiff Lake at very reasonable rates.

(A) between (B) along*
(C) below   (D) apart

적절한 전치사를 찾는 문제이다. '(특정 경로를) 따라' 가는 여행을 설명하는 데는 (B)가 알맞다. between ~사이에 along ~을 따라 below 아래에 apart 떨어져

정답 (B)

베터 시티 트래블은 스키프 호숫가를 따라 가는 자전거 여행을 매우 저렴한 가격대로 제공합니다.

어휘 offer 제공하다, 제안하다 reasonable 합리적인, (가격이) 알맞은 rate 요금

106

Of all snow tires, Marten's new MR-200 is, without a doubt, the most durable _____.

(A) that   (B) any
(C) one*   (D) either

〈정관사(the) + 최상급(most) + 형용사(durable) + _____〉의 빈칸에 들어갈 수 있는 것은 명사인데, 앞 부분에서 언급된 것을 받는 대명사 one은 형용사의 수식을 받을 수 있다. 따라서 (C)가 정답이 된다.

정답 (C)

모든 스노우 타이어 중에서, 마르텐의 신형 MR-200이 의심할 여지 없이 가장 내구성이 강합니다.

어휘 without a doubt 의심할 여지 없이, 분명히 durable 내구성이 있는, 오래가는

107

As the amount of orders increased significantly, Lawford's Coffee Shop was able to _____ new deals with its suppliers.

(A) negotiating (B) negotiates
(C) negotiated   (D) negotiate*

조동사 can과 같은 의미의 be able to 다음에는 동사원형 (D)가 들어갈 수 있다. negotiate 협상하다

* 빈출 to부정사 숙어

be ready to ~할 준비가 되다 be likely to ~되기 쉽다 be willing to 기꺼이 ~하다 be about to 막 ~하려고 하다 be supposed to ~하기로 되어 있다 be liable to ~할 의무가 있다 be eager to 간절히 ~하고 싶어 하다 be sure to 확실히 ~할 것이다

정답 (D)

주문량이 부쩍 늘어서, 로포드 커피 숍은 공급 업체들과 새로운 거래를 협상할 수 있었습니다.

어휘 amount 총액, 총계 order 주문(품) increase 늘다, 증가하다 significantly 상당히 deal 거래 supplier 공급 업체

108

Pandora Hair Design offers employees _____ opportunities to advance their careers.

(A) plenty (B) each
(C) very   (D) many*

빈칸 뒤에 가산명사 복수형이 있으므로 (D)가 들어가야 '많은 기회를 준다'라는 문맥을 적절히 완성한다. 참고로, (A)도 가산명사 및 불가산명사에 쓸 수 있지만 전치사 of가 필요하다. 단, 구어체에서는 문법을 무시한 채 plenty time처럼 쓰기도 한다. plenty 풍부한, 충분한

정답 (D)

판도라 헤어 디자인은 직원들에게 경력을 향상시킬 수 있는 많은 기회를 제공합니다.

어휘 opportunity 기회 advance 전진시키다, 향상시키다, 개선하다

그린빌과 트렌턴 사이의 56번 고속도로는 쓰러진 전신주 때문에 막혀 있습니다.

어휘 block off 막다, 차단하다
power pole 전신주

109

Highway 56 between Greenville and Trenton has been blocked off _____ fallen power poles.

(A) so that (B) as a result
(C) in order to (D) because of*

문맥상 빈칸 이하는 고속도로 폐쇄의 '원인'이므로 (D)가 정답이 된다. 참고로, (A)는 〈주어 + 동사〉의 절이, (C)는 동사원형이 이어져야 한다. 또, (B)는 원인을 나타낼 때 as a result of가 되어야 한다. so that ~하도록 as a result 결과적으로 in order to ~하기 위해서

* 이유를 나타내는 전치사구
due to / thanks to / owing to / as a result of / because of

정답 (D)

현재 세입자의 소개 없이는 도체스터 빌딩 내 아파트를 임대하기란 불가능합니다.

어휘 rent 임대하다 tenant 세입자

110

It is impossible to rent an apartment in the Dorchester Building without a _____ from a current tenant.

(A) referring (B) referred
(C) referral* (D) refer

〈전치사(without) + 부정관사(a) + _____〉의 빈칸에 들어갈 수 있는 것은 명사 (C)뿐이다. refer 참조, 조회하다, 위탁하다 referral 소개, 위탁

* -al로 끝나는 명사 (형용사로 혼동 주의)
arrival 도착 proposal 제안 denial 부인, 거부 refusal 거절 survival 생존

정답 (C)

초록색 스티커는 차량 점검이 완전히 끝난 후에만 차량 앞 유리에 붙일 수 있습니다.

어휘 windshield 바람막이 창 inspection 점검, 검사 vehicle 차량, 탈 것 complete 완벽한

111

A green sticker will be placed on the windshield _____ after the inspection of the vehicle is complete.

(A) when (B) only*
(C) still (D) most

빈칸 이하는 문맥상 스티커를 붙일 수 있는 '유일한 경우'에 해당된다. 따라서 (B)가 가장 적절하다.

정답 (B)

매니저 두 명이 조기 은퇴를 선택했으므로 7월 30일까지 후임자들을 찾아야 합니다.

어휘 opt 택하다 retirement 은퇴
replacement 교체, 후임자

112

Since two managers have opted for early retirement, it is _____ to find replacements by July 30.

(A) necessitating (B) necessary*
(C) necessarily (D) necessities

〈가주어(it) + be동사(is) + _____ + 진주어(to ~)〉 구조의 2형식 구문이므로 빈칸에는 주격 보어로 형용사 (B)나 명사 (D)가 가능하지만 문맥상 (B)가 자연스럽다. It is important to ~, It is impossible to ~도 자주 사용되는 가주어 구문이다. necessitate 필요로 하게 만들다 necessary 필요한, 필수적인 necessarily 필연적으로 necessity 필요(성)

정답 (B)

113

The cargo elevator in the south end of the building will not be in operation _____ further notice.

(A) until*
(B) onto
(C) since
(D) all

건물 남단의 화물 엘리베이터는 추후 공지가 있을 때까지 운영되지 않을 예정입니다.

어휘 cargo 화물 in operation 가동 중인 notice 공지

'다음 통지가 있을 때까지'라는 의미의 관용 어구 until further notice를 알면 쉽게 해결할 수 있는 문제이다. onto ~로, 쪽으로

정답 (A)

114

The weight indicated on the outside of this package is _____ accurate.

(A) fairness
(B) fairest
(C) fairly*
(D) fair

이 포장 밖에 적힌 무게는 꽤 정확합니다.

어휘 weight 무게 indicate 가리키다, 나타내다 accurate 정확한, 정밀한

빈칸은 문장의 주격 보어인 형용사 accurate를 수식하는 자리이므로 부사 (C)가 들어갈 수 있다. fairness 공정성 fairly 상당히, 꽤 fair 공정한

정답 (C)

115

David sent a link to a website that has a _____ of information on engine repair.

(A) wealth*
(B) height
(C) labor
(D) fame

데이비드가 엔진 수리에 관해 풍부한 정보가 실린 웹사이트 링크를 보내 줬습니다.

어휘 repair 수리, 수선

문맥상 '풍부한 양의 정보'라는 의미를 완성해야 타당하다. 따라서 빈칸에 적절한 명사는 (A)이다. (a wealth of = a lot of) wealth 풍부한 양, 다량 height 높이 labor 노동 fame 명성

정답 (A)

116

To find the easiest route to Simmons, Darthmouth, and nearby towns, be sure to look at an _____ map.

(A) update
(B) updated*
(C) updates
(D) updating

시몬스, 다스마우스, 그리고 인근 도시들로 가는 가장 편한 노선을 찾으려면, 갱신된 지도를 꼭 확인하십시오.

어휘 route 노선 nearby 인근의

〈부정관사(an) + _____ + 명사(map)〉의 빈칸에는 형용사 역할을 하는 (B)나 (D)가 들어갈 수 있는데 지도는 '갱신되는' 것이므로 수동을 나타내는 과거분사 (B)가 정답이 된다. update (최근 정보로) 갱신, 갱신하다

정답 (B)

지원서 마감일이 지났으므로 고용 위원회가 이력서 검토를 시작할 것입니다.

어휘 committee 위원회 résumé 이력서 application 지원(서) deadline 마감 pass 지나다

117

The hiring committee will start reviewing résumés _____ the application deadline has passed.

(A) how (B) nor
(C) now that* (D) whether

이력서 검토를 시작한 '계기, 이유'가 이어지므로 빈칸에는 이유를 나타내는 접속사 (C)가 가장 적절하다. now that ~이므로, ~이기 때문에 whether ~인지 아닌지

정답 (C)

텔레비전 쇼에서, 유명 미술 비평가인 글로리아 반 신겔은 다양한 시기의 회화 작품들을 분석합니다.

어휘 critic 비평가 a variety of 온갖 period 기간

118

On her television show, Gloria Van Cingel, the well-known art critic, _____ paintings from a variety of periods.

(A) analysis (B) analyzer
(C) analyzes* (D) analyzing

〈주어(Gloria Van Cingel) + 주어 동격(the well-known art critic) + _____ + 목적어(paintings)〉 구문에 필요한 것은 동사 (C)이다. analysis 분석 analyzer 분석자 analyze 분석하다

정답 (C)

레드포드 슈퍼마켓에 몇몇 셀프 계산대가 설치되면 직원 수에 변화를 만들 것으로 보입니다.

어휘 installation 설치 several 몇몇의 self-checkout kiosk 셀프 계산대

119

The installation of several self-checkout kiosks in the Redford Supermarket is expected to create changes _____ the number of employees.

(A) in* (B) again
(C) positions (D) ultimately

'~의 변화'를 나타내는 어구는 changes in 또는 changes to이다. 따라서 정답은 (A)이다. position 직(책) ultimately 궁극적으로, 결국

*명사 change의 다양한 용례
a change of address 주소 변경
make/create changes 변화를 만들다
Don't forget your change. 거스름돈 잊지 마세요. (이때 change는 불가산명사)

정답 (A)

다른 모든 사람과 비교해서, 도널드는 놀라울 정도로 짧은 기간 내에 부동산 면허 시험을 준비했습니다.

어휘 compared to ~와 비교하여 prepare 준비하다 real estate 부동산 exam 시험

120

Compared to everyone else, Donald prepared himself for the real estate license exam in a _____ short period of time.

(A) surprised (B) surprise
(C) surprisingly* (D) surprising

〈부정관사(a) + _____ + 형용사(short) + 명사(period)〉의 구조이다. 빈칸에 들어갈 단어가 형용사(short)를 수식하는지 명사(period)를 수식하는지를 판단하기 위해 의미를 따져 보아야 한다. '놀라울 정도로 짧은'이란 의미로 형용사(short)를 수식하므로 빈칸에는 부사 (C)가 들어가야 한다. surprised 놀란, 놀라는 surprise 놀라움, 놀라게 하다 surprisingly 놀랄 만큼 surprising 놀라운, 놀랄

정답 (C)

121

The production supervisor of Gleason Shoes is _____ of all the factory's operations.

(A) aware*
(B) current
(C) serious
(D) alert

글리슨 슈즈의 생산 관리자는 공장의 모든 운영 체제를 알고 있습니다.

어휘 production 생산, 제작 supervisor 관리자, 상사

'~을 알다'라는 의미의 관용 어구 be aware of를 알면 쉽게 해결할 수 있는 문제이다. aware ~을 알고 있는 serious 심각한, 진지한 alert 기민한, 알리다, 경보를 발하다

정답 (A)

122

The tourism _____ of Cape Breton Island has dramatically improved ever since the harbor was reopened last year.

(A) economical
(B) economic
(C) economize
(D) economy*

케이프 브레턴 아일랜드의 관광 경기는 작년에 항구를 다시 연 이후로 부쩍 개선되었습니다.

어휘 dramatically 극적으로 improve 개선되다, 나아지다 harbor 항구, 항만

〈정관사(the) + _____ + 전치사(of)〉의 빈칸에 들어갈 수 있는 것은 tourism과 복합명사를 이룰 명사 (D)뿐이다. economical 경제적인 economic 경제의, 경제성 있는 economize 아끼다, 절약하다 economy 경기, 경제

* 빈출 복합명사:
account number 계좌 번호 enrollment form 입학 신청서 construction delay 공사 지연 return policy 반환 정책 expiration date 만기일 product information 상품 정보 information distribution 정보 배포 retail sales 소매 판매 client satisfaction 고객 만족 recommendation letter 추천서

정답 (D)

123

Someone from Renforth Building Supplies asked us to _____ the type of lumber needed for the project.

(A) personify
(B) magnify
(C) specify*
(D) testify

렌포스 건설 용품점에서 나온 사람이 우리에게 그 프로젝트에 필요한 판재 유형을 명시해 달라고 요청했습니다.

어휘 supplies 용품, 비품 lumber 재목, 판재

빈칸은 the type of lumber ~를 목적어로 취하는 동사가 들어갈 자리이다. 특정한 타입/종류를 '명시하다'가 가장 적절하므로 (C)가 정답이 된다. personify 의인화하다, 전형적으로 보여 주다 magnify 확대하다 specify 명시하다 testify 증언하다, 진술하다

정답 (C)

124

Fitzgerald Air offers flights to over 200 destinations _____ northern Canada.

(A) toward
(B) throughout*
(C) regarding
(D) aboard

피츠제럴드 에어는 캐나다 북부 곳곳의 200군데가 넘는 목적지로 비행편을 제공합니다.

어휘 flight 비행(편) destination 목적지

비행편 200여 대가 어느 한 방향으로(toward) 가기보다 지역 곳곳(throughout) 두루 다니는 것이 맥락상 타당하므로 (B)가 정답이다. toward ~쪽으로 throughout 도처에 regarding ~에 관하여 aboard (비행기 따위의) 안에, 탑승한

정답 (B)

레스터빌 아카데미의 초보자 기타 강습은 금세 마감되니 온라인 등록 서식을 작성하실 것을 권합니다.

어휘 fill up 가득 차다 recommend 권하다 fill out 기입하다, 작성하다 form 서식

125

The beginners' guitar class at the Lesterville Academy fills up quickly, so we recommend filling out an online _____ form.

(A) enrollment* (B) inventory
(C) complaint (D) solicitation

'강습 신청'에 적절한 서식 종류는 (A)이다. enrollment 등록 inventory 재고 complaint 불평, 불만 solicitation 간청

정답 (A)

금요일에, 랭커스터 주식회사의 새로 임명된 부사장님이 직원들에게 처음으로 연설할 예정입니다.

어휘 address 말을 걸다, 연설하다

126

On Friday, Lancaster Incorporated's newly _____ vice-president will address his staff for the first time.

(A) appoint (B) appoints
(C) appointed* (D) appointing

〈부사(newly) + _____ + 명사(vice-president)〉의 빈칸에는 명사를 수식할 형용사가 들어갈 수 있는데, 분사도 형용사 역할을 할 수 있다. (C)와 (D) 중에서 답을 찾아보면, 문맥상 '임명된 부사장'이 적절하므로 수동태를 나타내는 과거분사 (C)가 정답이 된다. appoint 임명하다

정답 (C)

홍보 부장은 언론사들과 계속 연락을 해야 하므로 랜돌프 인더스트리즈는 커뮤니케이션 능력이 우수한 사람을 찾고 있습니다.

어휘 head 수석, 장 public relations 홍보, 선전 continually 계속 be in contact with ~와 접촉하고 있다, 연락하고 있다 exceptional 이례적일 정도로 우수한

127

The head of public relations must be continually in contact with the media so Randolph Industries _____ someone with exceptional communication skills.

(A) seeking (B) is seeking*
(C) are sought (D) have been sought

접속사 so로 연결된 절에서 주어인 Randolph Industries를 서술할 동사가 빈칸에 필요하다. 기업이 직원을 구하는(seek) 것은 능동태로 나타내야 타당하므로 (B)가 정답이다. 회사 이름은 -s로 끝나도 단수 취급(1개의 회사이므로)한다는 점에 유의하자. seek 찾다, 구하다

정답 (B)

라포트 씨가 모금 행사를 준비하는 방식은 할로웨이 씨와 무척 다릅니다.

어휘 approach 접근법, 처리 방법 organize (회합 등을) 준비하다 fundraising 모금 event 행사

128

Ms. Laporte's approach to organizing a fundraising event is _____ different from Ms. Halloway's.

(A) haltingly (B) intimately
(C) permissibly (D) markedly*

문맥상 '방식의 차이'가 '두드러진다'는 것을 나타내야 하므로 제시된 부사들 중 (D)가 가장 적절하다. haltingly 머뭇거리며 intimately 친밀히 permissibly 무방하여 markedly 현저하게

* markedly의 용례
differ markedly (= considerably, greatly, radically) 크게 차이 나다
markedly (= noticeably) improved 크게 개선된
markedly + 비교급: 현저하게 더 ~한

정답 (D)

129

Recently, Kingston has experienced a huge increase in the number of residents, _____ are international students.

(A) inasmuch as
(B) the reason being
(C) because of them
(D) most of whom*

최근 킹스턴의 주민 수가 급증했는데 대부분이 외국 학생들입니다.

어휘 huge 막대한, 거대한 increase 증가, 인상 resident 주민

빈칸은 콤마 이하 절의 주어가 들어갈 자리이다. 따라서 and most of the residents를 의미하는 (D)가 정답이다. 선행사인 residents가 사람이므로 who를 써야 하지만 of의 목적어가 되므로 목적격인 whom을 쓴다. inasmuch as ~이므로, ~인 점을 고려하면

정답 (D)

130

To help the staff of the Carrington Inn make your stay more _____, please fill out a guest feedback form and leave it at the front desk.

(A) knowledgeable
(B) considerable
(C) enjoyable*
(D) available

캐링턴 인의 직원들이 여러분의 숙박을 좀 더 즐겁게 해 드릴 수 있도록 고객 피드백 서식을 작성하신 후 프런트 데스크에 남겨 주시기 바랍니다.

어휘 stay 머무름, 방문 leave 남기다

문맥상 호텔 직원들이 고객들의 체류/숙박을 '더욱 즐거운 경험으로 만들 수 있는' 상황에 대한 설명이어야 타당하므로 (C)가 가장 적절하다. 이때 stay가 명사로 쓰였다는 점에 유의해야 한다. knowledgeable 아는 것이 많은 considerable 상당한, 많은 enjoyable 즐거운 available 이용 가능한

* make의 용례
make + A + 동사원형: A가 ~하게 시키다/만들다
make + A + 형용사/과거분사: A가 ~되게 하다
make + A + B: A를 B로 만들다

정답 (C)

PART 6

수신: sandrabae@gladstoneresearch.com.au
발신: markjohnson@sydneyunienergy.au
날짜: 5월 15일
제목: 고맙습니다!

배 박사님 귀하,

지난주 금요일 저희 주 연구 센터에 방문해 주셔서 대단히 감사합니다. 귀하의 전문적인 조언도, 언제나처럼, 감사했습니다. 기술 팀 전원이 산업 시설들을 위한 에너지 생산 및 소비 시스템의 흥미롭고 새로운 발전상에 대한 귀하의 발표에 많은 도움을 받았습니다. 이번 가을, 저희 부서는 기술 연구원을 다섯 명 더 고용할 계획입니다. 지난주에 말씀하신 주제에 대해서 교육 세션을 진행해 주시겠습니까? ---134---. 세부 사항을 논의할 수 있게 바로 답변 주시기를 고대합니다.

그럼 이만,

마크 존슨

어휘 expert 전문적인 entire 전체의 benefit 득을 보다 greatly 크게, 대단히 advance 발전, 진전 generation 발생 consumption 소비, 소모 facility 시설 department 부서 hire 고용하다 mind 꺼리다 lead 이끌다 training 교육, 훈련 look forward to ~을 고대하다 prompt 즉각적인 response 반응, 대답 so that ~하도록

Questions 131-134 refer to the following e-mail.

To: sandrabae@gladstoneresearch.com.au
From: markjohnson@sydneyunienergy.au
Date: 15 May
Subject: Thank you!

Dear Dr. Bae,

Thank you very much for ---**131**--- our main research center last Friday. Your expert advice, as always, ---**132**---. Our entire engineering team benefited greatly from your presentation on the exciting new advances in energy generation and consumption systems for industrial facilities. This fall, our department plans to hire five more engineering researchers. Would ---**133**--- mind leading a training session on the topic you spoke of last week? ---**134**---. We will look forward to your prompt response so that details can be discussed.

Sincerely,

Mark Johnson

131
(A) calling
(B) opening
(C) visiting*
(D) staffing

본 지문은 '초대 강사에게 감사를 전하는 이메일이다. 이는 뒤에 나오는 Our entire engineering team benefited greatly from your presentation과 the topic you spoke of last week에서 드러난다. 따라서 (C)가 정답이다. staff 직원으로 일하다, 직원을 제공하다

정답 (C)

132
(A) appreciates
(B) will be appreciated
(C) is appreciating
(D) was appreciated*

'지난주 금요일 (바로 앞 문장에서 last Friday라고 언급) 방문'에 대한 감사 인사이므로 과거시제 (D)가 정답이 된다. appreciate ~에 대해 감사하다

정답 (D)

133

(A) his (B) yours
(C) you* (D) he

빈칸은 Would로 시작하는 의문문의 주어가 들어갈 자리이므로 문법상 (C)나 (D)가 가능한데, '~해 주시겠습니까'라는 의미로 '상대'에게 부탁하는 맥락이니 (C)가 가장 적절하다. Would you mind ~?라는 표현으로 암기해 두자.

정답 (C)

134

(A) All engineers must adhere to our center's strict regulations.
(B) A large number of candidates have impressive résumés.
(C) If you can, it would undoubtedly prove beneficial to the new staff.*
(D) With your feedback, we will be able to build it quickly.

(A) 모든 기술자는 우리 센터의 엄밀한 규정을 지켜야 합니다.
(B) 많은 지원자의 이력서가 인상적입니다.
(C) 가능하시다면, 신입사원들에게 분명 유익할 것입니다.
(D) 귀하의 피드백으로, 저희는 빨리 그것을 지을 수 있을 겁니다.

새로 연구원들을 뽑을 계획인데 교육 세션을 맡아 주겠냐는 부탁에 이어지는 문장으로, '그래 주면 큰 도움이 될 것'이라는 요지의 (C)가 맥락상 가장 적절하다. adhere to ~을 고수하다, 충실하다 strict 엄격한, 엄밀한 regulation 규정 candidate 지원자 impressive 인상적인 résumé 이력서 undoubtedly 의심할 여지 없이, 확실히 prove ~로 판명되다, 입증되다 beneficial 유익한, 이로운

정답 (C)

Questions 135-138 refer to the following article.

GEARY (April 5) – This morning, the National Transportation Authority announced that a $41 million grant has been awarded to Weston Valley Air Travel Network. Thanks to this ---**135**---, the dream of having two airports in Weston Valley will soon be realized. Many residents in the region welcome news of this expansion to the current air service. ---**136**---. Business owners throughout the Weston Valley are truly delighted. Jennifer Rossignol, a local business owner, expressed her delight with the grant earlier today. "This is fantastic news for someone like myself ---**137**--- has to travel to Toronto frequently on business," says Rossignol. "We have had no choice ---**138**--- years but to endure a four-hour bus ride into the city, but soon, I will be able to board a plane and be there in under an hour."

135

(A) funding*
(B) policy
(C) design
(D) strategy

바로 앞 문장에서 기금($41 million grant)이 언급되었으므로 (A)가 정답이다. 참고로 fund는 가산명사, funding은 불가산명사라는 점도 익혀 두자. funding 자금 policy 정책 strategy 전략

정답 (A)

136

(A) Weston Valley Air Travel Network confirmed that the project must be delayed.
(B) Passengers will have access to more parking spaces at one of the airports.
(C) This development is expected to create over 500 jobs at both airports.*
(D) Air fares for most regional flights, however, will most likely be raised.

'지역 주민의 긍정적인 반응' 다음에 이어질 문장으로는, '일자리 창출'을 다룬 (C)가 가장 적절하다. confirm 확실히 하다 delay 지체시키다, 지연시키다 passenger 승객 access 접근, 이용 fare 요금 flight 비행(편) raise (들어) 올리다

정답 (C)

137
(A) likewise (B) another
(C) then (D) who*

빈칸은 has to travel이라는 서술어의 주체가 되어야 하므로 주격 관계대명사 (D)만 들어갈 수 있다. likewise 똑같이, 또한

정답 (D)

138
(A) for* (B) with
(C) about (D) on

적절한 전치사를 찾는 문제이다. 기간을 나타내는 years가 바로 뒤에 이어지니 '~동안'을 나타내는 (A)가 정답이다. for 다음에는 종종 〈숫자 + 시간 명사〉가 이어지지만, '수년, 며칠, 몇 시간 동안이나'라는 의미로 for years, for days, for hours로 사용할 때는 중간에 숫자를 넣지 않고도 사용한다. during 다음에는 특정 기간을 나타내는 명사(the vacation, the winter 등)가 나온다는 점도 참고로 알아 두자.

정답 (A)

수신: 아놀드 말로리 [amallory@channel6new.net]
발신: 멜린다 캘훈 [mcalhoun@channel6news.net]
제목: 환상적인 평가
날짜: 3월 21일

아놀드 귀하,

채널 6 뉴스 경영진은 몽크턴 가젯과 업타운 엔터테인먼트에 실린 우리 프로그램에 대한 선풍적인 평가를 읽고 정말 기뻤습니다. 우리 모두 귀하가 일을 그야말로 훌륭히 해내셨다는 데 동의합니다. 이런 이유로, 채널 6 뉴스는 진짜 기쁘게도 3월 30일에 드릴 귀하의 다음 월급에 연례 보너스를 더 드리기로 했습니다. 또한, 귀하의 현재 급여는 4월 1일 자로 12% 인상될 예정입니다. 작년 11월에 수석 뉴스 앵커 직을 맡으신 후로, 정규 시청자 수가 세 배 늘었습니다. ——142——. 귀하의 뛰어난 실적이 아니었다면 이 중 어느 것도 이루지 못했을 겁니다. 채널 6 뉴스의 모두를 대신해, 귀하의 노고와 헌신에 감사 드립니다.

멜린다

어휘 managerial 관리의, 경영진의 division 부서 positively 긍정적으로 sensational 선풍적인 agree 동의하다 reason 이유 add 추가하다 paycheck 급료 salary 임금 effective 시행되는, 발효되는 take over 인수하다 triple 3배가 되다 achieve 달성하다, 성취하다 outstanding 뛰어난 performance 실적, 성과 on behalf of ~을 대신해 dedication 전념, 헌신

Questions 139-142 refer to the following e-mail.

To: Arnold Mallory [amallory@channel6new.net]
From: Melinda Calhoun [mcalhoun@channel6news.net]
Re: Fantastic reviews
Date: March 21

Dear Arnold,

The managerial division here at Channel 6 News was positively excited to read sensational reviews of our program in both the Moncton Gazette and Uptown Entertainment. All of us agree that your work here has been nothing but ---**139**---. For this reason, Channel 6 News is truly delighted ---**140**--- you a yearly bonus that will be added to your next monthly paycheck on March 30. ---**141**---, your current salary will be raised by 12% effective April 1. Since you took over as Head News Anchor last November, our number of regular viewers has tripled. ---**142**---. We could not have achieved any of this without your outstanding performance. On behalf of everyone at Channel 6 News, thank you for your hard work and dedication.

Melinda

139

(A) withdrawn   (B) matched
(C) affordable   (D) exceptional*

앞서 '프로그램에 대한 평가가 선풍적이다'라고 했으므로 '업무 평가로서 (D)가 알맞다. withdrawn 내성적인, 내향적인 matched 잘 맞는 affordable (가격이) 알맞은 exceptional 이례적일 정도로 우수한

정답 (D)

140

(A) to award*   (B) an award
(C) it awarded   (D) that awards

award는 수여동사로서 〈award + 간접목적어 + 직접목적어〉로 쓰인다. 빈칸 뒤에 간접목적어 you와 직접목적어 a yearly bonus가 나와 있으므로 빈칸의 award는 수여동사로 쓰였음을 확인할 수 있다. 빈칸 앞에 be delighted가 있으므로 '~해서 기쁘다'란 의미의 〈be delighted to부정사〉를 완성할 수 있도록 (A)가 들어가야 한다. award 상, 수여하다

정답 (A)

488 해설집

141

(A) For example
(B) In addition*
(C) Nevertheless
(D) On the other hand

'연례 보너스' 외에 '임금 인상'도 주어진다는 흐름으로 볼 때 빈칸에 적절한 연결어(구)는 (B)이다. for example 이를테면, 예를 들어 in addition 게다가, 더욱이 nevertheless 그럼에도 불구하고 on the other hand 반면

정답 (B)

142

(A) Channel 6 has also received fabulous reviews in national newspapers.*
(B) An assistant news anchor will be hired sometime next month.
(C) Our team will meet next week to discuss changes to your show.
(D) You are one of two employees who are entitled to an annual bonus.

(A) 채널 6는 국내 신문들에서도 대단한 호평을 받았습니다.
(B) 보조 뉴스 앵커를 다음 달 중으로 고용할 것입니다.
(C) 저희 팀은 다음 주에 모여 귀하의 방송 변경 사항을 논의할 것입니다.
(D) 귀하는 연례 보너스를 받는 직원 두 명 중 한 사람입니다.

지문 맨 앞에서는 '잡지사 두 곳으로부터 우수한 평을 받았다'고 언급했으며, 빈칸 전후로는 '시청자 수가 세 배가 되었다'와 '이 모든 실적은 당신 덕이다'라는 내용이 앞뒤로 이어져 있다. 따라서 문맥상 '또 다른 실적'인 (A)가 들어가야 적절하다. fabulous 기막히게 좋은 entitle 자격/권리를 주다 annual 연례의

정답 (A)

전자 제품 무역 박람회
(8월 25일) 5년 연속으로 연례 세계 전자 제품 무역 박람회가 8월 23일 토요일 도쿄에서 개최되었다. ——143——. 작년 경우처럼, 중국은 가장 많은 관심을 받은 나라다. 더욱이 주최측은 남미 회사들 수가 이전 해들보다 상당히 많아졌다고 보고했다. 올해 행사의 두드러진 변화 중 또 하나는 대부분 회사가 일상적인 여흥용 전자 제품들보다 주방 가전들을 소개했다는 사실이다.

어휘 electronics 전자 제품 trade 무역, 거래 consecutive 연이은 represent 대표하다 organizer 조직은 significantly 상당히 previous 이전의 noticeable 뚜렷한, 현저한 the majority of 대부분의 showcase (신제품 등을) 소개하다 appliance 기기 rather than ~보다는

(A) 행사 자원봉사자들은 등록비를 낼 필요가 없었다.
(B) 제품 시연은 강당 세 군데에서 열릴 예정이다.
(C) 행사에는 전 세계 곳곳의 500여 회사가 참석했다.
(D) 채용자들은 참석한 대학생들에게서 이력서를 받았다.

Questions 143-146 refer to the following article.

Electronics Trade Show
(25 August) The annual Global Electronics Trade Show came to Tokyo on Saturday, 23 August for the fifth consecutive year. ---**143**---. As was the case last year, China was the most ---**144**--- represented nation. ---**145**---, organizers reported that the number of South American companies was significantly higher than previous years. Another noticeable change at this year's ---**146**--- was the fact that the majority of companies showcased kitchen appliances rather than the usual entertainment electronics.

143

(A) Volunteers at the event were not required to pay the registration fee.
(B) Product demonstrations will be held in three different auditoriums.
(C) The event featured over 500 companies from every corner of the world.*
(D) Recruiters collected résumés from university students in attendance.

이어지는 내용에서 다양한 참가국들이 언급되므로 빈칸에는 '참가 상황'을 전체적으로 설명해 준 (C)가 들어가야 맥락상 자연스럽다. require 필요로 하다 registration 등록 fee 수수료, 요금 recruiter 모집자 attendance 출석, 참석

정답 (C)

144

(A) heavy   (B) heavily*
(D) heavier   (D) heaviness

〈정관사(the) + 최상급(most) + _____ + 과거분사(represented) + 명사(nation)〉의 구조가 제시되어 있다. 빈칸에 들어갈 단어가 과거분사를 수식하는지 명사를 수식하는지 따져 보고 답을 찾아야 한다. heavy nation(무거운 나라?)은 의미가 통하지 않고, heavily represented(많이 대표된 → 발표자가 많이 나온)는 자연스러운 문맥을 형성하므로 (B)가 정답이다. heavy 무거운, 많은 heavily 아주 많이 heaviness 무거움, 중량

정답 (B)

490 해설집

145
(A) Moreover* (B) Rather
(C) Instead (D) Thus

참가국의 상황을 차례로 열거하는 맥락으로 보는 것이 가장 적절하다. 따라서 빈칸에 알맞은 연결어는 (A)이다. moreover 게다가, 더욱이 rather 약간, 상당히 instead 대신에 thus 따라서

정답 (A)

146
(A) class (B) demonstration
(C) event* (D) ceremony

본 지문은 제목에 언급된 무역 박람회(Trade Show)를 다룬 기사이므로 '올해 행사'라는 의미를 완성해 줄 (C)가 정답이 된다. ceremony (의)식

정답 (C)

PART 7

147 고객 여러분께,

10월부터 주간 장기 자랑의 밤을 열게 되었음을 기쁜 마음으로 발표합니다. 이 행사는 매주 수요일 저녁 6시부터 8시까지 진행되며 **147** 무대는 저희 카페 1층에 설치될 예정입니다.

참가자들께서는 노래하거나 악기를 연주하거나 시를 낭송하실 수 있습니다. 20분 간의 배정 시간을 등록하시려면 일찍 와 주시기 바랍니다. **148** 행사가 진행되는 동안 참가자 전원에게 무료 커피나 차를 드릴 것입니다.

더 많은 정보를 원하시면, 저희 웹사이트 www.cafemaria.com을 방문하시거나 777-4367로 전화 주시기 바랍니다.

Questions 147-148 refer to the following notice.

147 To our dear customers,

We are happy to announce that we will be hosting a weekly talent night starting in October. The event will be held every Wednesday from 6:00 P.M. until 8:00 P.M. and **147** the stage will be set up on the first floor of our café.

Participants may sing, play instruments, or read poetry. Make sure to arrive early to sign up for a twenty-minute slot. **148** All participants will be allowed free coffee or tea for the duration of the event.

For more information, please visit our website at www.cafemaria.com or call us at 777-4367.

어휘 announce 발표하다 host 주최하다 talent 재능, 장기 event 행사 be held 열리다 set up 설치하다 participant 참가자 instrument 기구, 악기 make sure 확실히 ~하다 arrive 도착하다 sign up for ~에 등록하다 slot 시간(대) allow 허용하다, 허락하다 free 무료의 duration 기간

본 공지는 어디에 있겠는가?
(A) 지하철 역에
(B) 음악 책에
(C) 커피 전문점에
(D) 진료소에

어휘 appear 나타나다

147

Where would the notice most likely appear?
(A) In a subway station
(B) In a music book
(C) At a coffee house*
(D) At a doctor's office

공지의 수신자를 나타내는 To our dear customers와 첫째 문단의 the stage will be set up on the first floor of our café에 언급된 장소 정보를 통해 정답 (C)를 유추할 수 있다.

정답 (C)

본 공지에 따르면, 참가자들은 무엇을 받을 것인가?
(A) 할인 쿠폰
(B) 소정의 비용
(C) 참가 증명서
(D) 무료 음료

어휘 payment 납부(금), 결제 participation 참가 certificate 증명(서) beverage 음료

148

According to the notice, what will participants receive?
(A) Discount coupons
(B) A small payment
(C) A participation certificate
(D) Free beverages*

'수령물'이 포인트이다. 둘째 문단에서 All participants will be allowed free coffee or tea for the duration of the event.라며 행사 중 무료로 커피나 차가 제공된다고 하므로 (D)가 정답이다.

* paraphrasing: coffee or tea → beverage

정답 (D)

Questions 149-150 refer to the following invoice.

Eastview Convention Center
55 Lakeview Road
Seattle, Washington

Date: April 12
Invoice number: 9800032

Bill To:
Trisha Baxter
Pure Motorcycles
90 Yamer Street
Orlando, Florida

Invoice for the Eastview Convention Center's Annual Automotive Show from June 25 - June 27.

Item:	Rate:	Total:
Convention Booth (30 square feet)	$100.00/day	$300.00
149 **Additional Services:**		
3 display tables	$10.00/unit	$30.00
Storage	$30.00/unit	$120.00
Computer rental	$20.00/unit	$20.00
55-inch television rental	$30.00/unit	$30.00
Show passes	$20.00/person	$200.00
	Subtotal	$700.00
	Tax	$45.50
	Total	$745.50*

150 *Please visit your online account to arrange payment by April 20.

---

149 What is NOT included in the cost of the event?
(A) Passes to the show
(B) Display tables
(C) Television rental
(D) Set up and clean up*

150 What is Ms. Baxter asked to do?
(A) Sign up for a membership
(B) Mail a check to the venue
(C) Settle an invoice*
(D) Confirm the number of participants

제니퍼 포터 [오전 11:23]
안녕하세요, 라파엘. 이번 주말에 릭터 애비뉴에 있는 부동산에 들르셨어요?

라파엘 모레즈 [오전 11:25]
네, 토요일에 갔어요. 151 우리 사진가 대부분이 날마다 행사장에서 일을 할건데, 정말 그렇게 큰 공간이 필요할까요?

제니퍼 포터 [오전 11:27]
방들이 크긴 하지만, 우리가 사업을 확장하면 그 공간이 필요할 거예요.

라파엘 모레즈 [오전 11:28]
그래도 몇 년 후에나 일어날 일이에요.

제니퍼 포터 [오전 11:30]
네, 그렇지만 회사의 장기 목표들에 대해 생각해야 해요. 152 릭터 애비뉴의 건물이 결국엔 151 현장 스튜디오를 개발하는 데 기회가 될 거예요.

라파엘 모레즈 [오전 11:32]
당신 말이 맞아요. 151 초상 사진 서비스를 시작하면 추가 공간이 분명 필요할 거예요.

이 사람들은 어떤 업체에서 일하겠는가?
(A) 사진 회사
(B) 패션 디자인 하우스
(C) 행사 기획 업체
(D) 예술 화랑

오전 11시 32분에, 모레즈 씨가 "당신 말이 맞아요"라고 쓸 때 의미하는 바는?
(A) 장소가 도시에서 너무 멀다.
(B) 그 건물이 회사 목표를 충족시키는 데 도움이 될 것이다.
(C) 그 건물 안에 많은 실내 디자인 작업이 필요하다.
(D) 그 부동산에는 심각한 결점들이 있다.

어휘 location 위치, 소재지 meet 충족시키다 significant 커다란, 상당한 flaw 결점, 흠

Questions 151-152 refer to the following text message chain.

Jennifer Porter [11:23 A.M.]
Hi, Raphael. Were you able to stop by the Rickter Avenue property this weekend?

Raphael Morez [11:25 A.M.]
Yes, I went on Saturday. 151 Since most of our photographers will be working at events every day, are you sure we need such a big place?

Jennifer Porter [11:27 A.M.]
The rooms are large, but as we expand, we'll need the space.

Raphael Morez [11:28 A.M.]
That might not happen for a few years, though.

Jennifer Porter [11:30 A.M.]
Yes, but we should be thinking about our long-term goals for the company. 152 The Rickter Avenue property will give us a chance to finally develop 151 an on-site studio.

Raphael Morez [11:32 A.M.]
You're right. We'll definitely need the extra space once 151 we start offering portrait services.

어휘 stop by 잠시 들르다 property 부동산, 재산 expand 확장하다 on-site 현장의, 현지의 definitely 분명히 offer 제공하다, 제안하다 portrait 초상화, 인물 사진

151

At what kind of business do the people most likely work?
(A) A photography company*
(B) A fashion design house
(C) An event planning business
(D) An art gallery

오전 11시 25분 메시지의 photographers, 11시 30분 메시지의 an on-site studio, 11시 32분 메시지의 portrait services를 통해 정답 (A)를 확인할 수 있다.

정답 (A)

152

At 11:32 A.M., what does Mr. Morez most likely mean when he writes, "You're right"?
(A) A location is too far from the city.
(B) The building will help the company meet its goals.*
(C) Much interior design work is needed in the building.
(D) The property has some significant flaws.

바로 앞서 포터 씨가 그곳이 스튜디오를 개발할 기회가 되리라(The Rickter Avenue property will give us a chance to finally develop an on-site studio.)고 말한 데 대한 동의이므로 (B)가 가장 적절하다. 제시문의 의미를 묻는 문제가 나오면 전후 맥락을 파악하는 데 집중해야 한다.

정답 (B)

Questions 153-155 refer to the following e-mail.

To: Tristan Starr
From: Emilia Simpson
Date: June 2
Re: Walton Shopping Center contract

Hi Tristan,

I just got an e-mail from Marcus Pine about the budget proposal you sent him yesterday. [153] Apparently, several of the figures are incorrect. It seems you included the initial figures we presented to him during our first advertising pitch on May 6 and [154] not the figures we later agreed on during negotiations on May 20.

Mr. Pine was hoping to present the advertising plan to his superiors on June 5. He mentioned that there are several other agencies that have sent him proposals, and he will select one of them instead if we cannot get this paperwork done by June 3. Since I'm just about to fly to our Chicago office, I'm hoping you can handle this right away. [155] Please send Mr. Pine the revised proposal and e-mail me when you get his response.

Sincerely,
Emilia

---

153. Why was the e-mail written?

(A) To request a vacation
(B) To introduce an applicant
(C) To announce a policy change
(D) To point out some mistakes*

첫째 문단에서 Apparently, several of the figures are incorrect.라며 수치가 잘못되었다고 하므로 (D)가 가장 적절하다. 글의 목적에 대한 결정적인 단서는 대체로 전반부에서 확인할 수 있다.

정답 (D)

제안서는 언제 수정되었는가?
(A) 5월 6일
(B) 5월 20일
(C) 6월 3일
(D) 6월 5일

어휘 modify 수정하다, 변경하다

154

When was the proposal modified?
(A) On May 6th
(B) On May 20th*
(C) On June 3rd
(D) On June 5th

첫째 문단에서 (A)에 처음 발표하고 더 나중인 (B)에 협상했다(not the figures we later agreed on during negotiations on May 20)고 한다. 따라서 (B)가 정답이 된다. 참고로, (C)는 수정안 마감 기한이고, (D)는 파인 씨의 상사에게 보고하겠다고 언급된 날짜이다.

정답 (B)

심슨 씨는 스타 씨가 무엇을 하기를 바라는가?
(A) 전화할 것
(B) 환불할 것
(C) 서류를 보낼 것
(D) 매니저에게 이야기할 것

어휘 make a phone call 전화하다 issue 발행하다, 발부하다 refund 환불

155

What would Ms. Simpson like Mr. Starr to do?
(A) Make a phone call
(B) Issue a refund
(C) Send a document*
(D) Speak with a manager

심슨 씨와 스타 씨가 각각 본 이메일의 발신자 및 수신자임을 파악해야 한다. 발신자의 요청 및 제안 사항은 대체로 후반부에서 확인할 수 있다. 둘째 문단에서 Please send Mr. Pine the revised proposal이라고 하므로 (C)가 정답이다.

* paraphrasing: the revised proposal → a document

정답 (C)

Questions 156-157 refer to the following article.

Restaurant sales are down in Plymouth County. According to a report in the Plymouth Journal, sales have dropped by more than fifteen percent this winter. The drop has shocked many restaurant owners, especially since the winter holidays usually increase restaurant business. [156] Bob Fulton, owner of Little Italy Eatery, attributed the drop to an increase in wholesale prices as one factor of the drop. "With the prices of everything going up, we've had to increase our prices as well," Mr. Fulton said in an interview. "Most customers just don't want to pay that much for a meal." [157] To encourage more business, many local restaurants have joined forces to develop membership programs. These programs provide customers with discounts at numerous restaurants in the county.

어휘 drop 하락, 하락하다 owner 소유주 increase 증가, 증가시키다 attribute A to B A의 요인이 B라고 보다 wholesale 도매의, 대량의 factor 요소 pay 결제하다, 지불하다 meal 식사 encourage 고무하다, 격려하다 join forces 힘을 합치다 numerous 무수한

156

According to the article, why have restaurant sales dropped?

(A) The weather has become unpleasant.
(B) The costs have risen too high.*
(C) Newer restaurants have been built.
(D) Many local jobs have been lost.

중반부의 Bob Fulton, owner of Little Italy Eatery, attributed the drop to an increase in wholesale prices as one factor of the drop.에서 도매가 인상을 판매 하락의 원인으로 보므로 (B)가 가장 적절하다.

정답 (B)

플리머스 카운티의 식당 수익이 하락했다. 플리머스 저널에 실린 기사에 따르면, 올 겨울 판매가 15% 이상 떨어졌다. 이 하락세는 많은 식당 소유주에게 충격을 줬다. 특히 겨울 휴가철에는 대체로 식당에 손님이 많기 때문이다. 156 리틀 이탈리 이터리 주인인 밥 풀턴은 이 하락세의 요인을 도매가 증가로 본다. "모든 가격이 올라가니, 우리도 가격을 올려야 했습니다," 풀턴 씨는 인터뷰에서 이렇게 말했다. "대부분 고객은 식사에 그렇게 많은 돈을 내고 싶지 않아 하죠." 157 사업 활성화를 위해서, 많은 지역 식당들이 협력해 멤버십 프로그램을 개발했다. 이 프로그램은 시내 많은 식당에서 고객들에게 할인을 제공해 줄 것이다.

본 기사에 따르면, 식당 판매가 왜 감소했는가?
(A) 날씨가 안 좋아져서
(B) 물가가 너무 비싸져서
(C) 더 새로운 식당들이 생겨서
(D) 많은 지역 일자리가 없어져서

어휘 unpleasant 불쾌한, 불편한 lose 잃다

157

How are restaurant owners responding to the trend?

(A) By improving the quality of the food
(B) By decreasing the number of workers
(C) By working with other restaurants*
(D) By launching television advertisements

'식당 주인들의 대응책'이 포인트임을 파악하고 지문을 살펴보면, 후반부의 To encourage more business, many local restaurants have joined forces to develop membership programs.를 통해 정답 (C)를 확인할 수 있다.

* paraphrasing: join → work with

정답 (C)

식당 주인들은 최신 경향에 대해 어떻게 대응하고 있는가?
(A) 음식 품질을 개선하는 것으로
(B) 직원 수를 줄이는 것으로
(C) 다른 식당들과 협업하는 것으로
(D) 텔레비전 광고를 내는 것으로

어휘 respond to ~에 대응하다, 대답하다 trend 경향 improve 개선하다, 향상시키다 quality (품)질 decrease 감소시키다 launch 출시하다, 발표하다, 공개하다

Questions 158-161 refer to the following online chat discussion.

Rita Frasier [2:23 P.M.]	Ms. Norton, do you have a minute? Thomas and I are unclear about our assignments. Last year, I was in charge of developing the seasonal training program, but Thomas was assigned the exact same job this year.
Patrina Norton [2:25 P.M.]	Yes, [158] everyone needs a chance to work on developing their own programs for human resources.
Rita Frasier [2:26 P.M.]	So, we will no longer use the materials I developed last year?
Patrina Norton [2:28 P.M.]	That's right. Thomas is expected to develop new materials that will be used this year.
Thomas Woods [2:30 P.M.]	But [160] what if I would like to use some of Rita's ideas?
Patrina Norton [2:33 P.M.]	Program development is part of the job.
Thomas Woods [2:35 P.M.]	Yes, but [159] Rita's program was excellent last year. I would hate all her hard work to go to waste.
Patrina Norton [2:39 P.M.]	If Rita is okay with it, I think you could use some of her materials so long as you update them where appropriate. [161] Let me review last year's materials first and get back to you.
Rita Frasier [2:41 P.M.]	What if Thomas and I worked together on the project?
Patrina Norton [2:44 P.M.]	I don't think that will be necessary.
Rita Frasier [2:45 P.M.]	Okay, I understand.
Thomas Woods [2:46 P.M.]	Let us know when you've decided. Thanks.

어휘 assignment 임무, 배정 be in charge of ~하는 것을 책임지다 training 교육, 훈련 assign 배정하다 human resources 인적 자원 no longer 더는 ~않는 material 재료, 자재 waste 낭비하다 so long as ~하는 한 appropriate 적절한

158
Who most likely is Ms. Norton?
(A) A financial planner
(B) A human resources manager *
(C) A company intern
(D) An advertising consultant

오후 2시 25분 노튼 씨의 메시지 everyone needs a chance to work on developing their own programs for human resources를 통해 인적 자원부를 위한 업무를 지시하고 있음을 알 수 있으므로 정답 (B)를 유추할 수 있다.

정답 (B)

노튼 씨는 누구이겠는가?
(A) 재정 기획가
(B) 인적 자원부 과장
(C) 회사 인턴
(D) 광고 컨설턴트

어휘 financial 재정의, 금융의

159
What is suggested about Ms. Frasier?
(A) She developed a successful training program last year. *
(B) She usually works with Mr. Woods on projects.
(C) She is pleased with this year's assignment.
(D) She will take over Ms. Norton's job next year.

핵심 인명 Ms. Frasier(Rita Frasier)에 유념해 지문을 살펴보면, 오후 2시 35분 메시지에서 Rita's program was excellent last year라며 작년 리타의 프로그램이 훌륭했다고 하므로 (A)가 가장 적절하다.
* paraphrasing: excellent → successful

정답 (A)

프레이저 씨에 대해 드러나는 사항은?
(A) 작년에 성공적인 교육 프로그램을 개발했다.
(B) 대체로 우즈 씨와 프로젝트를 함께 작업한다.
(C) 올해 임무에 만족한다.
(D) 노튼 씨의 일을 내년에 인수할 것이다.

어휘 take over 인계 받다

160
At 2:33 P.M., what does Ms. Norton most likely mean when she writes, "Program development is part of the job"?
(A) Her job duties include program development.
(B) She believes Ms. Frasier is better suited for the job.
(C) She disagrees with Mr. Woods' suggestion. *
(D) Her contract with the company needs revising.

직전에 어떤 내용이 나왔는지 보자. 우즈 씨가 리타의 아이디어를 써도 되냐(what if I would like to use some of Rita's ideas?)고 물은 데 이어진 반응이다. 따라서 시사하는 바로 가장 적절한 것은 (C)이다.

정답 (C)

오후 2시 33분에, 노튼 씨가 "프로그램 개발도 업무의 일부예요"라고 쓸 때 의미하는 바는?
(A) 자신의 임무에 프로그램 개발이 포함된다.
(B) 프레이저 씨가 그 일에 더 적합하다고 본다.
(C) 우즈 씨의 제안에 동의하지 않는다.
(D) 회사와의 계약을 수정해야 한다.

어휘 suit ~에게 맞다, 괜찮다, 어울리다 disagree 동의하지 않다 suggestion 제안 revise 수정하다

161
What will most likely happen next?
(A) Ms. Frasier will contact a supervisor.
(B) Mr. Woods will begin working on a project.
(C) Mr. Woods and Ms. Frasier will have a meeting.
(D) Ms. Norton will look at some old materials. *

~ next? 문제의 단서는 대체로 후반부에서 확인할 수 있다. 작년 자료를 그냥 버리자니 아까울 듯하다는 말에, 노튼 씨가 오후 2시 39분에 Let me review last year's materials first and get back to you.라며 먼저 살펴보고 다시 연락하겠다고 하므로 (D)가 정답이 된다.

정답 (D)

다음에 어떤 일이 생기겠는가?
(A) 프레이저 씨가 상사에게 연락할 것이다.
(B) 우즈 씨가 프로젝트 작업을 시작할 것이다.
(C) 우즈 씨와 프레이저 씨가 회의를 할 것이다.
(D) 노튼 씨가 옛날 자료를 검토할 것이다.

수신: 타미카 케인스
발신: 마르셀 벤트루
제목: 정보
날짜: 4월 22일

162 고객님이 저희 웹사이트에서 요청하신 서비스 견적에 관해 메일을 드립니다. 론 앤 가든 케어의 광범위한 서비스에 관심을 가져 주셔서 기쁩니다. —[1]— 저희 회사가 시내 최고의 조경 회사라는 것을 장담할 수 있습니다. 저희는 호텔 및 컨트리 클럽 등 많은 지역 업체들에 서비스합니다. —[2]— 또한 시내에 있는 메모리얼 스테디엄의 넓은 잔디밭도 관리 중입니다.

고객님이 요청하신 서비스 견적서를 첨부합니다. —[3]— 163 이 견적서는 레놀즈 갤러리의 잔디를 일주일에 한 번 관리하는 것을 기본으로 하여 작성했습니다. 하지만, 165 정원 식재나 벌목 같은 추가 서비스가 필요하실 경우, 추가 요금이 청구될 수 있습니다. —[4]— 견적서를 검토하시길 바랍니다. 164 제가 다음 주초에 연락 드려 궁금하신 사항들에 대해 답변을 드리겠습니다.

그럼 이만,
마르셀 벤트루

Questions 162-165 refer to the following e-mail.

To: Tamika Keynes
From: Marcel Ventrue
Re: Information
Date: April 22

162 I'm writing in regards to the service quote you requested on our website. I'm delighted you're interested in Lawn and Garden Care's extensive range of services. --[1]-- I can assure you that we are the top landscaping company in the city. We service many local businesses, such as hotels and country clubs. --[2]-- We also maintain the extensive lawns at Memorial Stadium downtown.

I have attached the service quote you requested. --[3]-- 163 The quote is based on weekly lawn maintenance services for The Renolds Gallery. However, 165 in the event that you require additional services, such as garden planting or tree removal, you would be charged extra. --[4]-- Have a look at the quote and 164 I will be in touch early next week to answer any questions you might have.

Sincerely,
Marcel Ventrue

어휘 in regards to ~에 관해서 quote 견적(서) request 요청하다 be interested in ~에 관심 있다 lawn 잔디 extensive 광범위한, 폭넓은 range 범위 assure 장담하다, 확언하다 landscaping 조경 maintain (점검 보수해 가며) 유지하다 memorial 기념비 attach 첨부하다 maintenance 유지 보수, 관리 in the event that ~할 경우에는 require 필요로 하다 additional 추가의, 가외의 removal 제거 charge 청구하다

본 이메일의 목적은 무엇인가?
(A) 일정을 변경하기 위해서
(B) 요청에 응답하기 위해서
(C) 설계도를 보내기 위해서
(D) 지원서를 제출하기 위해서

어휘 respond to ~에 응답하다, 대답하다 blueprint 설계도 submit 제출하다 application 지원(서)

162 What is the purpose of the e-mail?
(A) To change a schedule
(B) To respond to a request*
(C) To send a blueprint
(D) To submit an application

첫 문장 I'm writing in regards to the service quote you requested on our website.를 통해 정답 (B)를 확인할 수 있다. 글의 목적은 대체로 전반부에 나온다.

정답 (B)

163

For what kind of business does Ms. Keynes most likely work?

(A) An art gallery*
(B) A stadium
(C) A country club
(D) A hotel

둘째 문단의 The quote is based on weekly lawn maintenance services for The Renolds Gallery.에 언급된 업체명(Renolds Gallery)을 통해 (A)가 정답임을 알 수 있다. 나머지 선택지는 첫째 문단에서 발신자 측이 서비스하는 업체들로 다뤄졌다.

정답 (A)

케인스 씨는 어떤 업체를 운영하겠는가?
(A) 예술 갤러리
(B) 경기장
(C) 컨트리 클럽
(D) 호텔

164

What is mentioned in the e-mail?

(A) Ms. Keynes is a new employee at Lawn and Garden Care.
(B) Lawn and Garden Care is a new business.
(C) Ms. Keynes will hear from Mr. Ventrue next week.*
(D) Mr. Ventrue visited Ms. Keynes' business.

각 선택지들과 지문을 대조하면서 정답을 가려 내자. 후반부에서 I will be in touch early next week to answer any questions you might have.라며 발신자(Mr. Ventrue)가 다음 주에 연락하겠다고 하므로 (C)가 가장 적절하다.

정답 (C)

본 이메일에서 언급된 사항은?
(A) 케인스 씨는 론 앤 가든 케어의 신입 사원이다.
(B) 론 앤 가든 케어는 신생 업체이다.
(C) 케인스 씨는 다음 주에 벤트루 씨로부터 연락을 받을 것이다.
(D) 벤트루 씨는 케인스 씨의 업체에 방문했다.

어휘 new employee 신입 사원
hear from ~에서 연락을 받다, ~의 소식을 듣다

165

In which of the positions marked [1], [2], [3], and [4] does the following sentence best belong?

"However, all additional services will be discounted should you sign a two-year contract with us."

(A) [1]
(B) [2]
(C) [3]
(D) [4]*

제시문의 포인트가 '추가 서비스 할인'이므로 앞서 '추가 서비스'에 대한 언급이 있어야 흐름상 자연스럽다. 따라서 둘째 문단의 in the event that you require additional services, such as garden planting or tree removal, you would be charged extra 다음인 (D)가 정답이다.

정답 (D)

[1], [2], [3], [4] 중 다음 문장이 들어가기에 가장 적절한 곳은?
"하지만, 저희와 2년짜리 계약을 맺으시면 모든 추가 서비스가 할인될 것입니다."
(A) [1]
(B) [2]
(C) [3]
(D) [4]

어휘 contract 계약(서)

파커 월러스, 어드벤처 소프트웨어에 합류하다
166 작성 에이미 스완슨, 데일리 챗

뉴욕 (2월 24일) – 파커 월러스가 새 스타트업 어드벤처 소프트웨어에 합류할 것이라고 발표했다. 5년째 소프트웨어 응용 프로그램을 개발해 온 월러스는 음악 공유 프로그램인 마블 FM 제작자로 가장 유명하다. 마블 FM은 불과 2년 만에 3백만 다운로드를 기록해 월러스를 업계에서 가장 인기 있는 개발자로 만들었다.

리퀴드 앱스와 T&B 개발 회사의 일을 거절했으나, 월러스는 놀라운 행보로 2년이 채 안 되는 회사에 합류해 달라는 제의를 받아들였다. "166 어드벤처 소프트웨어의 알란 파이크를 만났을 때, 저는 그와 같은 목표를 갖고 있다는 걸 알았습니다." 167 월러스는 최근 자신의 최신 앱 발표장에서 이렇게 말했다. "그와 저 둘 다 음악에 열정적이며, 그는 앞으로의 프로젝트들에 대해 대단한 아이디어를 갖고 있었습니다. 우리가 내년에 굉장한 신제품들을 만들어 낼 것이라고 확신합니다."

167 월러스의 최신 앱, 마블 비디오는 한 달도 안 됐는데 벌써 50만여 다운로드를 기록했다. 기술 업계는 월러스가 파이크와 동업함으로써 엄청난 상품들이 나올 것으로 기대하는데, 3월 30일에 168 재출시되는 파이크의 스마트 심포니 개정판이 그 시작이 될 것이다.

파이크 씨는 누구이겠는가?
(A) 영화 감독
(B) 교향곡 작곡가
(C) 뮤직 비디오 프로듀서
(D) 소프트웨어 회사 소유주

어휘 composer 작곡가 producer 생산자, 제작자, 프로듀서 owner 소유주

Questions 166-168 refer to the following article.

Parker Wallace to Join Adventure Software
166 By Amy Swanson, The Daily Chat

NEW YORK (24 February) – Parker Wallace has announced he will join the new start-up Adventure Software. Wallace, who has been developing software applications for five years now, is best known as the creator of Marble FM, a music sharing application. Marble FM accumulated over three million downloads in just two years, leading Wallace to become one of the most sought-after developers in the industry.

Despite turning down jobs at Liquid Apps and T&B Developers, Wallace has made the surprising move and accepted an offer to join a company that is less than two years old. "When I met 166 Alan Pike of Adventure Software, I knew he and I shared the same goals," 167 Wallace recently said at the launch of his latest app. "He and I are both passionate about music, and he had some great ideas for future projects. I am extremely confident that we'll be putting out hot new products in the next year."

167 Wallace's newest app, Marble Video, has already generated over 500,000 downloads in less than a month. The tech world will be expecting big things from the partnership between Wallace and Pike, starting with 168 the rerelease of an upgraded version of Pike's Smart Symphony on March 30.

어휘 announce 발표하다 application 응용 프로그램 (=app) share 공유하다 accumulate 모으다, 축적하다 sought-after 수요가 많은, 인기 있는 industry (산업) 분야 despite ~에도 불구하고 turn down ~을 거절하다, 거부하다 accept 받다 offer 제안 launch 출시, 발표 passionate 열정적인, 열렬한 extremely 매우, 몹시 confident 자신감 있는, 확신하는 put out (상품을) 생산하다, 내놓다 generate 창출하다 rerelease 재발매

---

166 Who most likely is Mr. Pike?
(A) A film director
(B) A symphony composer
(C) A music video producer
(D) A software company owner*

핵심 인명 Mr. Pike에 유의해 지문을 살펴보면, 소프트웨어 개발 회사들을 언급한 둘째 문단의 Alan Pike of Adventure Software를 통해 정답 (D)를 유추할 수 있다.

정답 (D)

167

What most likely is true about Ms. Swanson?

(A) She was formerly employed at Liquid Apps.
(B) She attended the launch of Marble Video.*
(C) She purchased a copy of Marble FM.
(D) She met with Mr. Pike at an event.

핵심 인명 Ms. Swanson은 본 기사를 작성한 사람이다. 둘째 문단에 실린 인터뷰를 보면 신제품 출시장(Wallace recently said at the launch of his latest app)에 갔었다는 점이 드러나며 셋째 문단의 Wallace's newest app, Marble Video에서 신제품을 확인할 수 있으므로 (B)가 정답이 된다.

정답 (B)

스완슨 씨에 대해 무엇이 사실이겠는가?
(A) 이전에 리퀴드 앱스에서 일했다.
(B) 마블 비디오 발표장에 참석했다.
(C) 마블 FM을 구입했다.
(D) 파이크 씨와 행사장에서 만났다.

어휘 formerly 이전에 employ 고용하다 attend 참석하다 purchase 구입하다

168

What is indicated about Smart Symphony?

(A) It is an already existing app.*
(B) It was originally developed by T&B Developers.
(C) It will be limited to 500,000 copies.
(D) It will feature elements of Marble FM.

핵심 어구 Smart Symphony가 언급된 곳을 찾아보자. 마지막 문단에서 개정판으로 재발매된다(the rerelease of an upgraded version of Pike's Smart Symphony)고 한다. 따라서 현재에 존재하고 있는 것임을 알 수 있으므로 (A)가 가장 적절하다.

정답 (A)

스마트 심포니에 대해 드러나는 사항은?
(A) 이미 존재하고 있는 앱이다.
(B) 원래 T&B 개발 회사에서 개발했다.
(C) 50만 부 판매로 제한될 것이다.
(D) 마블 FM의 특징들을 포함할 것이다.

어휘 existing 존재하는 limited 제한된 feature 특징으로 하다 element 요소

Questions 169-171 refer to the following brochure.

Energy Savers

Are you paying high utility bills during the summer or winter months? [169] With Energy Savers, you can find the energy solutions that will save you money. Contact us for your free four-step consultation.

1. Determine your energy needs

Our qualified energy consultants will visit your home to determine what your energy needs are. [170 (A), (B)] You will be asked to complete a detailed survey regarding the number of hours you spend at home, your desired temperatures during each season, and your cooking and cleaning habits.

2. Home inspection

Once our consultants determine your needs, they will inspect the windows, walls, and doors of your home to ensure proper insulation. [170 (C)] They will also test your heating, cooling, and lighting systems for weaknesses. Unlike other companies, Energy Savers will prepare a detailed report of flaws and make suggestions for improvements.

3. Choose your upgrades

Our consultants will discuss the recommended upgrades for your home while keeping your budget in mind. We can help you choose and install everything from double-paned glass for your windows to solar panels on your roof.

4. Installations

Our team will work around your schedule to install your upgrades. [171] However, most installations take several days to complete. You will see instant savings on your utility bills and the best part is those savings never end. You will continue to save money for years to come. Should you have problems with your upgrades within the first year, Energy Savers will fix them free of charge.

169

What is the purpose of the brochure?

(A) To announce a new type of energy
(B) To compare two energy companies
(C) To advertise a company's services*
(D) To discuss the benefits of insulation

첫째 문단에서 공과금이 많이 나온다며 해결책이 있다(With Energy Savers, you can find the energy solutions that will save you money.)고 한 뒤 회사의 서비스 단계들을 설명하고 있다. 따라서 (C)가 가장 적절하다. 광고 업체의 성격은 이처럼 서두에서 질의응답 식으로 제시되는 경우가 많다.

정답 (C)

본 브로셔의 목적은 무엇인가?
(A) 새로운 에너지 유형을 발표하기 위해서
(B) 두 에너지 회사들을 비교하기 위해서
(C) 회사의 서비스를 광고하기 위해서
(D) 단열의 혜택을 논의하기 위해서

어휘 compare 비교하다 advertise 광고하다 benefit 혜택, 이득

170

What is NOT examined during the home consultation?

(A) The number of hours the home is occupied
(B) The home owner's preferred temperatures
(C) The efficiency of heating systems
(D) The current cost of monthly utilities*

home consultation에 관련된 부분을 찾아 각 선택지와 대조하면서 지문에 언급되지 않은 사항을 소거하는 식으로 문제를 해결한다. 둘째 문단의 You will be asked to complete a detailed survey regarding the number of hours you spend at home, your desired temperatures during each season에서 (A)와 (B)를, 셋째 문단의 They will also test your heating, cooling, and lighting systems for weaknesses.에서 (C)를 확인할 수 있다. 따라서 본 문제의 정답은 (D)가 된다.

* paraphrasing: desired → preferred

정답 (D)

주택 방문 상담 동안 검토되지 않는 것은?
(A) 주택이 사용되는 시간
(B) 주택 소유주가 선호하는 온도
(C) 난방 시스템의 효율성
(D) 현재의 월 공과금

어휘 occupied 사용 중인 efficiency 효율 cost 값, 비용

171

What does the brochure suggest is one disadvantage of the upgrades?

(A) The upgrades are costly to purchase.
(B) It takes time to install all the features.*
(C) Home owners must be present during the installations.
(D) Monthly bills will not decrease for a year.

키워드 disadvantage에 유의해 지문을 살펴보면, 마지막 문단에서 However, most installations take several days to complete.이라며 설치하는 데 며칠 걸린다고 하므로 (B)가 가장 적절하다. however 뒤에는 답이 잘 나온다.

정답 (B)

본 브로셔는 업그레이드의 한 가지 단점으로 무엇을 제시하는가?
(A) 업그레이드 구입비가 많이 든다.
(B) 모든 것이 설치되는 데 시간이 걸린다.
(C) 설치하는 동안 주택 소유주들이 집에 있어야 한다.
(D) 월 공과금이 1년간은 줄지 않을 것이다.

어휘 disadvantage 단점 costly 많은 돈이 드는 decrease 줄다, 감소하다

뉴몽 테크놀로지 컨벤션, 세계 투어를 시작하다

3월 5일 – 뉴몽 테크놀로지 컨벤션(NTC)이 다음 달 세계 투어의 첫 발을 내디딜 예정이다. 이 컨벤션은 세계 최대의 기술 전람회로 의료 기술부터 항공 우주 기술 시연까지 모든 것을 다룬다. 172 NTC는 뉴몽 인더스트리즈와 그 회사의 CEO인 배럿 마이클스가 호주 시드니에 설립했다. —[1]—173 매년, 30,000명이 넘는 사람들이 시장에 아직 나오지 않은 획기적인 기술들을 보고자 시드니 컨벤션을 방문한다.

NTC는 대개 전 세계에서 오는 과학자들을 맞이했지만, 이번에는 처음으로 해외 투어를 나가는 전람회가 될 것이다. —[2]—마이클스 씨는 인터뷰에서 이렇게 말했다. "이번 확장에 저희는 굉장히 들떠 있습니다. 십 년 전 컨벤션을 시작할 때만 해도, 세계에서 가장 큰 기술 행사가 될 지는 전혀 몰랐습니다. —[3]— 174 6개국을 도는 투어를 다음 달 영국 런던에서 시작하게 되어 매우 기쁩니다. 관객이 엄청나게 몰릴 것이라 기대합니다."

미국, 브라질, 일본, 독일, 남아프리카도 NTC의 이번 투어에 포함된다. 투어 일정의 대부분 티켓은 벌써 매진이다. —[4]— 175 "캐나다와 프랑스의 업계 전문가들도 이미 저희에게 제안서를 보냈습니다." 마이클스 씨가 덧붙였다. "다른 나라들도 비슷한 제안을 해 올 것이라고 낙관합니다."

Questions 172-175 refer to the following article.

Newmont Technology Convention to Launch World Tour

March 5 – The Newmont Technology Convention (NTC) is scheduled to make the first stop on its world tour next month. The convention is one of the world's largest technology exhibitions and features everything from medical technology to aerospace engineering demonstrations. 172 The NTC was founded in Sydney, Australia by Newmont Industries and its CEO, Barret Michaels. --[1]-- 173 Every year, over 30,000 people visit the Sydney convention to see some of the most innovative technologies that have not yet reached the market.

The NTC commonly hosts scientists from all over the world, but this is the first year it will become an international traveling exhibition. --[2]-- Mr. Michaels stated in an interview, "We're very excited about this expansion. When we started the convention ten years ago, we had no idea it would grow to be the biggest technology event in the world. -- [3]-- 174 We're extremely happy to kick off our six-country tour in London, England next month. We're already expecting a huge crowd."

The U.S., Brazil, Japan, Germany, and South Africa will also host the NTC during its tour. Tickets to most of the tour dates are already sold out. --[4]-- 175 "Industry professionals in both Canada and France have already reached out to us with proposals," Mr. Michaels said. "We're optimistic that other countries will make similar proposals."

어휘 exhibition 전시 aerospace 항공 우주 found 설립하다 innovative 획기적인 reach 도달하다, 이르다 market 시장 commonly 흔히, 보통 host 주최하다 state 진술하다, 말하다 expansion 확대, 확장 kick off 개시하다, 시작하다 huge 거대한, 막대한 crowd 군중, 무리 sold out 매진된 proposal 제안(서) optimistic 낙관적인 similar 비슷한, 유사한

뉴몽 인더스트리즈에 대해 사실인 것은?
(A) 뉴몽 테크놀로지 컨벤션을 설립하는 데 도움을 줬다.
(B) 영국, 브라질, 일본에 지사가 있다.
(C) 선두적인 의료 기술 개발 회사이다.
(D) 항공 우주 기술 장비를 사고 판다.

어휘 establish 설립하다 leading 선두적인, 내로라하는 equipment 기기, 장비

172

What is true about Newmont Industries?
(A) It helped establish the Newmont Technology Convention.*
(B) It has offices in England, Brazil, and Japan.
(C) It is the leading developer of medical technology.
(D) It buys and sells aerospace engineering equipment.

Newmont Industries에 유의해 지문을 살펴보면, 첫째 문단의 The NTC was founded in Sydney, Australia by Newmont Industries and its CEO, Barret Michaels.를 통해 (A)가 정답임을 알 수 있다.

* paraphrasing: found → establish

정답 (A)

173

What is stated about the convention in Sydney?

(A) It took five years to become popular.
(B) It employs over 30,000 workers.
(C) It features technologies that cannot be purchased.*
(D) It was the second location for the exhibition.

Sydney에 유의해 살펴보면, 첫째 문단에서 Every year, over 30,000 people visit the Sydney convention to see some of the most innovative technologies that have not yet reached the market.라며 '시장에 아직 나오지 않은 획기적인 기술들을 보러 많은 이가 방문했다'고 한다. 따라서 (C)가 가장 적절하다.

* paraphrasing: not yet reached the market → cannot be purchased

정답 (C)

시드니 컨벤션에 대해 뭐라고 하는가?
(A) 유명세를 얻는 데 5년이 걸렸다.
(B) 직원이 3만 명 이상이다.
(C) 구입할 수 없는 기술들을 특징으로 한다.
(D) 전람회의 두 번째 장소였다.

어휘 location 위치, 소재지

174

Where will the next Newmont Technology Convention be held?

(A) In France
(B) In England*
(C) In Brazil
(D) In Japan

'다음 개최지'가 포인트이다. 둘째 문단의 We're extremely happy to kick off our six-country tour in London, England next month.를 통해 정답 (B)를 확인할 수 있다.

정답 (B)

다음 뉴몬 테크놀로지 컨벤션은 어디에서 열릴 것인가?
(A) 프랑스에서
(B) 영국에서
(C) 브라질에서
(D) 일본에서

어휘 be held 열리다, 진행되다

175

In which of the positions marked [1], [2], [3], and [4] does the following sentence best belong?

"If the NTC tour is successful, Mr. Michaels plans to add additional locations to next year's tour."

(A) [1]
(B) [2]
(C) [3]
(D) [4]*

문맥상 '올해 투어의 성공 기대'가 언급된 다음 이어져야 자연스럽다. 또 제시문에서 내년 투어에 다른 나라가 추가될 가능성을 말하고 있으므로 뒤에 캐나다와 프랑스를 언급하는 (D)가 정답이 된다.

정답 (D)

[1], [2], [3], [4] 중 다음 문장이 들어가기에 가장 적절한 곳은?

"NTC 투어가 성공한다면, 마이클스 씨는 내년 투어에 몇 군데 추가할 계획이다."

(A) [1]
(B) [2]
(C) [3]
(D) [4]

Questions 176-180 refer to the following letter and survey.

Grand Palace Hotel
Koh Samui, Thailand

Bethanie Sparks
44 Brock Road,
Toronto, ON L1T 4W2

Dear Ms. Sparks,

Thank you for choosing the Grand Palace Hotel as your accommodation from October 12 to October 25. According to our records, 177 you purchased your stay as part of our Vacation in Thailand package, which celebrated our hotel's 50th anniversary. We are 178 conducting a short survey regarding this package. 176 We would appreciate you completing the enclosed survey and returning it in the self-addressed envelope. 179 If you respond by January 2, you will receive a 10% discount on your next trip as our thanks. However, should you send it back after that deadline, we would still like to enter you into a draw for a free night's stay in any of our hotels.

Sincerely,

Rita Lao
Grand Palace Hotel

Grand Palace Hotel, Thailand
By participating in this survey, you can assist us in providing the best possible services to all our guests.

Name: Bethanie Sparks   179 **Date:** 28 November

1. May we call you to discuss your answers further?
   - Yes, phone number_____ • **NO**

2. How would you rate the quality of our facilities and services?
   • Poor   • Fair   • Average   • **Good**   • Excellent

Please explain your response: I found my room to be luxurious and clean. The food in the restaurant was also excellent. However, when I ordered room service, the food was always delivered quite late.

3. How would you rate our amenities?
   • Poor   • Fair   • Average   • Good   • **Excellent**

Please explain your response: 180 I enjoyed the variety of the activities you had to offer. During my stay, I was able to go scuba diving, cave exploring, attend a dance lesson, and even take a tour of the local markets. There were so many exciting things to do!

176
Why did Ms. Lao write to Ms. Sparks?
(A) To notify of a late payment
(B) To reschedule a hotel stay
(C) To request some customer feedback*
(D) To respond to a complaint

177
What is indicated about the Grand Palace Hotel?
(A) Its head office is located in Thailand.
(B) It plans to build a hotel in Toronto.
(C) It wants to expand its recreational activities.
(D) It launched a promotion to celebrate an anniversary.*

편지에서, 첫째 문단 셋째 줄에 있는 "conducting"과 의미상 가장 유사한 단어는?
(A) 집행하다
(B) 인가하다
(C) 행동하다
(D) 이동하다

어휘 administer 관리하다, 운영하다, 집행하다 authorize 인가하다, 허가하다, 권한을 부여하다 behave 처신하다, 행동하다 transfer 옮기다, 이동하다, 이전하다

178

In the letter, the word "conducting" in paragraph 1 line 3 is closest in meaning to

(A) administering* (B) authorizing
(C) behaving (D) transferring

해당 부분은 '설문 조사를 하고 있다'는 요지이므로 대신 들어가 가장 유사한 문맥을 만들어줄 수 있는 단어는 (A)이다. conduct a survey = administer a survey = carry out a survey

정답 (A)

스파크스 씨는 그랜드 팰리스 호텔에서 무엇을 받겠는가?
(A) 할인 쿠폰
(B) 경연 대회 입장
(C) 스쿠버 다이빙 무료 강습
(D) 무료 1박 숙박권

179

What will Ms. Sparks most likely receive from the Grand Palace Hotel?

(A) A discount coupon*
(B) Entrance into a contest
(C) Free scuba diving lessons
(D) A free night's stay

Grand Palace Hotel 측의 편지(지문 1)에서 '혜택'에 관련된 부분을 찾아보면, 설문을 1월 2일까지 보낼 경우 10% 할인을 받을 수 있다(If you respond by January 2, you will receive a 10% discount on your next trip as our thanks.)고 한다. 이에 유념해 설문지(지문 2)에서 날짜를 보면, 할인 대상자가 되므로 (A)가 정답이 된다.

정답 (A)

스파크스 씨는 그랜드 팰리스 호텔에 대해 뭐라고 언급하는가?
(A) 문제 해결에 대해 직원이 도와주지 않았다.
(B) 손님들을 위한 활동이 다양하다.
(C) 음식 품질이 형편없었다.
(D) 대도시에 좋은 위치에 있다.

어휘 solve 해결하다 a wide range of 광범위한, 다양한 location 위치, 소재지

180

What does Ms. Sparks mention about the Grand Palace Hotel?

(A) Its staff did not help her solve a problem.
(B) It has a wide range of activities for guests.*
(C) Its food was of poor quality.
(D) It has a great location in a large city.

Ms. Sparks가 작성한 Grand Palace Hotel 설문지(지문 2)를 중점적으로 살펴보자. 마지막 답변에서 I enjoyed the variety of the activities you had to offer.라며 다양한 활동을 즐겼다고 한다. 따라서 (B)가 정답이다.

* paraphrasing: the variety of → a wide range of

정답 (B)

Questions 181-185 refer to the following notice and form.

To: Employees of Tombes Financial Monthly
From: Tombes Publications Acquisition Board
Re: Tombes-Parker Business and Finance
Date: 6 March

As you have been made aware, Tombes Financial Monthly plans to officially merge with Parker Business Magazine on April 27. [181] This merger will be an exciting opportunity for both companies. [182] Parker Business Magazine is one of the top three business publications and specializes in reporting on international business issues and trends. This merger will allow us to create the first-ever business and finance magazine, which we're sure will boost our publication to the number one spot. In addition, with our larger staff, we'll now be able to put out biweekly editions and generate more sales.

[183] Department managers will meet during the week of April 2 to work out some of the details of the merger as well as the renovation of our brand-new office space downtown. [184] If you have any concerns you'd like to raise during the meetings, please send an e-mail to the relevant department manager in advance.

Tombes Publications Acquisitions Board

어휘 financial 재정의, 금융의 publication 출판(물) acquisition 습득, 인수 board 위원회, 이사회 aware 알고 있는 merge 합병하다 merger 합병 opportunity 기회 specialize in ~을 전문으로 하다 trend 경향 issue 문제, 사안 boost 신장시키다, 북돋우다 in addition 게다가 biweekly 격주의 edition (잡지 등의) 호 generate 창출하다 renovation 개조 concern 우려 사항, 걱정 raise (들어) 올리다 relevant 관련 있는 in advance 미리, 사전에

Department	Date / Time	Department Managers
Editorial	Monday, April 2 9:00 A.M. – 1:00 P.M.	Joanne Steele, Editorial Director (Tombes Financial Monthly) / Tommy Renaldo, Editor-in-Chief (Parker Business Magazine)
Design	Tuesday, April 3 10:00 A.M. – 2:00 P.M.	[184] Samuel Westford, Lead Designer (Tombes Financial Monthly) / Wendy Skeller, Head of Design (Parker Business Magazine)
Administrative	Wednesday, April 4 11:00 A.M. – 4:00 P.M.	Annabelle Cordel, Office Manager (Tombes Financial Monthly) / Steven Parinon, Office Manager (Parker Business Magazine)
Public Relations	Thursday, April 5 09:30 A.M. – 12:00 P.M.	Laini Peterson, Lead Advertiser (Tombes Financial Monthly) / Sandy Baxter, Head of Advertising (Parker Business Magazine)

*모든 미팅은 톰베스 파이낸셜 먼슬리의 해당 부서에서 진행될 예정입니다.
*스티븐 파리논은 합병 전에 은퇴할 예정입니다. 애나벨 고델이 합병 이후 새 사무실의 관리를 맡게 됐습니다. 185 모든 부서 매니저들은 4월 4일 회의에 참석해 주시기 바라며, 참가자들의 수를 수용할 수 있도록 컨퍼런스 룸 A에서 진행합니다.

*All meetings will take place at Tombes Financial Monthly in the relevant department.
*Steven Parinon will retire prior to the merger. Annabelle Cordel has been selected to run the new office following the merger. 185 All department managers are expected to attend the meeting on April 4, which will be in conference room A to accommodate the number of attendees.

어휘 editorial 편집의 editor-in-chief 편집장 administrative 관리의, 행정의 public relations 홍보 take place 개최되다 retire 은퇴하다 prior to ~이전에 following ~에 이어 accommodate 수용하다 attendee 참가자

메모의 한 가지 목적은 무엇인가?
(A) 재정 계획의 변경 사항을 상기시키기 위해서
(B) 일부 직원을 보내는 이유를 설명하기 위해서
(C) 사무장의 은퇴를 발표하기 위해서
(D) 다음 합병의 혜택들을 설명하기 위해서

어휘 remind 상기시키다 retirement 은퇴 benefit 혜택 upcoming 다가오는 note 언급하다

181

What is one purpose of the memo?
(A) To remind of changes to a financial plan
(B) To explain why some employees were let go
(C) To announce the retirement of an office manager
(D) To note the benefits of an upcoming merger*

첫째 문단에서 합병 계획을 알리며 두 회사에 좋은 기회가 될 것(This merger will be an exciting opportunity for both companies.)이라고 한 후 상세 사항들을 설명한다. 따라서 (D)가 가장 적절하다.

정답 (D)

메모에 따르면, 파커 비즈니스 매거진의 전문 분야는?
(A) 지역 금융
(B) 기업 합병
(C) 정부 정책
(D) 국제 사업

어휘 government 정부 trade 무역, 거래

182

According to the memo, what is Parker Business Magazine's area of expertise?
(A) Local finance   (B) Company mergers
(C) Government policies   (D) International business*

첫째 문단의 Parker Business Magazine is one of the top three business publications and specializes in reporting on international business issues and trends.를 통해 정답 (D)를 확인할 수 있다.

정답 (D)

톰베스-파커 비즈니스 앤 파이낸스 직원들에 대해 드러나는 사항은?
(A) 조기 은퇴를 권고 받았다.
(B) 경영직에 지원할 수 있다.
(C) 새로운 사무 건물로 옮길 것이다.
(D) 모두 4월 6일 회의에 참석해야 한다.

어휘 apply for ~에 지원하다, 신청하다 management 경영, 운영 position 직책 relocate 이전하다

183

What is suggested about the employees of Tombes-Parker Business and Finance?
(A) They have been asked to retire early.
(B) They will be able to apply for management positions.
(C) They will relocate to a new office building.*
(D) They all need to attend the meeting on April 6.

메모(지문 1) 둘째 문단에서 Department managers will meet during the week of April 2 to work out some of the details of the merger as well as the renovation of our brand-new office space downtown.이라며 새 사무 공간 개조에 대해 언급한다. 따라서 (C)가 가장 적절하다.

정답 (C)

184

What is indicated about Mr. Westford?

(A) He plans to take over the position of office manager.
(B) He will discuss some e-mailed questions at his meeting.*
(C) He organized the merger between the two magazines.
(D) He chose the location for the new company headquarters.

핵심 인명 Mr. Westford는 서식(지문 2)의 Samuel Westford, Lead Designer에서 수석 디자이너로서 매니저 회의에 참석하는 사람임을 알 수 있다. 선택지들 중 가장 연관성이 있는 내용을 찾으려면 메모(지문 1)도 살펴봐야 한다. 둘째 문단에서 직원들은 매니저 회의에 상정하고 싶은 내용이 있으면 이메일로 미리 알려 달라(If you have any concerns you'd like to raise during the meetings, please send an e-mail to the relevant department manager in advance.)고 했으므로 이들을 연계했을 때 (B)가 정답이 된다.

정답 (B)

웨스트포드 씨에 대해 드러나는 사항은?
(A) 사무장 직을 인수할 계획이다.
(B) 이메일로 받은 질문들을 회의에서 다룰 것이다.
(C) 두 잡지 회사의 합병을 준비했다.
(D) 새 회사 본사가 들어갈 위치를 선택했다.

어휘 take over 인수하다 organize (회합 등을) 준비하다 headquarters 본사

185

What will happen at a meeting on April 4?

(A) A greater number of participants will be present.*
(B) Mr. Parinon will be absent from the discussion.
(C) The CEO of Parker Business Magazine will give a presentation.
(D) Employees will be informed of their new job assignments.

회의 일정을 다룬 서식(지문 2)에서 April 4에 관련된 부분을 찾아보자. 마지막 부분에서 All department managers are expected to attend the meeting on April 4, which will be in conference room A to accommodate the number of attendees.라며 모든 부서 매니저들이 참석하므로, 그 인원을 수용하기 위해 컨퍼런스룸에서 회의를 한다고 하므로 (A)가 가장 적절하다.

정답 (A)

4월 4일 미팅에 어떤 일이 생길 것인가?
(A) 더 많은 참석자들이 있을 것이다.
(B) 파리논 씨가 논의에서 빠질 것이다.
(C) 파커 비즈니스 매거진 CEO가 발표할 것이다.
(D) 직원들에게 새로운 업무들을 배정할 것이다.

어휘 participant 참석자 present 참석한 absent 결석한, 결근한 inform 알리다 assignment 배정, 배치

Questions 186-190 refer to the following announcement, instructions, and e-mail.

Individuals Needed for Mini Focus Groups

Dressler Marketing, the biggest market research company in Edmonton, is recruiting people between the ages of 21 and 70 for a study focused on travel. The event will take place in the conference center of the Sanderson Hotel, 48 Emery Avenue, during the second week of June. The study begins by viewing a series of short travel-related videos followed by small group discussions that are facilitated by our moderators. The entire session will last three hours and [186 (A)] compensation will be provided for all who participate. Anyone interested can phone Dressler at 409-5321-8082. Be sure to mention study 73. [186 (B)] To determine if a caller is eligible to take part in this study, he or she will be asked to remain on the line and respond to a few screening questions.

Roland,

Dressler Marketing really appreciates you taking time out from your busy work schedule to assist with our market research project for Pacific Adventures at the Sanderson Hotel. [188] You will be facilitating four mini focus groups composed of five people each. Since the focus is travelling along Canada's west coast, [186 (C)] our client insists that we [187] locate individuals with extensive travel experience, either for business or leisure, in that region.

Schedule of Sessions from 3:00 to 6:00 P.M.
Age Range/Date
21-35 Tuesday, June 9
36-45 Wednesday, June 10
46-60 Thursday, June 11
61-70 Friday, June 12

Upon arrival, participants will be given yellow name tags. Make sure their name tags are clearly visible at all times during the study; especially when making the video recordings of the members' discussions. [189] This will allow Dressler to refer to individuals by their names when submitting our findings and recommendations to Pacific Adventures.

Each of the four video clips centers on a different aspect of Pacific Adventures:

Video Clip 1: Group Discounts for Whale-watching tours
Video Clip 2: One-Day Kayaking Adventures

¹⁹⁰ Video Clip 3: Popular Mountain Resorts
Video Clip 4: Hiking Adventures in Whistler Mountain

Nina Hernandez

To: rothschild@pacificadventures.ca
From: nhernandez@dressler.ca
Date: 28 June
Subject: Study 73
Attachment: Study 73 findings

Dear Mr. Rothschild

I am contacting to notify you that the research you requested last month for a specific target market has been completed. As the attached report indicates, one theme was the favorite of all focus groups. ¹⁹⁰ This theme represents an overview of the most popular places for travelers to stay. To ensure that we have covered all the key aspects in our findings, we would like to view the video with you and your representatives and have a lengthy discussion on it. Please inform us of a convenient time and date to meet.

Best regards,

Nina Hernandez
Head of Client Services, Dressler Marketing

소규모 포커스 그룹 참가자들에 대해 드러나지 않는 사항은?
(A) 급여를 받을 것이다.
(B) 전화할 때 질문에 답해야 한다.
(C) 경험 있는 여행가들이어야 한다.
(D) 호텔 직원들이다.

어휘 payment 결제(금) experienced 노련한, 경험이 있는

186
What is NOT suggested about the participants of the mini focus groups?
(A) They will receive a payment.
(B) They need to answer questions when they call.
(C) They must be experienced travelers.
(D) They are hotel employees.*

'그룹 참가자 자격'에 유념해 지문들을 살펴보면, (A)와 (B)는 공지문(지문 1) 후반부의 compensation will be provided for all who participate와 To determine if a caller is eligible to take part in this study, he or she will be asked to remain on the line and respond to a few screening questions.에서 확인할 수 있다. (C)는 안내문(지문 2) 첫째 문단의 our client insists that we locate individuals with extensive travel experience, either for business or leisure, in that region을 통해 확인할 수 있다. 따라서 본 문제의 정답은 (D)이다.

정답 (D)

안내문에서, 첫째 문단 넷째 줄에 있는 "locate"와 의미상 가장 유사한 단어는?
(A) 논평하다
(B) 믿다
(C) 찾다
(D) 확인하다

어휘 remark 발언하다, 논평하다

187
In the Instructions, paragraph 1, line 4, the word "locate" is the closest in meaning to
(A) remark   (B) believe
(C) find*   (D) check

해당 부분을 찾아 문장 요지를 파악한 후 각 선택지들로 바꿨을 때 의미 전개가 가장 유사해지는 단어를 정답으로 택한다. 여행을 자주 한 사람을 '찾기'를 바란다는 문맥을 완성하려면 (C)가 적절하다.

정답 (C)

연구 73에 대해 드러나는 사항은?
(A) 드레슬러 본사에서 진행될 것이다.
(B) 동일 규모의 그룹 네 개가 포함된다.
(C) 수상 레저에만 집중한다.
(D) 이틀 안에 끝날 것이다.

어휘 be held 열리다 headquarters 본사 solely 오로지

188
What is indicated about study 73?
(A) It will be held at Dressler's headquarters.
(B) It includes four groups of the same size.*
(C) It centers solely on water leisure.
(D) It will be completed in two days.

회의 진행자에게 보낸 안내문(지문 2)에서 You will be facilitating four mini focus groups composed of five people each.라고 하는데, 5명으로 구성된 그룹이 4개라는 뜻이므로 (B)가 정답임을 알 수 있다.

정답 (B)

189 According to the instructions, why were the participants provided with name tags?

(A) So that the marketing company can identify them easily.*
(B) So that each registration number matches with the correct name.
(C) So that they would be able to find their seats quickly.
(D) So that they would be permitted to enter the conference center.

안내문에 따르면, 참가자들은 왜 명찰을 받았는가?
(A) 마케팅 회사가 그들을 쉽게 확인할 수 있도록
(B) 각 등록 번호가 정확한 이름과 짝지어지도록
(C) 좌석을 빨리 찾을 수 있도록
(D) 컨퍼런스 센터 입장이 허용되도록

어휘 identify 확인하다, 알아보다 registration 등록 permit 허용하다, 허락하다

name tags에 유념해 안내문(지문 2)을 살펴보자. 셋째 문단에서 명찰을 항상 잘 보이게 해 달라고 한 뒤 This will allow Dressler to refer to individuals by their names when submitting our findings and recommendations to Pacific Adventures.라며 연구 결과를 제출할 때 이름으로 각 참석자를 지칭할 수 있다고 덧붙인다. 따라서 (A)가 가장 적절하다.

정답 (A)

190 Based on the results of the study, what video clip was the most popular?

(A) Video Clip 1
(B) Video Clip 2
(C) Video Clip 3*
(D) Video Clip 4

연구 결과를 볼 때, 어떤 비디오 클립이 가장 인기가 좋았는가?
(A) 비디오 클립 1
(B) 비디오 클립 2
(C) 비디오 클립 3
(D) 비디오 클립 4

결과를 언급한 이메일(지문 3)과 비디오 클립들을 상세히 설명한 안내문(지문 2)을 연계해서 파악해야 해결할 수 있는 문제이다. 지문 3에서 모든 그룹이 가장 좋아했던 주제가 하나 있었다며 This theme represents an overview of the most popular places for travelers to stay.라고 설명한다. '여행가들의 인기 체류지'에 유념해 지문 2에서 비디오 클립에 관련된 부분을 보면 정답 (C)를 찾아낼 수 있다.

정답 (C)

Questions 191-195 refer to the following schedule and two e-mails.

St. John Art Gallery
Upcoming Exhibitions

Dates	Title of Exhibition	Brief Description
11 April – 20 August	Recycled Materials as Sculptures	People usually see recycled materials as mere scrap piles. However, as this exhibition featuring the works of 10 artists throughout [191] South America shows, any material can be transformed into breathtaking sculptures.
28 April – 3 October	The Portraits of Athletes	This watercolor collection features beautiful paintings of professional athletes by [191] artists from every corner of the globe.
5 June – 29 November	More than Just Trees	This remarkable collection of photographs and paintings by artists throughout [191] Africa and several Mediterranean nations captures the mesmerizing power of forests.
[193] 11 June – 14 July	The History of Food in Art	Through video recordings, sculptures, photographs, and paintings, this unique exhibition traces the history of food in the 15th to 19th century [191] Europe.

Tickets can be purchased through our website or by sending an e-mail to banderson@stjohnartgallery.org. To learn about our wonderful membership plans, simply go to our website and click on 'Become a St. John Art Gallery Member'! [192] Members receive two free tickets to the exhibition of their choice.

From: Chevon Jabar <CJabar@rogerstalent.ca>
To: Belinda Anderson <banderson@stjohnartgallery.org>
Subject: thank you
Date: March 10

[192] I am e-mailing to say thank you for the two free tickets to 'The History of Food in Art.' I also need another ticket for this event for my division head, Helena Lafleur. I assume the gallery has a record of my credit card details so please bill the same card and send the tickets to the same address.

I would like to thank your staff for providing such fantastic exhibitions.

Chevon Jabar

From: Belinda Anderson <banderson@stjohnartgallery.org>
To: Chevon Jabar <CJabar@rogerstalent.ca>
Subject: a cancelled exhibition
Date: March 14

Dear Mr. Jabar,

St. John Art Gallery would like to thank you for your patronage during the past seven years. We are truly sorry that the exhibition you and your colleague planned to see was cancelled due to circumstances beyond our control. However, we have already scheduled a replacement exhibition of black and white photographs. ¹⁹³ It is scheduled to ¹⁹⁴ run during the exact same dates (11 June – 14 July) and is called 'The Working Classes of Latin America'. ¹⁹⁵ I have already sent a new program guide in the mail to your office. Please let me know which exhibition you would like to see instead.

Thank you for your understanding in this matter.

Sincerely yours,

Belinda Anderson
St. John Art Gallery

---

191. According to the website, what do all of the exhibitions have in common?

(A) They showcase works from various nations.*
(B) They showcase paintings from Mediterranean countries.
(C) They include video presentations.
(D) They include sculptures.

192. What is indicated about Mr. Jabar?

(A) He donated a collection for an exhibition.
(B) He is currently employed as an art instructor.
(C) He has already seen three of the exhibits.
(D) He is a paid member of the art gallery.*

어떤 전시가 취소되었는가?
(A) 재활용 재료 조각품
(B) 운동 선수들의 초상화
(C) 단순한 나무 이상의 것
(D) 예술 작품에서 음식의 역사

어휘 recycled 재활용 portrait 초상화

193
Which exhibition has been canceled?
(A) Recycled Materials as Sculptures
(B) The Portraits of Athletes
(C) More Than Just Trees
(D) The History of Food in Art*

'전시 취소'에 관해 전시 주최측인 갤러리의 웹사이트(지문 1)와 두 번째 이메일(지문 3)을 연계해 파악해야 한다. 지문 3 중반부에서 취소된 전시를 대신해 같은 날짜에 다른 전시가 운영될 예정(It is scheduled to run during the exact same dates (11 June - 14 July))이라고 한다. 이 날짜에 해당되는 전시 제목을 지문 1에서 찾아보면, (D)가 정답임을 알 수 있다.

정답 (D)

두 번째 이메일에서, 첫째 문단 넷째 줄에 있는 "run"과 의미상 가장 유사한 단어는?
(A) 감독하다
(B) 제거하다
(C) 보여지다
(D) 발표되다

어휘 remove 제거하다, 없애다

194
In the second e-mail, the word "run" in paragraph 1, line 4 is closest in meaning to
(A) direct
(B) remove
(C) be shown*
(D) be announced

해당 부분은 '전시를 진행할 예정'이라는 요지이므로 이를 대신하기에 의미 전개상 가장 적절한 것은 (C)이다.

정답 (C)

앤더슨 씨는 자바 씨를 위해 무엇을 했는가?
(A) 신용 카드로 청구했다.
(B) 업데이트된 프로그램 가이드를 보냈다.
(C) 회원권을 업그레이드했다.
(D) 사교 행사 일정을 조정했다.

어휘 reschedule 일정을 조정하다

195
What did Ms. Anderson do for Mr. Jabar?
(A) Bill his credit card
(B) Mail an updated program guide*
(C) Upgrade his membership
(D) Reschedule a social event

Ms. Anderson이 작성한 이메일(지문 3) 후반부에서 I have already sent a new program guide in the mail to your office.라며 새 프로그램 가이드를 이미 보냈다고 하므로 (B)가 정답이다.

* paraphrasing: send → mail, new → updated

정답 (B)

Questions 196-200 refer to the following e-mails and the attachment.

To: Marcus Lount; Gabriella Sanchez; Daniel Wilkes
From: Shelly Dorcas
Date: July 16, 9:09 A.M.
Subject: business space
Attachment: available properties

Hi everyone,

198 I really enjoyed last Friday's lunch with you at the Davisville Grill. I am truly excited about opening our first Miami branch of Ebbet Construction Equipment Rentals. As Miami's housing market grows more and more each day, I am sure that we are all eager to attract our very first customers and start advising companies on the equipment that is most suitable for their projects and objectives.

I appreciate all the input you offered on the most appropriate business space. Using the budget and criteria you suggested, I searched for spaces at www.vanzylerealty.com. I found several possible spaces and compiled them into a list. That document is attached. Please have a look at it and get back to me with any comments you may have.

196 Shelly Dorcas, Ebbet Construction Equipment Rentals

13990 Gifford Way
Suburban two-story rental facility. Second floor office suites. Parking lot can accommodate up to 100 automobiles. Located across from Devon City's main bus terminal and near a large number of hotels used by business travelers. Half an hour from downtown Miami.
Monthly lease: $975

1389 Singleton Highway
200 Large retail space located in the heart of downtown Miami. Large sign on building makes it high visible to highway motorists. Building includes large storage facilities for parts and equipment. The newly installed air conditioning unit is guaranteed to keep you comfortable during the hot summers.
Monthly lease: $1,150

7643 Beckford Avenue
Third-floor retails and office space. Located uptown within Miami's main business district. Located on the same street as two major shopping centers. Facility includes state-of-the-art security alarm system. Printer/scanner/fax/color copier on-site for company use.
Monthly lease: $1,050

6094 Wilmot Drive
Single-story building. Comes with small office space. Land contract is also offered for property immediately behind facility. 197 Located on the city's east side in lovely Ryerson Park, a prime Miami development site for condominium towers.

Monthly lease: $825

어휘 suburban 교외의 parking lot 주차장 accommodate 수용하다 automobile 자동차 lease 임대차 계약 retail 소매(상) visible (눈에) 보이는, 알아볼 수 있는 storage 저장, 보관 part 부품 install 설치하다 comfortable 편안한 district 지구, 구역 state-of-the-art 최신의 security 보안, 안전 on-site 현장의 come with 딸려 있다 contract 계약(서) immediately 즉시, 바로

To: Shelly Dorcas; Marcus Lount; Gabriella Sanchez
From: Daniel Wilkes
Date: July 20, 11:23 A.M.
Re: business space

Hi everyone,

Thank you very much, Shelly, for all your work in narrowing our search to the options in the list you provided. I'm certain the strategy meeting held last Friday was quite productive. 198 My apologies for not being there, but I was called to Boston all of a sudden on an urgent business matter. Also, I have to say thank all of you for being patient in waiting for my response to this important e-mail discussion.

Marcus, while I truly appreciate the need to save money on an inexpensive suburban facility, 200 our company should not ignore the significance of having a facility conveniently located downtown as more and more homes are being built in that area.

199 I am also in agreement with Gabriella's idea that our company needs a booth at Miami's upcoming housing fair. Next week, I will be flying to Miami to visit relatives so I will look into the matter then. Also, while in Miami, I am scheduled to have lunch with a local realtor who worked for our company up until two years ago. Thank you, Shelly, for reminding me that Helen Richardson now resides in Miami. I'm sure she will have useful insights for us.

Daniel Wilkes, Ebbet Construction Equipment Rentals

어휘 narrow 좁히다 option 선택(권) strategy 전략 quite 패, 상당히 productive 생산적인 apology 사과 all of a sudden 갑자기 urgent 긴급한 matter 문제 response 응답 inexpensive 비싸지 않은 ignore 무시하다 significance 중요성 conveniently 편리하게 agreement 동의 relative 친척 realtor 부동산업자 remind 상기시키다 reside 살고 있다, 거주하다

---

196 Who most likely is Ms. Dorcas?
(A) A real estate expert
(B) An official in Miami Housing Bureau
(C) A construction equipment specialist*
(D) A cook at Davisville Grill

Ms. Dorcas는 첫 번째 이메일(지문 1)의 발신인이다. 끝 부분의 Shelly Dorcas, Ebbet Construction Equipment Rentals에서 정답 (C)를 확인할 수 있다.

정답 (C)

197 What is one property feature mentioned in the attachment?

(A) An energy-efficient heating system
(B) A newly-installed carpet in the office
(C) A large cafeteria for employees
(D) A location close to housing development*

첨부 파일(지문 2)에 제시된 각 부지들에 대한 설명에서 선택지 중 언급된 내용을 찾아야 하는데, 마지막 부지의 입지 조건 중 Located on the city's east side in lovely Ryerson Park, a prime Miami development site for condominium towers.에서 (D)가 언급된다.

정답 (D)

첨부 파일에서 언급된 한 가지 부동산의 특징은 무엇인가?
(A) 에너지 효율이 좋은 난방 시스템
(B) 사무실에 새로 설치된 카펫
(C) 직원들을 위한 대형 구내 식당
(D) 주택 개발지에 가까운 위치

어휘 energy-efficient 에너지 효율이 좋은

198 What is suggested about Mr. Wilkes?

(A) He will fly to Miami tomorrow morning.
(B) He is renting some property in Boston.
(C) He did not make it to the Davisville Grill meeting.*
(D) He plans to apply for a managerial position.

Mr. Wilkes가 작성한 이메일(지문 3)부터 살펴보자. 지문 3 첫째 문단에서 '지난주 금요일' 회의가 정말 생산적이었을 것이라 한 뒤 자신은 일이 생겨 참석하지 못했다며 사과한다(My apologies for not being there, but I was called to Boston all of a sudden on an urgent business matter.). there의 위치를 확인하기 위해 지난주 금요일에 관련된 정보를 첫째 이메일(지문 1)에서 보면, 첫 문장 I really enjoyed last Friday's lunch with you at the Davisville Grill.과 연계해 정답 (C)를 확인할 수 있다.

정답 (C)

윌크스 씨에 대해 드러나는 사항은?
(A) 내일 오전 마이애미로 갈 예정이다.
(B) 보스턴의 부동산을 임대 중이다.
(C) 데비스빌 그릴 회의 때 참석하지 못했다.
(D) 관리직에 지원할 계획이다.

어휘 rent 임대하다 make it to (시간 내에) 이르다, 도착하다

199 What is indicated about Ms. Sanchez?

(A) She suggested an idea to her colleagues by e-mail.*
(B) She used to live in downtown Miami.
(C) She will meet a former colleague.
(D) She started her own equipment rental business.

Ms. Sanchez(가브리엘라 산체스)에 유념해 지문들을 살펴보면, 일단 이들은 이메일로 논의를 이어 가고 있다는 것을 알 수 있고 두 번째 이메일(지문 3) 셋째 문단에서 I am also in agreement with Gabriella's idea that our company needs a booth at Miami's upcoming housing fair.라고 하므로 (A)가 가장 적절하다.

정답 (A)

산체스 씨에 대해 드러나는 사항은?
(A) 동료들에게 이메일로 아이디어를 제시했다.
(B) 마이애미 시내에 산 적이 있다.
(C) 이전 동료를 만날 것이다.
(D) 자신만의 장비 임대 사업을 시작했다.

어휘 colleague 동료 former 이전의

200 Which property does Mr. Wilkes most likely favor?

(A) 13990 Gifford Way   (B) 1389 Singleton Highway*
(C) 7643 Beckford Avenue (D) 6094 Wilmot Drive

Mr. Wilkes가 작성한 이메일(지문 3)과 부동산 목록이 실린 첨부 파일(지문 2)을 연계해서 파악해야 한다. 지문 3 둘째 문단의 our company should not ignore the significance of having a facility conveniently located downtown as more and more homes are being built in that area를 통해 '시내에서 편리한 접근성'을 강조함을 알 수 있다. 지문 2에서 이와 관련해 찾아보면(Large retail space located in the heart of downtown Miami.) (B)가 정답이 된다.

정답 (B)

윌크스 씨는 어떤 부동산을 가장 선호하겠는가?
(A) 13990 기포드 웨이
(B) 1389 싱글턴 하이웨이
(C) 7643 벡포드 애비뉴
(D) 6094 윌못 드라이브